Targeted Public Distribution System

Published by Academic Foundation
in association with the

National Council of Applied Economic Research

The Work is Sponsored by

Department of Food and Public Distribution,
Ministry of Consumer Affairs, Food and Public Distribution,
Government of India

Targeted Public Distribution System

Performance and Inefficiencies

PARMOD KUMAR

ACADEMIC FOUNDATION

NEW DELHI

First published in 2010 by

Academic Foundation

4772-73 / 23 Bharat Ram Road, (23 Ansari Road), Darya Ganj, New Delhi - 110 002 (India).
Phones : 23245001 / 02 / 03 / 04. Fax : +91-11-23245005.
E-mail : books@academicfoundation.com
www : academicfoundation.com

Cataloging in Publication Data--DK
Courtesy: D.K. Agencies (P) Ltd. <Docinfo@dkagencies.com>

Kumar, Parmod, 1966-
Targeted public distribution system : performance an inefficiencies/Parmod Kumar.
p. cm.
In Indian context.
Includes bibliographical references.

ISBN 13: 978-81-7188-798-9
ISBN 10: 81-7188-798-8

1. Food supply--Government policy--India--Evaluation. 2. Rationing--Government policy--India--Evaluation. 3. Poor--Government policy--India. 4. Food supply--Corrupt practices--India. 5. Rationing--Corrupt practices--India. I. Title.

DDC 363.8560954 22

Typeset by Italics India, New Delhi.
Printed and bound in India.

Contents

Part I

Part II

List of Tables, Figures and Annexures

Part I

Tables

Figures

Annexures

Part II

Tables

Figures

Annexures

Foreword

The Public Distribution System (PDS) continues to be a major instrument for ensuring food security for the poor. The basic objective of shifting from a universal PDS to targeted PDS (TPDS) was to benefit the poor at acceptable budgetary cost. The success of the TPDS in meeting its stated objectives depends largely on the ability of the State Governments to identify the genuinely poor families, restricting the number of poor families to the number estimated by the Planning Commission and in putting in place an effective and efficient delivery system. In a number of recent studies, it has been highlighted that there are large-scale errors in the identification of targeted families, low off-take of food grains by the poor and there are weaknesses in the delivery system.

In view of these concerns, the National Council of Applied Economic Research (NCAER) was entrusted with the study to examine the extent to which food grains disbursed under the TPDS are actually reaching the Antyodaya and below poverty population in the country and to find out the incidence as well as the mode of irregularities in the system. The Department of Food and Public Distribution, Government of India sponsored the study.

The study is based on a large primary survey. The two phases of the study covered six states in each phase. The first phase evaluated PDS functioning in Rajasthan, Bihar, Uttar Pradesh, Chhattisgarh, Assam and Mizoram. In the second phase, the six states covered were Delhi, Jharkhand, Kerala, Madhya Pradesh, Maharashtra and Uttarakhand. From each state, 1000 households were surveyed over six consecutive months.

The evaluation findings about the efficiency of the PDS system are mixed. The performance of PDS in terms of delivery of food to the poor was satisfactory except the cases of Bihar and Assam in the first phase and Jharkhand and Madhya Pradesh in the second phase. However, the study observed huge identification errors and some incidence of diversion of food, especially in the case of BPL households in both phases. The issue of gross failure of identification of the right beneficiaries found in both phases raises the question whether this is the right methodology to identify poor families on the basis of income cut-off, identified through household expenditure as is practiced by the Planning Commission. The other idiosyncrasies observed were excess cards issued/unidentified families, diversion of PDS food, no system of inspection of entitlements, etc.

These issues need to be corrected if the functioning of the PDS system is to be improved. The correct identification of the beneficiaries is the first step in that direction. The study has also found a large number of inclusion and exclusion errors due to imperfect information, arbitrariness and interference by vested interests in the identification of BPL and AAY beneficiaries. The problem of identification error arises because of lack of information/unawareness among the poor about the eligibility criteria for the AAY or BPL and other welfare schemes. The people in the lower strata are by and large unaware of the criteria being followed in issuing AAY, BPL and APL card. It would not be possible to improve this system unless the consumers are properly educated on these issues. Proper monitoring of the system and effective punishment against the culprit including the *panchayat* officials for wrong identification would be needed.

I hope that the findings and policy suggestions in this book will lead to a better-informed debate and will help those concerned to come up with new and innovative approaches for making the PDS system much more effective and pro-poor. The book will be helpful to the planners, policy makers, researchers, students and the academia.

Suman Bery
(Director General)
NCAER

Acknowledgements

I wish to express sincere thanks to the officials of the Ministry of Food and Public Distribution System. The Report would not have been possible without special aid in terms of suggestions of Shri R.N. Das and Shri T. Nand Kumar, (both Former Secretary, Ministry of Food), Dr. Bhagwan Sahai (Joint Secretary), Mrs. Anita Chaudhary (Former Joint Secretary), Mr. P. Kalyanasundaram (Former Deputy Secretary) and Shri I.S. Kalijai (Under Secretary). Sincere thanks to all of them for their keen interest and interaction during the course of this study. Thanks are also due to the other officials who attended various presentations on the progress of the work held from time to time in the Ministry of Food and Public Distribution and provided their valuable suggestions.

I duly acknowledge the efficient support extended by the field staff and the networking institutions in carrying out the primary survey for this project. I highly appreciate the cooperation extended to our team by the fair price shop owners and households in our primary survey. I express sincere thanks to all the respondents. My special thanks are due to the officials of the Food and Civil Supplies Departments of all states. The project team benefited from the interaction with various state, district and block officials during the course of this study. The list is too long to be spelt out here. I would like to express my sincere thanks to all of them.

Ms. Deepti Sethi in the first phase and Shri Sudhir Kumar Singh in the second phase helped in data processing with deft handling of stata. I wish to thank both of them for being team members and putting up serious efforts for this study intermittently. Finally, I wish to thank my NCAER colleague, Dr. Hari K. Nagarajan for his constructive suggestions especially on the issue of consumption smoothening. I also thank Shri Deborishi for being team member for this study for a very short period.

Parmod Kumar

About the Study

The study is based on a large primary survey conducted in two phases. A total number of 12 states (six in each phase) were selected to evaluate the Targeted Public Distribution System (TPDS). From each state, 1000 households were surveyed over six consecutive months. The 12 states evaluated are Assam, Bihar, Chhattisgarh, Rajasthan, Mizoram and Uttar Pradesh in the first phase and Delhi, Jharkhand, Kerala, Madhya Pradesh, Maharashtra and Uttarakhand in the second phase. A total number of 60 districts were shortlisted for the survey in the two phases. A total number of 12000 (6000+6000) households were surveyed for six months consecutively.

The main objectives of the study are as follows: (i) Find out deviations (if any) in the selection process of beneficiaries from the norms laid down by the Central government. (ii) To examine whether food grains are distributed by the FPSs regularly and as per the requirement of the beneficiaries and adhering to the norms prescribed by the government. (iii) Find out the underlying reasons for not lifting food grains from FPSs. (iv) To investigate the quality of food grains distributed through FPSs in the light of supplies received from FCI depots. (v) The analysis would focus on the availability of food grains at FCI depots in the states. The distribution system of food grains from the FCI depots to the FPSs would be evaluated on the basis of its regularity. (vi) Analysis pertaining to the income pattern and consumption volatility of cardholders will be carried out to gauge the inability of income to cover consumption and the magnitude of risk.

The book comprises the following eight chapters (each) in two volumes: Chapter 1: Introduction; Chapter 2: The Socio-Economic Background of the Selected States; Chapter 3: Occupational Distribution and Income Patterns; Chapter 4: Consumption Pattern and Role of PDS; Chapter 5: Consumption Smoothing and Insurance against the Income Risks; Chapter 6: Performance of TPDS—Errors of Inclusion and Exclusion; Chapter 7: Functioning of the Fair Price Shops; Chapter 8: Concluding Remarks and Policy Suggestions.

On the efficacy of Public Distribution System (PDS), the survey findings portray a mixed picture. On the one hand, households below poverty did obtain their entitlement quite regularly with a few exceptions. Deeper probing however, revealed gross irregularities indicating large-scale identification errors, excess cards issued/unidentified families, diversion of PDS food, no system of inspection of entitlements, etc. The policy suggestions include educating people about the criterion followed in fixing up the entitlement; making the monitoring compulsory and punishing the culprit including the *panchayats*; making the FPS more viable by giving them fair margin; and multi-tier checking of the quality of grains supplied.

Part I

1 Introduction

1.1 Need for Public Distribution System

Public distribution system (PDS) in India is essentially designed for the equitable distribution of commodities that are indispensable for endurance. At times the fee market mechanism fails to satisfy the requirements of the poorer sections of the society. As demand for food grains for poor people is highly inelastic, they have to spend a disproportionate amount of their income on food grains when food prices are on the rise. Therefore, to maintain the minimum living standard of all sections of society, it becomes essential for the State to interfere with the market mechanism. The question that arises is whether the government should maintain a dual system, i.e., running a separate market parallel to the free market mechanism, or supplement the free market by meeting the excess demand for food. The Government of India has adopted the dual market mechanism to meet the situation (Suryanarayana, 1985: 13). This distribution policy of the Government of India aims at regulating prices to safeguard consumers, particularly the poorer sections to improve their welfare.

1.2 Historical Perspective

The origin of public distribution can be traced back to the period of Second World War and the great famine when this system was employed in many countries as a weapon of inflationary control that arose out of the global food security. In India, the system of public distribution, commonly known as price control and rationing, also came into force during the period of Second World War. In the course of war, food shortage led to rapid increase in prices of food grains.[1] These developments compelled the government to resort to controls to check the scarcity conditions and to have a fair distribution of the available supplies. Thus, rationing in times of crisis like war and famine was the historical precursor to the national policy of stabilisation and management of food grains. Policies kept changing with the decontrol announced in December 1947, reintroduction of controls in September 1948, shift to decontrol during 1952-1954 and recourse to controls in 1957 (Planning Commission, 2005). With the beginning of the planning era, the system was assigned a significant role for achieving more equitable distribution of the available supplies at reasonable prices. The policy however, was relaxed to some extent during the late fifties and early sixties on account of favourable food positions in the country. These controls were however, again enforced with greater vigour following the occurrence of the two successive drought years in the mid-sixties.

The Green Revolution led the country to achieve self-sufficiency in food grains that brought about a new dimension in the food grains management. The Food Corporation of India (FCI) was established in 1965 as the public sector agency responsible for implementing government price policy through procurement and public distribution operations. The main objective was to provide fair procurement price to the farmers to insulate them from market vagaries, to operate buffer stocking, control of market prices and public distribution of essential commodities. Thus, the main functioning of FCI was to work as an autonomous organisation, working on commercial lines, to undertake purchase, storage, movement, transport, distribution and sale of food grains and other food stuff (Planning Commission, 2005). Until the 1960s, the public distribution system remained an ad hoc programme with no clear role defined for it on a continuous basis. However, the system had substantially contributed to the containment of rise in food grains prices and ensured access of food to urban consumers.

1. The index numbers of prices for wheat and rice rose to 156 and 114 respectively by 1943 from the base year 1939 (Famine Commission Report on Bengal, p.17).

A new phase of public distribution system emerged in 1969 with the beginning of the Fourth Five Year Plan. The plan document envisaged "the public distribution system was needed on regular basis for the country to provide help to the rural people and to some extent for generating a downward pressure on the open market prices. Buffer stocks needed to be built up and the requirements of the PDS should be met mostly though internal procurement". Whereas the Fourth Plan visualised PDS to be a regular mechanism, the Sixth Five Year Plan (1980-1985) envisioned that the PDS would "have to be so developed that it remains hereafter a stable and permanent feature of our strategy to control prices, reduce fluctuations and achieve an equitable distribution of essential consumer goods". As the national agricultural production had grown in the aftermath of Green Revolution, the outreach of PDS was extended to tribal blocks and areas of high incidence of poverty in the 1970s and 1980s. Thus, the PDS system has not only existed in India since the war time but also enforced, at times, in greater vigour and the rationale for the system has been mainly from the points of view of its distributional efficiency and economic equity (Mishra, 1985).

PDS, till 1992, was a general entitlement scheme for all consumers without any specific target. Revamped Public Distribution System (RPDS) was launched in June 1992 in 1775 blocks throughout the country. RPDS was launched with a view to strengthen and streamline the PDS as well as to improve its reach in the far-flung, hilly, remote and inaccessible areas where a substantial section of the poor live. It covered area specific programmes such as, the Drought Prone Area Programme (DPAP), Integrated Tribal Development Projects (ITDP), Desert Development Programme (DDP) and certain Designated Hill Areas (DHA) identified in consultation with State Governments for special focus, with respect to improvement of the PDS infrastructure. Food grains for distribution in RPDS areas were issued to the states at 50 paise below the Central Issue Price. The scale of issue was up to 20 kilograms per card. The RPDS included area approach for ensuring effective reach of the PDS commodities, their delivery by State Governments at the doorstep of FPSs in the identified areas, additional ration cards to the left out families, infrastructure requirements like additional FPSs, storage capacity etc., and additional commodities such as tea, salt, pulses, soap, etc., for distribution through PDS outlets.

1.3 Targeted Public Distribution System (TPDS)

The PDS as it was being implemented earlier had been criticised for its urban bias and its failure to serve effectively the poorer sections of the population, its limited coverage in the states with high concentration of the rural poor and lack of transparent and accountable arrangements for delivery. A need was felt for quite some time to review the PDS and make it more focused. The Targeted Public Distribution System (TPDS) replaced the erstwhile PDS from June 1997. Under the new system, two-tier subsidised pricing system was introduced to benefit the poor. The essential features of TPDS are: Government of India is committed to making available food grains to the states to meet the requirement of food grains at the scale of 10 kilogram per month per family at specially subsidised prices to population falling below the officially estimated poverty line (BPL families). The states would also receive the quantity needed for transitory allocation to above poverty line (APL) population. The State Governments were to streamline the PDS by issuing special cards to BPL families and selling essential articles under TPDS to them at specially subsidised prices, with better monitoring of the delivery system. Under the system, states are required to formulate and implement foolproof arrangements for identification of the poor for delivery of food grains and for its distribution in a transparent and accountable manner at the FPS level. The scheme, when introduced, was intended to benefit about 6 crore poor families for whom a quantity of about 72 lakh tonnes of food grains was earmarked annually.

The TPDS was implemented in the states of Haryana and Tripura with effect from May 1997 and in all other states/UTs from June 1997 except in the states of Delhi, Goa, Punjab and the Union Territory of Lakshadweep. By 1999, the scheme came in operation in all states/UTs except, Delhi and Lakshadweep as in these two states no distinction was made between the BPL and APL households for the purpose of PDS coverage. In 1999, this system (TPDS) was introduced in Delhi also. The system is now in operation in Lakshadweep as well, thereby at present the whole of India is covered by the TPDS.

The identification of the poor under the scheme is done by the states as per state-wise poverty estimates of the Planning Commission for 1993-94 based on the methodology of the "Expert Group on Estimation of Proportion and Number of Poor" chaired by Late Prof. Lakdawala. The total number of BPL households so determined were 596.23 lakh. Guidelines for implementing the TPDS were issued in which the State Governments had been advised to identify the BPL families by involving the *gram panchayats* and *nagar palikas*. While doing so, the thrust should be to include the really poor and vulnerable sections of the society such as landless agricultural labourers, marginal farmers, rural artisans/craftsmen such as potters, tappers, weavers, blacksmith, carpenters etc., in the rural areas and slum dwellers and persons earning their livelihood on daily basis in the informal sector like potters, rickshaw-pullers, cart-pullers, fruit and flower sellers on the pavement etc., in urban areas. The *gram panchayats* and *gram sabhas* should also be involved in the identification of eligible families. The number of BPL families has been increased w.e.f. 1.12.2000 by shifting the base to the population projections of the Registrar General as on 1.3.2000 instead of the earlier population projections of 1995. With this increase, the total number of BPL families is 652.03 lakh as against 596.23 lakh families originally estimated when TPDS was introduced in June 1997.

The allocation of food grains to the states/UTs was made on the basis of average consumption in the past i.e., average annual off-take of food grains under the PDS during the past 10 years at the time of introduction of TPDS. The quantum of food grains in excess of the requirement of BPL families was provided to the state as 'transitory allocation' for which a quantum of 103 lakh tonnes of food grains was earmarked annually. Over and above the TPDS allocation, additional allocation to states was also given. The transitory allocation was intended for continuation of benefit of subsidised food grains to the population above the poverty line (APL) as any sudden withdrawal of benefits existing under PDS from them was not considered desirable. The transitory allocation was issued at prices, which were subsidised but were higher than the prices for the BPL quota of food grains. Keeping in view the consensus on increasing the allocation of food grains to BPL families and to better target the food subsidy, Government of India increased the allocation to BPL families from 10 kilograms to 20 kilograms of food grains per family per month at 50 per cent of the economic cost w.e.f. 1.4.2000. The allocation of APL families was retained at the same level as at the time of introduction of TPDS but the Central Issue Prices (CIP) for APL were fixed at 100 per cent of economic cost from that date so that the entire consumer subsidy could be directed to the benefit of the BPL population.

The end retail price is fixed by the states/UTs after taking into account margins for wholesalers/retailers, transportations charges, levies, local taxes etc. Under the TPDS, the states were requested to issue food grains at a difference of not more than 50 paise per kilogram over and above the CIP for BPL families. Flexibility to states/UTs has been given in the matter of fixing the retail issue prices by removing the restriction of 50 paise per kilogram over and above the CIP for distribution of food grains under TPDS except with respect to Antyodaya Anna Yojana where the end retail price is to be retained at Rs. 2.0 per kilogram for wheat and Rs. 3.0 per kilogram for rice.

1.4 Antyodaya Anna Yojana (AAY)

A National Sample Survey (NSS) exercise points towards the fact that about 5 per cent of the total population in the country sleeps without two square meals a day. This section of the population can be called as "hungry". In order to make TPDS more focused and targeted towards this category of population, the Antyodaya Anna Yojana (AAY) was launched in December 2000 for one crore poorest of the poor families. AAY contemplates identification of one crore poorest of the poor families from amongst the BPL families covered under TPDS within the states and providing them food grains at a highly subsidised rate of Rs. 2.0 per kilogram for wheat and Rs. 3.0 per kilogram for rice. The states/UTs are required to bear the distribution cost, including margin to dealers and retailers as well as the transportation cost. Thus, the entire food subsidy is being passed on to the consumers under the scheme. The estimated annual allocation of food grains for Antyodaya families was 30 lakh tonnes, involving a subsidy of Rs. 2,315 crore at the beginning.

The scheme was started with one crore families but was expanded from time to time mostly during the presentation of annual budgets by the Union Finance Minister. With the third expansion in 2005-06, the scheme now covers around 2.5 crore households. The identification of the Antyodaya families and issuing of distinctive ration cards to these families is the responsibility of the concerned state governments. Detailed guidelines were issued to the states/UTs for identification of the Antyodaya families under the AAY and additional Antyodaya families under the expanded AAY. Allocation of food grains under the scheme is being released to the states/UTs on the basis of issue of distinctive AAY ration cards to the identified Antyodaya families. The present monthly allocation of food grains under AAY is around 7.27 lakh tonnes per month. The state-wise estimated number of AAY families and the families identified and ration cards issued under AAY by the state governments/ UTs are given in Table 1.1.

1.5 Scale of Issue of Food Grains under TPDS

Since 1997, the scale of issue of the BPL families has been gradually increased from 10 kilograms to 35 kilograms per family per month. The scale of issue was increased from 10 kilograms to 20 kilograms per family per month with effect from 1.4.2000. The allocation for APL families has been retained at the same level as at the time of introduction of TPDS (i.e. 10 kilograms per family per month). The allocation of food grains for the BPL families has been further increased from 20 kilograms to 25 kilograms per family per month with effect from July 2001. Initially, the Antyodaya families were provided 25 kilograms of food grains per family per month at the time of launching of the scheme. The scale of issue under APL, BPL and AAY has been revised to 35 kilograms per family per month with effect from 1.4.2002 with a view to enhancing the food security at the household level.

Table 1.1 Number of Households Identified and Ration Cards Issued to AAY Families in Different States (as on 02.08.2005)

S.N.	Name of the State/UT	Estimated No. of AAY Households (in lakhs)	No. of AAY Households Identified and Ration Cards Issued by the State Govts./UTs (in lakhs)
1	Andhra Pradesh	15.578	12.336
2	Arunachal Pradesh	0.380	0.301
3	Assam	7.040	4.115
4	Bihar	25.010	10.000
5	Chhattisgarh	7.189	5.693
6	Delhi	1.568	0.555
7	Goa	0.184	0.110
8	Gujarat	8.128	6.437
9	Haryana	3.025	1.815
10	Himachal Pradesh	1.971	1.543
11	J&K	2.822	2.181
12	Jharkhand	9.179	7.268
13	Karnataka	11.997	9.500
14	Kerala	5.958	4.718
15	Madhya Pradesh	15.816	12.447
16	Maharashtra	25.053	19.838
17	Manipur	0.636	0.504
18	Meghalaya	0.702	0.556
19	Mizoram	0.261	0.261
20	Nagaland	0.475	0.376
21	Orissa	12.645	10.013
22	Punjab	1.794	0.717
23	Rajasthan	9.321	7.355
24	Sikkim	0.165	0.099
25	Tamil Nadu	18.646	14.765
26	Tripura	1.131	0.679
27	Uttaranchal	1.909	1.145
28	Uttar Pradesh	40.945	32.423
29	West Bengal	19.857	14.207
30	A&N Islands	0.107	0.043
31	Chandigarh	0.088	0.035
32	D&N Haveli	0.069	0.037
33	Daman & Diu	0.015	0.006
34	Lakshdweep	0.012	0.004
35	Pondicherry	0.322	0.255
Total		250.000	182.337

Source: Economic Survey, 2005-06.

1.6 Central Issue Price

Wheat and rice are issued by the Central government at uniform central issue prices (CIPs) to states and union territories for distribution under TPDS. The difference between the economic cost and issue price of food grains is reimbursed to the FCI by the Central government in the form of subsidy. Any changes in the Minimum Support Prices (MSP) and economic cost of food grains affect the level of subsidy. The CIPs for APL were last fixed in July 2001 and for BPL were last fixed in July 2000 (Table 1.2).

Table 1.2 PDS Issue Prices of Wheat and Rice

(Rs./quintal)

Year	Wheat	Per cent Change	Rice	Per cent Change
1997-98				
BPL	250	-	350	-
APL	450	-	700	-
1998-99				
BPL	250	0.0	350	0.0
APL	650	44.4	905	29.3
1999-2000				
BPL	250	0.0	350	0.0
APL	682	4.9	905	0.0
2000-01				
BPL	415	66.00	565	61.40
APL	830	21.70	1130	24.90
2001-02				
BPL	415	0.00	565	0.00
APL	610	-26.50	830	-26.50
2002-03				
		April		
BPL	415	0.00	565	0.00
APL	510	-16.40	730	-12.00
July				
BPL	415	0.00	565	0.00
APL	610	19.6	830	13.7

Source: *Economic Survey*.

1.7 Procurement of Food Grains, Off-take and Stocks

Food Grains Procurement

Procurement of food grains is one of the essential aspects of the food security policy of the Government. It serves the objective of providing price security to the farmers, which induces them to sustain production levels besides meeting the Government's objective of PDS as an instrument to protect the vulnerable sections against price volatility. Procurement prices are based on support prices announced by the Government. The Central government maintains food stocks which commensurate with the requirements of: (i) the prescribed minimum buffer stock for food security, (ii) operational stock for monthly releases of food grains for supply through the PDS, and (iii) market intervention stock for release in the open market to help moderate the open market prices.

Food Corporation of India is the Central government's nodal agency for food grains procurement, whereas National Agricultural Federation (NAFED) is the agency for undertaking price support for pulses, oilseeds and other products. Food grains trade is free and farmers are free to sell to private traders in case they receive prices higher than the Minimum Support Price. Each year, the Food Corporation procures roughly 15-20 per cent of India's wheat production and 12-15 per cent of rice production. Major contributors to central procurement are Punjab, Andhra Pradesh, Haryana and Uttar Pradesh. Andhra Pradesh, Punjab and Haryana are the major rice procuring states, while Punjab, Haryana and Uttar Pradesh account for the bulk of wheat procurement. Quantity procured under the central pool for different years is listed in Table 1.3.

Table 1.3 Procurement of Wheat and Rice (Central Pool)

(Million Tonnes)

Marketing Year	Wheat (April–March)		Rice (Oct.–Sept.)	
	Qty	% Change	Qty	% Change
1997-98	9.30	13.97	15.59	20.20
1998-99	12.65	36.02	12.60	19.18
1999-2000	14.14	11.78	18.23	44.68
2000-01	16.35	15.63	21.28	16.73
2001-02	20.63	26.18	22.13	3.99
2002-03	19.05	-7.66	16.42	-25.80
2003-04	15.80	-17.06	22.83	39.04
2004-05	16.80	6.33	14.34	-37.19
2005-06	14.79	-11.96	15.88*	10.74

Note: * As on January 18, 2006.

Source: Economic Survey.

It is evident from the above trends that procurement of wheat and rice increased from 1997-98 to 2001-02. Unusually high procurement of rice and wheat by FCI resulted in huge surplus stocks much above the buffer stock norms during the early years of 2000. Poor off-take of food grains under TPDS also aggravated this situation. However, the stocks eased in following years due to fall in procurement of both the commodities subsequently. In February 2006, the Government had to import five lakh tonnes of wheat to augment the domestic supplies because of fall in supply for the procurement. For better regional spread, procurement of rice was extended to non-traditional surplus states such as Chhattisgarh, Orissa and Tamil Nadu. As a result, the share of rice procurement from four traditional states of Andhra Pradesh, Haryana, Punjab and Uttar Pradesh declined to 71.5 per cent in 2004-05 down by 2 per cent points over 2003-04 (Table 1.4). Procurement of wheat, on the other hand, did not see such sharp trends towards non-traditional states.

Off-take and Measures to Liquidate Stocks

Over the last few years, while there had been excessive procurement of rice and wheat due to higher MSPs, off-take of food grains from the central pool had remained very poor. This led to the accumulation of huge surplus stocks of food grains. In an effort to encourage off-take and to liquidate the surplus stocks of food grains, various measures were adopted during 2001-02, which included open market sale at prices much below economic cost, lowering of issue price under targeted public distribution system (TPDS) for APL families, increasing of monthly allocation for APL, BPL and Antyodaya families to 35 kg per month per family and utilisation of food grains for various welfare schemes. The off-take situation thus improved from 2001-02 (Table 1.5).

Buffer Stocks

In addition to the requirements of wheat and rice under the Targeted Public Distribution System (TPDS), the central pool is required to have sufficient stocks in order to meet emergencies like drought/failure of crops, and undertake open market sale in case of sharp rise in market prices. Maintaining a buffer stock is an important constituent of the Government's food policy, as agriculture in India still remains dependent on the vagaries of nature. The buffer stock provides the basic and most flexible instrument for moderating short-term effects of supply or production shortfalls. The concept of a buffer stock was first introduced during the 4th Five Year Plan (1969-1974) and a buffer stock of five million tonnes of food grains was envisaged. The buffer stock figures are normally reviewed after every five years. The minimum buffer stock norms as well as actual stocks in the central pool at the beginning of the four quarters for 1997-2005 are given in Table 1.6.

Table 1.4 Procurement of Wheat and Rice from Different States

State/U.T.	Quantity (Lakh Tonnes)			Percentage Share		
	2002-03	2003-04	2004-05	2002-03	2003-04	2004-05
			Rice			
Andhra Pradesh	26.35	42.30	39.04	16.04	18.53	15.82
Bihar	1.59	3.63	3.43	0.97	1.59	1.39
Chhattisgarh	12.91	23.74	28.37	7.86	10.40	11.49
Haryana	13.24	13.34	16.62	8.06	5.84	6.73
Maharashtra	1.52	3.08	2.05	0.93	1.35	0.83
Orissa	8.90	13.73	15.90	5.42	6.02	6.44
Punjab	79.40	86.62	91.06	48.35	37.94	36.89
Tamil Nadu	1.07	2.07	6.52	0.65	0.91	2.64
Uttar Pradesh	13.60	25.54	29.71	8.28	11.19	12.04
West Bengal	1.26	9.25	9.44	0.77	4.05	3.82
Others	6.39	4.98	4.69	2.67	2.18	1.9
Total	166.23	228.28	246.83	100.00	100.00	100.00
			Wheat			
	2003-04	2004-05	2005-06	2003-04	2004-05	2005-06
Bihar	0.01	0.15	0.01	0.01	0.09	0.0
Haryana	51.22	51.15	45.30	32.42	30.46	30.6
Himachal Pradesh	0.01	0.00	0.00	0.01	0.00	0.0
Madhya Pradesh	1.88	3.49	4.80	1.19	2.08	3.3
Punjab	89.38	92.40	90.10	56.57	55.02	60.9
Rajasthan	2.59	2.79	1.60	1.64	1.66	1.1
Uttaranchal	0.67	0.54	0.40	0.42	0.32	0.3
Uttar Pradesh	12.13	17.41	5.60	7.68	10.37	3.8
Delhi	0.12	0.02	0.02	0.08	0.01	0.0
Total	158.01	167.95	147.83	100.00	100.00	100.0

Source: *Economic Survey.*

Table 1.5 Food Grains Allocation and Off-take under PDS

(Million Tonnes)

	Wheat		Rice	
Year	Allocation	Off-take	Allocation	Off-take
1997-98	10.11	7.08	12.83	9.90
1998-99	10.11	7.95	12.93	10.74
1999-2000	10.37	5.76	13.89	11.31
2000-01*	11.57	4.07	16.26	7.97
2001-02*	13.14	5.68	17.23	8.16
2002-03*	38.66	9.78	36.02	10.35
2003-04*	37.11	10.71	34.46	12.08
2004-05*				

Note: * Including Antyodaya.
Source: *Economic Survey.*

Table 1.6 Central Food Grain Stocks and Minimum Buffer Stock Norms

(Million Tonnes)

Beginning of the Month	Wheat		Rice		Total (Wheat & Rice)	
	Buffer Norm	Actual Stock	Buffer Norm	Actual Stock	Buffer Norm	Actual Stock
January 1997	7.7	7.1	7.7	12.9	15.4	20.0
April	3.7	3.2	10.8	13.2	14.5	16.4
July	13.1	11.4	9.2	11.0	22.3	22.4
October	10.6	8.3	6.0	7.0	16.6	15.3
January 1998	7.7	6.8	7.7	11.5	15.4	18.3
April	3.7	5.1	10.8	13.1	14.5	18.2
July	13.1	16.5	9.2	12.0	22.3	28.5
October	10.6	15.2	6.0	9.0	16.6	24.2
January 1999	8.4	12.7	8.4	11.7	16.8	24.4
April	4.0	9.7	11.8	12.2	15.8	21.9
July	14.3	22.5	10.0	10.6	24.3	33.1
October	11.6	20.3	6.5	7.7	18.1	28.0
January 2000	8.4	17.2	8.4	14.2	16.8	31.4
April	4.0	13.2	11.8	15.7	15.8	21.7
July	14.3	27.8	10.0	14.5	24.3	42.2
October	11.6	26.9	6.5	13.2	18.1	40.1
January 2001	8.4	25.0	8.4	20.7	16.8	45.7
April	4.0	21.5	11.8	23.2	15.8	44.7
July	14.3	38.9	10.0	22.8	24.3	61.7
October	11.6	36.8	6.5	21.5	18.1	58.3
January 2002 (P)	8.4	32.4	8.4	25.6	16.8	58.0
April	4.0	26.0	11.8	24.9	15.8	50.9
July	14.3	41.1	10.0	21.9	24.3	63.0
October	11.6	35.6	6.5	15.8	18.1	51.4
January 2003 (P)	8.4	28.8	8.4	19.4	16.8	48.2
April	4.0	15.6	11.8	17.2	15.8	32.8
July	14.3	24.2	10.0	11.0	24.3	35.2
October	11.6	18.4	6.5	5.2	18.1	23.6
January 2004(P)	8.4	12.7	8.4	11.7	16.8	24.4
April	4.0	6.9	11.8	13.1	15.8	20.0
July	14.3	19.1	10.0	10.8	24.3	29.9
October	11.6	14.2	6.5	6.0	18.1	20.2
January 2005(P)	8.4	8.9	8.4	12.8	16.8	21.7
April	4.1	4.0	12.2	13.3	16.2	17.4
July	17.1	14.5	9.8	10.1	26.9	24.5
October	11.0	10.3	5.2	4.8	16.2	15.1

Note: P: Figures from 2002 onwards provisional.
Source: *Economic Survey*.

In a normal year, higher level of stock buildup leads to higher subsidies through higher carrying costs. Therefore, the buffer stock policy of the Government should ensure that the food grains stocks do not cross the norms for that year beyond a reasonable margin. Actual stocks of wheat and rice have consistently remained higher than the corresponding buffer stock norms during 2001-02, 2002-03, 2003-04 and the first three-quarters of 2004-05. During July 2005, for the first time since 2001-2002, the actual stocks of food grains fell short of the buffer norms by almost 2.4 million tonnes. The shortfall in stocks however, came down to only 1.1 million tonnes in October 2005. This shortfall is due to a shortfall of 0.7 million tonnes in wheat and 0.4 million tonnes in rice. However, the present shortfall in the stocks over the buffer stocks norms is not considered alarming and appears sufficient to meet the requirements under TPDS, welfare schemes and open market sales during the current financial year. This shortfall is expected to lead to a reduction in carrying costs and the subsidies' bill of the government.

1.8 Food Subsidy

The food security system in the country, which has the dual objective of providing minimum nutritional support to the poor at an affordable price and ensuring price stability in different parts of the country (by supplying food grains to the deficient areas), involves subsidy from the exchequer. Producers and consumers and, within this group the vulnerable sections of the society are the major beneficiaries of food subsidy. The subsidy incurred on the supply of food grains through the PDS at below FCI's economic cost constituents the consumer subsidy while the producer subsidy is the direct offshoot of the price support based procurement operations of the Government. The producer subsidy together with the cost of maintaining the buffer stock accounts for the cost of buffer stock operations. The consumer subsidy together with the buffer carrying cost constitutes the food subsidy.

Food subsidy shows an annual increase of above 27 per cent during each of the three years namely 2000-01, 2001-02 and 2002-2003. The annual increase came down to 4.1 per cent during 2003-04 and is expected to further decelerate to 2.54 per cent in 2004-05 (RE) (Table 1.7). Attainment of self-sufficiency in food grains production (with implication for reduced need for price stabilisation operations) and reduction in the proportion of people belonging to the BPL category should actually lead to decline in the levels of food subsidy. There is also unanimity that the targeting of food subsidy leaves a lot of scope for improvement.

Table 1.7 Growth of Food Subsidy in India

Year	Food Subsidy*(Rs. Crore)	Annual Growth (per cent)	As Per cent of GDP
1997-98	7900	30.23	0.52
1998-99	9100	15.19	0.52
1999-2000	9434	3.67	0.48$
2000-01	12060	27.84	0.57$
2001-02	17499	45.10	0.77$
2002-03	24176	38.16	0.98$
2003-04	25160	4.07	0.91$
2004-05 (RE)	25800	2.54	0.83$
2003-04 (BE)	26200	1.55	-

Note: * Other than that on sugar.
$ As a per cent of GDP (new series based on 1999-2000).

Source: *Economic Survey*.

1.9 Need for an Evaluation of PDS[2]

Public Distribution System (PDS) evolved as a major instrument of the Government's economic policy for ensuring availability of food grains to the public at affordable prices. This was with the express objective of providing food security for the poor. The system is also an important constituent of the strategy for poverty eradication and is intended to serve as a safety net for the poor whose number is substantially high and who are nutritionally at risk. PDS with a network of about 4.77 lakh Fair Price Shops (FPS) is perhaps the largest distribution network of its type in the world.

PDS is operating under the joint responsibility of the Central and the State Governments. The Central government has taken the responsibility for procurement, storage, transportation and bulk allocation of food grains. The responsibility for distributing the same to the consumers through the network of FPSs lies with the State Governments. The operational responsibilities including allocation within the states, identification of beneficiaries, issuance of ration cards, supervision and monitoring the functioning of FPSs rest with the State Governments. While responsibility of supplying the essential commodities, *viz.*, wheat, rice, sugar, kerosene, edible oils and soft coke remains with the Central government, the State Governments have the option to add other items considered essential by them. There are three types of cardholder categories, *viz.*, Above Poverty Line (APL), Below Poverty Line (BPL) and Antyodaya Anna Yojana (AAY—the poorest of the poor).

2. For review of literature, see Annexture A-1.1.

Certain inadequacies have been identified in the system. It has been alleged by some quarters that the allotted food grains fail to reach the identified cardholders. In view of these allegations, the Department of Food and Public Distribution, Government of India decided to verify the veracity of such a charge. In this respect, the Department entrusted a study to the NCAER to carry out a concurrent evaluation of TPDS in selected districts of some states in two phases.

1.10 Main Objectives

The main objective of the evaluation study is to examine the extent to which food grains disbursed under the TPDS are actually reaching the BPL and AAY categories of population in the country and the incidence as well as the mode of irregularities in the system. The proposed research study focuses on the following issues involving specific research queries:

1. *Identification of BPL and AAY beneficiaries*: Attempts will be made to find out deviations (if any) in the selection process of beneficiaries from the norms laid down by the Central government. Analysis pertaining to the income pattern and consumption volatility of cardholders will be carried out to gauge the inability of income to cover consumption and the magnitude of risk.
2. *The distribution system of food grains to the consumers by fair price shop dealers:* The main thrust of analysis would be to examine whether food grains are distributed by the FPSs regularly and as per the requirement of the beneficiaries and adhering to the norms prescribed by the Government. The analysis will throw light on simple questions: (a) how good or how bad are the FPSs in providing insurance (in the form of regular supply of food grains) to the beneficiaries against severe income fluctuations? (b) Is there any diversion of food grains from the distribution system?
3. *Off-take of food grains from FPSs by BPL and AAY categories of households*: It has been seen that BPL/AAY cardholders often purchase food grains from shops in the market and not from FPSs. The analysis would cull out the underlying reasons for not lifting food grains from FPSs.
4. *Quality of food grains at FPSs*: The study would investigate into the quality of food grains distributed through FPSs in the light of supplies received from FCI depots.
5. *Availability of food grains at FCI depots*: The analysis would focus on the availability of food grains at FCI depots in the states. The distribution system of food grains from the FCI depots to the FPSs would be evaluated on the basis of its regularity. Attempts will be made to capture the incidence of diversion of food grains (if any) from the FCI depots.

1.11 Approach and Methodology

The study is carried out with the help of primary survey. The target groups for the survey include: (a) APL, BPL and AAY cardholders, (b) FPSs, (c) State Food and Civil Supplies Department, (d) Food Corporation of India. Survey of the APL, BPL and AAY cardholders captures the irregularities at the micro-level in terms of identification of beneficiaries and timeliness of the supply. This also captures whether the beneficiaries are supplied with food grains according to the prescribed norms. This in turn will help in identifying the deviations (if any) within the supply mechanism. Monthly survey for a period of consecutive six months enables us to capture the time variants with regard to requirement of the beneficiaries (income pattern and consumption volatility) as well as access and availability of the food security. The supply chain mechanism and its effectiveness and efficiencies is studied through information collected through interactions with selected FPSs, State Food and Civil Supplies Department and Food Corporation of India. These interactions try to identify the anomalies between the prescribed norms and the real life situation exiting in case of PDS in terms of quality and quantity of supply of food grains. An in-depth survey of the APL, BPL and AAY cardholders was conducted with the help of structured questionnaire which addresses the above mentioned issues of the proposed study. The methodology details of field survey are explained in the following paragraphs.

Sampling Design

The present study is based on a large primary survey. In consonance with the Ministry, the following six states are selected for the study: Assam, Mizoram, UP, Bihar, Chhattisgarh and Rajasthan. From each selected state, five districts in the geographical regions of North, South, East, West and Central were selected for drawing the sample. After selecting districts, one block was selected from each district. The selection criterion for the block was based on the issuance of number of BPL cards. After collecting the list of all blocks in the selected districts, a particular block that had issued the largest number of BPL cards was selected for our sampling purpose. In this way, we selected 5 blocks from each state, thus total 30 blocks were selected for drawing sample. A total number of 200 households were surveyed for detailed information from each selected block. In this fashion, a total number of 6000 households (30*200) were surveyed for a consecutive six months' period. The proportion of BPL and APL households are done in the ratio of 80 and 20. Thereby, 4800 selected households belong to BPL and rest 1200 are APL. Out of the selected BPL households, the proportion of BPL and AAY is in the ratio of 77 and 23 (as that is the ratio of total existing number of BPL and AAY card holders in the country). Thus, the approximate number of BPL households is 3700, AAY is 1100 and APL is 1200 (there are minor changes in the numbers depending on the field circumstances). Keeping into account the proportion of rural and urban population in the country, an approximate ratio of 80/20 is adopted for drawing sample from the rural and urban areas. Thus, out of 6000 households, 4800 are selected from the village areas and 1200 are selected from the urban areas. The distribution of sample in APL, BPL and AAY for the urban and rural is done following the same criterion mentioned above. For selecting village and households, the following procedure was followed.

Selection of Village and Households

From each selected block, the list of villages with the number of BPL cards was obtained from the respective block officers. From each block, four villages were selected based on geographic location of the villages as well as the number of cards issued at the village level. Forty households were selected from each village. In the case of urban areas, one big city or two small towns were chosen for drawing a sample of 40 households from the selected city or two towns of each block. After selecting village, the list of cardholders was obtained from the District Rural Development Agency (DRDA) or village head or *gram sabha* etc., (whoever was the designated authority). The households from each strata (APL, BPL, AAY) were selected on a random basis. Additional information on different aspects of the study was also obtained from the FPS and Civil Supplies Departments in the states.

In each state, 5 blocks were selected from 5 districts. A sample of 200 BPL/AAY cardholders in each block was interviewed. Districts and blocks were selected based on the number of cardholders in these two categories. In each block, cardholders were selected randomly on the basis of the list provided by the concerned state government departments. The sample cardholders represent both rural and urban population. Information was collected on monthly basis and the evaluation process was carried out for a period of 6 months. A total number of 6000 sample cardholders were interviewed consecutively for 6 months during the entire survey period. Interactions with FCI, State Food and Civil Supplies Department and FPSs were based on semi-structured questionnaire addressing the relevant issues mentioned in the preceding section. The survey was carried during the financial year 2006-07. The details of district and blocks selected and the sample drawn is given in Annexure Table A-1.1.

Figure 1.1 Rajasthan District Map

Figrue 1.2 Chhattisgarh District Map

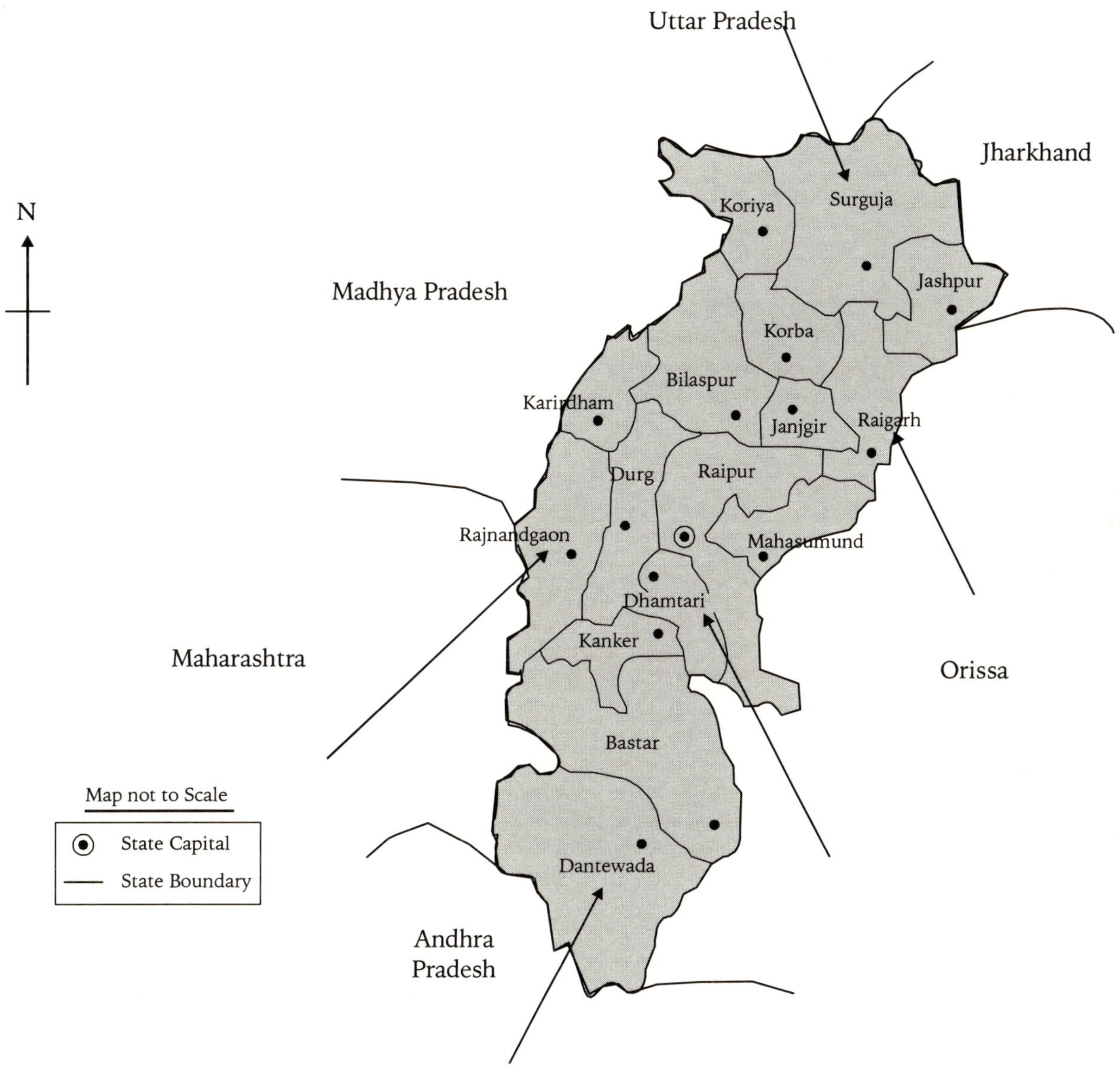

Figure 1.3 Bihar District Map

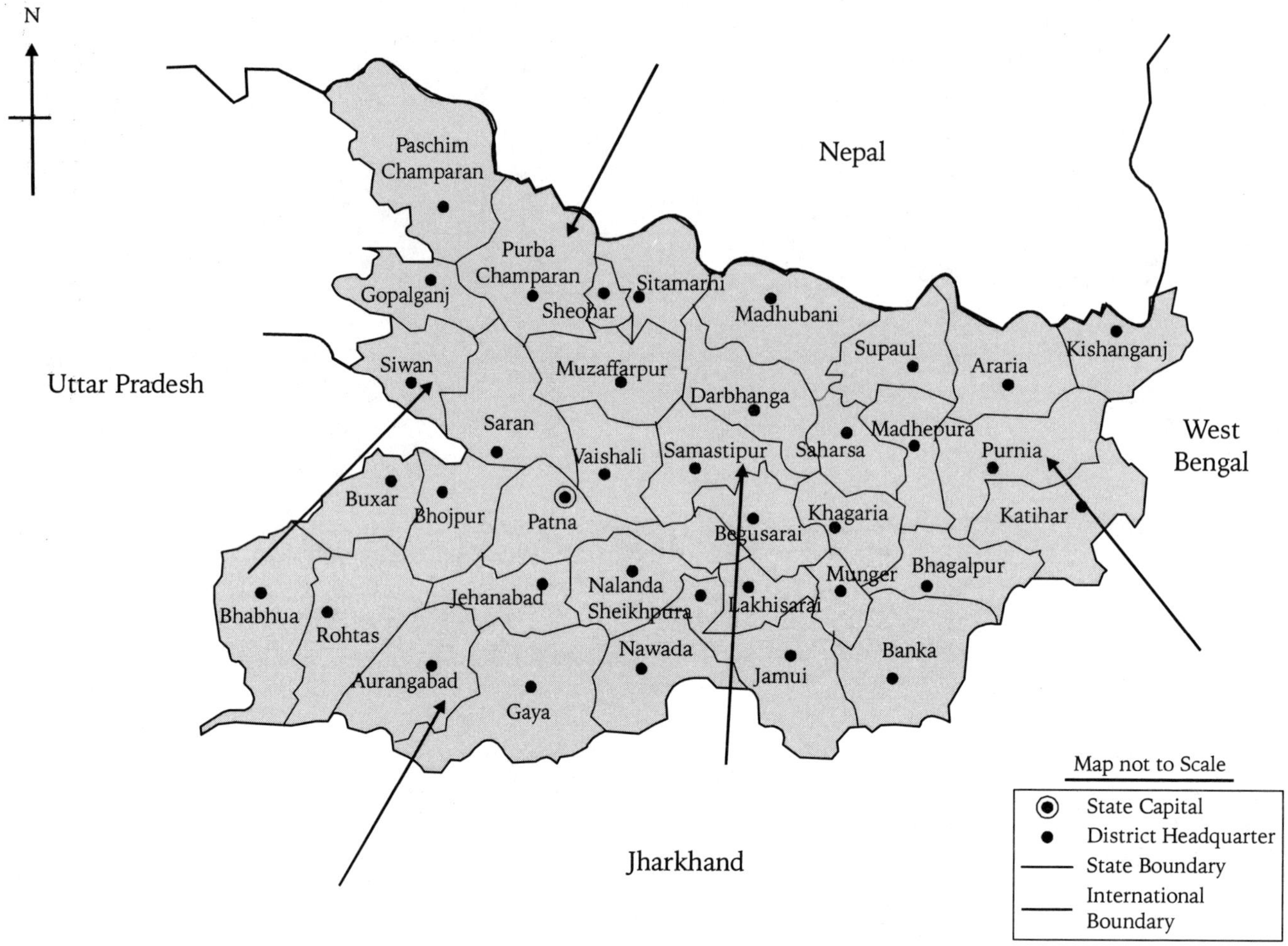

Figure 1.4 Uttar Pradesh District Map

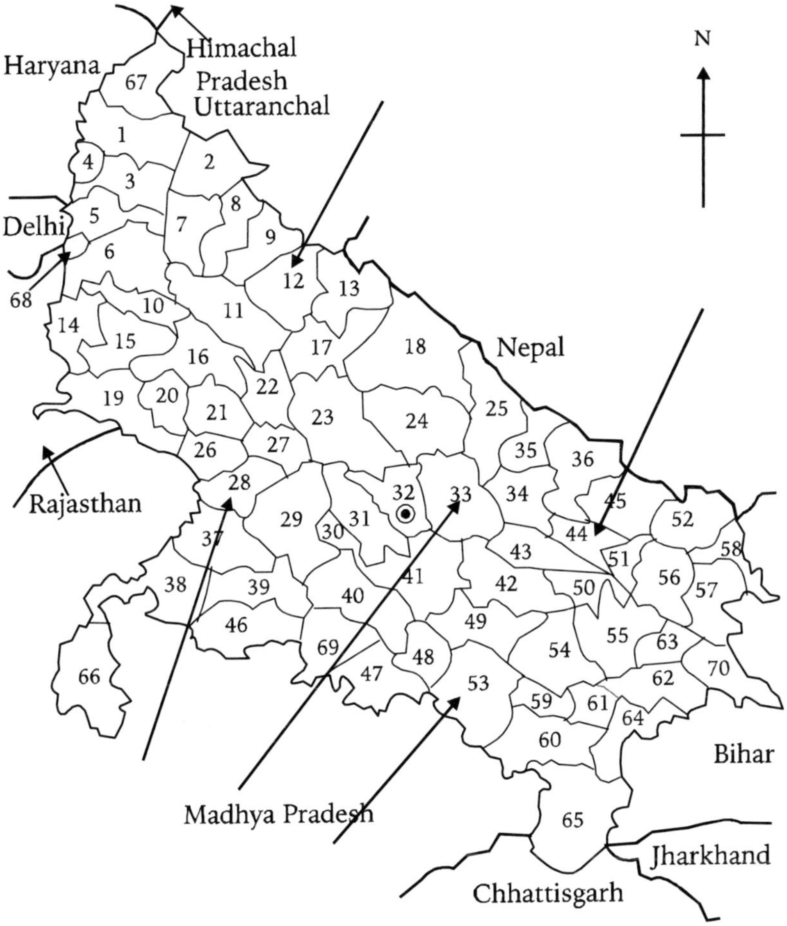

1. Muzaffarnagar
2. Bijnor
3. Meerut
4. Baghpat
5. Ghaziabad
6. Bulandshahar
7. Jyotiba Phule Nagar
8. Moradabad
9. Rampur
10. Aligarh
11. Budaun
12. Bareilly
13. Pilibhit
14. Mathura
15. Hathras
16. Etah
17. Shahjahanpur
18. Lakhimpur Kheri
19. Agra
20. Firozabad
21. Mainpuri
22. Farrukhabad
23. Hardoi
24. Sitapur
25. Bahraich
26. Etawah
27. Kannauj
28. Auraiya
29. Kanpur(Rural)
30. Kanpur(Urban)
31. Unnao
32. Lucknow
33. Barabanki
34. Gonda
35. Shravasti
36. Balrampur
37. Jalaun
38. Jhansi
39. Hamirpur
40. Fatehpur
41. Rae Bareli
42. Sultanpur
43. Faizabad
44. Basti
45. Siddharth Nagar
46. Mahoba
47. Chitrakoot
48. Kaushambi
49. Pratapgarh
50. Ambedkar Nagar
51. Sant Kabir Nagar
52. Maharajganj
53. Allahabad
54. Jaunpur
55. Azamgarh
56. Gorakhpur
57. Deoria
58. Kushi Nagar
59. Sant Ravidas Nagar
60. Mirzapur
61. Varanasi
62. Ghazipur
63. Mau (Maunath Bhanjan)
64. Chandauli
65. Sonbhadra
66. Lalitpur
67. Saharanpur
68. Gautam Buddha Nagar
69. Banda
70. Ballia

Map not to Scale

◉	State Capital
—— (thin)	State Boundary
—— (thick)	International Boundary

Figure 1.5 Assam District Map

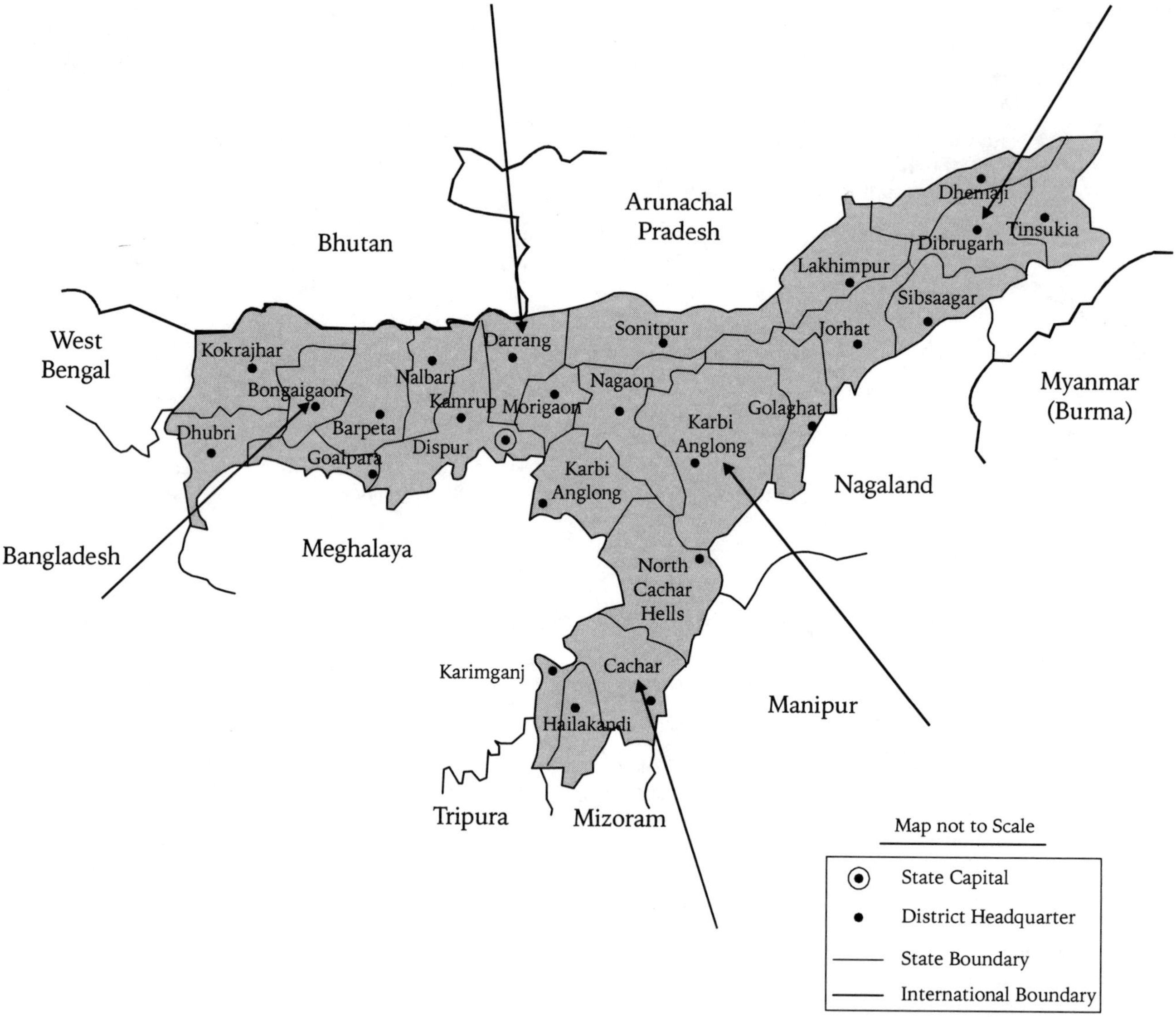

Figure 1.6 Mizoram District Map

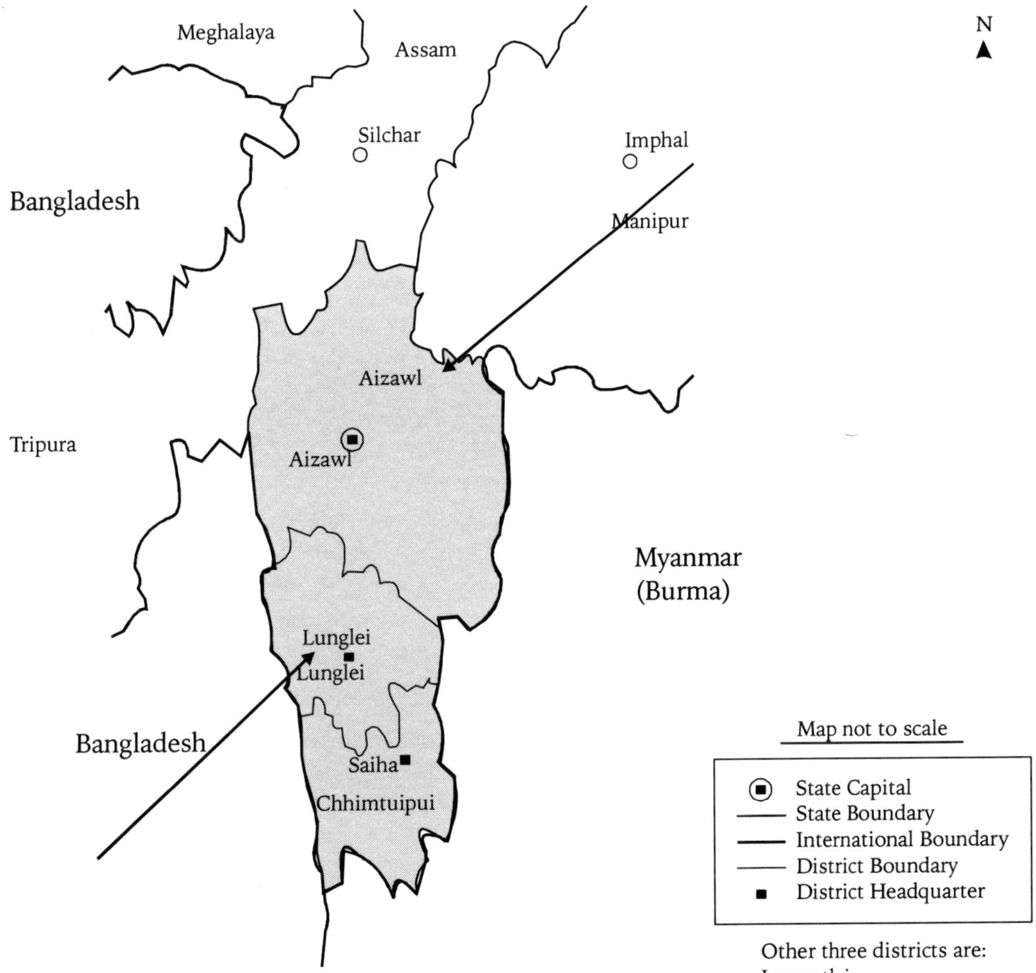

Other three districts are:
Lawngtlai
Mamit
Champhai

Annexure A-1.1: Review of Literature

Public Distribution System (PDS) has remained an important instrument of the government food policy. A vast literature is available on different aspects of PDS. To begin with, on the issue of the rationale of public distribution system in food grains, while scholars like Pigou (1952), Johnston (1953), Mellor (1966), Gulati and Krishnan (1975), Saran (1975), Jha (1976) and Houthakar (1976) have advocated for the system on grounds of social equity and economic efficiency, the critics like Cummings (1967), Lele (1973), Shenoy (1974) and a few others demonstrated the superior efficiency of the market mechanism in distributing the available supplies of food grains. More recent studies on PDS in India especially in the 1980s and 1990s have concentrated on the issues bringing on regional variations in the supply of food grains through PDS (Tyagi, 1990), urban bias in PDS (Howes and Jha, 1992), targeting of PDS (Jha, 1991; Dev and Suryanarayana, 1992) and growing cost of food subsidy (Parikh, 1994). Some other studies measured the welfare gains from PDS. The welfare gains include the extent of income transfer to the poor through PDS and the consequential reduction in poverty and the extent of nutritional support to the poor. Some of the relevant studies done in the recent past are reviewed in the following paragraphs.

Kirit Parikh (1994) in his study on effectiveness of PDS used NSS 42nd Round data (1986-87) to examine the coverage of cereals distributed through the PDS. The study also estimated the implicit subsidy involved. He observed that cereals distributed through PDS were not targeted to the poor. In almost all states, persons belonging to the bottom 70 per cent of the population got more or less the same amount. There was a large difference across various states in coverage under the PDS. In states like Punjab, Haryana, UP, Bihar, Orissa and MP, more than 90 per cent of the population did not purchase any cereals from the PDS. Barring AP and Kerala, the levels of implicit subsidy were very low except for a small fraction of the households in a few more states. On cost effectiveness, he observed that for every rupee spent, less than 22 paise reached the poor in all states, except in Goa, Daman and Diu where 28 paise reached the poor. The study observed that PDS was a blunt instrument for providing income support to the poor and unless effective targeting was carried out, it would continue to remain so. The author suggests that providing income support to the poor would be more effective if we combine the Employment Guarantee Scheme (EGS) with the PDS by giving food stamps in addition to normal wages only to those who are employed in EGS. He pinpointed that there was a strong case for withdrawing all subsidies from PDS excepting for those who work on employment schemes, and putting the money saved in additional allocation for self-targeting schemes such as JRY.

Radhakrishna and Subbarao (1997) estimated the impact of PDS on poor households in terms of income gains, reductions in the incidence and severity of poverty as well as nutritional improvements. They also assessed the cost effectiveness of PDS and evaluated the rice subsidy programme in Andhra Pradesh. Their findings suggest that the welfare gains of PDS in terms of income transfer were very meagre and its impact on poverty and nutritional status was abysmal. Even the meagre transfer benefits were realised at an exorbitant cost. They observed that only in four states, namely Andhra Pradesh, Karnataka, Kerala and Gujarat, the income gains to the poor were substantially higher than the national average but some of these states had expended additional resources of their own on the PDS programme. On the cost efficiency of PDS, they observed that at Central government costs, an amount of Rs. 4.27 was incurred to transfer one rupee of income to the poor. With combined state and Central level costs, one rupee of income was transferred at a cost of Rs. 6.35 in AP while the cost could be even higher in administratively weaker states. In comparison to with other anti-poverty programmes like ICDS and various employment programmes, PDS turned out to be the costliest. Reviewing the cross-country experience, they observed that no particular targeting method was found to be perfect but even the imperfectly targeted programmes proved better in reaching the poor and keeping the costs down than completely open-ended programmes. Tying beneficiary participation to food transfers lowers not only leakage but may also lower the economic costs associated with work disincentives. The study recommended to introduce food stamps or vouchers and link such food voucher programme with other employment and nutrition programmes for better targeting without incurring additional costs.

Raghbendra Jha *et al.* (1999) evaluated the policy and rationale for the then allocation pattern of rice and wheat through PDS in India on the basis of the notion of providing a real consumption subsidy. They found that the policy of food grains allocation was very ad hoc with allocation being fixed on a historical basis. The paper used four sets of pooled equations for predicting stable levels of per capita consumption of rice and wheat in physical terms in rural and urban India using NSS data for the 45th Round, 47th Round and 48th Round. Food grain demand and the own-price, cross-price and income elasticities of demand were estimated for all states. They observed that the allocation pattern appeared to ignore the structure of consumption demand in the country. The paper therefore, proposed an alternative formulation based on the concept of subsidising real consumption through PDS.

Dutta and Ramaswami (2001) in their paper on targeting and efficiency of the PDS, compared distribution of rice and wheat in Andhra Pradesh and Maharashtra based on the 50th Round NSS household data on consumption. The authors examined differences in utilisation, extent of targeting, magnitude of income transfers and the costeffectiveness of food subsidies. The major findings of the studies were the following: A significantly greater proportion of the population used the PDS in AP as compared to Maharashtra. The geographical coverage was universal in the case of AP whereas 30 per cent of the poor in Maharashtra were excluded because of lack of coverage. Errors of exclusion were much lower in AP especially in rural parts and poor people received a substantially higher subsidy per capita than the poor in Maharashtra. Errors of inclusion were highest in rural Andhra as non-poor received sizeable subsidy benefits. In urban Andhra Pradesh, the higher income groups received negligible subsidies and errors of inclusion were lowest. In Maharashtra also, the errors of inclusion were lowest in urban areas. The non-poor in urban and rural Maharashtra received subsidies of about the same magnitude as the poor. In terms of targeting, urban AP was the only sector that appeared ideal although that was not because of the targeting schemes but because of the lower utilisation of the PDS by higher income group, as compared to the poor. The relatively rich voluntarily opted out of the programme because of a number of reasons such as transaction costs, preference for higher quality grain available from private traders etc. The paper questions whether the PDS is an efficient mechanism for redistribution as the cost of delivering a rupee of subsidy to the bottom 40 per cent was more than Rs. 3 in both states. About the (targeted) TPDS, the authors argue that the task of State Governments to identify and distinguish between below and above poverty line households seems formidable if not impossible since many of the poor receive incomes from activities that are irregular, seasonal and unrecorded. The authors expressed apprehension about the success of the new strategy of targeted PDS in improving the efficiency of food subsidies in reaching the poor. The authors suggested that if subsidies were restricted to inferior goods, the relatively rich will voluntarily opt out of the programme and no costly and necessarily imperfect administrative mechanism is required to implement targeting. Therefore, they emphasised on self-targeting to minimise errors of inclusion.

Analysing the vagaries in the system of public distribution in Bihar, Jos Mooij (2001) found that there was large-scale misappropriation of food grains. The distribution of cards to BPL families was unsatisfactory. The author observed that corruption was the main problem in Bihar and almost all sections of society including the civil servants and politicians were all afflicted with this malady. The author argued that while many people benefited from the present set-up, there were also people within almost all categories of stakeholders who were dissatisfied with the large-scale misappropriation of food grains. The author admitted that there was a lot of scope for change, but change required strategic political manoeuvering and initially a low-key approach was to be maintained in order not to awaken and antagonising strong vested interests.

The paper by Jha and Srinivasan (2001) examines the costs and benefits of PDS. The authors find that in spite of incurring enormous tangible and intangible costs, the effectiveness of PDS in providing food security to the poor has been low under the system of universal provision of food subsidies. A large proportion of food subsidy goes to the non-poor and a large amount of grain leaks into the open market due to corruption. The rising costs of operation also make the system increasingly fiscally unsustainable. Even in the case of targeted PDS, the authors observed that the cost effectiveness of this (new) system appeared to be low partly due to the fact that several indirect benefits of the system went unaccounted. The introduction of TPDS has added to the rising food subsidy bill as off-take to the APL families has fallen because of narrow gap between the ration price and market price. The off-take from the BPL allocation has been impressive but a large part of the grains are diverted to the black market. TPDS has thus neither succeeded in reducing the food subsidy bill, nor in reaching food subsidies to a greater proportion of the poor. The paper examines the inefficiencies in the system by comparing costs of public storage and distribution operations with those of private agents and discusses how the rising government costs can be curtailed by making administration more efficient and relying on market forces for spatial distribution of grain. The paper also examines the potential for geographic targeting.

Ravi Srivastava (2001) in his study on rural Uttar Pradesh brought out some of the dilemmas confronting PDS policy. He suggested that the system might need some significant changes to effectively meet the challenge of providing food security to the rural poor. He observed that the evidence from rural UP showed that the percentage of excluded households was indeed very high in the state. About the universal PDS, he observed that as the government mounts an all or nothing strategy, the costs of exclusion mounted for those households who were left out of the net. He suggested that Antyodaya scheme should be used in conjunction with a more broad-based PDS scheme, which can use some other self-selecting criteria such as distribution of low quality rice to keep diversions low. Further, food stamps or grain passbooks could meet the poor's need more flexibly, with less distortion and leakage and therefore, could be tried out.

Kripa Shankar (2004) examined the efficiency of TPDS (targeted public distribution system) in tribal belts of southeastern Uttar Pradesh. This study was based on a primary survey of 593 households from 21 villages with majority of households belonging to BPL cards and a few others with Antyodaya and Annapurna cards. The author observed that despite acute poverty 73 per cent of the BPL cardholders did not purchase any food grains from PDS. As majority of the households were casual workers, they could not afford to visit the fair price shop that hardly opened for a few days in a month and at times even if it was opened, there was nothing in the stock. Another principal reason for not buying from the PDS was that households consumed what is locally called *khudi*, a small broken rice that was cheaper than the PDS rice. In the case of Antyodaya households also, only 28 per cent of the households succeeded in getting food grains every month of the year. Rest of the households got it less than 11 months in a year's time. Annapurna faired better with all households getting 90 per cent of their entitlement. The author concluded that the TPDS has not helped to provide food security to vulnerable households in the absence of assured regular income. Therefore, the policy measures should be directed at providing income opportunities in the vulnerable areas.

ORG (2005) completed a recent study on evaluation of TPDS and AAY. This study was based on a large survey of 25004 respondents across 35 states and union territories. The study observed that 27 per cent of APL ration cardholders were actually designated BPL in the village list. The error was much less in the case of BPL and AAY households, 1.3 and 1.1 per cent, respectively. About the accessibility, 30 per cent APL households, 3/4th BPL households and more than 90 per cent AAY households reported purchasing all commodities (food grains, sugar and kerosene) from ration shops. About the extent of diversion, the study found that overall diversion of rice and wheat at all India level was 39 and 53 per cent, respectively. The diversion was high in northeastern states, *viz.*, Manipur, Nagaland, Meghalaya and Mizoram and low in southern states, *viz.*, Andhra Pradesh, Tamil Nadu, Karnataka and Kerala. The authors observed that less than 50 per cent of the households' requirement is being supplied through PDS, not because of low quota but because in most cases, full quota is not being made available. The study suggests to encourage community-based storage facilities so that distribution and availability problem can be tackled from the grassroots. The study finds that AAY scheme has been fairly successful with 85 per cent households lifting rice and therefore, the scheme needs to be further highlighted and expanded. Finally, the policy suggestions are that for better utilisation TPDS distribution should be linked more with food for work schemes, thus getting more supplies to the needy and saving cash outflow on wage payments.

Another recent study by the Planning Commission (2005) evaluated the performance of TPDS system. The relevant data for the study was collected from 3600 households spread over 18 states in 60 districts throughout the country. In addition, information was collected from the village *panchayats* and 240 fair price shops. The major findings of the study are summarised below. Taking into account all the inefficiencies of PDS the study observed that the Government of India spends Rs. 3.65 to transfer Re. 1 to the poor. The study observed that about 57 per cent of subsidised grains do not reach the target group and around 36 per cent of that siphon off the supply chain. The implementation of PDS was found to be plagued by large errors of exclusion and inclusion. The researchers found that PDS was a less efficient mode of income transfer to the poor. The economic cost of grains was higher than the market price in most of the states. About the viability of the fair price shops (FPS), only 23 per cent of sample FPS were found to be viable while rest of all survived only through leakage and diversions of subsidised grains. The major problem faced by FPS was the irregular delivery of quota. The study suggested that to make the delivery system effective and efficient, the following steps were needed: ensure timely door step delivery of FPS quota; rationalising the cost structure of handling food grains though public agencies; make FPS functionally viable; involve PRIs effectively; and bring in transparency through e-governance.

Besides these studies on functioning of the PDS, some other studies have focused on risk and insurance, bringing forth the spotlight on the fact that income risks are pervasive in poor rural economies. These studies including Alderman and Paxson (1992), Deaton (1992), Fafchamps (1992), Grimard (1997), Morduch (1995) and Townsend (1994, 1995) lead to the question of how well households in rural economies are able to insure consumption against such shocks to income. They have concluded that households take action aimed at protecting consumption by drawing on both private and social risk sharing arrangements. Townsend (1994) lists five potential risk bearing mechanisms as: (i) Spatial diversification of land holdings; (ii) Storage of grains from one year to the next; (iii) Purchases and sales of assets such as bullocks and land; (iv) Credit from formal and informal sources; and (v) Gifts and transfers within the family networks. However, not all households are equally able to insure consumption against income shocks and differentiated access to markets, particularly financial markets result in differential ability of households to insure against income shocks.

Different versions of empirical specifications of risk and insurance have been tested by the researchers using household level data from both developed and developing countries. Mace (1991) in her study on risk sharing in the US economy finds that the evidence is conditional on the preference specification. Results are mostly consistent with consumption insurance for the exponential utility specification but not for the power utility specification. Townsend (1995) finds overwhelming rejection of the null hypothesis of no insurance for different regions in Thailand. His results confirm that consumption in one region or state tracks income in that region indicating some sort of insurance does exist. Deaton (1992) using data from Cote d'Ivoire finds that marginal propensities to consume out of current income are always positive and significant. In somewhat a similar case, Jalan and Ravallion (1999) using data from rural China, observe evidences of partial insurance of certain wealth groups while evidences of rejection of full insurance were strongest for the poorest wealth groups. In the case of rural India, Townsend (1994) using ICRISAT data for three villages to study risk and insurance observed that full consumption insurance was a fairly good benchmark. He observed that landless households were less well insured than their counterpart cultivators. However, in the case of rural Punjab, Maitra (1998) observed no evidence in favour of consumption insurance against income shocks. Yet another study by Maitra (2003) using ARIS-NCAER data show that the null hypothesis of full insurance is rejected both for the population as a whole and for the different land classes. The estimated marginal propensity to consume out of idiosyncratic changes in income is significantly higher for the poorer households compared to the richer households.

The implications of the income and consumption insurance are quite significant for the policy matter in the case of targeted public distribution system (TPDS). The purpose of making PDS system targeted was implicitly to reduce the risk of income shock being transferred into consumption shocks. In other words, aim of such welfare-oriented programmes was to provide a safety net to the poor households. In our analysis part, we make an attempt to find out how successful have been the policy of TPDS in the selected states in mitigating such risks and providing safety net to the vulnerable sections of our society, namely that of BPL and AAY cardholders.

Annexure Table A-1.1 Details of Districts, Blocks and Households Selected

State	District	Block	Village/Town	APL	BPL	AAY	Total
	1. Baran	Kishanganj	Chinod	8	25	7	40
			Ranibrod	8	25	7	40
			Bhanwargarh	8	25	7	40
			Jalwara	8	25	7	40
			Kishanganj	8	25	7	40
	2. Ganganagar	Anupgarh	27 A	8	25	7	40
			1 LSM (Panda Colony)	8	25	7	40
			22 A	8	25	7	40
			4 KAM (Khal)	8	25	7	40
			Anupgarh	8	25	7	40
Rajasthan	3. Jodhpur	Mandore	Keru	8	25	7	40
			Jajiwal	8	25	7	40
			Khokhriya	8	25	7	40
			Banad	8	25	7	40
			Jodhpur	8	25	7	40
	4. Pali	Bali	Dhani	8	25	7	40
			Boya	8	25	7	40
			Khudala	8	25	7	40
			Sesali	8	25	7	40
			Bali	8	25	7	40
	5. Banswara	Garhi	Sagwadiya	8	25	7	40
			Bhimsaur	8	25	7	40
			Karanpur	8	25	7	40
			Babisaredi	8	25	7	40
			Partapur	8	25	7	40
	Gross Total			200	625	175	1000

State	District	Block	Village/Town	APL	BPL	AAY	Total
	1. Dhamtari	Dhamtari	Chaati	8	25	7	40
			Kandel	8	25	7	40
			Gangrel	8	25	7	40
			Khartuli	8	25	7	40
			Dhamtari	8	25	7	40
	2. Surguja	Ambikapur	Sargawa	8	25	7	40
			Manikprakashpur	8	25	7	40
			Darina	8	25	7	40
			Labji	8	25	7	40
			Ambikapur	8	25	7	40
Chhattisgarh	3. Raigarh	Raigarh	Gerwani	8	25	7	40
			Kotmar	8	25	7	40
			Kotra	8	25	7	40
			Kashichua	8	25	7	40
			Raigarh	8	25	7	40
	4. Rajnandgaon	Rajnandgaon	Sukuldehan	8	25	7	40
			Amlidihit Dhaba	8	25	7	40
			Bharregaon	8	25	7	40
			Baghera	8	25	7	40
			Rajnandgaon	8	25	7	40
	5. Dantewada	Dantewada	Teknar	8	25	7	40
			Metapal	8	25	7	40
			Dhurli	8	25	7	40
			Keshavpur	8	25	7	40
			Dantewada	8	25	7	40
	Gross Total			200	625	175	1000

State	District	Block	Village/Town	APL	BPL	AAY	Total
	1. Bareilly	Alampur Jafrabad	Kaemua	8	24	8	40
			Chakarpur	8	24	8	40
			Champatpur	8	24	8	40
			Bamiyana	8	24	8	40
			Aampur Jasrabad	8	24	8	40
	2. Auraiya	Auraiya	Kakhawatu	8	24	8	40
			Khanpur	8	24	8	40
			Jaitapur	8	24	8	40
			Madhupur	8	24	8	40
			Auraiya	8	24	8	40
Uttar Pradesh	3. Barabanki	Haidergarh	Gaura	8	24	8	40
			Rithi Sikanderpur	8	24	8	40
			Bara	8	24	8	40
			Pecharuwa	8	24	8	40
			Haidergarh	8	24	8	40
	4. Basti	Harriya	Thanakhas	8	24	8	40
			Mauadabad	8	24	8	40
			Barapur	8	24	8	40
			Gangarpur	8	24	8	40
			Harriya	8	24	8	40
	5. Allahabad	Kaurihar	Kanjia	8	24	8	40
			Chasri Uparhar	8	24	8	40
			Hathigahan	8	24	8	40
			Samhai	8	24	8	40
			Kaurihar	8	24	8	40
	Gross Total			200	600	200	1000

State	District	Block	Village/Town	APL	BPL	AAY	Total
	1. Aurangabad	Rafiganj	Kerap	8	25	7	40
			Dhasila	8	25	7	40
			Chew	8	25	7	40
			Chrkawan	8	25	7	40
			Rafiganj	8	25	7	40
	2. East Champaran	Chiraiya	Madhopur	8	25	7	40
			Mishruliya	8	25	7	40
			Mirpur	8	25	7	40
			Harihare	8	25	7	40
			Chiraiya	8	25	7	40
Bihar	3. Purnia	Banmankhi	Kachery Baluwa	8	25	7	40
			Mahadevpur	8	25	7	40
			North Rupali	8	25	7	40
			Dhima	8	25	7	40
			Banmankhi	8	25	7	40
	4. Samastipur	Bibhutipur	Patpara	8	25	7	40
			North Kalyanpur	8	25	7	40
			South Mahthi	8	25	7	40
			Tabhka Khas	8	25	7	40
			Narhan	8	25	7	40
	5. Siwan	Barharia	Mahadavpur	8	25	7	40
			Suraiya	8	25	7	40
			Paharpur	8	25	7	40
			Sauna	8	25	7	40
			Barharia	8	25	7	40
	Gross Total			200	625	175	1000

State	District	Block	Village/Town	APL	BPL	AAY	Total
	1. Darrang	Sipajhar	Boguribari	8	25	7	40
			Dakhin Chuburi	8	25	7	40
			Chungapara	8	25	7	40
			2 No.	8	25	7	40
			Siphajhar (baniya para)	8	25	7	40
	2. Dibrugarh	Khawang	Siloibari (Bengali Gaon)	8	25	7	40
			Photika Chutia (Abhyapuri Gaon)	8	25	7	40
			Chutia (Nepali Gaon)	8	25	7	40
			Ikarani	8	25	7	40
			Moran Hat	8	25	7	40
Assam	3. Cachar	Narsingpur	Panibhara	8	25	7	40
			Dhalai	8	25	7	40
			Kabuganj	8	25	7	40
			Nutan Para	8	25	7	40
			Kazir Road (Manipuri Basti)	8	25	7	40
	4. Bongaigaon	Tapatary	Lathimara	8	25	7	40
			Arimara	8	25	7	40
			Abhyapuri	8	25	7	40
			Piradhara	8	25	7	40
			Bagekhati	8	25	7	40
	5. Karbi Anglong	Bokajan	Paise Engti	8	25	7	40
			Khorialdubi	8	25	7	40
			Matipul	8	25	7	40
			Kathalguri	8	25	7	40
			Bokajan	8	25	7	40
	Gross Total			200	625	175	1000

State	District	Block	Village/Town	APL	BPL	AAY	Total
	1. Aizawl	Tlanganuam	Sarawrtichun	8	25	7	40
			Tangril	8	25	7	40
			Tuigamic	8	25	7	40
			Chawlhhmun	8	25	7	40
			Luangmual	8	25	7	40
	2. Champhai	Khawzawi	Hamonbeng	8	25	7	40
			Zucchitbeng	8	25	7	40
			Bengthar	8	25	7	40
			Solombeng	8	25	7	40
			Khazawl	8	25	7	40
Mizoram	3. Lawngtlai	Lawngtlai	Thingkah, Doiltlang	8	25	7	40
			Kawlchaw	8	25	7	40
			Ngengpuilang	8	25	7	40
			Lawngtlai	8	25	7	40
			Bazaar	8	25	7	40
	4. Mamit	West Phaileng	Lallen	8	25	7	40
			Damparempui	8	25	7	40
			Phuldengsui	8	25	7	40
			Dingphar	8	25	7	40
			West Phaileng	8	25	7	40
	5. Lunglei	Lunglei	Thualthu	8	25	7	40
			Tawipui N-2	8	25	7	40
			Bualte	8	25	7	40
			Thaizawl	8	25	7	40
			Lunglai	8	25	7	40
	Gross Total			200	625	175	1000

2 The Socio-Economic Background of the Selected States

Rajasthan

Rajasthan was formed on 30 March 1949, when all erstwhile princely states ruled by Rajputs, known as Rajputana, merged into the Dominion of India. Rajasthan is the largest state of the Republic of India in terms of area. It encompasses most of the area of the large, inhospitable Great Indian Desert (Thar Desert), which has an edge paralleling the Sutlej-Indus river valley along its border with Pakistan. Th2e region borders Pakistan to the west, Gujarat to the southwest, Madhya Pradesh to the southeast, Uttar Pradesh and Haryana to the northeast and Punjab to the north. Rajasthan covers an area of 342,239 square kilometres (Table 2.1). The state capital is Jaipur. Geographical features include the Thar Desert along northwestern Rajasthan and the termination of the Ghaggar river near the archaeological ruins at Kalibanga, which are the oldest in the subcontinent discovered so far. One of the world's oldest mountain ranges, the Aravalli Ranges, cradles the only hill station of Rajasthan, Mount Abu and its world-famous Dilwara temples, a sacred pilgrimage for Jains. Eastern Rajasthan has two national tiger reserves, Ranthambore and Sariska, as well as Keoladeo National Park near Bharatpur, once famous for its bird life.

About three-fifths of Rajasthan lies northwest of the Aravallis, leaving two-fifths on the east and south. The northwestern portion of Rajasthan is generally sandy and dry. Most of the region is covered by the Thar Desert, which extends into adjoining portions of Pakistan. The Aravalli Range intercepts the moisture-giving southwest monsoon winds of the Arabian Sea, leaving the northwestern region in a rain shadow. The Thar Desert is thinly populated; the town of Bikaner is the largest city in the desert. The northwestern thorn scrub forests lie in a band around the Thar Desert, between the desert and the Aravallis. This region receives less than 400 mm of rain in an average year. Summer temperatures can exceed 45°C in the summer months and drop below freezing in the winter. The Luni river and its tributaries are the major river system of Godwar and Marwar regions, draining the western slopes of the Aravallis and emptying southwest into the great Rann of Kutch wetland in neighbouring Gujarat. This river is saline in the lower reaches and remains potable only up to Balotara in Barmer district. The Ghaggar river, which originates in Haryana, is an intermittent stream that disappears into the sands of the Thar Desert in the northern corner of the state and is seen as a remnant of the primitive Saraswati river. The Aravalli Range and the lands to the east and southeast of the range are generally more fertile and better watered. This region is home to the Kathiarbar-Gir dry deciduous forests eco-region, with tropical dry broadleaf forests that include teak, *Acacia* and other trees.

In Rajasthan, Hindus account for 88.8 per cent of the population. Muslims make up 8.5 per cent, Sikhs 1.4 per cent and Jains 1.2 per cent of the population. Rajasthan state is also populated by Sindhis, who came to Rajasthan from Sindh province (now in Pakistan) during the India-Pakistan separation in 1947. The mother tongue of the majority of people in Rajasthan is Rajasthani. Rajasthani and Hindi are the most widely used languages in Rajasthan. Some other languages used in Rajasthan are Sindhi and Punjabi. Rajasthan is culturally rich and has artistic and cultural traditions which reflect the ancient Indian way of life. Highly cultivated classical music and dance with its own distinct style is part of the cultural tradition of Rajasthan. The Ghoomar dance from Udaipur and Kalbeliya dance of Jaisalmer have gained international recognition. Folk music is a vital part of Rajasthani culture. Kathputali, Bhopa, Chang, Teratali, Ghindar, Kachchhighori, Tejaji, etc., are examples of the traditional Rajasthani culture. Rajasthan is known for its traditional, colorful art. The block prints, tie and dye prints, Bagaru prints, Sanganer prints, Zari embroidery are major export products from Rajasthan. Handicraft items like wooden furniture and handicrafts, carpets, blue pottery are some of the things commonly found here. Rajasthani dresses are usually designed in bright colours like blue, yellow and orange. Rajasthan is famous for the majestic forts, intricately carved temples and decorated *havelis*, which were built by kings in previous ages. Jantar Mantar, Dilwara temples, Chittorgarh Fort, Lake Palace Hotel, city palaces, Jaisalmer *havelis* are part of the true architectural heritage of India. Jain temples dot Rajasthan from north to south and east to west. Dilwara temples of Mount Abu, Ranakpur temple dedicated to Lord Adinath near Udaipur, Jain temples in the fort complexes of Chittor, Jaisalmer and Kumbhalgarh, Lodurva Jain temples, Bhandasar temple of Bikaner are some of the best examples. Rajasthan is often called a shopper's paradise. Rajasthan is famous for textiles, semi-precious stones and handicrafts. Rajasthani furniture has intricate carvings and bright colours. Rajasthani handicrafts are in demand due to the intricate work on them. Though a large percentage of the total area is desert and even though there is little forest cover, Rajasthan has a rich and varied flora and fauna. Some wildlife species, which are fast vanishing in other parts of India, are found in the desert in large numbers such as the Indian bustard *(Ardeotis nigriceps)*, the blackbuck *(Antilope cervicapra)*, the Indian gazelle *(Gazella bennettii)* and the Indian wild ass. Rajasthan's economy is primarily agricultural and pastoral. Wheat, *bajra* and barley are cultivated over large areas, as are pulses, sugarcane and oilseeds. Cotton and tobacco are cash crops. Rajasthan is among the largest producers of edible oils in India and the second largest producer of oilseeds. Rajasthan is also the biggest wool-producing state in India. There are mainly two crop seasons. The water for irrigation comes from wells and tanks. The Indira Gandhi Canal irrigates northwestern Rajasthan. The main industries are mineral based, agriculture based and textiles. Rajasthan is the second largest producer of polyester fibre in India. Several prominent chemical and engineering companies are located in the town of Kota, in western Rajasthan. Rajasthan is pre-eminent in quarrying and mining in India. The state is the second largest source of cement in India. It has rich salt deposits at Sambhar, copper mines at Khetri, zinc mines at Dariba and Zawarmala and *rampura aghucha* (opencast) near Bhilwara. Dimensional stone mining is also undertaken in Rajasthan. Jodhpur sandstone is mostly used in monuments, important buildings, residential buildings, etc. This stone is termed *chittar patthar*.

Endowed with natural beauty and a great history, tourism is a flourishing industry in Rajasthan. The palaces of Jaipur, lakes of Udaipur and desert forts of Jodhpur, Bikaner and Jaisalmer are among the most preferred destinations of many tourists, Indian and foreign. Tourism accounts for eight per cent of the state's domestic product. Many old and neglected palaces and forts have been converted into heritage hotels. Tourism has increased employment in the hospitality sector. Rajasthan is now the preferred destination for IT companies and north India's largest integrated IT park is located in Jaipur and is named as Mahindra World City. Some of the companies operating in Rajasthan include Infosys, Genpact, Wipro, Truworth, Deutsche Bank, NEI, MICO, Honda Siel Cars, Coca-Cola, Gillette, etc.

Chhattisgarh

Chhattisgarh was formed when the 16 Chhattisgarhi-speaking southeastern districts of Madhya Pradesh gained statehood on November 1, 2000. Raipur serves as its capital. It is the 10th largest state of India by area of 135,191 square kilometres (Table 2.1). Chhattisgarh takes its name from 36 princely states in this region from very old times (*Chattis* is 36 in Hindi and *garh* is fort). It borders Madhya Pradesh on the northwest, Maharashtra on the west, Andhra Pradesh on the south, Orissa on the east, Jharkhand on the northeast and Uttar Pradesh on the north.

The Chhattisgarhi language, part of the East Central group of Indo-Aryan languages, is the predominant language in the region. It is often regarded by linguists to be a dialect of western Hindi, which is the official language of the state. Other languages spoken in Chhattisgarh are Hindi, Oriya, Marathi and tribal languages. The state hosts many religious sects like Satnami Panth, Kabir Panth, Ramnami Samaj and others. Chhattisgarh has a very rich cultural heritage. Chhattisgarh has its unique style of dance, cuisine and music. This has made Chhattisgarh a favourite of anthropologists and sociologists due to its relevant profile. Several saints have their origin in Chhattisgarh, such as Parsurama Ramnami and Vallabha Acharya. Maharishi Mahesh Yogi, a noted Hindu leader and founder of Transcendental Meditation was from Raipur.

The gender ratio (number of females per 1000 males) has been steadily declining over the century in Chhattisgarh: 1046 in year 1901, 1032 in 1941, 996 in 1981 and 989 in 2001; but is better than the ratio for India: 972 in 1901, 945 in 1941, 934 in 1981 and 933 in 2001. In many ways, the women of Chhattisgarh enjoy a unique position within India. The proportion of women in the population is second highest among the states in India. Further, the female-male ratio is in favour of women in rural population. Most of the old temples/shrines here are related to 'women power' (e.g., Shabari, Mahamaya, Danteshwari) and existence of these temples gives insight into the historical and current social fabric of the state.

Geographically, the north and south parts of the state are hilly, while the central part is a fertile plain. Forests cover roughly 44 per cent of the state. The northern part of the state lies on the edge of the great Indo-Gangetic plain: The Rihand river, a tributary of the Ganges, drains this area. The eastern end of the Satpura Range and the western edge of the Chota Nagpur Plateau form an east-west belt of hills that divides the Mahanadi river basin from the Indo-Gangetic plain. The central part of the state lies in the fertile upper basin of the Mahanadi and its tributaries, with extensive rice cultivation. The upper Mahanadi basin is separated from the upper Narmada basin to the west by the Maikal range, part of the Satpuras and from the plains of Orissa to the east by ranges of hills. The southern part of the state lies on the Deccan plateau, in the watershed of the Godavari river and its tributary, the Indravati river. The Mahanadi is the chief river of the state. Other main rivers are Hasdo (a tributary of Mahanadi), Rihand, Indravati, Jonk and Arpa. It is situated in the east of Madhya Pradesh.

Chhattisgarh is one of the rapidly developing states of India. The per capita income was around Rs. 15073 (Table 2.1) in 2004-2005 that was around 65 per cent of the all India average. However, after separation the per capita income of the state grew at a rapid rate of around 9 per cent per annum. Only 20 per cent of population lives in urban areas. After partition, this mineral-rich state produces 30 per cent of the output of the old Madhya Pradesh state. The state's economy is fuelled by the presence of the Bhilai Steel Plant, S.E.C. Railway Zone, BALCO Aluminum Plant (Korba), and NTPC Korba (National Thermal Power Corporation Ltd.) and S.E.C.L. (South Eastern Coalfields Limited). The city of Korba is a hub for power generation, from where the electricity is supplied to several other Indian states. Chhattisgarh's southern area consists of iron ore available where NMDC is excavating to meet the iron demand in India and as well sending to countries like Japan. NMDC is located in Dantewara district. Recently ESSAR has started transporting iron ore through pipe lines to Vizag. The state is also launching an ambitious plan to become biofuel self-sufficient by 2015 by planting crops of jatropha.

Table 2.1 Socio-Economic Indicators of Selected States, *vis-à-vis* All India

	Area ('000 sq kms)	Population (Million)	Sex Ratio (Female per 1000 males)	Density (Population per sq. kms)	Percentage of Urban Population	Percentage of Population Below Poverty Line*	Literacy Rate	Percentage of SC Population to Total Population	Percentage of ST Population to Total Population	Per Capita NSDP (Current Prices in Rs.)**
	(2001 census)	(2001 census)	(2001 census)	(2001 census)	(2001 census)	(2004-05)	(2001 census)	(2001 census)	(2001 census)	(2004-05)
Rajasthan	342.239	56.51	922	165	23.4	17.5	60.4	17.2	12.6	16212
Chhattisgarh	135.191	20.83	989	154	20.1	32.0	64.7	11.6	31.8	15073
Bihar	94.163	83.00	919	881	10.5	32.5	47.0	15.7	0.9	5772
Uttar Pradesh	240.928	166.20	898	690	20.8	25.5	56.3	21.1	0.1	11477
Assam	78.438	26.66	935	340	12.9	15.0	63.3	6.9	12.4	13633
Mizoram	21.087	0.89	935	42	49.6	9.5	88.8	0.0	94.5	22207$
All India	3287.26	1028.74	933	325	27.8	21.8	65.4	16.2	8.1	22946

Note: * Estimates correspond to 30-day recall period (Source – Planning Commission)
** *Economic Survey, 2006-07*
$ for 2002-03.

Bihar

Bihar is the 12th largest state in terms of geographical size (94,163 square km) and 3rd largest by population. The state is situated in the eastern part of the country. Close to 85 per cent of the population lives in the rural countryside. Almost 58 per cent of Biharis are below the age of 25, which is the highest in India (Kaul, 2003). Bihar lies mid-way between the humid West Bengal in the east and the sub-humid Uttar Pradesh in the west which provides it with a transitional position in respect of climate, economy and culture. It is bounded by Nepal in the north and by Jharkhand state in the south. The Bihar plain is divided into two unequal halves by the river Ganga which flows through the middle from west to east. Bihar has notified forest area of 6,764.14 square km, which is 7.1 per cent of its geographical area. Hindi and Urdu are the official languages of the state, whilst the majority of the people speak one of the Bihari languages (once considered to be dialects of Hindi)—Bhojpuri, Magadhi, Maithili or Angika. Ancient Bihar, known as Magadha, was a centre of power, learning and culture in ancient and classical India. From Magadha arose India's first empire, the Maurya empire as well as one of the world's greatest pacifist religion, Buddhism. Magadha empires, notably under the Maurya and Gupta dynasties, unified large parts of South Asia under a central rule. Its capital Patna, earlier known as Patliputra, was an important centre of Indian civilisation.

Bihar is mainly a vast stretch of very fertile flat land. It is drained by the Ganges river, including northern tributaries Gandak and Koshi, originating in the Nepal Himalayas and the Bagmati, originating in the Kathmandu Valley that regularly flood parts of the Bihar plains. The state is located between 21°-58'-10" N ~ 27°-31'-15" N latitude and between 82°-19'-50" E ~ 88°-17'-40" E longitude. Its average elevation above sea level is 173 feet (53 metres). The Bihar plain is divided into two unequal halves by the river Ganga. Other Ganges tributaries are the Son, Budhi Gandak, Chandan, Orhani and Falgu. The Himalayas begin at the foothills in Nepal but influence Bihar's landforms, climate, hydrology and culture. Central parts of Bihar have some small hills, for example the Rajgir hills. The Himalayan mountains are to the north of Bihar, in Nepal. To the south is the Chota Nagpur plateau, which was part of Bihar until 2000 but now is part of a separate state called Jharkhand. Bihar is mildly cold in the winter (the lowest temperatures being around 5 to 10 degrees celsius) while hot in the summer (with average highs around 35-40 degree celsius). The monsoon months of June, July, August and September see good rainfall. The most important trees are *shorea robusta* (sal), shisham, *cedrela toona*, khair and semal.

Bihar is the third most populated state of India with a total population of 82,998,509 (43,243,795 males and 39,754,714 females). Hinduism is practiced by 83.2 per cent of the population and forms the majority religion in the state. Islam is practiced by 16.5 per cent of the population and other religions less than 0.5 per cent. Bihar's total literacy rate is 47 per cent (59.7 per cent for males and 33.1 per cent for females). Life expectancy in Bihar (61 years) is almost on par with the national life expectancy of 62.7 years. Historically, Bihar has been a major centre of learning, home to the ancient universities of Nalanda University and Vikramshila University. Today, Bihar lags behind the other Indian states in terms of human and economic development (see Table 2.1). In 2004, *The Economist* magazine quoted that, "Bihar has become a byword for the worst of India, of widespread and inescapable poverty, of corrupt politicians indistinguishable from mafia-dons they patronise, caste-ridden social order that has retained the worst feudal cruelties". In 2005, the World Bank believed that issues faced by the state was "enormous" because of "persistent poverty, complex social stratification, unsatisfactory infrastructure and weak governance" (World Bank, 2008). The current State Government has however made significant strides in improving governance. The improved governance has led to an economic revival in the state through increased investment in infrastructure, better health care facilities, greater emphasis on education and a reduction in crime and corruption (Goswami, 2008; Sharma and Jha, 2008, Jha, 2008).

The economy of Bihar is largely service-oriented but it also has a significant agricultural base. The state also has a small industrial sector. As of 2008, agriculture accounts for 35 per cent, industry 9 per cent and service 55 per cent of the economy of the state. Bihar has the lowest GDP per capita in India but there are pockets of higher than the average per capita income. Between 1999 and 2008, GDP grew by 5.1 per cent a year, which was below the Indian average of 7.3 per cent (*The Economist*, 2008). In actual terms, Bihar's GDP is ranked 14th out of 28 states. Corruption is an important hurdle for the government to overcome according to Transparency International, India, who highlighted Bihar as the Union's most corrupt state in a 2005 report. Despite many recent economic gains, significant challenges remain to do business in the state and the government has also stated that combating corruption is now the biggest challange facing the administration. Bihar accounts for 65 per cent of India's annual litchi production. Bihar has significant levels of production for the products of mango, guava, litchi, pineapple, brinjal, cauliflower, *bhindi* and cabbage in India. Despite the state's leading role in food production, investment in irrigation and other agriculture facilities has been inadequate in the past.

Uttar Pradesh

Uttar Pradesh is located in the northern part of India. With a population of over 166 million people, it is India's most populous state, as well as the world's most populous sub-national entity, and only 5 nations including India itself have more people than Uttar Pradesh. With an area of 240,928 square kilometres, Uttar Pradesh covers a large part of the highly fertile and densely populated upper Gangetic plain. It shares an international border with Nepal and is bounded by the states of Uttarakhand, Himachal Pradesh, Haryana, Delhi, Rajasthan, Madhya Pradesh, Chhattisgarh, Jharkhand and Bihar. The administrative and legislative capital of Uttar Pradesh is Lucknow and the financial and industrial capital is Kanpur. The state's high court is based at Allahabad. It is home to many historical cities like Agra and Varanasi.

Uttar Pradesh has an important place in the culture of India; as it is considered to be the birthplace of Hinduism and has many important sites of Hindu pilgrimage. It also holds much of the heritage of the Mughal empire, including both the famous Taj Mahal and the tomb of the great Mughal Emperor Akbar in Agra and Akbar's capital-palace in Fatehpur Sikri. The Indo-Gangetic plain, that spans most of the state, has been the ancient seat of Hindu religion, learning and culture, the birthplace of the Indo-Islamic syncretic culture of the medieval period, a centre of nationalism during the colonial period and has continued to play a prominent role in Indian political and cultural movements. The state has a rich heritage of traditional crafts and cottage industries of various types that employ highly skilled craftsmen and artisans. Uttar Pradesh forms part of the Hindi heartland of India, with Hindi and Urdu (which are mutually intelligible) being the principal and official languages of the state. While standard Hindi (*Khari boli*) is one of the official languages, several important regional Hindi dialects are spoken in the state, including Awadhi, Bhojpuri, Braj, Bagheli and Bundeli, besides several local dialects that do not have a formal name.

Nearly 75 per cent of Uttar Pradeshi's are Hindu, while Muslims make up 18 per cent of the population. The remaining population consists of Sikhs, Buddhists, Christians and Jains. The Brahmins, Kshatriyas and Vaishyas, the three upper castes people of the state who have dominated the political and economic scene over the centuries are in a minority. A major group comprises the backward classes and scheduled castes. The state can be divided into two distinct hypsographical regions. The larger Gangetic plain in the north includes the Ganga-Yamuna Doab, the Ghaghra plains, the Ganga plains and the Terai. It has highly fertile alluvial soils and flat topography broken by numerous ponds, lakes and rivers. The smaller Vindhya Hills and plateau region in the south is characterised by hard rock strata, varied topography of hills, plains, valleys and plateau with limited availability of water. The climate of Uttar Pradesh is predominantly sub-tropical but weather conditions change significantly with location and season. Rainfall in the state ranges from 1,000–2,000 mm (40–80 inches) in the east to 600–1,000 mm (24–40 inches) in the west. About 90 per cent of the rainfall occurs during the southwest monsoon, lasting from about June to September. With most of the rainfall concentrated during this four-month period, floods are a recurring problem and cause heavy damage to crops, life and property, particularly in the eastern part of the state, where the Himalayan-origin rivers flow with a very low north-south gradient. Periodic failure of monsoons results in drought conditions and crop failure.

Uttar Pradesh is the second largest state economy in India after Maharashtra, contributing 8.17 per cent to India's total GDP. Between 1999 and 2008, the economy grew only 4.4 per cent per year, one of the lowest rates in India (*The Economist*, 2008). The major economic activity in the state is agriculture. In 1991, 73 per cent of the population in the state was engaged in agriculture and 46 per cent of the state income was accounted for by agriculture. Uttar Pradesh has retained its pre-eminent position in the country as a food-surplus state. Uttar Pradesh is home to largest number of small scale units in the country, with 12 per cent of over 2.3 million units. The largest shoe-manufacturing centre in the country is Kanpur. The state is one of the top tourist destinations in India, with more than 71 million domestic tourists (in 2003) and almost 25 per cent of the all India foreign tourists visiting Uttar Pradesh. Lucknow and Noida are among the top IT destinations of the country.

Assam

Assam is a northeastern state of India with its capital at Dispur, in the outskirts of the city Guwahati. Located south of the eastern Himalayas, Assam comprises the Brahmaputra and the Barak river valleys and the Karbi Anglong and the North Cachar Hills with an area of 78,438 square kilometres. Assam is surrounded by the rest of the Seven Sister States: Arunachal Pradesh, Nagaland, Manipur, Mizoram, Tripura and Meghalaya. These states are connected to the rest of India via a narrow strip in West Bengal called the Siliguri Corridor or Chicken's Neck. Assam also shares international borders with Bhutan and Bangladesh and cultures, peoples and climate with South East Asia. Assam became a part of British India after the British occupied the region following the Treaty of Yandaboo of 1826.

Assam is known for its rich biodiversity. It has successfully conserved the one-horned Indian rhinoceros from near extinction; tiger; numerous species of birds; and provides one of the last wild habitats for the Asian elephant. It is increasingly becoming a popular destination for wildlife tourism, notably Kaziranga and Manas which are both World Heritage Sites. Assam was also known for its sal tree forests and forest products, much depleted now. A land of high rainfall, Assam is endowed with lush greenery and the mighty river Brahmaputra, whose tributaries and oxbow lakes provide the region with a unique hydrogeomorphic and aesthetic environment.

With the tropical monsoon rainforest climate, Assam is temperate (summer max. at 35-38°C and winter min. at 6-8°C) and experiences heavy rainfall and high humidity. The climate is characterised by heavy monsoon downpours reducing summer temperature and foggy nights and mornings in winter. Thunderstorms known as *Bordoicila* are frequent during the afternoons. Spring (March-April) and Autumn (September-October) are usually pleasant with moderate rainfall and temperature. Assam is one of the richest biodiversity zones in the world and consists of tropical rainforests, deciduous forests, riverine grasslands, bamboo orchards and numerous wetland ecosystems. Many are now protected as national parks and reserved forests. Kaziranga, home of the rare Indian rhinoceros, and Manas are two UNESCO World Heritage Sites in Assam. The state is the last refuge for numerous other endangered species such as golden langur (*Trachypithecus geei*), white-winged wood duck or *Deohanh* (*Cairina scutulata*), Bengal florican, black-breasted parrotbill, pygmy hog, greater adjutant and so on. Some other endangered species with significant population in Assam are tiger, elephant, hoolock gibbon, jerdon's babbler. Assam is also known for orchids. The region is prone to natural disasters with annual floods and frequent mild earthquakes.

Total population of Assam was 26.66 million with 4.91 million households in 2001. The census recorded literacy in Assam at 63.30 per cent with male literacy at 71.30 and female at 54.60 per cent. Urbanisation rate was recorded at 12.90 per cent (Table 2.1). Assam has many ethnic groups. Major religions are Hinduism (64.9 per cent) and Islam (30.9 per cent). Others include Christianity (3.7 per cent), Sikhism, Animism, Buddhism (Khamti, Phake, Aito, etc.). Assamese culture in its hybrid form and nature is one of the richest, still developing and in true sense is a 'cultural system' with sub-systems. It is interesting that many source-cultures of Assamese cultural system are still surviving either as sub-systems or as sister entities, for e.g., Bodo, Khasi or Missing. Assamese and Bodo are the major indigenous and official languages while Bengali holds official status in three districts in the Barak Valley. There are several important traditional festivals in Assam. Bihu is the most important and common and celebrated all over Assam. Assam has a rich tradition of performing arts and music. Folk songs and music related to Bihu and other festivals dates back to time immemorial. Assam has large numbers of traditional musical instruments including several types of drums, string instruments, flutes, cymbals, pipes, etc.

Economy of Assam today represents a unique juxtaposition of backwardness amidst plenty. Growth rate of Assam's income has not kept pace with that of India's; differences increased rapidly since the 1970s. In the post-liberalised era (after 1991), the differences widened further. According to the recent estimates (Table 2.1), per capita income in Assam has reached Rs. 13633 in 2004-05, which is still much lower than India's. The average annual growth rate of agriculture, which was only 2.6 per cent per annum over the 1980s has unfortunately fallen to 1.6 per cent in the 1990s (UNDP, 2004). Manufacturing sector has shown some improvement in the 1990s with a growth rate of 3.4 per cent per annum than 2.4 per cent in the 1980s. Since past five decades, the tertiary sector has registered the highest growth rates than the other sectors, which even has slowed down in the 1990s than in the 1980s (UNDP, 2004).

Agriculture accounts for more than a third of Assam's income and employs 69 per cent of workforce (Economic Survey of Assam, 2001-02). Assam's biggest contribution to the world is tea. It produces some of the finest and expensive teas, and has its own variety, *Camellia assamica*. Assam also accounts for a fair share of India's production of rice, rapeseed, mustard, jute, potato, sweet potato, banana, papaya, areca nut and turmeric. It is also a home of large varieties of citrus fruits, leaf vegetables, vegetables, useful grasses, herbs, spices, etc.

Apart from tea and petroleum refineries, Assam has few industries of significance. Industrial development is inhibited by its physical and political isolation from neighbouring countries such as Myanmar, China and Bangladesh and from other growing Southeast Asian economies. The region is landlocked, situated in the eastern periphery of India and is linked to the mainland by a flood and cyclone prone narrow corridor with weak transport infrastructure. The international airport in Guwahati is yet to find airlines providing direct international flights. The Brahmaputra suitable for navigation does not possess sufficient infrastructure for international trade and success of such a navigable trade route will be dependent on proper channel maintenance and diplomatic and trade relationships with Bangladesh.

Assam is a major producer of crude oil, exploited by the Assam Oil Company Ltd., and natural gas in India and is the second place in the world (after Titusville in the United States) where petroleum was discovered. Most of the oilfields are located in the Upper Assam region. Assam has four oil refineries located in Guwahati, Digboi, Numaligarh and Bongaigaon with a total capacity of 7 million metric tonnes per annum. Assam is endowed with petroleum, natural gas, coal, limestone and other minor minerals such as magnetic quartzite, kaolin, sillimanites, clay and feldspar. A small quantity of iron ore is available in western districts. Discovered in 1889, all the major petroleum gas reserves are in Upper Assam. A recent USGS estimate shows 399 million barrels of oil, 1,178 billion cubic feet of gas and 67 million barrels of natural gas liquids in Assam geologic province.

Although having a poor overall industrial performance, several other industries have nevertheless been started, including a chemical fertiliser plant at Namrup, petrochemical industries at Namrup and Bongaigaon, paper mills at Jagiroad, Panchgram and Jogighopa, sugar mills at Barua Bamun Gaon, Chargola, Kampur, cement plant at Bokajan and Badarpur, cosmetics plant (HLL) at Doom Dooma, etc. Moreover, there are other industries such as jute mill, textile and yarn mills, silk mill, etc. Unfortunately many of these industries are facing loss and closure due to lack of infrastructure and improper management practices.

Mizoram

Mizoram is one of the Seven Sister States in northeastern India. It shares land borders with the states of Tripura, Assam, Manipur, Bangladesh and Burma. Mizoram became the 23rd state of India on 20 February 1987. Its population at the 2001 census stood at 888,573. Mizoram ranks second in India with a literacy rate of 88.79 per cent. Mizoram has the most variegated hilly terrain in the eastern part of India. The hills are steep (average height 1000 metres) and separated by rivers which flow either to the north or south creating deep gorges between the hill ranges. The highest peak in Mizoram is the Blue Mountain with a height of 2210 metres. Its tropical location combined with the high altitude gives it a mild climate all year round.

Mizoram is a land of rolling hills, rivers and lakes. As many as 21 major hills ranges or peaks of different heights run through the length and breadth of the state, with plains scattered here and there. The average height of the hills to the west of the state are about 1,000 metres. These gradually rise up to 1,300 metres to the east. Some areas, however, have higher ranges which go up to a height of over 2,000 metres. Phawngpui, or the Blue Mountain, situated in the southeastern part of the state, is the highest peak in Mizoram. The biggest river in Mizoram is the River Kaladan, also known as Chhimtuipui Lui in local Mizo language. It originates from Chin state in Burma and passes through Saiha and Lawngtlai districts in southern tip of Mizoram and goes back to Burma's Rakhine state. Finally it enters Bay of Bengal at Akyab, a very popular port in Sittwe, Burma. Although many more rivers and streams drain the hill ranges, the most important and useful rivers are the Tlawng (also known as Dhaleswari or Katakhal), Tut (Gutur), Tuirial (Sonai) and Tuivawl which flow through the northern territory and eventually join the Barak river in Cachar district. The Koldoyne (Chhimtuipui) which originates in Burma, is an important river in the south of Mizoram. It has four tributaries and the river is in patches. The western part is drained by Karnaphuli (Khawthlang tuipui) and its tributaries.

Mizoram is rich in flora and fauna and many kinds of tropical trees and plants thrive in the area. Mizoram literally means land of the highlanders. Mizoram has a mild climate, not very warm in summer and not very cold in winter. During winter, the temperature varies from 11°C to 21°C and in summer it varies between 20°C to 29°C. The entire area is under the regular influence of monsoons. It rains heavily from May to September and the average rainfall is 254 cm, per annum. The average annual rainfall in Aizawl and Lunglei are 208 centimetres and 350 centimetres, respectively. Winter in Mizoram is normally rain-free. The Mizos are divided into numerous tribes, the largest of which is possibly the Lushais, which comprises almost two-thirds of the state's population. Other Mizo tribes include Hmar, Mara, Paite, Lai, Ralte. The Riang, a subtribe of Tripuri and the Chakma of Arakanese origin, are non-Mizo tribes living in Mizoram. Some 87 per cent of the population (including all ethnic Mizos) is Christian. Other faiths include Hindus who form a small minority in the state, at 3.6 per cent of the population following the religion. Muslims also form a small minority with 1.1 per cent of the population. People who believe in this faith are from other states but living in Mizoram.

Music and the society of Mizo's go together. Mizos are very fond of music, they sing in a funeral and in a wedding. Mizo traditional tunes are very soft and gentle, with locals claiming that they can be sung the whole night without the slightest fatigue. Even without musical instruments, the Mizos can enthusiastically sing together by clapping hands or any material which can produce complementary sound. All these informal instruments are called *chhepchher*. The Mizos in the early period were very close to nature and music was the tune of their life. Even today, the Mizos use a drum known locally as *khuang*, made from wood and animal hide, to accompany their singing in church services as well as cultural festivities. Western influence is evident from the contemporary music scene though, with experiments in genres such as rock (punk, emos cream, metal), pop and hiphop, R&B to name a few.

In terms of economic development, Mizoram lags behind in comparison to the rest of the country. Cottage industry and other small scale industries play an important role in its current economy. The people of Mizoram have not taken a keen responsibility for the development of industry due to the lack of market raw materials. The industry is wanting but lately there is a much wider chance for the development of forest products. The 9th Five Year Plan (1997–2002) gives much priority to the agro-based industry as nearly 70 per cent of the population is engaged in agriculture. 30 per cent of Mizoram is covered with wild bamboo forests, many of which are largely unexploited. Mizoram harvests 40 per cent of India's 80 million tonne annual bamboo crop. The current state administration wishes to increase revenue streams from bamboo and aside from uses as a substitute for timber, there is research underway to utilise bamboo more widely such as using bamboo chippings for paper mills, bamboo charcoal for fuel and a type of bamboo vinegar.

Agriculture is the mainstay of the people of Mizoram. More than 70 per cent of the total population is engaged in some form of agriculture. The age-old practice of *Jhum* cultivation is carried out annually by a large number of people living in rural areas. The climatic conditions of the state, its location in the tropic and temperate zones, and its various soil types along with well-distributed rainfall of 1900 mm to 3000 mm spread over 8 to 10 months in the year, have all contributed to a wide spectrum of rich and varied flora and fauna in Mizoram. These natural features and resources also offer opportunities for growing a variety of horticultural crops.

The agro-climatic conditions of Mizoram are conducive to agricultural and horticultural crops. As this is the case, a strong and effective food processing sector should play a significant supportive role in the economy. The total production of fruits, vegetables and spices will be increasing year by year as the number of farmers are weaned away from *Jhum* cultivation and are taking up diversification towards cash crops. Recently, Godrej Agrovet Limited has entered for a new venture wherein oil palm and jatropha cultivation is their main theme in Mizoram.

With its abundant scenic beauty and a pleasant climate, Mizoram hopes to develop its tourist-related industries. Specific tourist projects can be developed to put Mizoram on the tourist map of India. With the development of Reiek resort centre and a number of other resort centres in and around Aizawl, as well as establishment of tourist huts across the entire state, tourism has been much developed. The ever smiling faces of the Mizos is an experience to cherish and gives new meaning to life.

Table 2.2 Production, Procurement and Distribution of Food Grains—Selected States

(Lakh Tonnes)

	Production	Procurement	Current Stock in Central Pool*	Allotment Under TPDS	Off-take Under TPDS	As a Percentage of Production		
	(TE 2005-06)	(TE 2005-06)	As on Sept. 2006	(TE 2005-06)	(TE 2005-06)	Procurement	Allotment	Off-take
Rice								
Rajasthan	0.00	0.22	0.45	5.17	0.07	0.00	0.00	0.00
Chhattisgarh	50.10	27.97	6.05	10.93	6.31	55.83	21.83	12.60
Bihar	35.00	5.21	1.54	20.71	2.62	14.89	59.16	7.50
UP	111.30	28.92	6.06	43.89	16.80	25.98	39.43	15.10
Assam	35.50	0.06	1.05	13.23	8.96	0.17	37.28	25.24
Mizoram	0.00	0.00	0.10	0.90	0.77	0.00	0.00	0.00
All India	917.90	251.83	78.21	362.52	162.64	27.44	39.49	17.72
Wheat								
Rajasthan	58.70	2.32	2.19	34.45	10.12	3.96	58.68	17.25
Chhattisgarh	0.00	0.00	0.27	5.07	1.28	0.00	0.00	0.00
Bihar	32.40	0.06	1.37	28.60	8.50	0.17	88.27	26.22
UP	240.70	11.71	2.25	65.91	19.49	4.87	27.38	8.10
Assam	0.50	0.00	0.50	3.36	3.01	0.00	671.35	601.01
Mizoram	0.00	0.00	0.03	0.12	0.10	0.00	0.00	0.00
All India	693.50	157.93	67.17	352.73	118.66	22.77	50.86	17.11

Note: * With FCI State Agencies

Source: *Agricultural Statistics at a Glance, 2007* and Ministry of Food and Public Distribution, Government of India.

2. For review of literature, see Annexture 1.1.

3 Occupational Distribution and Income Patterns

3.1 Profile of Respondents

For the evaluation of public distribution system, a total number of 6000 households were selected from six states. Apart from the selected households, information was also gathered from the fair price shops as well as from district and state civil supply officials who were the real executors of the PDS scheme. The detailed selection procedure for the households and the fair price shops is already discussed in Chapter 1. In this chapter, we present a brief overview of the selected households followed by a detailed discussion on the occupation and income structure of the selected respondents. It is made clear at the outset that the Antyodaya Anna Yojana (AAY) households actually belong to the below poverty households who lie at the bottom in the list of below poverty line (BPL). In other words, among the poor, they are the poorest of the poor households. Therefore, the BPL households actually can be divided into two categories, i.e., AAY households and rest of the BPL households. For our convenience in the study, we make our analysis for the three categories namely, AAY, BPL and APL households, without using the nomenclature of rest of the BPL to keep the analysis simple and easy. Therefore, our analysis throughout this study would be classified in three categories of households, i.e., AAY, below poverty line (BPL) and above poverty line (APL) and a cross comparison will be done across the six selected states.

Tables 3.1 to 3.6 present demographic profile of the households by different states. It is apparent from the statistics that household size varied from 3.3 to 5.4 in different states with an average around 4.5 to 5 members per family. The household size was generally higher for the APL families and lower in the case of AAY families. The reason for the same seems to be that APL families generally had combined property in terms of land, tractor etc., and thereby they had a combined family system. The AAY families were mostly ad hoc earners generally not owning any land and had a nuclear family system. These facts are supported by the occupation structure presented in the next pages. Out of the average five members in a family, around one to two were earning members, as is apparent from the results presented in the tables. The AAY and BPL families had slightly higher number of earning members compared to APL families. As was mentioned above, households below poverty were dependent on non-regular (ad hoc) means of earnings, thereby in their case higher number of family members had to work to support their families as compared to the above poverty households who had more regular means of earnings.

The demographic profile of households indicates their socio-economic characteristics. Looking at the caste distribution, majority of households belonged to the scheduled castes (SC) and scheduled tribes (ST) in the case of AAY households, whereas other backward castes (OBC) along with the previous two classes formed the majority in the case of BPL households. Comparing these two categories, comparatively more number of forward castes (FC) households were found in the case of APL category. However, Mizoram made an exception where 93 to 99 per cent selected households were all schedule tribes in all the three categories and hardly any forward caste member was found in any category. The forward castes in the AAY category were less than 5 per cent in all the states except that of Assam and Uttar Pradesh where their proportion was around 24 and 12 per cent, respectively. Among the BPL households, the proportion of forward castes was around 8 per cent in Bihar and Rajasthan, 2 per cent in Chhattisgarh, 10 per cent in Uttar Pradesh and 32 per cent in Assam. Compared to these statistics, among the APL households, the percentage of forward castes was comparatively higher, around 4 per cent in Chhattisgarh, 24 per cent in Rajathan, 31 to 33 per cent in Assam and Uttar Pradesh and 39 per cent in Bihar. In terms of religion, except the case of Mizoram, where predominant number of respondents were Christians and Muslims, in all other states around 90 per cent respondents were Hindus. Looking at the gender of the selected family members, the distribution was on an average even around males and females. On the age factor, around half to two-third members of all households in all the cases were in the working age while rest of them were either children below working age or they were senior citizens.

Table 3.1 Demographic Profile of the Respondents (Rajasthan)

Characteristics		AAY	BPL	APL
No. of HH		180	606	214
Household size		4.26	4.76	4.79
Average no. of earners		1.34	1.35	1.28
Gender	Male	51.69	51.71	53.64
	Female	48.31	48.29	46.36
Age group	<16	39.97	41.36	37.34
	16-60	55.08	54.59	58.78
	>60	4.95	4.05	3.88
Identity of respondent	Head	92.78	79.54	82.71
	Others	7.22	20.46	17.29
Religion	Hindu	95.48	88.56	91.55
	Muslim	2.82	4.31	2.35
	Christian	0.56	1.33	1.41
	Sikh	1.13	5.64	4.69
	Others	0.00	0.17	0.00
Caste	SC	43.58	43.70	36.97
	ST	41.34	22.52	13.27
	OBC	10.06	26.05	25.59
	FC_Brahmin	2.23	1.51	11.85
	FC_Non-Brahmin	2.79	6.22	12.32

Table 3.2 Demographic Profile of the Respondents (Bihar)

Characteristics		AAY	BPL	APL
No. of HH		194	626	180
Household size		4.79	5.32	5.06
Average no. of earners		1.48	1.56	1.39
Gender	Male	54.70	53.33	55.95
	Female	45.30	46.67	44.05
Age group	<16	18.38	17.67	22.08
	16-60	67.65	62.04	59.09
	>60	13.97	20.29	18.83
Identity of respondent	Head	97.94	95.53	91.67
	Others	2.06	4.47	8.33
Religion	Hindu	87.37	88.65	87.21
	Muslim	12.63	11.35	11.63
	Christian	0.00	0.00	1.16
	Sikh	0.00	0.00	0.00
	Others	0.00	0.00	0.00
Caste	SC	44.57	35.5	12.5
	ST	11.41	8.33	1.19
	OBC	39.67	47.83	47.62
	FC_Brahmin	1.09	2.17	9.52
	FC_Non-Brahmin	3.26	6.17	29.17

Table 3.3 **Demographic Profile of the Respondents (Chhattisgarh)**

Characteristics		AAY	BPL	APL
No. of HH		208	599	193
Household size		4.00	4.46	5.07
Average no. of earners		1.44	1.52	1.60
Gender	Male	50.12	51.41	52.65
	Female	49.88	48.59	47.35
Age group	<16	32.25	31.87	23.38
	16-60	62.70	63.59	72.13
	>60	5.05	4.54	4.50
Identity of respondent	Head	95.19	93.99	90.67
	Others	4.81	6.01	9.33
Religion	Hindu	96.15	96.31	95.34
	Muslim	1.44	2.68	2.59
	Christian	2.40	0.67	2.07
	Sikh	0.00	0.17	0.00
	Others	0.00	0.17	0.00
Caste	SC	29.95	37.84	23.32
	ST	36.71	25.00	26.94
	OBC	30.92	35.45	46.11
	FC_Brahmin	0.00	0.34	0.00
	FC_Non-Brahmin	2.42	1.37	3.63

Table 3.4 **Demographic Profile of the Respondents (Uttar Pradesh)**

Characteristics		AAY	BPL	APL
No. of HH		205	597	198
Household size		5.22	4.67	4.83
Average no. of earners		1.19	1.14	1.13
Gender	Male	52.85	55.12	55.30
	Female	47.15	44.88	44.70
Age group	<16	42.92	38.58	33.51
	16-60	54.06	57.04	60.52
	>60	3.02	4.37	5.98
Identity of respondent	Head	92.20	91.79	89.39
	Others	7.80	8.21	10.61
Religion	Hindu	89.66	89.00	89.74
	Muslim	10.34	10.66	9.74
	Christian	0.00	0.17	0.00
	Sikh	0.00	0.17	0.00
	Others	0.00	0.00	0.51
Caste	SC	46.53	40.99	17.44
	ST	1.98	2.04	0.51
	OBC	39.60	46.60	48.72
	FC_Brahmin	7.92	7.65	26.15
	FC_Non-Brahmin	3.96	2.72	7.18

Table 3.5 Demographic Profile of the Respondents (Assam)

Characteristics		AAY	BPL	APL
No. of HH		190	609	201
Household size		4.07	4.03	4.21
Average no. of earners		1.11	1.21	1.14
Gender	Male	55.30	54.02	54.20
	Female	44.70	45.98	45.80
Age group	<16	30.08	25.47	21.24
	16-60	67.51	72.13	76.88
	>60	2.41	2.40	1.88
Identity of respondent	Head	68.42	64.86	64.68
	Others	31.58	35.14	35.32
Religion	Hindu	74.60	73.06	79.00
	Muslim	17.99	19.83	17.50
	Christian	7.41	6.61	3.50
	Sikh	0.00	0.50	0.00
	Others	0.00	0.00	0.00
Caste	SC	39.78	30.69	27.64
	ST	2.15	1.82	3.02
	OBC	33.87	34.82	38.19
	FC_Brahmin	1.61	3.80	8.54
	FC_Non-Brahmin	22.58	28.88	22.61

Table 3.6 Demographic Profile of the Respondents (Mizoram)

Characteristics		AAY	BPL	APL
No. of HH		175	569	256
Household size		3.24	3.65	3.82
Average no. of earners		1.37	1.48	1.31
Gender	Male	58.17	53.12	54.36
	Female	41.83	46.88	45.64
Age group	<16	20.59	23.19	21.95
	16-60	76.47	74.53	77.56
	>60	2.94	2.29	0.50
Identity of respondent	Head	96.94	98.16	94.64
	Others	3.06	1.84	5.36
Religion	Hindu	0.00	1.58	1.79
	Muslim	21.43	29.74	25
	Christian	78.57	68.16	73.21
	Sikh	0.00	0.00	0.00
	Others	0.00	0.53	0.00
Caste	SC	0.00	3.95	2.68
	ST	98.98	93.42	97.82
	OBC	1.02	1.84	0.00
	FC_Brahmin	0.00	0.26	0.00
	FC_Non-Brahmin	0.00	0.53	0.00

3.2 Occupation Structure

Distribution of sample family members in different occupations for AAY, BPL and APL households across the six states is given in Tables 3.7 to 3.12. The age distribution in the previous section indicated that around half to two-third members of the selected households were in the working age. However, out of the working population, some members were full-time students, either in college/university or doing other professional courses. A significant number of family members in all the states belonged to housewives engaged in household activities without yielding any economic remuneration. A few other members were unemployed or disabled/retired persons not having any active participation in any economic activities. Thus, the data presented in the tables gives us occupational distribution of the members who were truly active and were engaged in some earning activities either in agriculture and related activities or in the secondary and tertiary sectors.

Table 3.7 Main Occupation (% of Total Man-Days) (Rajasthan)

Occupation	AAY	BPL	APL
Self-employed in agriculture	17.32	17.64	17.72
Self-employed in livestock	21.39	29.75	19.16
Self-employed in non-agriculture	4.92	5.11	10.03
Agricultural casual labour	29.28	24.30	9.98
Non-agricultural casual labour	15.43	15.76	6.93
Work for public work programmes	0.00	0.25	0.17
Worked as a migrant worker	0.75	0.61	0.06
Other self construction work etc.	2.08	2.42	2.33
Work in common property res.	1.29	0.58	1.10
Regular/salary job	7.54	3.58	32.52
Total	100.00	100.00	100.00

Table 3.8 Main Occupation (% of Total Man-Days) (Bihar)

Occupation	AAY	BPL	APL
Self-employed in agriculture	2.34	2.83	17.99
Self-employed in livestock	10.55	9.90	17.22
Self-employed in non-agriculture	12.22	4.83	12.06
Agricultural casual labour	56.99	57.85	12.82
Non-agricultural casual labour	10.69	10.10	4.30
Work for public work programmes	0.17	0.11	0.22
Worked as a migrant worker	5.14	8.90	5.95
Other self construction work etc.	1.12	1.43	1.63
Work in common property res.	0.00	0.13	0.00
Regular/salary job	0.78	3.92	27.82
Total	100.00	100.00	100.00

The trends in occupation depict that majority of working members of AAY and BPL households depended on ad hoc means of income as they were engaged in wage earnings, either in agriculture or in non-agricultural activities. APL households, on the other hand, had more assured means of earnings, as they were either engaged in agriculture with having some ownership of cultivable land or were employed in business or salaried jobs. A glance on the statistics reveals that wage earnings in agriculture was the principal source of earnings for AAY and BPL households in almost all the states that occupied around 25 to 50 per cent of their man-days. Non-agricultural casual wages, self-employment in agriculture and livestock were the other major sources of employment for the below poverty households (including that of AAY). Self-employment in non-agriculture sector that includes small business within the village or in the surrounding villages, towns, e.g., village shop, huller or sheller, commission agents (*arhatias*), shops etc., provided significant employment to below poverty households only in the states of Assam, Uttar Pradesh and Mizoram. Similarly, permanent/temporary jobs with the private/government sector contributed significantly only in the case of Mizoram for the respective households.

Table 3.9 Main Occupation (% of Total Man-Days) (Chhattisgarh)

Occupation	AAY	BPL	APL
Self-employed in agriculture	27.50	19.05	28.27
Self-employed in livestock	9.80	8.30	12.97
Self-employed in non-agriculture	5.96	5.08	13.28
Agricultural casual labour	32.72	40.43	13.86
Non-agricultural casual labour	14.74	18.37	3.79
Work for public work programmes	0.27	1.09	0.26
Worked as a migrant worker	0.45	0.90	0.33
Other self construction work etc.	1.60	1.07	1.23
Work in common property res.	3.35	0.63	0.42
Regular/salary job	3.60	5.09	25.58
Total	100.00	100.00	100.00

Table 3.10 Main Occupation (% of Total Man-Days) (Uttar Pradesh)

Occupation	AAY	BPL	APL
Self-employed in agriculture	20.08	25.36	29.59
Self-employed in livestock	18.52	16.21	17.53
Self-employed in non-agriculture	16.17	16.95	12.39
Agricultural casual labour	16.01	14.80	6.21
Non-agricultural casual labour	21.68	11.91	4.20
Work for public work programmes	1.15	0.90	0.05
Worked as a migrant worker	0.13	0.21	0.52
Other self construction work etc.	1.06	1.05	1.17
Work in common property res.	0.00	0.01	0.03
Regular/salary job	5.18	12.60	28.31
Total	100.00	100.00	100.00

In the case of above poverty households, regular or salary job with government, semi-government or private sector was the major activity that provided employment to the majority of families in Assam and Mizoram. Among the APL households, this single activity contributed around 83 per cent man-days employment in Assam and 53 per cent in Mizoram. Self-employment in agriculture and livestock was the principal activity in rest of the four states that engaged around 47 per cent APL man-days in Uttar Pradesh, 41 per cent in Chhattisgarh and 37 per cent each in Rajasthan and Bihar. In the latter four states, salaried job was the second most important employment activity for the APL households as it engaged around 25 to 32 per cent of total workforce. Self-employment in business, shops or small factory also contributed significantly towards earnings of the APL households. The share of man-days employed in the latter activity among above poverty members was around 10 to 15 per cent in all the six states. Public work programmes, work in common property resources, other self-construction works and working as a migrant workers were the other minor occupations across all the three categories in the six states.

Table 3.11 Main Occupation (% of Total Man-Days) (Assam)

Occupation	AAY	BPL	APL
Self-employed in agriculture	13.26	26.15	4.36
Self-employed in livestock	3.86	13.65	1.00
Self-employed in non-agriculture	22.54	27.19	8.26
Agricultural casual labour	28.48	13.22	1.03
Non-agricultural casual labour	5.96	2.85	1.04
Work for public work programmes	18.32	9.60	1.00
Worked as a migrant worker	0.24	0.64	0.01
Other self construction work etc.	0.41	0.38	0.04
Work in common property res.	0.00	0.00	0.00
Regular/salary job	6.93	6.31	83.27
Total	100.00	100.00	100.00

Table 3.12 Main Occupation (% of Total Man-Days) (Mizoram)

Occupation	AAY	BPL	APL
Self-employed in agriculture	20.72	23.28	16.01
Self-employed in livestock	15.56	15.27	11.29
Self-employed in non-agriculture	15.99	13.41	6.33
Agricultural casual labour	17.38	12.01	8.77
Non-agricultural casual labour	9.56	8.42	4.46
Work for public work programmes	0.32	0.21	0.06
Worked as a migrant worker	0.00	0.00	0.00
Other self construction work etc.	0.92	0.53	0.20
Work in common property res.	0.00	0.15	0.00
Regular/salary job	19.54	26.72	52.88
Total	100.00	100.00	100.00

Thus, occupation structure was significantly different among below and above poverty households. Whereas above poverty households depended mostly on agriculture/allied activities and regular salaried jobs to eke out their daily earnings, below poverty households depended mostly on casual earnings in agriculture, non-farm activities or as migrant workers. As higher number of APL households depended on salary, self-business or agriculture, they had assured regular earnings. Whereas, BPL and AAY households were more vulnerable as they did not have any regular means of employment and in most of the cases they were not employed for the whole month. However, comparing occupation structure within BPL and AAY households, no significant differences appear in the pattern of occupation of these two categories.

Comparing occupation pattern across six states, the two northeastern states namely, Assam and Mizoram presented a contrasting occupational structure as compared to rest of the four states in a number of ways. Among the APL households, whereas agriculture and livestock combined together was a principal activity in rest of the four states, this activity was less important in Assam and Mizoram. Similarly, regular employment in fixed salary jobs contributed significantly in the case of BPL and AAY households only in the case of Mizoram, while its contribution was much lower in all other states. Yet in another case, public work programmes provided significant employment to AAY and BPL households only in the state of Assam. Some differences in occupation structure were also observed in the case of Bihar. Among AAY and BPL households, agriculture contributed very little in Bihar, whereas it was one of the significant employment provider in rest of five states even for the below poverty households. Last but not the least, the number of man-days employed as migrant workers (intra or inter state) was maximum in Bihar.

3.3 Household Income (Annual)

The main sources of earnings of the selected households were, agriculture income also known as farm business income; income from livestock activities namely, dairy and poultry farming; self-employment in non-agricultural activities, such as small business, shop or factory etc.; earnings through casual labour; regular salary or pension; and remittances obtained from outside, i.e., income from transfers. Besides these major sources, there were also minor inflows of income in terms of sale or renting out of assets, renting out of land (rentals) and income from dividends. These earnings were mostly intermittent in nature and were sighted in a very few households.

Tables 3.13 to 3.18 present distribution of household income by activity classifications for AAY, BPL and APL households for the selected six states. All earnings from different activities are in terms of net income that are obtained by subtracting material cost from the gross earnings for each activity. The tables also present the respective percentage share of each activity in the total household income. The coefficient of variation is calculated for each activity across the households in each category, i.e., AAY, BPL and APL. The data on household income pertains to the year 2005-06. A glance on the household income statistics reveals that by and large, estimated income of above and below poverty households was on expected lines. In all the six states, income was highest for the APL households and lowest for the AAY households without any exception. On an average, the selected AAY households earned around Rs. 12 thousand in Mizoram and Chhattisgarh each, 16 thousand in UP, 18 thousand in Bihar, 20 thousand in Rajasthan and 24 thousand in Assam from all sources during the financial year 2005-06. Thus, average household income was lowest in Mizoram and highest in Assam. The latter was highest income state among BPL and APL households as well, while lowest state was Chhattisgarh among BPL and Uttar Pradesh among the APL households. Among the BPL households, average earnings during the year were 15 thousand in Chhattisgarh, 20 thousand in UP, 22 thousand in Bihar, 26 thousand in Rajasthan, 27 thousand in Mizoram and 30 thousand in Assam. For the above poverty households, average earnings ranged from 50 to 55 thousand in three states, namely UP, Chhattisgarh and Rajasthan, 75 in Bihar and above 75 thousand to one lakh in the two northeastern states of Mizoram and Assam.

Comparing household income across the three categories of AAY, BPL and APL it is clearly evident from the data that on an average, BPL households earned 33 per cent higher income compared to AAY households. The AAY households belonged to the poorest of the poor category and thereby their income probably represented the bottom income group. Average above poverty households earned two and a half times higher income compared to BPL households and more than three times higher income compared to the poorest of the poor households. Excess of BPL over AAY income ranged from 21 per cent to 133 per cent among the six states. The difference was highest in the case of Mizoram followed by Chhattisgarh, Rajasthan, Assam, Bihar and Uttar Pradesh. Comparing BPL and APL income, APL income was three and a half times higher than BPL income in Chhattisgarh, Bihar and Assam, three times in Mizoram, two and a half times in Uttar Pradesh and twice in Rajasthan. Thus, the difference between the above and below poverty income was higher in poor states like Chhattisgarh and Bihar than that of comparatively better off states like Rajasthan.

Comparing the sources of income across different activities, it is clearly evident from the results that in all the states, wage income constituted a lion's share in the income of AAY and BPL households. It was observed in the last section that casual labour in agriculture and non-agricultural activities was the prominent occupation among the below poverty households. Dominant share of wages in BPL and AAY income further verifies our results of occupational distribution. In the case of above poverty households, in consonance with the occupational structure, earnings from agriculture and salary and pension constituted the highest share of income of these households in all the states without any exception. Income from self-employment was the third most important constituent of earnings for the APL households. For the BPL and AAY households, agriculture income and self-employment income were the other major sources of earning. As was mentioned at the outset, income from transfer, assets and rents were the minor source for all the three category of households in all the six states.

Table 3.13 **Household Income (Annual) (Rs. per Household) (Rajasthan)**

	Average Income	Per cent Share	COV(across HH)
	AAY		
Income from agriculture	7553	37.1	121.8
Income from livestock	500	2.5	89.9
Wage income	9787	48.0	55.2
Income from self-employment	1089	5.3	60.6
Income from salary	1200	5.9	60.6
Income from pension	202	1.0	22.0
Income from transfer	39	0.2	24.7
Total	20370	100.0	—
	BPL		
Income from agriculture	10224	39.8	66.8
Income from livestock	1306	5.1	70.5
Wage income	11586	45.1	55.4
Income from self-employment	1769	6.9	45.1
Income from salary	563	2.2	54.8
Income from pension	188	0.7	104.6
Income from rents	46	0.2	43.0
Income from transfer	4	0.0	—
Total	25686	100.0	—
	APL		
Income from agriculture	11921	22.5	63.6
Income from livestock	1898	3.6	190.9
Wage income	6422	12.1	65.0
Income from self-employment	9221	17.4	110.5
Income from salary	22303	42.1	58.0
Income from pension	668	1.3	139.1
Income from assets	327	0.6	—
Income from rents	270	0.5	77.9
Total	53030	100.0	—

Table 3.14 **Household Income (Annual) (Rs. per Household) (Bihar)**

	Average Income	Per cent Share	COV(across HH)
	AAY		
Income from agriculture	1552	8.7	135.0
Income from livestock	782	4.4	70.1
Wage income	12599	70.6	101.2
Income from self-employment	2463	13.8	52.3
Income from salary	309	1.7	—
Income from assets	113	0.6	115.7
Income from rents	26	0.1	—
Total	17844	100.0	—
	BPL		
Income from agriculture	1157	5.3	70.6
Income from livestock	585	2.7	124.5
Wage income	16377	75.0	69.9
Income from self-employment	2021	9.3	173.5
Income from salary	747	3.4	69.7
Income from pension	154	0.7	146.1
Income from assets	556	2.5	192.9
Income from rents	190	0.9	68.1
Income from transfer	40	0.2	28.3
Total	21827	100.0	—
	APL		
Income from agriculture	20267	26.7	104.9
Income from livestock	2250	3.0	52.5
Wage income	8653	11.4	72.6
Income from self-employment	21911	28.9	193.3
Income from salary	20339	26.8	64.0
Income from pension	2100	2.8	35.7
Income from assets	39	0.1	20.2
Income from rents	333	0.4	—
Total	75892	100.0	—

Table 3.15 **Household Income (Annual) (Rs. per Household) (Chhattisgarh)**

	Average Income	Per cent Share	COV (across HH)
	AAY		
Income from agriculture	2990	25.1	140.0
Income from livestock	439	3.7	91.3
Wage income	7089	59.6	88.2
Income from self-employment	374	3.1	77.1
Income from salary	740	6.2	36.2
Income from pension	249	2.1	108.3
Income from assets	13	0.1	113.7
Income from dividend	9	0.1	—
Total	11903	100.0	—
	BPL		
Income from agriculture	2585	17.0	65.9
Income from livestock	311	2.0	100.8
Wage income	10687	70.3	95.2
Income from self-employment	748	4.9	242.9
Income from salary	619	4.1	75.2
Income from pension	195	1.3	165.7
Income from assets	2	0.0	—
Income from rents	13	0.1	—
Income from transfer	37	0.2	12.9
Total	15197	100.0	—
	APL		
Income from agriculture	22086	42.2	146.7
Income from livestock	1280	2.4	132.6
Wage income	6000	11.5	83.5
Income from self-employment	8116	15.5	76.1
Income from salary	13429	25.7	66.6
Income from pension	1416	2.7	56.6
Income from assets	10	0.0	0.0
Income from transfer	5	0.0	—
Total	52342	100.0	—

Table 3.16 Household Income (Annual) (Rs. per Household) (Uttar Pradesh)

	Average Income	Per cent Share	COV(across HH)
	AAY		
Income from agriculture	3953	24.5	78.0
Income from livestock	862	5.3	149.5
Wage income	6413	39.8	53.0
Income from self-employment	4075	25.3	63.3
Income from salary	537	3.3	59.5
Income from pension	292	1.8	144.8
Total	16132	100.0	
	BPL		
Income from agriculture	5716	29.3	76.8
Income from livestock	537	2.8	104.4
Wage income	6536	33.5	74.6
Income from self-employment	4544	23.3	74.3
Income from salary	1597	8.2	49.9
Income from pension	575	2.9	95.4
Income from assets	17	0.1	—
Income from transfer	3	0.0	—
Total	19525	100.0	—
	APL		
Income from agriculture	20115	39.6	216.7
Income from livestock	2350	4.6	125.0
Wage income	3547	7.0	60.2
Income from self-employment	5937	11.7	65.9
Income from salary	13960	27.5	63.2
Income from pension	3262	6.4	54.2
Income from assets	1591	3.1	20.8
Income from transfer	91	0.2	94.3
Total	50853	100.0	—

Table 3.17 Household Income (Annual) (Rs. per Household) (Assam)

	Average Income	Per cent Share	COV(across HH)
	AAY		
Income from agriculture	3279	13.9	112.8
Wage income	11818	50.0	39.4
Income from self-employment	6652	28.2	40.6
Income from salary	1860	7.9	142.5
Income from pension	9	0.0	0.0
Total	23618	100.0	
	BPL		
Income from agriculture	8417	28.5	112.9
Wage income	8597	29.1	61.5
Income from self-employment	10135	34.4	34.7
Income from salary	1855	6.3	58.3
Income from pension	501	1.7	111.1
Total	29505	100.0	
	APL		
Income from agriculture	4055	4.0	144.0
Income from livestock	100	0.1	616.4
Wage income	1816	1.8	76.6
Income from self-employment	8234	8.1	71.4
Income from salary	82951	82.0	57.3
Income from pension	4030	4.0	12.9
Total	101186	100.0	

Table 3.18 Household Income (Annual) (Rs. per Household) (Mizoram)

	Average Income	Per cent Share	COV(across HH)
	AAY		
Income from agriculture	2048	17.9	22.8
Wage income	7277	63.5	38.9
Income from self-employment	335	2.92	36.6
Income from salary	1798	15.7	54.5
Total	11458	100.0	
	BPL		
Income from agriculture	6768	25.3	56.0
Income from livestock	341	1.28	229.7
Wage income	7881	29.5	95.3
Income from self-employment	5946	22.3	71.2
Income from salary	5691	21.3	74.0
Income from transfer	79	-	-
Total	26706	100.0	
	APL		
Income from agriculture	5179	6.57	48.9
Income from livestock	303	0.4	121.4
Wage income	1170	1.48	53.7
Income from self-employment	14438	18.3	46.9
Income from salary	57761	73.3	42.7
Total	78851	100.0	

The coefficient of variation indicates the dispersion of income across various households for the respective economic activities. Comparing the value of coefficient among the four major economic activities that constituted the highest share of income of all households namely, income from agriculture, wage income, income from self-employment and income from salary, the dispersion of income across households was highest for agriculture in almost all the categories and in all the states. High variability of agricultural income across households was prompted by three factors namely, seasonal nature of agricultural occupation, diversified cropping pattern across households and different amount of land cultivated by different households. Comparing across categories, dispersion in agriculture was highest among the APL households in all the states, except Rajasthan. The value of coefficient exceeded 200 per cent in Uttar Pradesh for the APL households. The percentage of households dependent on agriculture was highest for the APL category and that might be the reason for the highest dispersion across households in their case. For the other three economic activities, dispersion was lowest for salary, followed by wage income and self-employment earnings. Although the number of people engaged in salary and casual earnings was quite large as was discussed in the last section, these two activities had lowest dispersion in income across the households. These statistics indicate that wage and fixed salary differential across households were far less than the earnings through agriculture and self-employment. These results are not surprising as people engaged in casual labour (in agriculture and in non-agriculture) and in fixed salary draw a fixed amount for their work and remuneration do not fluctuate too much across various households. In the case of self-employment as well as agriculture, the returns are directly proportional to the amount of investment made in the business/factory etc., or the number of acres being operated by the households. Thereby, variation in wages and salaries represent dispersion across the households engaged in these activities, whereas dispersion in income from self-employment or agriculture, in addition to inter-personal differences, also include the variation that takes place due to differences in land area cultivated and the amount of capital invested by the households in business and other activities.

3.4 Household Income (Monthly)

An inimitable advantage of the present database is that being a longitudinal data, it not only provides information across households but also over time. As survey was repeated over six points of time, income by various economic activities is available not only for the year 2005-06 (as presented above) but also for a period of consecutive six months beginning from July 2006 onwards. The monthly data contains monthly income from various economic activities. The results are presented in Tables 3.19 to 3.24 for the selected states. In the previous section, we presented coefficient of variation in annual income across households for the same point of time. In the analysis of monthly income, we present coefficient of variation of monthly income across six months for every economic activity for the same households. While COV in the annual income presented dispersion across households, COV in monthly income presents dispersion in income across time.

Table 3.19 Monthly Income and its COV across Six Months (Rs. per Household) (Rajasthan)

	Month 1	Month 2	Month 3	Month 4	Month 5	Month 6	Avg.	COV
			AAY					
Income from agriculture	61.1	45.0	434.4	304.2	1192.2	92.2	354.9	123.6
Income from livestock	49.7	60.3	57.6	68.7	53.8	44.5	55.8	15.2
Wage income	988.0	956.0	1049.8	1091.2	1072.3	1190.2	1057.9	7.8
Income from self-emp.	106.7	112.7	112.5	131.4	121.7	125.6	118.4	7.9
Income from salary	100.0	100.0	94.4	94.4	83.9	86.1	93.1	7.3
Income from pension	16.8	16.8	16.8	16.8	16.8	15.7	16.7	2.7
Income from transfer	6.1	6.7	6.1	7.2	7.8	7.8	6.9	11.0
Total	1328.4	1297.6	1771.7	1714.0	2548.4	1562.1	1703.7	26.8
			BPL					
Income from agriculture	495.3	114.0	890.6	744.6	871.6	262.9	563.2	57.9
Income from livestock	138.8	137.5	148.6	166.3	161.1	125.4	146.3	10.6
Wage income	1124.5	1113.7	1138.7	1130.6	1183.0	1233.6	1154.0	4.0
Income from self-emp.	147.4	149.3	151.3	167.2	180.8	172.0	161.3	8.6
Income from salary	52.2	52.3	48.8	56.2	54.2	54.0	53.0	4.8
Income from pension	15.7	15.7	15.7	15.7	15.7	15.7	15.7	0.1
Income from transfer	1.2	3.8	1.3	1.5	1.2	1.2	1.7	62.3
Income from rental	3.8	3.8	3.8	3.8	3.8	3.8	3.8	0.0
Total	1979.0	1590.2	2398.7	2285.8	2471.3	1868.7	2098.9	16.4
			APL					
Income from agriculture	1311.2	91.1	2274.3	1637.9	990.7	175.2	1080.1	78.5
Income from livestock	159.6	118.5	130.4	155.4	214.7	84.5	143.8	30.7
Wage income	624.4	550.2	592.5	610.7	637.0	658.9	612.3	6.2
Income from self-emp.	887.1	813.1	857.2	884.3	929.4	907.7	879.8	4.6
Income from salary	1903.3	1879.9	1861.2	2300.5	1893.9	1856.5	1949.2	8.9
Income from pension	60.1	60.1	61.9	61.9	61.9	61.9	61.3	1.6
Income from transfer	0.0	0.0	4.7	0.0	0.0	0.0	0.8	244.9
Income from rental	18.9	17.1	17.1	17.1	17.1	17.1	17.4	4.4
Total	4964.6	3529.9	5799.4	5667.7	4744.8	3761.8	4744.7	19.9

Table 3.20 Monthly Income and its COV across Six Months (Rs. per Household) (Bihar)

	Month 1	Month 2	Month 3	Month 4	Month 5	Month 6	Avg.	COV
				AAY				
Income from agriculture	74.5	26.8	176.8	28.4	22.7	54.1	63.9	92.1
Income from livestock	25.0	27.3	23.2	23.5	23.5	23.5	24.3	6.6
Wage income	1170.9	1196.8	1337.4	1340.8	1445.1	1456.8	1324.6	9.1
Income from self-emp.	216.8	219.8	225.8	239.2	247.2	275.2	237.3	9.2
Income from salary	25.8	25.8	25.8	25.8	25.8	25.8	25.8	0.0
Income from pension	1.0	1.0	1.0	6.2	0.0	0.0	1.5	150.6
Income from transfer	0.0	0.0	1.0	0.5	0.3	0.5	0.4	101.1
Income from rental	11.3	11.9	11.9	11.9	24.7	21.1	15.5	38.2
Income from assets	9.3	6.7	8.8	7.7	19.1	0.0	8.6	71.5
Total	1534.6	1516.1	1811.6	1683.8	1808.2	1856.9	1701.9	8.7
				BPL				
Income from agriculture	117.5	70.4	75.4	50.5	56.3	59.6	71.6	33.9
Income from livestock	82.2	57.8	55.3	55.0	53.8	54.6	59.8	18.5
Wage income	1722.6	1527.5	1576.3	1570.4	1592.8	1641.8	1605.2	4.3
Income from self-emp.	218.6	148.9	144.1	157.8	151.1	154.5	162.5	17.2
Income from salary	91.9	72.0	100.5	81.1	79.9	79.9	84.2	12.1
Income from pension	12.8	14.2	15.7	15.7	31.8	13.1	17.2	42.2
Income from transfer	23.0	3.8	4.0	24.1	4.2	4.2	10.5	95.7
Income from rental	14.5	12.6	11.7	10.7	12.6	12.5	12.4	10.2
Income from assets	25.1	9.3	8.8	17.9	10.7	6.1	13.0	55.1
Income from dividends	0.0	0.0	0.0	0.0	134.2	0.0	22.4	244.9
Total	2308.1	1916.6	1991.7	1983.1	2127.4	2026.1	2058.8	6.8
				APL				
Income from agriculture	1793.1	1210.0	1197.2	1279.7	1199.4	1246.7	1321.0	17.7
Income from livestock	192.8	181.7	166.1	178.9	178.3	175.6	178.9	4.8
Wage income	967.2	958.9	974.7	1031.1	838.9	914.7	947.6	6.9
Income from self-emp.	1335.6	1428.9	1347.8	1400.6	1309.4	1371.1	1365.6	3.2
Income from salary	1916.7	1877.8	1788.9	2218.9	1824.4	2430.0	2009.4	12.8
Income from pension	175.0	175.0	180.6	180.6	180.6	180.6	178.7	1.6
Income from rental	0.0	55.6	0.0	0.0	0.0	0.0	9.3	244.9
Income from assets	1111.1	11.1	5.6	0.0	1.7	0.0	188.2	240.2
Total	7491.4	5898.9	5660.8	6289.7	5532.8	6318.6	6198.7	11.4

3.21 Monthly Income and its COV across Six Months (Rs. per Household) (Chhattisgarh)

	Month 1	Month 2	Month 3	Month 4	Month 5	Month 6	Avg.	COV
			AAY					
Income from agriculture	148.7	207.4	260.4	226.7	242.5	230.5	219.4	17.7
Income from livestock	27.5	23.9	26.0	34.4	36.5	38.5	31.1	19.6
Wage income	769.8	650.4	653.4	659.8	742.2	759.3	705.8	8.1
Income from self-emp.	33.7	30.3	39.2	46.0	43.0	55.8	41.3	22.1
Income from salary	76.9	123.8	134.6	137.5	96.2	86.5	109.3	23.8
Income from pension	23.2	18.0	17.3	22.7	23.4	21.3	21.0	12.8
Total	1079.7	1053.8	1130.9	1127.0	1183.9	1191.9	1127.9	4.9
			BPL					
Income from agriculture	89.1	138.5	125.6	122.1	119.5	129.4	120.7	14.0
Income from livestock	28.0	20.3	22.1	19.6	19.1	17.1	21.1	17.9
Wage income	982.4	981.4	965.9	1040.3	1064.9	1064.8	1016.6	4.4
Income from self-emp.	44.3	42.4	47.5	45.0	60.2	59.9	49.9	16.1
Income from salary	50.8	69.7	84.1	94.6	62.5	82.7	74.1	21.7
Income from pension	17.8	16.8	19.7	19.5	17.5	19.8	18.5	7.0
Income from rental	1.3	16.4	1.8	0.4	1.7	2.1	4.0	155.6
Total	1213.8	1285.6	1266.6	1341.5	1345.5	1375.8	1304.8	4.6
			APL					
Income from agriculture	665.0	707.4	705.7	720.2	1558.3	874.9	871.9	39.5
Income from livestock	55.9	46.8	52.1	56.6	46.8	36.6	49.1	15.1
Wage income	601.2	575.5	666.9	579.1	562.8	545.6	588.5	7.2
Income from self-emp.	721.2	640.9	642.5	664.2	567.8	602.8	639.9	8.2
Income from salary	1086.0	1183.4	1021.8	1242.0	1313.1	1746.6	1265.5	20.4
Income from pension	126.4	105.2	126.9	105.2	128.0	105.2	116.1	10.4
Total	3255.8	3259.2	3215.9	3367.4	4176.8	3911.8	3531.1	11.6

Table 3.22 Monthly Income and its COV across Six Months (Rs. per Household) (UP)

	Month 1	Month 2	Month 3	Month 4	Month 5	Month 6	Avg.	COV
			AAY					
Income from agriculture	337.1	345.9	463.4	312.2	354.4	325.6	356.4	15.3
Income from livestock	72.7	72.3	82.2	71.2	71.0	85.4	75.8	8.3
Wage income	641.1	647.8	663.3	838.8	772.2	698.9	710.4	11.2
Income from self-emp.	345.4	380.2	391.5	348.3	345.1	338.0	358.1	6.2
Income from salary	45.9	46.8	46.8	48.3	54.1	57.1	49.8	9.3
Income from pension	25.6	25.6	24.4	24.4	24.4	14.6	23.2	18.2
Income from transfer	2.4	2.9	1.5	2.9	1.5	2.0	2.2	30.6
Income from assets	0.0	0.0	0.0	19.5	0.0	0.0	3.3	244.9
Total	1470.2	1521.6	1673.1	1665.6	1622.7	1521.6	1579.1	5.4
			BPL					
Income from agriculture	534.3	583.1	558.6	485.0	500.7	474.9	522.8	8.2
Income from livestock	65.1	70.3	77.9	79.9	76.6	73.0	73.8	7.4
Wage income	665.1	594.7	632.7	606.1	579.2	592.4	611.7	5.2
Income from self-emp.	513.2	456.8	459.5	435.1	423.5	446.3	455.7	6.9
Income from salary	130.1	140.4	138.5	140.1	141.4	138.7	138.2	3.0
Income from pension	45.2	45.3	45.4	45.3	45.3	45.1	45.3	0.2
Income from transfer	1.3	0.0	0.8	0.0	0.0	0.0	0.4	161.0
Income from assets	0.0	8.4	0.0	25.6	0.0	0.0	5.7	182.4
Total	1954.5	1899.1	1913.6	1817.1	1766.6	1770.4	1853.5	4.3
			APL					
Income from agriculture	1482.8	1862.6	1382.3	1251.3	1361.5	1189.9	1421.7	16.8
Income from livestock	219.5	207.4	193.4	121.4	109.6	114.6	161.0	31.7
Wage income	342.8	365.4	336.7	344.2	327.0	349.2	344.2	3.7
Income from self-emp.	572.7	604.3	604.6	495.7	470.7	525.3	545.5	10.4
Income from salary	1058.8	1208.8	1142.2	1218.9	1158.3	1149.2	1156.1	5.0
Income from pension	364.8	355.8	353.8	360.4	353.9	380.1	361.4	2.8
Income from transfer	0.0	0.0	0.0	0.0	50.5	30.3	13.5	162.0
Income from assets	0.0	0.0	0.0	70.7	0.0	0.0	11.8	244.9
Total	4041.5	4604.4	4012.9	3862.5	3831.5	3738.6	4015.2	7.7

Table 3.23 **Monthly Income and its COV across Six Months (Rs. per Household) (Assam)**

	Month 1	Month 2	Month 3	Month 4	Month 5	Month 6	Avg.	COV
				AAY				
Income from agriculture	321.6	314.2	323.2	0.0	337.9	347.7	274.1	49.2
Income from livestock	0.0	0.0	0.5	0.0	0.0	0.0	0.1	244.9
Wage income	1075.4	1080.2	1129.6	1163.9	1064.2	1291.3	1134.1	7.6
Income from self-emp.	717.4	538.2	592.4	631.6	643.5	706.3	638.2	10.6
Income from salary	88.9	60.0	60.0	49.5	49.5	49.5	59.6	25.7
Income from pension	0.8	0.0	0.0	0.0	0.0	0.0	0.1	244.9
Total	2204.1	1992.5	2105.7	1845.0	2095.1	2394.8	2106.2	8.9
				BPL				
Income from agriculture	679.7	678.0	696.6	0.0	861.7	791.8	618.0	50.4
Income from livestock	0.0	0.0	0.3	0.0	0.0	0.0	0.1	240.6
Wage income	830.0	717.7	713.1	728.1	676.5	818.9	747.4	8.3
Income from self-emp.	960.7	926.0	902.4	863.3	980.5	1051.1	947.3	6.9
Income from salary	144.5	155.0	161.6	156.7	156.7	156.7	155.2	3.7
Income from pension	47.5	47.5	47.4	47.4	47.1	54.7	48.6	6.1
Total	2662.4	2524.3	2521.4	1795.4	2722.5	2873.1	2516.5	15.0
				APL				
Income from agriculture	329.4	362.7	360.2	0.0	609.0	434.3	349.3	56.9
Income from livestock	10.0	10.0	9.0	9.0	9.0	9.0	9.3	5.5
Wage income	178.5	126.0	172.6	160.9	154.5	161.2	159.0	11.5
Income from self-emp.	731.8	636.8	642.3	450.2	737.7	609.0	634.6	16.5
Income from salary	5826.1	7085.8	6536.7	6431.2	5517.3	6173.5	6261.8	8.8
Income from pension	338.8	338.8	338.8	338.8	338.8	338.8	338.8	0.0
Total	7414.6	8560.1	8059.6	7390.1	7366.1	7725.7	7752.7	6.2

Table 3.24 Monthly Income and its COV across Six Months (Rs. per Household) (Mizoram)

	Month 1	Month 2	Month 3	Month 4	Month 5	Month 6	Avg.	COV
			AAY					
Income from agriculture	231.1	360.7	202.6	189.9	119.4	114.8	203.1	44.4
Income from livestock	2.0	2.5	2.5	2.0	2.0	2.0	2.2	9.7
Wage income	639.5	628.2	628.0	633.7	638.6	654.3	637.0	1.5
Income from self-emp.	27.6	26.5	29.6	30.6	31.6	30.6	29.4	6.7
Income from salary	151.5	151.5	151.5	151.5	151.5	151.5	151.5	0.0
Total	1051.7	1169.4	1014.1	1007.8	943.2	953.3	1023.2	8.0
			BPL					
Income from agriculture	657.8	781.3	794.0	536.7	500.0	500.1	628.3	21.7
Income from livestock	31.3	32.1	30.7	30.2	30.3	28.2	30.5	4.4
Wage income	671.2	674.0	656.7	621.4	644.2	645.9	652.2	3.0
Income from self-emp.	464.6	496.3	485.3	477.5	488.3	491.0	483.8	2.3
Income from salary	520.9	520.9	520.9	520.9	520.9	520.9	520.9	0.0
Income from transfer	7.1	7.1	7.1	7.1	7.1	7.1	7.1	0.0
Total	2352.9	2511.8	2494.6	2193.8	2190.7	2193.2	2322.9	6.6
			APL					
Income from agriculture	544.6	683.0	375.0	218.8	218.8	254.5	382.4	50.5
Income from livestock	24.6	24.6	23.7	22.8	23.7	21.9	23.5	4.4
Wage income	91.1	92.9	98.2	95.5	102.7	100.0	96.7	4.5
Income from self-emp.	1327.7	1320.5	1260.7	1255.4	1250.0	1269.6	1280.7	2.7
Income from salary	4716.1	4762.5	4762.5	4726.8	4762.5	4762.5	4748.8	0.5
Total	6704.0	6883.5	6520.1	6319.2	6357.6	6408.5	6532.1	3.4

The monthly income estimates presented in the tables commensurate well with the annual income presented in the last section. On an average, monthly income for AAY, BPL and APL categories was quite closer to the annual income, if one divides the annual estimates by 12 to make it comparable with the monthly income. The estimates of monthly income were a little bit on the higher side for the AAY and BPL categories while annual income was higher in the case of APL households. Nonetheless, the difference between the two was not very high and significant. Therefore, for the purpose of comparison of poverty estimates we can use any one or both of these estimates.[1] Monthly income across the six states further verifies our earlier findings that Assam constituted the highest income while lowest income was observed by and large in the case of Chhattisgarh. For the AAY households, monthly (household) income was above Rs. two thousand for Assam, about one and a half thousand each for Rajasthan, Bihar and Uttar Pradesh, and around one thousand for Chhattisgarh and Mizoram. The monthly household income estimates for BPL population were very close to the AAY estimates. BPL income was estimated as Rs. two and a half thousand for Assam and Mizoram, around two thousand each for Rajasthan, Bihar and Uttar Pradesh and one and a half thousand for Chhattisgarh.

The APL income varied from Rs. eight thousand in Assam, above six thousand in Mizoram and Bihar and between three and a half to five thousand each in Chhattisgarh, Uttar Pradesh and Rajasthan. From the income estimates (monthly as well as annual), it does not appear that the AAY income belonged to the poorest of the poor households, especially those who were not able to get two square meals a day, that was the sole criteria for issuing separate BPL and AAY cards and that was also the principal theme of the targeted PDS system.[2] The BPL and AAY income estimates were very close denying the argument that former estimates belonged to the upper or average strata of income among the BPL population and the latter one representing the bottom most stratum. The distribution across different economic activities was almost same as was discussed in the case

1. We use both monthly and annual estimates to compare the official estimates of number of people below poverty in different states (See Chapter 6).

2. This issue will be probed in further details in the forthcoming chapters.

of annual income. The major constituents of monthly income were wages, agriculture and self-employment in the ascending order for the AAY and BPL households and agriculture, salary and self-employment in that order for APL households.

Comparing the dispersion of income across time period, it is apparent from the coefficient of variation results that agriculture income fluctuated the most across six months as was also expected because of seasonal nature of agriculture income. Dispersion was very high in Rajasthan, Bihar and Assam, while the variation was comparatively less in Mizoram, Chhattisgarh and Uttar Pradesh. It is noteworthy that agriculture earnings happen only during few months at the time of *kharif* and *rabi* harvest. However, in our survey data, the income figures are collected the way farmers receive their payments for the sale of crop from the buyer. Mostly, the buyer of the crop is an intermediary in the form of *arhatia* or commission agent in the *mandi*, or the landlord-moneylender-*sahukar* in the village. In most of the cases, buyer not only purchases crop from the farmer but also is the lender for the farmers on whom they depend for their day-to-day expenditure during the off-season. Generally, payments for the sale of crop are not mostly made immediately but deferred for the whole season. Therefore, our monthly earnings from agriculture in all the states do not truly reflect the seasonal nature of such earnings in the agriculture and consequently value of coefficient is very small in some of the states. Dispersion was particularly low in the case of salary as income for this item was almost fixed over time. Wages and self-employment income also varied less compared to agriculture and livestock income. Last and the least, because of the irregular nature of income from pension, transfer, rental and dividend, their dispersion was quite high in most of the cases.

To validate our estimates on income in the six selected states, we compare our below poverty income data with the Planning Commission poverty estimates of income released recently. The state-wise rural and urban poverty lines as released by the Planning Commission for the year 2004-05 are given in Table 3.25. The poverty line is estimated by the Planning Commission using the original state-specific poverty lines identified by the Expert Group and updating them to the current prices using the Consumer Price Index of Agricultural Labourers (CPIAL) for the rural poverty lines and Consumer Price Index for Industrial Workers (CPIIW) for the urban poverty lines. As our estimates of average household income coincide with the Planning Commission figure that are released for the year 2004-05, we can check whether the sampled families who owned below poverty ration cards were truly poor or not according to the definition of Planning Commission, Government of India. Table 3.2 presents per capital monthly income defined by the official poverty line and the observed per capita monthly income by our selected households. In our estimates, we have used both annual as well as monthly income estimates. Comparing our survey data with the Planning Commission, it is observed from the results that our income estimates were more or less very close to that of Planning Commission, except the two northeastern states, namely Mizoram and Assam where survey income was higher for BPL households in both the states and for AAY households in Assam. In other states, our observed income estimates were comparable with the official poverty line. However, it is worth mentioning that the official poverty line income is the upper bound cut-off, whereas our estimated income (presented in the table) is the arithmetic mean (central value).

Table 3.25 Comparison of Our Observed Income with the Official Poverty Line Income Defined by the Planning Commission

	Our Survey Data Estimates				Planning Commission Estimates[$]	
State	Based on Annual Income		Based on Monthly Income		Rural	Urban
	AAY	BPL	AAY	BPL		
Chhattisgarh	248	284	282	293	322	560
Uttar Pradesh	258	348	303	397	366	483
Bihar	311	342	355	387	354	435
Rajasthan	399	450	400	441	375	560
Assam	484	611	518	625	388	379
Mizoram	295	610	316	636	388[#]	379[#]

Note: 1. $ - The poverty line is worked out from the expenditure class-wise distribution of persons based on Uniform Recall Period consumption, i.e., consumption data collected from 30-day recall period for all items.

2. # - Poverty line of Assam is used for Mizoram as no separate poverty line was defined for Mizoram.

Source: Planning Commission, Government of India.

4 Consumption Pattern and Role of PDS

4.1 Introduction

Food being the basic necessity for living, gets the highest priority in the family expenditure of households, especially the poor ones who have very limited means of livelihood. Access to food demands affordability, which depends upon the twin factors, namely income of the people and prices prevailing in the country (Nasurudeen *et al.*, 2006). According to one estimate, food grains account for about four-fifth of the calorie intake of the poor. Therefore, food availability for such people is much more susceptible to any changes in their income as well as food prices. Consequently, the dietary pattern differs not only among various income groups but it also undergoes transition over time that includes both quantitative and qualitative changes in the diet. According to WHO (2003), the dietary consumption pattern is a complex process that is determined by many factors, such as income, prices, individual preferences, beliefs, cultural traditions as well as geographical, environmental, social and other economic factors.

India became food self-sufficient following tremendous achievement in food grains' productivity after the successful adoption of the green revolution. However, availability of food at the national level does not automatically ensure food security at the household level. The problem of transitory food insecurity is associated with issues related to either access or availability of food whereas chronic food insecurity is associated primarily with poverty and arises due to continuously inadequate diet (Radhakrishna, 2002). Though India's achievement in combating transitory food insecurity has remained impressive, the issue of chronic food insecurity still continues and is widespread in the country. The physical access to food have not been able to ensure economic access to food at the micro level indicating distorting trends in the food and nutrition security.

The available statistics on food consumption data through various rounds of National Sample Survey (NSS) portraits a baffling picture on food and nutrition security in India.[1] On the one hand, per capita food grains consumption and total calorie intake are declining and on the other, grain surpluses reached to the peak levels in the recent past and real per capita expenditure on food is rising among all income groups. There are numerous factors responsible for the falling per capita food consumption. The more sensible ones are, the reduction in calorie requirement due to a more sedentary lifestyle among the rural masses and diversification of the Indian diet to include more high value commodities in the form of fruits, vegetables, diary products, sugar, oil, eggs, fish and meat products and consequently fall in the required intake of calories in the form of cereals (Ray, 2005).

This chapter analyses the dynamics of consumption among the selected AAY, BPL and APL households in the six states. The chapter is divided into six sections. The chapter begins with a discussion on consumption of major food items by the selected households during the period of six months for which survey was carried out. A comparison of our survey results is made with that of NSS consumption data for the latest quinquennial round of NSS. Section two presents food and non-food expenditure where percentage is worked out for each item in the total consumption expenditure. Section three presents the amount delivered to the households by the PDS and the percentage of population obtaining PDS commodities. The next section makes a comparison of the percentage shares of PDS and that of market in the total quantity consumed by the households. The last section earmarks the actual prices paid by the households for the commodities purchased from PDS *vis-à-vis* from the market.

1. For details on this issue, see a special section on "Trends in Food Consumption and Nutrition—Food Security Concerns" published in *Indian Journal of Agricultural Economics* 61(3): 362-98, Conference Number, July-September 2006.

4.2 Food Consumption Pattern

Food consumption expressed in kilocalories (Kcal) per capita is used for measuring the level of nutrition. In defining poverty, the Planning Commission uses the calorie requirement norm of 2400 Kcal per capita for the rural areas and 2100 Kcal per capita for the urban areas. It further emphasises that 50 per cent of calories to be derived from carbohydrate and the remaining from the protein and fat with 25 per cent each. Fifty per cent of the required calorie means drawing 1200 calorie from cereals in rural India and 1050 in the urban India. To get the requisite 1200 calories, 10.44 kg cereals per capita per 30 days or 348 gms per capita per day are required by the rural people and 9.12 kg cereals per capita per 30 days or 304 gms per capita per day are required by the urban people to obtain 1050 calories.[2]

Tables 4.1 to 4.6 present per capita monthly consumption of food items, *viz.*, cereals, pulses, edible oils, sugar and milk by our selected households in the six states. It is evident from the results that on an average, per capita cereal consumption surpassed the 1200 calorie norm, i.e., the total cereal consumption was above 10.45 kgs in all the states and all the categories, except Chhattisgarh, where all the three category of households fell short of this target. Among the cereals, wheat and rice constituted the principal share. Wheat was the major cereal consumed in Rajasthan with average consumption of 9.5 kgs. Rice occupied the principal place in Chhattisgarh, Assam and Mizoram with an average quantity of 9 kgs, 11 kgs and 10 kgs, respectively. In the other two states namely, Uttar Pradesh and Bihar, both wheat and rice were consumed almost in the same ratio. The average quantity of wheat and rice consumed in Uttar Pradesh was 5.5 and 6 kgs, respectively. In Bihar, the average quantity was 6.5 and 5.5, for rice and wheat, respectively. The other coarse cereals consumed namely, *jowar*, *bajra*, maize, barley and *ragi* were around 1.5 kgs in Rajasthan, less than a kg each in Uttar Pradesh, Bihar and Chhattisgarh and almost nil in Assam and Mizoram. At the overall, total cereal consumption in the six states was around 11.5 kgs, that varied from 9.5 to 10 kgs in the case of Chhattisgarh and Mizoram to 11 kgs in Rajasthan and Assam, 12 kgs in Uttar Pradesh and 12.5 kgs in Bihar.

The tables also contain consumption of cereals as revealed by various rounds of National Sample Survey (NSS). Three rounds of large sample survey, i.e., 50th Round (1993-94), 55th Round (1999-2000) and 61st Round (2004-05) consumption results are presented in the tables along with the observed consumption for the average of AAY, BPL and APL households. The NSS figures represent average consumption of all households for rural areas as 80 per cent of our sample households are drawn from the rural area. The NSS consumption quantities are not presented for AAY, BPL and APL households separately, because the consumption in physical quantities was not readily available for different expenditure classes at the state level. However, while comparing consumption expenditure for AAY, BPL and APL households, the NSS figures are taken separately for the same income brackets as will be seen in the next section.

It was mentioned in the beginning that per capita consumption of cereals and total calorie intake in India has started declining in the recent past. It is evident from the NSS data presented in the tables that total cereal consumption has also declined in all our selected states, except Mizoram. Total cereals consumption declined from 14.9 kgs to 12.7 kgs in Rajasthan, 14.3 kgs to 13 kgs in Bihar, 13.9 kgs to 12.9 kgs in Uttar Pradesh while it remained stagnant at 13 kgs in Assam and slightly increased from 12 kgs to 13 kgs in Mizoram during the period from 1993-94 to 2004-05. The explanation provided for such a phenomenon in the literature centres around the theory of diversification in food basket as well as changing income and lifestyle of the rural and urban masses. On the one hand, due to change in work nature, the requirement of calorie intake has declined overtime and on the other, the changes in the composition of diet have increased the cost of calories (Radhakrishna and Ravi, 1991; Murty, 1999). Convergence between rural and urban patterns of calorie consumption also provides an explanation to this phenomenon. The per capita calorie intake declined by 5.3 per cent in rural areas whereas it increased at 2.3 per cent in the urban areas for the period from 1972-73 to 1999-2000 (Nasurudeen *et al.*, 2006). Whereas cereals and pulses were the main source of protein in both rural and urban areas in the previous rounds, the contribution of milk and milk products as source of protein is consistently increasing in the more recent rounds of NSS and the increase is observed much more in the urban areas. The contribution from meat, fish and eggs to protein has slightly increased. The urban consumers also often prefer foods that offer variety and convenience rather than maximum calorie content (Delgado *et al.*, 1999).[3]

---

2. The above calculations are based on Planning Commission (1977) calculations that 100 gms cereal on an average produce 345 calories.

3. There is however, an opposite view in other quarters that argues that consumption of cereals is declining due to fall in real purchasing power of a vast section, reduction in state intervention, increasing stocks of food grains along with starvation and failure of the public distribution system, see e.g., Patnaik, 2001, 2003, 2004; Sen and Himanshu, 2004; Ray and Lancaster, 2005; and Meenakshi and Vishwanathan, 2003.

Table 4.1 **Household Consumption of Food Items (Kgs Per Capita Per Month)—Rajasthan**

	Month 1	Month 2	Month 3	Month 4	Month 5	Month 6	Average	NSS[2] 1993-94	NSS[2] 1999-2000	NSS[2] 2004-05
					AAY					
Rice	0.45	0.46	0.51	0.62	1.12	0.99	0.69	-	-	-
Wheat	9.47	10.19	10.58	9.21	9.46	9.62	9.76	-	-	-
Other cereals	0.19	0.09	0.19	2.05	1.75	1.84	1.02	-	-	-
Total cereals	10.11	10.74	11.28	11.88	12.33	12.45	11.47	-	-	-
Total pulses	0.52	0.52	0.54	0.50	0.53	0.55	0.53	-	-	-
Sugar	1.09	0.94	0.92	0.90	0.96	0.95	0.96	-	-	-
Edible oils	0.42	0.45	0.45	0.47	0.49	0.47	0.46	-	-	-
Liquid milk[1]	3.08	3.10	3.16	3.33	3.39	3.35	3.24	-	-	-
					BPL					
Rice	0.44	0.49	0.48	0.59	1.12	1.10	0.70	-	-	-
Wheat	8.83	9.50	9.81	8.63	8.29	8.51	8.93	-	-	-
Other cereals	0.37	0.24	0.24	1.92	1.78	1.81	1.06	-	-	-
Total cereals	9.65	10.24	10.53	11.13	11.19	11.42	10.69	-	-	-
Total pulses	0.50	0.52	0.54	0.53	0.52	0.53	0.52	-	-	-
Sugar	1.12	1.07	0.99	1.00	0.95	0.94	1.01	-	-	-
Edible oils	0.42	0.47	0.46	0.49	0.50	0.47	0.47	-	-	-
Liquid milk[1]	3.91	3.79	3.78	4.03	3.86	3.97	3.89	-	-	-
					APL					
Rice	0.61	0.51	0.46	0.62	0.62	0.63	0.58	-	-	-
Wheat	9.13	9.36	9.64	8.64	9.57	9.60	9.32	-	-	-
Other cereals	0.17	0.19	0.29	1.62	1.76	2.28	1.05	-	-	-
Total cereals	9.92	10.05	10.40	10.87	11.94	12.51	10.95	-	-	-
Total pulses	0.58	0.59	0.61	0.65	0.61	0.56	0.60	-	-	-
Sugar	1.27	1.15	1.08	1.09	1.10	1.02	1.12	-	-	-
Edible oils	0.48	0.53	0.52	0.57	0.55	0.53	0.53	-	-	-
Liquid milk[1]	5.09	4.40	4.73	4.38	4.34	4.17	4.52	-	-	-
					Average					
Rice	0.50	0.49	0.48	0.61	0.95	0.91	0.66	0.22	0.22	0.18
Wheat	9.15	9.68	10.01	8.83	9.11	9.24	9.34	9.44	9.79	8.49
Other cereals	0.24	0.17	0.24	1.86	1.76	1.98	1.04	5.19	4.05	4.02
Total cereals	9.89	10.34	10.74	11.30	11.82	12.13	11.04	14.85	14.19	12.69
Total pulses	0.54	0.54	0.57	0.56	0.55	0.55	0.55	0.52	0.67	0.50
Sugar	1.16	1.05	1.00	1.00	1.00	0.97	1.03	1.17	1.17	-
Edible oils	0.44	0.48	0.48	0.51	0.51	0.49	0.48	0.26	0.43	-
Liquid milk[1]	4.03	3.76	3.89	3.91	3.86	3.83	3.88	10.41	9.62	-

Note: 1. Liquid milk is in litres.

2. The NSS consumption figures are taken from the respective rounds of NSS reports and the quantities represent all classes for the rural areas.

Table 4.2 Household Consumption of Food Items (Kgs Per Capita Per Month)—Bihar

	Month 1	Month 2	Month 3	Month 4	Month 5	Month 6	Average	NSS[2] 1993-94	NSS[2] 1999-2000	NSS[2] 2004-05
					AAY					
Rice	6.48	6.33	6.23	6.56	6.30	6.54	6.41	-	-	-
Wheat	6.42	5.76	5.05	5.41	4.98	5.03	5.44	-	-	-
Other cereals	0.20	0.65	0.72	0.59	0.76	0.75	0.61	-	-	-
Total cereals	13.10	12.74	12.00	12.56	12.04	12.33	12.46	-	-	-
Total pulses	0.60	0.61	0.65	0.77	0.63	0.62	0.65	-	-	-
Sugar	0.34	0.34	0.38	0.61	0.43	0.40	0.42	-	-	-
Edible oils	0.47	0.45	0.45	0.60	0.47	0.45	0.48	-	-	-
Liquid milk[1]	0.56	0.73	0.84	1.10	0.90	1.08	0.87	-	-	-
					BPL					
Rice	6.42	6.38	5.76	6.09	6.21	6.52	6.23	-	-	-
Wheat	5.68	5.03	4.69	4.92	4.78	4.88	5.00	-	-	-
Other cereals	0.17	0.67	0.77	0.64	0.72	0.69	0.61	-	-	-
Total cereals	12.28	12.08	11.21	11.66	11.71	12.09	11.84	-	-	-
Total pulses	0.64	0.63	0.67	0.79	0.64	0.62	0.66	-	-	-
Sugar	0.32	0.32	0.35	0.59	0.43	0.40	0.40	-	-	-
Edible oils	0.48	0.46	0.45	0.61	0.47	0.45	0.49	-	-	-
Liquid milk[1]	0.68	0.82	1.17	1.29	1.10	1.19	1.04	-	-	-
					APL					
Rice	7.19	6.75	6.34	6.36	6.52	6.56	6.62	-	-	-
Wheat	6.65	6.03	6.14	6.50	6.29	6.23	6.31	-	-	-
Other cereals	0.11	0.99	1.07	1.09	1.18	1.03	0.91	-	-	-
Total cereals	13.95	13.76	13.56	13.95	13.98	13.82	13.84	-	-	-
Total pulses	1.04	0.98	0.91	0.92	0.90	0.89	0.94	-	-	-
Sugar	0.69	0.67	0.72	1.00	0.79	0.75	0.77	-	-	-
Edible oils	0.87	0.86	0.77	0.88	0.71	0.62	0.79	-	-	-
Liquid milk[1]	4.43	4.28	4.67	4.15	4.23	4.33	4.35	-	-	-
					Average					
Rice	6.70	6.48	6.11	6.34	6.34	6.54	6.42	7.95	7.89	7.20
Wheat	6.25	5.61	5.29	5.61	5.35	5.38	5.58	5.58	5.21	5.45
Other cereals	0.16	0.77	0.85	0.78	0.88	0.82	0.71	0.78	0.46	0.00
Total cereals	13.11	12.86	12.26	12.72	12.58	12.75	12.71	14.31	13.75	13.04
Total pulses	0.76	0.74	0.74	0.82	0.72	0.71	0.75	0.63	0.78	0.61
Sugar	0.45	0.44	0.48	0.73	0.55	0.52	0.53	0.38	0.44	-
Edible oils	0.61	0.59	0.56	0.70	0.55	0.51	0.59	0.29	0.40	-
Liquid milk[1]	1.89	1.94	2.23	2.18	2.08	2.20	2.09	2.39	2.41	-

Note: 1. Liquid milk is in litres.

2. The NSS consumption figures are taken from the respective rounds of NSS reports and the quantities represent all classes for the rural areas.

Table 4.3 Household Consumption of Food Items (Kgs Per Capita Per Month)—Chhattisgarh

	Month 1	Month 2	Month 3	Month 4	Month 5	Month 6	Average	NSS[2] 2004-05
				AAY				
Rice	9.42	9.88	9.47	10.31	9.80	10.25	9.85	-
Wheat	0.15	0.12	0.06	0.28	0.25	0.34	0.20	-
Other cereals	0.03	0.00	0.00	0.12	0.10	0.07	0.05	-
Total cereals	9.60	10.00	9.54	10.71	10.15	10.66	10.11	-
Total pulses	0.42	0.39	0.37	0.53	0.49	0.50	0.45	-
Sugar	0.37	0.38	0.42	0.45	0.43	0.42	0.41	-
Edible oils	0.70	0.26	0.25	0.33	0.31	0.32	0.36	-
Liquid milk[1]	0.16	0.15	0.18	0.28	0.36	0.34	0.25	-
				BPL				
Rice	8.03	8.03	7.87	8.76	8.62	8.81	8.35	-
Wheat	0.29	0.61	0.72	0.91	0.93	0.98	0.74	-
Other cereals	0.26	0.02	0.00	0.36	0.28	0.28	0.20	-
Total cereals	8.58	8.66	8.59	10.02	9.83	10.07	9.29	-
Total pulses	0.38	0.38	0.37	0.56	0.51	0.51	0.45	-
Sugar	0.48	0.48	0.50	0.53	0.51	0.55	0.51	-
Edible oils	2.11	0.30	0.29	0.38	0.35	0.35	0.63	-
Liquid milk[1]	0.42	0.48	0.44	0.62	0.63	0.54	0.52	-
				APL				
Rice	8.24	8.61	8.59	8.93	8.81	8.94	8.69	-
Wheat	0.74	0.79	0.74	0.93	0.86	1.10	0.86	-
Other cereals	0.02	0.00	0.00	0.18	0.23	0.18	0.10	-
Total cereals	9.01	9.40	9.33	10.04	9.90	10.23	9.65	-
Total pulses	0.63	0.57	0.52	0.68	0.64	0.63	0.61	-
Sugar	0.59	0.58	0.55	0.60	0.57	0.60	0.58	-
Edible oils	0.41	0.40	0.37	0.42	0.39	0.39	0.40	-
Liquid milk[1]	0.94	1.15	0.99	1.18	1.21	1.07	1.09	-
				Average				
Rice	8.56	8.84	8.64	9.33	9.08	9.34	8.97	12.60
Wheat	0.39	0.50	0.51	0.71	0.68	0.81	0.60	0.51
Other cereals	0.10	0.01	0.00	0.22	0.20	0.18	0.12	0.06
Total cereals	9.06	9.35	9.15	10.26	9.96	10.32	9.68	13.17
Total pulses	0.47	0.44	0.42	0.59	0.55	0.55	0.50	0.73
Sugar	0.48	0.48	0.49	0.53	0.51	0.53	0.50	-
Edible oils	1.07	0.32	0.30	0.38	0.35	0.35	0.46	-
Liquid milk[1]	0.51	0.59	0.54	0.69	0.73	0.65	0.62	-

Note: 1. Liquid milk is in litres.

2. The NSS consumption figures are taken from the respective rounds of NSS reports and the quantities represent all classes for the rural areas.

Table 4.4 Household Consumption of Food Items (Kgs Per Capita Per Month)—Uttar Pradesh

	Month 1	Month 2	Month 3	Month 4	Month 5	Month 6	Average	NSS[2] 1993-94	NSS[2] 1999-2000	NSS[2] 2004-05
					AAY					
Rice	5.22	5.83	5.74	5.87	5.65	5.20	5.58	-	-	-
Wheat	4.03	5.18	5.19	6.37	6.35	5.86	5.50	-	-	-
Other cereals	0.03	0.03	0.09	0.00	0.02	0.01	0.03	-	-	-
Total cereals	9.28	11.04	11.01	12.25	12.02	11.07	11.11	-	-	-
Total pulses	0.82	0.82	0.74	0.74	0.71	0.65	0.75	-	-	-
Sugar	0.34	0.43	0.45	0.50	0.43	0.38	0.42	-	-	-
Edible oils	0.37	0.37	0.33	0.32	0.32	0.32	0.34	-	-	-
Liquid milk[1]	0.78	0.93	0.73	0.68	0.55	0.53	0.70	-	-	-
					BPL					
Rice	5.52	6.07	6.39	6.11	5.97	5.51	5.93	-	-	-
Wheat	4.40	5.52	5.69	6.45	6.33	6.39	5.80	-	-	-
Other cereals	0.03	0.02	0.24	0.01	0.01	0.02	0.05	-	-	-
Total cereals	9.94	11.61	12.33	12.57	12.31	11.91	11.78	-	-	-
Total pulses	0.84	0.95	0.92	0.96	0.83	0.79	0.88	-	-	-
Sugar	0.42	0.52	0.55	0.63	0.52	0.43	0.51	-	-	-
Edible oils	0.42	0.43	0.41	0.39	0.38	0.36	0.40	-	-	-
Liquid milk[1]	1.15	1.26	1.20	1.13	0.73	0.74	1.04	-	-	-
					APL					
Rice	5.19	5.55	5.87	5.24	5.09	5.25	5.36	-	-	-
Wheat	6.23	7.30	7.35	7.30	7.14	7.68	7.17	-	-	-
Other cereals	0.08	0.08	0.79	0.15	0.06	0.02	0.20	-	-	-
Total cereals	11.50	12.94	14.01	12.68	12.29	12.96	12.73	-	-	-
Total pulses	1.15	1.20	1.15	1.16	1.08	1.04	1.13	-	-	-
Sugar	0.53	0.61	0.70	0.73	0.70	0.59	0.64	-	-	-
Edible oils	0.51	0.53	0.53	0.51	0.48	0.49	0.51	-	-	-
Liquid milk[1]	2.22	2.84	2.48	2.04	1.97	1.70	2.21	-	-	-
					Average					
Rice	5.31	5.82	6.00	5.74	5.57	5.32	5.63	4.00	4.28	4.09
Wheat	4.89	6.00	6.08	6.71	6.61	6.64	6.15	9.16	8.92	8.55
Other cereals	0.05	0.04	0.37	0.05	0.03	0.02	0.09	0.74	0.22	0.28
Total cereals	10.24	11.86	12.45	12.50	12.21	11.98	11.87	13.90	13.62	12.91
Total pulses	0.94	0.99	0.94	0.95	0.88	0.83	0.92	0.90	1.07	0.82
Sugar	0.43	0.52	0.57	0.62	0.55	0.46	0.53	0.89	0.95	-
Edible oils	0.43	0.44	0.42	0.40	0.39	0.39	0.42	0.38	0.50	-
Liquid milk[1]	1.38	1.68	1.47	1.29	1.09	0.99	1.32	5.44	4.52	-

Note: 1. Liquid milk is in litres.

2. The NSS consumption figures are taken from the respective rounds of NSS reports and the quantities represent all classes for the rural areas.

Table 4.5 Household Consumption of Food Items (Kgs Per Capita Per Month)—Assam

	Month 1	Month 2	Month 3	Month 4	Month 5	Month 6	Average	NSS[2] 1993-94	NSS[2] 1999-2000	NSS[2] 2004-05
					AAY					
Rice	11.85	11.13	11.28	10.98	8.98	11.18	10.90	-	-	-
Wheat	0.01	0.10	0.02	0.03	0.02	0.01	0.03	-	-	-
Other cereals	0.00	0.00	0.00	0.00	0.00	0.00	0.00	-	-	-
Total cereals	11.86	11.24	11.31	11.01	9.01	11.18	10.93	-	-	-
Total pulses	0.59	0.59	0.59	0.60	0.50	0.60	0.58	-	-	-
Sugar	0.43	0.38	0.47	0.43	0.37	0.46	0.42	-	-	-
Edible oils	0.56	0.53	0.50	0.44	0.38	0.46	0.48	-	-	-
Liquid milk[1]	0.14	0.09	0.21	0.16	0.20	0.48	0.21	-	-	-
					BPL					
Rice	12.04	11.61	11.73	11.30	8.98	11.35	11.17	-	-	-
Wheat	0.00	0.03	0.05	0.04	0.02	0.02	0.03	-	-	-
Other cereals	0.00	0.00	0.00	0.00	0.00	0.00	0.00	-	-	-
Total cereals	12.04	11.64	11.79	11.34	9.00	11.37	11.20	-	-	-
Total pulses	0.75	0.72	0.67	0.67	0.57	0.68	0.68	-	-	-
Sugar	0.52	0.46	0.51	0.52	0.45	0.52	0.50	-	-	-
Edible oils	0.60	0.56	0.55	0.52	0.42	0.53	0.53	-	-	-
Liquid milk[1]	0.14	0.08	0.15	0.25	0.27	0.59	0.25	-	-	-
					APL					
Rice	12.23	11.74	11.84	11.56	9.48	12.01	11.47	-	-	-
Wheat	0.09	0.20	0.33	0.13	0.08	0.06	0.15	-	-	-
Other cereals	0.01	0.00	0.00	0.00	0.00	0.00	0.00	-	-	-
Total cereals	12.32	11.94	12.17	11.69	9.57	12.07	11.63	-	-	-
Total pulses	0.89	0.84	0.85	0.98	0.83	0.89	0.88	-	-	-
Sugar	0.61	0.56	0.63	0.65	0.52	0.60	0.59	-	-	-
Edible oils	0.73	0.77	0.69	0.71	0.54	0.60	0.67	-	-	-
Liquid milk[1]	1.58	1.24	1.17	0.96	0.89	0.88	1.12	-	-	-
					Average					
Rice	12.04	11.49	11.62	11.28	9.15	11.51	11.18	12.53	11.93	12.43
Wheat	0.03	0.11	0.13	0.07	0.04	0.03	0.07	0.64	0.57	0.61
Other cereals	0.00	0.00	0.00	0.00	0.00	0.00	0.00	0.00	0.00	0.00
Total cereals	12.07	11.60	11.75	11.35	9.19	11.54	11.25	13.17	12.63	13.04
Total pulses	0.74	0.72	0.70	0.75	0.63	0.72	0.71	0.49	0.51	0.61
Sugar	0.52	0.47	0.54	0.53	0.45	0.53	0.50	0.42	0.46	-
Edible oils	0.63	0.62	0.58	0.56	0.45	0.53	0.56	0.30	0.35	-
Liquid milk[1]	0.62	0.47	0.51	0.46	0.45	0.65	0.53	1.21	1.11	-

Note: 1. Liquid milk is in litres.

2. The NSS consumption figures are taken from the respective rounds of NSS reports and the quantities represent all classes for the rural areas.

Table 4.6 Household Consumption of Food Items (Kgs Per Capita Per Month)—Mizoram

	Month 1	Month 2	Month 3	Month 4	Month 5	Month 6	Average	NSS[2] 1993-94	NSS[2] 1999-2000	NSS[2] 2004-05
					AAY					
Rice	8.36	7.74	9.78	10.87	11.13	11.01	9.81	-	-	-
Wheat	0.05	0.05	0.05	0.05	0.05	0.05	0.05	-	-	-
Other cereals	0.01	0.00	0.03	0.03	0.00	0.00	0.01	-	-	-
Total cereals	8.42	7.79	9.86	10.95	11.18	11.06	9.87	-	-	-
Total pulses	0.72	0.77	0.79	0.80	0.83	0.77	0.78	-	-	-
Sugar	1.29	1.87	0.95	1.16	1.30	1.15	1.28	-	-	-
Edible oils	4.45	0.70	0.46	0.51	1.06	0.42	1.27	-	-	-
Liquid milk[1]	1.11	1.10	1.02	0.95	0.99	0.95	1.02	-	-	-
					BPL					
Rice	9.13	8.63	9.20	10.27	10.17	10.28	9.61	-	-	-
Wheat	0.00	0.00	0.02	0.01	0.04	0.02	0.01	-	-	-
Other cereals	0.00	0.00	0.03	0.00	0.03	0.00	0.01	-	-	-
Total cereals	9.13	8.63	9.25	10.28	10.23	10.30	9.64	-	-	-
Total pulses	0.64	0.73	0.76	0.80	0.81	0.71	0.74	-	-	-
Sugar	1.29	1.23	1.03	1.16	1.18	1.10	1.17	-	-	-
Edible oils	0.47	0.49	0.45	1.81	2.71	0.47	1.07	-	-	-
Liquid milk[1]	0.78	1.13	0.96	0.98	1.00	0.96	0.97	-	-	-
					APL					
Rice	9.45	9.44	9.91	10.46	10.61	10.52	10.06	-	-	-
Wheat	0.00	0.00	0.00	0.03	0.02	0.05	0.02	-	-	-
Other cereals	0.00	0.00	0.01	0.01	0.01	0.01	0.01	-	-	-
Total cereals	9.45	9.44	9.92	10.51	10.64	10.58	10.09	-	-	-
Total pulses	0.76	0.81	1.11	1.13	0.91	0.79	0.92	-	-	-
Sugar	1.35	1.22	1.06	1.18	1.27	1.26	1.22	-	-	-
Edible oils	0.40	0.51	0.46	0.49	0.47	0.48	0.47	-	-	-
Liquid milk[1]	1.02	1.27	1.20	1.14	1.17	1.03	1.14	-	-	-
					Average					
Rice	8.98	8.60	9.63	10.54	10.64	10.60	9.83	12.02	12.25	13.00
Wheat	0.00	0.00	0.02	0.01	0.02	0.02	0.01	0.04	0.29	0.16
Other cereals	0.00	0.00	0.02	0.01	0.01	0.01	0.01	0.00	0.00	0.09
Total cereals	8.98	8.60	9.67	10.56	10.67	10.63	9.85	12.06	12.64	13.24
Total pulses	0.71	0.77	0.89	0.91	0.85	0.76	0.81	0.46	0.84	0.57
Sugar	1.31	1.44	1.01	1.17	1.25	1.17	1.22	0.63	7.00	-
Edible oils	1.77	0.57	0.46	0.94	1.42	0.46	0.93	0.35	3.77	-
Liquid milk[1]	0.97	1.17	1.06	1.02	1.05	0.98	1.04	0.69	0.44	-

Note: 1. Liquid milk is in litres.

2. The NSS consumption figures are taken from the respective rounds of NSS reports and the quantities represent all classes for the rural areas.

The shift of calories from cereals and pulses towards edible oils, fats and high value products is also visible from the trends presented by our survey data. The quantity of cereals consumed by AAY households was higher than that of APL and BPL households in Rajasthan, Chhattisgarh and Bihar. On the other hand, the quantity of edible oils, sugar and milk consumed portrays trends that are opposite to the above trends. In all the states, without any exception, the above poverty households were consuming much higher quantity of milk, edible oils and sugar in comparison to both below poverty households as well as Antyodaya households. Therefore, the statistics depicted above substantiate the argument that with the rising level of income, people have a tendency to diversify their palate towards more nutritious and high value commodities. Comparing the consumption pattern revealed by our survey data with that of NSS, our average consumption pattern stands more or less in line with the NSS. Total cereal consumption was slightly less than the NSS figures in almost all the states, probably because our data was more slanting towards the below poverty households whereas the NSS figures depicted average figures for all classes. Pulses, sugar and edible oils however, were closer to the NSS figures. The next section will present a more clear picture in terms of consumption expenditure of different food and non-food items. Because NSS data for consumption expenditure is available by various expenditure categories, that enables us to make a comparison for the contiguous income groups.

Comparing variability in the food consumption, Annexure Table A-4.1 presents results of coefficient of variation across households and across time period (six months) for each category. Variations in consumption were higher across households than for the same households over time. Among different categories, consumption variation was higher among the below poverty households compared to the above poverty households. Higher variation in food consumption by the poor households puts forth the question of affordability of food by such people and raises the need for some sort of income insurance for them.[4] Among AAY households, coefficient of variation was high for milk in almost all the states, indicating its high cost for the poor that was beyond purchasing capacity of all the (AAY) households. Coarse cereals also displayed higher variability among the poorest households as the coarse cereals were an alternate to superior cereals in the event of fall in income of these households. Among the APL households, variability was high among the minor cereals namely, rice in Rajasthan, wheat in Chhattisgarh and Assam and coarse grains in Uttar Pradesh, Bihar and Chhattisgarh, as these were consumed by a few households in their category. Across time, variation was higher for coarse cereals across all the categories in all the states. At the overall, coefficient of variation of consumption over time was lower than that of coefficient of variation in income supporting the well-documented phenomenon of consumption smoothing by the households (see Chapter 5).[5]

4.3 Food and Non-Food Consumption Expenditure

According to the NSS data, the share of non-cereal items in the monthly per capita expenditure (all India) has been consistently increasing in both rural and urban areas. The share of non-food consumption expenditure increased from 27 per cent in 1972-1973 to 41 per cent in 1999-2000 in rural areas, while it increased from 36 per cent to 52 per cent in the urban areas during the same time period. In 1999-2000, about 59 per cent of the total consumption expenditure (all India) was on food items in rural areas, while it was 48 per cent in the urban areas. For our six selected states, monthly consumption expenditure per capita for each category and their comparative amount according to the NSS 2004-05 (61st Round) for the respective expenditure groups for food and non-food items is given in Tables 4.7 to 4.12. In the NSS 61st Round, two separate estimates are made for the monthly per capita non-food consumption expenditure with 30-day recall period in the first estimates and 365-day recall period in the second one. Presenting our tables, we tried to maintain uniformity with the NSS expenditure and therefore, our tables also present two respective separate estimates for per capita monthly non-food consumption expenditure. The NSS consumption expenditure for the AAY, BPL and APL were drawn by equating the per capita monthly income for these categories as given in Table 3.7 (previous chapter) with the respective MPCE classes for the rural areas as given in the NSS reports.[6,7] The percentage distribution of each food item in total food expenditure, each non-food item in total non-food expenditure and percentage of total food items and total non-food items in total expenditure for the three categories in all the six states is given in Tables 4.13 to 4.18.

4. We address this issue in detail in the next chapter.

5. See for example, Townsend (1994; 1995); Morduch (1990); Grimard (1997).

6. See for example, Level and Pattern of Consumer Expenditure, 2004-05—NSS 61st Round, Report No. 508 (61/1.0/1), National Sample Survey Organisation, Ministry of Statistics and Programme Implementation, Government of India, December 2006.

7. The NSS consumption figures are taken for the rural areas to maintain parity with our selected sample, as our sample is drawn with more than 80 per cent households from the rural areas.

Table 4.7 Monthly Consumption Expenditure of Households (Average of Six Months)—Rajasthan

	Monthly Per Capita (Rs.)	Coefficient of Variation	NSS 2004-05 (Rs.)	Monthly Per Capita (Rs.)	Coefficient of Variation	NSS 2004-05 (Rs.)	Monthly Per Capita (Rs.)	Coefficient of Variation	NSS 2004-05 (Rs.)
		AAY			BPL			APL	
				Food Items					
Rice	4.85	71.8	1.45	5.85	103.6	2.03	8.27	159.0	5.29
Wheat	46.30	96.9	52.33	56.17	73.4	49.98	86.23	51.1	77.14
Other cereals	8.20	69.5	22.03	8.71	81.2	29.47	9.19	94.0	19.35
Total cereals	59.35	-	75.81	70.74	-	81.48	103.70	-	101.78
Pulses	22.05	50.6	9.34	21.89	50.2	9.89	25.12	47.6	16.13
Sugar etc	19.45	76.8	14.85	20.66	84.4	15.50	22.63	81.4	27.53
Cooking oil	21.56	57.5	18.65	22.24	57.1	20.40	25.76	63.3	29.78
Spices	14.03	104.3	12.65	13.42	106.8	13.91	15.41	110.1	20.13
Milk & milk products	62.44	167.9	63.45	98.22	189.7	77.49	108.47	163.3	213.46
Poultry & meat	4.18	72.8	3.85	3.65	79.1	3.63	4.53	76.3	7.15
Fruits	6.45	62.1	3.10	6.53	61.2	3.53	10.66	91.2	16.01
Vegetables	20.28	66.8	21.91	20.58	66.3	24.19	24.25	69.7	39.17
Confectionery	3.42	76.1	14.53	3.56	67.0	16.68	7.15	141.2	31.56
Total food	292.58	-	238.35	352.22	-	266.78	451.37	-	503.43
				Non-food (30-day recall period)					
Education	91.29	211.8	16.39	42.14	161.4	18.66	70.74	189.3	105.58
Clothing	72.49	210.3	11.48	24.02	153.3	17.74	36.61	185.4	70.50
Footwear	28.10	194.7	4.68	9.61	162.1	5.20	14.62	182.5	19.72
Other items	109.86	206.1	69.17	41.32	90.0	75.08	62.91	110.6	210.22
Fuel	74.51	294.5	47.60	30.04	146.9	51.14	54.23	113.5	89.61
Total non-food	376.25	-	149.32	147.12	-	167.82	239.11	-	495.63
Gross total	668.83	-	387.67	499.34	-	434.60	690.48	-	999.06
				Non-food (365-day recall period)					
Education	28.04	94.14	9.31	30.95	101.62	9.7	62.19	166.48	50.88
Clothing	24.75	76.00	33.5	25.89	72.81	37.76	40.27	90.17	69.80
Footwear	9.08	70.30	6.83	9.37	84.63	7.68	14.64	81.48	13.79
Other items	33.70	95.08	69.17	32.65	89.24	75.08	66.65	124.96	210.22
Fuel	22.63	141.52	47.60	26.15	117.11	51.14	57.44	88.04	89.61
Total non-food	118.20	-	166.41	125.01	-	181.36	241.19	-	434.3
Gross total	410.77	-	404.76	477.22	-	448.14	692.56	-	937.73

Table 4.8 **Monthly Consumption Expenditure of Households (Average of Six Months)—Chhattisgarh**

	Monthly Per Capita (Rs.)	Coefficient of Variation	NSS 2004-05 (Rs.)	Monthly Per Capita (Rs.)	Coefficient of Variation	NSS 2004-05 (Rs.)	Monthly Per Capita (Rs.)	Coefficient of Variation	NSS 2004-05 (Rs.)
		AAY			BPL			APL	
				Food Items					
Rice	42.40	69.97	94.57	61.39	55.07	104.82	87.14	49.07	137.93
Wheat	1.46	63.67	0.65	4.31	80.34	1.74	9.11	60.54	14.76
Other cereals	0.42	57.68	0.26	1.35	73.68	0.19	0.97	53.68	0.00
Total cereals	44.28	-	95.48	67.06	-	106.75	97.22	-	152.69
Pulses	12.22	56.90	7.79	12.63	61.17	9.43	17.27	80.36	26.58
Sugar etc.	6.46	61.47	4.97	8.45	63.05	6.65	11.34	59.79	17.07
Cooking oil	16.60	52.92	14.31	18.37	53.44	16.00	22.44	68.46	32.91
Spices	9.61	121.88	6.98	9.75	94.40	8.16	11.42	157.56	13.77
Milk & milk products	3.52	109.00	2.64	7.00	116.34	1.90	17.61	102.72	23.17
Poultry & meat	7.60	118.44	6.28	9.63	88.94	7.01	14.64	98.48	19.15
Fruits	4.10	90.92	2.19	4.56	97.67	2.34	7.04	83.23	11.14
Vegetables	21.09	72.42	25.97	21.96	86.05	29.67	25.75	100.71	54.54
Confectionery	1.12	71.26	5.98	1.13	65.14	8.25	2.47	131.01	24.96
Total food	126.61	-	172.75	160.52	-	196.36	227.22	-	376.53
				Non-food (30-day recall period)					
Education	11.80	200.16	11.98	14.22	183.97	15.56	29.12	183.97	102.82
Clothing	20.53	188.87	2.43	22.76	176.40	5.51	32.57	176.40	52.93
Footwear	6.01	200.29	0.47	6.47	210.51	0.97	9.25	210.51	2.81
Other items	31.90	99.42	33.35	36.74	97.49	40.62	56.48	97.49	161.48
Fuel	29.80	120.55	32.52	32.28	91.38	36.70	59.15	91.38	68.64
Total non-food	100.05	-	80.75	112.48	-	99.36	186.57	-	388.68
Gross total	226.65	-	253.50	272.99	-	295.72	413.79	-	765.21
				Non-food (365-day recall period)					
Education	15.64	111.63	3.73	16.24	127.03	5.7	33.47	157.28	34.36
Clothing	10.47	107.19	25.25	10.31	75.38	30.24	23.52	95.80	57.48
Footwear	2.83	113.52	2.59	3.22	95.83	3.36	7.14	103.05	8.54
Other items	20.43	81.71	33.35	19.85	85.13	40.62	39.00	127.78	161.48
Fuel	18.60	111.18	32.52	17.36	99.14	36.70	47.33	68.64	68.64
Total non-food	67.97	-	97.44	66.98	-	116.62	150.46	-	330.50
Gross total	194.58	-	270.19	227.50	-	312.98	377.68	-	707.03

Table 4.9 Monthly Consumption Expenditure of Households (Average of Six Months)—Bihar

	Monthly Per Capita (Rs.)	Coefficient of Variation	NSS 2004-05 (Rs.)	Monthly Per Capita (Rs.)	Coefficient of Variation	NSS 2004-05 (Rs.)	Monthly Per Capita (Rs.)	Coefficient of Variation	NSS 2004-05 (Rs.)
		AAY			BPL			APL	
				Food Items					
Rice	49.53	85.49	61.59	59.10	69.81	66.00	68.67	48.07	115.43
Wheat	42.07	86.61	38.75	47.79	74.94	41.24	60.83	49.05	47.51
Other cereals	4.45	56.60	3.50	4.53	68.41	3.22	7.05	53.04	1.83
Total cereals	96.05	-	103.84	111.42	-	110.46	136.56	-	164.77
Pulses	17.37	68.98	10.57	18.35	67.12	12.42	27.39	62.50	31.60
Sugar etc.	8.23	81.55	4.90	8.14	72.11	6.03	15.96	67.37	19.61
Cooking oil	24.44	64.38	18.63	25.18	57.66	20.39	42.43	55.27	45.53
Spices	12.69	97.58	8.59	13.66	124.25	9.30	18.78	91.33	21.33
Milk & milk products	18.52	216.88	13.72	26.38	204.20	22.11	138.64	155.13	124.36
Poultry & meat	11.50	118.78	6.83	12.26	89.50	9.16	30.93	90.83	30.10
Fruits	7.06	84.88	1.54	7.58	88.99	2.10	22.54	132.99	24.52
Vegetables	33.55	103.18	27.24	34.81	103.68	29.53	48.79	105.11	60.57
Confectionery	2.42	75.34	8.79	2.54	79.54	10.77	8.97	92.12	71.12
Total food	231.82	-	205.69	260.32	-	233.91	490.97	-	596.95
				Non-food (30-day recall period)					
Education	32.43	181.58	6.48	34.66	160.86	8.48	115.40	156.44	286.39
Clothing	30.54	197.66	6.44	28.43	205.31	9.19	62.72	195.43	261.01
Footwear	6.05	222.81	0.65	6.33	231.86	1.05	13.00	268.89	21.48
Other items	30.29	127.68	34.82	29.96	122.01	43.30	99.48	91.57	290.40
Fuel	38.68	75.97	40.96	27.88	80.13	44.97	85.18	51.17	77.53
Total non-food	137.99	-	89.35	127.26	-	106.99	375.78	-	936.81
Gross total	369.80	-	295.04	387.57	-	340.90	866.75	-	1533.76
				Non-food (365-day recall period)					
Education	36.95	114.16	5.86	42.63	171.42	8.46	140.18	137.63	84.60
Clothing	22.52	111.01	24.05	20.25	132.90	29.94	67.95	103.23	84.12
Footwear	6.45	90.46	1.94	5.94	108.89	2.56	18.89	137.97	9.76
Other items	22.53	97.23	34.82	19.34	130.98	43.30	133.26	487.02	290.40
Fuel	25.37	127.15	40.96	26.51	173.81	44.97	63.35	73.34	77.53
Total non-food	113.82	-	107.63	114.66	-	129.23	423.64	-	546.41
Gross total	345.64	-	313.32	374.98	-	363.14	914.61	-	1143.36

Table 4.10 **Monthly Consumption Expenditure of Households (Average of Six Months)—Uttar Pradesh**

	Monthly Per Capita (Rs.)	Coefficient of Variation	NSS 2004-05 (Rs.)	Monthly Per Capita (Rs.)	Coefficient of Variation	NSS 2004-05 (Rs.)	Monthly Per Capita (Rs.)	Coefficient of Variation	NSS 2004-05 (Rs.)
		AAY			BPL			APL	
				Food Items					
Rice	28.51	75.86	31.86	44.77	52.26	32.52	51.18	63.10	36.03
Wheat	36.92	121.04	44.82	44.62	95.99	53.38	64.82	56.21	63.93
Other cereals	0.27	87.03	1.73	0.45	129.58	0.85	1.60	160.99	1.87
Total cereals	65.71	-	78.41	89.83	-	86.75	117.61	-	101.83
Pulses	22.16	58.23	13.14	26.62	55.20	15.85	36.19	76.66	25.26
Sugar etc.	7.11	57.71	7.26	8.76	63.67	10.76	12.76	73.85	22.47
Cooking oil	17.42	51.90	14.88	20.59	49.79	19.15	26.60	56.86	29.35
Spices	7.88	88.06	8.45	9.29	88.58	9.90	10.23	105.90	14.89
Milk & milk products	9.54	124.71	10.75	13.50	101.55	25.05	39.11	127.45	99.46
Poultry & meat	0.73	112.12	3.43	1.74	98.78	6.08	2.94	111.11	11.74
Fruits	2.96	84.12	1.93	4.33	85.45	3.22	9.48	94.47	14.46
Vegetables	21.04	103.89	22.72	25.93	102.61	27.67	29.17	101.98	40.89
Confectionery	1.89	89.61	6.77	2.76	107.34	10.13	5.60	135.09	26.77
Total food	156.42	-	167.93	203.35	-	215.06	289.68	-	387.89
				Non-food items (30-day recall period)					
Education	20.67	219.82	14.91	23.60	187.01	27.00	18.10	191.06	110.91
Clothing	8.20	197.60	2.90	10.78	212.99	8.55	5.48	188.63	56.80
Footwear	3.31	258.28	0.64	4.04	267.33	1.81	2.20	224.31	10.96
Other items	16.00	77.78	33.18	20.58	91.65	48.41	10.29	94.99	139.08
Fuel	21.59	140.52	34.27	27.41	131.31	41.91	59.23	87.02	68.04
Total non-food	69.77	-	85.90	86.41	-	127.68	95.31	-	385.79
Gross total	226.19	-	253.83	289.77	-	342.74	384.99	-	773.68
				Non-food (365-day recall period)					
Education	9.83	119.45	9.06	9.87	111.66	17.92	18.47	111.40	49.08
Clothing	2.54	173.56	23.36	2.78	196.49	27.75	4.79	139.87	51.00
Footwear	1.08	188.85	2.97	0.94	228.66	3.76	1.44	192.55	8.28
Other items	7.84	77.17	33.18	8.63	99.08	48.41	14.37	92.86	139.08
Fuel	8.71	107.52	34.27	11.91	109.70	41.91	37.74	70.35	68.04
Total non-food	30.00	-	102.84	34.13	-	139.75	76.80	-	315.48
Gross total	186.42	-	270.77	237.49	-	354.81	366.48	-	703.37

Table 4.11 Monthly Consumption Expenditure of Households (Average of Six Months)—Assam

	Monthly Per Capita (Rs.)	Coefficient of Variation	NSS 2004-05 (Rs.)	Monthly Per Capita (Rs.)	Coefficient of Variation	NSS 2004-05 (Rs.)	Monthly Per Capita (Rs.)	Coefficient of Variation	NSS 2004-05 (Rs.)
		AAY			BPL			APL	
				Food Items					
Rice	88.86	74.81	128.11	102.24	62.43	139.97	138.23	33.46	155.26
Wheat	0.35	65.53	5.52	0.34	111.48	6.36	2.00	93.38	14.05
Other cereals	0.01	5.66	0.06	0.05	125.04	0.04	0.03	34.48	0.00
Total cereals	89.22	-	133.69	102.64	-	146.37	140.25	-	169.31
Pulses	21.29	46.80	16.25	25.26	47.01	22.50	33.06	43.59	31.54
Sugar etc.	9.34	52.42	8.04	10.99	53.63	10.43	13.75	48.69	15.77
Cooking oil	27.58	46.12	25.06	30.44	40.86	30.25	38.59	41.02	48.03
Spices	10.25	60.78	11.27	10.57	71.85	13.15	12.09	58.55	18.12
Milk & milk products	4.28	119.11	17.47	4.82	108.55	33.14	20.77	74.09	74.61
Poultry & meat	43.79	73.66	47.37	52.32	70.52	68.70	78.28	70.44	117.30
Fruits	3.56	91.74	3.94	5.33	98.51	6.86	14.70	80.50	20.64
Vegetables	26.82	78.10	47.14	28.11	77.28	62.04	34.18	83.68	77.28
Confectionery	4.01	76.07	20.49	4.71	82.81	28.59	11.07	84.59	51.45
Total food	240.15	-	330.93	275.20	-	422.37	396.74	-	624.89
				Non-food (30-day recall period)					
Education	16.82	152.26	12.21	19.44	309.25	18.80	66.39	875.65	129.76
Clothing	22.81	177.43	16.31	30.18	204.60	26.49	51.40	335.49	165.88
Footwear	8.63	161.94	2.04	11.41	262.89	3.59	18.44	181.97	31.35
Other items	17.30	79.76	68.09	19.90	93.06	94.83	40.45	87.25	418.58
Fuel	35.50	84.40	51.91	53.77	80.00	61.32	166.19	92.17	110.30
Total non-food	101.06	-	150.56	134.69	-	205.03	342.86	-	855.87
Gross total	341.21	-	481.49	409.89	-	627.40	739.60	-	1480.76
				Non-food (365-day recall period)					
Education	20.69	252.38	13.30	22.37	85.28	17.87	55.18	149.68	85.65
Clothing	19.89	74.73	36.48	26.87	79.74	44.54	39.74	74.30	84.96
Footwear	8.58	139.04	4.57	9.61	100.83	7.04	15.06	74.12	17.18
Other items	19.34	122.41	68.09	19.70	72.12	94.83	45.22	67.90	418.58
Fuel	20.43	104.95	51.91	43.89	80.98	61.32	86.85	35.27	110.30
Total non-food	88.92	-	174.35	122.43	-	225.60	242.06	-	716.67
Gross total	329.07	-	505.28	397.62	-	647.97	638.80	-	1341.56

Table 4.12 **Monthly Consumption Expenditure of Households (Average of Six Months)—Mizoram**

	Monthly Per Capita (Rs.)	Coefficient of Variation	NSS 2004-05 (Rs.)	Monthly Per Capita (Rs.)	Coefficient of Variation	NSS 2004-05 (Rs.)	Monthly Per Capita (Rs.)	Coefficient of Variation	NSS 2004-05 (Rs.)
		AAY			BPL			APL	
				Food Items					
Rice	78.31	84.7	144.23	87.04	73.4	136.99	106.11	81.7	144.23
Wheat	0.10	-	4.27	0.11	109.9	2.72	0.11	92.8	4.27
Other cereals	0.12	112.1	0.29	0.06	124.6	0.17	0.08	62.3	0.29
Total cereals	-	-	148.79	-	-	139.88	-	-	148.79
Pulses	22.34	72.8	21.04	20.32	67.6	17.03	23.59	63.90	21.04
Sugar etc.	15.77	62.5	14.51	17.25	68.7	14.26	18.43	77.7	14.51
Cooking oil	26.59	77.7	29.04	25.59	56.2	23.36	26.38	46.7	29.04
Spices	16.75	75.2	13.35	13.57	71.1	10.97	15.85	175.8	13.35
Milk & milk products	19.60	78.3	20.99	18.46	115.3	10.84	22.58	90.2	20.99
Poultry & meat	43.25	86.7	86.56	38.88	91.5	74.43	37.97	75.1	86.56
Fruits	11.10	110.4	10.08	10.75	104.6	7.17	13.82	118.5	10.08
Vegetables	41.76	91.0	99.36	48.53	112.4	83.12	49.77	166.0	99.36
Confectionery	10.14	106.4	27.41	11.88	97.8	20.96	13.87	99.1	27.41
Total food	285.81	-	472.60	292.44	-	402.02	328.55	-	472.60
				Non-food items (30-day recall period)					
Education	108.96	171.4	25.79	67.20	137.7	23.10	98.45	148.5	25.79
Clothing	49.45	130.9	29.58	40.07	125.4	16.51	56.97	110.7	29.58
Footwear	47.17	150.8	13.79	36.62	136.7	7.93	57.49	125.0	13.79
Other items	107.20	129.6	141.84	95.03	94.6	101.49	127.64	95.7	141.84
Fuel	93.52	42.8	89.35	96.94	42.7	83.86	94.78	32.3	89.35
Total non-food	406.31	-	300.35	335.86	-	232.89	435.34	-	300.35
Gross total	692.12	-	772.95	628.30	-	634.91	763.88	-	772.95
				Non-food (365-day recall period)					
Education	143.33	158.05	29.70	82.32	117.09	22.28	113.11	138.99	29.70
Clothing	55.54	96.25	57.43	48.29	80.72	52.29	61.22	75.53	57.43
Footwear	48.67	130.70	36.31	39.80	117.45	33.98	53.98	105.38	36.31
Other items	84.51	158.87	141.84	85.26	297.43	101.49	104.70	110.85	141.84
Fuel	59.69	57.81	89.35	73.99	46.24	83.86	74.84	46.96	89.35
Total non-food	391.73	-	354.63	329.66	-	293.90	407.85	-	354.63
Gross total	677.54	-	827.23	622.10	-	695.92	736.40	-	827.23

Table 4.13 Percentage Distribution of Monthly Consumption Expenditure (Average of Six Months)—Rajasthan

	AAY		BPL		APL	
	Our Survey	NSS 2004-05	Our Survey	NSS 2004-05	Our Survey	NSS 2004-05
			Food Items			
Rice	1.7	0.6	1.7	0.8	1.8	1.1
Wheat	15.8	22.0	15.9	18.7	19.1	15.3
Other cereals	2.8	9.2	2.5	11.0	2.0	3.8
Pulses	7.5	3.9	6.2	3.7	5.6	3.2
Sugar etc.	6.6	6.2	5.9	5.8	5.0	5.5
Cooking oil	7.4	7.8	6.3	7.6	5.7	5.9
Spices	4.8	5.3	3.8	5.2	3.4	4.0
Milk & milk products	21.3	26.6	27.9	29.0	24.0	42.4
Poultry & meat	1.4	1.6	1.0	1.4	1.0	1.4
Fruits	2.2	1.3	1.9	1.3	2.4	3.2
Vegetables	6.9	9.2	5.8	9.1	5.4	7.8
Confectionery	1.2	6.1	1.0	6.3	1.6	6.3
Total food items	43.7	61.5	70.5	61.4	65.4	50.4
			Non-food (30-day recall period)			
Education	24.3	11.0	28.6	11.1	29.6	21.3
Clothing	19.3	7.7	16.3	10.6	15.3	14.2
Footwear	7.5	3.1	6.5	3.1	6.1	4.0
Other items	29.2	46.3	28.1	44.7	26.3	42.4
Fuel	19.8	31.9	20.4	30.5	22.7	18.1
Total non-food	56.3	38.5	29.5	38.6	34.6	49.6
Gross total	100.0	100.0	100.0	100.0	100.0	100.0

Table 4.14 **Percentage Distribution of Monthly Consumption Expenditure (Average of Six Months)—Chhattisgarh**

	AAY		BPL		APL	
	Our Survey	NSS 2004-05	Our Survey	NSS 2004-05	Our Survey	NSS 2004-05
			Food Items			
Rice	33.5	54.7	38.2	53.4	38.4	36.6
Wheat	1.2	0.4	2.7	0.9	4.0	3.9
Other cereals	0.3	0.2	0.8	0.1	0.4	0.0
Pulses	9.6	4.5	7.9	4.8	7.6	7.1
Sugar etc.	5.1	2.9	5.3	3.4	5.0	4.5
Cooking oil	13.1	8.3	11.4	8.1	9.9	8.7
Spices	7.6	4.0	6.1	4.2	5.0	3.7
Milk & milk products	2.8	1.5	4.4	1.0	7.8	6.2
Poultry & meat	6.0	3.6	6.0	3.6	6.4	5.1
Fruits	3.2	1.3	2.8	1.2	3.1	3.0
Vegetables	16.7	15.0	13.7	15.1	11.3	14.5
Confectionery	0.9	3.5	0.7	4.2	1.1	6.6
Total food items	55.9	68.1	58.8	66.4	54.9	49.2
			Non-food (30-day recall period)			
Education	11.8	14.8	12.6	15.7	15.6	26.5
Clothing	20.5	3.0	20.2	5.5	17.5	13.6
Footwear	6.0	0.6	5.8	1.0	5.0	0.7
Other items	31.9	41.3	32.7	40.9	30.3	41.5
Fuel	29.8	40.3	28.7	36.9	31.7	17.7
Total non-food	44.1	31.9	41.2	33.6	45.1	50.8
Gross total	100.0	100.0	100.0	100.0	100.0	100.0

Table 4.15 Percentage Distribution of Monthly Consumption Expenditure (Average of Six Months)—Bihar						
	AAY		BPL		APL	
	Our Survey	NSS 2004-05	Our Survey	NSS 2004-05	Our Survey	NSS 2004-05
			Food Items			
Rice	21.4	29.9	22.7	28.2	14.0	19.3
Wheat	18.1	18.8	18.4	17.6	12.4	8.0
Other cereals	1.9	1.7	1.7	1.4	1.4	0.3
Pulses	7.5	5.1	7.1	5.3	5.6	5.3
Sugar etc.	3.5	2.4	3.1	2.6	3.3	3.3
Cooking oil	10.5	9.1	9.7	8.7	8.6	7.6
Spices	5.5	4.2	5.2	4.0	3.8	3.6
Milk & milk products	8.0	6.7	10.1	9.5	28.2	20.8
Poultry & meat	5.0	3.3	4.7	3.9	6.3	5.0
Fruits	3.0	0.7	2.9	0.9	4.6	4.1
Vegetables	14.5	13.2	13.4	12.6	9.9	10.1
Confectionery	1.0	4.3	1.0	4.6	1.8	11.9
Total food items	62.7	69.7	67.2	68.6	56.6	38.9
			Non-food (30-day recall period)			
Education	23.5	7.3	27.2	7.9	30.7	30.6
Clothing	22.1	7.2	22.3	8.6	16.7	27.9
Footwear	4.4	0.7	5.0	1.0	3.5	2.3
Other items	22.0	39.0	23.5	40.5	26.5	31.0
Fuel	28.0	45.8	21.9	42.0	22.7	8.3
Total non-food	37.3	30.3	32.8	31.4	43.4	61.1
Gross total	100.0	100.0	100.0	100.0	100.0	100.0

Table 4.16 **Percentage Distribution of Monthly Consumption Expenditure (Average of Six Months)—Uttar Pradesh**

	AAY		BPL		APL	
	Our Survey	NSS 2004-05	Our Survey	NSS 2004-05	Our Survey	NSS 2004-05
			Food Items			
Rice	18.2	19.0	22.0	15.1	17.7	9.3
Wheat	23.6	26.7	21.9	24.8	22.4	16.5
Other cereals	0.2	1.0	0.2	0.4	0.6	0.5
Pulses	14.2	7.8	13.1	7.4	12.5	6.5
Sugar etc.	4.5	4.3	4.3	5.0	4.4	5.8
Cooking oil	11.1	8.9	10.1	8.9	9.2	7.6
Spices	5.0	5.0	4.6	4.6	3.5	3.8
Milk & milk products	6.1	6.4	6.6	11.6	13.5	25.6
Poultry & meat	0.5	2.0	0.9	2.8	1.0	3.0
Fruits	1.9	1.1	2.1	1.5	3.3	3.7
Vegetables	13.4	13.5	12.8	12.9	10.1	10.5
Confectionery	1.2	4.0	1.4	4.7	1.9	6.9
Total food items	69.2	66.2	70.2	62.7	75.2	50.1
			Non-food (30-day recall period)			
Education	29.6	17.4	27.3	21.1	19.0	28.7
Clothing	11.8	3.4	12.5	6.7	5.8	14.7
Footwear	4.7	0.7	4.7	1.4	2.3	2.8
Other items	22.9	38.6	23.8	37.9	10.8	36.1
Fuel	30.9	39.9	31.7	32.8	62.1	17.6
Total non-food	30.8	33.8	29.8	37.3	24.8	49.9
Gross total	100.0	100.0	100.0	100.0	100.0	100.0

Table 4.17 **Percentage Distribution of Monthly Consumption Expenditure (Average of Six Months)—Assam**

	AAY		BPL		APL	
	Our Survey	NSS 2004-05	Our Survey	NSS 2004-05	Our Survey	NSS 2004-05
			Food Items			
Rice	37.0	38.7	37.2	33.1	34.8	24.8
Wheat	0.1	1.7	0.1	1.5	0.5	2.2
Other cereals	0.0	0.0	0.0	0.0	0.0	0.0
Pulses	8.9	4.9	9.2	5.3	8.3	5.0
Sugar etc.	3.9	2.4	4.0	2.5	3.5	2.5
Cooking oil	11.5	7.6	11.1	7.2	9.7	7.7
Spices	4.3	3.4	3.8	3.1	3.0	2.9
Milk & milk products	1.8	5.3	1.8	7.8	5.2	11.9
Poultry & meat	18.2	14.3	19.0	16.3	19.7	18.8
Fruits	1.5	1.2	1.9	1.6	3.7	3.3
Vegetables	11.2	14.2	10.2	14.7	8.6	12.4
Confectionery	1.7	6.2	1.7	6.8	2.8	8.2
Total food items	70.4	68.7	67.1	67.3	53.6	42.2
			Non-food (30-day recall period)			
Education	16.6	8.1	14.4	9.2	19.4	15.2
Clothing	22.6	10.8	22.4	12.9	15.0	19.4
Footwear	8.5	1.4	8.5	1.8	5.4	3.7
Other items	17.1	45.2	14.8	46.3	11.8	48.9
Fuel	35.1	34.5	39.9	29.9	48.5	12.9
Total non-food	29.6	31.3	32.9	32.7	46.4	57.8
Gross total	100.0	100.0	100.0	100.0	100.0	100.0

Table 4.18 Percentage Distribution of Monthly Consumption Expenditure (Average of Six Months)—Mizoram

	AAY		BPL		APL	
	Our Survey	NSS 2004-05	Our Survey	NSS 2004-05	Our Survey	NSS 2004-05
Food Items						
Rice	27.4	30.5	29.8	34.1	32.3	30.5
Wheat	0.0	0.9	0.0	0.7	0.0	0.9
Other cereals	0.0	0.1	0.0	0.0	0.0	0.1
Pulses	7.8	4.5	6.9	4.2	7.2	4.5
Sugar etc.	5.5	3.1	5.9	3.5	5.6	3.1
Cooking oil	9.3	6.1	8.7	5.8	8.0	6.1
Spices	5.9	2.8	4.6	2.7	4.8	2.8
Milk & milk products	6.9	4.4	6.3	2.7	6.9	4.4
Poultry & meat	15.1	18.3	13.3	18.5	11.6	18.3
Fruits	3.9	2.1	3.7	1.8	4.2	2.1
Vegetables	14.6	21.0	16.6	20.7	15.1	21.0
Confectionery	3.5	5.8	4.1	5.2	4.2	5.8
Total food items	41.3	61.1	46.5	63.3	43.0	61.1
Non-food (30-day recall period)						
Education	26.8	8.6	20.0	9.9	22.6	8.6
Clothing	12.2	9.8	11.9	7.1	13.1	9.8
Footwear	11.6	4.6	10.9	3.4	13.2	4.6
Other items	26.4	47.2	28.3	43.6	29.3	47.2
Fuel	23.0	29.7	28.9	36.0	21.8	29.7
Total non-food	58.7	38.9	53.5	36.7	57.0	38.9
Gross total	100.0	100.0	100.0	100.0	100.0	100.0

Monthly per capita food consumption expenditure varied from Rs. 171 to 365 among the selected households. Its value was highest in Rajasthan, followed by Mizoram, Bihar, Assam, Uttar Pradesh and Chhattisgarh. Among the food items, highest amount was spent on cereals in almost all the states. Total expenditure on cereals varied from Rs. 115 in Bihar, 111 in Assam, 91 in Uttar Pradesh, 78 in Rajasthan and 70 in Chhattisgarh. Whereas meat (including fish) was the second highest item in food consumption in Assam and Mizoram, milk constituted second highest priority in Rajasthan and Bihar while pulses and vegetables were next to cereals in Uttar Pradesh and Chhattisgarh. Comparing food and non-food expenditure, on an average, the latter was less than total food expenditure in all the states, except Mizoram and that was consistent with the all India NSS data as was mentioned above. On an average, the distribution of food and non-food expenditure for all the categories and all the states, except Mizoram was 60-40, respectively. Food expenditure was highest, 72 per cent in Uttar Pradesh and lowest, 43 per cent in Mizoram. In other states, the percentage of food in total expenditure was 64 per cent in Assam, 62 per cent in Bihar, 60 per cent in Rajasthan and 57 per cent in Chhattisgarh. Non-food expenditure (30-day recall period) was maximum in Mizoram (Rs. 392), followed by Rajasthan (Rs. 254), Bihar (Rs. 214), Assam (Rs. 193), Chhattisgarh (Rs. 133) and Uttar Pradesh (Rs. 84). Non-food expenditure based on 365-day recall period was generally less than 30-day recall period because of memory loss due to comparatively higher time interval. Nonetheless, the distribution of expenditure was almost similar to that of 30-day recall period. Among the non-food items, education and health involved the highest expenditure in almost all the states. Education was followed by fuel and light, clothing, other items (toiletry, entertainment, intoxicants, transport and other services) and footwear. Thus, total consumption expenditure for all categories topped in Mizoram (Rs. 678), followed by Rajasthan (Rs. 620), Bihar (Rs. 541), Assam (Rs. 497), Chhattisgarh (Rs. 304), while Uttar Pradesh (Rs. 300) was found at the bottom. The order remained almost same even if we considered non-food expenditure with 365-day recall period.

Comparing across AAY, BPL and APL categories, it is discernible from the results of the tables that, while food expenditure of AAY and BPL households was quite close to each other, these two categories lagged behind above poverty households. Whereas all the categories spent proportionately a higher amount on cereals, comparative amount spent on items like milk, edible oils, meat and fish, vegetables and fruits was higher by the APL households as compared to the other two category of households. This was more true in high per capita income states like Assam, Rajasthan and Mizoram than the lower income states like Uttar Pradesh , Chhattisgarh and Bihar. In the case of non-food expenditure, education and health was top priority among all categories in the all the states. Fuel also constituted a major item among non-food commodities. Comparing food and non-food items, unlike the general belief that rich people spend higher amount on non-food, in our case, APL households spent much higher amount on food compared to non-food items and that was true in all the six states, without any exception. The same was true in other two categories as well.

Comparing our consumption expenditure with the NSS, it is seen from the tables that our estimates of food and non-food consumption expenditure compared very well with that of the NSS figures. Our total food as well as non-food consumption for AAY and BPL households in Rajasthan were slightly higher than that of the NSS figures, while for APL households, our estimates were slightly lower than that of the NSS estimates. In Chhattisgarh, our survey expenditure was marginally less than that of NSS in the case of all the three categories and in both food as well as non-food items. In Bihar and Uttar Pradesh, our survey figures were more or less comparable with that of NSS, except the case of non-food expenditure for the APL category whereby the NSS estimates were three times higher than our estimates in both the states. In the two northeastern states namely, Assam and Mizoram, our food expenditure was less than the NSS figures for AAY and BPL households while non-food expenditure for APL households was significantly less than that of the NSS estimates.

Last and the least, comparing the variability in food and non-food expenditure, it is observed from the results that coefficient of variation was significantly higher for the non-food commodities as compared to food items in all the states and in all the categories. On an average, coefficient of variation was less than 100 per cent in the case of food items while it averaged around 150 to 200 per cent in the non-food items. Among food items, variability was higher in the case of milk and milk products, poultry and meat, fruits and vegetables, in addition to not common cereals, like wheat in Assam, rice in Rajasthan and coarse cereals in Uttar Pradesh and Assam (as was also found in the previous section while discussing the quantity consumed of cereals). In the case of non-food items, variability was higher for all items compared to food items, because of wide differences in the use of such items among the selected households, as we have clubbed households in each category, irrespective of the fact whether they belong to rural or urban areas.

4.4 Role of PDS in Ensuring Food to the Below Poverty

To provide subsidised food to the poor, to mitigate regional inequalities through moving the food from surplus to deficit areas and to stabilise agricultural prices, the Food Corporation of India (FCI) procures and distributes food grains. However, the universal coverage of the PDS was replaced by the targeted public distribution (TPDS) in 1997 in order to reduce subsidies and to provide food to the people below the poverty line. Thus, below poverty consumers now fulfil their demand for cereals (and few other essentials) through purchases in the open market and from supplies through the PDS. It is however, a controversial question, to what extent food requirement of the poor is met through the PDS and how much they have to depend on the vagaries of the market situation. This section presents statistics related to the proportion of cereals, sugar and kerosene oil supplied through the PDS system to the AAY and BPL (and also to the APL if any) households in the selected states. It is however, mentioned at the outset that the proportion of wheat and rice distributed varied among different states and among various categories, depending upon the food habits of the households among different states. However, the total amount of cereals entitlement (rice + wheat) was fixed at 35 kgs in almost all the states and for all the categories.[8] In order to see how many households were receiving the entitled quantity of 35 kgs of cereals every month among all the three categories, we clubbed rice and wheat together to check the extent of entitlement received by the households for these two cereals.

8. Among APL households only a few had the entitlement.

Tables 4.19 to 4.24 present the quantity of cereals (wheat + rice), sugar and kerosene oil received by the households from PDS in all the three categories. The percentage of population receiving such quantity is also given in parentheses in the tables. The entitlement was fixed at 35 kgs of cereals, irrespective of the family size, except Mizoram where in some districts food is being distributed in proportionate with the size of the family.[9] It is seen from the tables that in almost all the states, the quantity of cereals distributed was very close to the entitled quantity of 35 kgs. On an average, in Rajasthan the quantity distributed was around 32 kgs for AAY and BPL and around 19 kgs for the APL. In Chhattisgarh, the AAY quantity averaged around 34 kgs while BPL and APL quantity was much less around 28 and 26 kgs, respectively. In Uttar Pradesh, average quantity distributed was near to the entitlement in the case of AAY and BPL (around 34 kgs, each) while it was around 26 kgs for the APL households. Similar to Uttar Pradesh, in Assam the average quantity distributed was near to the entitlement for the AAY and BPL households while it was much lower around 20 kgs for the APL households. The deviations from the entitlement were much higher in Mizoram, where AAY received around 23 kgs of cereals (mainly rice) while BPL and APL households received 26 kgs of cereals (rice). In the case of Bihar, the entitlement received averaged around 32 kgs among AAY households, 29 kgs among BPL households and around 26 kgs among the APL households. Thus, the entitled quantity of cereals received by the households deviated from 25 to 35 kgs among all the states, and it averaged around 32 kgs. Therefore, deviations in the amount of cereals received from that of the stipulated amount appear to be quite moderate. However, the question that arises is how many people entitled for such quantity actually received it.

Table 4.19 Quantity Obtained from PDS (Kgs per Household)—Rajasthan

	Month 1	Month 2	Month 3	Month 4	Month 5	Month 6	Average	COV across Time
				AAY				
Cereals (Rice +Wheat)	33.25 (93.9)	34.20 (95.6)	33.50 (90.6)	34.67 (89.4)	30.09 (91.1)	31.49 (87.2)	32.88 (91.3)	5.30
Sugar	2.75 (2.2)	2.00 (0.6)	1.88 (4.4)	1.00 (0.6)	0.00 (0.0)	0.00 (0.0)	2.07 (1.3)	88.93
Kerosene oil	3.79 (87.8)	3.99 (84.4)	3.91 (70.6)	3.81 (71.7)	3.71 (60.0)	3.76 (68.9)	3.84 (73.9)	2.70
				BPL				
Cereals (Rice +Wheat)	33.28 (91.8)	34.15 (94.4)	32.56 (89.6)	31.99 (89.9)	31.06 (86.8)	29.69 (91.9)	32.14 (90.7)	4.96
Sugar	4.33 (0.5)	3.00 (0.5)	2.07 (4.8)	0.00 (0.0)	2.00 (0.2)	0.00 (0.0)	2.33 (1.0)	89.24
Kerosene oil	4.0 (88.8)	4.08 (85.0)	3.96 (75.4)	3.93 (79.5)	3.92 (69.1)	3.94 (77.9)	3.97 (79.3)	1.51
				APL				
Cereals (Rice +Wheat)	31.56 (7.5)	34.27 (5.1)	16.07 (20.6)	17.76 (23.8)	19.26 (15.9)	13.87 (21.0)	18.77 (15.6)	38.79
Sugar	2.50 (0.9)	1.33 (1.4)	1.89 (4.2)	0.00 (0.0)	0.00 (0.0)	0.00 (0.0)	1.86 (1.1)	116.22
Kerosene oil	4.05 (64.9)	4.31 (66.4)	4.14 (59.8)	4.03 (57.5)	4.12 (42.5)	4.06 (59.8)	4.12 (58.4)	2.50

Note: 1. Figures in parentheses are respective percentage of people who obtained the entitled quantity.
2. Kerosene quantity is in litres.

9. For more details, see Chapter 6.

Table 4.20 Quantity Obtained from PDS (Kgs per Household)—Chhattisgarh

	Month 1	Month 2	Month 3	Month 4	Month 5	Month 6	Average	COV across Time
				AAY				
Cereals (Rice + Wheat)	31.56 (96.2)	35.16 (94.8)	34.51 (94.7)	35.17 (95.7)	34.90 (95.7)	35.46 (91.4)	34.45 (94.7)	4.23
Sugar	1.70 (63.0)	1.69 (65.9)	1.71 (72.6)	1.70 (68.3)	1.72 (65.9)	1.72 (65.4)	1.70 (66.8)	0.71
Kerosene oil	3.34 (90.9)	3.08 (85.1)	3.18 (88.9)	2.87 (72.6)	2.83 (73.6)	2.74 (71.6)	3.03 (80.5)	7.69
				BPL				
Cereals (Rice + Wheat)	24.89 (96.5)	27.46 (94.5)	28.65 (96.7)	29.08 (97.0)	28.88 (96.7)	29.12 (93.3)	28.01 (95.8)	5.88
Sugar	1.85 (66.1)	1.79 (67.1)	1.83 (71.1)	1.81 (74.3)	1.81 (73.1)	1.85 (76.8)	1.82 (71.4)	1.33
Kerosene oil	3.00 (82.3)	3.07 (78.3)	3.15 (82.6)	2.88 (70.9)	2.77 (72.9)	2.74 (71.3)	2.94 (76.3)	5.64
				APL				
Cereals (Rice + Wheat)	28.86 (11.4)	28.30 (15.5)	30.42 (16.1)	25.30 (22.3)	22.60 (13.0)	21.13 (16.1)	26.02 (15.7)	14.20
Sugar	2.47 (8.8)	2.63 (8.3)	2.33 (12.4)	2.72 (15.0)	2.37 (16.1)	2.30 (16.6)	2.46 (12.4)	6.93
Kerosene oil	3.33 (66.3)	3.20 (63.2)	3.25 (65.8)	3.29 (53.9)	3.18 (56.0)	3.02 (54.9)	3.22 (60.0)	3.40

Note: 1. Figures in parentheses are respective percentage of people who obtained the entitled quantity.
2. Kerosene quantity is in litres.

Table 4.21 Quantity Obtained from PDS (Kgs per Household)—Bihar

	Month 1	Month 2	Month 3	Month 4	Month 5	Month 6	Average	COV across Time
				AAY				
Cereals (Rice + Wheat)	28.20 (73.7)	32.25 (67.5)	32.92 (58.3)	34.43 (56.7)	29.78 (37.6)	34.16 (38.1)	31.78 (55.3)	7.77
Sugar	0.00 (0.0)	1.00 (1.0)	0.00 (0.0)	1.00 (19.6)	0.00 (0.0)	0.00 (0.0)	1.00 (3.4)	154.92
Kerosene oil	3.32 (84.0)	3.20 (81.4)	3.28 (82.0)	2.98 (87.1)	3.14 (90.2)	3.30 (89.2)	3.20 (85.7)	4.02
				BPL				
Cereals (Rice + Wheat)	25.94 (35.5)	31.44 (37.7)	29.45 (45.4)	25.66 (51.6)	31.11 (24.0)	32.09 (24.0)	28.80 (36.3)	9.68
Sugar	1.17 (0.5)	1.17 (0.5)	1.68 (0.6)	1.03 (19.2)	5.00 (0.2)	0.00 (0.0)	1.08 (3.5)	102.67
Kerosene oil	3.23 (81.6)	3.18 (77.5)	3.28 (79.1)	3.10 (88.2)	3.19 (90.6)	3.22 (83.9)	3.20 (83.5)	1.89
				APL				
Cereals (Rice + Wheat)	24.02 (22.8)	23.83 (10.0)	28.39 (12.2)	35.67 (5.0)	24.44 (5.0)	30.38 (4.4)	26.38 (9.9)	16.90
Sugar	3.00 (0.6)	0.00 (0.0)	0.00 (0.0)	1.00 (1.1)	1.00 (1.1)	0.00 (0.0)	1.40 (0.5)	140.29
Kerosene oil	4.39 (74.4)	4.24 (72.8)	4.39 (76.7)	4.07 (76.7)	4.14 (81.1)	4.22 (75.6)	4.24 (76.2)	3.06

Note: 1. Figures in parentheses are respective percentage of people who obtained the entitled quantity.
2. Kerosene quantity is in litres.

Table 4.22 Quantity Obtained from PDS (Kgs per Household)—Uttar Pradesh

	Month 1	Month 2	Month 3	Month 4	Month 5	Month 6	Average	COV across Time
				AAY				
Cereals (Rice + Wheat)	34.35 (93.2)	35.57 (93.7)	35.33 (97.1)	35.07 (93.2)	34.82 (89.76)	30.85 (89.76)	34.36 (92.8)	5.12
Sugar	1.86 (55.6)	1.77 (56.6)	1.66 (50.2)	1.99 (72.2)	1.90 (46.8)	1.78 (39.0)	1.84 (53.4)	6.31
Kerosene oil	2.63 (64.4)	2.43 (79.0)	2.39 (66.3)	2.60 (81.0)	2.56 (95.1)	2.64 (91.7)	2.54 (82.9)	4.19
				BPL				
Cereals (Rice + Wheat)	34.12 (84.6)	35.11 (89.5)	35.28 (93.6)	34.65 (86.4)	34.82 (81.1)	22.61 (80.0)	32.92 (85.8)	15.23
Sugar	1.80 (48.6)	1.76 (60.0)	1.74 (50.3)	2.06 (70.9)	1.99 (49.4)	1.79 (37.9)	1.87 (52.8)	7.22
Kerosene oil	2.48 (58.8)	2.46 (75.7)	2.34 (82.1)	2.54 (94.3)	2.57 (93.6)	2.63 (92.1)	2.51 (82.7)	4.03
				APL				
Cereals (Rice + Wheat)	26.63 (12.12)	22.50 (12.12)	24.37 (9.60)	28.26 (5.56)	31.43 (3.54)	20.00 (2.53)	25.27 (7.6)	16.11
Sugar	2.00 (6.1)	2.43 (3.5)	3.20 (2.5)	1.80 (5.1)	2.17 (3.0)	0.00 (0.0)	2.20 (3.4)	55.07
Kerosene oil	2.52 (61.6)	2.58 (77.8)	2.31 (77.3)	2.57 (82.8)	2.60 (90.4)	2.61 (92.4)	2.54 (80.4)	4.46

Note: 1. Figures in parentheses are respective percentage of people who obtained the entitled quantity.
2. Kerosene quantity is in litres.

Table 4.23 Quantity Obtained from PDS (Kgs per Household)—Assam

	Month 1	Month 2	Month 3	Month 4	Month 5	Month 6	Average	COV across Time
				AAY				
Cereals (Rice + Wheat)	33.34 (81.6)	33.82 (77.4)	34.83 (55.3)	34.85 (59.0)	34.84 (40.5)	34.80 (57.9)	34.29 (61.9)	1.93
Sugar	1.75 (14.7)	2.00 (3.7)	1.82 (11.6)	1.93 (7.9)	1.87 (7.9)	1.80 (7.9)	1.83 (8.9)	4.92
Kerosene oil	3.12 (88.9)	3.03 (86.3)	2.65 (86.3)	2.70 (86.8)	2.64 (64.2)	2.68 (81.6)	2.81 (82.4)	7.61
				BPL				
Cereals (Rice + Wheat)	32.82 (80.3)	33.60 (77.3)	34.28 (62.4)	34.76 (65.5)	34.57 (47.5)	34.73 (66.3)	34.05 (66.7)	2.26
Sugar	1.78 (18.2)	1.96 (4.3)	1.91 (13.3)	1.98 (10.3)	1.78 (10.5)	1.90 (9.5)	1.87 (11.0)	4.60
Kerosene oil	3.23 (84.2)	3.06 (81.8)	2.70 (80.5)	2.81 (82.6)	2.72 (62.2)	2.77 (81.4)	2.89 (78.8)	7.44
				APL				
Cereals (Rice + Wheat)	6.08 (6.5)	34.75 (2.0)	25.67 (3.0)	42.80 (2.5)	48.00 (1.5)	23.50 (2.0)	19.83 (2.9)	40.15
Sugar	0.20 (5.0)	2.00 (0.5)	2.33 (1.5)	2.00 (0.5)	2.00 (0.5)	2.50 (1.0)	2.22 (0.7)	44.05
Kerosene oil	3.14 (83.1)	3.03 (84.1)	2.7 (84.6)	2.75 (83.6)	2.70 (66.7)	2.76 (86.7)	2.85 (81.4)	6.66

Note: 1. Figures in parentheses are respective percentage of people who obtained the entitled quantity.
2. Kerosene quantity is in litres.

Table 4.24 Quantity Obtained from PDS (Kgs per Household)—Mizoram

	Month 1	Month 2	Month 3	Month 4	Month 5	Month 6	Average	COV across Time
				AAY				
Cereals (Rice +Wheat)	22.78 (89.8)	23.01 (89.8)	22.70 (87.8)	23.05 (88.8)	23.03 (88.8)	22.94 (88.8)	22.92 (88.9)	0.63
Sugar	1.71 (92.9)	1.71 (93.9)	1.70 (92.9)	1.71 (88.8)	1.72 (88.8)	1.74 (88.8)	1.72 (91.0)	0.70
Kerosene oil	1.91 (79.6)	2.25 (73.5)	1.69 (71.4)	2.06 (72.5)	1.90 (68.4)	1.55 (71.4)	1.90 (72.8)	13.25
				BPL				
Cereals (Rice +Wheat)	25.63 (87.4)	25.85 (85.5)	25.69 (85.8)	25.60 (84.7)	25.58 (84.5)	25.58 (84.5)	25.65 (85.4)	0.40
Sugar	1.81 (86.8)	1.81 (86.1)	1.82 (86.3)	1.83 (84.2)	1.83 (83.7)	1.82 (83.4)	1.82 (85.1)	0.40
Kerosene oil	2.02 (68.7)	2.32 (64.5)	1.69 (59.5)	1.99 (62.1)	1.91 (62.4)	1.42 (57.1)	1.90 (62.4)	16.25
				APL				
Cereals (Rice +Wheat)	27.22 (16.1)	27.11 (17.0)	26.94 (16.1)	26.47 (15.2)	26.47 (15.2)	26.47 (15.2)	26.79 (15.8)	1.31
Sugar	2.24 (42.9)	2.22 (42.0)	2.22 (42.0)	2.30 (40.2)	2.27 (40.2)	2.18 (39.3)	2.24 (41.1)	1.81
Kerosene oil	2.31 (34.8)	2.21 (29.5)	1.63 (28.6)	1.97 (28.6)	2.12 (29.5)	1.59 (28.6)	1.99 (29.9)	15.31

Note: 1. Figures in parentheses are respective percentage of people who obtained the entitled quantity.
2. Kerosene quantity is in litres.

It is shown by the data in the tables that in Rajasthan, on an average, above 90 per cent AAY and BPL families received entitled cereals, namely wheat and rice. However, the share of wheat was dominant because the latter was the main staple diet of Rajasthan. In the case of APL, only 15 per cent of the households received some quantity of cereals of wheat and rice. Kerosene oil was the other commodity that was distributed uniformly among all consumers irrespective of one's being below or above poverty. Around 75 per cent of below poverty households and 60 per cent of above poverty households received around 4 litres of kerosene oil from the PDS. Besides these commodities, sugar was also distributed through PDS, although in Rajasthan its distribution was just negligible among all the category of households.

In Chhattisgarh, PDS system seems to be working quite effectively, as around 95 per cent of AAY and BPL households received their entitled quantity of cereals (rice and wheat) while the proportion of rice was dominant as the latter was also the main staple cereal consumed by most of the people. Along with wheat and rice, sugar was also distributed among the below poverty households in the state. Around 65 to 70 per cent AAY and BPL households received more than 1.5 kgs of sugar. Like in Rajasthan, kerosene oil was distributed in Chhattisgarh among all households universally. Around 75 to 80 per cent below poverty households and 60 per cent above poverty households received more than 3 litres of kerosene oil from the PDS outlets in the state. It is to be mentioned here that kerosene oil was available on a universal basis. However, lesser number of APL households purchased their entitled quantity because of their better living standard as they used other substitutes for the purpose of lighting (electricity) and cooking (LPG gas).

In Uttar Pradesh, both wheat and rice being the staple diet were being supplied in combination through the PDS shops. Around 93 per cent of AAY households received around 34 kgs of rice and wheat (combined) through the PDS outlets. Similarly, around 86 per cent BPL households also received their quantity of wheat and rice through the PDS. The entitled quantity of rice and wheat received by the APL households was around 8 per cent indicating the system being targeted towards the poor alone. Under the targeted system, sugar was also supplied to the AAY and BPL households alone. Around 50 to 55 per cent households from these two categories received around 2 kgs of sugar every month. However, like all other states, kerosene oil was distributed on universal basis in Uttar Pradesh also. Around 80 per cent of all category households received around 2.5 litres of kerosene oil. In Assam, the PDS system was not as efficient as it was observed in the case of

Chhattisgarh and Uttar Pradesh. Only 62 per cent of AAY and 67 per cent of BPL households obtained their entitled quantity of cereals through the PDS. Rice being the staple diet was the first choice among almost all the households in Assam and therefore, the distribution of cereals in the state was that of mostly rice. Apart from rice, only kerosene oil was distributed regularly on a universal basis without being targeted, as was the case with other states. Distribution of kerosene oil was more even across the households and across the time period as around 80 per cent households of all the categories obtained kerosene regularly. Sugar unlike in other states, was not being distributed regularly and also it was not targeted in Assam.

In Mizoram, the distributed quantity of cereals was less than in the other five selected states. Unlike other states where distributed quantity was close to the entitlement quantity of 35 kgs of cereals, in Mizoram in all the categories and during all the six months, distributed quantity of cereals (mainly rice) was close to only 25 kgs. On an average, 89 per cent of AAY and 85 per cent of BPL households received around 25 kgs of cereals while more than 15 per cent of APL households also received 27 kgs of cereals on regular basis. Besides food grains, more than 85 per cent below poverty households and 40 per cent above poverty households received around 2 kgs of sugar. Similarly, two-third below poverty households and one third above poverty households received around 2 litres of kerosene oil. Thus, in Mizoram, on the one hand, below poverty households received significantly less than 35 kgs of stipulated cereals, while on the other, around one-sixth of the APL households also received more than 25 kgs of cereals from the PDS along with wide coverage of other commodities like sugar and kerosene oil.

Performance of PDS was least effective in Bihar among the six selected states. The statistics presented in the tables on Bihar reveals that among the AAY families, only 55 per cent of them received the entitled quantity of cereals. The supply of rice and wheat was even worse in the case of BPL households as only 36 per cent of them received the entitled quantity of these two cereals. These figures should be seen in the light of the fact that Bihar is among those states that have the maximum number of poor and therefore, an effective PDS system is most needed in that state. Entitlement for APL household was lower as less than 10 per cent households received around 26 kgs of cereals (wheat and rice) from the fair price shops. Distribution of sugar was almost negligible among any category of households while kerosene oil was under the universal system whereby 3-4 litres of kerosene oil was being distributed among 75 to 85 per cent of all households through the PDS system. Thus, there was a lot of scope for improvement in performance of PDS system especially in the two states of Bihar and Assam.

Tables 4.25 to 4.30 present the share of food provided by the PDS and that purchased through the open market by the selected households. Assuming the average family size as 5 members and 10 kgs cereals as the bare minimum for healthy diet, per family requirement thus turns out to be 50 kgs. As PDS system was providing 35 kgs of cereals, thereby if all the households were receiving their entitled quantity, the share of PDS and that of market should turn out as 70 and 30 per cent, respectively. It is seen from our statistics presented in the tables that the ratio of PDS to market was in fact around 70/30 for the combination of wheat and rice in the case of AAY and BPL households in Rajasthan, Chhattisgarh, Uttar Pradesh and Mizoram. In Assam, the share of PDS in total food was around 50 per cent for the AAY and BPL households. The share of PDS was observed as minimum in the case of Bihar. Only around 30 per cent food of AAY households and 20 per cent of the BPL households was covered by the PDS in that state. Share of PDS in consumption of sugar varied from state to state while more than 80 per cent demand of kerosene oil was met by the PDS in almost all the states and in all the categories including that of above poverty households, except Mizoram where only half of the demand of AAY and BPL households for kerosene was met by the PDS.

4.5 Food Prices—Market *versus* PDS

The PDS system serves the dual objective of providing greater access of food to the poor and providing it at affordable prices. In the previous section, we noticed that around 60 to 70 per cent of food to the poor, especially those who are at the bottom of the income level, was being provided through the PDS. In this section, we make an attempt to find out to what extent the food being provided to the below poverty households is being subsidised. Under the TPDS system, the Central government has fixed the price of wheat at Rs. 2 per kgs and rice at Rs. 3 per kgs for the AAY households in all the states. In the case of BPL, however, the price varies from state to state and it is generally higher than the AAY price for these two cereals. The actual price paid by our selected households for food (and other commodities) obtained through PDS and bought through the market are given in Table 4.30 for the six selected states. The table contains (arithmetic) mean, median and mode[10] prices paid

10. Mean -The average of a group of numbers is called the mean; Median – The middle number of the group is called the median; Mode - The number that appears the most often in a listing of number.

by the households. As mean can be distorted by extreme values, mode prices make the ideal case as that represents the model price that is paid by the majority of the households.

Table 4.25 Percentage Share of PDS and Market in Consumption of PDS Commodities—Rajasthan

Commodity		Month 1	Month 2	Month 3	Month 4	Month 5	Month 6
				AAY			
Rice	PDS	82.9	81.7	71.2	73.6	88.8	86.3
	Market	17.2	18.3	28.8	26.4	11.2	13.7
Wheat	PDS	73.5	71.7	63.9	74.2	57.6	58.2
	Market	26.5	28.3	36.1	25.8	42.4	41.8
Rice + Wheat	PDS	73.9	72.1	64.3	74.1	60.9	60.8
	Market	26.1	27.9	35.7	25.9	39.1	39.2
Sugar	PDS	1.3	0.3	2.1	0.2	0.0	0.0
	Market	98.7	99.7	97.9	99.9	100.0	100.0
Kerosene oil	PDS	96.8	99.2	100.0	99.4	99.3	100.0
	Market	3.2	0.8	0.0	0.6	0.7	0.0
				BPL			
Rice	PDS	76.6	75.9	77.5	73.2	85.4	90.9
	Market	23.4	24.1	22.5	26.8	14.6	9.1
Wheat	PDS	68.8	67.3	58.7	65.1	56.8	55.6
	Market	31.2	32.7	41.3	34.9	43.2	44.4
Rice + Wheat	PDS	69.2	67.7	59.6	65.6	60.2	59.7
	Market	30.8	32.3	40.4	34.4	39.8	40.3
Sugar	PDS	0.4	0.3	2.1	0.0	0.1	0.0
	Market	99.6	99.7	97.9	100.0	99.9	100.0
Kerosene oil	PDS	98.6	99.2	99.7	98.6	98.9	97.2
	Market	1.4	0.8	0.3	1.4	1.1	2.8
				APL			
Rice	PDS	22.2	32.9	23.7	28.1	49.9	54.4
	Market	77.8	67.1	76.3	71.9	50.1	45.6
Wheat	PDS	3.9	2.1	6.0	8.2	3.5	2.7
	Market	96.1	97.9	94.0	91.8	96.5	97.3
Rice + Wheat	PDS	5.1	3.7	6.8	9.6	6.3	5.1
	Market	94.9	96.3	93.2	90.4	93.7	94.9
Sugar	PDS	0.4	0.3	1.6	0.0	0.0	0.0
	Market	99.6	99.7	98.5	100.0	100.0	100.0
Kerosene oil	PDS	98.8	98.9	99.6	97.1	98.2	97.7
	Market	1.2	1.1	0.4	2.9	1.8	2.3

Table 4.26 Percentage Share of PDS and Market in Consumption of PDS Commodities—Chhattisgarh

Commodity		Month 1	Month 2	Month 3	Month 4	Month 5	Month 6
				AAY			
Rice	PDS	80.1	83.6	85.8	80.4	84.0	77.9
	Market	19.9	16.4	14.2	19.6	16.0	22.1
Wheat	PDS	22.1	50.0	50.9	39.1	43.5	30.9
	Market	77.9	50.0	49.1	60.9	56.5	69.1
Rice + Wheat	PDS	79.2	83.2	85.6	79.3	83.0	76.4
	Market	20.8	16.8	14.4	20.7	17.0	23.6
Sugar	PDS	72.3	72.5	74.5	64.9	65.5	66.3
	Market	27.7	27.5	25.5	35.1	34.5	33.7
Kerosene oil	PDS	97.4	97.5	99.2	95.8	96.7	96.7
	Market	2.6	2.5	0.8	4.2	3.3	3.3
				BPL			
Rice	PDS	65.2	66.9	70.8	64.1	63.6	61.0
	Market	34.8	33.1	29.2	35.9	36.4	39.0
Wheat	PDS	52.9	73.3	89.5	79.1	83.5	73.8
	Market	47.1	26.7	10.5	20.9	16.5	26.2
Rice + Wheat	PDS	64.8	67.4	72.4	65.5	65.6	62.3
	Market	35.2	32.6	27.6	34.5	34.4	37.7
Sugar	PDS	56.9	56.4	58.4	56.9	57.8	58.1
	Market	43.1	43.6	41.6	43.1	42.2	41.9
Kerosene oil	PDS	87.5	89.9	94.7	89.8	90.7	90.6
	Market	12.5	10.1	5.3	10.2	9.3	9.4
				APL			
Rice	PDS	7.7	9.3	10.6	11.2	5.8	6.5
	Market	92.3	90.7	89.4	88.8	94.2	93.5
Wheat	PDS	2.1	8.4	7.2	12.3	8.0	7.7
	Market	97.9	91.6	92.8	87.7	92.0	92.3
Rice + Wheat	PDS	7.2	9.2	10.3	11.3	6.0	6.7
	Market	92.8	90.8	89.7	88.7	94.0	93.3
Sugar	PDS	7.3	7.4	10.4	13.5	13.1	12.5
	Market	92.7	92.6	89.6	86.5	86.9	87.5
Kerosene oil	PDS	89.3	90.1	92.6	86.4	89.1	82.5
	Market	10.7	9.9	7.4	13.6	10.9	17.5

Table 4.27 Percentage Share of PDS and Market in Consumption of PDS Commodities—Bihar

Commodity		Month 1	Month 2	Month 3	Month 4	Month 5	Month 6
				AAY			
Rice	PDS	29.1	33.0	38.6	35.1	20.3	24.1
	Market	70.9	67.0	61.4	64.9	79.7	75.9
Wheat	PDS	38.3	42.7	31.7	32.8	21.3	22.7
	Market	61.7	57.3	68.3	67.2	78.7	77.3
Rice + Wheat	PDS	33.7	37.6	35.5	34.1	20.7	23.5
	Market	66.3	62.4	64.5	65.9	79.3	76.5
Sugar	PDS	0.0	0.6	0.0	6.7	0.0	0.0
	Market	100.0	99.4	100.0	93.3	100.0	100.0
Kerosene oil	PDS	79.7	81.1	85.1	75.0	89.6	88.9
	Market	20.3	18.9	14.9	25.0	10.4	11.1
				BPL			
Rice	PDS	10.5	18.1	25.2	22.6	14.9	15.0
	Market	89.5	81.9	74.8	77.4	85.1	85.0
Wheat	PDS	18.6	21.4	22.7	22.7	10.0	9.7
	Market	81.4	78.6	77.3	77.3	90.0	90.3
Rice + Wheat	PDS	14.3	19.5	24.1	22.6	12.8	12.7
	Market	85.7	80.5	75.9	77.4	87.2	87.3
Sugar	PDS	0.3	0.3	0.5	6.3	0.3	0.0
	Market	99.7	99.7	99.5	93.7	99.7	100.0
Kerosene oil	PDS	76.8	78.1	83.7	77.1	87.3	84.3
	Market	23.2	21.9	16.3	22.9	12.7	15.7
				APL			
Rice	PDS	4.5	4.7	4.6	3.5	1.3	2.4
	Market	95.5	95.3	95.4	96.5	98.7	97.6
Wheat	PDS	11.4	2.5	6.4	2.0	2.5	1.8
	Market	88.6	97.5	93.6	98.0	97.5	98.2
Rice + Wheat	PDS	7.8	3.7	5.5	2.7	1.9	2.1
	Market	92.2	96.3	94.5	97.3	98.1	97.9
Sugar	PDS	0.5	0.0	0.0	0.2	0.3	0.0
	Market	99.5	100.0	100.0	99.8	99.7	100.0
Kerosene oil	PDS	73.0	74.9	78.9	65.3	79.8	77.7
	Market	27.0	25.1	21.1	34.7	20.2	22.3

Table 4.28 Percentage Share of PDS and Market in Consumption of PDS Commodities—Uttar Pradesh

Commodity		Month 1	Month 2	Month 3	Month 4	Month 5	Month 6
				AAY			
Rice	PDS	76.3	72.1	74.7	69.8	69.8	63.5
	Market	23.7	27.9	25.3	30.2	30.2	36.5
Wheat	PDS	53.5	42.1	44.1	33.9	32.2	34.2
	Market	46.5	57.9	55.9	66.1	67.8	65.8
Rice + Wheat	PDS	66.3	58.0	60.2	51.1	49.9	48.0
	Market	33.7	42.0	39.8	48.9	50.1	52.0
Sugar	PDS	57.6	44.1	35.2	54.7	39.6	35.3
	Market	42.4	55.9	64.8	45.3	60.4	64.7
Kerosene oil	PDS	96.7	98.5	97.0	98.6	100.0	99.0
	Market	3.3	1.5	3.0	1.4	0.0	1.0
				BPL			
Rice	PDS	72.7	72.9	72.1	68.3	66.2	33.2
	Market	27.3	27.1	27.9	31.7	33.8	66.8
Wheat	PDS	49.3	41.6	43.2	34.7	33.0	31.9
	Market	50.7	58.4	56.8	65.3	67.0	68.1
Rice + Wheat	PDS	62.3	58.0	58.5	51.0	49.1	32.5
	Market	37.7	42.0	41.5	49.0	50.9	67.5
Sugar	PDS	44.3	43.7	33.8	49.8	40.4	34.1
	Market	55.7	56.3	66.2	50.2	59.6	65.9
Kerosene oil	PDS	93.3	96.8	96.4	98.5	98.1	97.8
	Market	6.7	3.2	3.6	1.5	1.9	2.2
				APL			
Rice	PDS	7.4	4.7	4.8	3.4	2.1	1.2
	Market	92.6	95.3	95.2	96.6	97.9	98.8
Wheat	PDS	4.5	4.2	2.8	2.0	1.8	0.5
	Market	95.5	95.8	97.2	98.0	98.2	99.5
Rice + Wheat	PDS	5.9	4.4	3.7	2.6	1.9	0.8
	Market	94.1	95.6	96.3	97.4	98.1	99.2
Sugar	PDS	4.7	2.9	2.4	2.6	2.0	0.0
	Market	95.3	97.1	97.6	97.4	98.0	100.0
Kerosene oil	PDS	79.9	92.5	90.5	93.2	94.7	97.4
	Market	20.1	7.5	9.5	6.8	5.3	2.6

Table 4.29 Percentage Share of PDS and Market in Consumption of PDS Commodities—Assam

Commodity		Month 1	Month 2	Month 3	Month 4	Month 5	Month 6
				AAY			
Rice	PDS	56.4	57.7	41.9	46.0	38.6	44.3
	Market	43.6	42.3	58.1	54.0	61.4	55.7
Wheat	PDS	0.0	0.0	0.0	0.0	0.0	0.0
	Market	0.0	0.0	0.0	0.0	0.0	0.0
Rice + Wheat	PDS	56.4	57.4	41.9	45.9	38.5	44.3
	Market	43.6	42.6	58.1	54.1	61.5	55.7
Sugar	PDS	14.7	4.8	11.0	8.7	9.8	7.6
	Market	85.3	95.2	89.0	91.3	90.2	92.4
Kerosene oil	PDS	81.9	83.1	72.2	82.0	78.4	82.1
	Market	18.1	16.9	27.8	18.0	21.6	17.9
				BPL			
Rice	PDS	54.4	55.6	45.3	50.8	45.4	50.4
	Market	45.6	44.4	54.7	49.2	54.6	49.6
Wheat	PDS	0.0	0.0	0.0	0.0	0.0	0.0
	Market	0.0	0.0	0.0	0.0	0.0	0.0
Rice + Wheat	PDS	54.4	55.5	45.1	50.7	45.3	50.3
	Market	45.6	44.5	54.9	49.3	54.7	49.7
Sugar	PDS	15.6	4.6	12.3	9.9	10.3	8.7
	Market	84.4	95.4	87.7	90.1	89.7	91.3
Kerosene oil	PDS	81.8	81.6	70.5	79.4	77.6	83.6
	Market	18.2	18.4	29.5	20.6	22.4	16.4
				APL			
Rice	PDS	0.8	1.4	1.5	2.2	1.8	0.9
	Market	99.2	98.6	98.5	97.8	98.2	99.1
Wheat	PDS	0.0	0.0	0.0	0.0	0.0	0.0
	Market	0.0	0.0	0.0	0.0	0.0	0.0
Rice + Wheat	PDS	0.8	1.8	1.5	1.5	1.0	0.9
	Market	99.2	98.2	98.5	98.5	99.0	99.1
Sugar	PDS	0.4	0.4	1.3	0.4	0.5	1.0
	Market	99.6	99.6	98.7	99.6	99.5	99.0
Kerosene oil	PDS	83.6	86.1	72.5	81.3	79.6	87.1
	Market	16.4	13.9	27.5	18.7	20.4	12.9

Table 4.30 Percentage Share of PDS and Market in Consumption of PDS Commodities—Mizoram

Commodity		Month 1	Month 2	Month 3	Month 4	Month 5	Month 6
				AAY			
Rice	PDS	65.3	71.3	54.3	50.2	49.0	49.4
	Market	34.7	28.7	45.7	49.8	51.0	50.6
Wheat	PDS	0.0	0.0	0.0	0.0	0.0	0.0
	Market	0.0	0.0	0.0	0.0	0.0	0.0
Rice + Wheat	PDS	65.3	71.3	54.3	50.2	49.0	49.4
	Market	34.7	28.7	45.7	49.8	51.0	50.6
Sugar	PDS	32.9	22.9	44.5	35.1	31.2	36.0
	Market	67.1	77.1	55.5	64.9	68.8	64.0
Kerosene oil	PDS	43.6	36.4	29.0	48.9	45.4	26.6
	Market	56.4	63.6	71.0	51.1	54.6	73.4
				BPL			
Rice	PDS	61.8	64.6	60.3	53.2	53.6	53.0
	Market	38.2	35.4	39.7	46.8	46.4	47.0
Wheat	PDS	0.0	0.0	0.0	0.0	0.0	0.0
	Market	0.0	0.0	0.0	0.0	0.0	0.0
Rice + Wheat	PDS	61.8	64.6	60.3	53.2	53.6	53.0
	Market	38.2	35.4	39.7	46.8	46.4	47.0
Sugar	PDS	30.7	31.9	38.3	33.4	32.8	34.7
	Market	69.3	68.1	61.7	66.6	67.2	65.3
Kerosene oil	PDS	50.0	48.2	41.4	54.3	54.1	48.2
	Market	50.0	51.8	58.6	45.7	45.9	51.8
				APL			
Rice	PDS	11.1	11.6	10.4	9.2	9.1	9.1
	Market	88.9	88.4	89.6	90.8	90.9	90.9
Wheat	PDS	0.0	0.0	0.0	0.0	0.0	0.0
	Market	0.0	0.0	0.0	0.0	0.0	0.0
Rice + Wheat	PDS	11.1	11.6	10.4	9.2	9.1	9.1
	Market	88.9	88.4	89.6	90.8	90.9	90.9
Sugar	PDS	17.0	18.3	21.0	18.7	17.2	16.3
	Market	83.0	81.7	79.0	81.3	82.8	83.7
Kerosene oil	PDS	28.9	22.5	19.9	24.0	28.2	22.6
	Market	71.1	77.5	80.1	76.0	71.8	77.4

Comparing the actual prices paid for the PDS wheat and rice with the stipulated prices for these commodities in the AAY category, it is evidently clear from the table that on an average, the mode price was quite closer to the stipulated price of Rs. 2 per kg for wheat and Rs. 3 per kg for rice. The mode price for the staple commodity of wheat in Rajasthan, Bihar and Uttar Pradesh was just equal to the stipulated price. Similarly, for the main staple of rice in Chhattisgarh, Bihar, Uttar Pradesh and Mizoram, the mode price charged was equal to the stipulated price. Mode price of rice was slightly above the stipulated price in Assam and Rajasthan. Thus, mode prices indicate that the majority of AAY households were provided food at the stipulated prices. In the case of BPL households, the mode price charged for wheat was Rs. 4.0 per kgs in Rajasthan, Rs.4.70 per kgs in Uttar Pradesh and Rs. 6.0 per kgs in Bihar. Mode price for rice was Rs.6.0 per kgs in Mizoram, Rajasthan and Chhattisgarh, Rs. 6.16 per kg in Uttar Pradesh and Rs. 7.0 per kgs in Bihar and Assam. Thus, the range across various states for mode prices was higher for wheat as compared to rice for the BPL households. In the case of APL, the PDS prices were closer to the market prices and that commensurate well with the main PDS theme of selling PDS food at the economic cost in the case of APL households. That also explains widely observed incidence of lower lifting of the PDS food by the above poverty households.

The mode price represents the price that is paid by the majority of the households. However, comparing mode prices with the more common average, namely the mean, it is seen from the table that mean prices were mostly above the mode prices for both wheat as well as rice. This was also true in the case of Antyodaya families. Mean prices above the mode prices indicate that although a majority of the households paid the stipulated prices, some households were charged more than stipulated prices for the PDS food. In the case of AAY, a few households paid more than Rs. two per kg for wheat in Rajasthan, Bihar and Uttar Pradesh. Similarly, above Rs. three per kg were charged for rice from a few households in almost all the states. Our fair price shop analysis indicated that higher than the stipulated prices occurred because shopkeepers passed on the transportation charges to the households in few cases.

In the case of sugar, although this commodity was under targeted system and was being supplied only to below poverty households in Chhattisgarh and Uttar Pradesh while it was supplied universally to all households in Mizoram, there was no difference in price for the above and below poverty households in any of the six selected states. Similar was the case in kerosene oil that was also supplied on universal basis and no price differential were observed between below and above poverty households in all the six selected states.

Concluding the findings on consumption pattern, it was observed that on an average per capita cereal consumption surpassed the 1200 calorie norm, i.e., the total cereal consumption was above 10.45 kgs in all the states and all the categories, except Chhattisgarh, where all the three category of households fell short of the target. Among the cereals, wheat and rice constituted the principal share. The total cereal consumed was highest in Bihar at 12.7 kgs and lowest in Chhattisgarh at 9.7 kgs per capita. On an average, the distribution of food and non-food expenditure for all the categories and all the states was 60-40, respectively. Food expenditure was highest, 72 per cent in Uttar Pradesh and lowest, 42 per cent in Mizoram. In other states, the percentage of food in total expenditure was 64 per cent in Assam, 62 per cent in Bihar, 60 per cent in Rajasthan and 57 per cent in Chhattisgarh. The performance of PDS in terms of providing food to the poor was quite satisfactory in Chhattisgarh, Uttar Pradesh and Rajasthan. In Mizoram, although the PDS system provided food to the poor but the amount received by the households was only around 25 kgs that was far less than the amount received by other states as well as the stipulated amount of 35 kgs. The PDS performed below average in providing food to the poor in Assam and its performance was completely unsatisfactory in the case of Bihar.

Table 4.31 **Prices of PDS Commodities *vis-à-vis* Market Price (Rs./Kgs or Litre) (Six Months Average)**

	Rice - PDS	Rice - OM	Wheat – PDS	Wheat - OM	Sugar - PDS	Sugar - OM	Kerosene - PDS	Kerosene - OM
				Rajasthan				
AAY								
Mean	4.64	17.43	2.77	9.38	13.46	20.76	10.49	11.57
Median	4.00	20.00	2.00	10.00	13.50	21.00	10.00	10.00
Mode	4.00	20.00	2.00	10.00	13.50	21.00	10.00	10.00
BPL								
Mean	6.43	17.03	4.73	9.49	13.98	20.85	10.35	13.10
Median	6.30	16.00	4.60	10.00	13.50	21.00	10.00	10.00
Mode	6.00	20.00	4.00	10.00	13.50	21.00	10.00	10.00
APL								
Mean	8.54	20.30	6.56	10.14	15.38	20.75	10.74	14.18
Median	9.00	20.00	6.80	10.00	13.50	21.00	10.00	15.00
Mode	9.00	20.00	6.80	10.00	13.50	21.00	10.00	10.00
				Chhattisgarh				
AAY								
Mean	3.45	10.21	-	10.31	13.87	21.22	10.11	12.48
Median	3.00	10.00	-	10.00	14.00	22.00	10.00	12.00
Mode	3.00	10.00	-	10.00	14.00	22.00	10.00	10.00
BPL								
Mean	6.22	10.23	5.09	11.46	13.82	20.75	10.10	12.91
Median	6.24	10.00	5.00	10.00	14.00	21.00	10.00	12.00
Mode	6.00	10.00	5.00	10.00	14.00	22.00	10.00	10.00
APL								
Mean	7.91	11.00	7.77	11.91	14.05	19.97	10.06	12.43
Median	9.00	10.00	7.00	12.00	14.00	20.00	10.00	12.00
Mode	9.00	10.00	5.00	12.00	14.00	20.00	10.00	12.00
				Bihar				
AAY								
Mean	3.52	10.22	3.03	10.44	14.03	21.02	11.85	28.26
Median	3.00	10.00	3.00	10.00	14.00	21.00	12.00	30.00
Mode	3.00	10.00	2.00	10.00	14.00	20.00	12.00	30.00
BPL								
Mean	6.64	10.32	5.86	10.52	14.03	21.01	11.85	28.80
Median	7.00	10.00	6.00	10.00	14.00	21.00	12.00	30.00
Mode	7.00	10.00	6.00	10.00	14.00	20.00	12.00	30.00
APL								
Mean	9.10	11.69	7.02	10.82	14.00	21.06	11.79	28.77
Median	10.00	10.00	6.50	10.00	14.00	21.00	12.00	30.00
Mode	10.00	10.00	6.00	10.00	14.00	20.00	12.00	30.00

contd...

contd...

	Rice - PDS	Rice - OM	Wheat – PDS	Wheat - OM	Sugar - PDS	Sugar - OM	Kerosene - PDS	Kerosene - OM
				Uttar Pradesh				
AAY								
Mean	3.22	10.74	2.30	10.23	13.93	20.63	10.94	20.83
Median	3.00	10.00	2.00	10.00	14.00	21.00	11.00	25.00
Mode	3.00	10.00	2.00	10.00	14.00	20.00	11.00	25.00
BPL								
Mean	6.44	10.84	5.05	10.25	13.92	20.77	10.95	21.45
Median	6.50	10.00	5.00	10.00	14.00	21.00	11.00	25.00
Mode	6.16	10.00	4.70	10.00	14.00	20.00	11.00	25.00
APL								
Mean	-	10.91	6.10	10.08	14.60	20.89	10.93	20.12
Median	-	10.00	5.00	10.00	14.00	21.00	11.00	25.00
Mode	-	10.00	5.00	10.00	14.00	22.00	11.00	25.00
				Assam				
AAY								
Mean	3.73	11.45	-	15.26	12.87	23.06	11.28	26.29
Median	3.51	12.00	-	16.00	12.00	23.00	11.00	30.00
Mode	3.51	12.00	-	16.00	12.00	22.00	11.00	30.00
BPL								
Mean	6.81	11.60	-	15.51	12.78	23.10	11.21	26.72
Median	7.00	12.00	-	16.00	12.00	23.00	11.00	30.00
Mode	7.00	12.00	-	16.00	12.00	22.00	11.00	30.00
APL								
Mean	10.90	12.16	-	16.05	12.43	23.00	11.20	25.48
Median	10.00	12.00	-	16.00	12.00	22.00	11.00	26.00
Mode	10.00	12.00	-	16.00	12.00	22.00	11.00	30.00
				Mizoram				
AAY								
Mean	3.02	12.92	-	-	14.24	21.06	14.41	18.73
Median	3.00	13.00	-	-	14.00	20.00	15.00	18.00
Mode	3.00	13.00	-	-	13.00	20.00	15.00	18.00
BPL								
Mean	7.31	12.49	-	-	13.98	20.98	14.16	18.72
Median	6.00	13.00	-	-	14.00	20.00	15.00	18.00
Mode	6.00	13.00	-	-	14.00	20.00	15.00	18.00
APL								
Mean	8.86	12.59	-	-	14.57	21.08	14.18	19.11
Median	9.00	13.00	-	-	14.00	20.00	15.00	18.00
Mode	9.00	13.00	-	-	13.00	20.00	15.00	18.00

Note: OM – Open Market Price.

Table A-4.1 Variations in Food Consumption across Households and Over Time

	Coefficient of Variation across Households			Coefficient of Variation across 6 Months		
	AAY	BPL	APL	AAY	BPL	APL
			Rajasthan			
Rice	113.5	106.6	107.2	41.9	45.3	12.4
Wheat	34.3	36.4	36.8	5.3	6.7	4.1
Other cereals	77.8	86.4	78.5	93.5	80.3	89.6
Total cereals	30.3	31.5	33.8	8.1	6.3	9.7
Total pulses	54.9	46.8	42.8	3.2	2.6	4.9
Sugar etc.	49.7	58.3	45.5	6.9	7.0	7.8
Edible oils	47.2	45.7	44.9	5.5	5.9	5.5
Milk	67.3	66.5	66.3	4.2	2.5	7.4
			Bihar			
Rice	50.6	50.7	41.1	2.2	4.5	4.8
Wheat	40.4	42.1	35.5	10.4	7.1	3.7
Other cereals	68.6	74.5	76.4	34.4	35.7	43.9
Total cereals	40.0	40.3	32.5	3.4	3.3	1.2
Total pulses	59.1	48.5	49.5	9.6	9.4	6.2
Sugar etc.	67.2	57.3	55.2	24.9	25.0	15.5
Edible oils	49.9	44.0	41.9	12.4	13.0	13.2
Milk	122.3	116.8	93.5	23.9	22.9	4.2
			Chhattisgarh			
Rice	29.6	37.7	35.7	3.8	5.1	3.0
Wheat	86.9	61.3	66.6	53.6	35.5	16.2
Other cereals	121.4	112.1	74.4	94.0	74.8	102.6
Total cereals	29.9	36.3	33.8	5.0	8.1	4.9
Total pulses	47.5	47.6	56.9	14.6	19.2	9.2
Sugar etc.	50.4	49.0	53.4	7.2	5.4	3.2
Edible oils	206.4	503.5	65.6	46.5	115.5	5.0
Milk	110.6	116.8	112.3	38.1	17.1	9.8
			Uttar Pradesh			
Rice	33.6	33.8	55.0	5.4	5.9	5.5
Wheat	46.3	51.1	43.4	16.2	13.6	6.9
Other cereals	95.0	123.6	163.8	98.7	173.0	148.4
Total cereals	34.6	37.7	42.0	9.4	8.2	6.5
Total pulses	42.7	43.3	49.1	8.5	8.2	5.0
Sugar etc.	54.7	53.4	59.4	13.4	15.2	11.8
Edible oils	38.5	35.4	37.2	7.2	6.9	3.6
Milk	109.4	83.4	70.3	21.5	22.8	18.3
			Assam			
Rice	31.3	29.9	27.5	9.0	9.9	8.7
Wheat	114.1	140.3	99.0	115.3	65.7	68.0
Other cereals	-	-	-	-	-	-

contd...

contd...

	Coefficient of Variation across Households			Coefficient of Variation across 6 Months		
	AAY	BPL	APL	AAY	BPL	APL
Total cereals	31.2	29.9	27.4	9.0	9.9	8.9
Total pulses	38.7	32.3	30.0	6.4	9.2	6.4
Sugar etc.	42.5	37.3	28.9	9.7	6.5	7.8
Edible oils	42.5	36.4	29.5	13.5	11.3	12.8
Milk	103.4	99.4	84.1	65.5	74.4	24.1
Mizoram						
Rice	30.03	29.23	37.53	14.91	7.43	5.38
Wheat	-	94.94	56.53	-	103.51	125.18
Other cereals	130.56	116.72	138.06	117.23	128.35	78.08
Total cereals	30.42	29.33	37.37	14.90	7.52	5.58
Total pulses	102.11	110.74	167.16	4.53	8.18	17.65
Sugar etc.	127.52	67.47	57.14	24.42	7.83	7.91
Edible oils	555.45	1033.06	42.79	124.35	90.72	7.68
Milk	86.88	126.54	108.65	7.18	11.47	8.77

5 Consumption Smoothing and Insurance against the Income Risks

5.1 Introduction

Household income is subject to various fluctuations as we have seen in the last chapter. Such fluctuations are much higher among the poor households in rural areas in the developing economies because earning sources of rural poor are not regular. In addition to fluctuations in their earnings subject to availability of employment during a particular period, they are also vulnerable to the natural calamities like, flood, drought, crop damage caused by insects, etc. Therefore, in the event of income failure how are they able to sustain their consumption poses a paramount question. In the event of no public immunity of any kind, the households are left to their social underpinnings to manage their consumption. There is a wide literature available that indicates the existence of some sort of insurance among the poor, either through the social networking, ethnicity or through their management of income or assets in the long run. The subject matter of this chapter deals with such issues among our selected households. The chapter is divided into three sections. The first section presents the theoretical framework of the model on consumption smoothing through insurance. The second section presents some facts about the observed distribution pattern of households' income and consumption in our selected states. Finally in the third section, we present the results of the model estimated to measure the risk insurance among the selected households using our panel data generated though six rounds of household survey.

5.2 Literature on Risk Insurance

How well are households in rural economies able to insure consumption against shocks to income? In the recent past, this question has led to a substantial literature examining the success of households in insuring consumption and identifying the different mechanisms that could potentially enable households to do so. The literature on risk and insurance in poor rural economies has established three stylised facts—(i) income risk is pervasive; (ii) household behaviour is geared in part to protecting consumption from such risk; and (iii) the mechanism of doing so are both private and social, the latter comprising various informal risk sharing arrangements amongst two or more households (Jalan and Ravallion, 1999).

The studies including Alderman and Paxson (1992), Deaton (1992), Fafchamps (1992), Grimard (1997), Morduch (1995) and Townsend (1994, 1995) lead to the question of how well households in rural economies are able to insure consumption against such shocks to income? They have concluded that households take action aimed at protecting consumption by drawing on both private and social risk sharing arrangements. Townsend (1994) lists five potential risk bearing mechanisms as: (i) Spatial diversification of land holdings; (ii) Storage of grains from one year to the next; (iii) Purchases and sales of assets such as bullocks and land; (iv) Credit from formal and informal sources; and (v) Gifts and transfers within the family networks. However, not all households are equally able to insure consumption against income shocks and differentiated access to markets, particularly financial markets result in differential ability of households to insure against income shocks.

Different versions of empirical specifications of risk and insurance have been tested by the researchers using household level data from both developed and developing countries. Mace (1991) in her study on risk sharing in the US economy finds that the evidence is conditional on the preference specification. Results are mostly consistent with consumption insurance for the exponential utility specification but not for the power utility specification. Townsend (1995) finds overwhelming rejection of the null hypothesis of no insurance for different regions in Thailand. His results confirm that consumption in one region or state tracks income in that region indicating some sort of insurance does exist. Deaton (1992) using data from Cote d'Ivoire finds that marginal propensities to consume out of current income are always positive and significant. In a somewhat similar case, Jalan and Ravallion (1999) using data from rural China observe evidences of partial insurance of certain wealth groups while evidences of rejection of full insurance were strongest for the poorest wealth groups. In the case of rural India, Townsend (1994) using ICRISAT data for three villages to study risk and insurance observed that full consumption insurance was a fairly good benchmark. He observed that landless households were less well insured than their counterpart cultivators. However, in the case of rural Punjab, Maitra (1998) observed no evidence in favour of consumption insurance against income shocks. Yet another study by Maitra (2003) using ARIS-NCAER data show that the null hypothesis of full insurance is rejected both for the population as a whole and for the different land classes. The estimated marginal propensity to consume out of idiosyncratic changes in income is significantly higher for the poorer households compared to the richer households.

The implications of the income and consumption insurance are quite significant for the policy matter in the case of targeted public distribution system (TPDS). The purpose of making PDS system targeted was implicitly to reduce the risk of income shock being transferred into consumption shocks. In other words, aim of such welfare-oriented programmes was to provide a safety net to the poor households. In our analysis part, we make an attempt to find out how successful have been the policy of TPDS in the selected states in mitigating such risks and providing a safety net to the vulnerable sections of our society, namely that of BPL and AAY cardholders.

5.3 The Theoretical Framework of Risk Insurance

The theoretical framework of risk sharing stems from the fact that households try to mitigate risk by their combined actions. If risks are idiosyncratic, i.e., they are household-specific in nature, then households will pool together to share all risks. If risks are fully pooled then there is complete risk sharing among households and changes in household consumption will track changes in the community average consumption and nothing else. In other words, if households pool their risks together, then their consumption will be determined in a combined way rather than being an individual phenomenon. In those circumstances, changes in factors specific to the household like changes in household income will not have a statistically significant impact on changes in household consumption. The estimated marginal propensity to consume of a particular household out of changes in its own income should be equal to zero while response of changes in community consumption on individual consumption should be equal to one. If that happens, such occurrences indicate that the household consumption is fully insured against any risk. The amount of risk sharing that actually takes place could be compared with this benchmark of complete risk sharing.

In this chapter we examine, whether the incidence of consumption smoothing (risk sharing) works better among the rich households (APL) who have better means of getting insured or does it work more effectively among the poor households (BPL and AAY). The poor households are likely to be more vulnerable to various kinds of income risks and therefore, they should undertake such measures to reduce the much higher chances of variability in consumption. However, although the poor being more vulnerable should be more likely to undertake such risk aversion measures but they will also be constrained by their limited availability of credit and insurance coverage. Therefore, it is very difficult to predict *a priori* whether the consumption smoothing through risk insurance would be more among the poor or rich households.

Formal financial and insurance markets for the prevalent risks particularly in rural areas in developing economies are often deficient. There could be various reasons for that, like high transaction costs, lack of information about the income pattern of rural households, lack of institutions for proper enforcement, collateral, etc. In the given circumstances, households are left with the only option of informal risk sharing among the family ties (relatives), their community members within or outside the village, etc. There are evidences that informal risk sharing schemes exist and perform very well in some developing countries.[1] Because of proximity of geographical locations and because of close transactions among group members, these informal ties work very well as the monitoring and enforcement costs are next to nil in their cases. However, these informal arrangements are still subject to aggregate risks. The amount of such risk would be higher among those community members where the whole community members are engaged in seasonal activities like in agriculture. The cropping pattern in developing countries is not diversified sufficiently. If all the cultivating members in a village are growing the same crop, their income will co-vary putting them in a combined risk. The local covariant risk can be reduced either by diversifying the cropping pattern or

1. For a review of issues related to the performance of traditional system of social security and insurance in developing countries, refer to Platteau (1991).

by extending the informal arrangements outside the village. The third option could be pooling with relatives or persons with close ties who are not subject to the same risk.

Therefore, the central question in the discussion of insurance among households is the identification of the appropriate group within which the informal risk sharing takes place. These groups may differ according to countries and societies. In relatively homogeneous societies, geographic proximity may be the determinant of the formation of the insurance group. In a number of studies as is mentioned in the review of literature discussed above, village is assumed to form such a homogeneous group. However, in societies that are more diverse, either along ethnic groups or castes, the village may not be the appropriate unit of risk sharing. In one of the examples, Morduch (1990) examined the possibility that rural households in the ICRISAT data set from India insures consumption with members of their own caste within their village. In an another study from Cote d' Ivoire, Grimard (1997) examined whether households take part in spatially diversified risk sharing arrangements with members of their own ethnic group. In both these studies, evidences were found for risk sharing but the hypothesis of complete risk sharing was however rejected.

In yet another study on India, Townsend (1994) uses an optimal consumption allocation framework to derive a test for complete insurance among households in villages in rural India. Although he rejected the incidence of complete insurance, his results did suggest that an individual household's consumption was partly insured with the other households in the village. In addition to above studies, there are many more especially in the developing countries that analysed risk sharing, taking village as the unit of risk sharing.[2] Udry (1994) and Townsend (1994) pointed out that the village arrangements were vulnerable to aggregate village shocks and that research was needed to examine how these households dealt with such an aggregate risk. Rosenzweig (1988) argues that households in informal risk sharing schemes were aware of the covariant nature of the risks and they would attempt to diversify spatially to reduce such risks. Rosenzweig and Stark (1989) took an example from the practice in rural India of sending daughters as brides to families residing in other villages that helps to mitigate the effects of income risks by establishing ties to households in locations that are subject to uncorrelated income shocks. Following the example of Townsend and other studies, we use village as unit for exploring risk insurance among our selected households. However, Morduch observed that caste played a very important role forming uniform group in India as members preferred to transact within their own caste group. In our survey data, we have another uniform group in terms of ration card holding. The people issued with similar cards belonged to one uniform group from both social as well as economic point of view. From the economic point, they were all in the same income brackets and from social point of view, they mostly belonged to the same caste group. It was presented in Chapter 2 that in majority of cases, AAY people belonged to the scheduled caste and scheduled tribe group, the BPL people mostly belonged to the SC, ST and other backward caste (OBC) while in the APL it was mostly forward caste people. Therefore, in our analysis we try to evaluate risk sharing theory from this point of view as well.

5.4 The Econometric Model

A fairly general specification of the risk sharing test may be developed by proposing a risk sharing group and assuming that within each group, consumption is efficiently allocated in each period over the life time of the household. Let us assume that each household i of a risk sharing group g, has a constant absolute risk aversion utility function in terms of its consumption at time t, c_{igt} and household preferences x_{igt}: $U(c_{igt}) = -\exp[-A(c_{igt} - x_{igt})]$. One can then develop a test for the hypothesis of perfect insurance by directly using the first order condition of the group's optimisation problem to solve for consumption:

$$c_{igt} = \left(\frac{1}{A}\right)\ln(A) + \left(\frac{1}{A}\right)\ln(\omega_{ig}) - \left(\frac{1}{A}\right)\ln(\lambda_{gt}) + \chi_{igt} \qquad \text{(i)}$$

where ω_{ig} is a welfare weight group g uses in choosing the optimal sets of consumption for the households of group, λ_{gt} is the Lagrange multiplier on the group resource constraint. Equation (i) states that if household i perfectly insures with other households of group g, its consumption should be partly determined by the aggregate resources of the group. Except insofar as it enters the aggregate resource constraint, household i's income does not affect household i's consumption. Include an individual household's earning term, y_{igt} in equation (i) and make this a testable proposition by including an error term u_{igt}. This error term may contain measurement error as well as household-specific shocks which are unobservable:

2. See Townsend (1995) for a survey of the studies of consumption insurance in developing countries.

$$c_{igt} = \left(\frac{1}{A}\right)\ln(A) + \left(\frac{1}{A}\right)\ln(\omega_{ig}) - \left(\frac{1}{A}\right)\ln(\lambda_{gt}) + \chi_{igt} + by_{igt} + u_{igt} \quad \text{(ii)}$$

Estimating equation (ii) is problematic because it contains terms, especially weights and preferences that are not observed. However, if one has information on the household for two consecutive periods, one can assume that household specific characteristics stay the same every period. Alternatively, they may be assumed to change but are orthogonal to individual income and group resource constraints. In both cases, the effect of individual household preferences can be removed by first differencing equation (ii).

$$\Delta c_{igt} = b\Delta y_{igt} + \sum_{j=1}^{G} \gamma_j \delta j_{gt} + \varepsilon_{igt} \quad \text{(iii)}$$

where $\Delta c_{igt} = c_{igt+1} - c_{igt}$, $\varepsilon_{igt} = u_{igt+1} - u_{igt}$ is the error term and G is the total number of risk sharing groups. δ_{igt} is a dummy variable equal to 1 if g = j and zero otherwise. This term represents $\ln\{(\lambda_{gt+1}) - \ln(\lambda_{gt})\}$ and is proportional to the change in the group's marginal utility of total income. It is the same across all the members of a group under complete insurance and can consequently be treated as a fixed effect for a member of that group. Finally, ε_{igt} is an error term that may include measurement error and household specific preference shocks.

The hypothesis of complete risk sharing is tested in this chapter using Equation (iii).[3] If the coefficient on the earning term, b is found to be not significantly different from zero and the group dummies are significantly different from zero, this would indicate that the household's consumption does not vary with its individual income but rather varies with the variation in the group's resource constraint. Thus, in this case, complete risk sharing within groups could not be rejected. However, the null hypothesis would be rejected if b is different from zero and the group dummies are insignificant. These results would support the hypothesis of purely individualistic household behaviour. A third possibility is that the coefficient b and the group dummies could both be significantly different from zero. It is not clear what such results imply for risk sharing. This possibility is consistent with partial risk sharing within groups, with a household's consumption partly determined by its own income and the group's resource constraint. However, it may be the result of other factors, as pointed out by Deaton (1990).

5.5 The Distribution of Income and Consumption

Before presenting the results of the model, a brief outline of the distribution of observed income and consumption per capita of the selected households is given. The household consumption comprises of expenditure on food and non-food items.[4] Similarly, household income includes all income earned from agriculture, livestock, agriculture and non-agricultural wages, salaries, earnings from business and self-employment and all other transfer earnings. In the last two chapters, we presented the estimates of average income and consumption over six months time period. It was seen in the analysis that variation in consumption across the households and over time period (of six months) was less than that of income. In this section, we further probe this issue by looking at the distribution of per capita income and consumption to compare the level of concentration of these two variables. Figures 5.1 to 5.18 present the Lorenz curves of per capita income and consumption among the three categories of households in the six states. The plots of the Lorenz curve clearly indicate that across the categories, consumption was more symmetric compared to income. This was true in all the states without any exception. It is seen from the plots that graph of consumption always remained closer to the diagonal line compared to income graph and in most of the cases it was true for the whole range of the graph indicating symmetry in consumption more than income for all households in each category. However, the volume of concentration varied across the states and categories. The Gini coefficient displayed in a small box in the middle of the graph measures the amount of concentration. The value of Gini coefficient for income was higher than that of consumption in all the categories. However, difference between the Gini of income and consumption was

3. The theoretical framework could also be explained using a constant relative risk aversion (CRRA) utility function. Equation (iii) would then be expressed in terms of change in logarithms instead of changes in levels. In our estimations, we use both the frameworks.

4. The details of food and non-food items is already discussed in the previous chapter.

highest among APL households in almost all the states. This was the natural outcome as the range between the lowest and highest income was much higher among the above poverty households than that of AAY and BPL households. Between the BPL and AAY, no major differences in the distribution of income and consumption were observed as value of Gini coefficient did not vary much for income as well as consumption between these two category of households. Comparing the six states, Gini coefficient for both income and consumption was highest in Mizoram, while its magnitude was lowest in Assam. The value of Gini coefficient for income varied from 0.67 in Uttar Pradesh for the APL category to 0.22 in Assam for the BPL households. In consumption, the range of Gini coefficient lied between 0.40 for AAY in Mizoram to 0.22 for AAY in Assam. Thus, two factors emerge from this analysis. On the one hand, individual consumption followed individual income, which negates our hypothesis of consumption insurance by the households within the village or within their community or ethnic groups. On the other hand, consumption variations were more symmetric compared to income variations. In other words, when income observed fluctuations due to some internal or external shocks, consumption did not fluctuate to the same magnitude. This latter phenomenon is compatible with the hypothesis of consumption smoothing due to the presence of some formal or informal insurance among the households.

Figure 5.1 Lorenz Curve (AAY)—Rajasthan

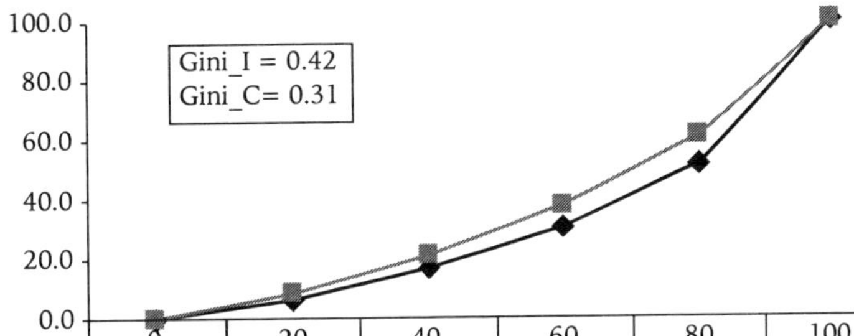

	0	20	40	60	80	100
Income	0.0	6.6	16.8	30.5	51.1	100.0
Consumption	0.0	8.0	20.6	37.8	61.5	100.0

Figure 5.2 Lorenz Curve (BPL)—Rajasthan

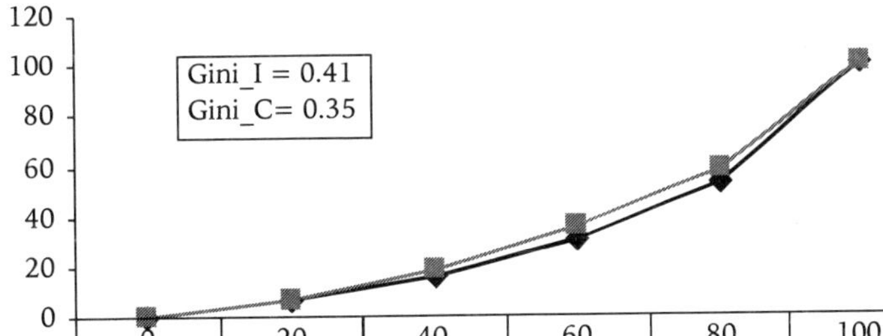

	0	20	40	60	80	100
Income	0.0	6.0	15.8	30.2	52.9	100.0
Consumption	0.0	7.1	18.8	35.2	58.4	100.0

Figure 5.3 Lorenz Curve (APL)—Rajasthan

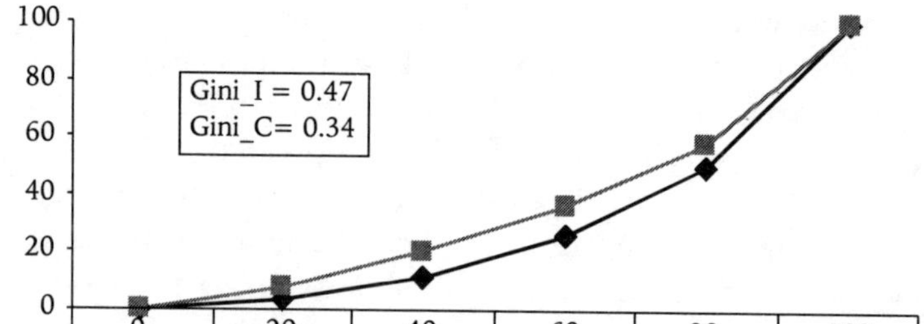

	0	20	40	60	80	100
Income	0.0	3.7	11.4	25.6	49.6	100.0
Consumption	0.0	7.7	20.0	36.0	57.6	100.0

Figure 5.4 Lorenz Curve (AAY)—UP

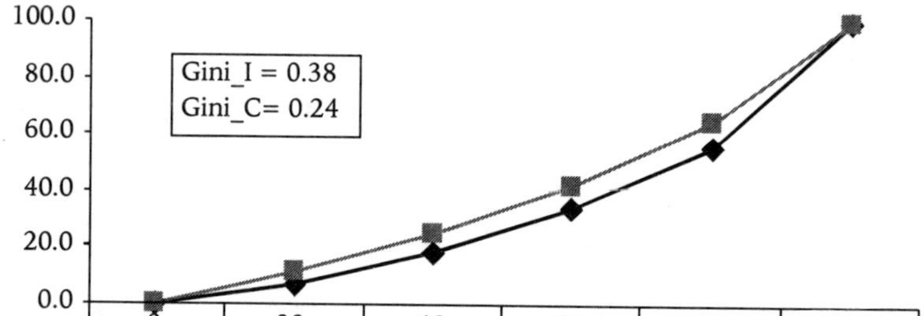

	0	20	40	60	80	100
Income	0.0	6.7	18.1	33.6	55.8	100.0
Consumption	0.0	11.1	25.5	42.6	65.1	100.0

Figure 5.5 Lorenz Curve (BPL)—UP

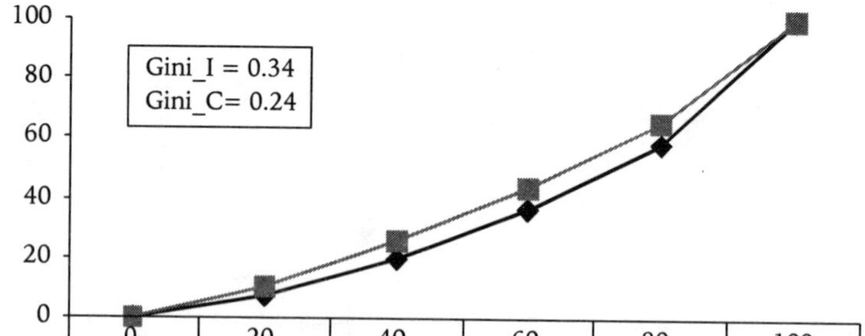

	0	20	40	60	80	100
Income	0.0	7.7	19.8	36.1	58.0	100.0
Consumption	0.0	10.8	25.6	43.2	65.3	100.0

Figure 5.6 Lorenz Curve (APL)—UP

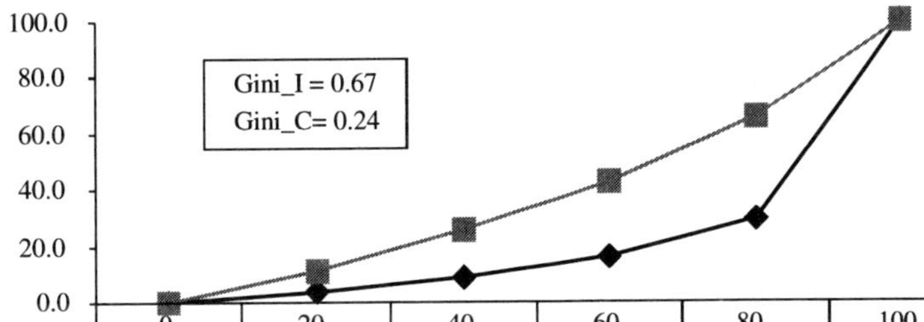

	0	20	40	60	80	100
Income	0.0	3.1	8.6	16.4	29.0	100.0
Consumption	0.0	10.8	25.0	42.4	65.7	100.0

Figure 5.7 Lorenz Curve (AAY)—Chhattisgarh

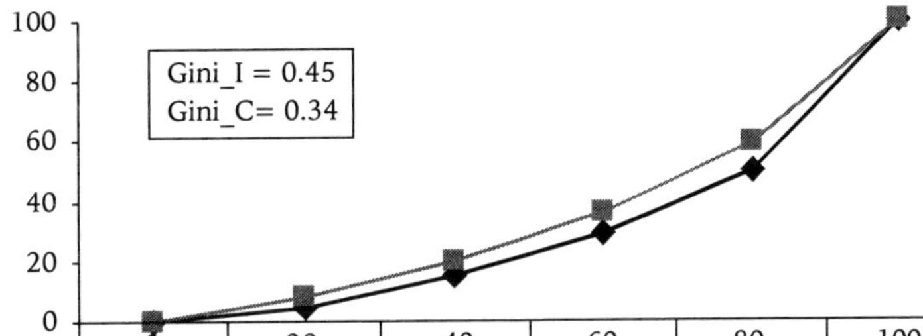

	0	20	40	60	80	100
Income	0.0	4.5	14.5	28.7	50.6	100.0
Consumption	0.0	7.6	19.5	35.8	59.0	100.0

Figure 5.8 Lorenz Curve (BPL)—Chhattisgarh

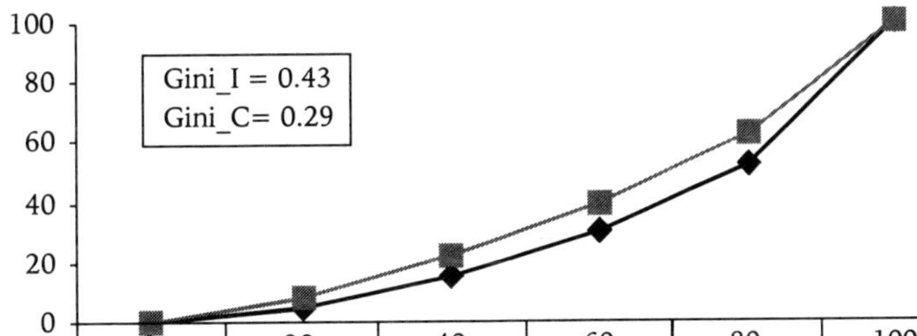

	0	20	40	60	80	100
Income	0.0	4.6	14.7	30.2	52.1	100.0
Consumption	0.0	8.5	21.9	39.6	62.7	100.0

Figure 5.9 Lorenz Curve (APL)—Chhattisgarh

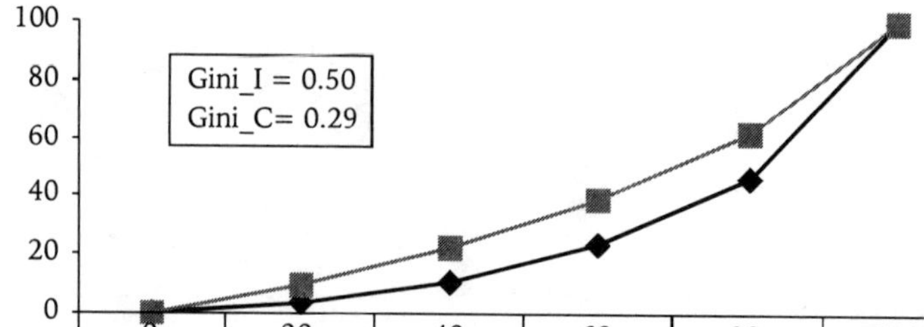

	0	20	40	60	80	100
Income	0.0	3.8	11.3	23.6	46.6	100.0
Consumption	0.0	9.0	22.4	39.8	62.4	100.0

Figure 5.10 Lorenz Curve (AAY)—Bihar

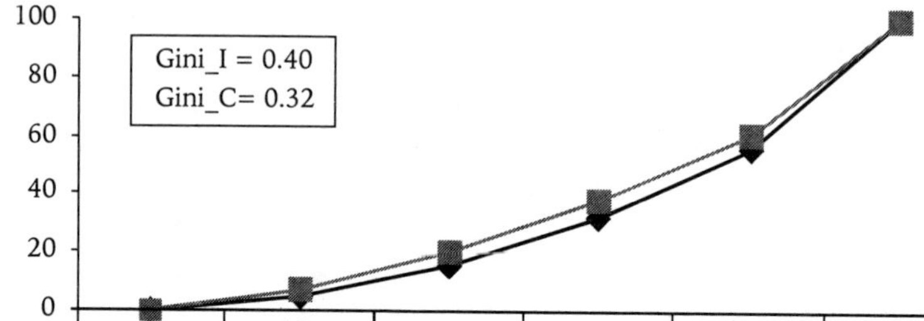

	0	20	40	60	80	100
Income	0.0	4.3	15.6	31.9	56.0	100.0
Consumption	0.0	7.4	20.0	37.8	61.1	100.0

Figure 5.11 Lorenz Curve (BPL)—Bihar

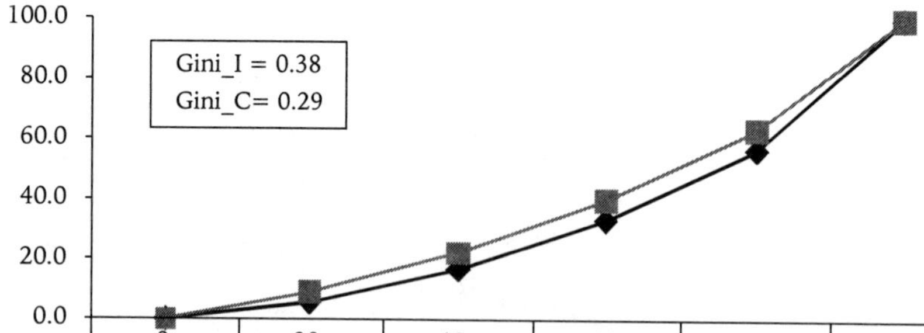

	0	20	40	60	80	100
Income	0.0	5.9	17.2	33.2	56.5	100.0
Consumption	0.0	9.2	22.8	40.1	63.0	100.0

Figure 5.12 Lorenz Curve (APL)—Bihar

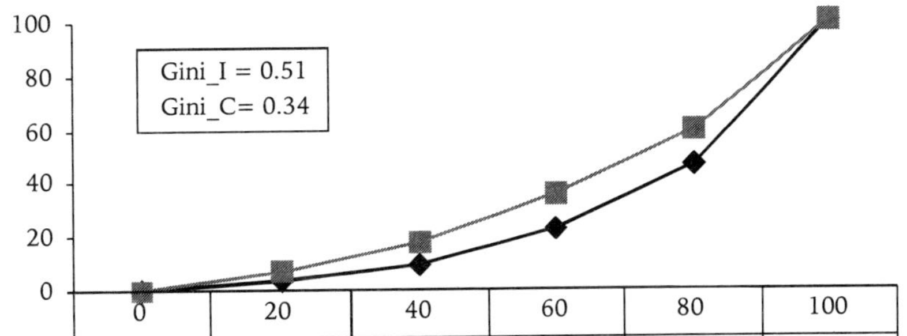

	0	20	40	60	80	100
Income	0.0	3.0	9.8	23.0	46.1	100.0
Consumption	0.0	6.7	17.8	35.2	59.7	100.0

Figure 5.13 Lorenz Curve (AAY)—Mizoram

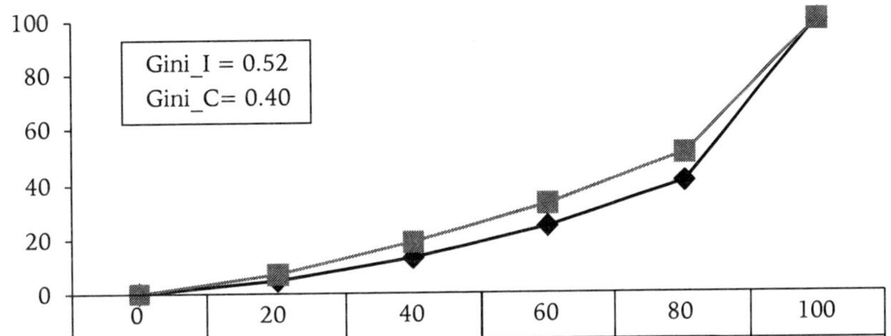

	0	20	40	60	80	100
Income	0.0	4.7	13.0	23.9	40.4	100.0
Consumption	0.0	7.3	18.2	32.1	51.3	100.0

Figure 5.14 Lorenz Curve (BPL)—Mizoram

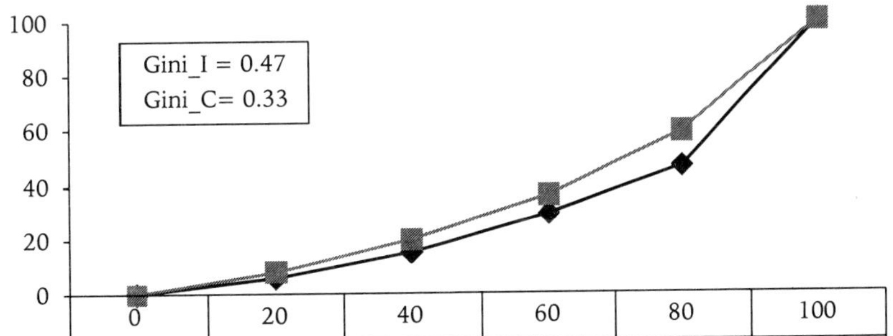

	0	20	40	60	80	100
Income	0.0	5.5	15.3	29.0	46.6	100.0
Consumption	0.0	7.8	19.9	35.9	59.2	100.0

Figure 5.15 Lorenz Curve (APL)—Mizoram

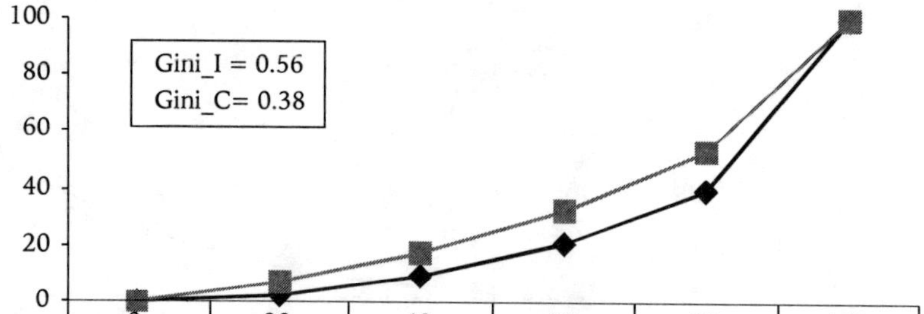

	0	20	40	60	80	100
Income	0.0	2.6	9.2	20.7	39.4	100.0
Consumption	0.0	7.2	17.8	32.0	53.7	100.0

Figure 5.16 Lorenz Curve (AAY)—Assam

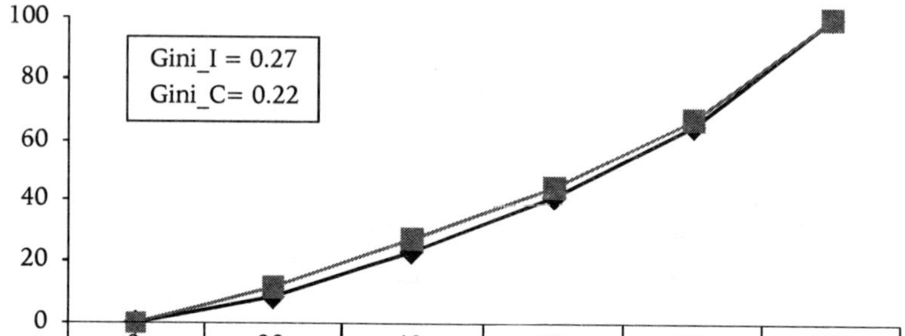

	0	20	40	60	80	100
Income	0.0	8.3	23.6	42.0	64.9	100.0
Consumption	0.0	11.6	27.3	45.2	66.8	100.0

Figure 5.17 Lorenz Curve (BPL)—Assam

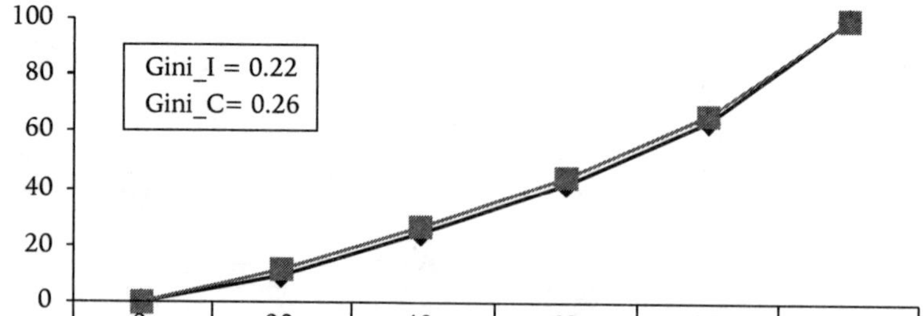

	0	20	40	60	80	100
Income	0.0	9.3	24.1	42.4	64.3	100.0
Consumption	0.0	11.7	26.9	44.5	66.0	100.0

Figure 5.18 Lorenz Curve (APL)—Assam

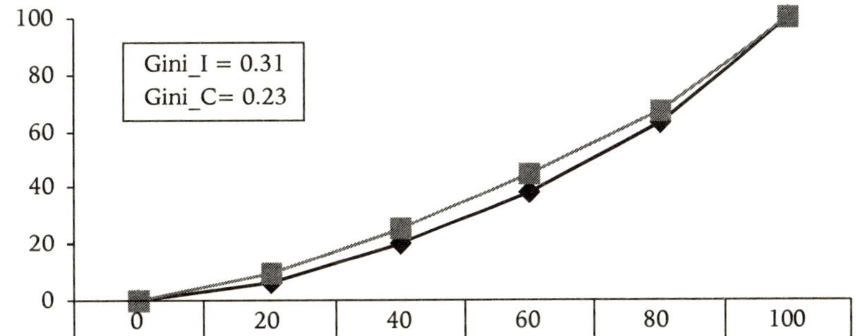

	0	20	40	60	80	100
Income	0.0	6.9	20.1	38.5	62.6	100.0
Consumption	0.0	9.9	25.6	44.6	66.9	100.0

5.6 Results of the Model

Before presenting the results of the model, it is essential to clarify the data we have used for building the model. The primary survey data collected over a period of six months for 6000 households in 6 states have been used for empirical estimation of this theoretical framework. In each state, data was collected from five districts, selecting five villages in each district. Thus, we have a total number of 25 villages in one state and 150 villages in all the six states.[5] In our estimation, therefore, we shall have 25 village dummies for each state. In addition, data was collected for three types of beneficiaries, i.e., AAY, BPL and APL. We also use this as a uniform group (as ethnic or caste group) and test whether households are undergoing some informal insurance within that group. Therefore, there will be two dummies in the ethnic groups. A total number of 1000 households were surveyed for a period of six months. However, in our estimation, we regress the change in consumption on change in income, therefore losing one month's information in the process of generating data for the first difference of income and consumption. By pooling the time series and cross section penal data, we shall have a total number of 5000 observations in each state. However, the number of observations would vary in the case of AAY, BPL and APL regressions in the proportion in which their numbers were selected in each state.

Equation (iii) is estimated using OLS in terms of first difference of levels and logarithms. We first estimate the regression of change in the level of consumption on the change in the level of income, for the state as a whole and separately for AAY, BPL and APL households without controlling for village level covariate risk (village dummies).[6] We then control for aggregate risk by adding (interacted) village dummies, as in equation (iii) and proceed with the same procedure estimating equations for the state as a whole and for the welfare groups of AAY, BPL and APL. In the next exercise, in place of village dummies, we attempt with the welfare group dummies and we call these dummies as ethnic or caste dummies. To test the hypothesis of consumption insurance, F test is used to test for the joint significance of village and ethnic dummies. Tables 5.1 to 5.6 present the results of regressions in levels (of first difference) and Tables 5.7 to 5.12 present the results for the regressions in logarithms.

The results of the regressions are mixed for different states and categories. In most of the cases, the hypothesis of full insurance was rejected. The income coefficient was significant in most of the states and categories. Similarly, the F test rejected the hypothesis that the combined value of coefficient of village dummy (accounting for the community effect on individual consumption) was equal to zero. In addition to village dummies, F test also rejected the hypothesis that value of dummies for ethnic groups was not significantly different from zero.

---

5. In our selection, we followed four villages and one city/town from each state. Therefore, our data consists of 120 villages and 30 towns/cities. However, for this exercise we do not differentiate between a village or a town. Therefore, we proceed with assuming there are a total number of 150 villages surveyed for this exercise alone.

6. Households' size is taken as additional variables, as consumption is also function of the number of members in the family. Number of earners is another variable that also determines the level of consumption and therefore, we have taken this as an additional variable.

Table 5.1 Regression Results—Rajasthan (Ordinary Least Square without Log) (Dependent Variable = ΔC)

	Δ Income	HH Size	Earners	Dummy Village	Dummy Caste	No. of Observations	R^{-2}	F
				Without Village Dummy				
State	0.03*	-43.08*	-26.61			4678	0.0312	51.29
	(11.06)	(-4.75)	(-1.06)					
AAY	0.03*	-25.42	-35.45			849	0.0182	6.24
	(3.77)	(-1.61)	(-0.82)					
BPL	0.02*	-34.31*	-35.99			2819	0.0082	8.76
	(3.32)	(-3.25)	(-1.24)					
APL	0.03*	-66.64**	-37.44			1010	0.0593	22.19
	(7.50)	(-2.43)	(-0.49)					
				With Village Dummy				
State	0.03*	-43.74*	14.28	1.89*		4678	0.0356	7.40
	(11.07)	(-4.71)	(0.50)					
AAY	0.03*	-23.67	-50.64	0.83		849	0.0135	1.43
	(3.77)	(-1.41)	(-0.89)					
BPL	0.02*	-32.66*	17.30	1.16		2819	0.0096	2.01
	(3.31)	(-2.97)	(0.49)					
APL	0.03*	-82.25*	36.33	1.53**		1010	0.0710	3.86
	(7.39)	(-2.79)	(0.44)					
				With Ethnic/Caste Dummy				
State	0.03*	-39.67*	-36.16		16.87*	4678	0.0378	37.73
	(10.96)	(-4.35)	(-1.44)					

Table 5.2 Regression Results—Rajasthan (Ordinary Least Square with Log) (Dependent Variable = ΔLogC)

	Δ Log Income	Log HH Size	Log Earners	Dummy Village	Dummy Caste	No. of Observations	R^{-2}	F
				Without Village Dummy				
State	0.07*	-0.04*	-0.01			4678	0.0085	14.35
	(5.43)	(-3.47)	(-0.44)					
AAY	0.07***	-0.03	-0.01			849	0.0035	1.98
	(2.19)	(-0.97)	(-0.18)					
BPL	0.05*	-0.04**	-0.01			2809	0.0048	5.54
	(2.98)	(-2.63)	(-0.46)					
APL	0.08*	-0.05	-0.01			1020	0.0161	6.57
	(3.94)	(-1.80)	(-0.43)					
				With Village Dummy				
State	0.06*	-0.03*	-0.003	1.85*		4678	0.0128	3.24
	(5.39)	(-2.89)	(-0.19)					
AAY	0.07***	-0.02	-0.03	0.67		849	-0.006	0.81
	(2.16)	(-0.80)	(-0.54)					
BPL	0.05*	-0.03	-0.002	1.47***		2809	0.0088	1.92
	(2.99)	(-1.76)	(-0.11)					
APL	0.08*	-0.05	-0.00	0.73		1020	0.0098	1.37
	(3.80)	(-1.77)	(-0.00)					
				With Ethnic/Caste Dummy				
State	0.07*	-0.04*	-0.01		4.23**	4678	0.0099	10.31
	(5.41)	(-3.28)	(-0.62)					

Table 5.3 Regression Results—Bihar (Ordinary Least Square without Log) (Dependent Variable = ΔC)

	Δ Income	HH Size	Earners	Dummy Village	Dummy Caste	No. of Observations	R_{-}^{2}	F
			Without Village Dummy					
State	0.01***	-13.36	-1.02			4744	0.0008	2.25
	(2.13)	(-1.34)	(-0.04)					
AAY	0.01	-11.42	16.46			865	-0.003	0.27
	(0.68)	(-0.59)	(0.33)					
BPL	0.004	-13.94	-8.73			3031	-0.00	0.98
	(0.5)	(-1.34)	(-0.34)					
APL	0.01	-12.62	-40.84			848	-0.001	0.77
	(1.42)	(-0.29)	(-0.36)					
			With Village Dummy					
State	0.008	-8.44	-12.67	1.41***		4744	0.0029	1.51
	(1.88)	(-0.78)	(-0.46)					
AAY	0.01	-6.50	-25.29	0.29		865	-0.023	0.29
	(0.61)	(-0.27)	(-0.41)					
BPL	0.002	-11.01	-18.16	0.91		3031	-0.001	0.92
	(0.30)	(-0.97)	(-0.62)					
APL	0.01	-23.38	-2.40	1.01		848	-0.002	0.94
	(1.24)	(-0.49)	(-0.02)					
			With Ethnic/Caste Dummy					
State	0.01***	-13.10	-7.03		5.28*	4744	0.0026	3.46
	(2.08)	(-1.31)	(-0.28)					

Table 5.4 Regression Results— Bihar (Ordinary Least Square with Log) (Dependent Variable = ΔLogC)

	Δ Log Income	Log HH Size	Log Earners	Dummy Village	Dummy Caste	No. of Observations	R_{-}^{2}	F
			Without Village Dummy					
State	0.06*	-0.03	-0.002			4739	0.0020	4.09
	(2.93)	(-1.71)	(-0.11)					
AAY	0.07	-0.03	0.01			865	0.0003	1.08
	(1.52)	(-0.95)	(0.29)					
BPL	0.06***	-0.03	-0.01			3026	0.0017	2.71
	(2.14)	(-1.38)	(-0.59)					
APL	0.04	-0.003	0.01			848	-0.002	0.39
	(1.07)	(-0.07)	(0.17)					
			With Village Dummy					
State	0.05**	-0.02	-0.01	1.80*		4739	0.0060	2.06
	(2.45)	(-1.09)	(-0.71)					
AAY	0.07	-0.03	-0.01	0.55		865	-0.012	0.61
	(1.31)	(-0.57)	(-0.21)					
BPL	0.05	-0.02	-0.03	1.45***		3026	0.0052	1.59
	(1.72)	(-0.74)	(-1.22)					
APL	0.04	-0.02	0.02	0.68		848	-0.011	0.65
	(0.87)	(-0.38)	(0.35)					
			With Ethnic/Caste Dummy					
State	0.06*	-0.03	-0.01		3.26**	4739	0.0029	3.76
	(2.85)	(-1.65)	(-0.29)					

Table 5.5 Regression Results—Chhattisgarh (Ordinary Least Square without Log) (Dependent Variable = ΔC)

	Δ Income	HH Size	Earners	Dummy Village	Dummy Caste	No. of Observations	$\bar{R}^2$	F
Without Village Dummy								
State	-0.01* (-3.15)	-7.95 (-1.27)	-4.00 (-0.25)			4549	0.0021	4.12
AAY	-0.03 (-1.11)	-2.70 (-0.27)	-18.91 (-0.72)			966	-0.001	0.74
BPL	0.02 (1.26)	-3.81 (-0.53)	3.08 (0.16)			2715	-0.0004	0.62
APL	-0.02*** (-2.24)	-11.46 (-0.53)	-10.15 (-0.20)			868	0.0029	1.84
With Village Dummy								
State	-0.013* (-3.06)	-14.73** (-2.25)	12.72 (0.75)	3.86*		4549	0.0169	3.90
AAY	-0.02 (-0.98)	-7.92 (-0.67)	3.55 (0.12)	1.02		966	-0.000	0.99
BPL	0.02 (1.36)	-8.58 (-1.13)	18.17 (0.89)	2.27*		2715	0.0107	2.08
APL	-0.01*** (-2.02)	-23.92 (-1.02)	2.41 (0.04)	1.32		868	0.0097	1.33
With Ethnic/Caste Dummy								
State	-0.01* (-0.27)	-4.89 (-0.78)	-4.43 (-3.07)		9.85*	4549	0.0059	6.42

Table 5.6 Regression Results—Chhattisgarh (Ordinary Least Square with Log) (Dependent Variable = ΔLogC)

	Δ Log Income	Log HH Size	Log Earners	Dummy Village	Dummy Caste	No. of Observations	$\bar{R}^2$	F
Without Village Dummy								
State	0.01 (0.39)	-0.02 (-1.54)	-0.002 (-0.10)			4549	0.000	1.07
AAY	0.004 (0.10)	-0.01 (-0.30)	-0.04 (-0.73)			966	-0.0020	0.35
BPL	0.01 (0.48)	-0.02 (-1.03)	0.02 (0.80)			2715	-0.0006	0.49
APL	-0.002 (-0.05)	-0.04 (-1.08)	-0.03 (-0.86)			868	0.0000	1.01
With Village Dummy								
State	0.01 (0.68)	-0.03 (-1.80)	0.02 (1.03)	5.12*		4549	0.0213	4.67
AAY	0.01 (0.23)	-0.03 (-0.67)	0.01 (0.11)	1.17		966	0.0023	1.08
BPL	0.02 (0.68)	-0.02 (-1.10)	0.04 (1.32)	3.06*		2715	0.0174	2.78
APL	0.002 (0.05)	-0.05 (-1.26)	-0.01 (-0.17)	1.29		868	0.0077	1.26
With Ethnic/Caste Dummy								
State	0.01 (0.36)	-0.02 (-1.29)	-0.003) (-0.14		3.63**	4549	0.0012	2.09

Table 5.7 Regression Results—Uttar Pradesh (OLS without Log) (Dependent Variable = ΔC)

	Δ Income	HH Size	Earners	Dummy Village	Dummy Caste	No. of Observations	$\bar{R}^2$	F
			Without Village Dummy					
State	-0.0003	-2.71	-8.11			4820	-0.0005	0.21
	(-0.08)	(-0.57)	(-0.39)					
AAY	-0.003	2.31	-4.71			1006	-0.0028	0.05
	(-0.24)	(0.26)	(-0.16)					
BPL	0.006	-2.52	-17.50			2858	-0.000	0.57
	(0.84)	(-0.48)	(-0.73)					
APL	-0.002	-9.35	25.47			956	-0.0027	0.13
	(-0.28)	(-0.56)	(0.29)					
			With Village Dummy					
State	0.001	-4.87	-3.81	5.74*		4820	0.0226	5.13
	(0.16)	(-0.97)	(-0.18)					
AAY	-0.002	-0.70	-24.99	1.20*		1006	0.0205	1.78
	(-0.16)	(-0.07)	(-0.77)					
BPL	0.009	-1.71	-9.52	5.90*		2858	0.0391	5.30
	(1.21)	(-0.31)	(-0.39)					
APL	-0.0014	-24.14	53.83	0.78		956	-0.008	0.71
	(-0.19)	(-1.29)	(0.57)					
			With Ethnic/Caste Dummy					
State	-0.00	-2.76	-8.80		3.72**	4820	0.0006	1.61
	(-0.10)	(-0.57)	(-0.42)					

Table 5.8 Regression Results—Uttar Pradesh (OLS with Log) (Dependent Variable = ΔLogC)

	Δ Log Income	Log HH Size	Log Earners	Dummy Village	Dummy Caste	No. of Observations	$\bar{R}^2$	F
			Without Village Dummy					
State	0.04***	-0.01	-0.01			4816	0.0005	1.83
	(2.17)	(-0.48)	(-0.66)					
AAY	0.06	0.003	-0.02			1006	-0.001	0.84
	(1.49)	(0.12)	(-0.55)					
BPL	0.03	-0.01	-0.02			2854	-0.000	0.86
	(1.39)	(-0.42)	(-0.63)					
APL	0.03	-0.02	0.01			956	-0.002	0.41
	(0.90)	(-0.61)	(0.27)					
			With Village Dummy					
State	0.04**	-0.01	0.001	6.60*		4816	0.0277	6.07
	(2.59)	(-1.22)	(0.03)					
AAY	0.06	-0.01	-0.03	2.68*		1006	0.0383	2.48
	(1.60)	(-0.48)	(-0.76)					
BPL	0.04	-0.01	-0.00	4.72*		2854	0.0303	4.30
	(1.74)	(-0.60)	(-0.03)					
APL	0.03	-0.04	0.04	0.83		956	-0.006	0.78
	(1.10)	(-1.21)	(0.68)					
			With Ethnic/Caste Dummy					
State	0.03***	-0.01	-0.01		1.19	4816	0.0006	1.57
	(2.13)	(-0.49)	(-0.69)					

Table 5.9 Regression Results—Assam (Ordinary Least Square without Log) (Dependent Variable = ΔC)

	Δ Income	HH Size	Earners	Dummy Village	Dummy Caste	No. of Observations	R-2	F
				Without Village Dummy				
State	0.004 (0.27)	-40.29 (-1.29)	63.82 (0.76)			3881	-0.0002	0.68
AAY	0.03 (1.44)	-39.54*** (-2.05)	25.24 (0.39)			726	0.0044	2.07
BPL	0.02 (1.18)	-41.19** (-2.43)	52.43 (1.23)			2377	0.0021	2.68
APL	-0.001 (-0.04)	-31.33 (-0.21)	104.00 (0.26)			778	-0.004	0.03
				With Village Dummy				
State	0.002 (0.15)	-18.90 (-0.56)	-8.76 (-0.10)	0.73		3881	-0.0019	0.73
AAY	0.02 (0.92)	-17.48 (-0.81)	-68.66 (-0.93)	1.26		726	0.0131	1.36
BPL	0.01 (0.63)	-19.63 (-1.08)	-22.53 (-0.47)	2.42*		2377	0.0163	2.45
APL	-0.0014 (-0.04)	-12.56 (-0.07)	14.83 (0.03)	0.13		778	-0.0316	0.12
				With Ethnic/Caste Dummy				
State	0.002 (0.18)	-38.90 (-1.24)	60.14 (0.72		1.55	3881	0.0000	1.03

Table 5.10 Regression Results—Assam (Ordinary Least Square with Log) (Dependent Variable = ΔLogC)

	Δ Log Income	Log HH Size	Log Earners	Dummy Village	Dummy Caste	No. of Observations	R-2	F
				Without Village Dummy				
State	0.05* (3.28)	-0.07* (-3.53)	0.04 (1.64)			3877	0.0056	8.31
AAY	0.11** (2.38)	-0.09** (-2.29)	0.02 (0.34)			726	0.0113	3.76
BPL	0.05** (2.62)	-0..06** (-2.34)	0.04 (1.45)			2373	0.0045	4.55
APL	0.01 (0.37)	-0.06 (-1.13)	0.05 (0.75)			778	-0.0016	0.59
				With Village Dummy				
State	0.04* (2.80)	-0.05*** (-2.09)	-0.02 (-0.67)	4.50*		3877	0.0267	4.94
AAY	0.08 (1.81)	-0.05 (-1.08)	-0.09 (-1.24)	1.41***		726	0.0247	1.68
BPL	0.04*** (2.11)	-0.04 (-1.41)	-0.02 (-0.53)	3.43*		2373	0.0284	3.57
APL	0.02 (0.42)	-0.01 (-0.14)	-0.02 (-0.33)	0.70		778	-0.011	0.68
				With Ethnic/Caste Dummy				
State	0.05* (3.05)	-0.07* (-3.42)	0.04 (1.68)		8.33*	3877	0.0094	8.34

Table 5.11 Regression Results—Mizoram (Ordinary Least Square without Log) (Dependent Variable = ΔC)

	Δ Income	HH Size	Earners	Dummy Village	Dummy Caste	No. of Observations	R^2	F
			Without Village Dummy					
State	0.02* (3.93)	-13.30 (-1.44)	6.51 (0.27)			3771	0.0039	5.90
AAY	0.08* (3.21)	-17.84 (-0.85)	14.94 (.20)			649	0.0127	3.79
BPL	0.01 (1.18)	-16.66 (-1.28)	17.82 (.56)			2119	0.0001	1.05
APL	0.05* (4.32)	-2.85 (-0.16)	-19.00 (-0.44)			1003	0.0190	6.43
			With Village Dummy					
State	0.02* (3.78)	-20.37 (-1.63)	-5.65 (-0.18)	5.13*		3771	0.0284	5.23
AAY	0.08* (3.08)	-35.85 (-1.01)	13.36 (.13)	1.24		649	0.0210	1.53
BPL	0.01 (1.22)	-25.31 (-1.44)	-2.77 (0.06)	2.80*		2119	0.0193	2.60
APL	0.04* (3.84)	-8.77 (-0.34)	-9.94 (-0.18)	2.27*		1003	0.0440	2.78
			With Ethnic/Caste Dummy					
State	0.02* (3.94)	-14.17 (-1.53)	5.63 (0.23)		0.70	3771	0.0037	3.82"

Table 5.12 Regression Results—Mizoram (Ordinary Least Square with Log) (Dependent Variable = ΔLogC)

	Δ Log Income	Log HH Size	Log Earners	Dummy Village	Dummy Caste	No. of Observations	R^2	F
			Without Village Dummy					
State	0.09* (4.13)	-0.09* (-5.88)	0.05** (2.77)			3771	0.0141	18.94
AAY	0.20* (4.49)	-0.08** (-2.67)	0.04 (0.83)			649	0.0416	10.37
BPL	0.06*** (2.19)	-0.10* (-4.43)	0.05*** (2.05)			2119	0.0110	8.83
APL	0.04 (0.80)	-0.08** (-2.68)	0.06 (1.78)			1003	0.0060	3.01
			With Village Dummy					
State	0.08* (3.87)	-0.07* (-3.67)	0.02 (0.80)	5.16*		3771	0.0385	6.80
AAY	0.20* (4.51)	-0.05 (-0.95)	-0.002 (-0.03)	1.11		649	0.0453	2.18
BPL	0.06*** (2.08)	-0.08* (-2.91)	-0.01 (0.36)	2.83*		2119	0.0303	3.54
APL	0.03 (0.64)	-0.09*** (-2.22)	0.04 (0.94)	2.84*		1003	0.0463	2.87
			With Ethnic/Caste Dummy					
State	0.09* (4.16)	-0.09* (-5.94)	0.05* (2.78)		0.48	3771	0.0138	11.55

Note: * significant at 1%, ** significant at 5%, *** significant at 10%.

Looking at the results for different states, it is seen from the tables that in Rajasthan, the coefficient of income was significant for the state as a whole and for all the three welfare groups of AAY, BPL and APL. This was true in all the cases, with or without village and ethnic dummies. The F test found that the village dummies were significantly different from zero only in the case of state as a whole and in APL households. In the case of ethnic dummies, F test clearly rejected the null hypothesis that their combined value was not significantly different from zero. The results were same for both the set of linear and log linear regressions. Thus, in the case of Rajasthan, the hypothesis of full insurance was clearly rejected. At the same time, it was observed that in the case of APL households, evidence was found supporting partial insurance for them, while AAY and BPL households supported the incidence of standalone. However, the hypothesis of consumption sharing within the ethnic, caste or religious groups was strongly supported by the F test.

In Chhattisgarh, Uttar Pradesh, Bihar and Assam, the linear regressions appear to be mis-specified as the sign of income coefficient was negative in few cases. The coefficient had a right sign in the case of logarithmic regressions and therefore, we consider only the log equations for these states. The coefficient of income was positive but insignificant for the state as well as for all the categories, with and without dummies in Chhattisgarh. In Uttar Pradesh, the coefficient of income was significant only in the case of state as a whole but insignificant for all the three categories when village dummies were excluded. The insignificant coefficients indicate that households' consumption was not dependent on their own income. Looking at the village dummies, the null hypothesis was rejected only in the case of state and BPL households in both the states. However, the hypothesis of ethnic/caste influencing the household consumption was accepted in both the states. Thus in some sense, the tests support the hypothesis of full insurance of consumption through the caste or ethnic grouping in the case of Chhattisgarh, while in Uttar Pradesh it makes a case of partial insurance.

In Bihar, like in Uttar Pradesh, the coefficient of income was significant only in the case of state as a whole. The village dummies were found significant in the state and in the case of BPL households alone, while in the latter case income coefficient was found insignificant, supporting the hypothesis of full insurance through village consumption. However, the dummy for ethnic/caste was significant along with the coefficient of income, thereby supporting the case of partial insurance in Bihar as well. In Assam, regression results were different in the sense that village dummies were significant in the state as well all the categories except that of above poverty households. Similarly, Mizoram, results provided evidence of some divergence from the other states, as the F test for ethnic dummies was not rejected while it was rejected for village dummies in most of the cases. The ethnic dummies provided the evidence of partial insurance in Assam, while village dummies supported partial insurance in Mizoram.

Comparing the results of AAY, BPL and APL households, it is evident that in most of the cases, the combined significance of village dummies was not rejected for AAY households. This was true in Rajasthan, Chhattisgarh, Bihar and Mizoram. On the other hand, for BPL households, F test accepted the combined significance of village in determining the individual consumption for all the states without any exception. In the case of APL households, combined significance was not rejected except Mizoram and Rajasthan. Thus, our results of village dummies point out that if at all any sort of partial insurance was available to the households, it was neither in the case of very poor households nor for the rich households. Only in the case of households in the middle income bracket, we could find some evidence of partial insurance. These results were further supported by the value of marginal propensities to consume (the coefficient of change in income). The value of income coefficients indicate the effect of idiosyncratic income shock on consumption. The value of the coefficient was slightly higher for the AAY group as compared to BPL or APL households and this was true in all the states without any exception. Last and the least, the household size had a negative impact on consumption that was significant in all the cases. The number of earners in each family, however, turned out insignificant in most of the cases.

In summary, our tests suggest that selected households were not fully insured against idiosyncratic income risks. The rejection of the full insurance model was for all the states and all the category of households, except one or two cases, where income coefficient was not found significant. The full insurance was earlier refuted by Townsend (1994), Udry (1994), Morduch (1990) and Deaton (1992). Our results suggest partial risk sharing activities between households either within the same village or within their same ethnic groups. The results of insurance through same ethnic groups were more robust than the results for the village insurance. These results are also valid from the socio-economic viewpoint. It is a well known fact that Indian society is strongly divided on caste and creed lines. The people in a particular caste group prefer to transact within their own ethnic group and these facts lend support to our above findings that risk sharing groups are more closely knit on the ethnic or caste basis. The results of insurance along the same caste line were found across the board whereas results for village insurance appeared in few cases, while it was rejected in other cases. Among our three categories, the results supported for partial insurance in the case of BPL households, while evidence for the AAY and APL was much weaker.

The implications of these results are quite significant. Government is running various schemes/programmes including the targeted public distribution system designed specifically to reduce the riskiness of rural incomes. The stated aim of such programmes is often to provide a safety net to the rural poor. Our results support the fact that such programmes are not being targeted adequately as the poorest of the poor (the AAY) households remain the most vulnerable. The results of this chapter strengthen the case for improved targeting and making some provision for the public insurance for the poorest of the poor.

6 Performance of Targeted Public Distribution System

Errors of Inclusion and Exclusion

6.1 Introduction

The basic objective of shifting from the universal PDS to targeted PDS was to benefit the poor and to keep the budgetary food subsidies under control to the desired extent. This objective was to be achieved through sale of food grains to APL households at economic cost and confining the food subsidy bill towards the identified BPL families whose number crossed 97 million families in 2006-07 (Government of India, 2006). Though the supply of the requisite quantity of food grains for distribution at BPL and AAY prices was to come from the central pool, the success of the TPDS in terms of meeting its stated objectives depended largely on the ability of State Governments in identifying the genuine poor families, restricting their numbers (of poor families) equal to the numbers estimated by the Planning Commission and putting in place an effective and efficient delivery system (Planning Commission, 2005). In the previous three chapters, we have provided the details of income and consumption pattern and their relationship for the selected AAY, BPL and APL households. In a number of recent studies, it has been highlighted that there are large-scale errors in the identification of BPL (and AAY) families, low off-take of food grains by the poor and there are weaknesses in the delivery system.[1] In the light of our observed per capita income and consumption of the below poverty households, it becomes essential to check the authenticity of identification of the beneficiaries and to further explore these issues in the light of information we have collected through our sample survey. This chapter deals with the matters related to efficiency of the targeted public distribution system. However, before discussing the topic of identification of BPL families and subject matter related to the number of duplicate or bogus cards issued, we present data related to entitlement, and ordering of consumer satisfaction among the selected below and above poverty households. This chapter is divided into five sections. The first section presents household entitlement for PDS grains and the actual delivery received (or not received) by the households. The next section presents indicators related to performance of PDS through our qualitative questions on the distribution of grains through fair price shops and the quality of grains distributed through PDS. Section 3 presents the criteria followed by State Governments in issuing BPL and AAY cards. We also check in this section if there is any diversions in the income or expenditure criterion followed by different states and that followed by the Planning Commission in estimating the number of poor in each state. Section 4 presents the issues related to identification of BPL and AAY households and the existence of excess cards if any in the selected six states. The last section makes comparison of income of the BPL and AAY households as defined by the Planning Commission norms and the actual income/expenditure observed through our sample survey.

6.2 Household Entitlement and the Amount of Grains Distributed

Tables 6.1 to 6.6 present the statistics related to household entitlement and the number of instalment preferred/received by the selected households during the reference year 2005-06 for wheat and rice in the six states. Similarly Tables 6.7 to 6.12 present data related to entitlement on the monthly basis for the six months of survey period. In the last chapter, we presented actual quantity of cereals received by the households from the PDS shops. In order to seek the household's perception about their entitlement, we asked them how much wheat and rice they were entitled to get from the PDS shops. On an average, households' perception was reasonably close to what they actually received from the fair price shops and most of the households were found to be aware about their entitlement. However, in the case of APL, entitlement and the actual amount received by

1. See for example, Planning Commission (2005), Radhakrishna and Subbarao (1997) and ORG (2005).

Table 6.1 Entitlement and Delivery under TPDS during 2005-06 (Rajasthan)

	Quantity Entitled (Kgs)	No. of Instalments Allowed (Per cent)				Your Preferred Instalments (Per cent)				No. of Months Entitlement Not Obtained during Last Year by the HHs who Obtained Irregular Supply				Reasons for Not Obtaining Entitlement by such HHs (Per cent)		
		1	2	>2	No Response	1	2	>2	No Response	1	2	>2	No Response	No Explanation Given	Less Supply to the FPS	No Response
AAY																
Rice	12.09	96.67	3.33	-	-	96.67	3.33	-	-	-	-	100.00	-	-	33.33	66.67
Wheat	31.87	99.43	0.57	-	-	95.95	2.89	1.16	-	21.43	50.00	28.57	-	20.00	66.67	13.33
BPL																
Rice	12.47	100.0	-	-	-	86.82	13.18	-	-	22.22	16.67	61.11	-	16.67	66.67	16.66
Wheat	31.24	99.83	0.17	-	-	90.27	8.19	0.51	1.03	44.00	12.00	44.00	-	35.48	51.61	12.91
APL																
Rice	10.00	100.0	-	-	-	100.00	-	-	-	-	-	-	100.00	-	-	-
Wheat	30.38	100.0	-	-	-	90.91	-	-	9.09	-	-	-	100.00	-	-	-

Table 6.2 Entitlement and Delivery under TPDS during 2005-06 (Chhattisgarh)

	Quantity Entitled (Kgs)	No. of Instalments Allowed (Per cent)				Your Preferred Instalments (Per cent)				No. of Months Entitlement Not Obtained during Last Year by the HHs who Obtained Irregular Supply				Reasons for Not Obtaining Entitlement by such HHs (Per cent)		
		1	2	>2	No Response	1	2	>2	No Response	1	2	>2	No Response	No Explanation Given	Less Supply to the FPS	No Response
AAY																
Rice	31.17	65.71	31.43	2.86	-	47.57	41.75	10.68	-	30.77	30.77	38.46	-	83.33	16.67	-
Wheat	6.22	58.33	41.67	-	-	54.55	36.36	9.09	-	50.00	50.00	-	-	100.00	-	-
BPL																
Rice	23.13	65.00	35.00	-	-	46.47	43.24	10.29	-	13.16	10.53	76.31	-	86.36	13.64	-
Wheat	4.54	69.45	30.55	-	-	67.95	30.13	1.92	-	5.71	17.14	77.15	-	86.11	13.89	-
APL																
Rice	15.20	38.46	61.54	-	-	53.85	38.46	7.69		-	-	-	100.00	-	-	-
Wheat	4.67	66.67	33.33	-	-	66.67	33.33	-		-	-	-	100.00	-	-	-

Table 6.3 Entitlement and Delivery under TPDS during 2005-06 (Bihar)

	Quantity Entitled (Kgs)	No. of Instalments Allowed (Per cent)				Your Preferred Instalments (Per cent)				No. of Months Entitlement Not Obtained during Last Year by the HHs who Obtained Irregular Supply				Reasons for Not Obtaining Entitlement by such HHs (Per cent)		
		1	2	>2	No Response	1	2	>2	No Response	1	2	>2	No Response	No Explanation Given	Less Supply to the FPS	No Response
AAY																
Rice	18.28	98.71	-	-	1.29	64.97	26.11	7.65	1.27	9.65	12.28	78.07	-	58.00	10.00	32.00
Wheat	15.50	98.72	-	-	1.28	64.97	26.75	7.01	1.27	10.53	7.89	81.58	-	57.43	39.60	2.97
BPL																
Rice	21.23	94.74	0.58	0.29	4.39	55.62	37.46	4.32	2.60	0.95	12.32	85.80	0.93	52.04	45.78	2.18
Wheat	13.44	94.52	0.58	1.16	3.75	56.82	36.08	4.54	2.56	0.94	7.31	90.81	0.94	51.75	46.36	1.89
APL																
Rice	8.60	83.33	-	-	16.67	78.26	17.39	4.35	-	5.71	2.86	91.43	-	56.00	44.00	-
Wheat	11.52	83.33	-	-	16.67	78.26	17.39	4.35	-	5.88	0.00	94.12	-	58.33	41.67	-

Table 6.4 Entitlement and Delivery under TPDS during 2005-06 (Uttar Pradesh)

	Quantity Entitled (Kgs)	No. of Instalments Allowed (Per cent)				Your Preferred Instalments (Per cent)				No. of Months Entitlement Not Obtained during Last Year by the HHs who Obtained Irregular Supply				Reasons for Not Obtaining Entitlement by such HHs (Per cent)		
		1	2	>2	No Response	1	2	>2	No Response	1	2	>2	No Response	No Explanation Given	Less Supply to the FPS	No Response
AAY																
Rice	22.79	98.96	-	-	1.04	94.85	3.09	0.52	1.54	100.00	-	-	-	100.00	-	-
Wheat	12.09	98.97	-	-	1.03	95.38	2.56	0.51	1.55	100.00	-	-	-	100.00	-	-
BPL																
Rice	22.38	98.22	-	0.71	1.07	96.06	2.5	0.72	0.72	66.67	7.14	11.42	14.77	70.00	23.33	6.67
Wheat	12.37	98.22	-	0.71	1.07	96.96	1.61	0.54	0.89	69.05	9.52	19.04	2.39	74.07	25.93	-
APL																
Rice	21.76	100.00	-	-	-	100.00	-	-	-	100.00	-	-	-	100.00	-	-
Wheat	12.00	100.00	-0	0.00	0.00	100.00	-	-	-	100.00	-	-	-	100.00	-	-

Table 6.5 Entitlement and Delivery under TPDS during 2005-06 (Assam)

	Quantity Entitled (Kgs)	No. of Instalments Allowed (Per cent)				Your Preferred Instalments (Per cent)				No. of Months Entitlement Not Obtained during Last Year by the HHs who Obtained Irregular Supply				Reasons for Not Obtaining Entitlement by such HHs (Per cent)		
		1	2	>2	No Response	1	2	>2	No Response	1	2	>2	No Response	No Explanation Given	Less Supply to the FPS	No Response
AAY																
Rice	33.78	28.04	70.37	1.59	0.00	0.65	77.27	13.64	8.44	33.33	33.33	0.00	33.34	78.57	7.14	14.29
Wheat	-	-	-	-	-	-	-	-	-	-	-	-	-	-	-	-
BPL																
Rice	33.57	25.99	72.20	1.48	0.33	0.37	61.58	24.26	13.79	38.10	4.76	2.38	54.76	76.74	0.00	23.36
Wheat	17.50	100.0	0.00	0.00	0.00	0.00	0.00	0.00	0.00	0.00	0.00	0.00	100.00	0.00	0.00	100.00
APL																
Rice	18.73	88.37	9.30	2.33	0.00	0.00	16.13	0.00	83.87	0.00	0.00	0.00	100.00	0.00	0.00	100.00
Wheat	-	-	-	-	-	-	-	-	-	-	-	-	-	-	-	-

Table 6.6 Entitlement and Delivery under TPDS during 2005-06 (Mizoram)

	Quantity Entitled (Kgs)	No. of Instalments Allowed (Per cent)				Your Preferred Instalments (Per cent)				No. of Months Entitlement Not Obtained during Last Year by the HHs who Obtained Irregular Supply				Reasons for Not Obtaining Entitlement by such HHs (Per cent)		
		1	2	>2	No Response	1	2	>2	No Response	1	2	>2	No Response	No Explanation Given	Less Supply to the FPS	No Response
AAY																
Rice	32.58	98.89		1.11	-	82.22	12.22	5.56	-	100.00	-	-	-	100.00	-	-
Wheat	-	-	-	-	-	-	-	-	-	-	-	-	-	-	-	-
BPL																
Rice	32.09	96.44	3.56	-	-	80.06	18.15	0.90	0.89	71.43	-	28.57	-	-	-	100.00
Wheat	-	-	-	-	-	-	-	-	-	-	-	-	-	-	-	-
APL																
Rice	22.27	95.45	2.27	2.28	-	86.05	4.65	-	9.30	-	-	-	100.00	-	-	-
Wheat	-	-	-	-	-	-	-	-	-	-	-	-	-	-	-	-

Table 6.7 Entitlement not Purchased Despite Availability Under TPDS during 2005-06 (Rajasthan)

	Entitled Qty. Not Purchased At Least Once during the Last Year (%)	Reasons by Such Households for Not Obtaining Entitlement (%)									
		Inferior Quality	No Difference in Price	Preference for Local Variety	Instalments Not Allowed	Standing in Queue a Problem	FPS Not Accessible	Grains Purchased from Other Food Programmes	Self Production	Scarcity of Income	Lack of Information
AAY											
Rice	1.11	50.00	-	-	-	-	-	-	-	50.00	-
Wheat	2.78	40.00	-	-	-	20.00	-	-	-	-	40.00
BPL											
Rice	0.33	-								100.00	
Wheat	2.15	45.45		18.18	9.09	27.27					
APL											
Rice	-	-	-	-	-	-	-	-	-	-	-
Wheat	-	-	-	-	-	-	-	-	-	-	-

Table 6.8 Entitlement not Purchased Despite Availability under TPDS during 2005-06 (Chhattisgarh)

	Entitled Qty. Not Purchased At Least Once during the Last Year (%)	Reasons by Such Households for Not Obtaining Entitlement (%)									
		Inferior Quality	No Difference in Price	Preference for Local Variety	Instalments Not Allowed	Standing in Queue a Problem	FPS Not Accessible	Grains Purchased from Other Food Programmes	Self Production	Scarcity of Income	Lack of Information
AAY											
Rice	12.98	9.09	4.55	0.00	36.36	0.00	0.00	0.00	18.18	31.82	0.00
Wheat	0.00	-	-	-	-	-	-	-	-	-	-
BPL											
Rice	12.52	1.67	1.67	1.67	56.67	1.67	0.00	0.00	23.33	13.33	0.00
Wheat	5.68	10.34	0.00	0.00	75.86	3.45	0.00	0.00	0.00	10.34	0.00
APL											
Rice	6.22	0.00	14.29	0.00	0.00	0.00	0.00	0.00	85.71	0.00	0.00
Wheat	-	-	-	-	-	-	-	-	-	-	-

Table 6.9 Entitlement not Purchased Despite Availability under TPDS during 2005-06 (Bihar)

	Entitled Qty. Not Purchased At Least Once during the Last Year (%)	Reasons by Such Households for Not Obtaining Entitlement (%)									
		Inferior Quality	No Difference in Price	Preference for Local Variety	Instalments Not Allowed	Standing in Queue a Problem	FPS Not Accessible	Grains Purchased from Other Food Programmes	Self Production	Scarcity of Income	Lack of Information
AAY											
Rice	11.86	5.00	0.00	10.00	0.00	35.00	0.00	10.00	0.00	20.00	20.00
Wheat	11.86	5.00	0.00	10.00	0.00	30.00	5.00	10.00	0.00	20.00	0.00
BPL											
Rice	14.37	22.22	8.89	14.44	0.00	14.44	0.00	1.11	0.00	22.22	16.67
Wheat	14.86	21.51	7.53	15.05	1.08	11.83	2.15	1.08	0.00	23.66	16.13
APL											
Rice	3.33	18.18	0.00	0.00	0.00	18.18	0.00	0.00	0.00	9.09	54.55
Wheat	3.33	18.18	0.00	0.00	0.00	18.18	0.00	0.00	0.00	9.09	54.55

Table 6.10 Entitlement not Purchased Despite Availability under TPDS during 2005-06 (Uttar Pradesh)

	Entitled Qty. Not Purchased At Least Once during the Last Year (%)	Reasons by Such Households for Not Obtaining Entitlement (%)									
		Inferior Quality	No Difference in Price	Preference for Local Variety	Instalments Not Allowed	Standing in Queue a Problem	FPS Not Accessible	Grains Purchased from Other Food Programmes	Self Production	Scarcity of Income	Lack of Information
AAY											
Rice	86.34	3.08				12.31	3.08	1.54	7.69	72.31	
Wheat	85.85	3.08				10.77	3.08	1.54	7.69	72.85	
BPL											
Rice	65.83	2.48	1.86	0.62	2.48	14.29	6.21	0.62	13.04	54.03	4.35
Wheat	65.66	2.48	1.86	0.62	2.48	14.29	6.21	0.62	13.04	54.03	4.35
APL											
Rice	4.04					33.33			33.33	33.33	
Wheat	4.04					33.33			33.33	33.33	

Table 6.11 Entitlement not Purchased Despite Availability under TPDS during 2005-06 (Assam)

	Entitled Qty. Not Purchased At Least Once during the Last Year (%)	Reasons by Such Households for Not Obtaining Entitlement (%)									
		Inferior Quality	No Difference in Price	Preference for Local Variety	Instalments Not Allowed	Standing in Queue a Problem	FPS Not Accessible	Grains Purchased from Other Food Programmes	Self Production	Scarcity of Income	Lack of Information
AAY											
Rice	55.78	67.59	0.93	0.00	30.56	0.93	0.00	0.00	0.00	0.00	0.00
Wheat	-	-	-	-	-	-	-	-	-	-	-
BPL											
Rice	54.51	93.39	0.00	0.00	3.90	2.70	0.00	0.00	0.00	0.00	0.00
Wheat	-	-	-	-	-	-	-	-	-	-	-
APL											
Rice	15.92	91.18	0.00	0.00	0.00	8.82	0.00	0.00	0.00	0.00	0.00
Wheat	-	-	-	-	-	-	-	-	-	-	-

Table 6.12 Entitlement not Purchased Despite Availability under TPDS during 2005-06 (Mizoram)

	Entitled Qty. Not Purchased At Least Once during the Last Year (%)	Reasons by Such Households for Not Obtaining Entitlement (%)									
		Inferior Quality	No Difference in Price	Preference for Local Variety	Instalments Not Allowed	Standing in Queue a Problem	FPS Not Accessible	Grains Purchased from Other Food Programmes	Self Production	Scarcity of Income	Lack of Information
AAY											
Rice	18.37	-	-	-	-	-	-	-	-	100.00	-
Wheat	-	-	-	-	-	-	-	-	-	-	-
BPL											
Rice	6.32	8.33	-	-	-	-	-	-	-	66.67	25.00
Wheat	0.79	50.00	-	-	-	-	-	-	-	50.00	-
APL											
Rice	90.18	77.78	5.56	16.67	-	-	-	-	-	-	-
Wheat	0.89	66.67	33.33	-	-	-	-	-	-	-	-

them did not tally in any state. In their case, most of the people replied with a disclaimer for any entitlement for food from the PDS, but in actual, a few households were able to receive some amount of grains distributed through fair price shops as was discussed in the last chapter. To our question, how many instalments in a month they were allowed to lift their entitled quantity, more than 90 per cent households in all the categories and in all states, except Assam, responded that they were allowed once in a month. In Assam, around 70 per cent households replied that they were allowed two instalments in a month to lift their entitled quantity of rice. More than 85 per cent households in Rajasthan, Uttar Pradesh and Mizoram also preferred one instalment in a month while 25 to 35 per cent households in Bihar wanted their entitled quantity in more than one instalments. In Assam, more than 60 per cent households preferred to lift their quantity twice in a month from the FPS.

In Chapter 4, we presented the amount of cereals received and the percentage of households receiving these cereals from the PDS. We further tried to check the regularity of cereal distribution among the households by asking households (who did not receive their entitlement regularly) for how many months they could not receive the cereals during the last year. A majority of such households (who did not receive their entitlements) in Bihar indicated that they did not receive regular supply for more than two months during the last year. In Chhattisgarh, among the households who did not receive their regular supply, a majority of them in the category of AAY households indicated not receiving their entitlements for one or two months and BPL households indicated more than two months. In Rajasthan and Uttar Pradesh, a majority of such households indicated one or two months when they did not receive their entitled quantity. In the two northeastern states, a majority of the households not receiving regular supply did not respond to our question. Among those who responded, around 1/3rd of them in Assam indicated irregular supply for only one or two months. In Bihar, around 50 per cent households (who obtained irregular supply) said they were not given any explanation for not being supplied the entitlement while the remaining households quoted the reason that the FPS did not receive the sufficient quantity from civil supply depots. Similar was the case in Rajasthan where majority of such households were told that irregular supply was due to less supply obtained by the FPS. In rest of the states, households quoted no explanation given by the FPS for irregular supply.

However, it was also noticed that in some cases respondents did not lift their entitlement even though supply was available at the FPS. Apart from the shortage of purchasing power in few cases there were other reasons like inferior quality at the FPS, preference for the local variety, home produced food available with the households, etc. Tables 6.7 to 6.12 present the details of households not lifting food from PDS despite its availability at the FPS. It is seen from the data that the phenomenon of not lifting the entitled quantity by the households during one or more months was highest in Uttar Pradesh, Assam and Mizoram while it was minimal in the case of Rajasthan and Chhattisgarh. In Uttar Pradesh, more than 60 per cent households did not lift their entitled quantity of wheat and rice and in Assam, more than 50 per cent households did not lift rice at least once during the last one year. In Mizoram, the phenomenon of not lifting at least once (or more) was above 90 per cent in the case of rice for above poverty households and it was around 18 per cent even among the Antyodaya households. The reason cited for the same in Assam was inferior quality of PDS rice (68 per cent of AAY and 93 per cent of BPL families) and instalments not allowed (31 per cent AAY and 4 per cent BPL families). In Uttar Pradesh, the main reason given for not lifting wheat and rice from FPS was scarcity of income by 72 per cent of AAY and 54 per cent of BPL households. In the case of Mizoram, 78 per cent APL households were of the view that quality of PDS rice was bad while 17 per cent preferred the local variety. The AAY households on the other hand, were found lacking money to buy the PDS food. Standing in queue, supply available from the self-production and FPS not accessible were the other reasons, specified by the households for not lifting their entitled grains. In Bihar, around 12 per cent of AAY and 14 per cent of BPL households did not buy from the FPS quoting the reason of scarcity of income, standing in queue and inferior quality for not buying from the PDS. In Chhattisgarh, 12 per cent of the households did not buy at least one month during the last year and the reason cited was instalments not allowed and scarcity of income by majority of them.

6.3 Performance of PDS—Qualitative Facts

We summarise here some qualitative facts about the performance of the PDS in the selected states. Tables 6.13 to 6.18 present facts related to PDS performance in terms of adherence to the prescribed norms, underweighment of the grains distributed and questions related to consumer satisfaction. Tables 6.19 to 6.24 present qualitative facts related to PDS specifically for the two main food crops, namely rice and wheat. To the question of adherence to the prescribed opening time and keeping the outlet opened for stipulated number of days by the FPS shopkeeper, around 80 per cent AAY and 85 per cent BPL households

Table 6.13 Qualitative Questions Related to TPDS (Rajasthan)

	AAY	BPL	APL
Q1: How do you rate adherence to the prescribed time of PDS outlet w.r.t. opening of the shop?			
Very good	13.89	13.41	21.56
Good	17.22	19.21	11.98
Satisfactory	49.44	50.33	40.12
Poor	6.11	7.45	9.58
Very poor	13.33	9.60	16.17
Q2: How do you rate adherence to the prescribed days of PDS outlet w.r.t. opening of the shop?			
Very good	15.00	14.55	21.69
Good	19.44	18.84	15.66
Satisfactory	44.44	48.43	36.14
Poor	11.11	9.75	13.86
Very poor	10.00	8.43	12.05
Q3: Do they underweigh grains while distributing?			
Yes	41.11	36.42	50.94
No	58.89	63.25	48.11
Q4: What is your perception about diversion of grains by ration shop owner?			
Very frequently	13.82	9.07	26.25
Frequently	19.74	21.36	32.50
Never	15.13	11.15	7.50
Sometimes	2.63	5.48	2.50
Cannot say	48.03	52.74	31.25
Q5: Are you satisfied with the quality of service at the FPS?			
Yes	71.02	76.35	70.44
No	28.98	23.65	29.56
Q6: If not what is the reason?			
Rude behaviour of the owner	19.51	26.77	23.26
Mismanagement in the shop	60.98	59.06	58.14
Preference given to known people in supply of grains	19.51	14.17	16.28
Q7: If the quality of service/grains is bad, do you know to whom to complain?			
Yes	37.85	36.18	44.44
No	62.15	63.65	54.94
Q8: Have you ever complained during the last year?			
Yes	23.46	14.52	21.69
No	76.54	85.06	77.11
Q9: Have you observed improvement in quality of service/grains after the complaint?			
Yes	0.00	5.26	5.00
No	100.00	94.74	95.00

Table 6.14 Qualitative Questions Related to TPDS (Chhattisgarh)

	AAY	BPL	APL
Q1: How do you rate adherence to the prescribed time of PDS outlet w.r.t. opening of the shop?			
Very good	35.00	37.08	43.55
Good	35.50	35.74	36.02
Satisfactory	28.00	25.50	19.89
Poor	1.00	0.84	0.54
Very poor	0.50	0.84	0.00
Q2: How do you rate adherence to the prescribed days of PDS outlet w.r.t. opening of the shop?			
Very good	33.5	36.58	45.7
Good	30	25.84	22.58
Satisfactory	36	36.74	31.72
Poor	0.00	0.5	0.00
Very poor	0.5	0.34	0.00
Q3: Do they underweigh grains while distributing?			
Yes	48.33	34.58	5.41
No	51.67	65.42	94.59
Q4: What is your perception about diversion of grains by ration shop owner?			
Very frequently	5.52	3.79	12.2
Frequently	13.81	14.63	4.88
Never	39.78	51.12	78.05
Sometimes	33.15	27.88	2.44
Cannot say	7.73	2.58	2.44
Q5: Are you satisfied with the quality of service at the FPS?			
Yes	80.87	79.73	87.92
No	19.13	20.27	12.08
Q6: If not what is the reason?			
Rude behaviour of the owner	14.71	47.2	16.67
Mismanagement in the shop	76.47	42.4	83.33
Preference given to known people in supply of grains	5.88	9.6	0.00
No response	2.94	0.80	0.00
Q7: If the quality of service/grains is bad, do you know to whom to complain?			
Yes	18.23	19.48	30.23
No	81.77	80.52	69.77
Q8: Have you ever complained during the last year?			
Yes	8.33	5.93	3.7
No	91.67	94.07	96.3
Q9: Have you observed improvement in quality of service/grains after the complaint?			
Yes	14.29	25	0.00
No	85.71	75	100

Table 6.15 Qualitative Questions Related to TPDS (Bihar)

	AAY	BPL	APL
Q1: How do you rate adherence to the prescribed time of PDS outlet w.r.t. opening of the shop?			
Good	6.04	5.53	10.13
Satisfactory	54.95	51.26	48.10
Poor	33.52	35.85	34.81
Very poor	5.49	7.37	6.96
Q2: How do you rate adherence to the prescribed days of PDS outlet w.r.t. opening of the shop?			
Very good	0.55	0.17	0.00
Good	6.59	4.03	5.06
Satisfactory	51.10	48.83	51.27
Poor	34.62	35.07	34.81
Very poor	7.14	11.91	8.86
Q3: Do they underweigh grains while distributing?			
Yes	82.32	73.39	68.25
No	17.68	26.61	31.75
Q4: What is your perception about diversion of grains by ration shop owner?			
Very frequently	26.22	27.11	34.85
Frequently	15.24	18.88	6.06
Never	45.73	45.98	54.55
Sometimes	1.83	3.01	0.00
Cannot say	10.98	5.02	1.52
No response	-	-	3.03
Q5: Are you satisfied with the quality of service at the FPS?			
Yes	39.23	41.2	62.96
No	60.77	58.8	37.04
Q6: If not what is the reason?			
Rude behaviour of the owner	3.51	2.29	8.2
Mismanagement in the shop	62.28	64.18	73.77
Preference given to known people in supply of grains	34.21	32.95	18.03
Q7: If the quality of service/grains is bad, do you know to whom to complain?			
Yes	30.91	25.44	52.48
No	69.09	74.56	47.52
Q8: Have you ever complained during the last year?			
Yes	71.43	70.71	69.81
No	28.57	29.29	30.19
Q9: Have you observed improvement in quality of service/grains after the complaint?			
Yes	4.88	10.10	0.00
No	95.12	89.90	100.00

Table 6.16 **Qualitative Questions Related to TPDS (Uttar Pradesh)**

	AAY	BPL	APL
Q1: How do you rate adherence to the prescribed time of PDS outlet w.r.t. opening of the shop?			
Very good	13.24	16.13	21.01
Good	26.47	19.86	23.91
Satisfactory	42.65	45.33	34.06
Poor	16.18	17.15	17.39
Very poor	1.47	1.53	3.62
Q2: How do you rate adherence to the prescribed days of PDS outlet w.r.t. opening of the shop?			
Very good	13.24	16.27	21.01
Good	27.45	20.51	18.84
Satisfactory	44.12	42.03	30.43
Poor	11.76	18.14	23.19
Very poor	3.43	3.05	6.52
Q3: Do they underweigh grains while distributing?			
Yes	16.42	16.78	21.33
No	83.58	82.87	78.67
Q4: What is your perception about diversion of grains by ration shop owner?			
Very frequently	15.12	9.26	20.00
Frequently	25.58	30.11	9.41
Never	28.49	25.68	21.18
Sometimes	22.67	28.42	28.24
Cannot say	8.14	6.53	21.18
Q5: Are you satisfied with the quality of service at the FPS?			
Yes	73.20	64.16	59.52
No	26.80	35.83	40.47
Q6: If not what is the reason?			
Rude behaviour of the owner	39.02	33.90	16.67
Mismanagement in the shop	39.02	39.83	41.67
Preference given to known people in supply of grains	21.95	23.73	41.67
No response	—	2.54	—
Q7: If the quality of service/grains is bad, do you know to whom to complain?			
Yes	32.04	35.59	7.55
No	67.96	64.41	92.45
Q8: Have you ever complained during the last year?			
Yes	25.86	14.04	20.00
No	74.14	85.96	80.00
Q9: Have you observed improvement in quality of service/grains after the complaint?			
Yes	88.89	3.13	0.00
No	5.56	90.63	100.00
No response	5.56	3.13	—

Table 6.17 **Qualitative Questions Related to TPDS (Assam)**

	AAY	BPL	APL
Q1: How do you rate adherence to the prescribed time of PDS outlet w.r.t. opening of the shop?			
Very good	1.06	3.28	1.04
Good	6.91	7.54	13.47
Satisfactory	83.51	74.1	76.17
Poor	2.13	8.36	4.66
Very poor	6.38	6.72	4.66
Q2: How do you rate adherence to the prescribed days of PDS outlet w.r.t. opening of the shop?			
Very good	2.13	3.11	1.04
Good	6.91	8.69	13.47
Satisfactory	82.45	73.28	76.17
Poor	2.66	8.36	4.66
Very poor	5.85	6.56	4.66
Q3: Do they underweigh grains while distributing?			
Yes	6.95	5.27	5.18
No	93.05	94.72	94.82
Q4: What is your perception about diversion of grains by ration shop owner?			
Very frequently	2.13	4.46	3.7
Frequently	72.87	66.5	55.56
Never	0.53	2.31	5.29
Sometimes	0.00	0.5	0.00
Cannot say	24.47	26.24	35.45
Q5: Are you satisfied with the quality of service at the FPS?			
Yes	81.38	74.88	77.2
No	18.62	25.12	22.80
Q6: If not what is the reason?			
Rude behaviour of the owner	86.11	81.94	90
Mismanagement in the shop	2.78	3.47	5.00
Preference given to known people in supply of grains	11.11	14.58	5.00
Q7: If the quality of service/grains is bad, do you know to whom to complain?			
Yes	52.94	55.19	49.74
No	47.06	44.81	50.26
Q8: Have you ever complained during the last year?			
Yes	77.57	76.47	65.63
No	20.56	23.24	34.38
No response	1.87	0.29	0.00
Q9: Have you observed improvement in quality of service/grains after the complaint?			
Yes	1.08	1.3	1.05
No	98.92	94.46	98.95
No response	-	4.24	-

Table 6.18 **Qualitative Questions Related to TPDS (Mizoram)**

	AAY	BPL	APL
Q1: How do you rate adherence to the prescribed time of PDS outlet w.r.t. opening of the shop?			
Very good	-	0.86	-
Good	12.90	9.77	5.66
Satisfactory	77.42	82.18	70.75
Poor	8.60	6.90	11.32
Very poor	1.08	0.29	12.26
Q2: How do you rate adherence to the prescribed days of PDS outlet w.r.t. opening of the shop?			
Very good	-	0.57	-
Good	12.90	8.62	5.66
Satisfactory	75.27	83.33	70.75
Poor	9.68	6.61	11.32
Very poor	2.15	0.87	12.26
Q3: Do they underweigh grains while distributing?			
Yes	21.50	26.15	21.9
No	78.50	73.85	78.10
Q4: What is your perception about diversion of grains by ration shop owner?			
Very frequently	1.19	4.33	2.15
Frequently	30.95	27.00	45.16
Never	5.95	10.33	11.83
Sometimes	29.76	24.33	18.28
Cannot say	32.14	34.00	22.58
Q5: Are you satisfied with the quality of service at the FPS?			
Yes	62.37	70.67	59.41
No	37.64	29.32	40.59
Q6: If not what is the reason?			
Rude behaviour of the owner	16.67	17.86	20.45
Mismanagement in the shop	33.33	35.71	45.45
Preference given to known people in supply of grains	50.00	46.43	34.09
Q7: If the quality of service/grains is bad, do you know to whom to complain?			
Yes	8.64	23.43	51.55
No	91.36	76.57	48.45
Q8: Have you ever complained during the last year?			
Yes	28.57	9.72	-
No	71.43	90.28	100.00
Q9: Have you observed improvement in quality of service/grains after the complaint?			
Yes	-	13.33	-
No	-	86.67	-
No response	100.00	-	-

Table 6.19 Qualitative Questions Related to TPDS for Rice and Wheat (Rajasthan)

	AAY	BPL	APL	AAY	BPL	APL
Q1: Is the local variety of grains considerably different from the PDS variety?						
	Rice			*Wheat*		
Yes	34.38	29.18	67.27	49.42	52.87	85.71
No	65.63	70.82	32.73	50.58	46.45	14.29
Q2: Do you strongly prefer the local variety of grains to the PDS variety?						
	Rice			*Wheat*		
Yes	35.05	34.14	40.00	46.24	52.46	51.79
No	64.95	65.56	60.00	53.76	45.84	48.21
Q3: Do they underweigh grains while distributing?						
	Rice			*Wheat*		
Yes	35.42	37.24	41.82	30.23	28.69	41.07
No	59.38	60.66	49.09	66.86	70.13	50
No response	5.21	2.1	9.09	2.91	1.17	8.93
Q4: If 'Yes' to above, what is the proportion?						
	Rice			*Wheat*		
<5%	55.81	47.73	92.59	45.9	48.13	77.78
5% to 10%	39.53	48.48	7.41	52.46	50.27	22.22
10% to 15%		0.76			0.53	
15% to 20%						
>20%	2.33	3.03		1.64	1.07	
No response	2.33					
Q5: Are you satisfied with the quality of grains?						
	Rice			*Wheat*		
Yes	65.63	71.6	49.09	69.82	70.71	51.79
No	34.38	28.4	50.91	30.18	29.30	48.21
Q6: If 'No' to above, how is the quality?						
	Rice			*Wheat*		
Presence of impurities	54.84	43.01	37.04	44	49.45	3.85
Rotten	9.68	12.9	7.41	14	11.54	15.38
Inferior quality	3.23	1.08		4	3.85	3.85
Broken grains	3.23	8.6	3.7	8	12.09	
Insect infested supply		12.9	14.81		0.55	3.85
Colour is not good	12.9	10.75	18.52	2	7.14	15.38
Taste is not good	16.13	8.6	14.81	16	10.99	42.31
Foul smell		1.08		12	3.3	15.38
Moisture content is more		1.08	3.7		0.55	
Q7: How do you rate the performance of TPDS with respect to supply of grains during times of distress?						
	Rice			*Wheat*		
Very good	19.59	23.65	3.64	10.40	12.65	5.36
Good	28.87	24.55	16.36	23.70	18.29	10.71
Satisfactory	25.77	29.64	30.91	46.82	51.62	32.14
Poor	3.09	4.49	1.82	4.62	6.67	5.36
Very poor	22.68	17.66	47.27	14.45	10.26	46.43

Table 6.20 Qualitative Questions Related to TPDS for Rice and Wheat (Chhattisgarh)

	AAY	BPL	APL	AAY	BPL	APL
Q1: Is the local variety of grains considerably different from the PDS variety?						
	Rice			*Wheat*		
Yes	40.21	42.74	5.41	12	42.55	2.86
No	59.79	57.26	94.59	88	57.45	97.14
Q2: Do you strongly prefer the local variety of grains to the PDS variety?						
	Rice			*Wheat*		
Yes	23.56	25.95	5.56	12.24	21.9	5.88
No	76.44	74.05	94.44	87.76	78.1	94.12
Q3: Do they underweigh grains while distributing?						
	Rice			*Wheat*		
Yes	41.54	34.02	5.41	14.00	33.15	2.86
No	57.95	65.98	94.59	86.00	66.85	97.14
No response	0.51	-	-	-	-	-
Q4: If 'Yes' to above, what is the proportion?						
	Rice			*Wheat*		
<5%	57.00	63.40	95.24	72.73	58.73	95.00
5% to 10%	38.00	33.96	4.76	27.27	38.10	5.00
10% to 15%	4.00	1.89	-	-	1.98	-
15% to 20%	-	0.75	-	-	0.79	-
>20%	-	-	-	-	-	-
No response	1.00	-	-	-	0.40	-
Q5: Are you satisfied with the quality of grains?						
	Rice			*Wheat*		
Yes	82.38	80.41	94.59	96.00	90.48	100.00
No	17.62	19.59	5.41	4.00	9.52	-
Q6: If 'No' to above, how is the quality?						
	Rice			*Wheat*		
Presence of impurities	71.43	73.17	100.00	50.00	57.14	100.00
Rotten	5.71	7.32	-	50.00	14.29	-
Inferior quality	2.86	2.44	-	-	1.79	-
Broken grains	5.71	3.66	-	-	10.71	-
Insect infested supply	-	-	-	-	1.79	-
Colour is not good		4.88	-	-	-	-
Taste is not good	8.57	7.32	-	-	12.50	-
Foul smell	2.86	1.22	-	-	1.79	
Moisture content is more	-	-	-	-	-	-
No response	2.86	-	-	-	-	-
Q7: How do you rate the performance of TPDS with respect to supply of grains during times of distress?						
	Rice			*Wheat*		
Very good	22.96	25.38	5.26	1.96	16.79	5.45
Good	38.27	38.84	84.21	58.82	40.71	83.64
Satisfactory	32.14	30.32	10.53	39.22	35	10.91
Poor	6.63	5.11	0.00	0.00	6.61	0.00
Very poor	0.00	0.34	0.00	0.00	0.89	0.00

Table 6.21 Qualitative Questions Related to TPDS for Rice and Wheat (Bihar)

	AAY	BPL	APL	AAY	BPL	APL
Q1: Is the local variety of grains considerably different from the PDS variety?						
	Rice			*Wheat*		
Yes	57.05	62.71	39.53	57.05	63.13	39.53
No	42.95	37.29	60.47	42.95	36.88	60.47
Q2: Do you strongly prefer the local variety of grains to the PDS variety?						
	Rice			Wheat		
Yes	68.15	68.54	46.51	68.15	68.54	46.51
No	31.85	31.46	53.49	31.85	31.46	53.49
Q3: Do they underweigh grains while distributing?						
	Rice			*Wheat*		
Yes	71.97	72.41	46.51	72.61	72.20	46.51
No	28.03	27.59	51.16	27.39	27.80	51.16
No response	-	-	2.33	-	-	2.33
Q4: If 'Yes' to above, what is the proportion?						
	Rice			*Wheat*		
<5%	5.26	4.27	9.09	5.26	4.27	13.04
5% to 10%	15.79	20.51	13.64	15.79	19.94	13.04
10% to 15%	51.75	46.44	72.73	51.75	46.72	69.57
15% to 20%	27.19	28.77	4.55	27.19	28.77	4.35
>20%	-	-	-	-	-	-
No response	-	-	-	-	0.28	-
Q5: Are you satisfied with the quality of grains?						
	Rice			*Wheat*		
Yes	8.92	8.77	16.28	32.48	31.11	37.21
No	91.08	91.23	83.72	66.88	68.89	62.79
No response	-	-	-	0.64	-	-
Q6: If 'No' to above, how is the quality?						
	Rice			*Wheat*		
Presence of impurities	32.41	37.81	63.89	5.52	12.76	36.11
Rotten	2.07	6.15	11.11	2.76	6.15	13.89
Inferior quality	8.28	6.15	16.67	8.28	5.69	-
Broken grains	16.55	10.71	5.56	6.21	5.24	-
Insect infested supply	24.83	21.64	-	33.79	25.97	19.44
Colour is not good	2.76	6.38	2.78	13.10	11.85	2.78
Taste is not good	13.10	10.93	-	29.66	29.61	25.00
Foul smell	-	0.23	-	0.69	2.51	-
Moisture content is more	-	-	-	-	0.23	2.78
Q7: How do you rate the performance of TPDS with respect to supply of grains during times of distress?						
	Rice			*Wheat*		
Very good	1.27	1.04	4.65	1.27	1.04	4.65
Good	5.73	7.92	4.65	6.37	7.29	4.65
Satisfactory	57.32	54.17	51.16	52.23	52.08	48.84
Poor	33.12	29.38	30.23	31.21	26.25	32.56
Very poor	2.55	7.50	9.30	8.92	13.34	9.30

Table 6.22 Qualitative Questions Related to TPDS for Rice and Wheat (Uttar Pradesh)

	AAY	BPL	APL	AAY	BPL	APL
Q1: Is the local variety of grains considerably different from the PDS variety?						
	Rice			*Wheat*		
Yes	32.97	29.29	9.30	30.56	29.24	4.76
No	67.03	70.71	90.70	69.44	70.77	95.24
Q2: Do you strongly prefer the local variety of grains to the PDS variety?						
	Rice			*Wheat*		
Yes	35.85	37.31	70.59	35.44	37.74	75.00
No	64.15	62.69	29.41	64.56	62.26	25.00
Q3: Do they underweigh grains while distributing?						
	Rice			*Wheat*		
Yes	15.90	16.67	23.29	15.98	16.70	23.94
No	84.10	83.16	76.71	84.02	83.13	76.06
No response	-	0.18	-	-	0.18	-
Q4: If 'Yes' to above, what is the proportion?						
	Rice			*Wheat*		
<5%	20.00	21.57	5.56	23.53	21.15	5.56
5% to 10%	65.71	56.86	83.13	52.94	36.54	55.56
10% to 15%	11.43	19.61	11.11	20.59	36.54	38.89
15% to 20%	-	0.98	-	2.94	3.85	
>20%	-	-	-	-		
No response	2.86	0.98	-	-	1.92	
Q5: Are you satisfied with the quality of grains?						
	Rice			*Wheat*		
Yes	62.30	65.59	14.89	63.49	67.93	13.04
No	37.17	34.41	85.11	36.51	32.07	86.96
No response	0.52	-	-	-	-	-
Q6: If 'No' to above, how is the quality?						
	Rice			*Wheat*		
Presence of impurities	21.05	13.83	66.67	16.22	15.00	66.67
Rotten	21.05	11.70	33.33	21.62	15.00	33.33
Inferior quality	15.79	3.19	-	13.51	2.50	-
Broken grains	36.84	37.23	-	10.81	1.25	-
Insect infested supply	2.63	2.13	-	21.62	33.75	-
Colour is not good	-	5.32	-	-	-	-
Taste is not good	-	8.51	-	2.70	6.25	-
Foul smell	-	13.83	-	5.41	2.50	-
Moisture content is more	-	1.06	-	5.41	21.25	-
No response	2.63	3.19	-	2.70	2.50	-
Q7: How do you rate the performance of TPDS with respect to supply of grains during times of distress?						
	Rice			*Wheat*		
Very good	24.69	25.44	76.47	24.69	25.00	79.59
Good	12.35	12.94	3.92	26.54	21.27	2.04
Satisfactory	54.32	48.68	7.84	33.33	35.75	8.16
Poor	6.79	11.40	3.92	12.96	15.13	4.08
Very poor	1.85	1.32	7.84	2.47	2.19	6.12
No response	-	0.22	-	-	0.66	-

Table 6.23 Qualitative Questions Related to TPDS for Rice and Wheat (Assam)

	AAY	BPL	APL	AAY	BPL	APL
Q1: Is the local variety of grains considerably different from the PDS variety?						
	Rice			*Wheat*		
Yes	93.51	95.02	92.76	100	100	75
No	6.49	4.98	7.24	0.00	0.00	25
Q2: Do you strongly prefer the local variety of grains to the PDS variety?						
	Rice			*Wheat*		
Yes	75.27	81.62	71.71	66.67	100.00	100.00
No	24.73	18.38	28.29	33.33	0.00	0.00
Q3: Do they underweigh grains while distributing?						
	Rice			*Wheat*		
Yes	5.98	4.80	4.61	20.00	50.00	25.00
No	94.02	95.20	94.08	80.00	50.00	75.00
No response			1.32			
Q4: If 'Yes' to above, what is the proportion?						
	Rice			*Wheat*		
<5%	7.14	20.00	12.50	-	-	-
5% to 10%	7.14	10.00	87.50	-	-	-
10% to 15%	42.86	32.50	-	-	-	-
15% to 20%	42.86	35.00	-	-	-	100.00
>20%	-	-	-	-	-	-
No response	-	2.50	-	100.00	100.00	-
Q5: Are you satisfied with the quality of grains?						
	Rice			*Wheat*		
Yes	72.28	66.67	61.84	100.00	100.00	25.00
No	27.72	33.33	37.50	-	-	75.00
No response	-	-	0.66	-	-	-
Q6: If 'No' to above, how is the quality?						
	Rice			*Wheat*		
Presence of impurities	60.00	23.85	3.45	-	-	-
Rotten	-	0.92	6.90	-	-	-
Inferior quality	20.00	7.34	44.83	-	-	100.00
Broken grains	6.67	65.14	44.83	-	-	-
Insect infested supply	-	-	-	-	-	-
Colour is not good	-	-	-	-	-	-
Taste is not good	-	-	-	-	-	-
Foul smell	-	-	-	-	-	-
Moisture content is more	-	-	-	-	-	-
No response	13.33	2.75	-	100.00	100.00	-
Q7: How do you rate the performance of TPDS with respect to supply of grains during times of distress?						
	Rice			*Wheat*		
Very good	1.07	0.17	0.00	0.00	0.00	0.00
Good	23.53	15.89	13.82	33.33	0.00	75
Satisfactory	66.31	67.38	73.68	66.67	100.00	25
Poor	1.6	14.4	11.18	0.00	0.00	0.00
Very poor	7.49	2.15	1.32	0.00	0.00	0.00

Table 6.24 Qualitative Questions Related to TPDS for Rice and Wheat (Mizoram)

	AAY	BPL	APL	AAY	BPL	APL
Q1: Is the local variety of grains considerably different from the PDS variety?						
	Rice			*Wheat*		
Yes	83.70	85.76	90.22	-	50.00	100.00
No	16.30	14.24	9.78	-	50.00	-
Q2: Do you strongly prefer the local variety of grains to the PDS variety?						
	Rice			*Wheat*		
Yes	58.70	58.24	88.04	40.00	100.00	-
No	41.30	41.76	11.96	60.00	-	100.00
Q3: Do they underweigh grains while distributing?						
	Rice			*Wheat*		
Yes	20.43	22.09	15.22	-	-	-
No	79.57	77.91	84.78	-	100.00	-
No response	-	0.22	-	-	-	-
Q4: If 'Yes' to above, what is the proportion?						
	Rice			*Wheat*		
<5%	40.00	42.53	28.57	-	-	-
5% to 10%	20.00	28.74	14.29	-	100.00	-
10% to 15%	25.00	24.14	35.71	-	-	-
15% to 20%	15.00	4.60	21.43	-	-	-
>20%	-	-	-	-	-	-
No response	-	-	-	100.00	-	100.00
Q5: Are you satisfied with the quality of grains?						
	Rice			*Wheat*		
Yes	64.13	65.59	56.67	-	-	-
No	35.87	34.41	43.33	-	100.00	100.00
No response	-	-	-	100.00	-	-
Q6: If 'No' to above, how is the quality?						
	Rice			*Wheat*		
Presence of impurities	70.59	53.13	52.94	-	20.00	-
Rotten	5.88	5.47	8.82	-	80.00	-
Inferior quality	17.65	26.56	29.41	-	-	100.00
Broken grains	5.88	4.69	2.94	-	-	-
Insect infested supply	-	3.13	-	-	-	-
Colour is not good	-	-	-	-	-	-
Taste is not good	-	7.03	5.88	-	-	-
Foul smell	-	-	-	-	-	-
Moisture content is more	-	-	-	-	-	-
No response		-	-	100.00	-	-
Q7: How do you rate the performance of TPDS with respect to supply of grains during times of distress?						
	Rice			*Wheat*		
Very good	4.40	1.79	-	-	-	-
Good	9.89	10.71	5.49	-	60.00	-
Satisfactory	68.13	75.30	65.93	-	-	100.00
Poor	16.48	11.31	14.29	-	40.00	-
Very poor	1.10	0.89	14.29	-	-	-
No response	-	-	-	100.00	-	-

were satisfied with the timings of opening of the shop in Rajasthan. Similarly, more than 85 per cent households in Assam, 90 per cent in Mizoram and more than 95 per cent in Chhattisgarh (including AAY and BPL) were satisfied with the openings of the FPS shops and the number of days food was being distributed. In Bihar and Uttar Pradesh, however, households faced problems in drawing their entitlement because of improper opening times and days of the FPS shop. Around 20 per cent AAY and BPL households in Uttar Pradesh and more than 40 per cent in Bihar rated the opening timings and number of days shop was opened as either poor or very poor. Many of the households had the perception that the cereals being supplied through the FPS were being underweighed. Around 40 per cent households in Rajasthan and Chhattisgarh and 80 per cent in Bihar were of the opinion that there was serious problem in food weighment at the FPS. In other states namely, Assam, Mizoram and Uttar Pradesh, the percentage of households who were satisfied with weighment at the FPS surpassed 80 to 90 per cent.

A majority of households in all the states opined that shop owners were indulging in diverting food to the open market or in other words, were involved in black marketing of PDS food. The frequency of such activities of the shop owners however, differed in different states. Around 70 per cent households in Assam felt that shop owners indulged in such activities frequently while 30 per cent households in Chhattisgarh thought they were doing such activities sometimes only. In other selected states around 30 to 40 per cent households gave an opinion that shopkeepers were diverting food frequently or quite frequently. Were the consumers satisfied with the quality of services offered at the FPS, around 60 per cent households in Bihar replied no. In other states, more than 70 per cent households were satisfied in Rajasthan, Chhattisgarh, Assam and Mizoram and above 65 per cent households indicated that they are satisfied in Uttar Pradesh. To the question, why the households were not satisfied, 64 per cent of the dissatisfied households in Bihar were of the opinion that there was mismanagement at the fair price shops while 32 per cent in Bihar and above 40 per cent in Mizoram replied that food was being distributed to the known people of the fair price shop owners. Among the dissatisfied households in the other states, majority of the households reasoned that there was mismanagement of food at the FPS in Mizoram, Rajasthan and Chhattisgarh. In Assam, majority of them quoted rude behaviour of the shop owner as the reason while in Uttar Pradesh households were equally divided on rude behaviour, mismanagement and preference given to the known people by the shop owners.

In almost all the states, majority of the households were not knowing whom to complain if the quality of grains offered from PDS was really bad. Around 60 to 80 per cent households in the selected states responded that they did not know how and where to complain. Even those who knew where to complain, around 80 to 90 per cent of them never complained on getting a bad quality during the last one year in all the states, except Assam and Bihar. In the latter two states, around 70 to 75 per cent dissatisfied households lodged a complaint at least once during the last year. But even after lodging the complaint, 90 per cent of them did not observe any improvement in the quality and they were not knowing how to get their problem redressed.

On the specific questions of quality and variety of wheat and rice distributed through PDS, a majority of households in Chhattisgarh, Rajasthan, Bihar and Uttar Pradesh responded that there was no difference between the PDS and local varieties. In the northeastern states namely, Assam and Mizoram, a majority of households stated that PDS rice was considerably different from the local varieties available. But among these two states also, a significant percentage of households in Mizoram did not prefer local variety over the PDS variety. Only in Assam and to some extent in Bihar, selected people preferred local variety over the PDS grains. Thus, majority of the selected households in different states did not observe the variety of grains offered at the PDS somewhat different from their preferred variety which they usually consumed. A related question was posed whether the households liked the quality of the grains supplied and if not, what was the lacuna in the grains supplied through PDS. Around 70 per cent households were satisfied with the quality of grain supplied in Rajasthan. Those who were not satisfied, a majority of them reasoned that there were impurities in the grain supplied. In Chhattisgarh, more than 85 per cent were satisfied with the quality of rice and wheat supplied through the FPS while presence of impurities in the grains was quoted as the biggest reason for the dissatisfaction by the others. In Bihar, around 90 per cent households in the case of rice and 70 per cent of wheat were not happy with the quality supplied through government shops. Presence of impurities, insect infested supply, broken grains and very bad taste of the grains were the common reasons for their outcries. Similar kind of complaints were found in Uttar Pradesh where around 35 per cent of households were dissatisfied with the quality of wheat and rice supplied through PDS. In Assam, impurities and broken rice were reasons quoted by 30 per cent of households who were not satisfied with the PDS quality of rice. Last and the least in Mizoram, around 35 to 40 per cent households were not happy with the quality of PDS rice. Presence of impurities, inferior quality, broken grains and the grains not being good in taste as well as in colour were the reasons cited for their dissatisfaction.

On the question of underweighment of the grains, we tried to find out what was the extent of such activities. Around 50 per cent of those households who answered that underweighment was happening were of the opinion that it was less than 5 per cent while the other 50 per cent opined that it was 5 to 10 per cent in Rajasthan. In Chhattisgarh, more than 60 per cent households pointed out that underweighment was less than 5 per cent only. In Bihar, more than 70 per cent families were of the opinion that grains were underweighed and majority of them said that its extent was between 10 to 20 per cent, that was the highest among all the selected states. Uttar Pradesh alongwith the two northeastern states faired better on this account, where less than 10 to 20 per cent households answered yes to the question of underweighment. Finally, to our question of how the households rate the performance of TPDS during the periods of distress, an overwhelming majority of them rated it satisfactory or highly satisfactory in Chhattisgarh, Assam and Mizoram. It was satisfactory in Rajasthan and Uttar Pradesh, while in Bihar around 40 per cent of them rated it poor or very poor.

6.4 Criterion Fixed for Identification of BPL and AAY Families

For the identification of BPL and AAY families, State Governments follow the guidelines issued by the Ministry of Rural Development, Government of India. For classifying people below poverty, State Governments have devised different methods for fixation of income norms to formulate some exclusion criteria. Most of the states have carried out some sort of income survey by involving District Rural Development Agencies (DRDA), rural development departments, panchayati raj institutions, *zilla panchayat* or muncipal committees etc. In addition to income criterion, some State Governments also have few additional exclusion criteria like families having assets as tractors, tillers, four or two wheelers, colour TV, telephone, etc.

Antyodaya Anna Yojana (AAY) was launched in December 2000 to ensure food security for all and to improve the PDS so as to serve the poorest of the poor in rural and urban areas. It was estimated at that time that there were around one crore families who were not able to get two square meals a day. The number of such families was worked out as 15.3 per cent of total families existing below poverty. The identification of these families was to be carried out by the State Governments/UT administrations, from amongst the number of BPL families within the state/UT. The number of Antyodaya families for each state/UT was calculated using the 15.3 per cent as the cut-out figure. These numbers were indicated to the State Governments/ UTs and were asked to distribute these numbers among various districts keeping in view the incidence of poverty and backwardness for which data should be available with each State Government from various sources. In the districts, the number of Antyodaya families was to be distributed among various *panchayats* and the municipal areas. The District Collectors would then start the process of identification after giving it wide publicity so that people should become aware of the process and procedure adopted for identification of beneficiaries under the scheme. The District Collectors were asked to use the services of district and block level officers, as well as the panchayati raj institutions for proper identification of beneficiaries. Once the tentative list for a *panchayat* was ready, in the second phase, a meeting of the *gram sabha* should be held. This meeting should be attended by the officer, who has been assigned the particular *panchayat*. The tentative list should be read out in the meeting of the *gram sabha* and the *gram sabha* should finalise the list of beneficiaries and arrange the names in the order of priority. In the case of urban areas, the State Governments were asked to undertake a similar exercise by involving the urban local bodies. After the identification of AAY families, distinctive ration cards would be issued by the designated authority. The ration card should contain the necessary details about the Antyodaya family, scale of ration, etc. Table 6.25 displays the identification criterion followed by the State Governments in the six selected states.

The income norms fixed by the State Governments in our selected states and the estimates obtained from the Planning Commission based on the 61st Round of National Sample Survey are given in Table 6.26. It is apparent from the income displayed by the table that on an average, the amount fixed by the State Governments as an exclusion criterion was less than that of the Planning Commission (rural as well as urban) in all the six states without any exception. However, it is important to mention that in fixing up the criterion for the BPL by the State Governments, in addition to the above cut-off income, various states have also laid down other indicators of well-being, like owning some specified acres of irrigated/unirrigated land, owning a tractor, four/two wheelers, telephone or having some movable or immovable property. Therefore, it is not justified comparing official cut-off income given by the states with the Planning Commission. However, the income limit set by the Planning Commission was based on the actual expenditure incurred by a household, which was worked out using the National Sample Survey Data (61st Round). Planning Commission have used this income to work out the percentage of poor existing in different states during the period 2004-05.[2] Therefore, for the sake of comparison, henceforth, we will use the Planning Commission income for rural areas as the official estimate of cut-off for the poverty line.[3]

Table 6.25 Criterion Adopted by the State Governments for BPL and AAY Cardholders

States	Criteria for BPL	Criteria for AAY
Mizoram	BPL Census 2002 based on a 'Score Based Ranking' of each household with 13 scorable indicators indicating their quality of life based on both economic and social indicators. Those families whose income level is below poverty line as per Indian Government norms. **Authority** The final authority rests with Rural Development Department and elected members of the village council in rural areas and local administrative department in the urban areas.	Those families whose income level is nil or negligible (Indian Government norms); Most of the cases widow, deprived, older aged, divorcee, separated, etc., should be preferred for the AAY category. Families from the bottom list of BPL should be chosen for issuing an AAY card.
Assam	As per survey by Department of Rural Development. Families whose income is not exceeding Rs. 15000 per annum.	Same as in the case of Mizoram.
Rajasthan	Urban BPL Survey 2003. Both economic and non-economic indicators are taken into account. Economic indicators: Annual income should not exceed Rs. 5591. Non-economic indicators: Should not own land more than one hectare of irrigated or two hectares of unirrigated. In the case of owned house, area should not exceed 400 square feet and in the case rented house, rent should not exceed Rs. 300-500. In addition, a household having telephone, mobile, three or four wheeler or tractor (or anyone of these) cannot be included in the BPL list.	Urban BPL Survey 1998. Under this survey, two categories were apportioned for the selection of AAY. First category: (i) Those families whose per capita income is almost nil. (ii) There is no member in the family in the working age (15-59 years). (iii) Due to handicap or old age the family is really in distress. Out of the above three criteria, those families should be preferred who are suffering by more than one of the above three criteria and their family size should also be large. Second category: All of BPL families who come under the first category. In the rest of the BPL families, those families who do not own any land and there one earning member and no other source of income. Out of is only the above, those families should be preferred who are living in rented houses. In rest of the cases, the AAY families should be chosen from the lowest order.
Uttar Pradesh	With five members as average family size, the income limit fixed for the BPL cut out for rural areas is Rs. 19884 and for urban areas, the limit set is Rs. 25546 per annum. The breakup of 106 lakh was achieved at the family income of Rs. 9000 only.	The requisite numbers should be chosen from the BPL list as those families who are the poorest in the list. The concerned authorities are desired to choose these families from the bottom of the BPL list.
Chhattisgarh	Those families whose annual household income falls below Rs. 11000 fall in the category of BPL. The verification is done by the committee constituted by the District Collector.	Local bodies in urban areas and *gram panchayat* in rural areas decide about the AAY families based on the bottom income groups in the BPL list. Generally, preference is given to people belonging to the class of cobblers, daily wagers, sweepers, ironsmith, landless labourers, potters, coolies, rikshaw pullers, petty traders, etc. The people who collect garbage, primitive tribes, etc., are given preference.
Bihar	Annual income should be less than Rs. 20000 (with the new circular while the previous circular of 1997 being Rs. 11500). Besides, the families should not own any vehicle etc.	As per Indian Government Order.

Comparing our observed income for BPL with that of the Planning Commission estimates, it is seen from Figure 6.1 that except Assam and Mizoram, in all other states, our average BPL income was lower than the cut-off estimates of the Planning Commission. However, our survey income is the average income of all the selected BPL households in each state. The actual distribution of BPL income will lie just above or below this income. On the other hand, the Planning Commission income

2. These income estimates are updated for the next year by the Planning Commission using the price index as a deflator. However, the current estimates were worked out by the Planning Commission for the year 2004-05, which almost coincides with the period of our survey data. Therefore, no adjustment is made in making comparison of our estimates with the Planning Commission figures.

3. As 80 per cent of our sample is drawn from the rural areas in each state, we will use Planning Commission poverty line as defined for the rural areas only.

Table 6.26 Divergence between State Government and Planning Commission Norms for BPL Cut-off (Rs. Per Household Per Annum)

State	Cut-off Income for BPL as per the State Government Norms	Cut-off as per Planning Commission's Norms		Average Income as Observed by our Survey Data	
		Rural	Urban	BPL	AAY
Rajasthan	5591[$]	27188	40620	25686	20370
Chhattisgarh	11000	19428	33744	15198	11903
Bihar	20000	25241	30984	21828	17845
Uttar Pradesh	9000	28323	37413	19525	16131
Assam	15000	25126	24555	29505	23618
Mizoram	15000[#]	25685	25102	26706	11459

Note: 1. The state income cut-off is not the only criterion for deciding the below poverty population. In many of the states in addition to the above given cut-off income, there were additional criterion related, e.g., family assets etc., for working the population below poverty line.

2. The Planning Commission (2004) estimates are worked out using NSS 61st Round data for expenditure class-wise distribution of persons (based on URP-consumption, that is, consumption data collected from 30-day recall period for all items).

3. The Planning Commission poverty line is given in terms of per capita monthly income. The household income estimates are calculated using the household size data as given in 'Census of India 2001, Analytical Report on Housing Amenities', Office of the Registrar General & Census Commissioner, New Delhi, India.

$ In addition to this economic indicator, there is also non-economic indicator according to which, a family should not own land more than one hectare of irrigated or two hectares of unirrigated land.

The criterion fixed by the Mizoram government is, as per Indian Government norms. For quantification, we have assumed the cut-off income for Mizoram equivalent to Assam.

displayed is the cut-off income that provides the upper limit for the poverty line. Those households who are just below or equal to this income would fall in the BPL list. In Assam and Mizoram, even our estimated average income was above the official cut-off income for poverty. To know how many households were truly above or below poverty compared to the official estimates, we would have to look at the actual distribution of income among our selected households, the analysis that is done in the next section. However, from this comparison it becomes clear that the identification process followed by the states had certain flaws in their mechanism.

6.5 Identification Problems—Errors of Targeting

The main reason for shifting from universal to targeted subsidies is to achieve the objective of resource transfer to the poor. It is well established in the targeting literature that design of interventions should be such that it leads to minimum leakage to the non-poor in order to provide maximum benefit to the poor households (Mateus, 1983; Grosh, 1992). According to Cornia and Stewart (1993), minimum leakage may not be practically possible because of administrative and efficiency costs, political factors and other general equilibrium effects like effects of alternative food interventions on food prices.[4] They particularly emphasised two errors of targeting, namely errors of omission of the poor from the scheme (exclusion error) and errors of inclusion of the non-poor (inclusion error). In statistical analysis, these two types of errors correspond to Type I and Type II errors.

In terms of efficiency of the targeting mechanism, the type I mistake refers to a situation where scheme fails to reach the target population. Cornia and Stewart describe this as an F-mistake indicating a failure in the prime objective of the intervention. The type II mistake refers to a situation where intervention reaches to the non-target population. This they called as E-mistake indicating excessive coverage. In designing targeted intervention, attention has tended to be focused on mistakes brought about by excessive coverage, with much less attention on mistakes resulting from failures to reach the target group. Narrowly targeted interventions often show apparently favourable cost-benefit ratios (Mateus, 1983; Pinstrup, 1991). According to Cornia and Stewart, in a pursuit to low E-mistakes tends to raise F-mistake as some of the target groups tend to be eliminated from the scheme along with the non-target population because of lack of information about the scheme among the

4. General food subsidies are more likely to affect food prices across the board than narrowly targeted schemes.

target group; costs of acquiring entitlements to targeted scheme; qualifications for entitlement which while excluding the non-poor, also almost invariably excludes some of the target group. The measurement of the two errors of targeting is important to understand whether and to what extent the benefits of TPDS are reaching the target group.

Figure 6.1 Comparison of Official Cut-off Income for BPL with Average BPL Income from Our Survey

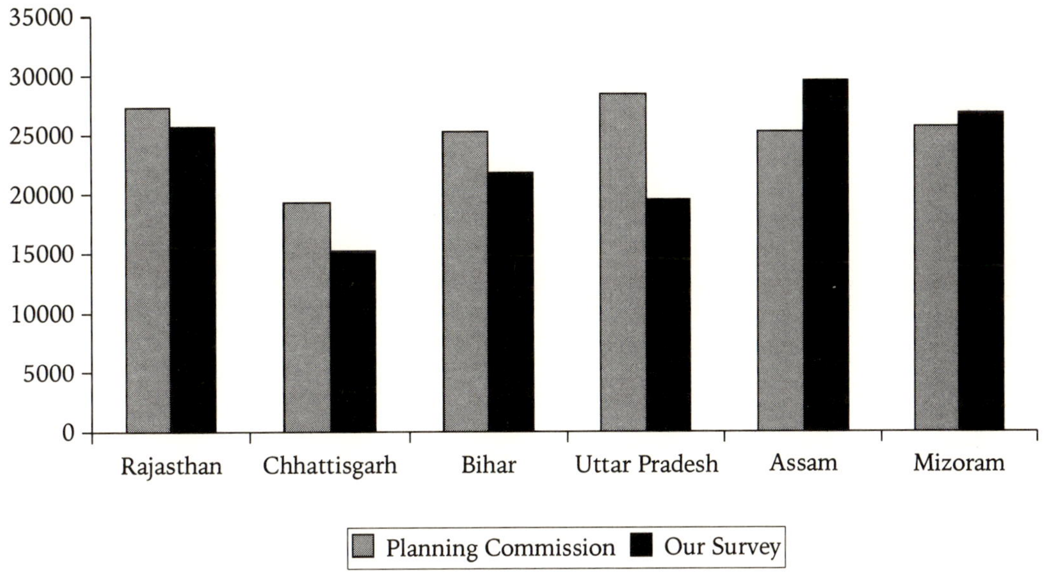

Measuring E (Inclusion) and F (Exclusion)-Mistakes

Let P belong to poor people in a given population M, who are the target group in the subsidy intervention scheme. Let us call the non-poor as N. Possible sets of combinations are given in the box below. Thus, the total population would be defined as:

$$P + N = M^c + M^{nc} = P^c + P^{nc} + N^c + N^{nc} = M$$

The ideal case where E and F mistakes are nil is defined as: $P^c + N^{nc} = M$

And in the case of total mistargeting when no member from the poor group is covered while all the non-poor are covered would be as: $N^c + P^{nc} = M$

Table 6.27 Identification Matrix: E and F-Mistakes

	Poor	Non-Poor	Total
All covered by subsidy scheme	P^c	N^c(E-Mistake, Inclusion error)	M^c
All non-covered by subsidy scheme	P^{nc}(F-mistake, Exclusion error)	N^{nc}	M^{nc}
Total	P	N	M

However, in the actual world, the above two situations would be rather rare. The actual situation lies in between these two extremes. F-mistake as defined above consists of exclusion of poor and is represented by P^{nc}. Dividing these numbers by the target population (P^{nc}/P) gives us the extent of F-mistake, which is a good measure of how far a scheme is failing in its primary intention to reach the target group. E-mistake, on the other hand, consists of non-poor covered and is represented by N^c. Dividing these numbers by the non-target population (N^c/N) gives us the extent of E-mistake, which also indicates the extra cost of the excess coverage.

Table 6.28 presents the number of ration cards issued and compares it with the projected number of households for each state and all India using data from various secondary sources. It is clearly evident from the data, that there are wider inter-state differences in the total number of card holdings and the total existing number of households. In many states, the total number of cards issued exceeded the number of total existing families indicating incidences of excess cards issued. The number of such excess cards was very high, more than one crore in Uttar Pradesh, 24 lakh in Rajasthan, more than 10 lakh in Madhya Pradesh and Haryana. At all India, the total number of excess cards issued was more than 2 crore. On the other hand, in a few states, the number of cards issued were less than the existing number of families and therefore, some families

Table 6.28 Number of Excess Cards Issued and the Number of Unidentified Households (Status as on 29.09.2006)

State/UT	AAY Cards Issued[1] (Lakhs)	BPL Cards Issued[1] (Lakhs)	APL Cards Issued[1] (Lakhs)	Total Cards Issued (Lakhs)	Projected No. of HH in 2006[2] (Lakhs)	Excess Cards Issed (Lakhs)	Unindentified HH(Lakhs)
Andhra Pradesh	15.58	126.24	34.24	176.06	180.37	-	4.31
Arunachal Pradesh	0.38	0.61	2.68	3.67	2.40	1.27	-
Assam	7.00	12.02	39.8	58.82	53.82	5.00	-
Bihar	15.00	49.99	15.53	80.52	158.58	-	78.06
Chhattisgarh	7.19	15.45	26.36	49.00	45.12	3.88	-
Delhi	0.56	3.82	21.96	26.34	30.97	-	4.63
Goa	0.15	0.13	3.16	3.44	2.99	0.45	-
Gujarat	8.10	26.92	83.32	118.34	106.81	11.53	-
Haryana	2.92	5.28	42.02	50.22	40.00	10.22	-
Himachal Pradesh	1.97	0.92	10.77	13.66	13.45	0.21	-
J&K	2.56	4.8	10.94	18.30	17.66	0.64	-
Jharkhand	7.27	16.68	5.15	29.10	54.01	-	24.91
Karnataka	12.00	58.22	43.15	113.37	110.92	2.45	-
Kerala	5.96	14.91	47.52	68.39	68.99	-	0.60
Madhya Pradesh	15.64	36.4	82.27	134.31	121.73	12.58	-
Maharashtra	19.84	53.15	148.34	221.33	211.19	10.14	-
Manipur	0.50	1.16	2.41	4.07	4.32	-	0.25
Meghalaya	0.70	1.13	2.66	4.49	4.80	-	0.31
Mizoram	0.26	0.42	1.8	2.48	1.83	0.65	-
Nagaland	0.47	0.77	1.83	3.07	4.26	-	1.19
Orissa	12.64	37.58	36.19	86.41	84.85	1.56	-
Punjab	1.39	4.79	49.37	55.55	46.74	8.81	-
Rajasthan	9.27	15.17	105.8	130.24	105.86	24.38	-
Sikkim	0.17	0.26	0.65	1.08	1.21	-	0.13
Tamil Nadu	18.65	149.65	0	168.30	149.82	18.48	-
Tripura	0.68	2.27	4.35	7.30	7.13	0.17	-
Uttar Pradesh	40.95	65.49	294.41	400.85	288.99	111.85	-
Uttaranchal	1.51	3.47	17.66	22.64	17.40	5.24	-
West Bengal	14.80	37.62	111.3	163.72	170.55	-	6.83
A&N Islands	0.04	0.12	0.75	0.91	0.82	0.09	-
Chandigarh	0.02	0.07	2.22	2.31	2.39	-	0.08
D&N Haveli	0.04	0.12	0.29	0.45	0.56	-	0.11
Daman & Diu	0.01	0.04	0.25	0.30	0.42	-	0.12
Lakshadweep	0.00	0.01	0.13	0.14	0.10	0.05	-
Pondicherry	0.32	0.87	1.82	3.01	2.29	0.72	-
All India	224.53	746.55	1251.10	2222.18	2116.18	230.36	121.54

Source: 1. Govt. of India, Ministry of Consumer Affairs, Food and Public Distribution, Dept. of Food & Public Distribution, New Delhi.

2. Calculated using population figures of 1991 and 2001 and household size of 2001 as given in 'Census of India 2001, Analytical Report on Housing Amenities', Office of the Registrar General & Census Commissioner, New Delhi, India.

were unindentified. It is not clear from the available data that these families belonged to which particular category. The number of such families who were not provided with any card were maximum in Bihar, followed by Jharkhand and West Bengal. The total number of such families at the all India, aggregated at 1.2 crore.

Table 6.29 Inclusion and Exclusion Errors in Identification (Status as on 29.09.2006)

State/UT	Projected No. of HH in 2006(Lakh)	Per cent Population Below Poverty Line[1]	Projected BPL HH in 2006 (Lakh)	BPL Cards Issued (Including AAY)(Lakh)	Projected APL HH in 2006	F-mistake (Exclusion Error)	E-mistake (Inclusion Error)
Andhra Pradesh	180.37	15.8	28.50	141.82	151.87	-	74.61
Arunachal Pradesh	2.40	17.6	0.42	0.99	1.98	-	28.71
Assam	53.82	19.7	10.60	19.02	43.22	-	19.48
Bihar	158.58	41.4	65.65	64.99	92.93	1.01	-
Chhattisgarh	45.12	40.9	18.45	22.64	26.67	-	15.69
Delhi	30.97	14.7	4.55	4.38	26.42	3.78	-
Goa	2.99	13.8	0.41	0.28	2.58	32.25	-
Gujarat	106.81	16.8	17.94	35.02	88.87	-	19.22
Haryana	40.00	14	5.60	8.20	34.40	-	7.56
Himachal Pradesh	13.45	10	1.35	2.89	12.11	-	12.76
J&K	17.66	5.4	0.95	7.36	16.70	-	38.35
Jharkhand	54.01	40.3	21.77	23.95	32.24	-	6.77
Karnataka	110.92	25	27.73	70.22	83.19	-	51.08
Kerala	68.99	15	10.35	20.87	58.64	-	17.94
Madhya Pradesh	121.73	38.3	46.62	52.04	75.11	-	7.21
Maharashtra	211.19	30.7	64.83	72.99	146.35	-	5.57
Manipur	4.32	17.3	0.75	1.66	3.57	-	25.52
Meghalaya	4.80	18.5	0.89	1.83	3.91	-	24.07
Mizoram	1.83	12.6	0.23	0.68	1.60	-	28.22
Nagaland	4.26	19	0.81	1.24	3.45	-	12.50
Orissa	84.85	46.4	39.37	50.22	45.48	-	23.85
Punjab	46.74	8.4	3.93	6.18	42.81	-	5.26
Rajasthan	105.86	22.1	23.40	24.44	82.47	-	1.27
Sikkim	1.21	20.1	0.24	0.43	0.97	-	19.24
Tamil Nadu	149.82	22.5	33.71	168.30	116.11	-	115.92
Tripura	7.13	18.9	1.35	2.95	5.78	-	27.71
Uttar Pradesh	288.99	32.8	94.79	106.44	194.20	-	6.00
Uttaranchal	17.40	39.6	6.89	4.98	10.51	27.73	-
West Bengal	170.55	24.7	42.13	52.42	128.43	-	8.01
A&N Islands	0.82	22.6	0.19	0.16	0.64	13.84	-
Chandigarh	2.39	7.1	0.17	0.09	2.22	47.03	-
D&N Haveli	0.56	33.2	0.18	0.16	0.37	13.25	-
Daman & Diu	0.42	10.5	0.04	0.05	0.38	-	1.47
Lakshadweep	0.10	16	0.02	0.01	0.08	10.24	-
Pondicherry	2.29	22.4	0.51	1.19	1.78	-	38.08
All India	2116.18	27.5	581.95	971.08	1534.23	-	25.36

Source: 1. Planning Commission, Govt. of India, 2004. The percentage below poverty is calculated by the Planning Commission using Uniform Recall Period consumption in which the consumer expenditure data for all the items are collected from 30-day recall period.

Using the E and F criterion devised by Cornia and Stewart (as discussed above), we calculated identification errors for all the states and for all India. The results in Table 6.29 clearly indicate that at the aggregate level, excessive targeting or inclusion error (E) was much higher than the exclusion error or failure of targeting the poor (F) error. The exclusion error was highest in Goa and Uttaranchal where the TPDS failed in targeting up to 30 per cent. Among our selected states, exclusion mistake was observed only in Bihar while the problem was not as severe in that state also. The inclusion of non-poor in the subsidised food was much more a serious problem and the incidence was found occurring in almost all the states. Inclusion error or excessive coverage was more than 100 per cent in Tamil Nadu, 75 per cent in Andhara Pradesh and 51 per cent in Karnataka. It is to be mentioned here that in Tamil Nadu, all the families were issued BPL (or AAY) card as no categorisation was done on the basis of BPL and APL. Among our selected states, inclusion (E) mistake was found up to 28 per cent in Mizoram, 19 per cent in Assam, 16 per cent in Chhattisgarh and 6 per cent in Uttar Pradesh. At the all India level, inclusion mistake was up to 25 per cent as number of BPL cards issued were 9.7 crore in comparison to only 5.8 crore existing families.

6.6 Authenticity of Identification and Diversion of PDS Food

In this section, we look into the distribution of observed income and expenditure per capita of our selected households and try to authenticate their identification in terms of holding AAY, BPL and APL cards. We compare the per capita income and expenditure of the selected AAY, BPL and APL households with the Planning Commission's cut-off income to validate whether the card they hold is true or false. In other words, if we re-designate the households as below or above poverty following the Planning Commission cut-off, then how many households would stand faulty in their present category. Table 6.30 provides such estimates for all the six selected states. However, it was not possible to check AAY identification, i.e., how many truely lied in the class of AAY and how many of them should have been in the BPL class, as there was no criterion fixed for that class neither by the Planning Commission nor by Central or any State Government. The only criterion for selecting AAY household was that they should come from the lowest income group among the BPL household list.

The results of Table 6.30 should be read in the following way. Among the AAY and BPL categories as given in the table, those households that are in the below percentage, are confirmed by the Planning Commission cut-off and these households are rightly designated as below poverty households. Similarly, among the APL families, those who appear in the above percentage are truly designated as above poverty households. However, those households among the AAY and BPL categories, who fall in the above percentage, are the controversial cases as following the Planning Commission criterion, they should have been designated as APL households. In technical terms, these households come under the inclusion error (E-mistake), as they are wrongly included in the BPL (or AAY) list whereas they should have been excluded from this list. The inclusion error highlights the extra cost that TPDS system is bearing because of wrong identification. On the other extreme, those APL households who appear in the below percentage are wrongly designated as APL households, whereas they should have been issued either a BPL or AAY card (cannot say definitely, to which category they belong to) as they are the cases of below poverty. In technical terms, this is the case of exclusion error (F-mistake), whereby the concerned authorities have failed in meeting the basic objective of striking the target group. The consequences of exclusion error are much more grave than the inclusion error. Whereas the occurrence of inclusion mistake raises the cost of the subsidy scheme, occurrence of exclusion mistake indicates failure in fulfilling the basic objective of the subsidy scheme, i.e., to target the poor in the TPDS system.

Looking at the extent of incidence of inclusion and exclusion errors among our selected households, it is clearly evident from the data that the percentage of inclusion error was much higher than the exclusion error as was also seen in the case of secondary data. It is to be clarified that to calculate these two types of errors (E- and F-mistakes), we have used both income as well as expenditure as observed by our selected households.[5] The average income and expenditure criterion indicate that inclusion error was highest around 75 per cent in Mizoram, 50 to 60 per cent in Assam, around 50 per cent in Rajasthan and Bihar, around 35 per cent in Chhattisgarh and 20 to 30 per cent in Uttar Pradesh. The more serious problem was the wrong identification of AAY households who should have been issued an APL card instead. Their proportion was around 70 per cent in the northeastern states (according to either income or expenditure criterion) and 30-35 per cent in the rest of the four selected states. Measuring the extent of exclusion error (F-mistake), the data indicate that the phenomenon of poor households being not issued a below poverty card was minimum in the northeastern states, less than 15 per cent, followed by Uttar Pradesh, Bihar, Chhattisgarh and Rajasthan.

5. In theory, income and expenditure should be equal if households are not saving (or dissaving).

Table 6.30 **The Percentage of Selected Households Below and Above the Cut-off Income of Poverty Line as Defined by the Planning Commission**

	Income Criterion[1]			Expenditure Criterion[1]		
	AAY	BPL	APL	AAY	BPL	APL
			Rajasthan			
% Below	62.78	50.33	**28.97***	50.56	45.87	**24.77***
% Above	**37.22****	**49.67****	71.03	**49.44****	**54.13****	75.23
			Chhattisgarh			
% Below	71.15	61.77	**26.94***	65.38	56.76	**30.05***
% Above	**28.85****	**38.23****	73.06	**34.62****	**43.24****	69.95
			Bihar			
% Below	64.43	60.22	**22.22***	40.72	35.30	**7.78***
% Above	**35.57****	**39.78****	77.78	**59.28****	**64.70****	92.22
			UP			
% Below	75.61	56.62	**19.19***	84.88	68.17	**28.79***
% Above	**24.39****	**43.38****	80.81	**15.12****	**31.83****	71.21
			Assam			
% Below	27.89	15.76	**4.48***	65.79	45.32	**14.93***
% Above	**72.11****	**84.24****	95.52	**34.21****	**54.68****	85.07
			Mizoram			
% Below	73.47	27.63	**3.57***	23.49	24.08	**18.36***
% Above	**26.53****	**72.37****	96.43	**76.51****	**75.92****	81.64

Note: 1. The income and expenditure per capita as observed by our selected households in our survey data.
2. The bold figures indicate that these households are issued a wrong card. The figures shown with ** are the cases of E – mistake (inclusion error) and that of * are the cases of F- mistake (exclusion error).

In the incidence of mistargeting, it is implicit that the food is being diverted to the non-poor due to identification problems. Even though food is being distributed and a very high percentage of households were found getting food in majority of states, it was actually being diverted to non-target population as has been indicated by showing the extent of occurrence of inclusion and exclusion errors among our selected sample. However, in addition to such diversions, there was some proportion of food that was not being actually distributed among any of the households but it was shown in the state records as uplifted. Therefore, we can presume that food grains not distributed but withdrawn from the state accounts are being diverted to the black market or in the open market or may be distributed among the non-poor people at a higher price.

In this section, we try to measure the extent of diversion of wheat and rice in our selected states. For arriving at the state level figures, we assume here that the percentage of households (six months average) obtaining amount of wheat and rice from the PDS in our sample on an average prevails over the whole state. Similarly, we assume that the quantity of wheat and rice received by the sample households for the six months sample period on an average also as the quantity for the whole state. With these assumptions, we calculate the total grains actually distributed through the PDS in our selected states using the total number of cards issued during 2006, as given by the Ministry of Food. We compare the distributed wheat and rice in our selected states with the total off-take as obtained from the secondary sources. The amount of diversion of rice and wheat in our six selected states is presented in Table 6.31.

Table 6.31 Diversion of Food (Rice and Wheat) in the Selected States

	Rajasthan	Chhattisgarh	Bihar	Uttar Pradesh	Assam	Mizoram
	AAY					
Rice						
Total cards issued in the state (lakh)	9.27	7.19	15.00	40.95	7.00	0.26
Percentage of beneficiaries receiving grain from FPS	21.39	94.55	49.14	91.63	61.93	88.95
Monthly amount received by the beneficiaries (kgs)	11.33	34.19	18.74	22.60	34.29	22.92
Total distributed grains per annum in the state (tonnes)	26955	278885	165765	1017393	178389	6385
Total off-take of grains by the state in 2005-06 (tonnes)	1450	229189	164070	884901	181090	10010
Percentage of diversion to off-take	0.00	0.00	0.00	0.00	1.49	36.21
Wheat						
Total cards issued in the state (lakh)	9.27	7.19	15.00	40.95	7.00	0.26
Percentage of beneficiaries receiving grain from FPS	88.52	6.33	53.26	91.95	0.00	0.00
Monthly amount received by the beneficiaries (kgs)	31.18	4.71	15.72	12.14	0.00	0.00
Total distributed grains per annum in the state (tonnes)	307002	2571	150727	548623	0	0
Total off-take of grains by the state in 2005-06 (tonnes)	299120	0	256990	553388	0	0
Percentage of diversion to off-take	0.00	0.00	41.35	0.86	0.00	0.00
	BPL					
Rice						
Total cards issued in the state (lakh)	15.17	15.45	49.99	65.49	12.02	0.42
Percentage of beneficiaries receiving grain from FPS	26.24	95.46	25.59	80.99	66.72	85.39
Monthly amount received by the beneficiaries (kgs)	10.49	25.40	22.68	22.11	34.05	25.65
Total distributed grains per annum in the state (tonnes)	50101	449595	348061	1407530	327686	11041
Total off-take of grains by the state in 2005-06 (tonnes)	19240	454003	145460	1535191	595480	17650
Percentage of diversion to off-take	0.00	0.97	0.00	8.32	44.97	37.44
Wheat						
Total cards issued in the state (lakh)	15.17	15.45	49.99	65.49	12.02	0.42
Percentage of beneficiaries receiving grain from FPS	87.95	54.90	33.55	84.95	0.00	0.00
Monthly amount received by the beneficiaries (kgs)	30.02	4.69	13.90	12.18	0.00	0.00
Total distributed grains per annum in the state (tonnes)	480726	47759	279776	813217	0	0
Total off-take of grains by the state in 2005-06 (tonnes)	450330	82800	526550	1025072	0	0
Percentage of diversion to off-take	0.00	42.32	46.87	20.67	0.00	0.00
	APL					
Rice						
Total cards issued in the state (lakh)	105.8	26.36	15.53	294.41	39.8	1.8
Percentage of beneficiaries receiving grain from FPS	6.54	12.44	5.37	3.87	2.90	15.77
Monthly amount received by the beneficiaries (kgs)	15.10	30.15	21.96	26.46	19.83	26.79
Total distributed grains per annum in the state (tonnes)	125378	118579	21975	361916	27484	9129
Total off-take of grains by the state in 2005-06 (tonnes)	0	2570	1320	2236	164340	48340
Percentage of diversion to off-take	0.00	0.00	0.00	0.00	83.28	81.12
Wheat						
Total cards issued in the state (lakh)	105.8	26.36	15.53	294.41	39.8	1.8
Percentage of beneficiaries receiving grain from FPS	9.97	4.40	7.04	6.23	0.00	0.00
Monthly amount received by the beneficiaries (kgs)	19.56	7.73	20.38	14.28	0.00	0.00
Total distributed grains per annum in the state (tonnes)	247592	10763	26729	314335	0	0
Total off-take of grains by the state in 2005-06 (tonnes)	204170	49680	24230	37930	280240	7550
Percentage of diversion to off-take	0.00	78.34	0.00	0.00	100.00	100.00

It is evident from the data that in the case of AAY cardholders, PDS wheat and rice were being distributed quite satisfactorily, except in two states, namely Bihar and Mizoram. In Bihar, only 50 per cent of the cardholders obtained their entitlements while in Mizoram, the quantity of rice distributed was about half of the stipulated quantity. The magnitude of diversion was estimated up to 41 per cent for wheat in Bihar and 36 per cent for rice in Mizoram. In the case of BPL, all states except Rajasthan indicated diversion of food. The diversion was highest in Assam and Mizoram in the case of rice and Bihar and Chhattisgarh in wheat. In all these four cases, diversion was up to 40 per cent of total off-take. In Uttar Pradesh, diversion was 20 per cent in wheat and slightly less than 10 per cent in rice for the BPL households. Among above poverty households, the whole amount of wheat uplifted was diverted in the two northeastern states of Assam and Mizoram. Even in the case of rice, more than 80 per cent uplifted amount was not distributed among the beneficiaries in these two states. In the other four states, diversion of food for APL households was found only in Chhattisgarh for wheat that was as high as 78 per cent. Rajasthan was the only state where it was observed that the whole amount of uplifted food was distributed among the beneficiaries in all the three cases of AAY, BPL and APL. The figures displayed in Table 6.31 indicate that the total amount of grains distributed in that state exceeded the total off-take for the study period. Last and the least, Annexure Table A-6.1 presents off-take as a percentage of allocation in the selected states. It is evident from the table that off-take percentage was very high in the category of AAY households, while in some cases, BPL off-take was comparatively less. The figures for Bihar off-take reconfirms our assertion that grains were not being distributed in that state.

Thus, diversion of food for the AAY category was not very high except the case of wheat in Bihar and rice in Mizoram. Similarly in the case of BPL, diversion of rice was found very high in the two northeastern states, while wheat diversion was found high in the case of Bihar and Chhattisgarh. The distribution of grains was found more satisfactory in the case of Rajasthan and Uttar Pradesh. Nonetheless, gross violations were observed in the identification of target groups and these were very high in all the states across the board as indicated by the exclusion and inclusion errors.

Table A-6.1 Percentage of Off-take of Rice and Wheat under TPDS

		2003-04			2004-005			2005-06		
		BPL	APL	AAY	BPL	APL	AAY	BPL	APL	AAY
Assam	Rice	92.1	26.4	95.0	95.7	25.2	92.7	95.2	26.6	103.4
	Wheat	-	83.9	-	-	97.9	-	-	83.2	-
Bihar	Rice	6.6	0.1	89.1	13.3	0.1	88.4	14.4	0.1	86.8
	Wheat	42.7	0.5	91.8	52.0	0.7	92.7	45.5	2.0	90.6
Chhattisgarh	Rice	91.5	0.2	94.0	99.0	0.3	89.8	101.9	0.4	89.9
	Wheat	84.2	5.1	116.9	77.2	9.6	-	95.1	14.2	-
Mizoram	Rice	102.3	94.3	90.2	101.9	71.2	95.4	96.6	80.7	96.2
	Wheat	-	90.8	-	-	97.2	-	-	62.3	-
Rajasthan	Rice	3.1	0.0	17.2	0.0	0.0	11.9	25.5	0.0	37.9
	Wheat	80.4	4.1	94.5	93.0	11.2	92.7	87.0	9.3	89.0
UP	Rice	51.0	0.0	108.5	93.2	0.0	117.6	87.1	0.1	94.3
	Wheat	61.8	0.2	91.2	78.2	0.2	83.4	86.7	1.1	92.1
All India	Rice	71.3	10.2	95.1	84.1	17.6	93.6	81.4	20.6	94.5
	Wheat	68.3	8.9	87.0	79.4	13.1	86.0	81.7	16.3	88.5

7 Functioning of the Fair Price Shops

7.1 Introduction

This chapter is devoted to the issues related to functioning of fair price shops, their monitoring, transparency and financial viability. The facts presented here are based on a separate questionnaire designed specially for the FPS and carried out twice during the longitudinal field survey. In total, 150 fair shops, one each for our selected village was surveyed. The selected fair price shop was the one that was catering to our selected households in each village. Discussion of this chapter is divided into 10 sections. The next section presents the profile of the fair price shops, their management and general functioning. Section 3 presents the issue that deal with entitlement of households from the PDS. The fourth section is devoted to the issues related to lifting of quota by the FPS. Section 5 discusses of transparency. Next section presents the monitoring system of the FPS followed by a section on the stocking pattern at the FPS. Section 8 presents the pattern of distribution of grains among the consumers by the FPS, followed by a section that puts forth the issues related to mode of transportation of grains. The chapter is concluded by a section that compares prices of grains as revealed by the FPS owners with the price paid by the consumers.

7.2 Profile of Fair Price Shops

The fair price shop owners selected for the field survey were mostly literate. A majority of them in all the states were educated up to secondary or higher secondary level. The shop they were running to sell PDS grains was exclusively for that purpose in most of the cases, except Assam and Mizoram where shop owners were also doing business for retailing with the same outlet. The ownership status was individual ownership in Mizoram, Bihar, Rajasthan and Assam among overwhelming majority of shops while in Chhattisgarh, the ownership status was mixed. The ownership status rested with the *gram panchayat* in 20 per cent cases, 36 per cent were being run under cooperative ownership and 20 per cent rested with the government. In Uttar Pradesh also, around 40 per cent shops were owned by the *gram panchayats*. The shops in all the cases were located in a periphery of around 5 to 20 kilometres from the godown from where the grains were being lifted. To the question of how many days the shop owners were keeping the shop opened for distribution of grains among the households, a majority of them replied more than 15 days, and the shop was opened the whole day in majority of the cases for the convenience of the beneficiaries.

7.3 Entitlement according to FPS

All shop owners indicated 35 kgs of entitlement of grains for the AAY category. It was only rice in the case of Mizoram, Chhattisgarh and Assam and wheat in the case of Rajasthan. In Bihar, it was a combination of wheat (14 kgs) and rice (21 kgs) and in Uttar Pradesh, it was a combination of wheat and rice in 10 and 25 kgs, respectively. In the BPL category, entitlement according to shop owners was 35 kgs of rice in Assam and Mizoram, 20 kgs of wheat and 15 kgs of rice in Rajasthan and 10 kgs of wheat and 25 kgs of rice in Uttar Pradesh. The shop owners in Chhattisgarh and Bihar quoted less than 35 kgs of grains as entitlement for the BPL. It was 5 and 25 kgs of rice and wheat, respectively in Chhattisgarh and 12 and 10 kgs of wheat and rice in Bihar. In the case of APL, no entitlement was quoted by the FPS except in Mizoram, where entitlement was 2 kgs of rice per family member. Thus, only in Mizoram in the case of APL, entitlement was not fixed per family; rather it was based on the number of family members as were entered in the ration card issued for the purpose of public distribution.

Table 7.1 **Profile of Fair Price Shop (%)**

	Mizoram	Bihar	Uttar Pradesh	Chhattisgarh	Rajasthan	Assam
Educational qualifications of the shop owner						
Literate without formal schooling	-	4.00	-	-	-	-
Upto primary	16.00	20.00	28.00	-	12.00	40.00
Upto secondary	76.00	64.00	24.00	8.00	40.00	28.00
Upto higher secondary	8.00	12.00	20.00	40.00	32.00	8.00
Above higher secondary	-	-	24.00	28.00	16.00	24.00
Illiterate	-	-	4.00	24.00	-	-
Type of shop						
Only PDS	64.00	84.00	96.00	94.00	100.00	56.00
PDS cum retailer	28.00	12.00	-	8.00	-	44.00
PDS cum wholesaler	8.00	-	4.00	-	-	-
No response	-	4.00	-	-	-	-
Ownership status						
Individual	100.00	100.00	52.00	8.00	76.00	72.00
Joint	-	-	-	4.00	-	-
Government	-	-	-	20.00	8.00	4.00
Corporate	-	-	-	36.00	16.00	24.00
Corporation	-	-	-	12.00	-	-
NGO	-	-	-	-	-	-
Gram panchayat	-	-	44.00	20.00	-	-
Others	-	-	4.00	-	-	-

Table 7.2 **Location and Functioning of the Shop**

	Mizoram	Bihar	Uttar Pradesh	Chhattisgarh	Rajasthan	Assam
Proximity of lifting godown from the ration shop						
Within 5 kms	32.00	32.00	36.00	24.00	24.00	72.00
5-10 kms	24.00	40.00	36.00	24.00	16.00	28.00
10-20 kms	28.00	28.00	24.00	36.00	28.00	-
>20 kms	16.00	-	4.00	16.00	28.00	-
No response	-	-	-	-	4.00	-
For how many days does your shop remain open in a month?						
Only 1 day	-	-	-	-	-	-
Upto 5 days	-	12.00	4.00	16.00	4.00	-
5-10 days	12.00	8.00	12.00	20.00	8.00	4.00
11-15 days	48.00	-	32.00	12.00	24.00	96.00
>15 days	40.00	80.00	52.00	52.00	64.00	-
What is the opening time of your shop?						
Forenoon	44.00	48.00	24.00	20.00	68.00	24.00
Afternoon	-	-	16.00	12.00	4.00	-
Evening	-	4.00	12.00	-	4.00	12.00
Whole day	56.00	36.00	48.00	68.00	24.00	60.00
No response	-	12.00	-	-	-	4.00

Table 7.3 Monthly Entitlement according to FPS (in Kgs)

	Wheat			Rice		
	AAY	BPL	APL	AAY	BPL	APL
Mizoram	0.00	0.00	0.00	35.00	35.00	2.00
Bihar	14.00	12.00	0.00	21.00	10.00	0.00
Uttar Pradesh	10.00	10.00	0.00	25.00	25.00	0.00
Chhattisgarh	0.00	5.00	0.00	35.00	25.00	0.00
Rajasthan	35.00	20.00	0.00	0.00	15.00	0.00
Assam	0.00	0.00	0.00	35.00	35.00	0.00

7.4 Lifting of Quota and Disposal of Remaining Stocks

During the last year, were there any instances when the FPS had lifted less than the allocated quota from the godown? Around 70 per cent of owners replied no to this question, while 30 per cent of the selected owners said that their lifted quota was less than the allotted quota up to 5 times during the last year. The reason pointed out for not lifting the quota were less availability at godown, insufficient opening stock, poor demand and lack of money with the shop owners. Against the phenomenon of lifting less than allotted quota from godown, fair price shops were also left with undistributed grains in many instances. Around 20 to 40 per cent of the interviewed shop owners accepted that sometimes entitlement was not lifted by some of the beneficiaries. To our question, how they were disposing off the unlifted stock, around 15 to 20 per cent of them replied that they adjust it in the next month supply, while a very few admitted that they distribute more grains to the beneficiaries while no one said that they sell in the open market. However, majority of the cases did not reply to this question indicating some foul play on the part of the shop owners.

Table 7.4 Instances of Lifting Less Than Quota by FPS from Godown

	Mizoram	Bihar	Uttar Pradesh	Chhattisgarh	Rajasthan	Assam
Wheat						
Are there instances during the 2005-06 when lifting by FPS from godown was less than the allotted quota?						
Yes	-	28.00	40.00	32.00	20.00	4.00
No	-	72.00	60.00	68.00	80.00	8.00
No response	100.00	-	-	-	-	88.00
If 'Yes' to above, how many times the lifted quota was less than the allotted quota?						
Never	-	-	24.00	8.00	-	-
1-5 times	-	16.00	24.00	16.00	-	-
5-10 times	-	-	8.00	4.00	-	4.00
>10 times	-	4.00	4.00	8.00	4.00	-
No response	100.00	80.00	60.00	64.00	96.00	96.00
What were the reasons for not lifting the grains?						
Less availability at godown	-	4.00	36.00	16.00	-	-
Insufficient opening stock	-	4.00	-	16.00	4.00	-
Due to poor demand	-	4.00	-	-	-	4.00
Lack of money	-	-	-	-	-	-
Bad quality	-	-	-	-	-	-
Others	-	4.00	4.00	-	-	-
No response	100.00	84.00	60.00	68.00	96.00	96.00

contd...

...contd...

	Mizoram	Bihar	Uttar Pradesh	Chhattisgarh	Rajasthan	Assam
			Rice			
Are there instances during the 2005-06 when lifting by FPS from godown was less than the allotted quota?						
Yes	-	28.00	28.00	16.00	4.00	20.00
No	100.00	72.00	72.00	84.00	72.00	80.00
No response	-	-	-	-	24.00	-
If 'Yes' to above, how many times the lifted quota was less than the allotted quota?						
Never	-	-	-	4.00	-	-
1-5 times	-	16.00	12.00	8.00	-	4.00
5-10 times	-	-	8.00	4.00	-	12.00
>10 times	-	4.00	8.00	4.00	-	-
No response	-	80.00	72.00	80.00	100.00	84.00
What were the reasons for not lifting the grains?						
Less availability at godown	-	4.00	24.00	12.00	-	16.00
Insufficient opening stock	-	4.00	-	8.00	-	-
Due to poor demand	-	-	-	-	-	-
Lack of money	-	4.00	-	4.00	-	-
Bad quality	-	-	-	-	-	-
Others	-	4.00	4.00	-	-	-
No response	-	84.00	72.00	76.00	-	84.00
			Wheat			
Are there instances during the last six months (July to December), when lifting by FPS from godown was less than the allotted quota?						
Yes	-	16.00	12.00	20.00	20.00	-
No	-	84.00	76.00	80.00	80.00	-
No response	100.00	-	12.00	-	-	100.00
If 'Yes' to above, how many times the lifted quota was less than the allotted quota?						
Never	-	-	-	-	-	-
1-5 times	-	8.00	12.00	12.00	-	-
5-10 times	-	8.00	-	4.00	-	-
>10 times	-	-	-	4.00	4.00	-
No response	-	84.00	88.00	80.00	96.00	100.00
What were the reasons for not lifting the grains?						
Less availability at godown	-	12.00	8.00	16.00	-	-
Insufficient opening stock	-	8.00	4.00	4.00	4.00	-
Due to poor demand	-	-	-	-	-	-
Lack of money	-	-	-	-	-	-
Bad quality	-	-	-	-	-	-
Others	-	4.00	-	-	-	-
No response	-	76.00	88.00	80.00	96.00	100.00
			Rice			
Are there instances during the last six months (July to December), when lifting by FPS from godown was less than the allotted quota?						
Yes	-	16.00	48.00	20.00	4.00	4.00
No	100.00	84.00	44.00	80.00	76.00	96.00
No response	-	-	8.00	-	20.00	-
If 'Yes' to above, how many times the lifted quota was less than the allotted quota?						
Never	-	-	-	-	-	-
1-5 times	-	8.00	52.00	16.00		
5-10 times	-	8.00	-	-	-	-
>10 times	-	84.00	-	4.00	-	-
No response	-	-	48.00	80.00	100.00	100.00

contd...

...contd...

	Mizoram	Bihar	Uttar Pradesh	Chhattisgarh	Rajasthan	Assam
What were the reasons for not lifting the grains?						
Less availability at godown	-	12.00	52.00	16.00	-	-
Insufficient opening stock	-	8.00	-	4.00	-	16.00
Due to poor demand	-	-	-	-	-	-
Lack of money	-	-	-	-	-	-
Bad quality	-	-	-	-	-	-
Others	-	4.00	-	-	-	-
No response	-	76.00	88.00	80.00	96.00	100.00
			Rice			
Are there instances during the last six months (July to December), when lifting by FPS from godown was less than the allotted quota?						
Yes	-	16.00	48.00	20.00	4.00	4.00
No	100.00	84.00	44.00	80.00	76.00	96.00
No response	-	-	8.00	-	20.00	-
If 'Yes' to above, how many times the lifted quota was less than the allotted quota?						
Never	-	-	-	-	-	-
1-5 times	-	8.00	52.00	16.00	-	-
5-10 times	-	8.00	-	-	-	-
>10 times	-	84.00	-	4.00	-	-
No response	-	-	48.00	80.00	100.00	100.00
What were the reasons for not lifting the grains?						
Less availability at godown	-	12.00	52.00	16.00	-	-
Insufficient opening stock	-	8.00	-	4.00	-	16.00
Due to poor demand	-	-	-	-	-	-
Lack of money	-	-	-	-	-	-
Bad quality	-	-	-	-	-	-
Others	-	4.00	-	-	-	-
No response	-	76.00	48.00	80.00	100.00	84.00

Table 7.5 Disposal of Remaining Stock

	Mizoram	Bihar	Uttar Pradesh	Chhattisgarh	Rajasthan	Assam
			Wheat			
Are there any instances during 2005-06 when your shop was left with some stock undistributed?						
Yes	-	24.00	20.00	16.00	40.00	-
No	16.00	64.00	80.00	80.00	60.00	100.00
No response	84.00	12.00	-	4.00	-	-
If 'Yes' to above, how did you dispose off the remaining stock?						
Adjusted in next month	-	28.00	16.00	16.00	44.00	-
Gave more to consumer	-	-	4.00	-	-	-
Sold in open market	-	-	-	-	-	-
Others	-	-	-	-	-	-
No response	-	72.00	80.00	84.00	56.00	100.00
Are there any instances during last six months (July to December) when your shop was left with some stock undistributed?						
Yes		16.00	16.00	36.00	44.00	4.00
No		84.00	76.00	64.00	56.00	96.00
No response		-	8.00	-	-	-

contd...

...*contd*...

	Mizoram	Bihar	Uttar Pradesh	Chhattisgarh	Rajasthan	Assam
If 'Yes' to above, how did you dispose off the remaining stock?						
Adjusted in next month	-	16.00	12.00	36.00	40.00	-
Gave more to consumer	-	-	-	4.00	-	-
Sold in open market	-	-	4.00	-	-	-
Others	-	-	-	-	-	-
No response	-	84.00	84.00	60.00	60.00	100.00
			Rice			
Are there any instances during 2005-06 when your shop was left with some stock undistributed?						
Yes	-	28.00	20.00	44.00	4.00	4.00
No	100.00	60.00	80.00	56.00	68.00	80.00
No response	-	12.00	-	-	28.00	16.00
If 'Yes' to above, how did you dispose off the remaining stock?						
Adjusted in next month	-	28.00	16.00	44.00	12.00	4.00
Gave more to consumer	-	4.00	4.00	-	-	-
Sold in open market	-	-	-	-	-	-
Others	-	-	-	-	-	-
No response	-	68.00	80.00	56.00	88.00	96.00
Are there any instances during last six months (July to December) when your shop was left with some stock undistributed?						
Yes	-	16.00	16.00	52.00	24.00	-
No	96.00	84.00	76.00	48.00	48.00	92.00
No response	4.00	-	8.00	-	28.00	8.00
If 'Yes' to above, how did you dispose off the remaining stock?						
Adjusted in next month	-	16.00	12.00	-	20.00	-
Gave more to consumer	-	-	-	52.00	-	-
Sold in open market	-	-	4.00	-	-	-
Others	-	-	-	-	-	-
No response	-	84.00	84.00	48.00	80.00	-

7.5 Records of Transparency

The performance of PDS also depends on the level of awareness of the beneficiaries as well as the transparency maintained at the fair price shop. Keeping proper records, displaying the list and entitlement of the beneficiaries, the timings of the distribution of grains, price, etc., keep the consumers vigilant. We propounded some questions related to transparency to the FPS owners and the details provided by them are summarised in Tables 7.6 and 7.7 below. To the question whether the FPS shop owners keep records of their transaction, more than 80 per cent of interviewed shop owners answered yes. On the type of records maintained, more than 60 per cent were of the opinion that they kept all the details of stocks handled as well as lifting details from the godown and distribution of grains among the beneficiaries by the number of cards and the total grains distributed of a particular commodity. To the question whether they just keep the records with themselves or do they display the information related to price, stock and the number of cards registered with the FPS on the notice board for public information, a majority of them replied yes in all the states, except Mizoram, where most of the interviewed shop owners denied displaying any such records on the notice board.

On further details of transparency, we tried to find out how systematically FPS were functioning, which were run mostly by the private owners. A majority of the shop owners in all the states indicated that they had displayed the list of beneficiaries outside the shop for public knowledge. They also opined that alongwith the list of beneficiaries, the amount of entitlement in each case and the scale of issue and the retail price at which food was being distributed were also displayed. Along with these details, shop owners also claimed that they were keeping the beneficiaries updated about the timings of opening and closing of the shop and stocks of essential commodities received and distributed. However, to the question whether they displayed the name and address of the authority for redressal of consumers' grievances, a majority of them either did not reply to this question or they said no. Similarly, on cross checking from the households, the replies of the shop owners were not found consistent and there were two opposite views on many of the above questions. Last and the least, do the shop owners provide samples of food they distribute among the consumers? Some of the shopkeepers replied that they keep all the samples on display, while some others said that they keep only some of the samples. However, a majority of them did not respond to this question, indirectly answering that they were not displaying any such samples.

Table 7.6 Maintenance of Records

	Mizoram	Bihar	Uttar Pradesh	Chhattisgarh	Rajasthan	Assam
Do you maintain updated records?						
Yes	84.00	96.00	100.00	96.00	96.00	100.00
No	12.00	-	-	4.00	-	
No response	4.00	4.00	-	-	4.00	
If 'Yes' to above, what type of records do you maintain?						
Stock details						
Yes	64.00	92.00	92.00	88.00	68.00	80.00
No	36.00	8.00	8.00	12.00	32.00	20.00
Lifting details (Commodity wise)						
Yes	64.00	92.00	92.00	80.00	96.00	80.00
No	36.00	8.00	8.00	20.00	4.00	20.00
Distribution details (Commodity wise)						
Yes	48.00	72.00	84.00	76.00	88.00	64.00
No	52.00	28.00	16.00	24.00	12.00	36.00
Distribution details (Card status wise)						
Yes	60.00	92.00	88.00	88.00	76.00	72.00
No	40.00	8.00	12.00	12.00	24.00	28.00
Display of prices of stock						
Yes	-	96.00	88.00	84.00	80.00	68.00
No	100.00	4.00	12.00	16.00	20.00	32.00
Display of stock						
Yes	24.00	96.00	68.00	92.00	84.00	64.00
No	76.00	4.00	32.00	8.00	16.00	36.00
Ration card register						
Yes	-	92.00	92.00	96.00	96.00	44.00
No	100.00	8.00	8.00	4.00	4.00	56.00
Any other (mention details)						
Yes	-	12.00	4.00	16.00	28.00	4.00
No	100.00	88.00	96.00	84.00	72.00	96.00

7.6 Monitoring System of the FPS

For the monitoring of the FPS functioning, there were multiple authorities that were supposed to check the functioning of the FPS and also could check the samples of grain being sold to the beneficiaries. Such authority was vested with the *gram panchayat* or its designated committee, vigilance committee from the block or district officials or the government officials from the Civil Supplies Department. Among our selected shop owners, the distribution was quite equal for the *gram panchayat*, the district officials and for the Civil Supplies Department as the designated authority who inspected their shops. A few shop owners also replied that their shops were not being monitored by any authority, while some shop owners did not reply to the question of who monitors their shop. To the question, what was the frequency of such inspection, a majority of the shop keepers replied atleast once in a month's time period while 10 per cent of the selected owners also replied that either their shop was not inspected last year or it was never inspected at all by any authority.

Table 7.7 Records of Transparency

	Mizoram	Bihar	Uttar Pradesh	Chhattisgarh	Rajasthan	Assam
List of BPL and AAY beneficiaries						
Yes	40.00	92.00	68.00	96.00	56.00	76.00
No	36.00	8.00	20.00	4.00	40.00	16.00
No response	24.00	-	12.00	-	4.00	8.00
Entitlement of essential commodities						
Yes	40.00	80.00	80.00	68.00	80.00	64.00
No	28.00	12.00	16.00	20.00	20.00	16.00
No response	32.00	8.00	4.00	12.00	-	20.00
Scale of issue						
Yes	32.00	92.00	80.00	84.00	80.00	64.00
No	20.00	4.00	16.00	8.00	20.00	16.00
No response	48.00	4.00	4.00	8.00	-	20.00
Retail issue price						
Yes	48.00	100.00	84.00	100.00	80.00	84.00
No	20.00	-	16.00	-	20.00	16.00
No response	32.00	-	-	-	-	-
Timings of opening and closing of the FPS						
Yes	32.00	92.00	80.00	100.00	80.00	84.00
No	28.00	8.00	20.00	-	20.00	16.00
No response	40.00	-	-	-	-	-
Stock of essential commodities received during the month						
Yes	-	80.00	92.00	72.00	72.00	72.00
No	28.00	20.00	4.00	16.00	24.00	16.00
No response	72.00	-	4.00	12.00	4.00	12.00
Opening and closing stock of essential commodities						
Yes	-	88.00	76.00	84.00	76.00	64.00
No	28.00	8.00	20.00	8.00	20.00	16.00
No response	72.00	4.00	4.00	8.00	4.00	20.00
The authority for redressal of grievances/lodging complaints w.r.t. quality and quantity of essential commodities under the PDS						
Yes		36.00	28.00	44.00	72.00	44.00
No	24.00	32.00	52.00	24.00	20.00	16.00
No response	76.00	32.00	20.00	32.00	8.00	40.00
Availability of sample on display						
Display all samples	48.00	32.00	20.00	56.00	40.00	48.00
Display some samples	16.00	8.00	28.00	8.00	32.00	28.00
No sample display	36.00	60.00	52.00	36.00	28.00	24.00

Table 7.8 **Monitoring of FPS Functioning**

	Mizoram	Bihar	Uttar Pradesh	Chhattisgarh	Rajasthan	Assam
			(Priority I)			
Who monitors the FPS						
Panchayat committee/ designated authority by the *panchayat* or village	16.00	-	24.00	44.00	28.00	40.00
Vigilance committee from the block/district level	20.00	32.00	44.00	24.00	36.00	20.00
Government officials/civil supply departments	24.00	64.00	20.00	32.00	20.00	40.00
Nobody monitors	-	4.00	-	-	16.00	-
Other	-	-	-	-	-	-
No response	40.00	-	12.00	-	-	-
			(Priority II)			
Who monitors the FPS						
Panchayat committee/ designated authority by the *panchayat* or village	40.00	8.00	-	4.00	8.00	12.00
Vigilance committee from the block/district level	12.00	16.00	12.00	20.00	12.00	8.00
Government officials/civil supply departments	28.00	32.00	48.00	28.00	32.00	-
Nobody monitors	-	-	-	-	20.00	-
Other	-	-	-	4.00	-	-
No response	20.00	44.00	40.00	44.00	28.00	80.00
What is the frequency of your inspection?						
Atleast once in a month	52.00	44.00	68.00	68.00	24.00	76.00
Four times in a year	12.00	24.00	8.00	20.00	48.00	16.00
Two times in a year	16.00	20.00	4.00	8.00	-	-
Once in a year	22.00	4.00	-	-	4.00	4.00
Did not visit last one year	-	4.00	4.00	-	4.00	4.00
Never	-	4.00	12.00	-	12.00	-
No response	8.00	-	4.00	4.00	-	-

7.7 Stocking Pattern at the FPS

What was the pattern of lifting food from the godowns and distributing it among the beneficiaries? Overwhelming majority of the shop owners were of the opinion that they were receiving their stock from the godown with a pre-set date and time period. It was either on a fixed date during a month, or it was fixed for the week during which the food was being distributed or in some cases after the distribution week so that the food should be available in the shop before hand for the next month. However, around 20 per cent of the shop owners replied that there was no such pre date fixed for lifting and they have to depend on the concerned officials' order for lifting grains every month which caused a great inconvenience for such shop owners and some times also delayed the distribution of food among the beneficiaries. Generally after receiving the release order from the godowns, the shop owners were given one week's time period to lift their quotas. However, in some cases it ranged up to 15 days. To our question whether the stocks were readily available when they visited the godown, a majority of them replied that stocks were available in the first week of the month or after the first week while 20 per cent in Bihar and 16 per cent in Rajasthan replied that stocks were not available regularly and they received their quota once in two to three months. However, to the question whether after getting the release order, whether or not the shopkeepers were getting their quota in a single lot, a majority of them replied always or sometimes while around 10 per cent replied that they never get their quota in a single lot which increases their transportation cost.

Table 7.9 Frequency of Lifting Ration from Godowns

	Mizoram	Bihar	Uttar Pradesh	Chhattisgarh	Rajasthan	Assam
When do you receive lifting/release order for lifting stock for FPS for current month?						
On a fixed date during a month	28.00	12.00	80.00	32.00	8.00	-
First week of distributing month	28.00	16.00	16.00	60.00	28.00	44.00
After first week of distributing month	16.00	20.00	-	-	36.00	20.00
Not get any such order	24.00	36.00	-	4.00	16.00	32.00
No response	4.00	16.00	4.00	4.00	12.00	4.00
			Wheat			
How many days are you allowed/actually to lift stock after receiving/releasing order?						
Less than 3 days	4.00	56.00	16.00	32.00	8.00	-
3 to 7 days	-	16.00	68.00	20.00	36.00	-
8 to 15 days	4.00	8.00	12.00	32.00	28.00	-
More than 15 days	-	20.00	4.00	12.00	28.00	-
No response	92.00	-	-	4.00	-	100.00
			Rice			
How many days are you allowed/actually to lift stock after receiving/releasing order?						
Less than 3 days	-	56.00	16.00	36.00	8.00	20.00
3 to 7 days	8.00	16.00	64.00	20.00	36.00	12.00
8 to 15 days	32.00	8.00	12.00	32.00	24.00	48.00
More than 15 days	44.00	20.00	8.00	4.00	20.00	20.00
No response	16.00	-	-	8.00	8.00	-

Table 7.10 Availability of Stocks at Godowns

	Mizoram	Bihar	Uttar Pradesh	Chhattisgarh	Rajasthan	Assam
			Wheat			
Readiness of stock availability at the godowns during 2005-06						
Available as and when required	-	48.00	28.00	20.00	16.00	-
Available only in first week of month	-	8.00	40.00	44.00	20.00	-
Available after first week of month	-	4.00	8.00	8.00	28.00	-
Available once in 2-3 months	-	8.00	8.00	4.00	8.00	-
Available irregularly	-	20.00	-	-	16.00	-
Rarely available	-	8.00	-	16.00	12.00	-
Not available at all	-	-	12.00	-	-	-
No response	100.00	4.00	4.00	8.00	-	100.00
Readiness of stock availability at the godowns during last six months (July to December)						
Available as and when required	-	32.00	44.00	28.00	24.00	-

contd...

...contd...

	Mizoram	Bihar	Uttar Pradesh	Chattisgarh	Rajasthan	Assam
Available only in first week of month	-	28.00	28.00	40.00	32.00	-
Available after first week of month	-	8.00	16.00	28.00	24.00	-
Available once in 2-3 months	-	4.00	-	-	12.00	-
Available irregularly	-	4.00	-	-	8.00	-
Rarely available	-	-	-	-	-	-
Not available at all	-	24.00	-	4.00	-	-
No response	100.00	-	12.00	-	-	100.00
How often you get the total allotted stock in a single lot after receiving releasing order?						
Always	-	60.00	96.00	52.00	60.00	-
Sometimes	-	36.00	4.00	36.00	20.00	-
Never	-	-	-	12.00	20.00	-
No response	100.00	4.00	-	-	-	100.00
			Rice			
Readiness of stock availability at the godowns during 2005-06						
Available as and when required	100.00	48.00	36.00	20.00	12.00	48.00
Available only in first week of month	-	8.00	36.00	52.00	16.00	16.00
Available after first week of month	-	4.00	8.00	4.00	28.00	24.00
Available once in 2-3 months	-	8.00	4.00	-	8.00	-
Available irregularly	-	20.00	-	-	12.00	-
Rarely available	-	-	-	16.00	12.00	-
Not available at all	-	8.00	12.00	-	-	12.00
No response	-	4.00	4.00	8.00	12.00	-
Readiness of stock availability at the godowns during last six months (July to December)						
Available as and when required	36.00	32.00	44.00	28.00	20.00	40.00
Available only in first week of month	52.00	28.00	28.00	40.00	28.00	40.00
Available after first week of month	8.00	8.00	16.00	28.00	24.00	
Available once in 2-3 months	4.00	4.00	-	-	12.00	-
Available irregularly	-	4.00	-	-	8.00	-
Rarely available	-	-	-	-	-	-
Not available at all	-	24.00	-	-	-	16.00
No response	-	-	12.00	4.00	8.00	4.00
How often you get the total allotted stock in a single lot after receiving releasing order						
Always	60.00	60.00	88.00	64.00	60.00	56.00
Sometimes	32.00	36.00	4.00	24.00	20.00	36.00
Never	8.00	-	8.00	12.00	16.00	8.00
No response	-	4.00	-	-	-	-

7.8 Pattern of Distribution among the Consumers

It is common opinion that grains are distributed once in a month through fair price shops. However, among our selected FPS, some of the shop owners pointed out that they are distributing grains weekly and fortnightly. The percentage of such shop owners was around 10 to 15 per cent in Mizoram, Chhattisgarh, Uttar Pradesh and Rajasthan. A majority of shop owners indicated that the frequency of grain distribution was monthly. In Bihar and Mizoram, a large number of shop owners replied that the distribution of grains among the beneficiaries depended on when the FPS received its stipulated quota from the godown. To an another question of how frequently the shop runs stock out situation, majority of FPS owners indicated that they run out of stock once or twice (less than five times) only in a year. To another question, how often they have to pay bribe to receive their allocated quota from the godown, 20 per cent selected shop owners in Bihar and 28 per cent in Chhattisgarh said that they bribe every time to receive their stipulated grains. However, 60 to 80 per cent of the shop owners in all the states, including Bihar and Chhattisgarh denied having paid any bribe for getting their entitled quota of grains.

7.9 Mode of Transportation of Grains

For transporting grains from the godown to the fair price shop, almost all shop owners in Bihar, Mizoram, Uttar Pradesh and Assam pointed out that they had to make their own arrangements while in Chhattisgarh and Rajasthan, a majority replied that these arrangements were being made either by the government sources or by some other institutions like *panchayat* etc. The mode of transportation used for this purpose was truck or tempo in Mizoram, Chhattisgarh and Rajasthan while tractor-trolley was generally used in Bihar and Uttar Pradesh. Around 60 per cent shop owners in Assam and 36 per cent in Mizoram pointed out that out-rickshaw or pedal rickshaw with a load carrier was also being used for transporting rice and other commodities from godown to the shop. To the question who bears the transportation cost, overwhelming majority in Mizoram, Bihar, Uttar Pradesh and Assam replied that it was borne out by the FPS, while in other cases it was being shared among the FPS, FCI, *panchayat,* etc. In some cases, transportation cost was paid by the FPS but they were reimbursed the same either at the time of lifting of grains or later. The reimbursement cases were highest in Mizoram and Chhattisgarh. A few shop owners from Rajasthan and Assam also indicated that they were getting some reimbursement for the transportation cost. However, in some of the cases, it was also found that FPS owners were charging higher than the stipulated price from the beneficiaries on account of recovering the transportation cost from the buyers. It was happening especially in those cases wherever transportation cost was not being reimbursed to the shop owners and therefore, they were passing it out to the consumer. It was learned through the surveyed shop owners that in most of the cases, food grains were being stored in the *kuccha/pucca* houses, as there was no provision for scientific storage or warehouse at the FPS. As a consequence, 5 per cent of the grains stored in the shop were getting spoiled or their quality was deteriorated by the time the grains were lifted by the consumer.

7.10 Price Charged by the FPS and the Number of Beneficiaries Catered

Before concluding the chapter, we present here the number of beneficiaries/consumers catered on an average by each shop in the selected states. It is evident from the data presented in the tables that the number of households catered each month varied in almost all the shops. The variation in number of households catered despite the number of ration cards registered with the shop being fixed indicates irregular nature of supply issued from the FPS on monthly basis. The reason for the same could be multiple. It might be due to unfair means at the part of the shopkeeper, irregular supply being received by them or irregular demand on the part of the consumers. The range of beneficiaries catered was quite high and it varied from less than a hundred to more than six thousand. The average number of households catered during the six months of survey period was lowest in Assam 553, followed by Rajasthan 1144, Mizoram 1471, Bihar 1811, Uttar Pradesh 2575 and highest in Chhattisgarh 4523. However, the coefficient of variation of number of households catered was highest in Rajasthan, followed by Bihar and Mizoram, while it was lowest in Assam and Chhattisgarh probably indicating more regular supply in the latter two states.

Last and the least, we tried to recheck the prices at which the food grains were being supplied to the households from FPS. We collected the retail prices at which food was being sold to the beneficiaries from the fair price shop owners during our survey period. The price details as given by the fair price shops are summarised in a Table 7.15. It is seen from the data that almost all fair price shop owners in all the states, stated that they were supplying wheat at the rate of Rs. 2 per kg and rice at Rs. 3 per kg to the AAY households. The mode prices as revealed by the households were quite close to the prices stated by the shop owners. However, a few households had to bear higher than prices indicated by the shop owners (the stipulated prices) as mean prices were mostly higher than the mode prices indicating higher price paid by some of the households (see Chapter 4).

Table 7.11 Frequency of Distribution to Consumer

	Mizoram	Bihar	Uttar Pradesh	Chhattisgarh	Rajasthan	Assam
			Wheat			
What was the frequency of distribution of stock to the consumers during 2005-06?						
Weekly	-	-	16.00	12.00	8.00	-
Fortnightly	-	-	12.00	-	4.00	-
Monthly	-	32.00	64.00	36.00	24.00	4.00
Once in 2 months	-	4.00	-	-	8.00	-
Once in 3-6 months	-	-	-	-	28.00	-
Depending on the availability of items	-	40.00	-	4.00	-	-
Not lifted	-	-	-	12.00	-	-
No response	100.00	24.00	8.00	36.00	28.00	96.00
			Rice			
What was the frequency of distribution of stock to the consumers during 2005-06?						
Weekly	12.00	-	16.00	28.00	8.00	-
Fortnightly	4.00	-	4.00	-	4.00	-
Monthly	32.00	32.00	72.00	36.00	24.00	88.00
Once in 2 months	-	4.00	-	-	4.00	-
Once in 3-6 months	-	-	-	-	16.00	-
Depending on the availability of items	24.00	40.00	-	4.00	12.00	-
Not lifted	-	-	-	-	-	-
No response	28.00	24.00	8.00	32.00	32.00	12.00
			Wheat			
How often did you face stock out situation during 2005-06?						
Once in a year	-	20.00	28.00	32.00	52.00	-
Less than 5 times in year	-	16.00	8.00	12.00	20.00	-
5 to 10 times in a year	-	12.00	4.00	12.00	8.00	-
More than 10 times in year	-	8.00	4.00	8.00	-	-
No response	100.00	44.00	56.00	36.00	20.00	100.00
			Rice			
How often did you face stock out situation during 2005-06?						
Once in a year	52.00	20.00	28.00	44.00	36.00	60.00
Less than 5 times in year	-	16.00	8.00	4.00	20.00	16.00
5 to 10 times in a year	12.00	12.00	4.00	8.00	-	8.00
More than 10 times in year	36.00	8.00	4.00	8.00	-	12.00
No response	-	44.00	56.00	36.00	44.00	4.00
			Wheat			
Have you ever paid bribe for lifting commodities from godowns?						
Paid bribe all the times	-	20.00	16.00	28.00	4.00	
Paid bribe most of the times	-	-	-	-	8.00	
Paid bribe sometimes	-	8.00	4.00	-	20.00	8.00
Never paid	-	68.00	80.00	72.00	64.00	4.00
No response	100.00	4.00	-	-	4.00	88.00
			Rice			
Have you ever paid bribe for lifting commodities from godowns?						
Paid bribe all the times	-	20.00	16.00	28.00	4.00	-
Paid bribe most of the times	-	-	-	-	8.00	-
Paid bribe sometimes	-	8.00	4.00	-	20.00	12.00
Never paid	100.00	68.00	80.00	72.00	64.00	88.00
No response	-	4.00	-	-	4.00	-

Table 7.12 Lifting and Transportation

	Mizoram	Bihar	Uttar Pradesh	Chhattisgarh	Rajasthan	Assam
Who makes the transportation arrangements for grains from godown to the FPS						
Own arrangements	92.00	100.00	96.00	8.00	24.00	100.00
Delivered by government	8.00	-	4.00	88.00	44.00	-
Others	-	-	-	4.00	28.00	-
No response	-	-	-	-	4.00	-
What mode of transportation is used for transporting commodities to FPS?						
Truck	100.00	-	-	76.00	80.00	32.00
Bus	32.00	-	-	-	-	-
Tempo/van/matador	16.00	4.00	-	36.00	12.00	48.00
Tractor trolley	28.00	76.00	88.00	20.00	24.00	-
Auto rickshaw	36.00	-	-	-	-	32.00
Animal drawn vehicle	8.00	28.00	12.00	4.00	-	12.00
Rickshaw with load carrier	-	4.00	-	-	-	28.00
Boats	-	-	-	-	-	4.00
Animal back	-	12.00	-	-	-	-
Head load	4.00	20.00	-	8.00	-	-
Any other	-	-	-	-	-	-
No response	-	-	-	-	-	-

Table 7.13 Storage of Food Grains by FPS

	Mizoram	Bihar	Uttar Pradesh	Chhattisgarh	Rajasthan	Assam
Where do you store food grains?						
Scientific storage/warehouse	4.00	-	4.00	-	8.00	-
***Pukka* house**	36.00	80.00	92.00	80.00	48.00	72.00
***Kuccha* house**	44.00	20.00	4.00	20.00	40.00	28.00
No response	16.00	-	-	-	4.00	-
What is the percentage of food grains damaged in the store?						
1% to 5 %	24.00	72.00	56.00	52.00	56.00	32.00
5% to 10%	-	20.00	-	-	4.00	-
> 10%	-	-	4.00	16.00	20.00	4.00
No response	76.00	8.00	40.00	32.00	20.00	64.00

Table 7.14 Transportation Charges

	Mizoram	Bihar	Uttar Pradesh	Chhattisgarh	Rajasthan	Assam
Who bears transportation cost?						
FPS	92.00	60.00	100.00	36.00	32.00	68.00
Panchayat raj institutions	-	8.00	-	4.00	-	-
Civil supplies departments	-	8.00	-	20.00	28.00	4.00
Food Corporation of India (FCI)	-	-	-	20.00	-	16.00
Any other agency	-	4.00	-	-	20.00	4.00
Jointly	-	20.00	-	20.00	20.00	-
No response	8.00	-	-	-	-	-
Do they get reimbursement from the government?						
Yes	92.00	4.00	-	40.00	12.00	20.00
No	-	64.00	100.00	4.00	36.00	80.00
No response	8.00	32.00	-	56.00	52.00	-
In what proportion you get reimbursement?						
In some proportion	60.00	4.00	-	24.00	12.00	-
Fully	40.00	8.00	-	-	8.00	20.00
Partially	-	-	-	-	-	-
No response	-	88.00	-	76.00	80.00	80.00
What is the average time taken for getting reimbursement amount (days)?						
No. of days	-	-	-	-	-	-
Less than one month	32.00	-	-	32.00	-	-
One month	-	-	-	-	-	-
One to six months	-	4.00	-	-	-	-
Year	-	-	-	-	-	-
More than a year	68.00	-	-	-	-	20.00
No response	-	96.00	-	68.00	100.00	80.00
Who bears jointly and in what proportion?						
Who bears?						
FPS and PRIs						
FPS and civil supplies depts.	20.00	-	-	16.00	-	-
FPS and FCI	-	4.00	-	4.00	-	-
Any other	-	4.00	-	20.00	-	-
No response	80.00	92.00	-	60.00	100.00	100.00
In what proportion?						
50:50	-	-	-	4.00	24.00	-
25:75	-	-	-	4.00	-	-
75:25	-	-	-	12.00	4.00	-
Any other ratio	-	8.00	-	-	12.00	-
No response	100.00	-	-	80.00	60.00	100.00

Table 7.15 Prices at which Grains were Sold from the FPS (Rs/Kg)

	July			August			September			October			November			December			Average		
	AAY	BPL	APL	AAY	BPL	APL	AAY	BPL	APL	AAY	BPL	APL	AAY	BPL	APL	AAY	BPL	APL	AAY	BPL	APL
Mizoram																					
Wheat	-	-	-	-	-	-	-	-	-	-	-	-	-	-	-	-	-	-	-	-	-
Rice	3.00	6.15	9.50	3.00	6.15	9.50	3.00	7.00		3.00	7.00		3.00	7.00		3.00	7.00		3.00	6.72	9.50
Bihar																					
Wheat	2.00	4.85	-	2.00	4.85	-	2.00	4.85	-	2.00	4.85	-	2.00	4.85	-	2.00	4.85	-	2.00	4.85	-
Rice	3.00	7.00	-	3.00	7.00	-	3.00	6.30	-	3.00	6.30	-	3.00	6.30	9.00	3.00	6.30	9.00	3.00	6.53	9.00
UP																					
Wheat	2.00	4.65	-	2.00	4.65	-	2.00	4.65	-	2.00	4.65	-	2.00	4.65	-	2.00	4.65	-	2.00	4.65	-
Rice	3.00	6.15	-	3.00	6.15	-	3.00	6.15	9.50	3.00	6.15	9.50	3.00	6.15	9.50	3.00	6.15	9.50	3.00	6.15	9.50
Chhattisgarh																					
Wheat	3.00	4.65	6.81	3.00	4.65	6.81	3.00	4.75	6.81	3.00	4.75	6.81	3.00	4.75	6.81	-	4.75	6.81	3.00	4.72	6.81
Rice	3.00	6.15	9.04	3.00	6.15	9.04	3.00	6.25	9.04	3.00	6.25	9.04	3.00	6.25	9.04	3.00	6.25	9.04	3.00	6.22	9.04
Rajasthan																					
Wheat	2.00	4.70	6.80	2.00	4.70	6.80	2.00	4.70	6.80	2.00	4.70	6.80	2.00	4.70	6.80	2.00	4.70	6.80	2.00	4.70	6.80
Rice	3.00	6.30	-	3.00	6.30	-	3.00	6.83	-	3.00	6.83	-	3.00	6.83	-	3.00	6.83	-	3.00	6.65	-
Assam																					
Wheat	-	-	-	-	-	-	-	-	-	-	-	-	-	-	-	-	-	-	-	-	-
Rice	3.50	7.00	10.00	3.50	7.00	10.00	3.00	7.00	-	3.00	7.00	-	3.00	7.00	-	3.00	7.00	-	3.17	7.00	10.00

Table 7.16 Number of Households Catered by the FPS

	July			August			September			October			November			December		
	AAY	BPL	APL	AAY	BPL	APL	AAY	BPL	APL	AAY	BPL	APL	AAY	BPL	APL	AAY	BPL	APL
Mizoram	429	985	1271	2491	978	1308	2498	976	1263	2469	973	1322	2514	951	1304	2527	962	1251
Bihar	2310	2895	587	2432	2895	657	2505	2777	303	1522	2953	303	2176	2905	483	2153	2260	483
Uttar Pradesh	1868	3053	2830	1880	3056	2830	1875	2959	2830	1801	3020	2830	1906	2946	2830	1915	3093	2835
Chhattisgarh	96	4823	6435	3066	4693	6228	3078	4757	6418	3092	4762	6355	3100	4597	5894	3129	4676	6213
Rajasthan	965	2148	195	1052	2172	178	1040	2166	146	1039	2119	184	1098	2239	184	1133	2288	239
Assam	181	571	660	329	717	660	329	717	660	329	717	660	329	717	660	329	720	660

8 Concluding Remarks and Policy Suggestions

8.1 Introduction

The PDS as it was being implemented earlier had been criticised for its urban bias and its failure to serve effectively the poorer sections of the population, its limited coverage in the states with high concentration of the rural poor and lack of transparent and accountable arrangements for delivery. A need was felt for quite some time to review the PDS and make it more focused. The targeted public distribution system (TPDS) replaced the erstwhile PDS from June 1997. Under the new system, a two-tier subsidised pricing system was introduced to benefit the poor. The State Governments were to streamline the PDS by issuing special cards to BPL families and selling essential articles under TPDS to them at specially subsidised prices, with better monitoring of the delivery system. Under the system, states were required to formulate and implement foolproof arrangements for identification of the poor for delivery of food grains and for its distribution in a transparent and accountable manner at the fair price shops (FPS).

A National Sample Survey (NSS) exercise pointed towards the fact that about 5 per cent of the total population in the country sleeps without two square meals a day. This section of the population can be called as "hungry". In order to make TPDS more focused and targeted towards this category of population, the Antyodaya Anna Yojana (AAY) was launched in December 2000 for one crore poorest of the poor families. AAY contemplates identification of one crore poorest of the poor families from amongst the BPL families covered under TPDS within the states and providing them food grains at a highly subsidised rate of Rs.2.0 per kilogram for wheat and Rs. 3.0 per kilogram for rice. The states/UTs were required to bear the distribution cost, including margin to dealers and retailers as well as the transportation cost. Thus, the entire food subsidy is supposed to be passed on to the consumers under the scheme. The estimated annual allocation of food grains for Antyodaya families was 30 lakh tonnes, involving a subsidy of Rs. 2,315 crore at the beginning. The scheme was started with one crore families but was expanded from time to time. The scheme now covers around 2.5 crore households. The identification of the Antyodaya families and issuing of distinctive ration cards to these families was the responsibility of the concerned State Governments. The present monthly allocation of food grains under AAY is around 7.27 lakh tonnes per month.

PDS with a network of about 4.77 lakh fair price shops (FPS) is perhaps the largest distribution network of its type in the world. However, in such a large distribution network certain inadequacies have been identified in the system. It has been alleged by some quarters that the allotted food grains fail to reach the identified cardholders. In view of these allegations, the Department of Food and Public Distribution, Government of India has decided to verify the veracity of such a charge. In this respect a concurrent evaluation of TPDS is carried out in selected districts of some states with financial support from the Department of Food and Public Distribution. The main objective of the evaluation study was to examine the extent to which food grains disbursed under TPDS were actually reaching the BPL and AAY categories of population in the country and to identify the incidence as well as the mode of irregularities in the system.

8.2 Main Findings

Demographic Profile

Looking at the demographic profile of the selected households, majority of households belonged to the scheduled castes (SC) and scheduled tribes (ST) in the case of AAY households, whereas other backward castes (OBC) along with the previous two classes formed the majority in the case of BPL households. Comparing these two categories, comparatively more number of forward castes (FC) households were found in the case of APL category. On the age factor, around half to two-third members of all households in all the cases were in the working age while rest of them were either children below working age or were the senior citizens. Household size varied from 3.3 to 5.4 in different states with an average around 4.5 to 5 members per family. The AAY and BPL families had slightly higher number of earning members compared to APL families. The households below poverty were comparatively much more dependent on irregular means of earnings and thereby in their case higher number of family members had to work to provide support to the family.

Income and Employment Structure

Occupation structure was significantly different among below and above poverty households. Whereas above poverty households depended mostly on agriculture/allied activities and regular salaried jobs to eke out their daily earnings, below poverty households depended mostly on casual earnings in agriculture, non-farm activities or as migrant workers. As higher number of APL households depended on salary, self-business or agriculture, they had assured regular earnings. Whereas BPL and AAY households were more vulnerable as they did not have any regular means of employment and in most of the cases they were not employed for the whole month. However, comparing occupation structure within BPL and AAY households, no significant differences appear in the pattern of occupation of these two categories. However, the northeastern states presented a contrasting picture, whereas agriculture and livestock was the principal activity in rest of the four states, this activity contributed very little to employment in Assam and Mizoram among the APL households. Similarly, regular employment in fixed salary jobs contributed significantly in the case of BPL and AAY households only in the case of Mizoram, while its contribution was much lower in all other states.

Comparing household income across the three categories of AAY, BPL and APL it was clearly shown by the data that on an average, BPL households earned 33 per cent higher income compared to AAY households. The AAY households belonged to the poorest of the poor category and thereby their income probably represented the bottom income group. Average above poverty households earned two and a half times higher income compared to BPL households and more than three times higher income compared to the poorest of the poor households. The difference between BPL and AAY income was highest in the case of Mizoram followed by Chhattisgarh, Rajasthan, Assam, Bihar and Uttar Pradesh. Comparing BPL and APL income, APL income was three and a half times higher than BPL income in Chhattisgarh, Bihar and Assam, three times in Mizoram, two and a half times in Uttar Pradesh and twice in Rajasthan. Thus, the difference between the above and below poverty income was higher in poor states like Chhattisgarh and Bihar than that of comparatively better off states like Rajasthan. Comparing the sources of income across different activities, wage income constituted a lion's share in the income of AAY and BPL households in all the states. Dominant share of wages in BPL and AAY income further verifies our results of occupational distribution. In the case of above poverty households, in consonance with the occupational structure, earnings from agriculture and salary and pension constituted the highest share of income of these households in all the states.

The dispersion of income across households was highest for agriculture and for the APL category in almost all the states. High variability of agricultural income across households was prompted by three factors namely, seasonal nature of agricultural occupation, diversified cropping pattern across households and different amount of land cultivated by different households. Dispersion was lowest for salary, followed by wage income and self-employment earnings. These statistics indicate that wage and fixed salary differential across households were far less than the earnings through agriculture and self-employment. The reason for the same seems to be that variations in wages and salaries represent dispersion across the households engaged in these activities, whereas dispersion in income from self-employment and agriculture, in addition to inter-personal differences, also include the variation that takes place due to differences in land area cultivated and the amount of capital invested by the households in business and other activities.

From the income estimates (monthly as well as annual), it did not appear that the AAY income belonged to the poorest of the poor households, especially those who were not able to get two square meals a day, the one sole criteria for issuing separate AAY cards and which was also the principal theme of the targeted PDS system. The BPL and AAY income estimates were very close denying the argument that former estimates belonged to the upper or average strata of income among the BPL population and the latter one representing the bottom most stratum. Comparing our income estimates with the Planning Commission, it was apparent that our income estimates were more or less very close to that of the Planning Commission, except the two northeastern states, namely Mizoram and Assam. In other states, our observed income estimates were mostly below the poverty line, as poverty line income was the upper bound whereas our estimated income was enumerated on average basis.

Food Consumption Pattern

On an average, per capita cereal consumption surpassed the 1200 calorie norms or 10.45 kgs per household per month (i.e., drawing 50 per cent of the 2400 calorie from carbohydrate and remaining from the protein and fat with 25 per cent each). The total cereal consumption was above 10.45 kgs in all the states and all the categories, except Chhattisgarh, where all the three categories of households fell short of this target. Among the cereals, wheat was the major cereal consumed in Rajasthan with average consumption of 9.5 kgs. Rice occupied the principal place in Chhattisgarh, Mizoram and Assam with an average quantity of 9 kgs, 10 kgs and 11 kgs, respectively. In the other two states namely, Uttar Pradesh and Bihar, both wheat and rice were consumed almost in the same ratio. The average quantity of wheat and rice consumed in Uttar Pradesh was 5.5 and 6 kgs, respectively. In Bihar, the average quantity was 6.5 and 5.5 kgs for rice and wheat, respectively. The other coarse cereals consumed namely, *jowar*, *bajra*, maize, barley and *ragi* were around 1.5 kgs in Rajasthan, less than a kg each in Uttar Pradesh, Bihar and Chhattisgarh and almost nil in Assam and Mizoram.

The shift of calories from cereals and pulses towards edible oils, fats and high value products as shown by the NSS data was also visible from the trends presented by our survey data. The quantity of cereals consumed by AAY households was higher than that of APL and BPL households as was seen in Rajasthan, Chhattisgarh and Bihar. On the other hand, the above poverty households were consuming much higher quantity of milk, edible oils and sugar in comparison to both below poverty households as well as Antyodaya households. Therefore, the statistics depicted above substantiate the argument that with the rising level of income, people have a tendency to diversify their palate towards more nutritious and high value commodities. Comparing the consumption pattern revealed by our survey data with that of NSS, our average consumption pattern stands more or less in line with the NSS. Total cereal consumption was slightly less than NSS figures in almost all the states, probably because our data was more slanting towards the below poverty households whereas the NSS figures depicted average figures for all classes. Pulses, sugar and edible oils however, were closer to the NSS figures.

Variations in consumption were higher across households than for the same households over time. Among different categories, consumption variation was higher among the below poverty households compared to above poverty households. Higher variation in food consumption by the poor households puts forth the question of affordability of food by such people and raises the need for some sort of income insurance for them. Among AAY households, coefficient of variation was high for milk in almost all the states, indicating its high cost for the poor that was beyond the purchasing capacity of the AAY households. Coarse cereals also displayed higher variability among the poorest households as the coarse cereals were an alternate to superior cereals in the event of fall in income of these households. At the overall, coefficient of variation of consumption over time was lower than that of coefficient of variation in income supporting the well-documented phenomenon of consumption smoothing by the households.

Monthly per capita food consumption expenditure varied from Rs. 171 to 365 among the selected households. Its value was highest in Rajasthan, followed by Mizoram, Bihar, Assam, Uttar Pradesh and Chhattisgarh. Among the food items, highest amount was spent on cereals in almost all the states. Whereas meat (including fish) was the second highest item in food consumption in Assam and Mizoram, milk constituted second highest priority in Rajasthan and Bihar, while pulses and vegetables were next to cereals in Uttar Pradesh and Chhattisgarh. Comparing food and non-food expenditure, on an average, the latter was less than total food expenditure in all the states, except Mizoram and that was consistent with the all India NSS figures. On an average, the distribution of food and non-food expenditure for all the categories and all the states was 60-40, respectively. Non-food expenditure (30-day recall period) was maximum in Mizoram (Rs. 392), followed by Rajasthan (Rs. 254), Bihar (Rs. 214), Assam (Rs. 193), Chhattisgarh (Rs. 133) and Uttar Pradesh (Rs. 84). Among the non-food items, education and health involved the highest expenditure in almost all the states. Education was followed by fuel and light, clothing, other items (toiletry, entertainment, intoxicants, transport and other services) and footwear.

Comparing across AAY, BPL and APL categories, while food expenditure of AAY and BPL households was quite close to each other, these two categories lagged behind above poverty households. Whereas all the categories spent proportionately higher amount on cereals, comparative amount spent on items like milk, edible oils, meat and fish, vegetables and fruits was higher by the APL households as compared to the other two category of households. This was more true in high per capita income states like Assam, Rajasthan and Mizoram as compared to lower income states like Uttar Pradesh and Chhattisgarh. In the case of non-food expenditure, education and health was top priority among all categories in all the states. Comparing food and non-food items, unlike the general belief that rich people spend higher amount on non-food, in our case, APL households spent much higher amount on food compared to non-food items and that was true in all the six states, without any exception. The same was true in other two categories as well.

Comparing variability in food and non-food expenditure, the coefficient of variation was significantly higher for the non-food commodities as compared to food items in all the states and in all the categories. On an average, coefficient of variation was less than 100 per cent in the case of food items while it averaged around 150 to 200 per cent in the non-food items. Among food items, variability was higher in the case of milk and milk products, poultry and meat, fruits and vegetables. In the case of non-food items, variability was higher for all items compared to food items, because of wide differences in the use of such items among the selected households.

Role of PDS in Ensuring Food to the Below Poverty

The statistics presented in tabular analysis revealed that in Rajasthan, on an average, above 90 per cent AAY and BPL households received around 32 kgs cereals, namely wheat and rice. However, the share of wheat was dominant because the latter was the main staple diet of Rajasthan. In the case of APL, only 15 per cent of the households received around 19 kgs of cereals. In Chhattisgarh, around 95 per cent of AAY and BPL households received their entitled quantity of cereals while the proportion of rice was dominant as the latter was also the main staple cereal consumed by most of the people. In Uttar Pradesh, both wheat and rice being the staple diet were being supplied in combination through the PDS shops. Around 93 per cent of AAY households received around 34 kgs of rice and wheat through the PDS outlets. Similarly, around 86 per cent BPL households also received the same quantity of wheat and rice through the PDS. The entitlement received by the APL households was only 26 kgs and around 8 per cent of the households received that quantity indicating the system being targeted towards the poor alone. In Assam, the PDS system was not as efficient as it was observed in the case of Chhattisgarh and Uttar Pradesh. Only 62 per cent of AAY and 67 per cent of BPL households obtained their entitled quantity of cereals (mainly rice) through the PDS.

Unlike other states where distributed quantity was close to the entitlement of 35 kgs cereals, in Mizoram, in all the categories and during all the six months, distributed quantity of cereals (mainly rice) was close to only 25 kgs. On an average, 89 per cent of AAY and 85 per cent of BPL households received around 25 kgs of cereals. Performance of PDS was least effective in Bihar among the six selected states. Among the AAY families, only 55 per cent of them received around 32 kgs of cereals that were distributed in the combination of wheat and rice in the state. The supply of cereals was even worse in the case of BPL households as only 36 per cent of them received around 29 kgs of these two cereals. These figures should be seen in the light of the fact that Bihar is among those states that have the maximum number of poor and therefore, an effective PDS system is most needed in that state. Entitlement for APL household was lower as less than 10 per cent households received around 26 kgs of cereals (wheat and rice) from the fair price shops. Thus, there was a lot of scope for improvement in the performance of PDS system especially in the two states of Bihar and Assam.

It is seen from our statistics presented in the tables that the ratio of PDS to market turns out to be around 70/30 for wheat or rice (or combination of wheat and rice) in the case of AAY and BPL households in Rajasthan, Chhattisgarh, Uttar Pradesh and Mizoram. In Assam, the share of PDS in total food was around 50 per cent for the AAY and BPL households. The share of PDS was observed as minimum in the case of Bihar. Only 30 per cent food of AAY households and 20 per cent of the BPL households was covered by the PDS in that state.

Comparing the actual prices paid for the PDS wheat and rice with the stipulated prices, it was seen that on an average, the mode price was quite closer to the stipulated price of Rs. 2 per kg for wheat and Rs. 3 per kg for rice indicating that majority of AAY households were provided food at the stipulated prices. In the case of BPL households, the mode price charged for wheat was Rs. 4.0 per kg in Rajasthan, Rs. 4.70 per kg in Uttar Pradesh and Rs. 6.0 per kg in Bihar. Mode price for rice was Rs.6.0 per kg in Mizoram, Rajasthan and Chhattisgarh, Rs. 6.16 per kg in Uttar Pradesh and Rs. 7.0 per kg in Bihar and Assam. However, comparing mode prices with the more common average—mean prices, it was seen that mean prices were mostly above the mode prices for both wheat as well as rice. This indicated that although a majority of the households paid the stipulated prices, some households were charged more than stipulated prices for the PDS food. Further analysis indicated that higher than the stipulated prices occurred because shopkeepers passed on the transportation charges to the households in a few cases.

Insurance against the Income Risks

We tested the hypothesis of consumption insurance by the households against the unforeseen income risks using regression tools on our penal data. Our test results suggested that our selected households were not fully insured against idiosyncratic income risks. The rejection of the full insurance model was for all the states and all the category of households with a few exceptions. Our results suggested partial risk sharing activities between households either within the same village or within their same ethnic groups. The results of insurance through same ethnic groups were more robust than the results for the village insurance. The results of insurance along the same caste line were found across the board whereas results for village insurance appeared in a few cases, while it was rejected in other cases. Among our three categories, the results supported for partial insurance in the case of BPL households, while evidence for the AAY and APL was much weaker. The absence of informal insurance for AAY households highlighted their vulnerability to the various income shocks and underlined the need for the government to make some provision for their social security.

Performance of Targeted Public Distribution System

We posed some qualitative questions to the households to assess the performance of the PDS system. On an average, households' perception about the entitlement was reasonably close to what they actually received from the fair price shops and most of the households were found to be aware about their entitlement. We tried to inquire the reasons for the irregularity of cereal distribution among those households who did not receive their entitlements regularly by asking them for how many months that happened during the last year. A majority of such households in Bihar indicated that they did not receive regular supply for more than two months during the last year. In Chhattisgarh, Rajasthan and Uttar Pradesh, majority of the households who did not receive regular supply indicated that they did not get it for one or two months. In the two northeastern states, a majority of the households not receiving regular supply did not respond to our question. In Bihar, around 50 per cent of the households who obtained irregular supply were not given any explanation for not being supplied the entitlement while remaining households quoted the reason that the FPS did not receive the sufficient quantity from civil supply depots. Similar was the case in Rajasthan where majority of such households were told that irregular supply was due to less supply obtained by the FPS. In rest of the states, households quoted no explanation given by the FPS for irregular supply. However, it was also noticed that in some cases respondents did not lift their entitlement even though supply was available at the FPS. Apart from the shortage of purchasing power, in few cases there were other reasons like inferior quality at the FPS, preference for the local variety, home produced food available with the households, etc. The phenomenon of not lifting the entitled quantity by the households during one or more months was highest in Uttar Pradesh, Assam and Mizoram while it was minimal in the case of Rajasthan and Chhattisgarh.

To the question of adherence to the prescribed opening time and keeping the outlet opened for stipulated number of days by the FPS shopkeeper, the households were mostly satisfied except in few states. In Bihar and Uttar Pradesh, households faced problems in drawing their entitlement because of improper opening times and days of the FPS shop. Most of the households had the perception that the cereals being supplied through the FPS were being underweighed. Around 40 per cent households in Rajasthan and Chhattisgarh and 80 per cent in Bihar were of the opinion that there was serious problem in food weighment at the FPS. A majority of households in all the states opined that shop owners were indulging in diverting food to the open market or they were involved in black marketing of PDS food. Were the consumers satisfied with the quality of services offered at the FPS, around 60 per cent households in Bihar replied no. In other states, more than 70 per cent households were satisfied in Rajasthan, Chhattisgarh, Assam and Mizoram and above 65 per cent households indicated that they are satisfied in Uttar Pradesh. To the question, why the households were not satisfied, 64 per cent of the dissatisfied households in Bihar were of the opinion that there was mismanagement at the fair price shops while 32 per cent in Bihar and above 40 per cent in Mizoram replied that food was being distributed to the known people by the fair price shop owners. In almost all the states, majority of the households, were not knowing whom to complain if the quality of grains offered from PDS was really bad. On the specific questions of quality and variety of wheat and rice distributed through PDS, a majority of households in Chhattisgarh, Rajasthan, Bihar and Uttar Pradesh responded that there was no difference between the PDS and local varieties. In the northeastern states namely, Assam and Mizoram, a majority of households stated that PDS rice was considerably different from the local varieties available. But among these two states also, majority in Mizoram did not prefer local variety over the PDS variety. Only in Assam and to some extent in Bihar, selected people preferred local variety over the PDS grains. A related question was posed whether the households liked the quality of the grains supplied and if not what was the lacuna in the grains supplied through PDS. Around 70 per cent households were satisfied with the quality of grain supplied in Rajasthan. In Chhattisgarh, more than 85 per cent were satisfied with the quality of rice and wheat supplied through the FPS. In Bihar, 90 per cent households in the case of rice and 70 per cent of wheat were not happy with the quality supplied through government shops. Presence of impurities, insect infested supply, broken grains and very bad taste of the grains were the common reasons for their outcries. Similar kind of complaints were found in Uttar Pradesh where around 35 per cent of households were dissatisfied with the quality of wheat and rice supplied through the PDS. In Assam, impurities and broken rice were reasons quoted by 30 per cent of households who were not satisfied with the PDS quality of rice. Last and the least, in Mizoram, around 35 to 40 per cent households were not happy with the quality of PDS rice. Presence of impurities, inferior quality, broken grains and the grains not being good in taste, as well as in colour, were the reasons cited for their dissatisfaction. Finally, to our question of how the households rate the performance of TPDS during the periods of distress, an overwhelming majority of them rated it satisfactory or highly satisfactory in Chhattisgarh, Assam and Mizoram. It was satisfactory in Rajasthan and Uttar Pradesh, while in Bihar around 40 per cent of them rated it poor or very poor.

Flaw in Identification of BPL and AAY Families—Errors of Targeting

For identification of BPL and AAY families, State Governments follow the guidelines issued by the Ministry of Rural Development, Government of India. For the identification of people below poverty, State Governments have devised different methods for fixation of income norms to formulate some exclusion criteria. Most of the states have carried out some sort of income survey by using its state machinery whatever way. It was however, demonstrated in the analysis that on an average, the amount fixed by the State Governments as an exclusion criterion was less than that of the Planning Commission (rural as well as urban) in all the six states without any exception. To further check the identification of our selected households, we compared our observed income/expenditure for BPL with that of the Planning Commission estimates. It was shown in Chapter 6 that except Assam and Mizoram, in all other states, our average BPL income was lower than the cut-off estimates of the Planning Commission. However, the survey income compared was the average income of all the selected BPL households in each state. The actual distribution of BPL income would lie just above or below this income. On the other hand, the Planning Commission income displayed was the cut-off income that provided the upper limit for the poverty line. Those households, who were just below or equal to the cut-off income would fall in the BPL list. In Assam and Mizoram, even our estimated average income was above the official cut-off income for poverty.

Using the methodology devised by Cornia and Stewart (1993), we estimated two errors of targeting, namely errors of omission of the poor from the scheme (exclusion error); and errors of inclusion of the non-poor (inclusion error). In terms of efficiency of the targeting mechanism, the first type mistake refers to a situation where the scheme fails to reach the target population. Cornia and Stewart describe this as an F-mistake indicating a failure in the prime objective of the intervention. The second type mistake refers to a situation where intervention reaches to the non-target population. This they called as E-mistake indicating excessive coverage. The measurement of the two errors of targeting is important to understand whether and to what extent the benefits of TPDS are reaching the target group.

Using various secondary sources, we showed that there are wider inter-state differences in the total number of card holdings and the total existing number of households. In many states, the total number of cards issued exceeded the number of total existing families indicating incidences of excess cards issued. The number of such excess cards was very high, more than one crore in Uttar Pradesh, 24 lakh in Rajasthan, more than 10 lakh in Madhya Pradesh and Haryana. At the all India level, the total number of excess cards issued was more than 2 crore. On the other hand, in a few states, the number of cards issued were less than the existing number of families and therefore, some families were unindentified. It is not clear from the available data that these families belonged to which particular category. The number of such families who were not provided with any card, were maximum in Bihar, followed by Jharkhand and West Bengal. The total number of such families at all India aggregated at 1.2 crore.

Using the E and F criterion as discussed above, we calculated identification errors for all the states and for all India using data from the secondary sources. At the aggregate level, excessive targeting error (E) was much higher than the failure of targeting the poor (F) error. The F-mistake was highest in Goa and Uttaranchal where the TPDS failed in targeting up to 30 per cent. Among our selected states, F-mistake was observed only in Bihar while the problem was not as severe in that state also. The inclusion of non-poor in the subsidised food was a much more severe problem and the incidence was found occurring in almost all the states. Excessive coverage was more than 100 per cent in Tamil Nadu, 75 per cent in Andhra Pradesh and 51 per cent in Karnataka. It is to be mentioned here that in Tamil Nadu, all the families were issued BPL (or AAY) card as no categorisation was done on the basis of BPL and APL. Among our selected states, E-mistake was found up to 28 per cent in Mizoram, 19 per cent in Assam, 16 per cent in Chhattisgarh and 6 per cent in Uttar Pradesh. At the all India level, exclusion mistake was up to 25 per cent as number of BPL cards issued were 9.7 crore in comparison to only 5.8 crore existing families.

Authenticity of Identification and Diversion of PDS Food

We looked into the distribution of observed income and expenditure per capita of our selected households and tried to authenticate their identification in terms of holding AAY, BPL and APL cards. We compared the per capita income and expenditure of the selected AAY, BPL and APL households with the Planning Commission's cut-off income to validate whether the card they held was true or false. In other words, if we re-designate the households as below or above poverty following the Planning Commission cut-off, then how many households would stand faulty in their present category? Looking at the extent of incidence of E and F-mistakes among our selected households, it was clearly evident from the data that the percentage of E-mistake (inclusion error) was much higher than F-mistake (exclusion error) as was also seen in the case of secondary data. The average income and expenditure criterion indicated that inclusion error (E-mistake) was highest around 75 per cent in Mizoram, 50 to 60 per cent in Assam, around 50 per cent in Rajasthan and Bihar, around 35 per cent in Chhattisgarh and 20 to 30 per cent in Uttar Pradesh. The more serious problem was the wrong identification of AAY households who should have been issued an APL card instead. Their proportion was around 70 per cent in the northeastern states and 30-35 per cent in the rest of the four selected states. Measuring the extent of exclusion error (F-mistake), the data indicated that the phenomenon of poor households being not issued a below poverty card was minimum in the northeastern states, less than 15 per cent, followed by Uttar Pradesh, Bihar, Chhattisgarh and Rajasthan.

In the incidence of mistargeting, it is implicit that food was being diverted to the non-poor due to identification problems. Even though food is being distributed and a very high percentage of households were found getting cereals in majority of states, it was actually being diverted to non-target population as has been shown by the extent of occurrence of E and F-mistake among our selected sample. However, in addition to such diversions, there was some proportion of food that was not being actually distributed among any of the households but it was shown in the state records as uplifted. Therefore, we can presume that food grains not distributed but withdrawn from the state accounts were being diverted to the black market or in the open market or may be distributed among the non-poor people at a higher price.

We tried to measure the extent of diversion of wheat and rice in our selected states. For arriving at the state level figures, we assumed that the percentage of households drawing food and the amount of wheat and rice drawn by them in our sample prevailed across the whole state. With these assumptions, we calculated the amount of diversion of rice and wheat in the selected states. It was shown by the data that in the case of AAY cardholders, PDS food was being distributed quite satisfactorily, except in the two states, namely Bihar and Mizoram. The magnitude of diversion was estimated up to 41 per cent for wheat in Bihar and 36 per cent for rice in Mizoram. In the case of BPL, almost all states had the incidence of diversion, except Rajasthan. The diversion was highest in Assam and Mizoram in the case of rice, and Bihar and Chhattisgarh in wheat. In all these cases, diversion was up to 40 per cent of total off-take. Among above poverty households, the whole amount of wheat uplifted was diverted in the two northeastern states of Assam and Mizoram. Even in the case of rice, more than 80 per cent uplifted amount was not distributed among the beneficiaries in these two states. In the other four states, diversion of food for APL households was found only in Chhattisgarh. Rajasthan was the only state where it was observed that the whole amount of uplifted food was distributed among the beneficiaries in all the three cases of AAY, BPL and APL. Thus, diversion of food for the AAY category was found in the case of Bihar and Mizoram and for BPL, in the two northeastern states and in Bihar and Chhattisgarh. The distribution of grains was found more satisfactory in the case of Rajasthan and Uttar Pradesh. Nonetheless, gross violations were observed in the identification of target groups and these were very high in all the states across the board as indicated by the exclusion and inclusion errors.

Functioning of the Fair Price Shops

We tried to assess the functioning of fair price shops, their system of monitoring and transparency through a separate questionnaire designed especially for the fair price shop owners. The questions were mostly in qualitative nature and replies were coded. A brief summary of findings is given here. The fair price shop owners selected for the field survey were mostly literate. The shop they were running to sell PDS grains was exclusively for that purpose in most of the cases. The ownership status was individual ownership in Mizoram, Bihar, Rajasthan and Assam among overwhelming majority of shops while in Chhattisgarh and Uttar Pradesh, the ownership status was mixed. The shops in all the cases were located in a periphery of around 5 to 20 kilometres from the godown from where the grains were being lifted. A majority of the shopkeepers were keeping their shop opened to supply grains for more than 15 days and shop was opened the whole day in majority of cases for the convenience of the beneficiaries.

Around 70 per cent of owners replied no to the question whether during the last year there were any instances when the FPS had lifted less than the allocated quota from the godown. The other 30 per cent said that their lifted quota was less than the allotted quota up to 5 times during the last year. The reasons pointed out for not lifting the quota were less availability at godown, insufficient opening stock, poor demand and lack of money with the shop owners. Against the phenomenon of lifting less than allotted quota from godown, fair price shops were also left with undistributed grains in many instances. Around 20 to 40 per cent of the interviewed shop owners accepted that sometimes entitlement was not lifted by some of the beneficiaries. To our question, how they were disposing off the unlifted stock, around 15 to 20 per cent of them replied that they adjusted it in the next month supply, while a very few admitted that they distributed more grains to the beneficiaries while no one said that they sold such grains in the open market.

We propounded some questions related to transparency to the FPS owners. To the question whether the FPS shop owners kept records of their transactions, more than 80 per cent of the interviewed shop owners answered yes. On the type of records maintained, more than 60 per cent were of the opinion that they kept all the details of stocks handled as well as lifting details from the godown and distribution of grains among the beneficiaries by the number of cards and the total grains distributed of a particular commodity. A majority of the shop owners pointed out that they were displaying this information on the notice board for the public knowledge, except Mizoram, where most of the interviewed shop owners denied displaying any such records on the notice board. On the question of transparency, a majority of the shop owners in all the states indicated that they had displayed the list of beneficiaries outside the shop for the public knowledge. They also opined that along with the list of beneficiaries, the amount of entitlement in each case and the scale of issues and the retail prices at which food was being distributed were also displayed. However, to the question whether they displayed the name and addresses of the authority for redressal of consumers' grievances, a majority of them either did not reply to this question or they said no. Similarly, on cross checking from the households, the replies of the shop owners were not found consistent and there were two opposite views on many of the above questions.

For the monitoring of the FPS functioning, there were multiple authorities that were supposed to check the functioning of the FPS and also could check the samples of grain being sold to the beneficiaries. Such authority was vested either with the *gram panchayat*, or its designated committee, or vigilance committee from the block/district officials or the government officials from the Civil Supplies Department. Among our selected shop owners, the distribution was quite equal for the *gram panchayat*, the district officials and the Civil Supplies Department officials, as the designated authority who were inspecting their shops. A few shop owners also replied that their shops were not being monitored by any authority. To the question, what was the frequency of such inspection, a majority of the shop keepers replied, at least once in a month's time period while 10 per cent of the selected owners also replied that either their shop was not inspected last year or it was never inspected at all by any authority.

It is common opinion that grains are distributed once in a month through fair price shops. However among our selected FPS, some of the shop owners pointed out that they are distributing grains weekly and fortnightly. The percentage of such shop owners was around 10 to 15 per cent in Mizoram, Chhattisgarh, Uttar Pradesh and Rajasthan. A majority of shop owners indicated that the frequency of grain distribution was monthly. In Bihar and Mizoram, a large number of shop owners replied that the distribution of grains among the beneficiaries depended on when the FPS received its stipulated quota from the godown. To an another question of how frequently the shop runs stock-out situation, majority of FPS owners indicated that they run out of stock once or twice (less than five times) only, in a year.

The number of households catered each month varied in almost all the shops. The variation in number of households catered despite the number of ration cards registered with the shop being fixed, indicates the irregular nature of supply issued from the FPS on monthly basis. The range of beneficiaries catered was quite high and it varied from less than a 100 to more than 6000. The average number of households catered during the six months of survey period was lowest in Assam 553, followed by Rajasthan 1144, Mizoram 1471, Bihar 1811, Uttar Pradesh 2575 and Chhattisgarh 4523. Last and the least, we tried to re-check the prices at which the food grains were being supplied to the households from FPS. We collected the retail prices at which food was being sold to the beneficiaries from the fair price shop owners during our survey period. Almost all fair price shop owners in all the states, stated that they were supplying wheat at the rate of Rs. 2 per kg and rice at Rs. 3 per kg to the AAY households. However, the mean price paid by the households was higher, indicating more than stipulated prices being charged from a few households for both wheat as well as rice.

8.3 Policy Suggestions

The evaluation findings for the six selected states about the efficiency of the PDS system are mixed ones. On the one hand, the delivery of food to the poor was found quite regular in majority of the selected states. For instance, among the poorest of the poor households, around 90 per cent or more of such households received their cereal entitlement quite regularly during the six months of survey period, except the case of Bihar and Assam. Similarly, among the other poor households (BPL), the delivery of food was above 80 per cent in Rajasthan, Chhattisgarh, Uttar Pradesh and Mizroam. On the other hand, deep probing into the subject brought forward the gross idiosyncrasies hidden behind the bright picture. The gross irregularities that came into view are highlighted below:

- *Identification Errors:* Although food was being distributed among the entitled beneficiaries, the entitlement itself was wrongly identified. We compared the observed income and expenditure of the AAY and BPL households with the Planning Commission's definition of poverty and observed a large amount of inclusion and exclusion errors. Exclusion error was up to the extent of 75 per cent in Mizoram, more than 50 per cent in Assam, Rajasthan and Bihar. So, in the circumstances even if food was being distributed, in actual terms it was a case of diversion. The basic criterion for the identification of AAY was that it should be meant for those people who are not able to have two square meals a day. In our questionnaire we posed this question to all our households (did they have days without two square meals per day in a month during the last one year?). The responses of the households are summarised in Table 8.1. It is clear from the results that on an average less than 5 per cent AAY households answered yes to the above question. Similarly, we have summarised the amount of assets held by our selected households in Table 8.2. The data clearly indicates that the average assets holding for AAY households was very high, especially in the case of Rajasthan, Uttar Pradesh and Chhattisgarh.
- *Excess Cards Issued and Unidentified Families:* By using secondary sources, we calculated the number of excess card as well as the families unidentified across various states. Excessive coverage was more than 100 per cent in Tamil Nadu, 75 per cent in Andhra Pradesh and 51 per cent in Karnataka. At the all India level, a total number of 9.7 crore BPL cards were issued whereas only 5.8 crore families existed below poverty.
- *Diversion of PDS Food:* Using our observations from the field, we calculated the total amount of diversion of food in our selected states. The diversion was found to be more than 40 per cent of off-take of wheat for the AAY in Bihar and 36 per cent of rice in Mizoram during the year 2005-06. The diversion of the BPL food was even more, around 45 per cent in Assam, 37 per cent in Mizoram (both rice) and 47 per cent in Bihar and 42 per cent in Chhattisgarh (both wheat) during that period. If we also keep into account the diversion that is taking place due to wrong identification, then the figures will turn much higher.
- *Viability of the FPS:* Although majority of the households paid the stipulated prices, in few cases FPS passed on the transportation cost to the consumers. For FPS, it was not possible to run their business if they would bear the transportation cost. To our question, an overwhelming majority of the FPS replied that they have to pick up the grains from the civil supply godowns at their own cost and nobody reimbursed them for the transportation cost. In order to make a recovery, they were forced to pass on the transportation cost to the consumers.
- *No System of Inspection of Entitlement:* The entitlement decision for the AAY and BPL card was by and large left to the local administration or to the *gram panchayats*. Such an authority (whoever it was vested with) was completely unquestionable. Moreover, there seems to be no monitoring of the system whether a person is issued a wrong or a right card.

Table 8.1 Percentage of the Population who Remained without Two Square Meals a Day in a Month

	Month 1	Month 2	Month 3	Month 4	Month 5	Month 6
			AAY			
Rajasthan	8.99	6.67	5.36	6.48	3.67	1.83
Bihar	18.88	2.91	1.14	2.70	1.60	1.63
UP	3.96	-	-	-	1.71	-
Chhattisgarh	5.69	2.50	1.67	0.55	0.57	-
Assam	0.53	0.56	-	-	-	-
Mizoram	1.21	-	-	-	-	0.62
			BPL			
Rajasthan	4.36	3.62	2.30	2.84	0.87	-
Bihar	13.00	1.33	1.41	2.19	0.49	0.33
UP	0.69	0.26	-	0.32	-	-
Chhattisgarh	4.15	2.14	1.36	0.78	0.80	-
Assam	1.49	0.34	0.18		-	-
Mizoram	0.20	-	-	0.18	-	-
			APL			
Rajasthan	2.40	0.63	0.77	0.77	-	-
Bihar	1.65	0.59	-	-	-	-
UP	0.51	-	-	-	-	-
Chhattisgarh	2.11	0.62	0.62	0.62	0.61	-
Assam	0.99	-	-	-	-	-
Mizoram	-	-	-	0.4	-	-

These issues need to be corrected if the functioning of the PDS system is to be improved. The right identification of the beneficiary is the first step in that direction. The whole discussion raises the question whether it is right methodology to identify poor families on the basis of income/expenditure criterion. Identifying sources of income at the household level and measuring them with precision on such a large scale are fraught with many problems (Planning Commission, 2005). Our study has found a large number of inclusion and exclusion errors due to imperfect information, arbitrariness and interference by the vested interests in the identification of BPL and AAY entitlement. There is a serious need to devise an appropriate criterion for the identification of BPL households. Attempt can be made to make the PDS system self-targeted, e.g., linking it with the employment guarantee programmes whereby wage rate is kept at such a level that only the poor people participate, thereby making the system self-targeted.

However, devising some alternate criterion as cut-off income/expenditure or some other method for the identification of poor is not going to be an easy task. A voice is raised from some quarters in favour of replacing the procurement and distribution system by food stamps whereby subsidy is transferred to the poor by means of stamps rather than handling the huge amount of food stocks. However, the international experience suggests the system of food stamps is also wrought with huge amount of inclusion and exclusion errors. As in our evaluation of the system, we have seen that the major drawback of the PDS system at present is not that of distribution (of food) but that of wrong identification. Even if we switch to the system of food stamp, the problem of wrong identification is going to increase rather than decrease. Another major problem that food stamps programme might have to face is the misuse of food stamps whereby poor people use stamps to buy commodities other than food or resell stamps to better-off people in lure of money.

Given the ground reality, it would not be possible to improve the PDS system unless the consumer, especially the poorest ones are made aware of their rights. The whole problem of identification error arises because of lack of information/unawareness of the poor about the fixation criteria for the AAY or BPL or any other welfare schemes for that matter. The people in the lower strata are by and large, unaware of the method that is being followed in fixing up the entitlement for holding an AAY, BPL or

APL card. The following steps might help in bringing more awareness among the poor and improving the functioning of the PDS system overall, in meeting the targets:

Table 8.2 Assets Holdings (Rs. Per Household)

	Rajasthan	Bihar	Uttar Pradesh	Chhattisgarh	Assam	Mizoram
			AAY			
Land	99061	10085	23358	53511	22297	8298
House property	26356	16271	17718	15462	4587	2000
Livestock	4497	1597	1079	4848	232	42
Agricultural implements	-	226	45	3000	307	-
Consumer assets	4599	370	1338	2697	2067	1952
Business assets	5000	57	162	500	-	30
Ornaments	9673	1393	1110	1502	1196	73
Utensils	913	273	705	551	471	245
Others	750	33	23	200	60	35
Total	150849	30305	45538	82271	31217	12675
			BPL			
Land	83628	15838	28875	115806	25999	16438
House property	35598	26929	22961	27258	6222	7561
Livestock	93936	1676	1168	5239	266	455
Agricultural implements	15500	48	102	32293	396	110
Consumer assets	4054	392	1275	3714	4143	2563
Business assets	12538	125	1103	5273	82	23
Ornaments	12634	1491	1150	2344	2793	97
Utensils	1339	367	720	689	654	378
Others	2972	80	19	850	117	220
Total	262199	46946	57373	193466	40672	27845
			APL			
Land	188367	317719	87984	211883	48932	21539
House property	112969	147312	53518	60935	26351	18263
Livestock	20938	5680	3177	8864	348	161
Agricultural implements	225000	24856	2551	26618	482	1479
Consumer assets	19826	12648	3908	10395	8650	4738
Business assets	48944	4885	2692	117817	-	8
Ornaments	24562	7725	6550	8611	5659	422
Utensils	2886	1463	1185	2078	1868	415
Others	3763	108	4	166667	389	1463
Total	647255	522396	161569	613866	92679	48488

Display the Criterion Followed in Fixing Up the Entitlement

It should be made mandatory on the part of the *gram panchayat*/civil supply authorities to display the main criterion followed for issuing a BPL or AAY card. The information should be written in the local language and it should be displayed on the notice board at the *panchayat* office as well as on all other important places, like school, primary health care centre, *choupal*, etc. It should also be made mandatory on the part of the *panchayat* to propagate the criterion among the villagers through a campaign or mass information system usually used for disseminating important information among the villagers.

Display the Entitled Quantity and Price for AAY and BPL Households

It should be made mandatory for the *panchayat* to educate people about the entitlement of grains fixed for the BPL and AAY households as well as the stipulated price. The mass information system should be used to keep the villagers informed and updated about the entitlement and price of grains as well as the grains received from the godown by FPS and timing of distribution of grains among the beneficiaries. This can also be done with the help of primary and secondary schools running within the village by educating the kids about the criterion followed in issuing cards and entitlement and price of grains for the AAY and BPL households. There is a need to include this within the curriculum of the schools. The medium of mass awareness, e.g., local language newspapers, regional radio and television stations can also be used for spreading general awareness about the criterion and the entitlement among the public.

Display the Criterion and Entitlement on the FPS and on the Ration Card

It would also help to educate the villagers to a great extent if the list of beneficiaries (AAY and BPL cardholders) is displayed on a notice board outside each and every fair price shop. In addition to beneficiary list, the information related to entitlement for each category, price of grains, the total amount of stock received from godown and distributed among the beneficiaries should be displayed in local language on daily basis. The criterion as well as entitlement and price information should also be printed on the back of the ration card. The same was being practiced in Barabanki in Uttar Pradesh and it was quite effective in making the beneficiaries informed about the entitlement. For the purpose of demonstration, a specimen copy of this information is given below.

Make the Monitoring Compulsory and Punish the Culprit including the Panchayats

It is essential to monitor the process of identification of card holding. At present, identification is done by the district/block supply officers on the recommendations of the concerned *panchayat* or local bodies in the village and urban areas, respectively. However, this power of identification is indisposed in most of the cases. There is no authority that cross checks the identification. In the given circumstances, a large number of E and F-mistakes are found as is confirmed by the results of this study. Even if the irregularities are observed at some level, there is no provision for any action against the authorities that have done wrong identification either deliberately or due to lack of proper information. Nonetheless, it becomes compulsory to make the system more full proof by making the provision of bringing the concerned officials as well as that of the *panchayat* or local bodies to book if such irregularities come into picture. It would be more appropriate if there are multiple authorities cross checking the identification.

Open a Grievance Cell for the Poor

In some cases, it has been observed that there is a nexus between the FPS owner, civil supplies inspector and the *sarpanch* in the village. There is a dire need to break this nexus. This can be done by taking various actions like, frequent monitoring of the FPS; opening up one grievance cell in every village or in a group of villages where people can lodge their complaints related to PDS; circulation of clear rules and regulations related to identification, entitlement, prices and quality norms and its mass publicity among the public; evaluation of PDS functioning in the village by a peer group within the village, including the headmaster/school teachers, doctor at the community health centre and other more aware members that may include some of the members from the *panchayat*, excluding the *sarpanch*.

Make the FPS more Viable by Giving them Higher Margin

In many cases it was observed that fair price shops were neither being provided with any transportation facility nor their transportation cost from godown to the fair price shop was being refunded. By and large, the fair price shop owners were of the opinion that if they did not pass on the transportation cost to the consumers, they would end up bearing huge losses. In many other cases, lower net margin also led the fair price shop owners to indulge in unfair means and black marketing. In order to improve efficiency and remove corruption in the system, it becomes compulsory to provide incentives to the FPS by giving them better margin between their purchase and sale price.

Computerisation of Records for Ccross Checking

All business at fair price shops and supply godowns was done on manual basis. In such a system, it becomes very difficult to cross check the records to maintain the transparency in the system. In the long run, it is highly desirable to computerise the whole system and prepare a network whereby all FPS and civil supply godowns should be connected online. This will bring more efficiency and transparency in the system.

Multi-tier Checking of the Quality of Grains Supplied

The grains supplied from godown to the FPS and ultimately to the consumers should be inspected at multi stages. A large number of households surveyed pointed out defects in the quality of grains supplied through fair price shops. In some of the cases even households were not buying their entitlements because of poor quality of the grains supplied. A clue can be taken from the three-tier inspection of the grains at the FPS by the supply inspector, village *panchayat* development officer and by the *gram panchayat,* currently being done in Lucknow district in Uttar Pradesh. The specimen copy of the format is given below.

Strengthening the Role of NGOs in Combating Corruption

NGOs can play a significant role in ensuring that FPS owners do not indulge in diverting PDS food to the open market or in black marketing. There are many examples whereby NGOs using Right to Information Act helped poor people in obtaining their entitled quantity at the stipulated price. Other means of awareness should also be used for spreading information among the poor people. Ignorance has been one of the major causes of diversion. More awareness regarding entitlements, prices stipulated by the Government for rice and wheat can be spread through street plays and documentary movies. These can be based on the real life instances. Also, information such as the prices stipulated by the Government must be there on the ration card so that each person can ensure that he/she is not being cheated.

मो. सलमान प्रारुप संख्या ६ ग्राम पौन्ड

वाल पैन्टिंग का प्रारुप

क्र. सं.	योजना का नाम		कार्ड सं.	कोटेदार का मासिक कोटा (कु.में)	प्रतिकार्ड मात्रा (कि.ग्रा.में)	दर रु. में	कुल धनराशि
१.	बी पी एल योजना (सफेद कार्ड)	गेहूँ	270	27.00 कु.	10 किग्रा.	4.65	46.50
		चावल	270	67.50 "	25 "	6.15	153.75
२.	अन्त्योदय योजना (लाल कार्ड)	गेहूँ	168	16.80 "	10 "	2.00	20.00
		चावल	168	42.00 "	25 "	3.00	75.00
3.	अन्नपूर्णा योजना (हरा कार्ड)	गेहूँ	12	1.20 "	10 "	निशुल्क	00.00
4.	ए.पी.एल. योजना (पीला कार्ड)		414				
5.	मिट्टी तेल		852	ली.22.00/ ड्रम 11	3 लीटर	10.10	30.30
6.	चीनी		438	15 कुन्टल	700 ग्रा. प्रति यूनिट	13.50	9.45

नोट:- ए.पी.एल. राशन कार्ड पर मिट्टी तेल, बी.पी.एल. व अन्त्योदय कार्ड पर खाद्यान्न, चीनी, मिट्टी तेल तथा अन्नपूर्णा कार्ड पर १० कि. खाद्यान्न निशुल्क उपलब्ध होगा।

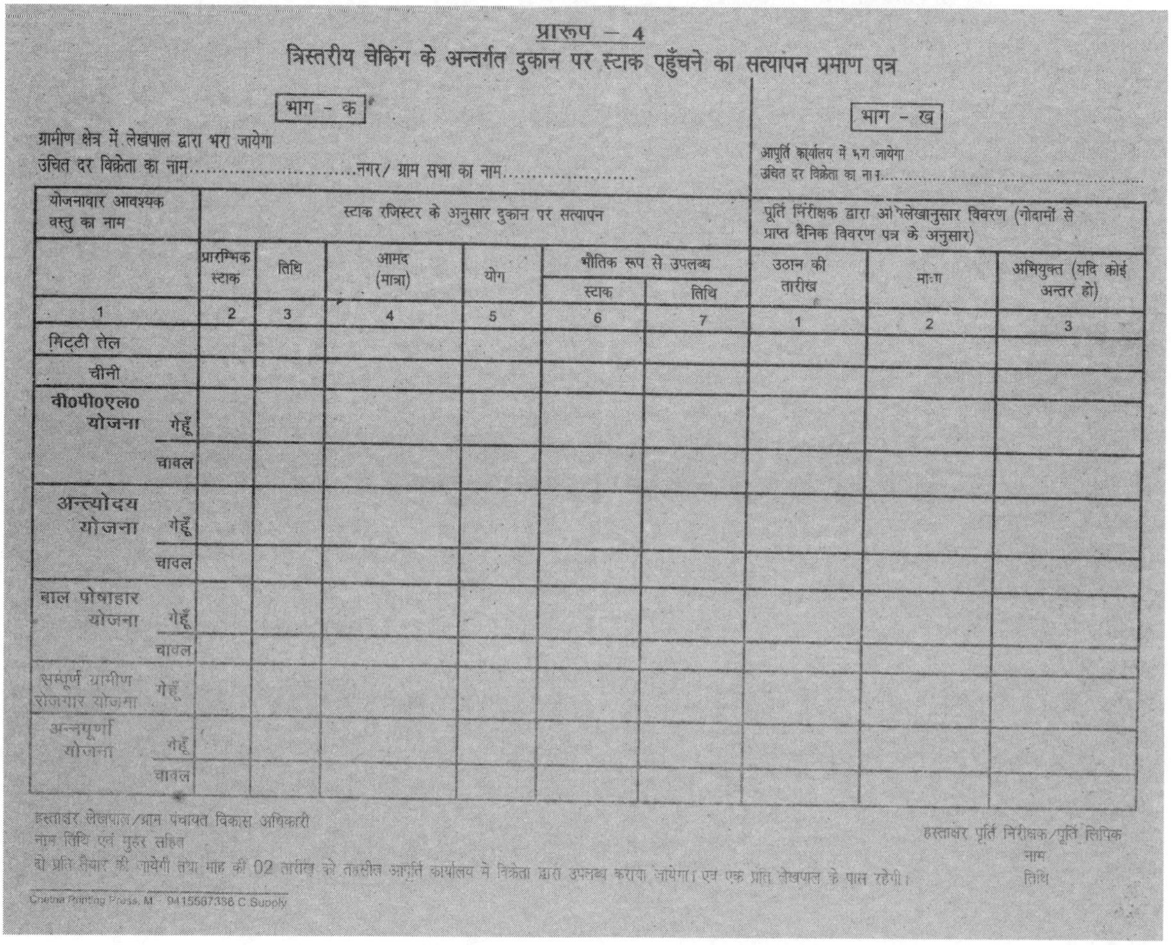

प्रारूप – 4

त्रिस्तरीय चेकिंग के अन्तर्गत दुकान पर स्टाक पहुँचने का सत्यापन प्रमाण पत्र

भाग - क

ग्रामीण क्षेत्र में लेखपाल द्वारा भरा जायेगा

उचित दर विक्रेता का नाम............................नगर/ ग्राम सभा का नाम......................

भाग - ख

आपूर्ति कार्यालय में भरा जायेगा

उचित दर विक्रेता का नाम............................

योजनावार आवश्यक वस्तु का नाम	स्टाक रजिस्टर के अनुसार दुकान पर सत्यापन						पूर्ति निरीक्षक द्वारा अभिलेखानुसार विवरण (गोदामों से प्राप्त दैनिक विवरण पत्र के अनुसार)		
	प्रारम्भिक स्टाक	तिथि	आमद (मात्रा)	योग	भौतिक रूप से उपलब्ध		उठान की तारीख	मात्रा	अभियुक्त (यदि कोई अन्तर हो)
					स्टाक	तिथि			
1	2	3	4	5	6	7	1	2	3
मिट्टी तेल									
चीनी									
बी0पी0एल0 योजना गेहूँ									
चावल									
अन्त्योदय योजना गेहूँ									
चावल									
बाल पोषाहार योजना गेहूँ									
चावल									
सम्पूर्ण ग्रामीण रोजगार योजना गेहूँ									
अन्नपूर्णा योजना गेहूँ									
चावल									

हस्ताक्षर लेखपाल/ग्राम पंचायत विकास अधिकारी

नाम तिथि एवं मुहर सहित

हस्ताक्षर पूर्ति निरीक्षक/पूर्ति लिपिक

नाम

तिथि

दो प्रति तैयार की जायेगी तथा माह की 02 तारीख को तहसील आपूर्ति कार्यालय में विक्रेता द्वारा उपलब्ध कराया जायेगा। एवं एक प्रति लेखपाल के पास रहेगी।

Chetna Printing Press, M - 9415567356 C Supply

References

Alderman, H. and C. Paxson (1994). "Do the Poor Insure?: A Synthesis of the Literature on Risk and Consumption in Developing Countries", in E. Bacha (ed.), *Economics in a Changing World*, Vol. 4. Proceedings of the 10th World Congress of the International Economic Association, Moscow, *Development, Trade and the Environment*, IEA Conference Volume No. 110. New York: St. Martin's Press; London: Macmilan Press in association with the International Economic Association.

———. (1992). "Do the Poor Insure?: A Synthesis of the Literature on Risk and Consumption in Developing Countries", Policy Research, *Working Paper* No.108. Washington D.C.: The World Bank.

Cummings, Jr., R.W. (1967). *Pricing Efficiency in Indian Wheat Market*. New Delhi. Impex India.

Cornia G.A. and Frances Stewart (1993). "Two Errors of Targeting", in M. Lipton and J. van der Gaag (eds.), *Including the Poor.* Washington DC.: World Bank.

Deaton, A., (1990). "On Risk, Insurance, Intra Village Consumption Smoothing, Research Program in Development Studies". Unpublished Manuscript. Princeton University.

———. (1992), "Saving and Income Smoothing in Cote d'Ivoire". *Mimeo*. Princeton University.

Delgado *et al.* (1999). "Livestock to 2020: The Next Food Revolution", Food, Agriculture and The Environment *Discussion Paper* 28, International Food Policy Research Institute, Washington D.C., U.S.A.

Dev, Mahendra S. and M.H. Suryanarayana (1992). "Is PDS Urban Biased and Pro-Rich?: An Evaluation", *Economic and Political Weekly* XXVI(41).

Dutta, Bhaskar and Bharat Ramaswami (2001). "Targeting and Efficiency in the Public Distribution System: Case of Andhra Pradesh and Maharashtra", *Economic and Political Weekly*, May 5.

Fafchamps, M. (1992). "Solidarity Networks in Pre Industrial Societies: Rational Peasants With a Moral Economy", *Economic Development and Cultural Change* 41: 147-76.

Grimard, F. (1997). "Household Consumption Smoothing Through Ethnic Ties: Evidence from Cote d'Ivoire", *Journal of Development Economics* 41: 391-422.

Grosh, M.E. (1992). "The Jamaican Food Stamps Program: A Case Study in Targeting", *Food Policy* 17(1): 23-40.

Gulati, I.S. and T.N. Krishnan (1975). "Public Distribution and Procurement of Foodgrains: A Proposal", *Economic and Political Weekly* 10, May 24.

Govt. of India (1943). *Famine Commission Report on Bengal.*

Goswami, Urmi A. (2008). "Biharis Get Work at Home, Bashers Realise Their Worth", *The Economic Times*, pp.6-17, 17 June.

Houthakar, H.S. (1976). "Do We Need A National Food Policy", *American Journal of Agricultural Economics* 54, February.

Howes, Stephen and S. Jha (1992). "Urban Bias in the Public Distribution System", *Economic and Political Weekly* XXVII, May 9.

http://www.undp.org.in/index.php?option=com_content&task=view&id=125&Itemid=83

http://www.reliefweb.int/library/documents/2004/undp-india

Jha, Abhay Mohan (2008). "English Makes Inroads in Bihar Villages", *NDTV.com*, 8 March.

Jalan, J. and M. Ravallion (1999). "Are the Poor Less Well Insured?: Evidence on Vulnerability to Income Risk in Rural China", *Journal of Development Economics* 58: 61-81.

Jha, L.K. (1976). *Shortages and High Prices: The Way Out*. New Delhi: The Indian Book Company.

Jha, S. (1991). *Consumer Subsidies in India: Is Targeting Effective*. Bombay: Indira Gandhi Institute of Development Studies.

Jha, R., K.V., B. Murthy, H.K. Nagarajan and Ashok K. Seth (1999). "Real Consumption Levels and Public Distribution System in India", *Economic and Political Weekly*, April 10.

Jha, Srinivasan and P. V. Srinivasan (2001). "Taking the PDS to the Poor: Directions for Further Reform", *Economic and Political Weekly*, September 29.

Johnston, B.F. (1953). *Japanese Food Management in World War II*. California: Stanford University Press.

Kaul, Abhishek (2003). *The Economic Strangulation of Bihar*. New Delhi: Centre for Policy Alternatives.

Lele, Uma J. (1971). *Foodgrains Marketing In India: Private Performance and Public Policy.* Corness University Prsss.

Mace, B.J. (1991). "Full Insurance in the Presence of Aggregate Uncertainty", *Journal of Political Economy* 99(5): 928-56.

Maitra, P. (1998). "Consumption Smoothing in Rural Punjab in the Green Revolution Years", *Indian Economic Review* 33(2): 185-96.

———. (2003). "Are the Poor More Vulnerable to Income Shocks? An Analysis of Consumption Insurance in Rural India", in Raghbendra Jha (ed.), *Indian Economic Reforms*. New York: Palgrave, Macmillan.

Mateus, A. (1983). "Targeting Food Subsidies for the Needy: The Use of Cost—Benefit Analysis and Institutional Design", *World Bank Staff Working Paper* 617. Washington DC: World Bank.

Mellor, J.W. (1966). *The Economics of Agricultural Development.* Bombay: Vora and Company.

Meenakshi, J.V. and Brinda Vishwanathan (2003). "Calorie Deprivation in Rural India, 1983-1999/00", *Economic and Political Weekly* 38(4): 369-75, January 25.

Mishra, Bhagabat (1985). *Economics of Public Distribution System in Foodgrains.* New Delhi: Ashish Publishing House.

Mooij, Jos (2001). "Food and Power in Bihar and Jharkhand: PDS and Its Functioning", *Economic and Political Weekly,* August 25.

Morduch, J. (1995). "Income Smoothing and Consumption Smoothing", *Journal of Economic Perspectives* 9(3): 103-14.

———. (1990). "Consumption Smoothing Across Space: Testing for Village Level Responses to Risk". Unpublished Manuscript. Harvard University.

Murty, K.N. (1999). "Decomposition of Changes in Cereals Demand into its Components in Semi-Arid Tropical Area", Paper presented at the 35th *Indian Econometrics Society Meeting* held at the Department of Economics, University of Rajasthan, Jaipur, March 11-13.

Nasurudeen *et al.* (2006). "The Dynamics and Inequality of Nutrient Consumption in India", *Indian Journal of Agricultural Economics.*

NSSO (2004-05). *Level and Pattern of Consumer Expenditure.* National Sample Survey Organisation, Government of India, December, Report No. 508.

———. (1993-94). *Consumption of Some Important Commodities in India.* National Sample Survey Organisation, Government of India, March, Report No. 404.

———. (1999-2000). *Consumption of Some Important Commodities in India.* National Sample Survey Organisation, Government of India, July, Report No. 461.

ORG (2005). *Evaluation Study of Targeted Public Distribution System and Antodaya Anna Yojana.* New Delhi: ORG Centre for Social Research.

Patnaik, Utsa (2004). "The Republic of Hunger", *Social Scientist* 32(9-10), September-October.

———. (2003). "Food Stocks and Hunger: Causes of Agrarian Distress", *Social Scientist* 32(7-8), July-August.

———. (2001). "Concentration of Regional Food Output and the PDS", *People's Democracy* 25(23), June.

Parikh, Kirit S. (1994). "Who Gets How Much from PDS: How Effectively Does it Reach the Poor", *Sarvekshna* XVII(3), January-March.

Pigou, A.C. (1952). *The Economics of Welfare.* 4th Edition. London: Macmillan and Comp.

Pinstrup, (1991). "Targeted Nutrition Interventions", *Food and Nutrition Bulletin* 13(3): 161-169.

Planning Commission (2005). *Performance Evaluation of Targeted Public Distribution System (TPDS).* New Delhi: Programme Evaluation Organisation, Planning Commission, Government of India.

Platteau, J.P. (1991). "Traditional System of Social Security and Hunger insurance: Some Lessons from the Evidence Pertaining to Third World Village Societies", in E. Ahmad, J. Dreze, A.K. Sen (eds.), *Social Security in Developing Countries.* Oxford: Oxford University Press.

Radhakrishna R., and K. Subbarao (1997). "India's Public Distribution System: A National and International Perspective", *World Bank Discussion Paper* No. 380. Washington D.C.: World Bank.

Radhakrishna, R. and Kirit S. Parikh (2002). *India Development Report.* Oxford University Press.

Radhakrishna, R. and C. Ravi (1991). *Food Demand Projection For India.* Hyderabad: Centre For Economic and Social Studies.

Ray, R. (2005). *Analysis of Changes in Food Consumption and their Implications for Food Security and Undernourishment: The Indian Experience in the 1990s,* University of Tasmania.

Ray, R. and G. Lancaster (2005). "On Setting the Poverty Line Based on Estimated Nutrient Prices: Condition of Socially Disadvantaged Groups during the Reform Period", *Economic and Political Weekly* 40(1): 46-56, January 1-7.

Rosenzweig, M.R. (1988). "Risk, Implicit Contracts and the Family in Rural Areas of Low-Income Countries", *The Economic Journal* 98: 1148-1170.

Rosenzweig, M.R. and O. Stark (1989). "Consumption Smoothing, Migration and Marriage: Evidence from Rural India", *Journal of Political Economy* 97(4): 905.27.

Saran, Ram (1975). "Management of Mass Consumption Goods Distribution With Special Reference to Foodgrains", *Agricultural Situation in India* 20, January.

Sen, A. and Himanshu (2004). "Poverty and Inequality in India", *Economic and Political Weekly* 39: 4247-4263, September 18-24.

Shankar, Kripa (2004). "How Efficient is TPDS in Tribal Areas?", *Economic and Political Weekly,* May 22.

Sharma, Supriya and Abhay Mohan Jha (2008). "Bihar Witnesses a Quiet Transformation", *NDTV.com,* 15 July.

Shenoy, B.R. (1968). *Indian Economic Policy.* Bombay: Popular Prakashan.

———. (1974). *PL 480 Aid and India's Food Problem.* New Delhi: Affiliate-East West Press.

Srivastava, Ravi (2001). "Public Distribution System in Rural Uttar Pradesh", in M.D. Asthana and Pedro Medrano (eds.), *Proceedings of National Consultation on "Towards Hunger Free India: Agenda and Imperatives".* Manohar Publications.

Suryanarayana, G. (1985). *Public Distribution in India.* Allahabad: Chugh Publications.

The Economist (2008). "A Special Report on India: Ruled by Lakshmi", *The Economist,* 11 December.

Townsend, R.M. (1994). "Risk and Insurance in Village India", *Econometrica* 62(3): 539-91.

———. (1995). "Consumption Insurance: An Evaluation of Risk Bearing Systems in Low Income Countries", *Journal of Economic Perspectives* 9(3): 83-102.

Tyagi, D.S (1990). *Managing India's Food Economy: Problems and Alternatives.* New Delhi: Sage Publications.

Udry, C. (1994). "Risk, Insurance and Default in a Rural Credit Market: An Empirical Investigation in Northern Nigeria", Unpublished Manuscript. Northwestern University.

World Bank (2008). *Bihar - Towards a Development Strategy.* World Bank Report.

World Health Organization (2003). *Diet Nutrition and the Prevention of Chronic Diseases.* Technical Report Series 916. Geneva.

Part II

1 Introduction

The public distribution system (PDS) is essentially a welfare programme that involves distribution of subsidised food grains to the needy. Simultaneously, it is also an instrument of food policy that influences the price mechanism and is a means to promote food grains production. The PDS came into existence in India during the Second World War as an anti-inflationary measure on a very limited scale. In its present form as a (producer) price-support-cum-consumer subsidy programme, the PDS has evolved in the wake of critical, national level food shortage of the 1960s (Radhakrishna and Subbarao, 1997). Even after more than 60 years of its inception, the PDS is still an issue in public debate and policy. It is presented and interpreted in different ways by different actors, even sometimes by the same actors in different contexts. For instance, on the one hand, the system is presented as very costly and inefficient. Since the beginning of the structural adjustment reforms in 1991, advocates of these policies have stressed the enormous waste of money implied in the PDS. On the other hand, the PDS is presented as the safety net par excellence to help the needy through difficult periods (Mooij, 1999).

The PDS thus, has evolved as a major instrument of the Government's economic policy for ensuring availability of food grains to the public at affordable prices and secure self-sustenance in food production on the supply side. The system is also an important constituent of the strategy for poverty eradication and is intended to serve as a safety net for the poor whose number is substantially high and who are nutritionally at risk. PDS with a network of about 4.77 lakh Fair Price Shops (FPS) is perhaps the largest distribution network of its type in the world. PDS is operated under the joint responsibility of the Central and the State Governments. The Central government has taken the responsibility for procurement, storage, transportation and bulk allocation of food grains. The responsibility for distributing the same to the consumers through the network of FPS lies with the State Governments. The operational responsibilities including allocation within the states, identification of beneficiaries, issuance of ration cards, supervision and monitoring the functioning of FPSs rest with the State Governments. Under the Targeted Public Distribution System (TPDS), food grains (wheat and rice) are disbursed by the State Governments/UTs to the identified cardholders. There are three types of cardholder categories, *viz.*, Above Poverty Line (APL), Below Poverty Line (BPL) and Antyodaya Anna Yojana (AAY—the poorest of the poor).

Certain inadequacies have been identified in the system. It has been alleged by some quarters that the allotted food grains fail to reach the identified cardholders. In view of these allegations, the Department of Food and Public Distribution, Government of India decided to verify the veracity of such charges. The Department started a series of concurrent evaluation of the 'Targeted Public Distribution System' in different states. The National Council of Applied Economic Research completed two phases of the evaluation in 12 states. This volume is second in that series for a set of six states namely, Delhi, Jharkhand, Kerala, Maharashtra, Madhya Pradesh, Maharashtra and Uttarakhand. The objectives of the study are already outlined in the first chapter of the first volume of this book. The objectives for this volume also remain same and need not be reported here to avoid the repetition.

1.1 Approach and Methodology

The study is carried out with the help of primary survey. The target groups for the survey include: (a) APL, BPL and AAY cardholders, (b) FPSs, (c) State Food and Civil Supplies Departments, (d) Food Corporation of India. Survey of the APL, BPL and AAY cardholders captures the irregularities at the micro level in terms of identification of beneficiaries and timeliness of the supply. This also captures whether the beneficiaries are supplied with food grains according to the prescribed norms. This in turn helps in identifying the deviations (if any) within the supply mechanism. Monthly survey for a period of consecutive six months enables us to capture the time variants with regard to requirement of the beneficiaries (income pattern and consumption volatility) as well as access and availability of the food security. The supply chain mechanism and its effectiveness and efficiency is studied with the help of information collected through interactions with selected FPSs, State Food and Civil Supplies Departments and Food Corporation of India. These interactions try to identify the anomalies between the prescribed norms and the real life situation exiting in case of PDS in terms of quality and quantity of supply of food grains. An in-depth survey of the APL, BPL and AAY cardholders was conducted with the help of structured questionnaire which addresses the above mentioned issues of the proposed study. The methodology details of field survey are explained in the following paragraphs:

Sampling Design

The present study is based on a large primary survey. In consonance with the Ministry, the following six states are selected for the study: Delhi, Jharkhand, Kerala, Madhya Pradesh, Maharashtra and Uttarakhand. From each selected state, five districts in the geographical regions of North, South, East, West and Central were selected for drawing the sample. After selecting the districts, one block was selected from each district. The selection criterion for the block was based on the issuance of number of BPL cards. After collecting the list of all blocks in the selected districts, a particular block that had issued the largest number of BPL cards was selected for our sampling purpose. In this way we selected 5 blocks from each state, thus total 30 blocks were selected for drawing the sample. A total number of 200 households were surveyed for detailed information from each selected block. In this fashion, a total number of 6000 households (30*200) were surveyed for a consecutive six months' period. The proportion of BPL and APL households are done in the ratio of 80 and 20. Thereby, 4800 selected households belong to BPL and the rest, 1200 are APL. Out of the selected BPL households, the proportion of BPL and AAY was in the ratio of 77 and 23 (as that is the ratio of total existing number of BPL and AAY cardholders in the country). Thus, the approximate number of BPL households is 3700, AAY is 1100 and APL is 1200 (there are minor changes in the numbers depending on the field circumstances). Keeping into account the proportion of rural and urban population in the country, an approximate ratio of 80/20 was adopted for drawing sample from the rural and urban areas. Thus out of 6000 households, 4800 are selected from the village areas and 1200 are selected from the urban areas. The distribution of sample in APL, BPL and AAY for the urban and rural is done following the same criterion mentioned above. For selecting villages and households, the following procedure was followed.

Selection of Village and Households

From each selected block, the list of villages with the number of BPL cards was obtained from the respective block officers. From each block, four villages were selected based on geographic location of the villages as well as the number of cards issued at the village level. Forty households were selected from each village. In the case of urban areas, one big city or two small towns were chosen for drawing a sample of 40 households from the selected city or two towns of each block. After selecting a village, the list of cardholders was obtained from the District Rural Development Agency (DRDA) or village head or *gram sabha* etc. (whoever was the designated authority). The households from each strata (APL, BPL, AAY) were selected on a random basis. Additional information on different aspects of the study was also obtained from the FPS and Civil Supplies Departments in the States.

In each state, 5 blocks were selected from 5 districts, one from each district. Districts and blocks were selected based on the number of BPL/AAY cardholders. Samples of 200 BPL/AAY/APL cardholders in each block were interviewed. In each block, cardholders were selected randomly on the basis of the list provided by the concerned State Government Departments. The sample cardholders represent both rural and urban population. Information was collected on monthly basis and the evaluation process was carried out for a period of 6 months. A total number of 6000 sample cardholders were interviewed consecutively for 6 months during the entire survey period. Interactions with FCI, State Food and Civil Supplies Departments and FPSs were based on semi-structured questionnaire addressing the relevant issues mentioned in the preceding section. The survey was carried out consecutively for six months beginning from January 2007. The collected data represents these six months period for the monthly data and the calendar year 2006 for the annual data. The details of district and blocks selected and the sample drawn is given in Annexure Table A-1.1.

Figure 1.1 Delhi District Map

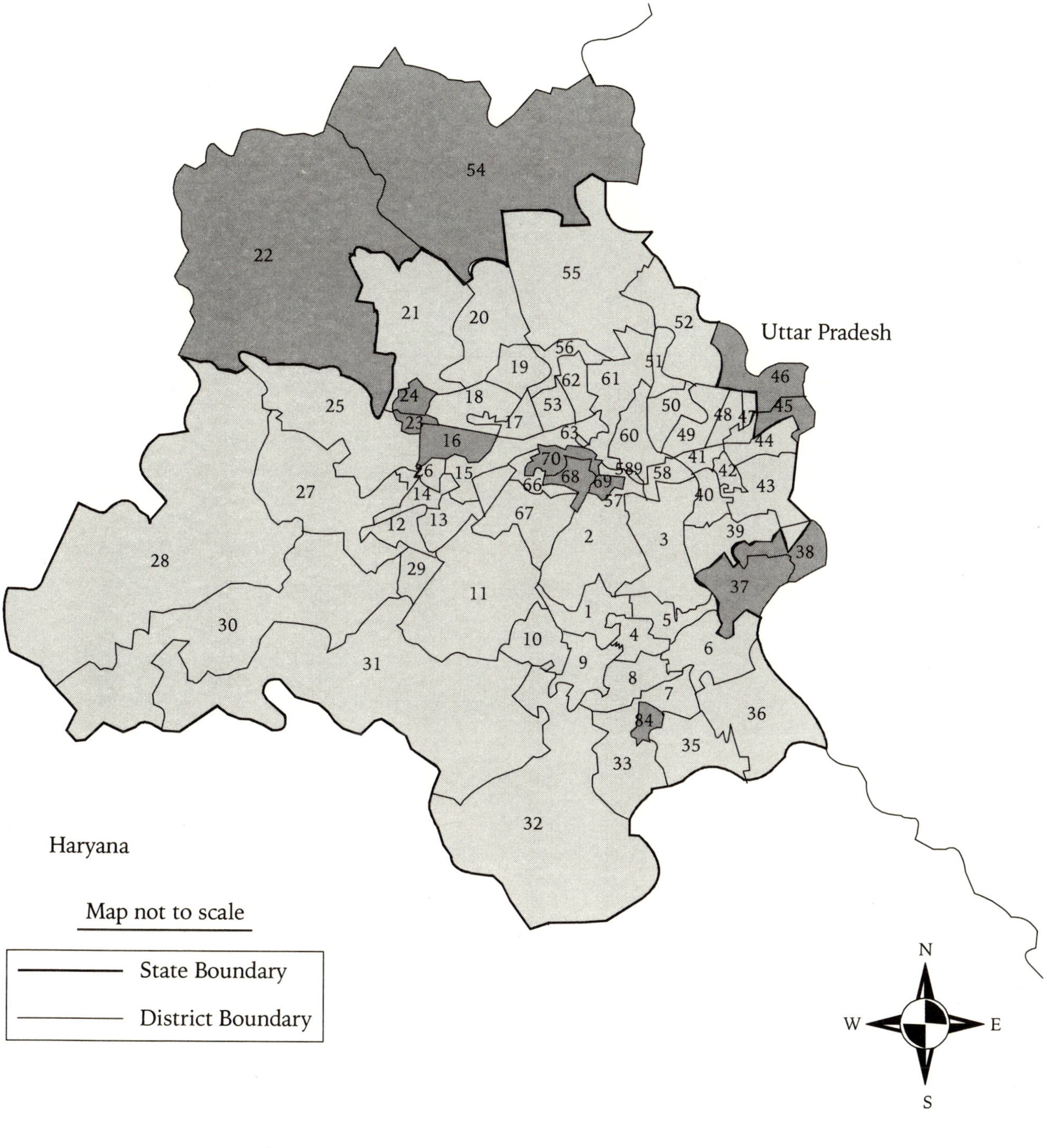

Figure 1.2 Jharkhand District Map

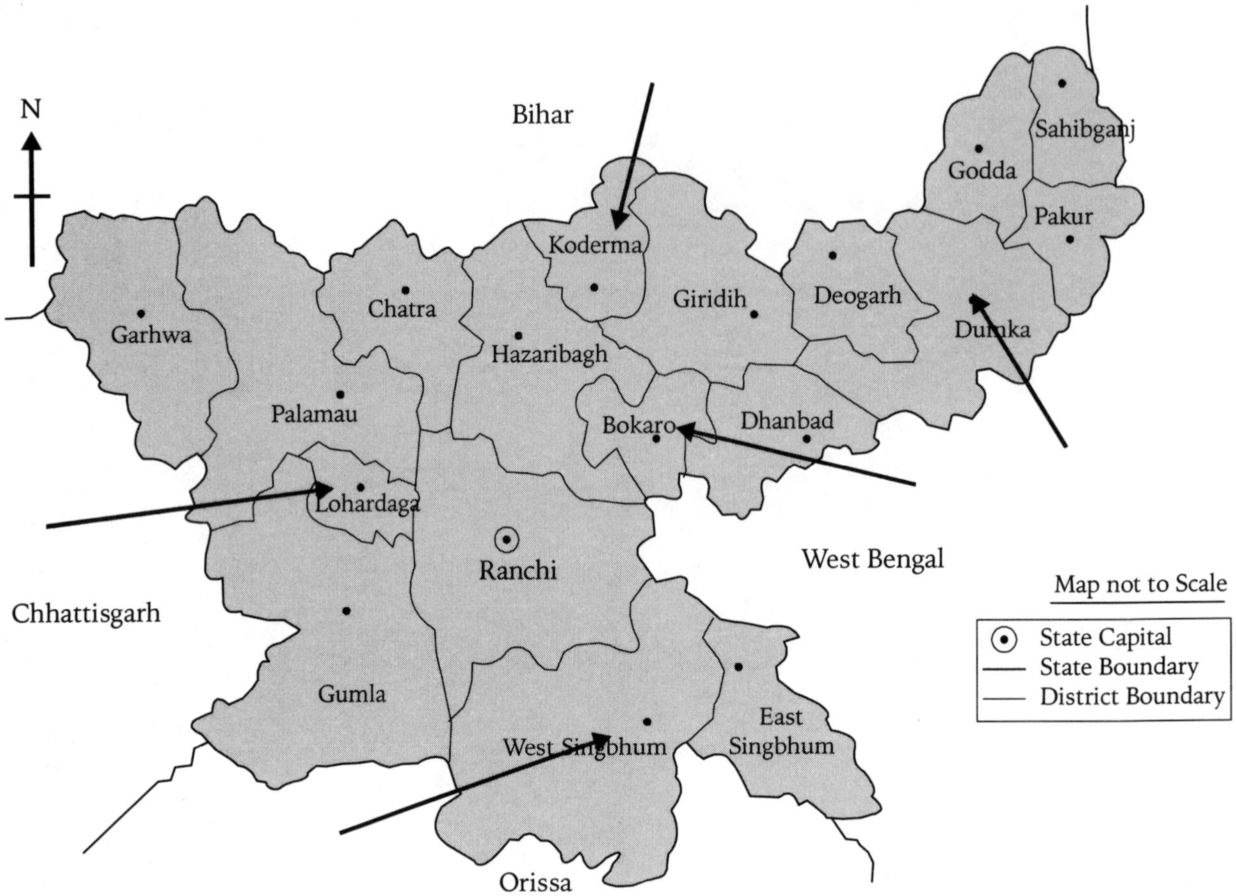

Figure 1.3 Kerala District Map

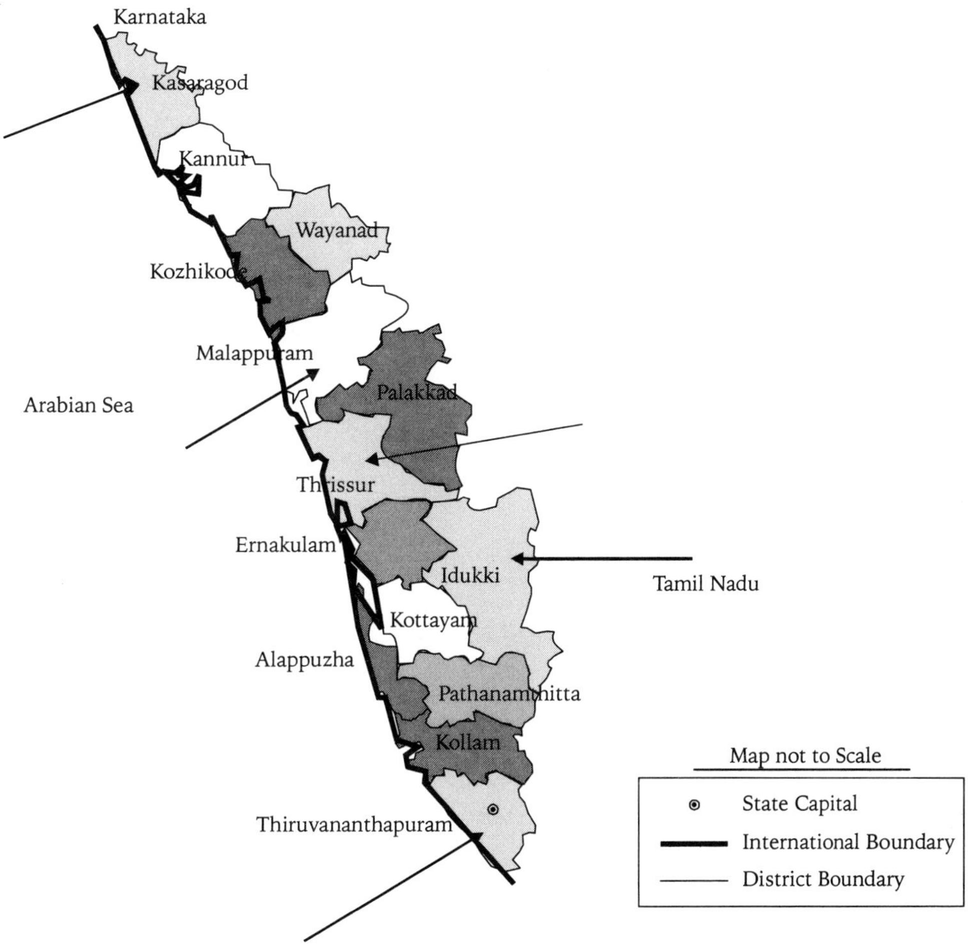

Figure 1.4 Madhya Pradesh District Map

Figure 1.5 Maharashtra District Map

Figure 1.6 Uttarakhand District Map

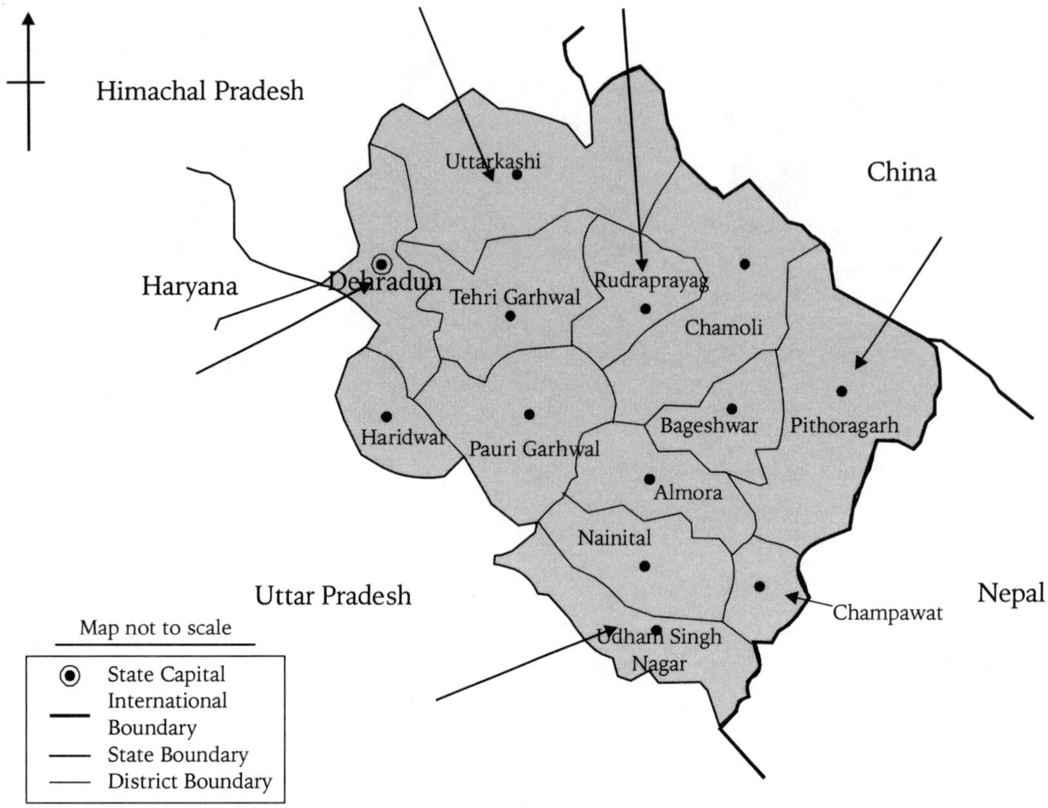

Table A-1.1 Details of Districts, Blocks and Households Selected

State: Delhi (Code: 07)

District/Block Name	Code	Village Name	Household's Code
Central	01	Baljeet Nagar	0001 - 0040
		Matia Mahal	0041 - 0080
		Paharganj	0081 - 0120
		Patel Nagar	0121 - 0160
		Ram Nagar	0161 - 0200
East	02	Geeta Colony	0201 - 0240
		Nand Nagari	0241 - 0280
		Patparganj	0281 - 0320
		Seelampur	0321 - 0360
		Shahdara	0361 - 0400
North	03	Adarsh Nagar	0401 - 0440
		Badli	0441 - 0480
		Karawal Nagar	0481 - 0520
		Narela	0521 - 560
		Sadar Bazar	0561 - 0600
South	04	Ambedkar Nagar	0601 - 0640
		Badarpur	0641 - 0680
		Mehrauli	0681 - 0720
		Mahipalpur	0721 - 0760
		Okhla	0761 - 0800
West	05	Bawana	0801 - 0840
		Hastal	0841 - 0880
		Madipur	0881 - 0920
		Nasirpur	0921 - 0960
		Nazafgarh	0961 - 1000

State: Jharkhand (Code: 08)

District/Block Name	Code	Village Name	Household's Code
Bokaro/Jaridih	06	Bandh Dih	1001 - 1040
		Gangjori	1041 - 1080
		Gaychhanda	1081 - 1120
		Tand Mohanpur	1121 - 1160
		Tantri	1161 - 1200
Dumka/Sikribada	07	Asna	1201 - 1240
		Dhaka	1241 - 1280
		Gamra	1281 - 1320
		Jamkadar	1321 - 1360
		Sarsajol	1361 - 1400
Koderma/Chindwada	08	Bhonso	1401 - 1440
		Chandwara	1441 - 1480
		Kanko	1481 - 1520
		Kanti	1521 - 1560
		Madan Gundi	1561 - 1600
Lohardaga/Kuru	09	Chandlaso	1601 - 1640
		Henjla	1641 - 1680
		Kolasimri	1681 - 1720
		Kuru	1721 - 1760
		Tati	1761 - 1800
West Singhbhum/Bangaon	10	Bandgaon	1801 - 1840
		Kangseya	1841 - 1880
		Katwa	1881 - 1920
		Lumbani	1921 - 1960
		Tokad	1961 - 2000

Table 3.12 Main Occupation (No. of Days per Annum) (Uttarakhand)

Occupation	AAY		BPL		APL	
	Days per HH	Percentage	Days per HH	Percentage	Days per HH	Percentage
Self-employed in agriculture/livestock	86	(25.4)	145	(31.6)	155	(33.4)
Self-employed in non-agriculture	34	(10.0)	37	(8.0)	30	(6.4)
Agricultural casual labour	41	(12.1)	47	(10.3)	37	(7.9)
Non-agricultural casual labour	137	(40.8)	186	(40.7)	101	(21.8)
Work for public work programmes	0	(0.0)	0	(0.0)	0	(0.0)
Worked as a migrant worker	0	(0.1)	3	(0.7)	2	(0.5)
Other self-construction work etc.	0	(0.0)	3	(0.6)	2	(0.4)
Work in common property resources	0	(0.1)	0	(0.0)	0	(0.0)
Regular/salary job	39	(11.5)	37	(8.1)	138	(29.7)
Total	337	(100.0)	458	(100.0)	465	(100.0)

The tables contain the number of days worked by households in each activity. The days are worked out on per annum basis, based on the information we collected for labour allocation during the six months of survey period. In addition to working days, the tables also display the percentage distribution of working days in each economic activity. Trends in occupation depict that the number of working days were highest in Jharkhand and Madhya Pradesh. These two states were at the bottom in per capita state domestic product (Chapter 2) among our six selected states. People have to toil hard to meet their two ends, as remuneration rate were lower in these states compared to better-off states, e.g., Kerala and Delhi. Comparing the major occupation of the selected households, it is visible from the tables that majority of the working members of AAY and BPL households depended on ad hoc means of income as they were engaged in wage earnings, mostly in non-agricultural activities. APL households, on the other hand, had more assured means of earnings, as they were engaged mostly in agriculture, self-employment/business or in salaried jobs. A glance on the statistics reveals that wage earnings in non-agriculture was the principal source of earnings for AAY and BPL households in almost all the states that occupied around 25 to 50 per cent of their man-days. Wage employment in agriculture among AAY and BPL households occupied principal place only in Maharashtra, while in other states, it occupied around 10 to 20 per cent of the total employment days. Self-employment in agriculture/ livestock and self-employment in non-agricultural activities were the other major sources of employment for the below poverty households (including that of AAY). Salaried job was a major employment for AAY and BPL households only in Delhi, where it contributed more than 45 per cent of their man-days. Among other states, salaried jobs contributed around 20 per cent of man-days in Kerala and around 10 per cent in Maharashtra and Uttarakhand for the AAY and BPL categories.

In the case of above poverty households, regular or salaried job with government, semi-government or private sector was the major activity that provided employment to the majority of families in Delhi, Kerala, Maharashtra and Uttarakhand. This single activity contributed around 30 to 60 per cent man-days employment in these four states for the APL households. Self employment in agriculture and livestock consumed around 30 per cent man-days among APL households in Jharkhand, Madhya Pradesh and Uttarakhand. Self-employment in non-agriculture sector that includes small business within the village or in the surrounding villages, towns, e.g., village shop, huller or sheller, commission agents (*arhatias*), shops etc., was the third most significant activity that provided employment to above poverty households. Self-employment engaged around 20 to 30 per cent man-days in Delhi, Madhya Pradesh and Maharashtra. Public work programmes, work in common property resources, other self-construction works and working as a migrant workers were the other minor occupations across all the three categories in the six states.

Thus, occupation structure was significantly different among below and above poverty households. Whereas above poverty households depended mostly on agriculture/livestock, regular salaried jobs and on employment in self-business to eke out their daily earnings, below poverty households depended mostly on casual earnings in non-agriculture, farming activities or as migrant workers. As higher number of APL households depended on salary or self-business, they had assured regular earnings. Whereas, BPL and AAY households were more vulnerable as they did not have any regular means of employment and in most of the cases they were not employed for the whole month. However, comparing occupation structure within BPL and AAY households, no significant differences appear in the pattern of occupation of these two categories.

Comparing occupation pattern across six states, some differences were observed in the occupational structure in various ways. Whereas agriculture and livestock combined together contributed around 1/3rd of the man-days in Jharkhand, Madhya Pradesh, Uttarakhand and slightly less numbers in Maharashtra, agriculture/allied activities contribution was almost negligible in Delhi and Kerala in all the three categories. Similarly, agricultural casual labour contributed quite significantly only in the case of Maharashtra among AAY and BPL households. Casual labour among APL households (agriculture + non-agriculture) was much higher in Kerala as compared to all other states. Yet in another case, migrant workers were found quite significant not only among AAY and BPL households but also among APL households, only in the state of Madhya Pradesh.

3.3 Household Income (Annual)

The household income is the sum total income earned by the family members who are sharing a common kitchen. It may include the transfer payments made by the household members who have migrated temporarily within the country (to a different city) or abroad. It also includes payments received in terms of dividend on the investment, income from sale of assets or rent for hiring out of assets, house or other property, etc. The main sources of earnings of our selected households were, agriculture income also known as farm business income; income from livestock activities namely, dairy and poultry farming; self-employment in non-agricultural activities, such as small business, shop or factory, etc; earnings through casual labour in agriculture or non-agriculture; regular salary or pension; and remittances obtained from outside, i.e., income from transfers. Besides these major sources, there were also minor inflows of income in terms of sale or renting out assets, renting out land (rentals) and income from dividends. These earnings were mostly intermittent in nature and were sighted among a very few households.

Tables 3.13 to 3.18 present distribution of household income by activity classifications for AAY, BPL and APL households for the selected six states. All earnings from different activities are in terms of net income that are obtained by subtracting material cost from the gross earnings for each activity. The tables also present the respective percentage share of each activity in the total household income. The coefficient of variation is calculated for each activity across the households in each category, i.e., AAY, BPL and APL. The data on household income presented in the above tables pertains to the calendar year 2006 for the annual income. A glance on the household income statistics reveals that by and large, estimated income of above and below poverty households was on expected lines. In all the six states, income was highest for the APL households and lowest for the AAY households without any exception. Across the six states, household income followed the trends as displayed by per capita State Domestic Product (SDP) presented in Chapter 2. On an average, the selected AAY households earned around Rs. 43 thousand in Kerala, 28 thousand in Delhi, 20 thousand in Maharashtra and around 15 thousand in other three states, namely Uttarakhand, Jharkhand and Madhya Pradesh from all sources during the calendar year 2006. Among the BPL households, average earnings during the year were Rs. 47 thousand in Kerala, 38 thousand in Delhi, 28 to 29 thousand in Maharashtra and Uttarakhand, while Jharkhand and Madhya Pradesh were at the bottom with 18 and 16 thousand, respectively. For the above poverty households, average earnings topped in Delhi at Rs. 80 thousand, followed by Maharashtra and Kerala with an average of Rs. 66 and 63 thousand, respectively. Uttarakhand lay in the middle with slightly above than Rs. 50 thousand and Jharkhand and Madhya Pradesh remained at the bottom in the case of APL also with an average income of Rs. 28 to 34 thousand. Thus, as expected, Jharkhand and Madhya Pradesh remained at the bottom in average household income, while Delhi and Kerala were at the top in the six selected states. Maharashtra and Uttarakhand occupied the middle position and this ranking was almost true for all the three categories.

Comparing household income across the three categories of AAY, BPL and APL, the difference between AAY and BPL income was highest in Uttarakhand and lowest in Kerala. The difference was more than 50 per cent in Uttarakhand, in the range of 25 to 50 per cent in Delhi, Maharashtra and Madhya Pradesh and less than 15 per cent in Jharkhand and Kerala. Comparing below and above poverty household income, the APL income was more than double that of BPL income in three states namely, Delhi, Maharashtra and Madhya Pradesh while in Uttarakhand, it was almost double. In the other two selected states, APL income was one and a half times more than that of BPL income in Jharkhand while in Kerala, their difference was less than 50 per cent. Comparing above poverty households with the bottom class of AAY households, the average income of APL households was more than thrice that of AAY households in Maharashtra and Uttarakhand. It was two to three times in Delhi and Madhya Pradesh and less than twice in rest of the two states, namely Jharkhand and Kerala. In summary, the differences in household income among different categories were lowest in Kerala and Jharkhand and higest in Delhi and Maharashtra. On an average, BPL income was 30 per cent higher compared to AAY income while APL income was around twice that of BPL income and thrice that of AAY income among all the selected states.

Table 3.13 Household Income (Annual) (Rs. per Household) (Delhi)

	Average Income	Per cent Share	COV(across HH)
	AAY		
Wage income (non-agriculture)	8149	28.72	36.17
Income from self-employment	6879	24.24	38.84
Income from salary	12887	45.42	59.16
Income from pension	396	1.40	41.36
Income from transfer payment	60	0.21	-
Income from sale/rent of assets/land/house etc.	5	0.02	-
Total	28376	100.00	-
	BPL		
Wage income (agriculture)	150	0.40	54.34
Wage income (non-agriculture)	12087	31.95	51.87
Income from self-employment	9485	25.07	47.38
Income from salary	15317	40.48	57.72
Income from pension	227	0.60	109.77
Income from transfer	121	0.32	-
Income from sale/rent of assets/land/house etc.	304	0.80	-
Income from migration	80	0.21	-
Income from other sources	64	0.17	-
Total	37835	100.00	-
	APL		
Wage income(agriculture)	296	0.37	-
Wage income(non-agriculture)	7920	9.92	74.22
Income from self-employment	27588	34.56	165.76
Income from salary	35319	44.25	64.83
Income from pension	1649	2.07	67.40
Income from transfer	118	0.15	-
Income from sale/rent of assets/land/house etc.	1576	1.97	-
Income from migration	207	0.26	-
Income from other sources	5153	6.45	-
Total	79826	100.00	-

Table 3.14 Household Income (Annual) (Rs. per Household) (Jharkhand)

	Average Income	Per cent Share	COV(across HH)
	AAY		
Income from agriculture	573	3.68	75.76
Income from livestock	15	0.10	69.03
Wage income(agriculture)	1263	8.10	77.83
Wage income(non-agriculture)	9457	60.68	60.95
Income from self-employment	1956	12.55	64.49
Income from salary	688	4.41	119.22
Income from pension	42	0.27	141.42
Income from transfer	83	0.53	-
Income from migration	931	5.97	-
Income from CPR etc.	357	2.29	-
Income from public work programme etc.	222	1.43	-
Total	15587	100.00	-
	BPL		
Income from agriculture	1270	7.10	110.55
Income from livestock	42	0.24	175.97
Wage income(agriculture)	1536	8.58	91.15
Wage income(non-agriculture)	9561	53.44	86.37
Income from self-employment	2375	13.27	66.49
Income from salary	657	3.67	65.23
Income from pension	80	0.45	139.92
Income from transfer	147	0.82	-
Income from sale/rent of assets/land/house etc.	19	0.10	-
Income from migration	1256	7.02	-
Income from CPR etc.	373	2.08	-
Income from public work programme etc.	485	2.71	-
Income from other sources	92	0.51	-
Total	17893	100.00	-
	APL		
Income from agriculture	2267	8.09	144.22
Income from livestock	32	0.12	94.08
Wage income(agriculture)	859	3.06	87.28
Wage income(non-agriculture)	5100	18.20	69.12
Income from self-employment	7474	26.67	88.40
Income from salary	10129	36.15	52.58
Income from pension	1040	3.71	66.65
Income from transfer	13	0.04	-
Income from sale/rent of assets/land/house etc.	85	0.30	-
Income from migration	802	2.86	-
Income from CPR etc.	8	0.03	-
Income from public work programme etc.	157	0.56	-
Income from other sources	57	0.20	-
Total	28023	100.00	-

Table 3.15 **Household Income (Annual) (Rs. per Household) (Kerala)**

	Average Income	Per cent Share	COV(across HH)
	AAY		
Income from agriculture	1178	2.71	127.32
Income from livestock	858	1.97	55.45
Wage income(agriculture)	5191	11.93	66.13
Wage income(non-agriculture)	24074	55.34	65.29
Income from self-employment	4006	9.21	106.68
Income from salary	6350	14.60	86.48
Income from pension	689	1.58	212.18
Income from transfer	257	0.59	-
Income from migration	129	0.30	-
Income from CPR etc.	771	1.77	-
Total	43503	100.00	-
	BPL		
Income from agriculture	471	1.00	87.21
Income from livestock	207	0.44	63.51
Wage income(agriculture)	7439	15.79	125.98
Wage income(non-agriculture)	26789	56.86	104.23
Income from self-employment	4005	8.50	214.60
Income from salary	6210	13.18	93.21
Income from pension	594	1.26	169.75
Income from transfer	413	0.88	-
Income from sale/rent of assets/land/house etc.	37	0.08	-
Income from migration	118	0.25	-
Income from CPR etc.	648	1.38	-
Income from other sources	184	0.39	-
Total	47115	100.00	-
	APL		
Income from agriculture	3116	4.93	95.34
Income from livestock	692	1.10	61.48
Wage income(agriculture)	4763	7.54	73.34
Wage income(non-agriculture)	16702	26.45	64.44
Income from self-employment	4424	7.01	50.61
Income from salary	26197	41.48	192.14
Income from pension	4132	6.54	126.04
Income from transfer	1325	2.10	-
Income from CPR etc.	1141	1.81	-
Income from other sources	657	1.04	-
Total	63149	100.00	-

Table 3.16 Household Income (Annual) (Rs. per Household) (Madhya Pradesh)

	Average Income	Per cent Share	COV(across HH)
	AAY		
Income from agriculture	452	3.58	82.70
Income from livestock	-43	-0.34	-
Wage income(agriculture)	1581	12.53	79.01
Wage income(non-agriculture)	5495	43.57	61.48
Income from self-employment	1528	12.12	72.00
Income from salary	594	4.71	56.40
Income from pension	231	1.83	115.64
Income from migration	2457	19.48	-
Income from public work programme etc.	252	2.00	-
Income from other sources	66	0.53	-
Total	12613	100.00	-
	BPL		
Income from agriculture	1295	8.02	128.81
Income from livestock	63	0.39	1314.45
Wage income(agriculture)	1928	11.94	81.65
Wage income(non-agriculture)	5609	34.74	68.09
Income from self-employment	2003	12.41	73.83
Income from salary	1556	9.64	112.92
Income from pension	87	0.54	153.79
Income from transfer	10	0.06	-
Income from migration	3323	20.58	-
Income from public work programme etc.	269	1.66	-
Income from other sources	2	0.01	-
Total	16145	100.00	-
	APL		
Income from agriculture	5961	17.73	119.43
Income from livestock	710	2.11	191.94
Wage income(agriculture)	1113	3.31	51.34
Wage income(non-agriculture)	4675	13.90	83.25
Income from self-employment	5426	16.14	82.06
Income from salary	10548	31.37	71.86
Income from pension	329	0.98	155.64
Income from transfer	456	1.36	-
Income from sale/rent of assets/land/house etc.	191	0.57	-
Income from migration	1687	5.02	-
Income from CPR etc.	36	0.11	-
Income from public work programme etc.	54	0.16	-
Income from other sources	2438	7.25	-
Total	33624	100.00	-

Table 3.17 Household Income (Annual) (Rs. per Household) (Maharashtra)

	Average Income	Per cent Share	COV(across HH)
	AAY		
Income from agriculture	1025	5.03	65.09
Income from livestock	215	1.05	147.53
Wage income(agriculture)	7080	34.72	77.88
Wage income(non-agriculture)	6273	30.76	63.63
Income from self-employment	2752	13.50	97.42
Income from salary	2538	12.45	87.77
Income from pension	401	1.97	136.24
Income from sale/rent of assets/land/house etc.	10	0.05	-
Income from CPR etc.	98	0.48	-
Total	20392	100.00	-
	BPL		
Income from agriculture	4040	13.99	102.03
Income from livestock	369	1.28	98.61
Wage income(agriculture)	7281	25.22	66.61
Wage income(non-agriculture)	8077	27.97	64.40
Income from self-employment	2559	8.86	88.16
Income from salary	5669	19.63	71.26
Income from pension	199	0.69	110.09
Income from transfer	25	0.09	-
Income from sale/rent of assets/land/house etc.	160	0.56	-
Income from migration	27	0.09	-
Income from CPR etc.	420	1.45	-
Income from other sources	49	0.17	-
Total	28875	100.00	-
	APL		
Income from agriculture	18866	28.38	99.27
Income from livestock	607	0.91	137.87
Wage income(agriculture)	3594	5.41	112.21
Wage income(non-agriculture)	3635	5.47	50.37
Income from self-employment	8057	12.12	55.78
Income from salary	27697	41.66	82.38
Income from pension	2248	3.38	40.62
Income from transfer	985	1.48	-
Income from sale/rent of assets/land/house etc.	369	0.56	-
Income from migration	212	0.32	-
Income from CPR etc.	163	0.24	-
Income from other sources	42	0.06	-
Total	66475	100.00	-

Table 3.18 Household Income (Annual) (Rs. per Household) (Uttarakhand)

	Average Income	Per cent Share	COV(across HH)
	AAY		
Income from agriculture	359	2.05	66.51
Income from livestock	723	4.14	134.89
Wage income(agriculture)	1891	10.83	78.31
Wage income(non-agriculture)	9717	55.68	70.44
Income from self-employment	1667	9.55	62.86
Income from salary	2309	13.23	71.36
Income from pension	755	4.33	70.93
Income from other sources	31	0.18	-
Total	17452	100.00	-
	BPL		
Income from agriculture	1429	5.18	130.89
Income from livestock	632	2.29	147.91
Wage income(agriculture)	2053	7.44	132.28
Wage income(non-agriculture)	15237	55.24	94.41
Income from self-employment	3524	12.78	93.37
Income from salary	3762	13.64	93.69
Income from pension	318	1.15	103.09
Income from transfer	182	0.66	-
Income from sale/rent of assets/land/house etc.	61	0.22	-
Income from migration	262	0.95	-
Income from other sources	120	0.43	-
Total	27580	100.00	-
	APL		
Income from agriculture	8213	15.59	168.45
Income from livestock	1122	2.13	93.59
Wage income(agriculture)	1650	3.13	68.57
Wage income(non-agriculture)	8369	15.89	76.97
Income from self-employment	2784	5.28	83.55
Income from salary	25426	48.27	65.52
Income from pension	3695	7.01	49.83
Income from transfer	394	0.75	-
Income from interest/dividend	18	0.03	-
Income from sale/rent of assets/land/house etc.	365	0.69	-
Income from migration	345	0.65	-
Income from other sources	300	0.57	-
Total	52681	100.00	-

Comparing the sources of income across different activities, it is clearly evident from the results that wage income, income from self-employment (non-agriculture) and income from salary/pension were the major activities that contributed a lion's share in the aggregate household income. Among different categories, wage income from non-agricultural activities dominated with its share in total income of AAY and BPL households. In the case of APL households, it was income from the regular employment in salary that contributed the major amount in most of the states. It was observed in the occupational distribution that casual labour in agriculture and non-agricultural activities was the foremost occupation among the below poverty households. Wage income from non-agriculture contributed the major income of AAY and BPL households in Jharkhand, Kerala, Madhya Pradesh and Uttarakhand. In Maharashtra, it was wage income from agriculture along with non-agriculture while in Delhi, it was the salary income from regular employment that dominated household income of these two categories. Significant share of wages in BPL and AAY income further verifies our results of occupational distribution. In the case of above poverty households, in consonance with the occupational structure, earnings from salary/pension and self-employment in non-agriculture constituted the highest share of income of these households in all the states without any exception. Income from agriculture/livestock was significant only in the case of Maharashtra and Madhya Pradesh. In rest of the states, very few people were engaged in agriculture as was also seen in the analysis of occupational distribution. For the BPL and AAY households, salary/pension and self-employment income were the other major sources of earning. The transfer earnings from the family members who migrated temporarily constituted a significant share especially among the AAY and BPL households in two states, namely Madhya Pradesh and Jharkhand. Last and the least, as was mentioned at the outset, income from dividends, hiring-out assets and rents were the minor sources for all the three category of households in all the six states.

The coefficient of variation indicates the dispersion of income across various households for the respective economic activities. Comparing the value of coefficient among the four major economic activities that constituted the highest share of income of all households namely, income from agriculture, wage income (agriculture and non-agriculture), income from self-employment and income from salary, the dispersion of income across households was highest for agriculture/livestock in most of the cases. High variability of agricultural and livestock income is quite natural because of the seasonal nature of these activities. For other activities, dispersion was lowest for salary, followed by wage income and self-employment earnings. Although the number of people engaged in salary and casual earnings was quite large as was discussed in the last section, these two activities had lowest dispersion in income across the households. These statistics indicate that wage and fixed salary differential across households (state-wise) were far less than the earnings through agriculture and self-employment. These results are not surprising as people engaged in casual labour (in agriculture and in non-agriculture) and in fixed salary draw a fixed amount for their work and remuneration do not fluctuate too much across various households. In the case of self-employment as well as agriculture, the returns are directly proportional to the amount of investment made in the business/factory etc., or the number of acres being operated by the households. Thereby, variation in wages and salaries represent dispersion across the households engaged in these activities, whereas dispersion in income from self-employment or agriculture, in addition to inter-personal differences, also include the variation that takes place due to differences in land area cultivated and the amount of capital invested by the households in business and other activities.

3.4 Household Income (Monthly)

An inimitable advantage of the present database is that being a longitudinal data, it not only provides information across households but also over time. In our household questionnaire, we collected information on income for the last one year and for every month of survey starting from January 2007. Thus, in addition to having information on household income for the calendar year 2006 as presented above, we also have data on each earning activity for the six months survey period, i.e., from January 2007 to June 2007. The monthly data contains monthly income from various economic activities. The results are presented in Tables 3.19 to 3.24 for the selected states. In the previous section, we presented coefficient of variation in annual income across households for the same point of time. In the present analysis, we present coefficient of variation of monthly income across six months for every economic activity for the same households. While COV in the annual income measured dispersion across households, COV in monthly income enumerates dispersion in income across time.

Table 3.19 Monthly Income and its COV across Six Months (Rs. per Household) (Delhi)

	Month 1	Month 2	Month 3	Month 4	Month 5	Month 6	Avg	COV
				AAY				
Wage income (agri.)	0	0	0	13	14	14	7	109.6
Wage income (non-agri.)	910	624	836	791	715	694	761	13.7
Income from self-emp.	582	738	454	830	648	573	638	20.8
Income from salary	1087	1152	724	704	914	768	891	21.6
Income from pension	35	38	20	29	42	36	33	23.8
Income from transfer	5	0	0	5	0	3	2	114.6
Income from sale/rent etc.	0	0	3	0	3	0	1	154.9
Income from other sources	0	11	4	3	0	3	3	122.1
Total	2619	2563	2041	2375	2336	2091	2336	-
				BPL				
Wage income (agri.)	9	2	2	2	1	1	3	103.7
Wage income (non-agri.)	1309	905	1125	962	908	884	1016	16.6
Income from self-emp.	851	675	583	810	642	598	693	16.2
Income from salary	1314	1412	1040	1226	1140	1103	1206	11.5
Income from pension	27	40	21	36	27	17	28	30.8
Income from transfer	10	0	0	0	0	0	2	244.9
Income from sale/rent etc.	22	9	7	0	5	0	7	114.7
Income from other sources	17	13	0	1	0	3	6	134.2
Total	3559	3056	2778	3037	2723	2606	2961	-
				APL				
Wage income (non-agri.)	767	419	575	430	378	362	488	32.0
Income from self-emp.	2316	1414	1752	1970	1251	1260	1661	25.9
Income from salary	2994	2720	2109	2528	2800	2487	2606	11.7
Income from pension	177	109	106	165	120	49	121	38.0
Income from transfer	10	0	0	0	0	0	2	244.9
Income from sale/rent etc.	118	89	20	69	59	0	59	73.9
Income from migration	18	0	0	0	0	0	3	244.9
Income from other sources	25	10	0	0	0	0	6	173.2
Total	6425	4761	4762	5162	4608	4158	4946	-

Table 3.20 Monthly Income and its COV across Six Months (Rs. per Household) (Jharkhand)

	Month 1	Month 2	Month 3	Month 4	Month 5	Month 6	Avg.	COV
				AAY				
Income from agriculture	32	16	3	2	13	7	12	92.9
Income from livestock	3	12	7	9	3	3	6	62.8
Wage income (agri.)	249	40	36	18	44	37	71	124.2
Wage income(non-agri.)	920	984	1210	1142	1243	1161	1110	11.6
Income from self-emp.	198	274	308	306	310	319	286	16.0
Income from salary	63	100	106	11	32	123	73	61.3
Income from pension	4	8	0	2	1	0	2	128.7
Income from migration	245	89	75	67	30	26	89	90.7
Income from CPR etc.	31	47	55	58	33	33	43	28.2
Income from public work	90	96	69	92	70	89	84	14.1
Total	1835	1666	1869	1707	1779	1798	1776	-
				BPL				
Income from agriculture	18	23	6	15	6	0	11	77.3
Income from livestock	1	15	15	12	5	8	9	61.0
Wage income (agri.)	307	45	32	35	47	66	89	121.4
Wage income(non-agri.)	942	1064	1261	1227	1190	1149	1139	10.4
Income from self-emp.	295	318	381	329	351	313	331	9.3
Income from salary	55	35	31	20	47	51	40	33.9
Income from pension	7	10	10	7	13	9	9	26.8
Income from transfer	0	13	28	25	8	0	12	99.2
Income from migration	246	56	56	51	23	20	75	113.0
Income from CPR etc.	38	43	54	58	47	34	46	19.8
Income from public work	104	104	90	82	100	107	98	9.8
Income from other sources	19	0	0	0	0	0	3	237.9
Total	2032	1726	1964	1861	1837	1757	1862	-
				APL				
Income from agriculture	6	80	46	52	26	15	38	72.6
Income from livestock	1	15	15	12	5	8	9	61.0
Wage income (agri.)	260	59	59	55	73	71	96	83.6
Wage income(non-agri.)	498	822	824	832	937	834	791	19.0
Income from self-emp.	814	765	972	712	873	887	837	11.1
Income from salary	861	554	508	651	646	745	661	19.4
Income from pension	87	107	48	41	29	34	58	55.0
Income from transfer	0	9	0	0	0	0	2	244.9
Income from interest/div.	0	9	47	0	0	0	9	200.0
Income from sale/rent etc.	0	22	0	0	0	0	4	244.9
Income from migration	206	22	19	19	13	13	49	158.4
Income from CPR etc.	1	9	26	20	19	3	13	76.8
Income from public work	43	65	66	78	13	4	45	67.4
Total	2777	2538	2630	2472	2634	2614	2612	-

Table 3.21 Monthly Income and its COV across Six Months (Rs. per Household) (Kerala)

	Month 1	Month 2	Month 3	Month 4	Month 5	Month 6	Avg.	COV
AAY								
Income from agriculture	252	0	792	51	2	36	189	164.2
Income from livestock	362	55	18	31	4	9	80	174.9
Wage income (agri.)	477	478	510	490	499	423	479	6.3
Wage income(non-agri.)	2163	2090	2403	2439	2379	2490	2327	7.0
Income from self-emp.	285	214	209	103	209	106	188	37.5
Income from salary	542	414	417	330	445	355	417	17.9
Income from pension	56	36	38	46	65	17	43	39.4
Income from transfer	21	0	0	35	0	0	9	161.6
Income from interest/div.	0	0	0	15	0	0	2	244.9
Income from migration	34	82	12	0	12	13	25	117.3
Income from CPR etc.	61	50	153	103	161	166	116	44.8
Total	4253	3419	4552	3643	3776	3615	3875	-
BPL								
Income from agriculture	50	42	330	37	24	3	81	151.5
Income from livestock	25	28	22	25	17	15	22	22.8
Wage income (agri.)	589	516	552	507	537	464	528	8.1
Wage income (non-agri.)	2487	2055	2429	2557	2404	2439	2395	7.3
Income from self-emp.	273	214	182	193	253	213	221	15.9
Income from salary	500	447	383	446	480	429	448	9.1
Income from pension	50	50	106	109	106	28	75	48.3
Income from transfer	29	61	344	122	0	7	94	138.7
Income from interest/div.	0	32	0	1	0	0	5	239.6
Income from sale/rent etc.	0	2	20	15	0	0	6	147.0
Income from migration	18	56	7	2	0	0	14	156.1
Income from CPR etc.	66	40	138	134	133	138	108	40.3
Income from other sources	5	3	10	2	0	0	3	111.6
Total	4092	3546	4523	4150	3954	3736	4000	-
APL								
Income from agriculture	144	33	135	144	95	56	101	47.6
Income from livestock	114	44	25	46	20	0	42	94.3
Wage income (agri.)	443	579	507	512	482	445	495	10.2
Wage income(non-agri.)	1541	1440	1522	1533	1466	1453	1492	3.0
Income from self-emp.	352	273	235	229	435	324	308	25.6
Income from salary	2188	1327	1436	1321	1691	1678	1607	20.4
Income from pension	440	319	310	171	451	215	317	35.9
Income from transfer	110	142	384	189	3	177	167	75.0
Income from interest/div.	0	40	0	0	0	66	18	161.4
Income from migration	18	60	15	16	0	0	18	121.1
Income from CPR etc.	96	56	142	138	142	131	118	29.5
Income from other sources	149	0	38	6	8	6	35	167.8
Total	5595	4313	4749	4305	4793	4551	4718	-

Table 3.22 **Monthly Income and its COV across Six Months (Rs. per Household) (Madhya Pradesh)**

	Month 1	Month 2	Month 3	Month 4	Month 5	Month 6	Avg.	COV
				AAY				
Income from agriculture	7	0	47	0	0	0	9	208.5
Income from livestock	-6	-1	8	15	16	15	8	117.6
Wage income (agri.)	160	151	151	188	232	334	203	35.2
Wage income(non-agri.)	697	612	612	1000	1027	1015	827	25.0
Income from self-emp.	155	163	163	280	214	269	208	27.1
Income from salary	49	8	28	24	39	30	30	46.2
Income from pension	26	2	17	12	10	9	12	65.1
Income from transfer	0	10	24	3	0	0	6	156.8
Income from migration	419	470	470	352	423	199	389	26.4
Income from public work	18	33	33	36	4	3	21	71.0
Income from other sources	44	0	0	0	0	0	7	244.9
Total	1569	1448	1553	1910	1965	1874	1720	-
				BPL				
Income from agriculture	28	0	70	14	0	0	19	147.0
Income from livestock	4	0	11	19	19	16	12	70.7
Wage income (agri.)	148	183	183	173	172	281	190	24.5
Wage income(non-agri.)	701	734	734	1102	1124	1089	914	23.0
Income from self-emp.	183	189	189	305	300	474	273	41.6
Income from salary	129	72	94	99	133	118	107	21.8
Income from pension	10	6	12	12	11	8	10	24.5
Income from migration	553	463	463	321	474	230	417	28.4
Income from public work	49	26	26	16	5	15	23	66.0
Income from other sources	91	1	24	2	0	0	20	184.6
Total	1896	1674	1806	2063	2238	2231	1985	-
				APL				
Income from agriculture	36	0	144	270	0	0	75	147.7
Income from livestock	67	23	55	69	69	63	58	30.7
Wage income (agri.)	127	204	204	73	114	144	144	35.9
Wage income(non-agri.)	536	482	482	751	757	768	629	22.8
Income from self-emp.	740	630	630	934	974	1816	954	46.9
Income from salary	1003	771	1185	1019	1046	786	968	16.6
Income from pension	31	34	55	118	34	65	56	59.4
Income from transfer	0	5	412	29	10	0	76	216.8
Income from interest/div.	0	0	28	8	0	0	6	189.1
Income from sale/rent etc.	5	0	31	0	0	0	6	205.8
Income from migration	537	287	287	178	189	81	260	60.1
Income from public work	16	9	9	4	0	0	6	99.5
Income from other sources	57	38	119	0	0	23	39	113.3
Total	3155	2483	3641	3453	3193	3746	3277	-

Table 3.23 Monthly Income and its COV across Six Months (Rs. per Household) (Maharashtra)

	Month 1	Month 2	Month 3	Month 4	Month 5	Month 6	Avg.	COV
AAY								
Income from agriculture	0	26	63	0	0	0	15	173.8
Income from livestock	17	11	27	12	17	10	16	41.1
Wage income (agri.)	752	641	645	879	781	938	773	15.6
Wage income(non-agri.)	598	621	609	574	553	562	586	4.7
Income from self-emp.	199	167	111	138	254	219	181	29.2
Income from salary	212	225	148	152	191	197	188	16.8
Income from pension	36	10	5	87	48	42	38	78.3
Income from migration	25	13	19	32	31	31	25	30.8
Income from CPR etc.	10	10	10	11	12	7	10	18.8
Income from other sources	89	0	2	37	4	0	22	163.5
Total	1938	1724	1639	1922	1891	2006	1854	-
BPL								
Income from agriculture	20	130	196	140	0	0	81	104.7
Income from livestock	63	41	52	32	37	30	42	29.7
Wage income (agri.)	802	697	680	990	962	1039	862	18.1
Wage income(non-agri.)	781	685	716	723	720	725	725	4.3
Income from self-emp.	258	238	156	181	241	244	220	18.6
Income from salary	477	462	240	425	429	446	413	21.0
Income from pension	27	4	5	13	6	7	10	83.7
Income from transfer	0	31	0	26	0	25	14	110.4
Income from migration	32	3	25	7	11	12	15	76.5
Income from CPR etc.	36	37	38	35	30	39	36	8.3
Income from other sources	217	25	0	63	0	0	51	167.2
Total	2713	2353	2108	2635	2436	2567	2469	-
APL								
Income from agriculture	121	0	136	738	0	0	166	173.2
Income from livestock	136	92	54	191	42	93	101	54.4
Wage income (agri.)	250	254	229	434	360	419	324	28.1
Wage income(non-agri.)	392	330	349	351	340	329	348	6.6
Income from self-emp.	792	900	414	764	833	705	735	23.2
Income from salary	2311	2194	1219	2169	2485	2325	2117	21.4
Income from pension	205	171	86	319	181	251	202	38.9
Income from transfer	0	0	0	12	0	6	3	167.3
Income from interest/div.	0	0	7	30	0	0	6	192.2
Income from sale/rent etc.	0	0	0	15	0	0	2	244.9
Income from migration	35	12	20	20	9	20	19	47.4
Income from CPR etc.	10	12	12	13	7	18	12	29.5
Income from other sources	345	0	25	76	0	16	77	174.7
Total	4597	3965	2551	5132	4257	4182	4112	-

Table 3.24 **Monthly Income and its COV across Six Months (Rs. per Household) (Uttarakhand)**

	Month 1	Month 2	Month 3	Month 4	Month 5	Month 6	Avg.	COV
				AAY				
Income from agriculture	0	0	0	31	0	3	6	220.7
Income from livestock	43	11	65	60	60	42	47	42.1
Wage income (agri.)	227	64	178	247	283	365	227	44.6
Wage income(non-agri.)	1164	855	1109	1098	951	913	1015	12.3
Income from self-emp.	299	260	204	284	203	234	247	16.3
Income from salary	199	373	288	256	258	276	275	20.6
Income from pension	75	141	70	140	100	113	107	29.0
Income from transfer	0	67	30	0	0	10	18	150.4
Income from migration	12	0	0	0	0	0	2	244.9
Income from CPR etc.	0	0	2	3	4	7	3	98.4
Income from other sources	2	0	24	3	0	0	5	193.0
Total	2021	1771	1970	2122	1859	1963	1952	-
				BPL				
Income from agriculture	45	0	0	416	0	0	77	217.8
Income from livestock	165	17	101	96	76	70	87	55.5
Wage income (agri.)	223	50	206	373	358	398	268	49.9
Wage income(non-agri.)	1550	1514	1454	1341	1289	1224	1395	9.4
Income from self-emp.	221	181	275	256	247	298	247	16.7
Income from salary	338	302	249	310	339	359	316	12.3
Income from pension	66	80	37	26	36	24	45	50.4
Income from transfer	15	253	129	10	10	56	79	123.0
Income from interest/div.	0	35	0	0	0	0	6	244.9
Income from sale/rent etc.	2	0	17	0	1	1	3	201.0
Income from migration	55	13	16	0	8	8	17	117.1
Income from other sources	84	0	154	2	2	0	40	161.7
Total	2764	2445	2638	2830	2366	2438	2580	-
				APL				
Income from agriculture	300	0	69	1647	59	0	346	187.1
Income from livestock	181	17	119	132	93	84	104	52.7
Wage income (agri.)	155	72	168	303	293	309	217	45.6
Wage income(non-agri.)	899	793	882	611	618	641	741	18.1
Income from self-emp.	310	269	244	247	215	226	252	13.5
Income from salary	2138	1880	1979	2560	2328	2433	2220	12.0
Income from pension	696	411	406	417	192	414	423	37.9
Income from transfer	0	83	2660	20	0	52	469	228.9
Income from interest/div.	0	20	177	39	0	20	43	158.3
Income from sale/rent etc.	0	59	305	0	0	0	61	201.1
Income from migration	57	25	0	0	0	0	14	171.5
Income from other sources	70	26	133	0	15	59	50	96.0
Total	4806	3655	7142	5976	3813	4238	4940	-

Whereas annual income estimates are based on respondents' memory recall of last one year, the monthly estimates should be more closer to reality as these estimates have much shorter memory recall. However, some activities, e.g., agricultural income, which is seasonal in nature might be better captured by the annual estimates as that would cover both *kharif* and *rabi* estimates rather than the monthly estimates that are based on only six months' survey period and these estimates might skip one of the two harvest seasons in agriculture. Our monthly income estimates compare very well with the annual income presented in the last section. On an average, monthly income for AAY, BPL and APL categories was quite closer to the annual income.[2] The monthly income estimates were slightly less than the annual income in Jharkhand, Madhya Pradesh and Uttarakhand while they were pretty close to that of annual income for all the categories in Delhi, Kerala and Maharashtra. Nonetheless, in the former three states also the difference between the two was not very high and significant. Therefore, for the purpose of comparison of poverty estimates we will use both these estimates.[3] Monthly income across the six states further verifies our earlier findings on the ranking of different states in terms of household income. Like in annual income, Delhi and Kerala were also on top in monthly income while Madhya Pradesh and Jharkhand lay at the bottom, leaving Maharashtra and Uttarakhand in the middle similar to as was observed in the case of annual income. On an average, monthly income was 3.5 to 5 thousand per household in Delhi and Kerala, it was around 3 thousand in Maharashtra and Uttarakhand and less than 2.5 thousand in Madhya Pradesh and Jharkhand.

The BPL monthly income, on an average, was one and a quarter times that of AAY income. The APL income was one and a half times that of BPL income and twice or more than twice that of AAY income. The difference between the three was highest in Uttarakhand and Maharashtra and lowest in Kerala and Jharkhand. Delhi and Madhya Pradesh had the moderate wedge between AAY, BPL and APL monthly household income. The BPL and AAY income estimates were very close denying the argument that former estimates belonged to the upper or average strata of income among the BPL population and the latter one representing the bottom most stratum.[4] The distribution across different economic activities was almost same as was discussed in the case of annual income. The major constituent of monthly income was wage from the non-griculture sector in the case of AAY and BPL households, except Maharashtra where agriculture wages contributed the highest share. In the case of APL households, salary and income from self-employment contributed the major share in their case.

Comparing the dispersion of income across time period, it is apparent from the coefficient of variation results that agriculture income as well as income from agricultural wages fluctuated the most across six months as was also expected because of the seasonal nature of agriculture income. It is noteworthy that agriculture earnings happen only during few months at the time of *kharif* and *rabi* harvest. The seasonal nature of agriculture causes fluctuations in income not only for the cultivators who are working for their self-production but also for the labourers who work as wage earners in agriculture. Dispersion was low in the case of salary as income for this item was almost fixed over time. Wages and self-employment income also varied less compared to agriculture and livestock income. Last and the least, because of the irregular nature of income from pension, transfer, rental and dividend, their dispersion was quite high in most of the cases.

Before concluding the chapter, we compare our below poverty income data with the Planning Commission poverty estimates of income based on 61st Round of National Sample Survey released in 2004-05. The state-wise rural and urban poverty lines as released by the Planning Commission for the year 2004-05 are given in Table 3.25. The poverty line is estimated by the Planning Commission using the original state-specific poverty lines identified by the Expert Group and updating them to the current prices using the Consumer Price Index of Agricultural Labourers (CPIAL) for the rural poverty lines and Consumer Price Index for Industrial Workers (CPIIW) for the urban poverty lines. By comparing our estimates with the official poverty line, we can check whether the sampled families who owned below poverty ration cards were truly poor or not according to the definition of Planning Commission, Government of India. It is however, noted that the Planning Commission estimates were available for the year 2004-05. We have updated these estimates to 2006-07 using the CPI AL for the rural and CPI IW for the urban cut-off. Table 3.25 presents per capita monthly income defined by the official poverty line and the observed per capita monthly income by our selected households. In our estimates, we have used both annual as well as monthly income estimates. Comparing our survey data with the Planning Commission, it is observed from the results that our income

2. For comparison, we have to convert the annual estimates into monthly by dividing annual estimates by 12.

3. We use both monthly and annual estimates to compare the official estimates of number of people below poverty in different states (See Chapter 6).

4. This issue will be probed in further details in the forthcoming chapters.

estimates were more or less very close to that of the Planning Commission. Our BPL income estimates were above the official poverty line in Delhi, Kerala and Maharashtra based on both annual estimates as well as monthly estimates.[5] In these three states, even our AAY per capita income exceeded the Rural Poverty Line defined by the Planning Commission. In Madhya Pradesh, our BPL estimates based on monthly income were almost equal to the official figure for rural areas while annual BPL income was less than that of official figure. In Uttarakhand and Jharkhand, our BPL income based on annual as well as monthly was less than that of official poverty line. However, it is worth mentioning that the official poverty line income is the upper bound cut-off, whereas our estimated income is only the average income, thereby some households would fall below this income but some will be above this average income and thereby they would be wrongly defined as below poverty households.

Table 3.25 Comparison of our Observed Income Per Capita with the Official Poverty Line Income Defined by the Planning Commission

State	Our Survey Data Estimates				Planning Commission Estimates$ #	
	Based on Annual Income		Based on Monthly Income		Rural	Urban
	AAY	BPL	AAY	BPL		
Delhi	537	658	531	618	466	697
Jharkhand	260	287	356	359	434	505
Kerala	710	792	759	807	458	614
Madhya Pradesh	221	260	361	384	385	663
Maharashtra	415	475	453	488	416	814
Uttarakhand	338	439	454	493	569	761

Note: 1. $ - The poverty line is worked out from the expenditure class-wise distribution of persons based on Uniform Recall Period consumption, i.e., consumption data collected from 30-day recall period for all items.

2. # - The Planning Commission Estimates of 2004-05 have been updated to 2006-07 using Consumer Price Index Numbers for Agricultural Labourers for the rural income and Consumer Price Index Numbers for Industrial Workers for the urban income.

Source: Planning Commission, Government of India.

5. As our field survey contains 80 per cent samples from the rural areas, one should compare our estimates with that of official rural poverty line.

4 Consumption Pattern and Food Distribution under PDS

4.1 Introduction

In the previous chapter, we presented trends in the occupation pattern and income earnings of the selected households. This chapter analyses the dynamics of consumption among the selected AAY, BPL and APL households in the six states. The chapter is divided into six sections. The chapter begins with a discussion on consumption of major food items by the selected households during the period of six months for which survey was carried out. A comparison of our survey results is made with that of NSS consumption data for the latest three quinquennial rounds of NSS. Section 3 presents food and non-food expenditure where percentage is worked out for each item in the total consumption expenditure. Section 4 presents the amount delivered to the households by the PDS and the percentage of population obtaining PDS commodities. This section also makes a comparison of the percentage shares of PDS and that of market in the total quantity consumed by the households. The last section earmarks the actual prices paid by the households for the commodities purchased from PDS, *vis-à-vis* from the market.

4.2 Food Consumption Pattern

Food consumption expressed in kilocalories (Kcal) per capita is used for measuring the level of nutrition. In defining poverty, the Planning Commission uses the calorie requirement norm of 2400 Kcal per capita for the rural areas and 2100 Kcal per capita for the urban areas. It further emphasises that 50 per cent of calories to be derived from carbohydrate and the remaining from the protein and fat with 25 per cent each. Fifty per cent of the required calorie means drawing 1200 calorie from cereals in rural India and 1050 in the urban India. To get the requisite 1200 calories, 10.44 kg cereals per capita per 30 days or 348 gms per capita per day are required by the rural people and 9.12 kg cereals per capita per 30 days or 304 gms per capita per day are required by the urban people to obtain 1050 calories.[1]

Tables 4.1 to 4.6 present per capita monthly consumption of food items, *viz.*, cereals, pulses, edible oils, sugar and milk by our selected households in the six states. It is evident from the results that on an average, per capita cereal consumption was more or less in consonance with the 1200 calorie norm, i.e., total cereal consumption was around 10.5 kgs in Delhi, Madhya Pradesh, Maharashtra and Uttarakhand. It far exceeded the 1200 calorie norm in Jharkhand where average cereal consumption was found 13.5 kgs while cereal consumption was found much lower than the norm, around 8.5 kgs in Kerala. In Jharkhand, all categories of households, *viz.*, AAY, BPL and APL had much above the minimum requirement norm while in Kerala, all categories fell short of this target. Among the cereals, wheat and rice constituted the principal share while coarse grains were minor cereals. Wheat was the major cereal consumed in Delhi with average consumption of 7.7 kgs and in Madhya Pradesh with average quantity of 6 kgs. Rice occupied the principal place in Kerala and Jharkhand with an average quantity of 7.8 kgs and 11.4 kgs, respectively. In the other two states namely, Maharashtra and Uttarakhand, both wheat and rice were consumed almost in the same ratio. The average quantity of rice and wheat consumed in Maharashtra was 5.6 and 3.7 kgs, respectively. In Uttarakhand, the average quantity of rice and wheat was 6.9 and 4.3 kgs, respectively. In Delhi and Madhya Pradesh, about 3 kgs of rice quantity per capita was also consumed along with the above-mentioned quantity of wheat. Similarly, in Kerala less than a kg and in Jharkhand, 2 kgs of wheat per capita was also consumed. The other coarse cereals consumed namely,

1. The above calculations are based on Planning Commission (1977) calculations that 100 gms cereal on an average produce 345 calories.

jowar, bajra, maize, barley and *ragi* (combined) were around 1.5 kgs in Maharashtra and one kg in Madhya Pradesh. In the other four states namely, Delhi, Jharkhand, Kerala and Uttarakhand, coarse cereal consumption was almost negligible. At the overall, average cereal consumption in the six states was around 11 kgs, that varied from 8.6 kgs in Kerala, between 10 to 11 kgs in Delhi, Madhya Pradesh and Maharashtra each, a little more than 11 kgs in Uttarakhand and as high as 13.5 kgs in Jharkhand.

Table 4.1 Household Consumption of Food Items (Kgs. Per Capita per Month)—Delhi

	Month 1	Month 2	Month 3	Month 4	Month 5	Month 6	Average	NSS[2] 1993-94	NSS[2] 1999-2000	NSS[2] 2004-05
					AAY					
Rice	2.84	3.05	3.35	3.05	3.25	3.24	3.13	-	-	-
Wheat	7.54	7.64	7.67	8.11	8.40	8.13	7.91	-	-	-
Other cereals	0.06	0.00	0.03	0.01	0.00	0.03	0.02	-	-	-
Total cereals	10.44	10.69	11.04	11.56	11.65	11.40	11.07	-	-	-
Total pulses	0.75	0.74	0.96	0.84	0.81	0.75	0.81	-	-	-
Sugar	1.16	1.13	1.21	1.14	1.10	1.13	1.14	-	-	-
Edible oils	0.42	0.37	0.42	0.42	0.44	0.42	0.41	-	-	-
Liquid milk[1]	1.97	1.91	2.48	2.46	2.38	2.31	2.25	-	-	-
					BPL					
Rice	2.99	2.94	3.23	3.07	3.19	3.04	3.08	-	-	-
Wheat	7.41	7.29	7.45	7.89	8.19	7.99	7.70	-	-	-
Other cereals	0.02	0.00	0.05	0.01	0.02	0.00	0.02	-	-	-
Total cereals	10.42	10.23	10.73	11.34	11.40	11.03	10.80	-	-	-
Total pulses	0.78	0.72	0.91	0.85	0.81	0.75	0.80	-	-	-
Sugar	1.15	1.09	1.14	1.08	1.06	1.06	1.10	-	-	-
Edible oils	0.46	0.37	0.44	0.42	0.43	0.42	0.42	-	-	-
Liquid milk[1]	2.43	2.32	2.76	2.70	2.65	2.59	2.58	-	-	-
					APL					
Rice	3.00	3.08	3.15	2.85	2.90	2.81	2.96	-	-	-
Wheat	7.09	7.04	7.20	7.59	7.62	7.58	7.35	-	-	-
Other cereals	0.02	0.00	0.03	0.00	0.06	0.00	0.02	-	-	-
Total cereals	10.11	10.12	10.38	10.82	10.58	10.38	10.34	-	-	-
Total pulses	0.86	0.80	0.82	0.79	0.79	0.77	0.80	-	-	-
Sugar	1.12	1.00	1.07	0.94	0.91	0.91	0.99	-	-	-
Edible oils	0.58	0.47	0.53	0.49	0.48	0.52	0.51	-	-	-
Liquid milk[1]	4.28	3.83	4.15	3.80	3.79	3.76	3.93	-	-	-
					Average					
Rice	2.97	2.99	3.23	3.02	3.13	3.02	3.06	2.76	1.75	2.43
Wheat	7.36	7.30	7.43	7.86	8.10	7.92	7.66	7.75	6.11	6.80
Other cereals	0.02	0.00	0.04	0.01	0.02	0.01	0.02	0.00	0.00	0.00
Total cereals	10.36	10.29	10.71	11.26	11.26	10.96	10.74	10.51	7.86	9.23
Total pulses	0.79	0.74	0.90	0.83	0.81	0.76	0.80	1.12	0.92	0.75
Sugar	1.15	1.08	1.13	1.06	1.03	1.04	1.08	1.46	1.00	-
Edible oils	0.48	0.39	0.46	0.43	0.45	0.44	0.44	0.74	0.53	-
Liquid milk[1]	2.76	2.58	3.02	2.90	2.85	2.80	2.82	8.69	6.34	-

Note: 1. Liquid milk is in litres.

2. The NSS consumption figures are taken from the respective rounds of NSS reports and the quantities represent all classes for the rural areas.

Table 4.2 Household Consumption of Food Items (Kgs. Per Capita per Month)—Jharkhand

	Month 1	Month 2	Month 3	Month 4	Month 5	Month 6	Average	NSS[2] [3]1993-94	NSS[2] [3]1999-2000	NSS[2] 2004-05
					AAY					
Rice	11.78	10.67	10.97	10.83	11.15	10.70	11.02	-	-	-
Wheat	2.87	2.40	2.85	2.67	2.50	2.47	2.63	-	-	-
Other cereals	0.02	0.01	0.00	0.00	0.00	0.02	0.01	-	-	-
Total cereals	14.67	13.08	13.82	13.59	13.65	13.19	13.65	-	-	-
Total pulses	0.32	0.28	0.29	0.29	0.26	0.26	0.29	-	-	-
Sugar	0.21	0.20	0.25	0.20	0.20	0.22	0.21	-	-	-
Edible oils	0.26	0.24	0.25	0.23	0.23	0.25	0.24	-	-	-
Liquid milk[1]	0.21	0.09	0.21	0.22	0.18	0.12	0.17	-	-	-
					BPL					
Rice	12.08	10.54	12.18	11.71	11.54	11.57	11.60	-	-	-
Wheat	1.90	1.87	1.92	1.91	2.02	1.97	1.93	-	-	-
Other cereals	0.03	0.01	0.02	0.01	0.01	0.01	0.02	-	-	-
Total cereals	14.02	12.43	14.11	13.71	13.56	13.56	13.55	-	-	-
Total pulses	0.41	0.28	0.29	0.29	0.26	0.27	0.30	-	-	-
Sugar	0.19	0.19	0.25	0.20	0.21	0.22	0.21	-	-	-
Edible oils	0.25	0.21	0.24	0.23	0.23	0.24	0.23	-	-	-
Liquid milk[1]	0.18	0.10	0.35	0.32	0.23	0.12	0.22	-	-	-
					APL					
Rice	10.42	11.95	11.49	11.26	10.52	10.33	11.00	-	-	-
Wheat	3.14	2.15	1.83	2.39	2.39	2.45	2.39	-	-	-
Other cereals	0.04	0.02	0.02	0.01	0.01	0.01	0.02	-	-	-
Total cereals	13.61	14.11	13.33	13.79	12.92	12.79	13.41	-	-	-
Total pulses	0.43	0.33	0.35	0.35	0.34	0.34	0.35	-	-	-
Sugar	0.31	0.24	0.31	0.27	0.27	0.28	0.28	-	-	-
Edible oils	0.33	0.27	0.31	0.28	0.28	0.29	0.29	-	-	-
Liquid milk[1]	0.51	0.31	0.84	0.87	0.84	0.72	0.68	-	-	-
					Average					
Rice	11.74	10.81	11.83	11.46	11.29	11.19	11.39	7.95	7.89	9.59
Wheat	2.30	2.02	2.08	2.14	2.18	2.15	2.14	5.58	5.21	2.83
Other cereals	0.03	0.01	0.01	0.01	0.00	0.01	0.01	0.78	0.65	0.39
Total cereals	14.07	12.84	13.92	13.70	13.47	13.35	13.54	14.31	13.75	12.81
Total pulses	0.40	0.29	0.30	0.30	0.28	0.28	0.31	0.72	0.78	0.49
Sugar	0.22	0.20	0.26	0.21	0.22	0.23	0.22	0.38	0.44	-
Edible oils	0.27	0.23	0.26	0.24	0.24	0.25	0.25	0.29	0.40	-
Liquid milk[1]	0.24	0.14	0.41	0.40	0.33	0.22	0.29	2.39	2.41	-

Note: 1. Liquid milk is in litres.

2. The NSS consumption figures are taken from the respective rounds of NSS reports and the quantities represent all classes for the rural areas.

3. 1993-94 and 1999-2000 figures belong to Bihar.

Table 4.3 Household Consumption of Food Items (Kgs. Per Capita per Month)—Kerala

	Month 1	Month 2	Month 3	Month 4	Month 5	Month 6	Average	NSS[2] 1993-94	NSS[2] 1999-2000	NSS[2] 2004-05
					AAY					
Rice	9.41	9.37	8.56	8.48	8.05	7.82	8.62	-	-	-
Wheat	0.48	0.65	0.15	0.14	0.08	0.08	0.26	-	-	-
Other cereals	0.01	0.00	0.01	0.00	0.00	0.00	0.00	-	-	-
Total cereals	9.89	10.02	8.73	8.81	8.13	7.90	8.88	-	-	-
Total pulses	0.21	0.21	0.20	0.20	0.19	0.20	0.20	-	-	-
Sugar	0.67	0.68	0.66	0.65	0.66	0.71	0.67	-	-	-
Edible oils	0.34	0.35	0.36	0.35	0.33	0.32	0.34	-	-	-
Liquid milk[1]	0.94	0.81	0.65	0.69	0.54	0.56	0.70	-	-	-
					BPL					
Rice	8.47	8.11	7.33	7.32	6.93	6.80	7.49	-	-	-
Wheat	0.98	1.16	0.86	0.88	0.84	0.86	0.93	-	-	-
Other cereals	0.00	0.00	0.00	0.01	0.00	0.00	0.00	-	-	-
Total cereals	9.45	9.27	8.19	8.41	7.77	7.66	8.43	-	-	-
Total pulses	0.21	0.22	0.21	0.22	0.20	0.21	0.21	-	-	-
Sugar	0.71	0.75	0.68	0.67	0.71	0.71	0.70	-	-	-
Edible oils	0.37	0.38	0.40	0.39	0.38	0.43	0.39	-	-	-
Liquid milk[1]	0.92	0.92	0.90	0.89	0.84	0.81	0.88	-	-	-
					APL					
Rice	8.71	8.58	7.55	7.28	6.93	6.80	7.64	-	-	-
Wheat	1.04	1.04	0.85	0.88	0.86	0.83	0.92	-	-	-
Other cereals	0.00	0.01	0.01	0.01	0.01	0.02	0.01	-	-	-
Total cereals	9.75	9.62	8.41	8.42	7.79	7.65	8.57	-	-	-
Total pulses	0.27	0.26	0.25	0.25	0.25	0.24	0.25	-	-	-
Sugar	0.87	0.87	0.77	0.77	0.75	0.77	0.80	-	-	-
Edible oils	0.53	0.49	0.49	0.47	0.47	0.45	0.48	-	-	-
Liquid milk[1]	1.99	1.82	1.78	1.80	1.81	1.60	1.80	-	-	-
					Average					
Rice	8.71	8.46	7.63	3.02	7.16	7.01	7.75	9.29	8.89	8.61
Wheat	0.89	1.03	0.71	0.73	0.69	0.70	0.79	0.82	0.91	0.92
Other cereals	0.00	0.00	0.00	0.01	0.00	0.01	0.00	0.00	0.09	0.00
Total cereals	9.60	9.49	8.35	8.49	7.85	7.71	8.55	10.11	9.89	9.53
Total pulses	0.22	0.23	0.21	0.22	0.21	0.21	0.22	0.43	0.55	0.49
Sugar	0.73	0.76	0.69	0.68	0.70	0.72	0.72	0.86	0.85	-
Edible oils	0.40	0.39	0.41	0.39	0.39	0.41	0.40	0.26	0.42	-
Liquid milk[1]	1.13	1.07	1.01	1.02	0.96	0.91	1.02	2.61	2.97	-

Note: 1. Liquid milk is in litres.

2. The NSS consumption figures are taken from the respective rounds of NSS reports and the quantities represent all classes for the rural areas.

Table 4.4 Household Consumption of Food Items (Kgs. Per Capita per Month)—MP

	Month 1	Month 2	Month 3	Month 4	Month 5	Month 6	Average	NSS[2] 1993-94	NSS[2] 1999-2000	NSS[2] 2004-05
					AAY					
Rice	2.85	2.88	2.92	2.52	2.46	2.53	2.69	-	-	-
Wheat	6.00	6.48	6.81	7.37	7.35	7.53	6.92	-	-	-
Other cereals	0.94	0.65	0.82	0.89	0.99	1.06	0.89	-	-	-
Total cereals	9.78	10.01	10.55	11.05	10.80	11.12	10.50	-	-	-
Total pulses	0.43	0.39	0.44	0.55	0.52	0.52	0.47	-	-	-
Sugar	0.35	0.35	0.40	0.43	0.43	0.44	0.40	-	-	-
Edible oils	0.25	0.22	0.26	0.31	0.33	0.32	0.28	-	-	-
Liquid milk[1]	0.17	0.12	0.18	0.70	0.69	0.66	0.42	-	-	-
					BPL					
Rice	3.77	3.70	3.84	3.24	3.13	3.13	3.47	-	-	-
Wheat	4.59	5.07	5.53	6.11	6.15	6.21	5.61	-	-	-
Other cereals	1.09	0.87	0.95	1.05	0.91	1.15	1.00	-	-	-
Total cereals	9.45	9.64	10.33	10.71	10.19	10.49	10.08	-	-	-
Total pulses	0.49	0.46	0.49	0.55	0.54	0.54	0.51	-	-	-
Sugar	0.38	0.36	0.43	0.46	0.49	0.48	0.43	-	-	-
Edible oils	0.29	0.24	0.29	0.33	0.35	0.34	0.30	-	-	-
Liquid milk[1]	0.47	0.27	0.41	1.06	0.82	0.80	0.60	-	-	-
					APL					
Rice	3.58	3.92	3.83	3.43	3.29	3.26	3.55	-	-	-
Wheat	5.62	5.51	5.76	6.84	6.94	6.79	6.25	-	-	-
Other cereals	1.23	1.04	1.29	1.18	0.90	1.07	1.10	-	-	-
Total cereals	10.43	10.48	10.88	11.84	11.13	11.03	10.90	-	-	-
Total pulses	0.69	0.64	0.67	0.70	0.70	0.71	0.69	-	-	-
Sugar	0.64	0.55	0.58	0.67	0.66	0.67	0.63	-	-	-
Edible oils	0.40	0.35	0.36	0.43	0.43	0.43	0.40	-	-	-
Liquid milk[1]	1.69	1.18	1.46	2.46	2.26	2.18	1.87	-	-	-
					Average					
Rice	3.56	3.59	3.67	3.02	3.04	3.04	3.34	6.03	5.44	2.31
Wheat	5.05	5.42	5.81	6.49	6.53	6.57	5.98	5.81	6.20	7.64
Other cereals	1.09	0.86	1.00	1.04	0.93	1.10	1.00	2.36	1.30	1.81
Total cereals	9.71	9.87	10.48	11.00	10.49	10.71	10.32	14.20	12.94	11.76
Total pulses	0.52	0.48	0.52	0.58	0.57	0.57	0.54	0.97	0.87	0.74
Sugar	0.43	0.40	0.45	0.50	0.52	0.51	0.47	0.72	0.82	-
Edible oils	0.30	0.26	0.30	0.35	0.36	0.35	0.32	0.30	0.43	-
Liquid milk[1]	0.66	0.43	0.58	1.14	1.09	1.05	0.82	2.76	2.71	-

Note: 1. Liquid milk is in litres.

2. The NSS consumption figures are taken from the respective rounds of NSS reports and the quantities represent all classes for the rural areas.

Table 4.5 Household Consumption of Food Items (Kgs. Per Capita per Month)—Maharashtra

	Month 1	Month 2	Month 3	Month 4	Month 5	Month 6	Average	NSS[2] 1993-94	NSS[2] 1999-2000	NSS[2] 2004-05
					AAY					
Rice	6.83	6.10	6.71	6.56	6.58	6.46	6.54	-	-	-
Wheat	3.67	3.84	4.10	4.10	4.12	4.25	4.01	-	-	-
Other cereals	1.16	0.98	1.16	1.31	1.23	1.16	1.17	-	-	-
Total cereals	11.66	10.93	11.97	12.27	11.93	11.87	11.72	-	-	-
Total pulses	0.60	0.61	0.60	0.51	0.48	0.48	0.55	-	-	-
Sugar	0.63	0.63	0.65	0.70	0.71	0.69	0.67	-	-	-
Edible oils	0.38	0.40	0.38	0.41	0.43	0.44	0.41	-	-	-
Liquid milk[1]	0.67	0.86	0.78	0.92	0.88	0.85	0.82	-	-	-
					BPL					
Rice	5.77	5.37	5.95	5.47	5.36	5.42	5.56	-	-	-
Wheat	3.40	3.41	3.54	3.63	3.72	3.66	3.56	-	-	-
Other cereals	1.58	1.02	1.39	1.70	1.54	1.61	1.47	-	-	-
Total cereals	10.76	9.82	10.89	11.12	10.61	10.70	10.59	-	-	-
Total pulses	0.61	0.60	0.61	0.55	0.49	0.51	0.56	-	-	-
Sugar	0.64	0.60	0.65	0.73	0.73	0.73	0.68	-	-	-
Edible oils	0.43	0.40	0.41	0.44	0.45	0.45	0.43	-	-	-
Liquid milk[1]	0.93	0.80	1.07	1.06	1.76	0.97	0.97	-	-	-
					APL					
Rice	5.48	4.46	5.64	5.39	5.12	5.04	5.19	-	-	-
Wheat	4.21	3.99	4.34	4.25	3.69	3.93	4.07	-	-	-
Other cereals	1.66	1.02	1.72	1.66	1.46	1.53	1.52	-	-	-
Total cereals	11.34	9.47	11.69	11.75	10.27	10.57	10.77	-	-	-
Total pulses	0.83	0.75	0.82	0.68	0.60	0.64	0.72	-	-	-
Sugar	0.93	0.91	0.94	0.97	0.96	0.94	0.94	-	-	-
Edible oils	0.58	0.53	0.56	0.61	0.59	0.59	0.57	-	-	-
Liquid milk[1]	2.02	1.94	2.23	2.58	2.40	2.34	2.25	-	-	-
					Average					
Rice	5.88	5.30	6.01	5.63	5.51	5.52	5.64	2.97	3.12	2.97
Wheat	3.61	3.60	3.80	3.83	3.78	3.81	3.74	2.21	3.48	3.41
Other cereals	1.53	1.01	1.42	1.63	1.47	1.54	1.43	6.21	5.82	4.12
Total cereals	11.02	9.91	11.23	11.44	10.76	10.86	10.81	11.39	11.32	10.50
Total pulses	0.65	0.63	0.65	0.57	0.51	0.53	0.59	0.93	1.00	0.87
Sugar	0.70	0.67	0.71	0.77	0.77	0.76	0.73	1.09	1.07	-
Edible oils	0.45	0.42	0.43	0.47	0.47	0.48	0.45	0.30	0.59	-
Liquid milk[1]	1.11	1.04	1.26	1.35	1.26	1.23	1.21	2.50	2.66	-

Note: 1. Liquid milk is in litres.

2. The NSS consumption figures are taken from the respective rounds of NSS reports and the quantities represent all classes for the rural areas.

Table 4.6 Household Consumption of Food Items (Kgs. Per Capita per Month)—Uttarakhand

	Month 1	Month 2	Month 3	Month 4	Month 5	Month 6	Average	NSS[2] [3]1993-94	NSS[2] [3]1999-2000	NSS[2] 2004-05
					AAY					
Rice	7.95	7.79	7.88	7.43	7.30	7.46	7.63	-	-	-
Wheat	4.34	3.94	4.18	4.36	4.37	4.25	4.24	-	-	-
Other cereals	0.07	0.00	0.00	0.02	0.00	0.00	0.02	-	-	-
Total cereals	12.36	11.73	12.05	12.05	11.67	11.71	11.89	-	-	-
Total pulses	0.60	0.52	0.52	0.56	0.57	0.56	0.55	-	-	-
Sugar	0.81	0.74	0.74	0.69	0.69	0.70	0.73	-	-	-
Edible oils	0.58	0.43	0.47	0.41	0.39	0.39	0.44	-	-	-
Liquid milk[1]	1.24	0.94	1.21	1.48	1.51	1.37	1.29	-	-	-
					BPL					
Rice	7.20	6.96	7.15	6.64	6.47	6.43	6.81	-	-	-
Wheat	4.17	3.73	3.93	4.28	4.26	4.21	4.10	-	-	-
Other cereals	0.02	0.00	0.00	0.01	0.00	0.01	0.01	-	-	-
Total cereals	11.39	10.69	11.09	11.13	10.74	10.64	10.91	-	-	-
Total pulses	0.57	0.48	0.48	0.52	0.52	0.52	0.51	-	-	-
Sugar	0.80	0.68	0.72	0.64	0.67	0.68	0.70	-	-	-
Edible oils	0.44	0.41	0.45	0.39	0.39	0.38	0.41	-	-	-
Liquid milk[1]	1.04	0.90	1.16	1.75	1.76	1.70	1.38	-	-	-
					APL					
Rice	7.00	6.45	6.80	6.24	5.89	5.87	6.38	-	-	-
Wheat	4.81	4.30	4.90	5.07	5.20	4.97	4.88	-	-	-
Other cereals	0.12	0.05	0.02	0.01	0.00	0.02	0.04	-	-	-
Total cereals	11.94	10.80	11.72	11.61	11.10	10.86	11.29	-	-	-
Total pulses	0.81	0.66	0.65	0.66	0.64	0.63	0.67	-	-	-
Sugar	1.06	1.01	1.02	0.87	0.85	0.87	0.95	-	-	-
Edible oils	0.56	0.52	0.58	0.48	0.47	0.48	0.52	-	-	-
Liquid milk[1]	2.43	1.96	2.20	3.27	3.41	3.34	2.77	-	-	-
					Average					
Rice	7.30	7.00	7.21	6.70	6.50	6.51	6.87	4.00	4.28	5.01
Wheat	4.33	3.88	4.16	4.45	4.47	4.36	4.27	9.16	8.92	6.28
Other cereals	0.05	0.01	0.01	0.01	0.00	0.01	0.01	0.75	0.42	0.59
Total cereals	11.67	10.90	11.38	11.39	10.97	10.88	11.16	13.91	13.62	11.88
Total pulses	0.62	0.52	0.52	0.55	0.55	0.55	0.55	0.98	1.07	0.93
Sugar	0.85	0.75	0.78	0.69	0.71	0.72	0.75	0.89	0.95	-
Edible oils	0.49	0.43	0.48	0.41	0.41	0.40	0.44	0.38	0.50	-
Liquid milk[1]	1.35	1.11	1.37	2.00	2.04	1.97	1.64	5.44	4.52	-

Note: 1. Liquid milk in litres.

2. The NSS consumption figures are taken from the respective rounds of NSS reports and the quantities represent all classes for the rural areas.

3. 1993-94 and 1999-2000 figures belong to Uttar Pradesh.

We compare our consumption trends from six rounds of survey data with the consumption of cereals as revealed by various rounds of National Sample Survey (NSS). Three rounds of large sample survey, i.e., 50th Round (1993-94), 55th Round (1999-2000) and 61st Round (2004-05) consumption results are presented in the tables along with our observed consumption for the overall average of all category households. The NSS figures represent household consumption (aggregate of all expenditure classes) from the rural area. We have presented NSS figures for rural areas to maintain parity with our sample as 80 per cent of our sample households are drawn from the rural areas. The NSS consumption quantities are not presented for AAY, BPL and APL households separately, because the consumption in physical quantities was not readily available for different expenditure classes at the state level.[2] Comparing total cereal consumption in the selected states from our survey data with that of NSS, our average cereal consumption was slightly less than the latest round of NSS (2004-05) survey in Kerala, Madhya Pradesh and Uttarakhand. It was slightly higher in rest of the three states, namely Delhi, Jharkhand and Maharashtra. However, the difference between our survey data and the respective NSS data was generally less than 10 per cent.

In the first volume, it was discussed in detail that per capita consumption of cereals and total calorie intake in India has started declining in the recent past. It is evident from the NSS data presented in the tables that total cereal consumption has also declined in our current selected states without any exception. Total cereals consumption declined from 10.5 kgs to 9.2 kgs in Delhi, 14.3 kgs to 12.8 kgs in Jharkhand, 10.1 kgs to 9.5 kgs in Kerala, 14.2 kgs to 11.8 kgs in Madhya Pradesh, 11.4 kgs to 10.5 kgs in Maharashtra and 13.9 kgs to 11.9 kgs in Uttarakhand during a decade's time period from 1993-94 to 2004-2005. As was discussed in the previous volume, the declining cereals might have been caused by the diversification of the food basket and the changing income and lifestyle of the rural and urban masses. On the one hand, due to change in work nature, the requirement of calorie intake has declined overtime and on the other, the changes in the composition of diet have increased the cost of calories (Radhakrishna and Ravi, 1991; Murty, 1999). Convergence between rural and urban patterns of calorie consumption also provides an explanation to this phenomenon.

The food basket of an average Indian is diversifying with their rising income and improved living standards. Whereas cereals and pulses were the main source of protein in both rural and urban areas in the seventies and early eighties, the contribution of milk and milk products as source of protein is consistently increasing in the more recent rounds of NSS and the increase is observed much more in the urban areas. The contribution from meat, fish and eggs to protein has slightly increased (Delgado *et al.*, 1999). The diversification of consumption from cereals and pulses towards edible oils, milk and high value products is also visible from the trends presented by our survey data. Comparing the three categories of households, the quantity of cereals consumed by AAY households was generally higher than that of BPL and APL households. On the other hand, the quantity of edible oils, sugar and milk consumed was much higher for APL households as compared to BPL and AAY households in all the states without any exception. Therefore, the statistics depicted above substantiate the argument that with the rising level of income, people have a tendency to diversify their palate towards more nutritious and high value commodities. Comparing the consumption of milk, sugar and edible oil with that of the NSS, generally the quantity consumed in the NSS was slightly higher than that of our survey households. The possible reason could be that consumption of these items had higher income elasticity (as is seen above) and because our data was more slanting towards the below poverty households whereas the NSS figures depicted average quantity for all the classes.

Comparing variability in the food consumption, Annexure Table A-4.1 presents results of coefficient of variation across households and across time period (six months) for each category. Variations in consumption were higher across households than for the same households over time. Among different categories, consumption variation was higher among the below poverty households compared to above poverty households. Higher variation in food consumption by the poor households puts forth the question of affordability of food by such people and raises the need for some sort of income insurance for them.[3] Among AAY households, coefficient of variation was high for milk in almost all the states, indicating its high cost for the poor that was beyond purchasing capacity of all the (AAY) households. At the overall, coefficient of variation of consumption over time was lower than that of coefficient of variation in income supporting the well-documented phenomenon of consumption smoothing by the households (see Chapter 5).[4]

2. In the next section while comparing consumption expenditure for AAY, BPL and APL households, the NSS figures are taken separately for same income brackets, as per capita expenditure data from NSS is available for the respective expenditure classes at the state level.

3. We address this issue in detail in the next chapter.

4. See for example, Townsend (1994, 1995); Morduch (1990); Grimard (1997).

Table 4.7 Monthly Consumption Expenditure of Households (Average of Six Months)—Delhi

	AAY			BPL			APL		
	Monthly Per Capita (Rs.)	Coefficient of Variation	NSS 2004-05 (Rs.)	Monthly Per Capita (Rs.)	Coefficient of Variation	NSS 2004-05 (Rs.)	Monthly Per Capita (Rs.)	Coefficient of Variation	NSS 2004-05 (Rs.)
Food Items									
Rice	17.67	95.15	16.00	25.61	60.89	16.00	33.23	66.56	19.79
Wheat	40.01	97.38	54.00	55.14	60.12	54.00	69.40	61.99	57.98
Other cereals	0.13	78.14	0.00	0.09	47.29	0.00	0.14	54.55	0.01
Total cereals	57.80	-	70.00	80.84	-	70.00	102.76	-	77.78
Pulses	25.59	46.29	18.40	25.71	44.28	18.40	29.78	50.67	20.97
Sugar etc.	15.99	28.72	7.60	15.28	25.12	7.60	17.97	43.68	12.61
Cooking oil	21.92	46.38	22.00	22.46	43.71	22.00	26.50	49.56	31.75
Spices	12.62	99.13	15.40	12.84	97.68	15.40	13.82	107.66	14.49
Milk & milk products	44.83	47.08	14.00	50.96	48.49	14.00	79.23	58.33	69.46
Poultry & meat	7.45	75.09	16.00	9.72	76.57	16.00	10.88	82.35	6.65
Fruits	3.46	59.02	7.00	4.45	61.65	7.00	10.44	70.02	9.86
Vegetables	36.62	61.30	35.00	35.99	58.49	35.00	38.42	60.53	46.30
Confectionery	2.49	91.51	10.80	3.38	102.60	10.80	7.87	85.59	19.01
Total food	228.78	-	216.20	261.64	-	216.20	337.68	-	308.88
Non-food (30-day recall period)									
Education	8.34	218.90	10.00	9.26	94.72	10.00	19.21	199.25	6.52
Clothing	5.24	54.24	0.00	5.88	59.77	0.00	11.44	87.55	0.00
Footwear	2.50	80.06	0.00	2.81	58.55	0.00	4.20	89.69	1.65
Other items	37.37	273.40	75.00	39.79	161.78	75.00	53.41	222.16	142.92
Fuel	63.75	41.96	91.00	64.32	45.86	91.00	81.30	41.73	92.81
Total non-food	117.20	-	176.00	122.05	-	176.00	169.56	-	243.90
Gross total	345.98	-	392.20	383.70	-	392.20	507.24	-	552.78
Non-food (365-day recall period)									
Education	23.12	100.62	4.11	29.09	100.62	4.11	71.87	313.81	5.59
Clothing	22.89	62.70	26.71	26.14	62.70	26.71	37.19	70.75	28.41
Footwear	5.84	70.64	2.05	6.67	70.64	2.05	10.15	85.77	5.48
Other items	34.70	146.02	75.00	40.18	146.02	75.00	64.32	219.73	142.92
Fuel	72.75	39.91	91.00	70.43	39.91	91.00	85.94	93.97	92.81
Total non-food	159.31	-	198.87	172.52	-	198.87	269.47	-	275.21
Gross total	388.09	-	415.07	434.16	-	415.07	607.15	-	584.09

Table 4.8 Monthly Consumption Expenditure of Households (Average of Six Months)—Jharkhand

	Monthly Per Capita (Rs.)	Coefficient of Variation	NSS 2004-05 (Rs.)	Monthly Per Capita (Rs.)	Coefficient of Variation	NSS 2004-05 (Rs.)	Monthly Per Capita (Rs.)	Coefficient of Variation	NSS 2004-05 (Rs.)
		AAY			BPL			APL	
				Food Items					
Rice	82.40	101.91	65.94	103.94	73.87	74.91	109.77	64.87	90.38
Wheat	9.47	162.31	11.26	13.73	99.72	14.49	27.87	84.42	24.29
Other cereals	0.04	76.37	1.18	0.09	191.7	2.20	0.09	34.83	1.82
Total cereals	91.91	-	78.38	117.77	-	91.60	137.74	-	116.49
Pulses	9.06	71.13	5.61	8.85	62.02	8.03	11.30	67.77	10.38
Sugar etc.	4.20	63.45	3.97	4.15	62.17	4.71	5.53	69.43	6.35
Cooking oil	14.24	59.09	13.49	13.82	61.63	16.28	17.40	63.74	19.82
Spices	5.66	124.77	7.05	6.15	114.4	8.29	7.02	99.45	10.83
Milk & milk products	2.40	81.55	1.68	2.84	87.49	3.61	10.31	90.78	7.42
Poultry & meat	11.05	70.13	6.35	11.74	71.38	8.01	16.41	82.66	11.86
Fruits	0.86	83.60	0.38	0.85	79.91	0.62	2.14	107.35	1.72
Vegetables	23.15	95.11	19.86	22.10	95.41	24.15	24.00	100.33	33.97
Confectionery	2.06	134.49	5.12	1.85	86.32	7.68	3.61	126.83	11.78
Total food	164.60	-	142.19	190.12	-	173.33	235.46	-	231.28
				Non-food (30-day recall period)					
Education	6.89	338.71	4.74	6.64	429.03	7.97	13.32	143.13	9.84
Clothing	3.79	88.54	3.66	3.91	118.47	4.91	7.42	131.66	9.20
Footwear	1.73	61.83	0.60	1.56	101.36	0.80	2.71	111.56	1.87
Other items	30.92	547.78	25.26	29.82	423.26	32.91	38.56	128.29	45.30
Fuel	20.32	69.15	30.39	19.46	74.33	35.68	23.20	70.83	43.18
Total non-food	63.65	-	64.65	61.40	-	82.27	85.21	-	109.39
Gross total	228.25	-	206.84	251.51	-	255.60	320.66	-	340.67
				Non-food (365-day recall period)					
Education	10.03	106.01	2.52	10.56	151.85	3.69	20.40	145.50	6.77
Clothing	17.68	54.40	17.46	18.48	51.21	19.85	25.05	75.92	26.30
Footwear	2.87	66.78	1.35	3.59	77.43	1.87	4.47	69.53	3.07
Other items	23.11	147.02	25.26	25.67	281.22	32.91	35.61	371.71	45.30
Fuel	19.18	75.02	30.39	19.57	79.29	35.68	23.42	83.48	43.18
Total non-food	72.87	-	76.98	77.87	-	94.00	108.96	-	124.62
Gross total	237.47	-	219.17	267.99	-	267.33	344.42	-	355.90

Table 4.9 **Monthly Consumption Expenditure of Households (Average of Six Months)—Kerala**

	AAY			BPL			APL		
	Monthly Per Capita (Rs.)	Coefficient of Variation	NSS 2004-05 (Rs.)	Monthly Per Capita (Rs.)	Coefficient of Variation	NSS 2004-05 (Rs.)	Monthly Per Capita (Rs.)	Coefficient of Variation	NSS 2004-05 (Rs.)
Food Items									
Rice	51.43	92.77	54.95	54.25	106.49	54.95	80.89	63.36	79.84
Wheat	2.52	105.39	5.10	4.07	155.08	5.10	8.26	85.19	5.35
Other cereals	0.03	50.74	0.18	0.02	84.82	0.18	0.07	85.84	0.13
Total cereals	53.98	-	60.23	58.34	-	60.23	89.22	-	85.32
Pulses	6.98	55.55	6.02	7.37	59.39	6.02	8.87	58.53	7.66
Sugar etc.	10.65	77.51	9.59	11.09	76.49	9.59	13.55	67.74	13.40
Cooking oil	19.20	60.09	14.98	21.43	68.00	14.98	26.77	65.11	17.85
Spices	18.34	107.02	11.61	21.05	115.86	11.61	21.50	105.35	14.76
Milk & milk products	9.50	73.29	5.73	11.95	68.97	5.73	25.19	69.42	14.77
Poultry & meat	38.32	84.20	26.71	42.25	86.22	26.71	57.23	95.05	35.29
Fruits	4.03	75.67	16.21	4.86	80.37	16.21	7.79	91.28	25.59
Vegetables	20.62	87.46	14.44	21.88	89.28	14.44	26.16	86.04	18.39
Confectionery	3.29	88.10	16.42	3.91	88.96	16.42	7.30	191.05	29.30
Total food	184.91	-	186.26	204.13	-	186.26	283.56	-	266.26
Non-food (30-day recall period)									
Education	20.18	141.66	20.35	22.01	147.12	20.35	40.13	161.71	28.80
Clothing	1.56	57.65	1.66	1.82	72.86	1.66	3.82	115.50	9.42
Footwear	0.70	56.40	0.67	0.92	68.96	0.67	1.39	122.33	2.15
Other items	43.69	251.17	51.43	49.22	213.36	51.43	69.06	132.19	81.75
Fuel	24.51	89.89	32.40	31.00	95.79	32.40	49.92	70.66	43.77
Total non-food	90.64	-	106.51	104.97	-	106.51	164.33	-	165.89
Gross total	275.55	-	292.77	309.10	-	292.77	447.89	-	432.15
Non-food (365-day recall period)									
Education	34.66	268.25	20.43	30.24	176.56	20.43	64.25	236.11	26.40
Clothing	18.82	72.07	22.39	22.08	78.42	22.39	32.73	78.39	28.64
Footwear	3.87	70.57	3.72	4.47	71.05	3.72	7.20	178.56	4.46
Other items	59.87	122.18	51.43	69.16	156.99	51.43	103.25	175.69	81.75
Fuel	29.42	77.47	32.40	36.72	90.62	32.40	55.06	74.66	43.77
Total non-food	146.64	-	130.37	162.68	-	130.37	262.49	-	185.02
Gross total	331.55	-	316.63	366.81	-	316.63	546.05	-	451.28

Table 4.10 Monthly Consumption Expenditure of Households (Average of Six Months)—Madhya Pradesh

	Monthly Per Capita (Rs.)	Coefficient of Variation	NSS 2004-05 (Rs.)	Monthly Per Capita (Rs.)	Coefficient of Variation	NSS 2004-05 (Rs.)	Monthly Per Capita (Rs.)	Coefficient of Variation	NSS 2004-05 (Rs.)
	AAY			BPL			APL		
Food Items									
Rice	20.13	147.57	21.67	31.54	116.54	21.03	38.63	89.95	16.73
Wheat	31.86	109.31	32.74	45.35	97.96	38.13	62.82	70.69	45.65
Other cereals	7.61	64.81	8.09	8.70	76.62	11.71	9.47	76.08	12.62
Total cereals	59.60	-	62.50	85.58	-	70.87	110.93	-	75.00
Pulses	15.43	55.91	9.49	16.75	58.76	11.81	23.71	71.03	17.43
Sugar etc.	6.17	54.00	5.99	6.79	61.77	7.82	10.86	70.76	13.18
Cooking oil	14.69	55.00	11.52	15.99	56.72	13.84	20.64	59.35	20.20
Spices	10.93	86.63	7.41	11.06	92.36	8.94	13.96	87.10	11.08
Milk & milk products	5.66	103.70	6.32	8.33	90.07	11.14	26.81	81.88	33.78
Poultry & meat	9.66	66.47	2.36	9.17	68.12	2.87	9.37	68.05	5.54
Fruits	1.98	53.69	1.50	2.32	65.44	2.40	4.70	77.45	3.96
Vegetables	22.07	75.57	14.99	22.51	78.47	17.71	27.14	83.56	22.40
Confectionery	1.40	67.24	5.27	1.54	100.18	7.21	2.61	110.67	13.60
Total food	147.61	-	127.63	180.03	-	154.76	250.72	-	216.81
Non-food (30-day recall period)									
Education	2.75	90.95	8.18	3.86	184.77	13.78	11.59	128.43	28.05
Clothing	2.11	63.28	2.93	2.71	145.50	5.44	5.62	86.05	20.41
Footwear	1.14	70.10	0.63	1.09	68.71	1.27	2.23	108.91	3.75
Other items	27.92	129.74	30.81	32.77	268.90	40.32	63.68	117.93	67.37
Fuel	10.21	228.85	29.08	13.25	89.53	37.36	31.42	76.74	50.60
Total non-food	44.13	-	71.63	53.69	-	98.17	114.54	-	170.18
Gross total	191.74	-	199.26	233.72	-	252.93	365.26	-	387.00
Non-food (365-day recall period)									
Education	11.54	279.54	3.55	15.56	172.53	6.63	48.31	191.47	11.82
Clothing	13.97	62.54	22.61	19.04	123.85	26.74	30.32	103.31	32.29
Footwear	2.69	66.60	3.80	3.72	138.99	3.89	6.67	137.89	5.23
Other items	25.27	143.46	30.81	27.72	143.92	40.32	52.13	143.79	67.37
Fuel	15.02	120.76	29.08	17.85	105.42	37.36	37.08	82.68	50.60
Total non-food	68.49	-	89.85	83.89	-	114.94	174.51	-	167.31
Gross total	216.10	-	217.48	263.92	-	269.70	425.23	-	384.12

Table 4.11 Monthly Consumption Expenditure of Households (Average of Six Months)—Maharashtra

	AAY			BPL			APL		
	Monthly Per Capita (Rs.)	Coefficient of Variation	NSS 2004-05 (Rs.)	Monthly Per Capita (Rs.)	Coefficient of Variation	NSS 2004-05 (Rs.)	Monthly Per Capita (Rs.)	Coefficient of Variation	NSS 2004-05 (Rs.)
Food Items									
Rice	39.75	89.95	21.92	47.32	86.91	21.71	58.33	62.17	29.11
Wheat	15.04	70.69	13.99	25.18	86.07	16.46	42.38	63.26	26.72
Other cereals	11.15	76.08	26.28	14.25	68.81	27.68	15.47	83.27	26.79
Total cereals	65.94	-	62.19	86.75	-	65.85	116.18	-	82.62
Pulses	17.99	71.03	15.84	18.47	63.97	17.37	24.91	68.94	22.29
Sugar etc.	11.97	70.76	11.27	11.98	50.40	13.41	16.70	50.43	17.51
Cooking oil	21.39	59.35	20.19	22.65	51.25	21.99	30.72	55.07	33.56
Spices	15.06	87.10	9.47	15.39	92.85	11.09	18.57	88.97	15.07
Milk & milk products	12.45	81.88	10.06	14.97	88.06	10.05	37.58	79.58	31.27
Poultry & meat	20.93	68.05	6.13	20.36	78.76	7.45	27.26	82.95	13.64
Fruits	1.82	77.45	5.33	2.12	69.35	6.90	6.11	81.26	15.28
Vegetables	24.17	83.56	17.73	23.04	63.45	20.15	28.72	69.74	28.00
Confectionery	1.19	110.67	7.49	1.57	68.58	9.89	5.10	145.01	19.43
Total food	192.90	-	166.49	217.30	-	185.01	311.87	-	281.20
Non-food (30-day recall period)									
Education	6.92	135.66	10.32	6.54	105.85	11.83	17.77	182.28	31.90
Clothing	3.25	97.75	2.05	2.61	65.39	3.50	7.69	106.15	9.40
Footwear	1.41	87.04	0.52	1.25	117.99	0.94	2.60	114.24	1.88
Other items	36.39	155.86	43.10	38.17	89.71	55.66	60.94	159.56	94.72
Fuel	22.85	139.47	29.94	25.64	70.56	36.58	55.67	63.58	60.88
Total non-food	70.82	-	85.93	74.22	-	108.51	144.68	-	198.78
Gross total	263.72	-	252.42	291.52	-	293.52	456.54	-	479.98
Non-food (365-day recall period)									
Education	13.66	120.77	11.42	15.50	133.87	7.43	53.49	356.03	11.75
Clothing	21.99	111.19	27.04	21.61	86.02	29.19	34.80	89.34	41.92
Footwear	4.90	94.39	3.39	5.39	151.83	3.69	8.06	92.70	5.87
Other items	39.85	114.41	43.10	43.64	124.86	55.66	81.84	133.54	94.72
Fuel	18.12	205.12	29.94	18.03	151.88	36.58	36.66	136.48	60.88
Total non-food	98.53	-	114.89	104.17	-	132.55	214.84	-	215.14
Gross total	291.43	-	281.38	321.47	-	317.56	526.71	-	496.34

Table 4.12 Monthly Consumption Expenditure of Households (Average of Six Months)—Uttarakhand

	Monthly Pper Capita (Rs.)	Coefficient of Variation	NSS 2004-05 (Rs.)	Monthly Per Capita (Rs.)	Coefficient of Variation	NSS 2004-05 (Rs.)	Monthly Per Capita (Rs.)	Coefficient of Variation	NSS 2004-05 (Rs.)
		AAY			BPL			APL	
				Food Items					
Rice	41.52	81.70	30.30	56.51	45.60	30.30	70.69	50.77	43.20
Wheat	27.43	125.82	37.63	35.43	87.66	37.63	50.48	71.62	43.49
Other cereals	0.11	67.56	3.37	0.06	88.29	3.37	0.16	49.24	2.56
Total cereals	69.07	-	71.30	92.00	-	71.30	121.34	-	89.25
Pulses	20.83	70.67	16.05	19.40	55.39	16.05	26.36	65.41	20.55
Sugar etc.	10.80	55.27	13.69	10.43	54.79	13.69	15.20	72.43	18.46
Cooking oil	23.20	54.44	19.55	22.55	45.12	19.55	28.15	46.81	24.20
Spices	13.62	97.67	8.49	12.63	89.98	8.49	15.43	93.81	10.79
Milk & milk products	20.14	64.30	26.92	20.76	56.93	26.92	41.46	57.97	60.01
Poultry & meat	11.84	67.50	4.47	12.50	67.06	4.47	15.87	69.50	4.79
Fruits	2.32	69.26	2.76	1.78	70.56	2.76	5.02	70.85	4.38
Vegetables	29.80	78.09	23.29	28.04	78.47	23.29	35.53	83.42	29.72
Confectionery	2.08	97.15	11.00	1.87	91.75	11.00	3.97	84.89	16.86
Total food	203.70	-	197.90	221.95	-	197.90	308.34	-	279.54
				Non-food (30-day recall period)					
Education	11.61	188.94	13.36	10.75	204.29	13.36	29.02	230.29	20.30
Clothing	3.09	96.68	0.74	3.22	130.47	0.74	14.63	124.19	8.88
Footwear	1.91	204.23	0.73	1.73	76.62	0.73	5.65	116.02	2.00
Other items	30.06	92.51	36.31	29.65	266.61	36.31	44.70	198.48	55.27
Fuel	21.44	79.97	50.44	20.69	73.82	50.44	50.88	81.80	64.68
Total non-food	68.11	-	101.58	66.04	-	101.58	144.88	-	151.13
Gross total	271.81	-	299.48	287.99	-	299.48	453.21	-	430.67
				Non-food (365-day recall period)					
Education	31.36	181.64	13.21	27.59	146.64	13.21	56.51	217.36	20.29
Clothing	21.66	90.36	26.07	21.12	92.38	26.07	30.23	73.98	31.71
Footwear	5.14	86.64	6.69	4.90	89.76	6.69	7.88	85.58	7.24
Other items	36.50	128.47	36.31	45.02	409.87	36.31	51.46	213.08	55.27
Fuel	23.73	75.50	50.44	22.85	69.03	50.44	44.97	61.54	64.68
Total non-food	118.39	-	132.72	121.49	-	132.72	191.04	-	179.19
Gross total	322.09	-	330.62	343.44	-	330.62	499.38	-	458.73

Table 4.13 Percentage Distribution of Monthly Consumption Expenditure (Average of Six Months)—Delhi

	AAY		BPL		APL	
	Our Survey	NSS 2004-05	Our Survey	NSS 2004-05	Our Survey	NSS 2004-05
			Food Items			
Rice	7.72	7.40	9.79	7.40	9.84	6.41
Wheat	17.49	24.98	21.07	24.98	20.55	18.77
Other cereals	0.05	0.00	0.03	0.00	0.04	0.00
Total cereals	25.27	32.38	30.90	32.38	30.43	25.18
Pulses	11.19	8.51	9.83	8.51	8.82	6.79
Sugar etc.	6.99	3.52	5.84	3.52	5.32	4.08
Cooking oil	9.58	10.18	8.59	10.18	7.85	10.28
Spices	5.52	7.12	4.91	7.12	4.09	4.69
Milk & milk products	19.60	6.48	19.48	6.48	23.46	22.49
Poultry & meat	3.26	7.40	3.72	7.40	3.22	2.15
Fruits	1.51	3.24	1.70	3.24	3.09	3.19
Vegetables	16.01	16.19	13.76	16.19	11.38	14.99
Confectionery	1.09	5.00	1.29	5.00	2.33	6.15
Total food items	58.95	52.09	60.26	52.09	55.62	52.88
			Non-food (365-day recall period)			
Education	14.51	2.07	16.86	2.07	26.67	2.03
Clothing	14.37	13.43	15.15	13.43	13.80	10.32
Footwear	3.67	1.03	3.87	1.03	3.77	1.99
Other items	21.78	37.71	23.29	37.71	23.87	51.93
Fuel	45.67	45.76	40.83	45.76	31.89	33.72
Total non-food	41.05	47.91	39.74	47.91	44.38	47.12
Gross total	100.00	100.00	100.00	100.00	100.00	100.00

Table 4.14 Percentage Distribution of Monthly Consumption Expenditure (Average of Six Months)—Jharkhand

	AAY		BPL		APL	
	Our Survey	NSS 2004-05	Our Survey	NSS 2004-05	Our Survey	NSS 2004-05
			Food Items			
Rice	50.06	46.37	54.67	43.22	46.62	39.08
Wheat	5.76	7.92	7.22	8.36	11.84	10.50
Other cereals	0.02	0.83	0.05	1.27	0.04	0.79
Total cereals	55.84	55.12	61.94	52.85	58.50	50.37
Pulses	5.50	3.95	4.66	4.63	4.80	4.49
Sugar etc.	2.55	2.79	2.19	2.72	2.35	2.75
Cooking oil	8.65	9.49	7.27	9.39	7.39	8.57
Spices	3.44	4.96	3.23	4.78	2.98	4.68
Milk & milk products	1.46	1.18	1.50	2.08	4.38	3.21
Poultry & meat	6.71	4.47	6.18	4.62	6.97	5.13
Fruits	0.52	0.27	0.45	0.36	0.91	0.74
Vegetables	14.07	13.97	11.62	13.93	10.19	14.69
Confectionery	1.25	3.60	0.97	4.43	1.54	5.09
Total food items	69.31	64.88	70.94	64.84	68.36	64.98
			Non-food (365-day recall period)			
Education	13.76	3.27	13.57	3.93	18.72	5.43
Clothing	24.26	22.68	23.73	21.12	23.00	21.10
Footwear	3.94	1.75	4.61	1.99	4.11	2.46
Other items	31.72	32.81	32.96	35.01	32.68	36.35
Fuel	26.32	39.48	25.13	37.96	21.50	34.65
Total non-food	30.69	35.12	29.06	35.16	31.64	35.02
Gross total	100.00	100.00	100.00	100.00	100.00	100.00

Table 4.15 Percentage Distribution of Monthly Consumption Expenditure (Average of Six Months)—Kerala

	AAY		BPL		APL	
	Our Survey	NSS 2004-05	Our Survey	NSS 2004-05	Our Survey	NSS 2004-05
			Food Items			
Rice	27.81	29.50	26.57	29.50	28.53	29.99
Wheat	1.36	2.74	1.99	2.74	2.91	2.01
Other cereals	0.02	0.10	0.01	0.10	0.02	0.05
Total cereals	29.19	32.34	28.58	32.34	31.46	32.04
Pulses	3.77	3.23	3.61	3.23	3.13	2.88
Sugar etc.	5.76	5.15	5.43	5.15	4.78	5.03
Cooking oil	10.38	8.04	10.50	8.04	9.44	6.70
Spices	9.92	6.23	10.31	6.23	7.58	5.54
Milk & milk products	5.14	3.08	5.85	3.08	8.88	5.55
Poultry & meat	20.72	14.34	20.70	14.34	20.18	13.25
Fruits	2.18	8.70	2.38	8.70	2.75	9.61
Vegetables	11.15	7.75	10.72	7.75	9.22	6.91
Confectionery	1.78	8.82	1.92	8.82	2.58	11.00
Total food items	55.77	58.83	55.65	58.83	51.93	59.00
			Non-food (365-day recall period)			
Education	23.64	15.67	18.59	15.67	24.48	14.27
Clothing	12.84	17.17	13.57	17.17	12.47	15.48
Footwear	2.64	2.85	2.75	2.85	2.74	2.41
Other items	40.83	39.45	42.51	39.45	39.34	44.18
Fuel	20.06	24.85	22.57	24.85	20.98	23.66
Total non-food	44.23	41.17	44.35	41.17	48.07	41.00
Gross total	100.00	100.00	100.00	100.00	100.00	100.00

Table 4.16 Percentage Distribution of Monthly Consumption Expenditure (Average of Six Months)—Madhya Pradesh

	AAY		BPL		APL	
	Our Survey	NSS 2004-05	Our Survey	NSS 2004-05	Our Survey	NSS 2004-05
			Food Items			
Rice	13.63	16.98	17.52	13.59	15.41	7.72
Wheat	21.58	25.65	25.19	24.64	25.06	21.06
Other cereals	5.16	6.34	4.83	7.57	3.78	5.82
Total cereals	40.38	48.97	47.54	45.79	44.24	34.59
Pulses	10.45	7.44	9.30	7.63	9.46	8.04
Sugar etc.	4.18	4.69	3.77	5.05	4.33	6.08
Cooking oil	9.95	9.03	8.88	8.94	8.23	9.32
Spices	7.41	5.81	6.14	5.78	5.57	5.11
Milk & milk products	3.84	4.95	4.62	7.20	10.69	15.58
Poultry & meat	6.55	1.85	5.09	1.85	3.74	2.56
Fruits	1.34	1.18	1.29	1.55	1.87	1.83
Vegetables	14.95	11.74	12.51	11.44	10.82	10.33
Confectionery	0.95	4.13	0.85	4.66	1.04	6.27
Total food items	68.31	58.69	68.21	57.38	58.96	56.44
			Non-food (365-day recall period)			
Education	16.85	3.95	18.55	5.77	27.68	7.06
Clothing	20.40	25.16	22.69	23.26	17.37	19.30
Footwear	3.93	4.23	4.44	3.38	3.82	3.13
Other items	36.89	34.29	33.04	35.08	29.87	40.27
Fuel	21.93	32.37	21.28	32.50	21.25	30.24
Total non-food	31.69	41.31	31.79	42.62	41.04	43.56
Gross total	100.00	100.00	100.00	100.00	100.00	100.00

Table 417 Percentage Distribution of Monthly Consumption Expenditure (Average of Six Months)—Maharashtra

	AAY		BPL		APL	
	Our Survey	NSS 2004-05	Our Survey	NSS 2004-05	Our Survey	NSS 2004-05
			Food Items			
Rice	20.61	13.17	21.78	11.73	18.70	10.35
Wheat	7.79	8.40	11.59	8.90	13.59	9.50
Other cereals	5.78	15.78	6.56	14.96	4.96	9.53
Total cereals	34.18	37.35	39.92	35.59	37.25	29.38
Pulses	9.33	9.51	8.50	9.39	7.99	7.93
Sugar etc.	6.20	6.77	5.51	7.25	5.36	6.23
Cooking oil	11.09	12.13	10.42	11.89	9.85	11.93
Spices	7.81	5.69	7.08	5.99	5.95	5.36
Milk & milk products	6.46	6.04	6.89	5.43	12.05	11.12
Poultry & meat	10.85	3.68	9.37	4.03	8.74	4.85
Fruits	0.94	3.20	0.97	3.73	1.96	5.43
Vegetables	12.53	10.65	10.60	10.89	9.21	9.96
Confectionery	0.62	4.50	0.72	5.35	1.64	6.91
Total food items	66.19	59.17	67.60	58.26	59.21	56.65
			Non-food (365-day recall period)			
Education	13.86	9.94	14.88	5.61	24.90	5.46
Clothing	22.32	23.54	20.74	22.02	16.20	19.48
Footwear	4.97	2.95	5.18	2.78	3.75	2.73
Other items	40.45	37.51	41.89	41.99	38.09	44.03
Fuel	18.40	26.06	17.31	27.60	17.06	28.30
Total non-food	33.81	40.83	32.40	41.74	40.79	43.35
Gross total	100.00	100.00	100.00	100.00	100.00	100.00

Table 4.18 Percentage Distribution of Monthly Consumption Expenditure (Average of Six Months)—Uttarakhand

	AAY		BPL		APL	
	Our Survey	NSS 2004-05	Our Survey	NSS 2004-05	Our Survey	NSS 2004-05
			Food Items			
Rice	20.38	15.31	25.46	15.31	22.93	15.45
Wheat	13.47	19.01	15.96	19.01	16.37	15.56
Other cereals	0.06	1.70	0.03	1.70	0.05	0.92
Total cereals	33.91	36.03	41.45	36.03	39.35	31.93
Pulses	10.23	8.11	8.74	8.11	8.55	7.35
Sugar etc.	5.30	6.92	4.70	6.92	4.93	6.60
Cooking oil	11.39	9.88	10.16	9.88	9.13	8.66
Spices	6.69	4.29	5.69	4.29	5.00	3.86
Milk & milk products	9.89	13.60	9.35	13.60	13.45	21.47
Poultry & meat	5.81	2.26	5.63	2.26	5.15	1.71
Fruits	1.14	1.39	0.80	1.39	1.63	1.57
Vegetables	14.63	11.77	12.63	11.77	11.52	10.63
Confectionery	1.02	5.56	0.84	5.56	1.29	6.03
Total food items	63.24	59.86	64.63	59.86	61.74	60.94
			Non-food (365-day recall period)			
Education	26.49	9.95	22.71	9.95	29.58	11.32
Clothing	18.30	19.64	17.38	19.64	15.82	17.70
Footwear	4.34	5.04	4.04	5.04	4.12	4.04
Other items	30.83	27.36	37.06	27.36	26.94	30.84
Fuel	20.05	38.00	18.81	38.00	23.54	36.10
Total non-food	36.76	40.14	35.37	40.14	38.26	39.06
Gross total	100.00	100.00	100.00	100.00	100.00	100.00

4.3 Food and Non-Food Consumption Expenditure

According to the NSS data, the share of non-cereal items in the monthly per capita expenditure (all India) has been consistently increasing in both rural and urban areas. The share of non-food consumption expenditure increased from 27 per cent in 1972-1973 to 41 per cent in 1999-2000 in rural areas, while it increased from 36 per cent to 52 per cent in the urban areas during the same time period. In 1999-2000, about 59 per cent of the total consumption expenditure (all India) was on food items in rural areas, while it was 48 per cent in the urban areas. As our selected sample is dominated by the rural households, expenditure on food is expected to lead that of non-food expenditure to commensurate with the NSS trends as discussed above. Monthly consumption expenditure per capita for each category for our selected states along with the NSS 2004-05 (61st Round) figures for the respective expenditure groups for food and non-food items are given in Tables 4.7 to 4.12. In the NSS 61st Round, two separate estimates are made for the monthly per capita non-food consumption expenditure with 30-day recall period in the first estimates and 365-day recall period in the second one. Presenting our tables, we have maintained uniformity with the NSS data. The NSS consumption expenditure for the AAY, BPL and APL were drawn by equating the per capita monthly expenditure for the respective categories.[5,6] The percentage distribution of each food item in total food expenditure, each non-food item in total non-food expenditure and percentage of total food items and total non-food items in total expenditure for the three categories in all the six states are given in Tables 4.13 to 4.18.

Monthly per capita food consumption expenditure varied between Rs. 150 to Rs. 300 among our selected households. Although expenditure was lowest for the AAY households and highest for the APL households in all the states, the wedge between these three classes was not too wide. The consumption expenditure of BPL households was around 15 per cent higher against their AAY counterparts while it was 35 per cent higher in the case of APL households against that of BPL households. The wedge between APL and AAY households was little wider whereby the consumption expenditure of the former was more than 50 per cent higher compared to the latter. Comparing the six selected states, the consumption expenditure was highest in Delhi, followed by Uttarakhand, Maharashtra, Kerala, Jharkhand and Madhya Pradesh in the descending order. Among the food items, highest amount was spent on cereals in almost all the states. Total expenditure on cereals varied from Rs. 115 in Jharkhand, 94 in Uttarakhand, 89 in Maharashtra, 85 in Madhya Pradesh, 80 in Delhi and 67 in Kerala. Whereas expenditure on cereals was lowest in Kerala among all the states, the state had second highest expenditure on meat (including fish). In Delhi, milk products were the dominant items among food consumption after cereals, while in other states namely Madhya Pradesh, Maharashtra, Uttarakhand and Jharkhand, vegetables/pulses recorded the second highest priority in the items of food consumption. Comparing food and non-food expenditure, the latter was less than total food expenditure in all the states without any exception and that was consistent with the all India NSS data as was mentioned above. On an average, the distribution of food and non-food expenditure for all the categories and all the states was in the range of 60-70 per cent for food and 30-40 per cent for non-food. The food expenditure was slightly above 70 per cent of total expenditure in Jharkhand, Madhya Pradesh, Maharashtra and Uttarakhand, while it was 66 per cent in Delhi and 64 per cent in Kerala.

Non-food expenditure (365-day recall period) was highest in Delhi (Rs. 200), followed by Kerala (Rs. 191), Uttarakhand (Rs. 144), Maharashtra (Rs. 139), Madhya Pradesh (Rs. 109) and Jharkhand (Rs. 87). Non-food expenditure based on 30-day recall period was generally less than 365-day recall period because some of the expenses like clothing, footwear and some other payments, like tuition fee for professional courses etc., were generally based on annual payments. Nonetheless, the distribution of expenditure was almost similar to that of 365-day recall period. Among the non-food items, education and health involved the highest expenditure in almost all the states. Education expenditure was followed by fuel and light, clothing; other items (toiletry, entertainment, intoxicants, transport and other services); and footwear. Looking at the spread of total consumption expenditure across the selected states, it is revealed by the data in the tables that total consumption expenditure for all categories topped in Delhi (Rs. 476), followed by Kerala (Rs. 415), Uttarakhand (Rs. 388), Maharashtra (Rs. 380) while Madhya Pradesh and Jharkhand were on the bottom with per capita consumption expenditure around Rs. 300 and 283, respectively. The total expenditure with 30-day recall period was slightly less for the reasons mentioned above but the order remained same as in the case of 365-day recall period.

---

5. See for example, Level and Pattern of Consumer Expenditure, 2004-05—NSS 61st Round, Report No. 508(61/1.0/1), National Sample Survey Organisation, Ministry of Statistics and Programme Implementation, Government of India, December 2006.

6. The NSS consumption figures are taken for the rural areas to maintain parity with our selected sample, as our sample is drawn with more than 80 per cent households from the rural areas.

Comparing across AAY, BPL and APL categories, it is discernible from the tables that, whereas all the categories spent proportionately higher amount on cereals, comparative amount spent on items like milk, edible oils, meat and fish, vegetables and fruits was higher by the APL households as compared to the other two category of households. This was more true in high per capita income states like Delhi, Kerala, Maharashtra and Uttarakhand than in lower income states namely, Madhya Pradesh and Jharkhand. In the case of non-food expenditure, education, health and fuel constituted the highest expenditure among all categories in all the states. Comparing food and non-food expenditure among different category of households, there were no significant differences in percentage of amount spent on food and non-food across our three categories. This however, negates the general belief that rich people spend higher amount on non-food. In our case, APL households spent equal percentage of amount on food as compared to the other two categories, i.e., BPL and AAY.

Comparing our consumption expenditure with the NSS, it is seen from the tables that our estimates of food and non-food consumption expenditure compared very well with that of the NSS figures. Our estimates were slightly more in some cases and slightly less in other cases as compared to the expenditure for each class given by the NSS. Comparing our expenditure with the NSS for different commodities in different states, it seen from the data that in Delhi, our consumption of cereals was slightly lower than the NSS for the AAY households, while it was slightly higher for the BPL and APL households. In Jharkhand and Maharashtra, our cereal expenditure was higher than the NSS for all the categories. In Uttarakhand and Madhya Pradesh, our cereals expenditure was slightly higher for APL and BPL and lower for the AAY households as compared to the NSS expenditure. In Kerala, however, both estimates were more or less equal. Comparing percentage of expenditure on food from our data with that of the NSS, it is clear from the tables that our food estimates were around 10 per cent higher than the NSS in Delhi, Madhya Pradesh, Maharashtra and Uttarakhand, while difference was less than 5 per cent in Jharkhand and no major difference was found in Kerala.

Last and the least, comparing the variability in food and non-food expenditure, it is observed from the results that coefficient of variation was significantly higher for the non-food commodities as compared to food items in all the states and in all the categories. On an average, coefficient of variation was less than 100 per cent in the case of food items while it averaged around 150 to 200 per cent in the non-food items. Among food items, variability was higher in the case of milk and milk products, poultry and meat, fruits and vegetables, in addition to not common cereals, like coarse grains. Similarly, variation was found very high in the case of spices, edible oils and other high value commodities. In the case of non-food items, variability was higher for all items compared to food items, because of wide differences in the use of such items among the selected households, as we have clubbed households in each category, irrespective of the fact whether they belong to rural or urban areas.

4.4 The Delivery of Food to the Poor under TPDS

Before 1997, the public distribution system was open-ended and it was meant for all sections of society. From June 1997, the erstwhile PDS has been replaced by the 'Targeted Public Distribution System' (TPDS). Under the new system, a two-tier subsidised pricing system was introduced to benefit the poor. The scale of issue under BPL and AAY has been revised to 35 kilograms per family per month with effect from 1.4.2002 with a view to enhancing the food security at the household level. In addition, certain sections of APL households are also entitled for 35 kgs of grains. Thus, below poverty consumers now fulfil their demand for cereals through purchases in the open market and from supplies through the PDS. It is however, a controversial question, to what extent food requirement of the poor is met through the PDS and how much they have to depend on the vagaries of the market situation. Efficiency of the PDS delivery mechanism depends on two factors: (a) whether or not the stipulated amount of food is being distributed; and (b) what is the percentage of targeted population obtaining the stipulated amount. Now, the question that arises is out of BPL (and AAY) population, how many of them obtained their entitled quantity on a regular basis (during the six months of survey period). This section presents statistics related to the amount of cereals, sugar and kerosene oil supplied through the PDS system to the AAY and BPL (and also to the APL if any) households in the selected states.

Tables 4.19 to 4.24 present the quantity of rice, wheat, sugar and kerosene oil received by the households from PDS in all the three categories. The percentage of population receiving such quantity is given in parentheses in the tables. In the case of cereals, only wheat and rice were distributed. The proportion of these two cereals varied in different states depending upon the food habits of the households as was also mentioned in the previous section. The entitlement was fixed per family irrespective of the family size. It is shown by the data in the tables that in Delhi and Madhya Pradesh, wheat distribution dominated while rice was the principal cereal distributed in Kerala, Jharkhand and Uttarakhand. In Maharashtra, both these cereals were distributed nearly in the same proportion. The quantity of total cereals distributed among the AAY households averaged around 33 kgs in Delhi, Jharkhand and Uttarakhand and around 30 kgs in the other three states namely, Maharashtra, Madhya Pradesh and Kerala. The coverage of population was quite impressive with more than 98 per cent of household surveyed in the AAY category in Delhi and Uttarakhand, around 97 per cent in Kerala and Maharashtra, 93 per cent in Jharkhand and around 91 per cent in Madhya Pradesh. Thus, more than 90 per cent of the targeted AAY population obtained 30 kgs or more of rice and wheat during the six months of survey period without any exception in the six selected states.

Table 4.19 Quantity Obtained from PDS (Kgs. per Household)—Delhi

	Month 1	Month 2	Month 3	Month 4	Month 5	Month 6	Average	COV across Time
				AAY				
Rice	9.90	9.97	10.08	9.61	9.73	9.64	9.82	1.92
	(98.0)	(98.5)	(100.0)	(98.5)	(94.5)	(97.0)	(97.8)	1.91
Wheat	24.59	24.34	24.71	23.29	23.28	22.85	23.84	3.34
	(97.5)	(99.0)	(97.5)	(99.0)	(97.0)	(98.5)	(98.1)	0.88
Cereals (Rice+Wheat)	34.36	34.27	34.51	32.85	32.76	32.35	33.52	2.88
	(98.0)	(99.0)	(99.0)	(99.0)	(97.0)	(98.5)	(98.4)	0.81
Sugar	4.89	5.06	5.30	4.85	4.90	5.01	5.00	3.33
	(97.0)	(96.5)	(96.5)	(95.5)	(92.0)	(92.0)	(94.9)	2.43
Kerosene oil	19.51	20.21	20.56	19.68	20.12	19.51	19.94	2.16
	(86.5)	(93.5)	(95.5)	(94.0)	(93.0)	(91.0)	(92.3)	3.44
				BPL				
Rice	9.97	9.97	10.01	9.56	9.61	9.54	9.78	2.32
	(98.3)	(99.3)	(99.0)	(93.3)	(90.1)	(93.3)	(95.6)	4.01
Wheat	24.55	24.58	24.87	23.31	23.57	22.88	23.96	3.40
	(98.7)	(99.5)	(98.2)	(99.3)	(99.2)	(99.3)	(99.0)	0.52
Cereals (Rice+Wheat)	34.31	34.47	34.55	32.23	32.25	31.79	33.27	3.92
	(99.2)	(99.7)	(99.3)	(99.5)	(99.3)	(99.5)	(99.4)	0.18
Sugar	5.17	5.25	5.40	5.03	4.96	4.99	5.13	3.28
	(98.7)	(97.5)	(97.7)	(96.0)	(98.0)	(98.2)	(97.7)	0.94
Kerosene oil	20.23	20.31	20.58	19.83	19.93	19.54	20.07	1.87
	(84.9)	(90.1)	(90.3)	(91.0)	(91.6)	(92.1)	(90.0)	2.89
				APL				
Rice	9.58	9.08	9.19	8.98	9.11	9.04	9.14	2.351
	(52.7)	(59.1)	(66.5)	(77.3)	(80.3)	(79.3)	(69.2)	6.76
Wheat	23.22	22.33	22.60	21.26	21.44	21.23	21.90	3.74
	(58.1)	(64.5)	(73.4)	(87.7)	(88.7)	(92.1)	(77.4)	18.29
Cereals (Rice+Wheat)	31.91	30.19	30.71	29.19	29.53	29.01	30.09	3.64
	(58.1)	(65.5)	(73.9)	(87.7)	(89.2)	(92.1)	(77.8)	18.05
Sugar	5.39	5.50	5.50	5.21	5.17	5.50	5.37	2.84
	(9.4)	(6.9)	(3.9)	(6.9)	(5.9)	(4.9)	(6.3)	29.74
Kerosene oil	12.84	12.32	10.30	10.03	10.48	10.86	11.17	10.41
	(33.0)	(31.0)	(29.1)	(28.1)	(31.5)	(37.4)	(31.7)	10.48

Note: 1. Figures in parentheses are respective percentage of people who obtained the entitled quantity.

2. Kerosene quantity is in litres.

Table 4.20 Quantity Obtained from PDS (Kgs. per Household)—Jharkhand

	Month 1	Month 2	Month 3	Month 4	Month 5	Month 6	Average	COV across Time
				AAY				
Rice	21.34 (86.5)	21.64 (84.5)	21.68 (98.0)	21.40 (93.0)	22.36 (92.5)	22.15 (93.0)	21.77 (91.3)	1.87 5.40
Wheat	13.36 (84.0)	12.50 (81.0)	12.88 (97.5)	12.11 (94.5)	12.75 (93.0)	12.55 (92.0)	12.68 (90.3)	3.29 7.10
Cereals (Rice+Wheat)	33.54 (88.5)	32.47 (87.5)	34.15 (99.0)	832.15 (97.5)	34.44 (94.5)	34.38 (93.5)	33.52 (93.4)	2.97 4.98
Sugar	0.00 (0.0)	0.00 (0.0)	0.00 (0.0)	0.75 (1.0)	0.00 (0.0)	0.83 (1.5)	0.80 (0.4)	155.24 159.50
Kerosene oil	3.21 (98.0)	3.14 (97.5)	3.05 (99.0)	3.06 (99.0)	2.79 (100.0)	2.66 (100.0)	2.98 (98.9)	7.16 1.03
				BPL				
Rice	21.32 (39.5)	24.19 (73.3)	23.99 (74.7)	22.86 (60.7)	25.92 (61.5)	25.51 (86.6)	24.22 (66.0)	7.10 24.47
Wheat	9.65 (54.1)	9.49 (80.5)	9.47 (82.8)	9.53 (67.7)	9.06 (71.5)	9.19 (91.0)	9.38 (74.6)	2.41 17.44
Cereals (Rice+Wheat)	23.19 (58.8)	29.20 (86.9)	28.88 (89.2)	26.54 (76.6)	30.36 (73.8)	32.68 (93.1)	28.48 (79.7)	11.50 15.90
Sugar	0.00 (0.0)	0.00 (0.0)	0.00 (0.0)	0.50 (0.2)	0.00 (0.0)	0.75 (0.6)	0.70 (0.1)	159.50 192.25
Kerosene oil	3.17 (95.8)	3.07 (98.9)	3.12 (99.5)	3.03 (99.2)	2.82 (99.4)	2.56 (98.9)	2.96 (98.6)	7.71 1.43
				APL				
Rice	20.00 (1.9)	25.15 (12.6)	24.95 (13.8)	22.25 (5.0)	23.50 (1.3)	19.00 (1.9)	24.03 (6.1)	11.3 693.60
Wheat	8.83 (3.8)	10.84 (20.1)	12.93 (8.8)	10.67 (1.9)	15.50 (8.8)	14.17 (3.8)	12.20 (7.9)	20.42 84.63
Cereals (Rice+Wheat)	14.13 (5.0)	26.56 (20.1)	22.81 (20.1)	26.25 (5.0)	18.86 (8.8)	20.29 (4.4)	21.48 (10.6)	22.11 71.33
Sugar	0.00 (0.0)	0.00 (0.0)	0.00 (0.0)	0.00 (0.0)	0.00 (0.0)	0.00 (0.0)	0.00 (0.0)	—
Kerosene oil	3.36 (98.7)	3.18 (97.5)	3.30 (98.7)	3.26 (98.1)	2.87 (97.5)	2.84 (98.1)	3.14 (98.1)	7.23 0.57

Note: 1. Figures in parentheses are respective percentage of people who obtained the entitled quantity.
2. Kerosene quantity is in litres.

Table 4.21 Quantity Obtained from PDS (Kgs. per Household)—Kerala

	Month 1	Month 2	Month 3	Month 4	Month 5	Month 6	Average	COV across Time
				AAY				
Rice	30.71 (98.0)	29.22 (93.5)	28.60 (99.0)	28.69 (99.0)	28.55 (98.0)	29.51 (95.0)	29.21 (97.1)	2.83 2.35
Wheat	4.63 (4.0)	5.91 (17.4)	4.57 (3.5)	4.71 (3.5)	4.50 (4.0)	5.25 (2.0)	5.30 (5.7)	11.20 100.92
Cereals (Rice+Wheat)	30.90 (98.0)	30.00 (94.5)	28.76 (99.0)	28.86 (99.0)	28.73 (98.0)	29.62 (95.0)	29.48 (97.3)	2.94 2.04
Sugar	1.72 (80.6)	1.63 (77.1)	1.66 (88.1)	1.65 (88.6)	1.60 (85.6)	1.60 (87.1)	1.64 (84.5)	2.75 5.47
Kerosene oil	2.49 (98.5)	2.43 (95.5)	2.51 (99.5)	2.43 (99.5)	2.49 (98.5)	2.39 (98.5)	2.46 (98.3)	1.92 1.49
				BPL				
Rice	19.30 (98.0)	19.00 (90.2)	18.87 (99.5)	18.82 (99.7)	18.80 (99.2)	18.87 (98.3)	18.94 (97.5)	0.99 3.73
Wheat	4.87 (77.7)	5.27 (73.7)	4.49 (86.4)	4.65 (85.0)	4.49 (88.2)	4.66 (89.9)	4.72 (83.5)	6.21 7.62
Cereals (Rice+Wheat)	23.24 (97.7)	22.31 (94.2)	22.73 (99.7)	22.79 (99.7)	22.68 (99.7)	22.94 (99.2)	22.78 (98.3)	1.34 2.22
Sugar	1.64 (86.0)	1.63 (76.2)	1.61 (90.0)	1.60 (89.2)	1.60 (88.9)	1.58 (90.2)	1.61 (86.7)	1.34 6.20
Kerosene oil	2.51 (99.0)	2.44 (95.2)	2.44 (98.8)	2.40 (99.2)	2.83 (98.8)	2.42 (97.8)	2.44 (98.1)	6.42 1.56
				APL				
Rice	23.38 (56.6)	23.19 (58.1)	21.49 (71.7)	21.67 (71.7)	20.88 (72.2)	20.63 (72.2)	21.77 (67.1)	5.30 11.30
Wheat	6.92 (36.9)	6.85 (39.9)	5.50 (55.1)	5.63 (55.6)	5.72 (55.6)	5.83 (55.1)	5.98 (49.7)	10.47 17.70
Cereals (Rice+Wheat)	26.47 (59.6)	26.08 (62.1)	23.71 (77.8)	24.00 (77.8)	23.17 (78.8)	22.98 (78.8)	24.40 (72.5)	6.15 12.48
Sugar	1.49 (11.6)	1.41 (13.6)	1.51 (8.6)	1.73 (5.6)	1.33 (5.6)	1.35 (8.1)	1.46 (8.8)	9.92 36.81
Kerosene oil	2.42 (96.0)	2.54 (94.9)	2.42 (97.5)	2.44 (96.5)	2.59 (96.5)	2.47 (98.0)	2.47 (96.5)	2.79 1.12

Note: 1. Figures in parentheses are respective percentage of people who obtained the entitled quantity.
2. Kerosene quantity is in litres.

Table 4.22 **Quantity Obtained from PDS (Kgs. per Household)—Madhya Pradesh**

	Month 1	Month 2	Month 3	Month 4	Month 5	Month 6	Average	COV across Time
				AAY				
Rice	6.91 (90.3)	7.39 (88.2)	6.95 (87.7)	5.47 (77.4)	5.38 (79.5)	5.36 (75.9)	6.30 (83.2)	15.00 (7.5)
Wheat	24.25 (90.3)	24.43 (89.2)	24.60 (90.8)	26.90 (90.3)	25.82 (88.2)	25.71 (87.2)	25.28 (89.3)	4.09 1.56
Cereals (Rice+Wheat)	29.48 (95.4)	30.85 (91.8)	30.13 (94.4)	31.59 (90.3)	30.67 (88.2)	30.20 (87.7)	30.49 (91.3)	2.37 3.46
Sugar	1.70 (53.8)	1.65 (64.6)	1.74 (70.8)	2.09 (59.5)	2.01 (45.6)	2.15 (37.4)	1.86 (55.3)	11.63 22.27
Kerosene oil	2.36 (87.7)	2.47 (87.7)	2.42 (89.2)	3.20 (89.7)	2.83 (86.2)	3.24 (84.1)	2.75 (87.4)	14.46 2.37
				BPL				
Rice	7.49 (80.2)	8.15 (72.7)	8.22 (76.1)	7.71 (73.0)	8.93 (70.4)	8.07 (72.0)	8.08 (74.1)	6.13 4.78
Wheat	15.98 (81.2)	15.39 (73.0)	15.05 (78.6)	15.71 (81.3)	14.27 (77.9)	14.28 (76.1)	15.12 (78.0)	4.78 4.06
Cereals (Rice+Wheat)	22.01 (86.3)	22.40 (76.6)	22.59 (80.0)	22.36 (82.3)	21.26 (81.8)	20.93 (79.7)	21.92 (81.1)	3.09 3.97
Sugar	1.76 (51.2)	1.83 (59.4)	1.89 (61.5)	2.25 (52.5)	2.19 (43.9)	2.22 (36.2)	2.00 (50.8)	10.90 18.78
Kerosene oil	2.51 (84.6)	2.57 (84.0)	2.51 (87.9)	3.18 (84.0)	3.15 (90.7)	3.31 (86.1)	2.87 (86.2)	13.21 3.09
				APL				
Rice	10.39 (14.4)	13.71 (7.2)	9.58 (6.2)	11.92 (6.7)	13.41 (8.8)	14.00 (6.2)	11.97 (8.2)	15.23 38.53
Wheat	22.50 (12.4)	23.69 (6.7)	27.50 (9.3)	20.09 (5.7)	10.11 (9.3)	9.93 (7.2)	19.23 (8.4)	38.66 28.63
Cereals (Rice+Wheat)	25.97 (16.5)	27.78 (9.3)	33.89 (9.3)	26.86 (7.2)	20.50 (10.3)	18.06 (8.8)	25.51 (10.2)	22.04 31.64
Sugar	2.38 (10.8)	2.17 (10.8)	2.05 (10.8)	2.25 (2.1)	1.75 (4.1)	2.00 (2.1)	2.15 (6.8)	10.46 66.11
Kerosene oil	2.65 (63.9)	2.75 (69.1)	2.48 (74.7)	3.26 (84.0)	3.54 (82.5)	3.39 (76.3)	3.01 (75.1)	14.60 10.26

Note: 1. Figures in parentheses are respective percentage of people who obtained the entitled quantity.

2. Kerosene quantity is in litres.

Table 4.23 Quantity Obtained from PDS (Kgs. per Household)—Maharashtra

	Month 1	Month 2	Month 3	Month 4	Month 5	Month 6	Average	COV across Time
				AAY				
Rice	16.33 (95.3)	16.55 (94.8)	16.64 (97.9)	17.21 (96.9)	17.58 (96.4)	17.32 (96.4)	16.94 (96.3)	2.94 1.15
Wheat	12.69 (96.4)	13.25 (95.3)	14.56 (91.7)	14.37 (95.9)	15.09 (95.3)	15.56 (94.8)	14.25 (94.9)	7.66 1.74
Cereals (Rice+Wheat)	28.54 (97.4)	29.39 (96.4)	30.28 (97.9)	31.43 (96.9)	32.51 (96.4)	32.62 (96.4)	30.79 (96.9)	5.44 0.68
Sugar	1.00 (0.5)	0.00 (0.0)	0.00 (0.0)	0.00 (0.0)	2.00 (0.5)	0.00 (0.0)	1.50 (0.2)	167.33 154.92
Kerosene oil	3.22 (94.8)	3.24 (94.3)	3.28 (94.3)	3.52 (96.9)	3.62 (95.3)	3.63 (96.9)	3.42 (95.4)	5.65 1.26
				BPL				
Rice	14.17 (96.2)	14.40 (95.9)	14.54 (96.7)	14.46 (97.0)	14.66 (96.5)	14.60 (97.7)	14.47 (96.7)	1.19 0.66
Wheat	11.43 (95.9)	11.35 (92.4)	11.69 (90.2)	12.62 (94.0)	13.86 (95.2)	13.26 (96.0)	12.38 (94.0)	8.43 2.42
Cereals (Rice+Wheat)	25.01 (98.3)	25.17 (96.5)	25.15 (97.8)	26.46 (97.8)	28.08 (97.4)	27.36 (98.7)	26.20 (97.8)	4.99 0.78
Sugar	2.50 (1.7)	0.00 (0.0)	3.00 (0.5)	0.00 (0.0)	0.00 (0.0)	3.00 (0.2)	2.64 (0.4)	110.30 168.55
Kerosene oil	3.43 (92.1)	3.34 (95.9)	3.39 (97.5)	3.76 (97.7)	3.76 (98.2)	3.75 (98.3)	3.57 (96.6)	5.72 2.48
				APL				
Rice	12.42 (5.9)	15.81 (13.3)	16.29 (3.4)	19.69 (7.9)	22.00 (2.5)	16.15 (6.4)	16.56 (6.6)	19.59 58.61
Wheat	17.08 (6.4)	17.48 (15.3)	15.53 (8.4)	18.00 (7.4)	12.86 (3.4)	18.79 (6.9)	17.02 (8.4)	12.87 49.55
Cereals (Rice+Wheat)	26.50 (6.9)	27.69 (17.2)	22.24 (8.4)	30.79 (9.4)	25.00 (3.9)	23.65 (9.9)	25.98 (9.3)	11.77 47.90
Sugar	0.00 (0.0)	0.00 (0.0)	0.00 (0.0)	0.00 (0.0)	0.00 (0.0)	0.00 (0.0)	0.00 (0.0)	—
Kerosene oil	3.19 (84.2)	3.29 (82.8)	3.23 (85.2)	3.51 (93.1)	3.57 (92.6)	3.57 (92.1)	3.40 (88.3)	5.24 5.38

Note: 1. Figures in parentheses are respective percentage of people who obtained the entitled quantity.

2. Kerosene quantity is in litres.

Table 4.24 **Quantity Obtained from PDS (Kgs. per Household)—Uttarakhand**

	Month 1	Month 2	Month 3	Month 4	Month 5	Month 6	Average	COV across Time
				AAY				
Rice	23.08 (97.6)	23.28 (96.1)	23.50 (98.0)	23.24 (98.5)	23.06 (99.0)	23.26 (99.0)	23.24 (98.0)	0.69 1.13
Wheat	9.76 (95.1)	9.91 (92.2)	9.79 (96.6)	9.87 (98.0)	9.73 (96.6)	9.75 (96.6)	9.80 (95.9)	0.72 2.10
Cereals (Rice+Wheat)	32.28 (98.5)	32.45 (97.1)	33.14 (98.0)	32.74 (99.5)	32.55 (99.0)	32.77 (99.0)	32.66 (98.5)	0.92 0.89
Sugar	2.35 (97.6)	2.38 (95.1)	2.39 (94.1)	2.63 (96.6)	2.55 (93.2)	2.64 (96.1)	2.49 (95.4)	5.31 1.70
Kerosene oil	3.78 (87.8)	3.68 (94.6)	3.64 (94.6)	3.23 (99.0)	3.19 (99.5)	3.27 (96.6)	3.46 (95.4)	7.50 4.46
				BPL				
Rice	23.32 (95.3)	23.30 (93.8)	23.46 (95.6)	23.39 (92.2)	23.76 (91.2)	23.73 (90.2)	23.49 (93.0)	0.86 2.36
Wheat	10.10 (87.2)	10.11 (86.5)	10.07 (88.0)	10.04 (85.3)	9.76 (84.3)	9.98 (81.9)	10.01 (85.5)	1.30 2.58
Cereals (Rice+Wheat)	32.16 (96.5)	32.28 (94.8)	32.50 (96.3)	32.26 (93.4)	32.59 (91.7)	32.74 (90.4)	32.42 (93.8)	0.69 2.63
Sugar	2.79 (94.6)	2.72 (94.6)	2.75 (95.6)	2.90 (96.5)	2.80 (94.3)	2.95 (96.1)	2.82 (95.3)	3.19 0.96
Kerosene oil	3.97 (87.0)	3.92 (93.9)	3.91 (95.3)	3.52 (97.5)	3.46 (98.3)	3.49 (97.0)	3.70 (94.8)	6.55 4.37
				APL				
Rice	23.74 (28.6)	22.79 (27.6)	23.13 (25.1)	21.28 (24.6)	20.41 (24.1)	21.68 (28.1)	22.22 (26.4)	5.67 7.36
Wheat	10.29 (27.6)	10.44 (26.6)	10.93 (27.6)	11.31 (33.0)	8.37 (26.6)	8.38 (26.1)	9.95 (27.9)	12.82 9.18
Cereals (Rice+Wheat)	31.50 (30.5)	30.17 (30.0)	31.43 (28.1)	25.31 (35.5)	25.93 (27.6)	28.97 (28.6)	28.88 (30.0)	9.36 9.62
Sugar	2.79 (86.2)	2.74 (85.7)	2.90 (83.3)	2.79 (93.6)	2.69 (92.1)	2.81 (92.1)	2.78 (88.8)	2.52 4.83
Kerosene oil	3.84 (80.3)	3.75 (85.2)	3.90 (90.1)	3.41 (96.6)	3.34 (95.6)	3.31 (94.6)	3.58 (90.4)	7.46 7.19

Note: 1. Figures in parentheses are respective percentage of people who obtained the entitled quantity.

2. Kerosene quantity is in litres.

The quantity of cereals distributed among the BPL households, however, was far less than the stipulated amount in some of the selected states. Similarly, the targeted population among BPL households was also not as efficient as was found in the case of AAY households. The states where distributed quantity of cereals was closer to the stipulated amount were Delhi, 33 kgs covering 99 per cent of the households and Uttarakhand, 32 kgs distributed among 94 per cent of the selected households. In the other selected states, in Maharashtra, 26 kgs of cereals were distributed among 98 per cent of the selected households. Similar was the position of Kerala, where 98 per cent of BPL households obtained 23 kgs of cereals (mainly rice). Jharkhand and Madhya Pradesh were relatively less efficient in delivery as only 79 per cent population obtained 29 kgs of cereals in Jharkhand, while 81 per cent of selected BPL households obtained only 22 kgs of rice and wheat in Madhya Pradesh. Delhi and Kerala made an exception in APL targeting where more than 70 per cent of the selected APL households obtained 30 and 24 kgs of cereals, respectively. In Uttarakhand, around one-third of the selected households obtained around 29 kgs of cereals. In rest of the three states namely, Jharkhand, Maharashtra and Madhya Pradesh, APL targeting remained only nominal as less than 10 per cent of them obtained 20-25 kgs of cereals.

Sugar and kerosene oil were the other commodities that were being distributed in the selected states. In Delhi, around 95 per cent AAY and 98 per cent BPL households obtained 5 kgs of sugar regularly during the survey period. Among the APL families, only 6 per cent of them reported obtaining 5 kgs of sugar. Similarly, above 90 per cent BPL households (including that of AAY) obtained 20 litres of kerosene oil while 32 per cent of APL households obtained 11 litres of kerosene oil on a regular basis in Delhi during the 6 months of survey period. In Uttarakhand, both sugar and kerosene oils were distributed uniformly among all consumers irrespective of one's being below or above poverty. Above 95 per cent of below poverty households and around 90 per cent of above poverty households received around 2.8 kgs of sugar and 3.5 litres of kerosene oil in the state on a regular basis. Similar to Uttarakhand, kerosene oil was distributed on a uniform basis among all the selected households in rest of the four states. In Jharkhand and Kerala, around 98 per cent of all households obtained 3 and 2.5 litres of kerosene oil, respectively on a regular basis. Similarly, in Maharashtra, 96 per cent of below poverty and 88 per cent of above poverty households obtained 3.5 litres of kerosene oil. In Madhya Pradesh, around 87 per cent below poverty and 75 per cent above poverty households obtained 3 litres of kerosene oil through PDS shops. In Kerala and Madhya Pradesh, sugar was targeted only to below poverty households as only a handful of above poverty households reported obtaining sugar through PDS in these two states. In Kerala, 85 per cent of below poverty households (including that of AAY) obtained 1.6 kgs of sugar while in Madhya Pradesh, 55 per cent AAY and 50 per cent of BPL households obtained 2 kgs of sugar through PDS on a regular basis. In rest of the two states namely, Jharkhand and Maharashtra, sugar distribution was almost negligible among any category of selected households. Besides these four commodities, some selected households in Delhi also reported obtaining some quantity of pulses (not on a regular basis) at some concessional price during one or two months of the survey period.

To check the regularity of PDS distribution across six months time period, coefficient of variation across time is presented in the last column of the tables displaying distribution of PDS commodities. Lower value of the coefficient indicates that distribution of commodities was symmetric across six months while higher value indicates higher diversion across time. It is discernible from the values of the coefficient that distribution of cereals was most symmetric among AAY and BPL households whereby value of the coefficient lay below 5 per cent both in the case of quantity and percentage of targeted population. The only exception was found in the case of BPL households in Jharkhand where value of the coefficient exceeded 10 percentage points for both quantity as well as targeted population. On the other hand, the value of the coefficient was much higher for both quantity, as well as targeted population, for APL households in all the six states. Similarly, value of the coefficient in the case of sugar and kerosene oil was also lower for AAY and BPL households as compared to APL households in all the states. Lower coefficient for AAY and BPL for all commodities indicates more symmetric distribution of all commodities in the below poverty households as compared to above poverty households across time for all the states.

Tables 4.25 to 4.30 present the share of food provided by the PDS and that purchased through the open market by the selected households. The public distribution system does not incline to provide full requirement of food to the target (below poverty) population. It only supplies 35 kgs of cereals per family. Given the average family size, the entitlement through PDS turns out around 6-7 kgs cereals per capita, whereas requirement as was seen in the previous section ranges between 8.6 kgs in Kerala to 13.5 kgs in Jharkhand (see Tables 4.1 to 4.6). Thus, public distribution would cover 50 to 75 per cent of the total food requirement of the below poverty households, even when targeting is complete. It is seen from the statistics presented in the tables that the ratio of PDS to market was around two-third to one-third for the combination of wheat and rice in the case of AAY households in Delhi, Kerala, Maharashtra and Uttarakhand. It was slightly higher than 50 per cent for the PDS in

Madhya Pradesh and slightly less than 50 per cent in Jharkhand. In the case of other below poverty households, the ratio of PDS to market (for cereals) was 60/40 in Delhi, Kerala, Maharashtra and around 50/50 in Uttarakhand. In Madhya Pradesh, the ratio was measured one-third to two-third and in Jharkhand it was slightly more than 40/60. Share of PDS in consumption of sugar and kerosene varied from state to state. In the case of sugar, almost whole demand of below poverty households in Delhi was met by the PDS. In Uttarakhand, more than 80 per cent demand for sugar was fulfilled by PDS for the below poverty households. Similarly, in Kerala, 60 to 70 per cent requirement of sugar of the poor was met by PDS. In Madhya Pradesh, PDS supply was less than 50 per cent of sugar for the below poverty households. In rest of the two states namely, Jharkhand and Maharashtra, no sugar was supplied through public distribution. In the case of kerosene oil, more than 90 per cent demand was met by the PDS in almost all the states and in all the categories including that of above poverty households.

Table 4.25 Percentage Share of PDS and Market in Consumption of PDS Commodities—Delhi

Commodity		Month 1	Month 2	Month 3	Month 4	Month 5	Month 6
				AAY			
Rice	PDS	77.60	73.13	68.42	70.48	64.28	65.65
	Market	22.40	26.87	31.58	29.52	35.72	34.35
Wheat	PDS	72.24	71.68	71.42	64.64	61.08	62.91
	Market	27.76	28.32	28.58	35.36	38.92	37.09
Rice + Wheat	PDS	73.70	72.10	70.51	66.24	61.98	63.69
	Market	26.30	27.90	29.49	33.76	38.02	36.31
Sugar	PDS	93.04	97.99	96.33	92.70	92.99	93.13
	Market	6.96	2.01	3.67	7.30	7.01	6.87
Kerosene oil	PDS	100.00	100.00	100.00	99.52	99.36	98.67
	Market	0.00	0.00	0.00	0.48	0.64	1.33
				BPL			
Rice	PDS	68.30	70.21	64.09	60.69	56.70	61.12
	Market	31.70	29.79	35.91	39.31	43.30	38.88
Wheat	PDS	68.09	69.93	68.38	61.22	59.53	59.37
	Market	31.91	30.07	31.62	38.78	40.47	40.63
Rice + Wheat	PDS	68.15	70.01	67.09	61.07	58.74	59.85
	Market	31.85	29.99	32.91	38.93	41.26	40.15
Sugar	PDS	92.23	97.82	96.86	92.94	95.94	96.89
	Market	7.77	2.18	3.14	7.06	4.06	3.11
Kerosene oil	PDS	99.19	99.91	99.53	99.38	99.42	99.63
	Market	0.81	0.09	0.47	0.62	0.58	0.37
				APL			
Rice	PDS	31.95	33.08	36.80	46.29	47.93	48.52
	Market	68.05	66.92	63.20	53.71	52.07	51.48
Wheat	PDS	36.15	38.94	43.76	46.65	47.39	49.02
	Market	63.85	61.06	56.24	53.35	52.61	50.98
Rice + Wheat	PDS	34.90	37.16	41.64	46.55	47.54	48.88
	Market	65.10	62.84	58.36	53.45	52.46	51.12
Sugar	PDS	8.57	7.18	3.84	7.24	6.41	5.66
	Market	91.43	92.82	96.16	92.76	93.59	94.34
Kerosene oil	PDS	90.53	90.02	85.81	82.77	89.94	89.49
	Market	9.47	9.98	14.19	17.23	10.06	10.51

Table 4.26 Percentage Share of PDS and Market in Consumption of PDS Commodities—Jharkhand

Commodity		Month 1	Month 2	Month 3	Month 4	Month 5	Month 6
				AAY			
Rice	PDS	30.89	34.24	39.28	36.43	37.53	38.42
	Market	69.11	65.76	60.72	63.57	62.47	61.58
Wheat	PDS	72.65	79.94	88.03	85.32	93.59	93.96
	Market	27.35	20.06	11.97	14.68	6.41	6.04
Rice + Wheat	PDS	39.06	42.64	49.32	46.09	47.80	48.84
	Market	60.94	57.36	50.68	53.91	52.20	51.16
Sugar	PDS	0.00	0.00	0.00	0.75	0.00	1.13
	Market	100.00	100.00	100.00	99.25	100.00	98.87
Kerosene oil	PDS	98.19	97.85	99.10	98.47	99.40	99.73
	Market	1.81	2.15	0.90	1.53	0.60	0.27
				BPL			
Rice	PDS	13.18	31.71	28.27	22.76	26.44	36.33
	Market	86.82	68.29	71.73	77.24	73.56	63.67
Wheat	PDS	51.80	78.05	76.86	65.19	64.61	82.71
	Market	48.20	21.95	23.14	34.81	35.39	17.29
Rice + Wheat	PDS	18.43	38.69	34.88	28.70	32.12	43.09
	Market	81.57	61.31	65.12	71.30	67.88	56.91
Sugar	PDS	0.00	0.00	0.00	0.07	0.00	0.42
	Market	100.00	100.00	100.00	99.93	100.00	99.58
Kerosene oil	PDS	96.86	99.09	98.45	98.06	99.15	99.97
	Market	3.14	0.91	1.55	1.94	0.85	0.03
				APL			
Rice	PDS	0.68	4.61	5.31	1.97	0.69	0.69
	Market	99.32	95.39	94.69	98.03	99.31	99.31
Wheat	PDS	1.84	17.61	10.77	1.37	9.52	3.83
	Market	98.16	82.39	89.23	98.63	90.48	96.17
Rice + Wheat	PDS	0.95	6.59	6.06	1.87	2.32	1.29
	Market	99.05	93.41	93.94	98.13	97.68	98.71
Sugar	PDS	0.00	0.00	0.00	0.00	0.00	0.00
	Market	100.00	100.00	100.00	100.00	100.00	100.00
Kerosene oil	PDS	96.00	99.39	97.89	97.41	99.03	99.89
	Market	4.00	0.61	2.11	2.59	0.97	0.11

Table 4.27 Percentage Share of PDS and Market in Consumption of PDS Commodities—Kerala

Commodity		Month 1	Month 2	Month 3	Month 4	Month 5	Month 6
				AAY			
Rice	PDS	62.07	57.08	64.77	65.57	67.95	70.19
	Market	37.93	42.92	35.23	34.43	32.05	29.81
Wheat	PDS	7.55	30.90	20.38	23.57	43.90	24.42
	Market	92.45	69.10	79.62	76.43	56.10	75.58
Rice + Wheat	PDS	59.44	55.38	63.99	64.91	67.72	69.71
	Market	40.56	44.62	36.01	35.09	32.28	30.29
Sugar	PDS	40.64	36.06	43.17	43.56	40.97	38.71
	Market	59.36	63.94	56.83	56.44	59.03	61.29
Kerosene oil	PDS	99.20	98.94	100.00	100.00	100.00	100.00
	Market	0.80	1.06	0.00	0.00	0.00	0.00
				BPL			
Rice	PDS	44.90	42.59	51.63	51.69	54.25	55.07
	Market	55.10	57.41	48.37	48.31	45.75	44.93
Wheat	PDS	78.06	68.60	90.72	90.66	94.93	97.86
	Market	21.94	31.40	9.28	9.34	5.07	2.14
Rice + Wheat	PDS	48.33	45.84	55.75	55.87	58.66	59.90
	Market	51.67	54.16	44.25	44.13	41.34	40.10
Sugar	PDS	40.10	33.46	43.07	43.20	40.62	40.43
	Market	59.90	66.54	56.93	56.80	59.38	59.57
Kerosene oil	PDS	97.65	97.62	98.91	99.58	99.38	99.30
	Market	2.35	2.38	1.09	0.42	0.62	0.70
				APL			
Rice	PDS	31.93	33.09	43.20	44.91	45.81	46.12
	Market	68.07	66.91	56.80	55.09	54.19	53.88
Wheat	PDS	51.64	56.66	75.25	74.58	78.14	80.99
	Market	48.36	43.34	24.75	25.42	21.86	19.01
Rice + Wheat	PDS	34.03	35.64	46.46	48.12	49.37	49.93
	Market	65.97	64.36	53.54	51.88	50.63	50.07
Sugar	PDS	4.17	4.65	3.51	2.64	2.08	2.97
	Market	95.83	95.35	96.49	97.36	97.92	97.03
Kerosene oil	PDS	95.63	97.75	95.11	95.88	95.13	96.77
	Market	4.38	2.25	4.89	4.12	4.87	3.23

Table 4.28 **Percentage Share of PDS and Market in Consumption of PDS Commodities—Madhya Pradesh**

Commodity		Month 1	Month 2	Month 3	Month 4	Month 5	Month 6
				AAY			
Rice	PDS	44.68	47.66	43.76	35.43	36.55	33.80
	Market	55.32	52.34	56.24	64.57	63.45	66.20
Wheat	PDS	75.73	69.87	70.23	69.18	64.99	62.45
	Market	24.27	30.13	29.77	30.82	35.01	37.55
Rice + Wheat	PDS	65.73	63.04	62.28	60.59	57.87	55.26
	Market	34.27	36.96	37.72	39.41	42.13	44.74
Sugar	PDS	53.01	64.75	64.38	61.06	44.37	38.43
	Market	46.99	35.25	35.62	38.94	55.63	61.57
Kerosene oil	PDS	95.50	97.45	97.14	99.46	99.61	100.00
	Market	4.50	2.55	2.86	0.54	0.39	0.00
				BPL			
Rice	PDS	30.90	31.00	31.59	33.63	38.94	36.01
	Market	69.10	69.00	68.41	66.37	61.06	63.99
Wheat	PDS	53.73	42.66	42.16	40.50	35.03	33.88
	Market	46.27	57.34	57.84	59.50	64.97	66.12
Rice + Wheat	PDS	43.43	37.74	37.83	38.12	36.35	34.60
	Market	56.57	62.26	62.17	61.88	63.65	65.40
Sugar	PDS	45.31	58.11	53.24	49.37	0.00	32.56
	Market	54.69	41.89	46.76	50.63	100.00	67.44
Kerosene oil	PDS	94.28	97.13	96.19	97.59	98.51	98.31
	Market	5.72	2.87	3.81	2.41	1.49	1.69
				APL			
Rice	PDS	7.61	4.74	2.91	4.38	6.72	5.00
	Market	92.39	95.26	97.09	95.62	93.28	95.00
Wheat	PDS	8.97	5.33	8.33	3.09	2.50	1.98
	Market	91.03	94.67	91.67	96.91	97.50	98.02
Rice + Wheat	PDS	8.44	5.08	6.16	3.52	3.85	2.96
	Market	91.56	94.92	93.84	96.48	96.15	97.04
Sugar	PDS	7.54	8.06	7.15	1.30	2.05	1.16
	Market	92.46	91.94	92.85	98.70	97.95	98.84
Kerosene oil	PDS	79.09	89.40	89.55	99.07	99.26	99.80
	Market	20.91	10.60	10.45	0.93	0.74	0.20

Table 4.29 **Percentage Share of PDS and Market in Consumption of PDS Commodities—Maharashtra**

Commodity		Month 1	Month 2	Month 3	Month 4	Month 5	Month 6
				AAY			
Rice	PDS	55.61	62.81	59.16	62.26	63.01	63.27
	Market	44.39	37.19	40.84	37.74	36.99	36.73
Wheat	PDS	81.40	80.27	79.54	81.25	81.86	82.35
	Market	18.60	19.73	20.46	18.75	18.14	17.65
Rice + Wheat	PDS	64.62	69.56	66.90	69.56	70.26	70.83
	Market	35.38	30.44	33.10	30.44	29.74	29.17
Sugar	PDS	0.20	0.00	0.00	0.00	0.36	0.00
	Market	99.80	100.00	100.00	100.00	99.64	100.00
Kerosene oil	PDS	97.36	97.68	97.71	98.80	98.52	98.55
	Market	2.64	2.32	2.29	1.20	1.48	1.45
				BPL			
Rice	PDS	46.66	50.80	46.66	50.64	52.08	51.93
	Market	53.34	49.20	53.34	49.36	47.92	48.07
Wheat	PDS	63.65	60.80	58.72	64.45	70.08	68.55
	Market	36.35	39.20	41.28	35.55	29.92	31.45
Rice + Wheat	PDS	52.96	54.68	51.16	56.15	59.45	58.63
	Market	47.04	45.32	48.84	43.85	40.55	41.37
Sugar	PDS	1.27	0.00	0.45	0.00	20.79	0.13
	Market	98.73	100.00	99.55	100.00	79.21	99.87
Kerosene oil	PDS	95.82	97.88	98.33	98.62	99.24	99.15
	Market	4.18	2.12	1.67	1.38	0.76	0.85
				APL			
Rice	PDS	2.75	9.22	1.95	5.81	2.07	4.21
	Market	97.25	90.78	98.05	94.19	97.93	95.79
Wheat	PDS	5.32	13.72	6.15	6.41	2.47	7.15
	Market	94.68	86.28	93.85	93.59	97.53	92.85
Rice + Wheat	PDS	3.87	11.35	3.78	6.08	2.24	5.49
	Market	96.13	88.65	96.22	93.92	97.76	94.51
Sugar	PDS	0.00	0.00	0.00	0.00	0.00	0.00
	Market	100.00	100.00	100.00	100.00	100.00	100.00
Kerosene oil	PDS	94.44	97.19	95.71	97.65	97.96	96.95
	Market	5.56	2.81	4.29	2.35	2.04	3.05

Table 4.30 **Percentage Share of PDS and Market in Consumption of PDS Commodities—Uttarakhand**

Commodity		Month 1	Month 2	Month 3	Month 4	Month 5	Month 6
				AAY			
Rice	PDS	65.88	67.08	68.27	72.02	73.02	71.83
	Market	34.12	32.92	31.73	27.98	26.98	28.17
Wheat	PDS	49.93	54.10	52.81	51.79	50.22	51.64
	Market	50.07	45.90	47.19	48.21	49.78	48.36
Rice + Wheat	PDS	60.25	62.72	62.91	64.54	64.48	64.50
	Market	39.75	37.28	37.09	35.46	35.52	35.50
Sugar	PDS	65.77	71.41	70.79	86.26	80.08	84.75
	Market	34.23	28.59	29.21	13.74	19.92	15.25
Kerosene oil	PDS	97.54	98.62	99.58	100.00	100.00	100.00
	Market	2.46	1.38	0.42	0.00	0.00	0.00
				BPL			
Rice	PDS	58.97	60.04	59.93	62.11	64.03	63.61
	Market	41.03	39.96	40.07	37.89	35.97	36.39
Wheat	PDS	40.34	44.80	43.10	38.25	36.88	37.17
	Market	59.66	55.20	56.90	61.75	63.12	62.83
Rice + Wheat	PDS	52.14	54.72	53.96	52.76	53.25	53.16
	Market	47.86	45.28	46.04	47.24	46.75	46.84
Sugar	PDS	62.73	72.83	69.60	83.61	75.55	79.86
	Market	37.27	27.17	30.40	16.39	24.45	20.14
Kerosene oil	PDS	95.69	99.41	99.73	99.12	100.00	99.75
	Market	4.31	0.59	0.27	0.88	0.00	0.25
				APL			
Rice	PDS	20.11	20.46	17.92	17.61	17.53	21.75
	Market	79.89	79.54	82.08	82.39	82.47	78.25
Wheat	PDS	12.34	13.52	12.89	15.44	8.98	9.23
	Market	87.66	86.48	87.11	84.56	91.02	90.77
Rice + Wheat	PDS	16.95	17.68	15.82	16.64	13.52	16.01
	Market	83.05	82.32	84.18	83.36	86.48	83.99
Sugar	PDS	47.37	48.68	49.66	62.62	60.80	62.73
	Market	52.63	51.32	50.34	37.38	39.20	37.27
Kerosene oil	PDS	93.16	97.74	98.49	99.55	99.54	100.00
	Market	6.84	2.26	1.51	0.45	0.46	0.00

4.5 Comparative Price Analysis—Market *versus* PDS

The main objective of PDS is to provide food and other essentials to the poor at affordable prices. Among our selected states, around 50 to 70 per cent food requirement of the below poverty households was fulfilled by the fair price shops under PDS. However, the more pertinent question to ask is to what extent the food subsidy is being passed on to the poor (through concessional prices). Under the TPDS system, the Central government has fixed the price of wheat at Rs. 2 per kg and rice at Rs. 3 per kg for the AAY households in all the states. In the case of BPL, however, the price varies from state to state and it is generally higher than the AAY price for these two cereals. The actual prices paid by our selected households for food (and other commodities) obtained through PDS and that bought through the market are given in Table 4.6 for the six selected states. The table contains (arithmetic) mean, median and mode[7] prices paid by the households. The mean price is the average price whereas the median represents the middle value and the mode is the highest frequency price. However, mean can be distorted by extreme values while median is only the situational middle value. In the given circumstances, mode prices make the ideal case as that represents the model price that is paid by the majority of the households.

Comparing the actual prices paid for the PDS wheat and rice with the stipulated prices for these commodities in the AAY category, it is discernible from the table that mode price was exactly equal to the stipulated price of Rs. 2 per kg for wheat and Rs. 3 per kg for rice in all the selected states, except Kerala, where mode price for wheat and rice both was Rs. 3 per kg. Thus, mode prices indicate that the majority of AAY households were provided food at the stipulated prices and thereby, they were passed on the subsidy on account of concessional prices. In the case of BPL households, the mode price charged for rice was Rs. 7 per kg in Jharkhand, Rs. 6.50 per kg in Madhya Pradesh and Uttarakhand, Rs. 6.20 per kg in Delhi and Rs. 6 per kg in Maharashtra. In Kerala, peculiarly the price charged for rice and wheat both, for AAY as well as BPL households was Rs. 3 per kg. Price charged for wheat in all other states for the BPL households was uniformly Rs. 5 per kg. Thus, range across various states for mode price was higher for rice as compared to wheat for the BPL households. In the case of APL, the PDS prices were closer to the market prices and that commensurate well with the main PDS theme of selling PDS food at the economic cost in the case of APL households. That also explains widely observed incidence of lower lifting of the PDS food by the above poverty households.

Comparing mode prices with the more common average, namely the mean, it is seen from the table that mean prices were more or less equal to the mode prices in all the states for both wheat as well as rice. Mean prices were slightly higher for AAY households in Jharkhand and for BPL households in Maharashtra and Uttarakhand. Nonetheless, the difference between the mean and mode prices was only miniscule, not only for wheat and rice but also for kerosene oil and sugar. However, in the case of latter two commodities, namely sugar and kerosene, uniform price was charged from all the households as no significant difference in price was observed among above and below poverty households in any of the six selected states. Finally, in Kerala, in some places a few households obtained their entitled quantity of wheat and rice free of cost. Among the beneficiaries who obtained free entitlement were not only the Antyodaya and other below poverty families but ironically also some of the above poverty households.[8] In conclusion, in passing out the subsidy to the poor households in terms of lower (stipulated) price, no major distortions were observed in all the six selected states.

Concluding the findings on consumption pattern, it was observed that on an average, per capita cereal consumption surpassed the norm of 10.45 kgs in all the states across all categories, except Kerala. Among cereals, wheat and rice constituted the principal share whereas in Maharashtra and Madhya Pradesh, some amount of coarse grains were also consumed by all the three categories. The cereal consumption was highest in Jharkhand (13.5 kgs) and lowest in Kerala (8.6 kgs). On an average, the distribution of food and non-food expenditure for all the categories and all the states was in the range of 60-70 for food and 30-40 for non-food. Total consumption expenditure for all categories topped in Delhi (Rs. 476), followed by Kerala (Rs. 415), Uttarakhand (Rs. 388), Maharashtra (Rs. 380) while Madhya Pradesh and Jharkhand were on the bottom with per capita consumption expenditure around Rs. 300 and Rs. 283, respectively. The performance of PDS in terms of providing food to the poor was quite satisfactory in Delhi and Uttarakhand where near 35 kgs of cereals were distributed to more than 98 per cent targeted groups. In Kerala and Maharashtra, although coverage of targeted groups was above 96 per cent but the cereals distributed were far less than 35 kgs. Madhya Pradesh and Jharkhand, both fell short of target, both in terms of targeting population and the amount of cereals distributed. In both these states, only 80 per cent of BPL households were supplied 22 and 28 kgs of cereals, respectively.

7. Mean -The average of a group of numbers is called the mean; Median – The middle number of the group is called the median; Mode - The number that appears the most often in a listing of number.

8. Among our selected households, around 20-25 households among AAY and BPL and around 9 APL households obtained wheat/rice from fair price shops free of cost.

Table 4.31 **Prices of PDS Commodities *vis-à-vis* Market Price (Rs./Kgs or Litre) (Six Months Average)**

	Rice-PDS	Rice-OM	Wheat-PDS	Wheat-OM	Sugar-PDS	Sugar-OM	Kerosene-PDS	Kerosene-OM
				Delhi				
AAY								
Mean	3.00	11.84	2.00	11.40	13.78	18.00	9.54	20.00
Median	3.00	12.00	2.00	12.00	14.00	18.00	9.55	20.00
Mode	3.00	12.00	2.00	12.00	14.00	18.00	9.09	20.00
BPL								
Mean	6.31	11.93	4.84	11.40	13.78	18.17	9.56	19.31
Median	6.20	12.00	4.80	12.00	14.00	18.00	9.55	20.00
Mode	6.20	12.00	5.00	12.00	14.00	18.00	9.09	20.00
APL								
Mean	9.01	12.66	6.79	11.55	13.93	18.35	9.77	18.31
Median	9.00	12.00	6.96	12.00	14.00	18.00	10.00	20.00
Mode	9.00	12.00	7.00	12.00	14.00	18.00	10.00	20.00
				Jharkhand				
AAY								
Mean	3.16	9.94	2.16	11.95	15.60	20.15	11.00	27.81
Median	3.00	10.00	2.00	12.00	16.00	20.00	11.00	30.00
Mode	3.00	10.00	2.00	12.00	16.00	20.00	11.00	30.00
BPL								
Mean	6.79	9.78	5.10	11.98	16.00	20.17	11.00	25.80
Median	7.00	10.00	5.00	12.00	16.00	20.00	11.00	30.00
Mode	7.00	10.00	5.00	12.00	16.00	20.00	11.00	30.00
APL								
Mean	8.86	10.04	5.84	12.10		20.16	11.00	27.82
Median	9.00	10.00	5.00	12.00		20.00	11.00	30.00
Mode	9.00	10.00	5.00	12.00		20.00	11.00	30.00
				Kerala				
AAY								
Mean	3.00	11.48	2.90	12.30	13.90	17.40	10.13	26.00
Median	3.00	12.00	3.00	12.00	14.00	17.50	10.00	30.00
Mode	3.00	12.00	3.00	12.00	14.00	18.00	9.50	25.00
BPL								
Mean	2.99	11.64	3.04	12.72	13.90	17.35	10.15	19.17
Median	3.00	12.00	3.00	12.00	14.00	17.00	10.00	20.00
Mode	3.00	12.00	3.00	12.00	14.00	18.00	9.50	20.00
APL								
Mean	8.91	11.95	6.94	14.06	13.96	17.25	10.15	21.44
Median	9.00	12.00	7.00	12.00	14.00	17.00	10.00	20.00
Mode	9.00	12.00	7.00	12.00	14.00	16.00	9.50	20.00

contd...

contd...

	Rice-PDS	Rice-OM	Wheat-PDS	Wheat-OM	Sugar-PDS	Sugar-OM	Kerosene-PDS	Kerosene-OM
				Madhya Pradesh				
AAY								
Mean	3.01	10.73	2.00	10.28	13.75	17.86	10.08	13.79
Median	3.00	10.00	2.00	10.00	13.50	18.00	10.00	15.00
Mode	3.00	10.00	2.00	10.00	13.50	18.00	10.00	15.00
BPL								
Mean	6.55	10.68	4.97	10.28	13.78	17.85	10.09	13.86
Median	6.50	10.00	5.00	10.00	13.50	18.00	10.00	14.00
Mode	6.50	10.00	5.00	10.00	14.00	18.00	10.00	15.00
APL								
Mean	8.98	11.25	6.03	10.35	14.22	17.79	10.13	15.56
Median	9.00	11.00	5.00	10.00	14.00	18.00	10.00	15.00
Mode	9.00	10.00	5.00	10.00	14.00	20.00	10.00	15.00
				Maharashtra				
AAY								
Mean	3.03	10.96	2.11	10.72	14.50	17.93	11.23	19.74
Median	3.00	11.00	2.00	10.00	14.50	18.00	10.00	20.00
Mode	3.00	12.00	2.00	10.00	13.00	20.00	10.00	25.00
BPL								
Mean	6.20	11.08	5.09	10.54	14.12	17.86	11.29	22.36
Median	6.00	12.00	5.00	10.00	14.00	18.00	10.00	25.00
Mode	6.00	12.00	5.00	10.00	14.00	20.00	10.00	25.00
APL								
Mean	9.06	11.49	6.15	10.94		17.94	11.30	21.75
Median	9.00	12.00	5.80	10.00		18.00	10.00	24.00
Mode	9.00	12.00	5.00	10.00		20.00	10.00	25.00
				Uttarakhand				
AAY								
Mean	3.05	11.12	2.07	11.23	13.77	18.25	10.76	17.33
Median	3.00	10.00	2.00	11.00	14.00	18.00	11.00	15.00
Mode	3.00	10.00	2.00	10.00	14.00	18.00	11.00	15.00
BPL								
Mean	6.68	11.51	5.20	11.05	13.78	18.36	10.69	16.37
Median	6.52	10.00	5.00	10.00	14.00	18.00	11.00	15.00
Mode	6.52	10.00	5.00	10.00	14.00	18.00	11.00	20.00
APL								
Mean	9.08	11.70	6.45	11.04	13.78	18.71	10.71	19.45
Median	9.00	12.00	7.00	10.00	14.00	18.00	11.00	20.00
Mode	9.00	10.00	7.00	10.00	14.00	20.00	11.00	20.00

Table A-4.1 Variations in Food Consumption across Households and over Time

	Coefficient of Variation across Households			Coefficient of Variation across 6 Months		
	AAY	BPL	APL	AAY	BPL	APL
			Delhi			
Rice	27.98	33.80	51.33	5.87	3.59	4.61
Wheat	36.70	36.13	43.74	4.36	4.78	3.70
Other cereals	64.04	58.71	67.65	100.92	118.99	129.39
Total pulses	40.60	39.31	47.13	10.30	8.66	3.94
Sugar	29.85	26.48	40.20	3.14	3.61	8.95
Edible oils	45.92	42.94	91.61	5.69	6.73	7.75
Liquid milk	47.12	48.01	57.87	11.03	6.53	5.67
			Jharkhand			
Rice	63.74	63.70	64.46	3.76	5.03	6.05
Wheat	41.69	55.43	73.87	7.59	2.85	18.15
Other cereals	71.77	112.05	42.42	113.06	64.00	73.10
Total pulses	66.28	44.64	67.44	7.14	18.30	10.65
Sugar	62.58	62.44	68.76	8.54	9.96	9.59
Edible oils	58.00	60.24	62.37	5.56	5.93	7.69
Liquid milk	76.12	88.66	76.26	32.63	47.44	33.13
			Kerala			
Rice	47.68	53.40	53.70	7.65	8.87	10.78
Wheat	78.07	50.96	57.16	91.53	12.90	10.39
Other cereals	55.78	77.39	63.47	133.33	75.35	83.17
Total pulses	52.83	55.46	55.13	4.66	2.89	3.67
Sugar	71.37	78.32	68.80	2.76	4.18	7.00
Edible oils	58.94	62.17	63.48	3.36	4.88	5.95
Liquid milk	72.28	68.34	65.77	21.88	5.34	7.01
			Madhya Pradesh			
Rice	111.00	101.62	92.57	7.92	9.70	7.86
Wheat	48.13	71.16	68.81	8.71	11.95	10.88
Other cereals	58.53	65.32	72.88	16.26	10.78	12.76
Total pulses	65.56	66.00	70.96	13.43	7.64	3.79
Sugar	48.80	56.41	71.18	10.35	12.47	8.35
Edible oils	53.66	55.92	59.86	15.40	13.31	9.03
Liquid milk	99.38	86.96	84.76	69.27	49.87	26.93
			Maharashtra			
Rice	66.50	65.60	62.72	3.81	4.39	8.09
Wheat	59.47	60.03	61.54	5.32	3.73	5.99
Other cereals	70.80	67.84	74.95	9.14	16.72	16.86
Total pulses	61.95	63.26	67.91	11.83	8.84	13.19
Sugar	60.42	51.37	51.34	5.28	8.19	2.42
Edible oils	55.77	50.90	54.43	6.75	5.03	4.96
Liquid milk	95.51	84.28	74.14	10.85	34.84	10.62
			Uttarakhand			
Rice	34.90	36.33	47.46	3.54	5.00	7.29
Wheat	52.51	59.17	65.61	3.85	5.35	6.40
Other cereals	46.29	78.45	147.85	181.66	93.07	125.23
Total pulses	68.06	53.45	62.67	5.47	6.75	9.96
Sugar	54.11	51.57	60.82	6.56	8.20	9.84
Edible oils	178.89	45.39	47.45	15.95	7.46	9.28
Liquid milk	65.19	57.85	56.41	16.36	28.56	23.30

5 Risk Insurance and Intra-Village Consumption Smoothing

5.1 Introduction

In the event of income failure how poor households sustain their consumption poses a paramount question. There is a wide literature available that indicates the existence of some sort of insurance among the poor, either through the social networking, ethnicity or through their management of income or assets in the long run. How well are households in rural economies able to insure consumption against shocks to income? In the recent, past this question has led to a substantial literature examining the success of households in insuring consumption and identifying the different mechanisms that could potentially enable households to do so. The literature on risk and insurance in poor rural economies has established three stylised facts: (i) income risk is pervasive; (ii) household behaviour is geared in part to protecting consumption from such risk; and (iii) the mechanism of doing so are both private and social, the latter comprising various informal risk sharing arrangements amongst two or more households (Jalan and Ravallion, 1999).

The studies including Alderman and Paxson (1992), Deaton (1992), Fafchamps (1992), Grimard (1997), Morduch (1995) and Townsend (1994, 1995) lead to the question of how well households in rural economies are able to insure consumption against such shocks to income? They have concluded that households take action aimed at protecting consumption by drawing on both private and social risk sharing arrangements. Townsend (1994) lists five potential risk bearing mechanisms as: (i) Spatial diversification of land holdings; (ii) Storage of grains from one year to the next; (iii) Purchases and sales of assets such as bullocks and land; (iv) Credit from formal and informal sources; and (v) Gifts and transfers within the family networks. However, not all households are equally able to insure consumption against income shocks and differentiated access to markets, particularly financial markets result in differential ability of households to insure against income shocks.

Different versions of empirical specifications of risk and insurance have been tested by the researchers using household level data from both developed and developing countries. Mace (1991) in her study on risk sharing in the US economy finds that the evidence is conditional on the preference specification. Results are mostly consistent with consumption insurance for the exponential utility specification but not for the power utility specification. Townsend (1995) finds overwhelming rejection of the null hypothesis of no insurance for different regions in Thailand. His results confirm that consumption in one region or state tracks income in that region indicating some sort of insurance does exist. Deaton (1992) using data from Cote d'Ivoire finds that marginal propensities to consume out of current income are always positive and significant. In somewhat a similar case, Jalan and Ravallion (1999) using data from rural China observe evidences of partial insurance of certain wealth groups while evidences of rejection of full insurance were strongest for the poorest wealth groups. In the case of rural India, Townsend (1994) using ICRISAT data for three villages to study risk and insurance observed that full consumption insurance was a fairly good benchmark. He observed that landless households were less well insured than their counterpart cultivators. However, in the case of rural Punjab, Maitra (1998) observed no evidence in favour of consumption insurance against income shocks. Yet another study by Maitra (2003) using ARIS-NCAER data shows that the null hypothesis of full insurance is rejected both for the population as a whole and for the different land classes. The estimated marginal propensity to consume out of idiosyncratic changes in income is significantly higher for the poorer households compared to the richer households.

The implications of the income and consumption insurance are quite significant for the policy matter in the case of targeted public distribution system (TPDS). The purpose of making PDS system targeted was implicitly to reduce the risk of income shock being transferred into consumption shocks. In other words, aim of such welfare-oriented programmes was to provide a safety net to the poor households. In our analysis part, we make an attempt to find out how successful have been the policy of TPDS in the selected states in mitigating such risks and providing a safety net to the vulnerable sections of our society, namely that of BPL and AAY cardholders.

The subject matter of this chapter deals with such issues among our selected households. The chapter is divided into three sections. The first section introduces the concept of consumption smoothing through insurance. The second section presents some facts about the observed distribution pattern of households' income and consumption in our selected states. Finally in the third section, we present the results of the model estimated to measure the risk insurance among the selected households using our penal data generated though six rounds of household survey.

Econometric Model[1]

The theoretical framework of risk sharing stems from the fact that households try to mitigate risk by their combined actions. If risks are idiosyncratic, i.e., they are household-specific in nature, then households will pool together to share all risks. If risks are fully pooled then there is complete risk sharing among households and changes in household consumption will track changes in the community average consumption and nothing else. In other words, if households pool their risks together, then their consumption will be determined in a combined way rather than being an individual phenomenon. In those circumstances, changes in factors specific to the household like changes in household income will not have a statistically significant impact on changes in household consumption. The estimated marginal propensity to consume of a particular household out of changes in its own income should be equal to zero while response of changes in community consumption on individual consumption should be equal to one. If that happens, such occurrences indicate that the household consumption is fully insured against any risk. The amount of risk sharing that actually takes place could be compared with this benchmark of complete risk sharing.

In this chapter we examine, whether the incidence of consumption smoothing (risk sharing) works better among the rich households (APL) who have better means of getting insured or does it work more effectively among the poor households (BPL and AAY). The poor households are likely to be more vulnerable to various kinds of income risks and therefore, they should undertake such measures to reduce the much higher chances of variability in consumption. However, although the poor being more vulnerable should be more likely to undertake such risk aversion measures but they will also be constrained by their limited availability of credit and insurance coverage. Therefore, it is very difficult to predict *a priori* whether the consumption smoothing through risk insurance would be more among the poor or rich households.

Formal financial and insurance markets for the prevalent risks particularly in rural areas in developing economies are often deficient. There could be various reasons for that, like high transaction costs, lack of information about the income pattern of rural households, lack of institutions for proper enforcement, collateral, etc. In the given circumstances, households are left with the only option of informal risk sharing among the family ties (relatives), their community members within or outside the village, etc. There are evidences that informal risk sharing schemes exist and perform very well in some developing countries.[2] Because of proximity of geographical locations and because of close transactions among group members, these informal ties work very well as the monitoring and enforcement costs are next to nil in their cases. However, these informal arrangements are still subject to aggregate risks.

A fairly general specification of the risk sharing test may be developed by proposing a risk sharing group and assuming that within each group, consumption is efficiently allocated in each period over the life time of the household. Let us assume that each household i of a risk sharing group g, has a constant absolute risk aversion utility function in terms of its consumption at time t, c_{igt} and household preferences x_{igt}: $U(c_{igt}) = -\exp[-A(c_{igt} - x_{igt})]$. One can then develop a test for the hypothesis of perfect insurance by directly using the first order condition of the group's optimisation problem to solve for consumption:

$$c_{igt} = \left(\frac{1}{A}\right)\ln(A) + \left(\frac{1}{A}\right)\ln(\omega_{ig}) - \left(\frac{1}{A}\right)\ln(\lambda_{gt}) + \chi_{igt} \tag{i}$$

1. For details of theoretical framework and review of literature on the subject, see Report on the first phase of the PDS evaluation, NCAER.

2. For a review of issues related to the performance of traditional system of social security and insurance in developing countries, refer to Platteau (1991).

where ω_{ig} is a welfare weight group g uses in choosing the optimal sets of consumption for the households of group, λ_{gt} is the Lagrange multiplier on the group resource constraint. Equation (i) states that if household i perfectly insures with other households of group g, its consumption should be partly determined by the aggregate resources of the group. Except insofar as it enters the aggregate resource constraint, household i's income does not affect household i's consumption. Include an individual household's earning term, y_{igt} in equation (i) and make this a testable proposition by including an error term u_{igt}. This error term may contain measurement error as well as household-specific shocks, which are unobservable:

$$c_{igt} = \left(\frac{1}{A}\right)\ln(A) + \left(\frac{1}{A}\right)\ln(\omega_{ig}) - \left(\frac{1}{A}\right)\ln(\lambda_{gt}) + \chi_{igt} + by_{igt} + u_{igt} \qquad \text{(ii)}$$

Estimating equation (ii) is problematic because it contains terms, especially weights and preferences that are not observed. However, if one has information on the household for two consecutive periods, one can assume that household specific characteristics stay the same every period. Alternatively, they may be assumed to change but are orthogonal to individual income and group resource constraints. In both cases, the effect of individual household preferences can be removed by first differencing equation (ii).

Empirical Implications

The risk sharing implications are recast for empirical implementation. The major implication is that changes in individual consumption are determined by changes in aggregate consumption rather than by changes in idiosyncratic variables. Empirical specifications for individual observations are developed for exponential utility. For exponential preferences, there is a direct relationship between the change in individual j's consumption and change in aggregate consumption:

$$\Delta cjt = \Delta cta + (\Delta bjt - \Delta bat) \qquad \text{(iii)}$$

Where

$$\Delta cjt = Cjt - Cjt - 1,$$

$$\Delta cta = \frac{1}{j}\sum \Delta Cjt,$$

$$\Delta bta = \frac{1}{j}\sum \Delta bjt$$

Equation (iii) presents a non-trivial approach for testing the full insurance implications: regress the changes in individual consumption onto the changes in aggregate consumption and the right hand side variables such as changes in individual income, family size and earning members in a family. All variables other than the aggregate consumption variable are predicted to enter insignificantly. This reflects the key feature of risk sharing: individual consumption responds to aggregate risk but not to idiosyncratic risk. Formally, the empirical specification is

$$\Delta c_t^j = \beta_0 + \beta_1 \Delta Y^j{}_t + \beta_2 \Delta C^a{}_t + u^j{}_t \qquad \text{(iv)}$$

where ΔY^j_t is the change in individual j's income and ΔC^a_t is change in village combined consumption. The error term includes the time varying component of both individual and aggregate preference shocks and might also include measurement errors from the consumption and income data. The predictions of the risk sharing model are $\beta_1 = 0$ and $\beta_2 = 1$. The model also predicts a zero coefficient for the right hand side variables. The hypothesis of complete risk sharing is tested in this chapter using Equation (iv).[3]

5.2 The Distribution of Income and Consumption

Before presenting the results of the model, a brief outline of the distribution of observed income and consumption per capita for the selected households is given. The household consumption comprises of expenditure on food and non-food items.

3. The theoretical framework could also be explained using a constant relative risk aversion (CRRA) utility function. Equation (iv) would then be expressed in terms of change in logarithms instead of changes in levels. In our estimations, we use both the frameworks.

Similarly, household income includes all income earned from agriculture, livestock, agriculture and non-agricultural wages, salaries, earnings from business and self-employment and all other transfer earnings. In the last two chapters, we presented the estimates of average income and consumption over six months time period. It was seen in the analysis that variation in consumption across the households and over time period (of six months) was less than that of income. In this section, we further probe this issue by looking at the distribution of per capita income and consumption to compare the level of concentration of these two variables. Figures 5.1 to 5.18 present the Lorenz curves of per capita income and consumption among the three categories of households in the six states. The plots of the Lorenz curve clearly indicate that across the categories, consumption was more symmetric compared to income. This was true in all the states without any exception. It is seen from the plots that graph of consumption always remained closer to the diagonal line compared to income graph and in most of the cases it was true for the whole range of the graph indicating symmetry in consumption more than income for all households in each category. However, the volume of concentration varied across the states and categories. The Gini coefficient and COV displayed in a small box in the middle of the graph measure the amount of concentration. The value of Gini coefficient for income was higher than that of consumption in all the categories. However, difference between the Gini of income and consumption was highest among APL households in almost all the states. This was the natural outcome as the range between the lowest and highest income was much higher among the above poverty households than that of AAY and BPL households. Between the BPL and AAY, no major differences in the distribution of income and consumption were observed as value of Gini coefficient did not vary much for income as well as consumption between these two category of households. Comparing the six states, Gini coefficient for both income and consumption was comparatively higher in Maharahstra and Uttarakhand, while its magnitude was lowest in Jharkhand. The value of Gini coefficient for income varied from 0.45 in Maharashtra for the APL category to 0.22 in Jharkhand for the AAY households. In consumption, the range of Gini coefficient lied between 0.28 for APL in Madhya Pradesh to 0.15 for BPL in Maharashtra. Thus, two factors emerge from this analysis. On the one hand, individual consumption followed individual income, which negates our hypothesis of consumption insurance by the households. On the other hand, consumption variations were more symmetric compared to income variations. In other words, when income observed fluctuations due to some internal or external shocks, consumption did not fluctuate to the same magnitude. This latter phenomenon is compatible with the hypothesis of consumption smoothing due to the presence of some formal or informal insurance among the households.

Figure 5.1 Lorenz Curve (AAY)—Delhi

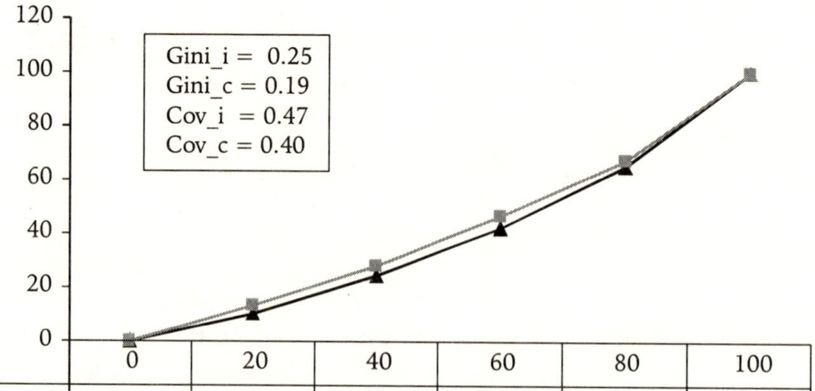

	0	20	40	60	80	100
Income	0.0	10.3	24.5	42.3	64.9	100.0
Consumption	0.0	13.11	28.5	46.3	67.1	100.0

Figure 5.2 Lorenz Curve (BPL)—Delhi

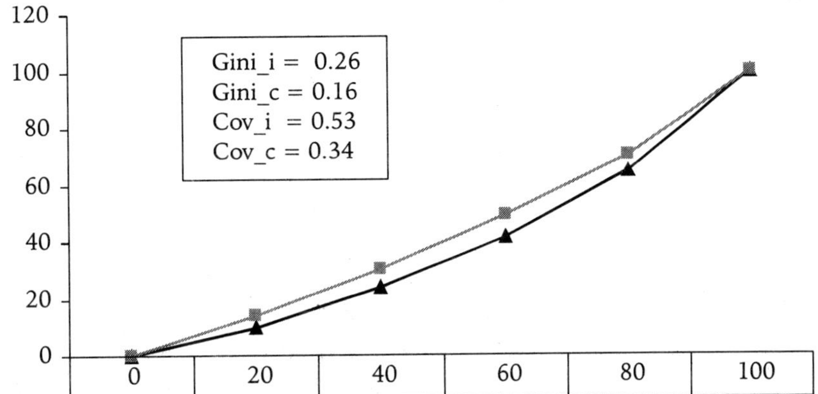

	0	20	40	60	80	100
Income	0.0	10.0	23.8	41.4	64.3	100.0
Consumption	0.0	14.0	30.4	48.8	70.3	100.0

Figure 5.3 Lorenz Curve (APL)—Delhi

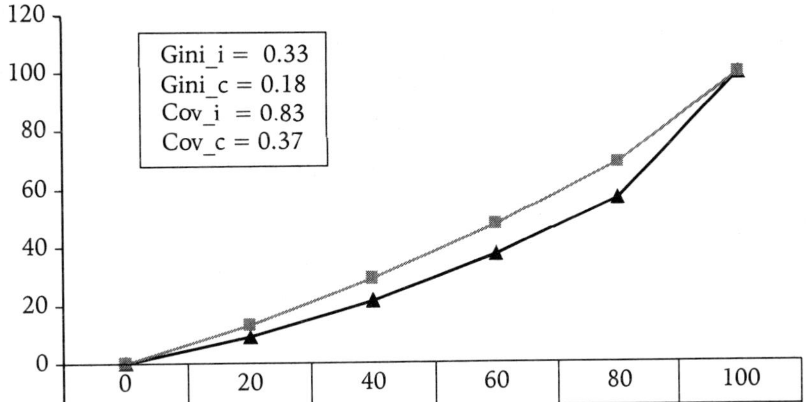

	0	20	40	60	80	100
Income	0.0	8.8	21.1	36.9	57.23	100.0
Consumption	0.0	13.2	29.1	47.65	69.0	100.0

Figure 5.4 Lorenz Curve (AAY)—Jharkhand

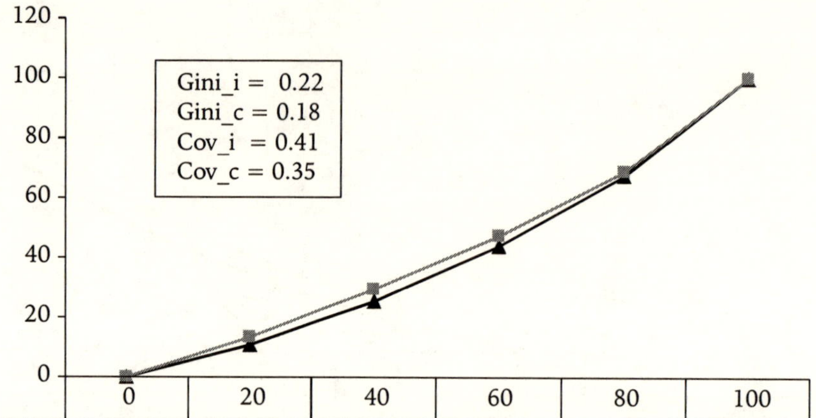

	0	20	40	60	80	100
Income	0.0	11.0	25.6	44.0	67.09	100.0
Consumption	0.0	13.3	29.2	47.44	68.9	100.0

Figure 5.5 Lorenz Curve (BPL)—Jharkhand

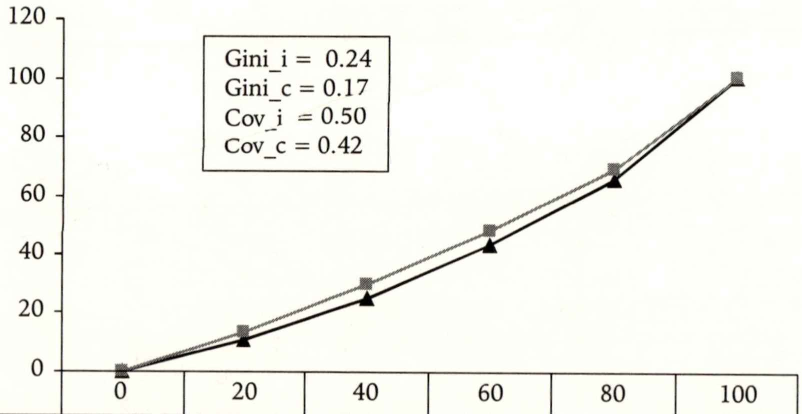

	0	20	40	60	80	100
Income	0.0	10.7	25.2	43.4	65.5	100.0
Consumption	0.0	13.5	29.7	48.0	69.0	100.0

Figure 5.6 Lorenz Curve (APL)—Jharkhand

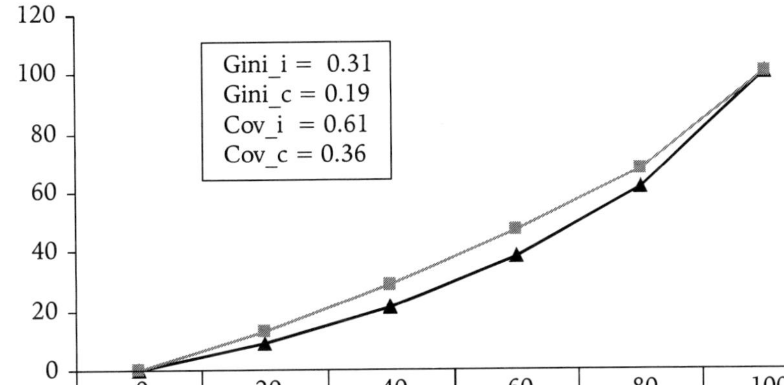

	0	20	40	60	80	100
Income	0.0	8.7	21.3	38.0	61.1	100.0
Consumption	0.0	12.8	28.6	46.8	67.8	100.0

Figure 5.7 Lorenz Curve (AAY)—Kerala

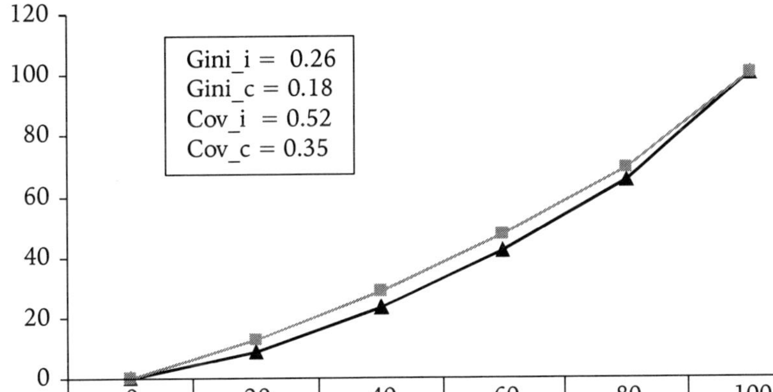

	0	20	40	60	80	100
Income	0.0	8.9	23.2	41.6	65.1	100.0
Consumption	0.0	12.9	28.8	47.1	68.9	100.0

Figure 5.8 Lorenz Curve (BPL)—Kerala

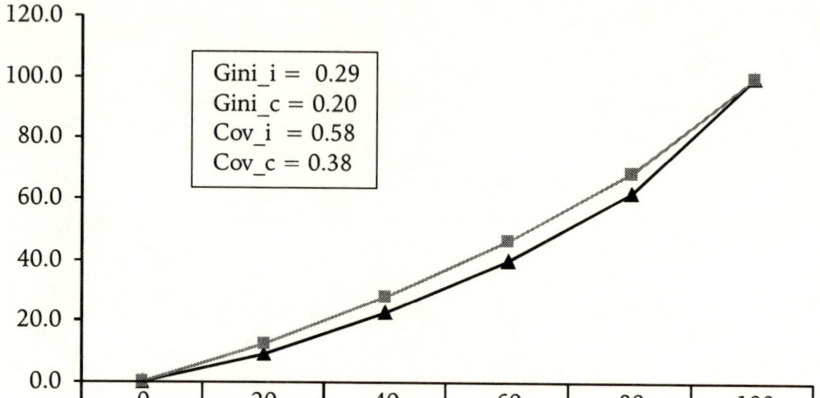

	0	20	40	60	80	100
Income	0.0	9.0	22.8	39.9	62.0	100.0
Consumption	0.0	12.1	28.0	46.2	68.2	100.0

Figure 5.9 Lorenz Curve (APL)—Kerala

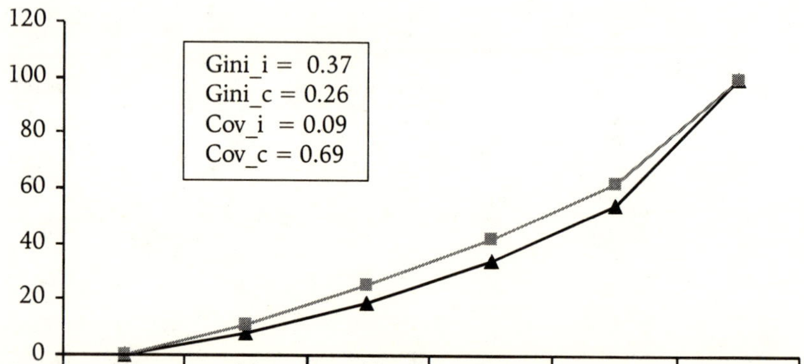

	0	20	40	60	80	100
Income	0.0	7.6	18.9	34.2	54.4	100.0
Consumption	0.0	10.9	25.06	41.9	61.9	100.0

Figure 5.10 Lorenz Curve (AAY)—Madhya Pradesh

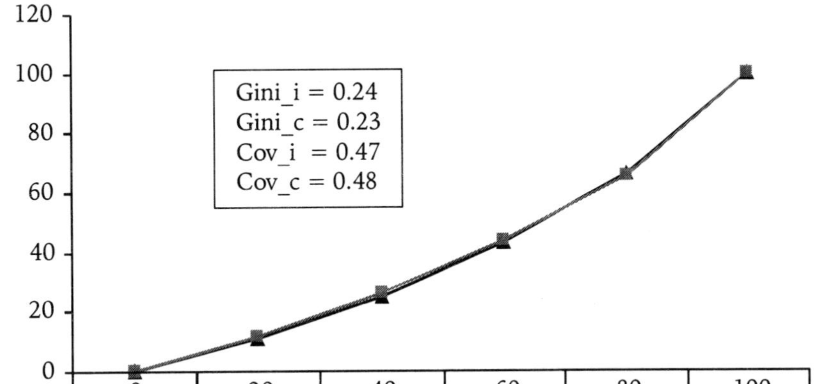

	0	20	40	60	80	100
Income	0.0	10.5	24.8	43.0	65.8	100.0
Consumption	0.0	11.6	26.3	43.9	65.2	100.0

Figure 5.11 Lorenz Curve (BPL)—Madhya Pradesh

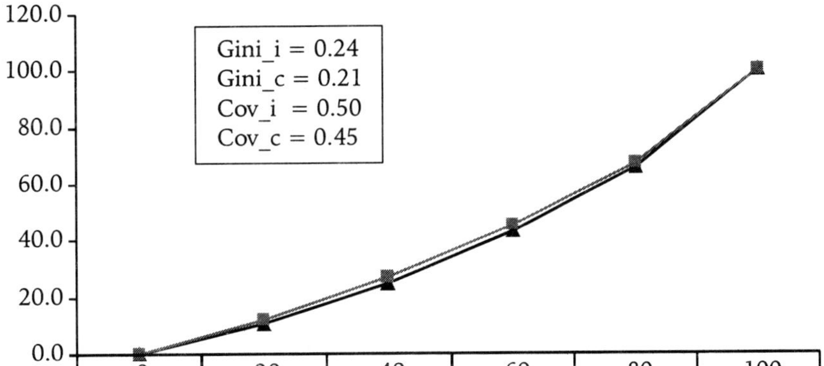

	0	20	40	60	80	100
Income	0.0	10.3	24.8	43.0	65.8	100.0
Consumption	0.0	11.7	27.0	45.0	67.0	100.0

Figure 5.12 Lorenz Curve (APL)—Madhya Pradesh

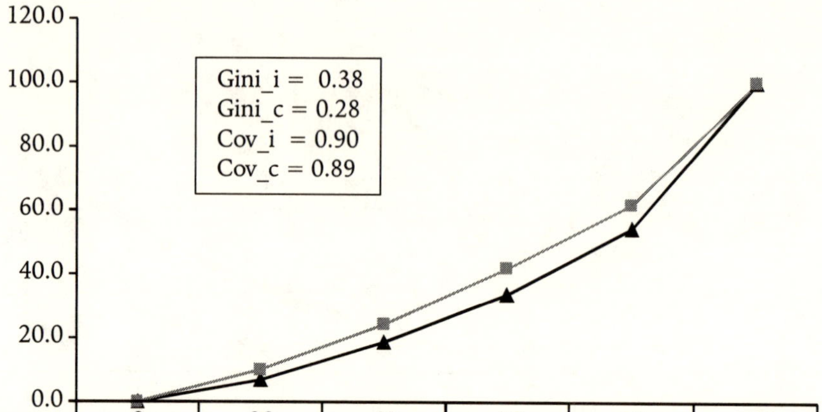

	0	20	40	60	80	100
Income	0.0	6.7	18.7	33.9	54.2	100.0
Consumption	0.0	10.0	24.7	41.8	61.9	100.0

Figure 5.13 Lorenz Curve (AAY)—Maharashtra

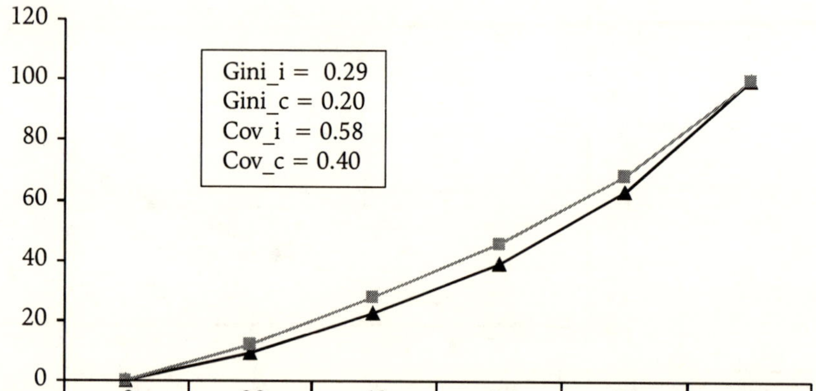

	0	20	40	60	80	100
Income	0.0	9.0	22.3	39.1	62.9	100.0
Consumption	0.0	12.2	27.7	45.6	68.3	100.0

Figure 5.14 Lorenz Curve (BPL)—Maharashtra

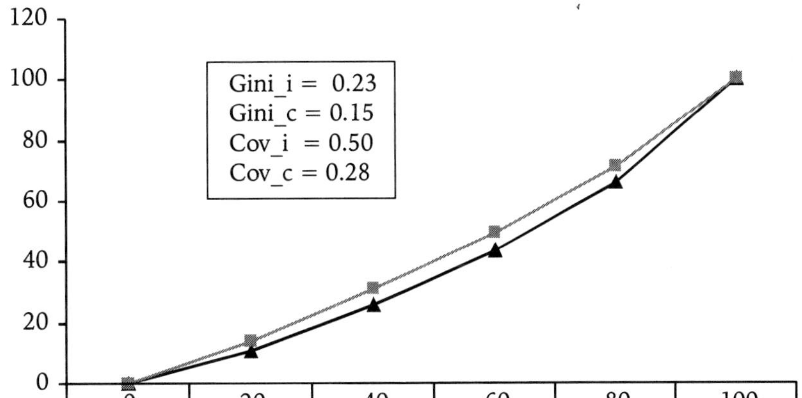

	0	20	40	60	80	100
Income	0.0	10.4	25.5	43.6	66.0	100.0
Consumption	0.0	13.9	30.7	49.7	71.5	100.0

Figure 5.15 Lorenz Curve (APL)—Maharashtra

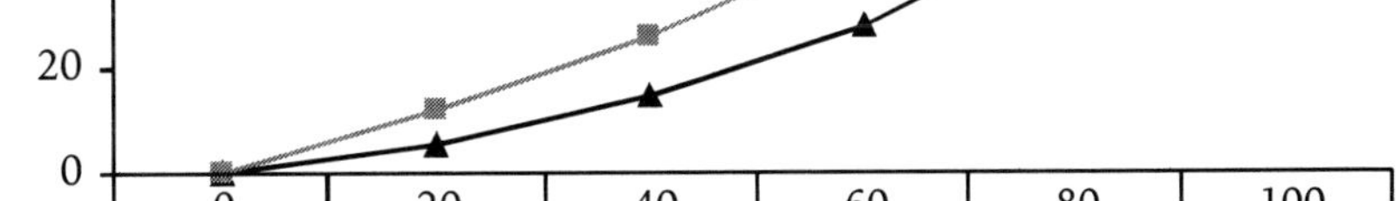

	0	20	40	60	80	100
Income	0.0	5.0	14.8	28.2	48.5	100.0
Consumption	0.0	11.7	26.3	44.6	66.0	100.0

Figure 5.16 Lorenz Curve (AAY)—Uttarakhand

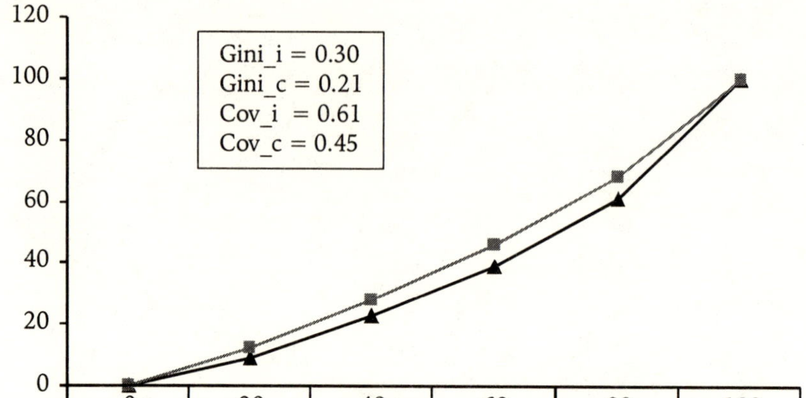

	0	20	40	60	80	100
Income	0.0	9.3	22.5	39.0	61.3	100.0
Consumption	0.0	12.0	27.6	45.8	67.8	100.0

Figure 5.17 Lorenz Curve (BPL)—Uttarakhand

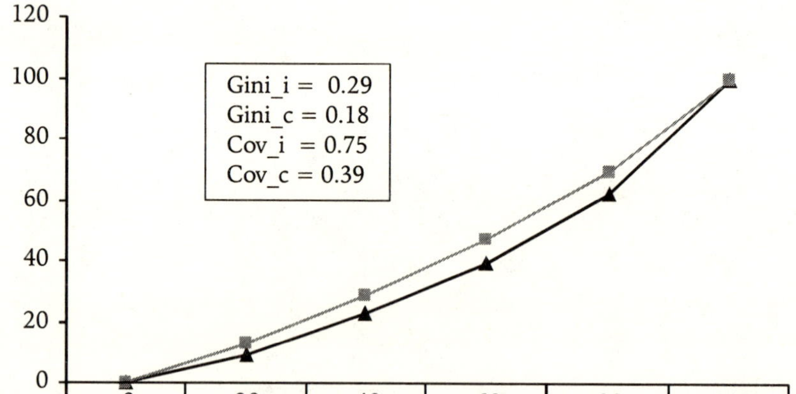

	0	20	40	60	80	100
Income	0.0	9.5	22.6	39.6	62.0	100.0
Consumption	0.0	12.8	29.0	47.3	69.4	100.0

Figure 5.18 Lorenz Curve (APL)—Uttarakhand

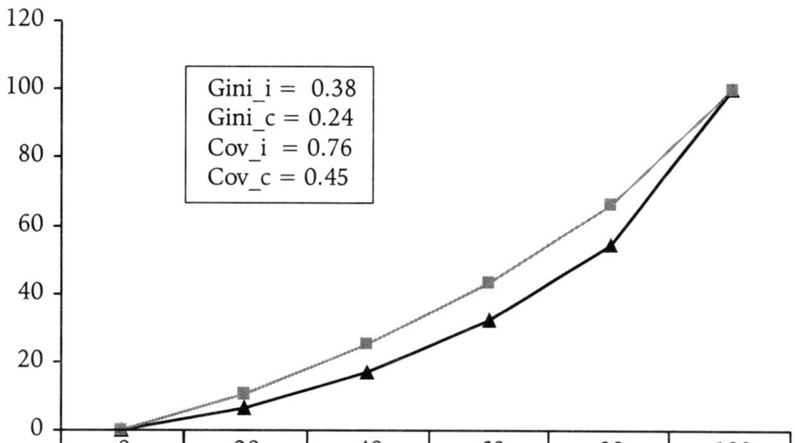

	0	20	40	60	80	100
Income	0.0	6.5	16.7	32.3	54.4	100.0
Consumption	0.0	10.5	24.9	43.18	65.9	100.0

5.3 Results of the Model

Before presenting the results of the model, it is essential to clarify the data we have used for building the model. The primary survey data collected over a period of six months for 6000 households in 6 states have been used for empirical estimation of this theoretical framework. In each state, data was collected from five districts, selecting five villages in each district. Thus, we have a total number of 25 villages in one state and 150 villages in all the six states.[4] The data was collected for three types of beneficiaries, i.e., AAY, BPL and APL. Our results include the regressions for the state as a whole as well as each of the sub-category (AAY, BPL and APL, separately). A total number of 1000 households were surveyed for a period of six months. However, in our estimation, we regress the change in consumption on change in income, therefore, losing one month's information in the process of generating data for the first difference of income and consumption. By pooling the time series and cross sectional, penal data, we shall have a total number of 5000 observations in each state. However, the number of observations would vary in the case of AAY, BPL and APL regressions in the proportion in which their numbers were selected in each state.

Equation (iv) is estimated using OLS in terms of the first difference of levels and logarithms. We first estimate the regression of change in the level of consumption on the change in the level of income and change in village consumption, for the state as a whole and then separately for each of the AAY, BPL and APL welfare groups. In an alternate specification, we test whether the risk sharing is taking place within caste or community (ethnic groups) rather than within the village.[5] We have data on four categories of castes, i.e., households either belong to SC, ST, OBC or to the Forward Caste (FC), that is Brahmin or non-Brahmin. To test the hypothesis of risk sharing within ethnic or caste groups, instead of rounding up consumption across the village, we rounded it up further for the four sub-castes within each village to form combined ethnic consumption. In another specification, we test whether insurance unit rather than based on ethnic, caste and creed grounds is actually based on

4. In our selection, we followed four villages and one city/town from each state. Therefore, our data consists of 120 villages and 30 towns/cities. However, for this exercise we do not differentiate between a village or a town. Therefore, we proceed with assuming there are a total number of 150 villages surveyed for this exercise alone.

5. The central question in the discussion of insurance among households is the identification of the appropriate group within which the informal risk sharing takes place. In relatively homogeneous societies, geographic proximity may be the determinant of the formation of the insurance group. In a number of studies, village is assumed to form such a homogeneous group. However, in societies that are more diverse, either along ethnic groups or castes, the village may not be the appropriate unit of risk sharing. Morduch (1990) examined the possibility that rural households (in the ICRISAT data set from India) insure consumption with members of their own caste within their village. In an another study from Cote d' Ivoire, Grimard (1997) examined whether households take part in spatially diversified risk sharing arrangements with members of their own ethnic group. In both these studies, evidences were found for risk sharing but the hypothesis of complete risk sharing was however rejected.

economic grounds. It is possible to have people interact within the same economic strata, i.e., belonging to same set of living standards rather than poor interacting with rich and vice versa. In our sampling, we have data on households holding AAY, BPL and APL cards. This stratification is based on economic criterion rather than on the basis of caste/ethnicity. Similar to ethnic grouping, for the economic categorisation within a village, we clubbed village consumption based on three economic categories of AAY, BPL and APL card holding by the households. Tables 5.1 to 5.6 present the results of regressions in levels (of first difference) and Tables 5.7 to 5.12 present the results for the regressions in logarithms. The tables present value of the coefficients of individual income and village consumption in column three and four, respectively. In column five, coefficient of beneficiary consumption (based on economic grouping) and in column six coefficient of ethnic consumption (based on caste grouping) is presented. The value of F-ratio is reported in column eight for testing the coefficient of individual income equal to zero. Column nine presents F-test for village/ethnic/beneficiary consumption equal to zero. The last three columns present F-ratio to test for the joint occurring of $\beta_1=0$ and $\beta_2=1$, which tests the hypothesis of complete risk sharing.

Table 5.1 Regression Results—Delhi (Ordinary Least Square Without Log) Dependent Variable = ΔC

	Constant	ΔY	ΔVC	ΔBC	ΔEC	R^2	F*	No of Obs.	F* ΔY=0	F* ΔVC=1 or ΔBC =1 or ΔEC =1	F* ΔY=0, ΔVC =1	F* ΔY=0, ΔBC =1	F* ΔY=0, ΔEC =1
							Aggregate						
1.	-31.1	0.01*				0.003	13.7*	5000	13.7*				
	(-4.8)	(3.7)											
2.	-22.3	0.01*	0.64*			0.145	426*	5000	12.5*	258.7*	134.7*		
	(-3.7)	(3.5)	(28.9)										
3.	-5.4	0.01*		0.80*		0.238	780*	5000	11.1*	96.2*		52.9*	
	(-1.0)	(3.3)		(39.3)									
4.	-6.1	0.01*			0.78*	0.185	565*	5000	14.7*	93.1*			53.5*
	(-1.0)	(3.8)			(33.3)								
							AAY						
5.	22.4	0.01				0.001	2.41	1000	2.41				
	(2.0)	(1.6)											
6.	28.7	0.01*	0.41*			0.110	62.7*	1000	7.5*	245*	132*		
	(2.8)	(2.7)	(11.1)										
7.	5.79	0.00		0.75*		0.224	145*	1000	0.99	30.7*		15.6*	
	(0.6)	(1.0)		(16.9)									
8.	39.9	0.01**			0.57*	0.156	93.6*	1000	5.9**	105*			57.2*
	(3.9)	(2.4)			(13.6)								
							BPL						
9.	-15.8**	0.01*				0.007	21.6*	2985	21.6*				
	(-2.3)	(4.64)											
10.	-6.60	0.012*	0.63*			0.196	364*	2985	23.56*	243.6*	132.7*		
	(-1.04)	(4.85)	(26.5)										
11.	-0.42	0.01*		0.91*		0.283	588.6*	2985	16.35*	12.4*		12.41*	
	(-0.07)	(4.04)		(33.9)									
12.	5.79	0.01*			0.72*	0.225	11.7*	2985	20.7*	23.6*			123.7*
	(0.92)	(4.85)			(28.9)								
							APL						
13.	-128.57	0.00				-0.000	0.28	1015	0.28				
	(-6.02)	(0.53)											
14.	-119	-0.00	0.95*			0.137	81.5*	1015	0.19	0.46	0.35		
	(-6.01)	(-0.43)	(12.8)										
15.	-36.97	0.00		0.71*		0.184	115*	1015	0.52	39.88*		20.24*	
	(-1.83)	(0.72)		(15.2)									
16.	-85.6	0.00			1.01*	0.175	108*	1015	0.07	0.77			0.653
	(-4.34)	(0.27)			(14.7)								

Table 5.2 **Regression Results—Jharkhand (Ordinary Least Square Without Log) Dependent Variable = ΔC**

	Constant	ΔY	ΔVC	ΔBC	ΔEC	R^2	F*	No of Obs.	F* ΔY=0	F* ΔVC=1 or ΔBC =1 or ΔEC =1	F* ΔY=0, ΔVC =1	F* ΔY=0, ΔBC =1	F* ΔY=0, ΔEC =1
							Aggregate						
1.	-19.77	0.02*				0.002	9.95*	5000	9.95*				
	(2.82)	(3.15)											
2.	-4.46	0.01*	0.75*			0.140	408.5*	5000	9.32*	86.48*	47.56*		
	(-0.68)	(3.05)	(28.4)										
3.	-2.56	0.02*		0.84*		0.272	936.4*	5000	13.2*	71.03*		42.08*	
	(-0.43)	(3.63)		(43.1)									
4.	-4.23	0.01**			0.76*	0.164	485.7*	5000	5.96**	92.6*			48.51*
	(-0.65)	(2.44)			(31.0)								
							AAY						
5.	27.01	0.01				0.000	1.31	1000	1.31				
	(-1.87)	(1.14)											
6.	-14.83	0.01	0.60*			0.102	57.9*	1000	0.34	52.51*	26.27*		
	(-1.08)	(0.58)	(10.7)										
7.	-9.30	0.00		0.66*		0.140	82.5	1000	0.10	44.61*		22.32*	
	(-0.69)	(0.32)		(12.8)									
8.	-14.02	0.00			0.51*	0.093	51.95*	1000	0.15	91.08*			45.61*
	(-1.00)	(0.39)			(10.1)								
							BPL						
9.	-16.38	0.033*				0.009	28.45*	3205	28.45*				
	(-2.20)	(5.33)											
10.	-1.68	0.31*	0.69*			0.165	316.4*	3205	29.44*	118.6*	73.11*		
	(-0.24)	(5.43)	(24.5)										
11.	-0.79	0.02*		0.89*		0.252	541.9*	3205	15.32*	14.72*		14.06*	
	(-0.12)	(3.91)		(32.4)									
12.	-4.19	0.028*			0.73*	0.182	354.3*	3205	25.02*	89.5*			55.89*
	(-0.62)	(5.00)			(25.9)								
							APL						
13.	-22.5	-0.01				-0.001	0.27	795	0.27				
	(-0.85)	(-0.52)											
14.	-3.59	-0.00	1.15*			0.153	72.6*	795	0.07	2.44	1.27		
	(-0.15)	(-0.27)	(12.0)										
15.	-2.42	0.014		0.84*		0.365	228.8*	795	1.72	15.44*		9.13*	
	(-0.11)	(1.31)		(21.4)									
16.	7.96	-0.01			1.05*	0.202	100.9*	795	0.40	0.48			0.44
	(0.33)	(-0.63)			(14.2)								

Table 5.3 Regression Results—Kerala (Ordinary Least Square Without Log) Dependent Variable = ΔC

	Constant	ΔY	ΔVC	ΔBC	ΔEC	R^2	F*	No of Obs.	F* ΔY=0	F* ΔVC=1 or ΔBC =1 or ΔEC =1	F* ΔY=0, ΔVC =1	F* ΔY=0, ΔBC =1	F* ΔY=0, ΔEC =1
							Aggregate						
1.	-50.12	0.02*				0.012	63.84	5000	63.84				
	(-5.98)	(7.99)											
2.	-53.94	0.02*	0.80*			0.1141	322.9*	5000	72.31*	34.32*	53.46*		
	(-6.8)	(8.5)	(23.9)										
3.	-11.02	0.02*		0.74*		0.167	503.2*	5000	92.8*	112*		105.6*	
	(-1.41)	(9.63)		(30.5)									
4.	-9.96	0.02*			0.76*	0.159	407.5*	5000	86.29*	81.56*			85.26*
	(-1.27)	(9.29)			(29.4)								
							AAY						
5.	-48.4	0.02*				0.006	7.08*	1005	7.08				
	(-2.84)	(2.66)											
6.	-52.14	0.01*	0.88*			0.150	89.6*	1005	7.84*	3.47***	5.63*		
	(-3.3)	(2.8)	(13.1)										
7.	-9.04	0.02*		0.77*		0.241	162.0*	1005	20.8*	27.5*		26.4*	
	(-0.60)	(4.56)		(17.7)									
8.	-8.41	0.02*			0.80*	0.171	102.4*	1005	10.1*	12.1*			11.3*
	(-0.53)	(3.17)			(14.0)								
							BPL						
9.	-38.7	0.01*				0.004	13.4*	3005	13.42*				
	(-3.89)	(3.66)											
10.	-42.2	0.02*	0.77*			0.116	197*	3005	20.6*	33.6*	28.01*		
	(-4.5)	(4.54)	(19.5)										
11.	-3.61	0.02*		0.88*		0.197	368.9*	3005	35.36*	13.86*		26.3*	
	(-0.4)	(5.95)		(26.8)									
12.	1.44	0.02*			0.79*	0.179	327.3*	3005	28.3*	46.93*			39.4*
	(0.16)	(5.32)			(25.3)								
							APL						
13.	-86.3	0.03*				0.030	32.04*	990	32.04*				
	(-3.6)	(5.66)											
14.	-91.4	0.03*	0.82*			0.094	52.3*	990	30.3*	3.20***	16.4*		
	(-3.94)	(5.5)	(8.4)										
15.	-38.6	0.03*		0.51*		0.100	55.6*	990	30.85*	68.5*		48.12*	
	(-1.63)	(5.6)		(8.8)									
16.	-46.1	0.03*			0.68*	0.121	68.4*	990	34.2*	22.2*			27.5*
	(-2.02)	(5.8)			(9.9)								

Table 5.4 Regression Results—Madhya Pradesh (Ordinary Least Square Without Log) Dependent Variable = ΔC

	Constant	ΔY	ΔVC	ΔBC	ΔEC	R^2	F*	No of Obs.	F* ΔY=0	F* ΔVC=1 or ΔBC =1 or ΔEC =1	F* ΔY=0, ΔVC =1	F* ΔY=0, ΔBC =1	F* ΔY=0, ΔEC =1
							Aggregate						
1.	47.6	0.05*				0.003	15.13*	5000	15.13*				
	(1.31)	(3.89)											
2.	26.4	0.05*	0.49*			0.015	39.5*	5000	13.6*	67.2*	39.6*		
	(0.73)	(3.68)	(8.00)										
3.	36.5	0.05*)		0.22*		0.001	24.3*	5000	13.25*	402.3*		204.9*	
	(1.00)	(3.64		(5.77)									
4.	35.6	0.05*			0.24*	0.001	22.8*	5000	13.9*	308.4*			159.5*
	(0.97)	(3.73)			(5.5)								
							AAY						
5.	61.1	0.01				-0.001	0.10	975	0.10				
	(2.36)	(0.31)											
6.	46.7	-0.01	0.35*			0.065	35.1	975	0.18	246.5*	1249*		
	(1.86)	(-0.43)	(8.4)										
7.	48.2	0.01		0.21*		0.001	3.86**	975	0.06	106.8*		53.4*	
	(1.84)	(0.24)		(2.76)									
8.	54.7	0.004			0.11*	0.010	5.78*	975	0.02	809.15*			405.4*
	(2.09)	(0.15)			(3.38)								
							BPL						
9.	52.9	0.01				-0.000	0.35	3055	0.35				
	(1.49)	(0.59)											
10.	29.7	0.004	0.55*			0.025	41.6*	3055	0.07	54.6*	27.3*		
	(0.85)	(0.27)	(9.1)										
11.	19.8	0.01		0.62*		0.042	67.2	3055	0.20	49.0*		24.6*	
	(0.57)	(0.45)		(11.6)									
12.	37.7	0.01			0.30*	0.018	28.1*	3055	0.14	295.3*			147.7*
	(1.06)	(0.37)			(7.5)								
							APL						
13.	20.8	0.07**				0.001	6.32**	970	6.32**				
	(0.14)	(2.51)											
14.	-2.28	0.07**	0.49**			0.008	5.10*	970	6.19**	4.08**	5.06*		
	(-0.02)	(2.49)	(1.97)										
15.	19.3	0.07**		0.05		0.004	3.35**	970	6.11**	126.3*		64.7*	
	(0.13)	(2.47)		(0.62)									
16.	13.3	0.07**			0.15	0.005	3.37**	970	6.06**	19.09*			12.3*
	(0.09)	(2.46)			(0.77)								

Table 5.5 Regression Results—Maharashtra (Ordinary Least Square Without Log) Dependent Variable = ΔC

	Constant	ΔY	ΔVC	ΔBC	ΔEC	R^2	F*	No of Obs.	F* ΔY=0	F* ΔVC=1 or ΔBC =1 or ΔEC =1	F* ΔY=0, ΔVC =1	F* ΔY=0, ΔBC =1	F* ΔY=0, ΔEC =1
							Aggregate						
1.	25.19	0.03*				0.015	76.9*	5000	76.9*				
	(3.3)	(8.7)											
2.	4.06	0.02*	0.83*			0.136	393.8*	5000	64.05*	31.3*	45.5*		
	(0.57)	(8.0)	(26.5)										
3.	5.41	0.02*		0.78*		0.215	686.8*	5000	51.3*	106.2*		73.7*	
	(0.79)	(7.2)		(35.7)									
4.	11.2	0.03*			0.55*	0.097	266.9*	5000	84.7*	288.6*			180.6*
	(1.52)	(9.2)			(20.8)								
							AAY						
5.	19.8	0.06*				0.030	30.9*	965	30.9*				
	(1.71)	(5.56)											
6.	1.96	0.05*	0.68*			0.205	124.9*	965	23.9*	46.1*	32.5*		
	(0.19)	(4.9)	(14.6)										
7.	3.53	0.04*		0.79*		0.326	234.3*	965	20.9*	29.1*		22.7*	
	(0.36)	(4.57)		(20.6)									
8.	13.37	0.06*			0.22*	0.076	39.8*	965	25.8	600.8*			304.2*
	(1.19)	(5.08)			(6.8)								
							BPL						
9.	28.56	0.02*				0.008	26.3*	3020	26.3*				
	(3.67)	(5.13)											
10.	13.02	0.02*	0.61*			0.116	198.9*	3020	24.24*	150.2*	85.7*		
	(1.76)	(4.92)	(19.2)										
11.	5.37	0.02*		0.81*		0.134	234.3*	3020	17.1*	25.5*		20.1*	
	(0.73)	(4.14)		(20.9)									
12.	16.2	0.02*			0.50*	0.095	158.6*	3020	22.9*	289.4*			154.6
	(2.16)	(4.79)			(17.1)								
							APL						
13.	19.9	0.03*				0.019	20.1*	1015	20.1*				
	(0.73)	(4.48)											
14.	-21.8	0.02*	1.65*			0.193	122.1*	1015	12.6*	34.1*	25.5*		
	(-0.88)	(3.55)	(14.8)										
15.	4.5	0.02*		0.76*		0.255	174.4*	1015	13.9*	31.7*		21.3*	
	(0.19)	(3.72)		(17.9)									
16.	-7.9	0.03*			1.28*	0.166	100.6*	1015	23.3*	8.36*			16.8*
	(-0.31)	(4.82)			(12.9)								

Table 5.6 Regression Results—Uttarakhand (Ordinary Least Square Without Log) Dependent Variable = ΔC

	Constant	ΔY	ΔVC	ΔBC	ΔEC	R^2	F*	No of Obs.	F* ΔY=0	F* ΔVC=1 or ΔBC =1 or ΔEC =1	F* ΔY=0, ΔVC =1	F* ΔY=0, ΔBC =1	F* ΔY=0, ΔEC =1
Aggregate													
1.	-34.6	0.01*				0.001	37.1*	5000	37.1*				
	(-4.4)	(6.09)											
2.	-23.3	0.01*	0.65*			0.127	363.2*	5000	26.4*	192.6*	106.1*		
	(-3.15)	(5.14)	(26.2)										
3.	-9.91	0.01*		0.72*		0.166	499.2*	5000	29.3*	134.5*		79.5*	
	(-1.37)	(5.41)		(30.9)									
4.	-10.1	0.01*			0.72	0.134	381.1*	5000	25.2*	109.6*			65*
	(-1.4)	(5.02)											
AAY													
5.	-29.4	0.06*				0.043	47.5*	1025	47.5*				
	(-2.30)	(6.9)											
6.	-20.8	0.05*	0.46*			0.153	93.6	1025	37.2*	179.1*	100.8*		
	(-1.7)	(6.1)	(11.6)										
7.	-12.0	0.04*		0.62*		0.159	98.4*	1025	28.3*	53.5*		35.5*	
	(-0.99)	(5.32)		(11.9)									
8.	-5.77	0.05*			0.63*	0.203	129.4*	1025	27.3*	73.1*			45.04*
	(-0.48)	(5.23)			(14.4)								
BPL													
9.	-27.6	0.01*				0.007	20.6*	2960	20.6*				
	(-3.4)	(4.54)											
10.	-17.0	0.01	*0.62*			0.170	304.3*	2960	12.4*	226.1*	116.5*		
	(-2.27)	(3.53)	(24.2)										
11.	-3.43	0.004*		0.88*		0.224	427.1*	2960	10.13*	16.2*		12.4*	
	(-0.47)	(3.18)		(28.8)									
12.	-5.4	0.01*			0.73*	0.192	349.1*	2960	13.0*	94.9*			52.2*
	(-0.73)	(3.61)			(25.9)								
APL													
13.	-64.6	0.02*				0.008	8.87*	1015	8.87*				
	(-2.34)	(2.98)											
14.	-48.5	0.02*	0.95*			0.108	62.1*	1015	8.44*	0.35	4.36**		
	(-1.9)	(2.91)	(10.7)										
15.	-26.8	0.02*		0.64*		0.137	81.1*	1015	10.9*	46.3*		28.8*	
	(-1.03)	(3.31)		(12.3)									
16.	-32.5	0.02*			0.76*	0.075	41.0*	1015	7.54*	7.1*			7.2*
	(-1.21)	(2.75)			(8.5)								

Table 5.7 Regression Results—Delhi (Ordinary Least Square With Log) Dependent Variable = ΔLC

	Constant	ΔLY	ΔLVC	ΔLBC	ΔLEC	R^2	F*	No of Obs.	F* ΔLY=0	F* ΔLVC=1 or ΔLBC =1 or ΔLEC =1	F* ΔLY=0, ΔLVC =1	F* ΔLY=0, ΔLBC =1	F* ΔLY=0, ΔLEC =1
							Aggregate						
1.	-0.01	0.01**				0.000	4.2**	4254	4.2**				
	(-2.8)	(2.1)											
2.	0.00	0.002	0.82*			0.188	494*	4254	0.50	49.4*	24.8*		
	(1.3)	(0.7)	(31.4)										
3.	-0.00	0.001		0.78*		0.224	616*	4254	0.47	101.4*		50.7*	
	(-0.4)	(0.7)		(35.0)									
4.	0.00	0.002			0.71*	0.175	450*	4234	1.10	146*			73.1*
	(0.4)	(1.0)			(29.9)								
							AAY						
5.	0.02	-0.00				-0.001	0.21	839	0.21				
	(2.67)	(-0.46)											
6.	0.03	-0.00	0.58*			0.096	45.53*	839	0.23	47.34*	23.78*		
	(4.28)	(-0.48)	(9.58)										
7.	0.01	-0.01		0.66*		0.180	92.8*	839	1.77	48.33*		25.71*	
	(1.32)	(-1.33)		(13.6)									
8.	0.03*	-0.00			0.56*	0.100	47.7*	839	0.08	59.25*			29.6*
	(4.04)	(-0.28)			(9.8)								
							BPL						
9.	-0.01	0.01*				0.005	13.03*	2559	13.03*				
	(-1.56)	(3.61)											
10.	0.01	0.01	0.87*			0.224	370*	2559	3.95**	16.38*	9.60*		
	(2.10)	(1.99)	(26.9)										
11.	0.00	0.01**		0.85*		0.242	409.3*	2559	4.62**	24.17*		13.72*	
	(0.16)	(2.15)		(28.3)									
12.	0.00	0.01**			0.72*	0.195	309*	2559	5.30**	83.37*			42.9*
	(0.91)	(2.30)			(24.5)								
							APL						
13.	-0.05	-0.00				-0.000	0.66	856	0.66				
	(-5.95)	(-0.82)											
14.	-0.03	-0.01	0.91*			0.215	118.5*	856	1.65	2.05	1.90		
	(-4.97)	(-1.29)	(15.4)										
15.	-0.02	-0.00		0.70*		0.205	111.6*	856	0.48	41.43		20.9*	
	(-2.27)	(-0.69)		(14.9)									
16.	-0.03	-0.01			0.79*	0.209	113.3*	856	1.40	15.38*			8.47*
	(-4.83)	(-1.18)			(15.0)								

Table 5.8 Regression Results—Jharkhand (Ordinary Least Square With Log) Dependent Variable = ΔLC

	Constant	ΔLY	ΔLVC	ΔLBC	ΔLEC	R^2	F*	No of Obs.	F* ΔLY=0	F* ΔLVC=1 or ΔLBC=1 or ΔLEC=1	F* ΔLY=0, ΔLVC=1	F* ΔLY=0, ΔLBC=1	F* ΔLY=0, ΔLEC=1
						Aggregate							
1.	-0.01	-0.00				-0.000	0.02	4942	0.02				
	(-3.15)	(-0.13)											
2.	-0.01	-0.00	0.50*			0.088	239.4*	4942	0.00	457.9*	229*		
	(-1.51)	(-0.02)	(21.9)										
3.	-0.01	-0.00		0.52*		0.127	360.2*	4942	0.05	608.45*		30426*	
	(-1.48)	(-0.21)		(26.8)									
4.	-0.01	-0.00			0.45*	0.084	224.9*	4942	0.03	651.9*			325.9*
	(-1.73)	(-0.17)			(21.2)								
						AAY							
5.	-0.02	-0.01				-0.001	0.48	994	0.48				
	(-1.72)	(-0.69)											
6.	-0.01	-0.01	0.41*			0.044	23.66*	994	0.47	95.38*	47.90*		
	(-1.2)	(-0.68)	(6.84)										
7.	-0.01	-0.01		0.37*		0.055	29.86*	994	0.77	177.34*		89.35*	
	(-1.04)	(-0.88)		(7.70)									
8.	-0.01	-0.01			0.33*	0.037	19.55*	994	0.44	165.3*			82.84*
	(-1.34)	(-0.66)			(6.22)								
						BPL							
9.	-0.01	0.01				0.001	2.61	3171	2.61				
	(-1.97)	(1.62)											
10.	-0.00	0.01	0.52*			0.106	189.7*	3171	2.00	310.3*	155.8*		
	(-0.66)	(1.41)	(19.4)										
11.	-0.00	0.00		0.56*		0.137	252.8*	3171	1.38	312.7*		156.6*	
	(-0.63)	(1.17)		(22.4)									
12.	-0.00	0.01			0.47*	0.096	168.3*	3171	2.05	428.8*			215.2*
	(0.40)	(1.43)			(18.3)								
						APL							
13.	-0.02	-0.01				0.003	3.41***	777	3.41***				
	(-1.88)	(-1.85)											
14.	-0.01	-0.01	0.54*			0.099	43.39*	777	1.73	59.69*	30.16*		
	(-0.94)	(-1.32)	(9.11)										
15.	-0.01	-0.01		0.59*		0.229	116.23*	777	1.30	112.16*		56.19*	
	(-1.31)	(-1.14)		(15.1)									
16.	-0.01	-0.01			0.58*	0.131	59.28*	777	2.52	62.42*			32.06*
	(-0.98)	(-1.59)			(10.7)								

Table 5.9 Regression Results—Kerala (Ordinary Least Square With Log) Dependent Variable = ΔLC

	Constant	ΔLY	ΔLVC	ΔLBC	ΔLEC	R^2	F*	No of Obs.	F* ΔLY=0	F* ΔLVC=1 or ΔLBC =1 or ΔLEC =1	F* ΔLY=0, ΔLVC =1	F* ΔLY=0, ΔLBC =1	F* ΔLY=0, ΔLEC =1
							Aggregate						
1.	-0.05	0.01*				0.002	8.86*	4668	8.86*				
	(-9.70)	(2.98)											
2.	-0.02	0.02*	0.81*			0.161	447.7*	4668	27.14*	50.48*	41.44*		
	(-4.47)	(5.21)	(29.8)										
3.	-0.02	0.02*		0.69*		0.164	457.9*	4668	23.33*	179.28*		105.0*	
	(-5.63)	(4.83)		(30.1)									
4.	-0.02	0.02*			0.67*	0.137	366.1*	4668	21.83*	177.5*			103*
	(-5.52)	(4.67)			(26.9)								
							AAY						
5.	-0.04	0.03**				0.003	4.22**	942	4.22**				
	(-3.64)	(2.1)											
6.	-0.01	0.01**	1.08*			0.229	140.9*	942	5.41**	1.67	3.54**		
	(-0.70)	(2.3)	(16.6)										
7.	-0.02	0.03*		0.75*		0.252	159.3*	942	7.88*	34.5*		21.5*	
	(-1.69)	(2.8)		(17.7)									
8.	-0.02	0.02***			0.83*	0.159	88.46*	942	2.78***	7.05*			4.72*
	(-1.64)	(1.67)			(13.1)								
							BPL						
9.	-0.04	0.01***				0.001	2.73***	2826	2.73***				
	(-6.94)	(1.65)											
10.	-0.01	0.02*	0.82*			0.171	292.2*	2826	14.2*	27.3*	22.5*		
	(-2.66)	(3.77)	(24.1)										
11.	-0.02	0.02*		0.77*		0.172	293.3*	2826	14.34*	53.7*		36.5*	
	(-4.02)	(3.79)		(24.2)									
12.	-0.02	0.02*			0.72*	0.158	263.6*	2826	14.1*	75.3*			47.6*
	(-3.37)	(3.75)			(22.9)								
							APL						
13.	-0.01	0.01***				0.002	2.92***	900	2.92***				
	(-6.32)	(1.71)											
14.	-0.05	0.02**	0.49*			0.070	35.04*	900	5.8**	74.4*	42.01*		
	(-4.9)	(2.41)	(8.2)										
15.	-0.05	0.01***		0.36*		0.046	22.8*	900	3.58***	136.6*		70.6*	
	(-4.71)	(1.89)		(6.5)									
16.	-0.05	0.02**			0.39*	0.066	32.2*	900	4.7**	149.2*			78.5*
	(-5.02)	(2.18)			(7.8)								

Table 5.10 Regression Results—Madhya Pradesh (Ordinary Least Square With Log) Dependent Variable = ΔLC

	Constant	ΔLY	ΔLVC	ΔLBC	ΔLEC	R^2	F*	No of Obs.	F* ΔLY=0	F* ΔLVC=1 or ΔLBC =1 or ΔLEC =1	F* ΔLY=0, ΔLVC =1	F* ΔLY=0, ΔLBC =1	F* ΔLY=0, ΔLEC =1
							Aggregate						
1.	0.08	0.01***				0.000	2.74***	4675	2.74***				
	(12.7)	(1.65)											
2.	0.01	0.00	0.24*			0.026	63.5*	4675	0.23	1312.8*	662.2*		
	(11.3)	(0.48)	(11.1)										
3.	0.07	0.00		0.25*		0.030	75.1*	4675	0.39	1384.9*		695.8*	
	(11.04)	(0.63)		(12.1)									
4.	0.07	0.00			0.23*	0.027	65.5*	4675	0.37	1465.3*			7375*
	(11.04)	(0.60)			(11.3)								
							AAY						
5.	0.11	-0.03**				0.004	4.7**	911	4.7**				
	(7.52)	(-2.17)											
6.	0.10	-0.04*	0.21*			0.025	12.5*	911	7.4*	288.1*	155.5*		
	(7.04)	(-2.71)	(4.5)										
7.	0.09	-0.04**		0.34*		0.051	25.4*	911	6.28*	1708*		90.1*	
	(5.86)	(-2.51)		(6.7)									
8.	0.10	-0.04**			0.19*	0.021	10.6*	911	6.39*	314.2*			165*
	(6.8)	(-2.53)			(4.0)								
							BPL						
9.	0.08	0.01				-0.000	0.66	2890	0.66				
	(9.7)	(0.81)											
10.	0.07	-0.002	0.26*			0.032	48.8*	2890	0.07	749.5*	380.3*		
	(8.62)	(-0.27)	(9.9)										
11.	0.01	0.001		0.26*		0.035	52.4*	2890	0.01	845.9*		424.9*	
	(8.40)	(0.10)		(10.2)									
12.	0.07	-0.002			0.26*	0.036	55.2*	2890	0.05	858.0*			434*
	(8.33)	(-0.023)			(10.4)								
							APL						
13.	0.06	0.03*				0.009	8.55*	874	8.55*				
	(4.02)	(2.92)											
14.	0.06	0.03**	0.19*			0.023	11.3*	874	6.58*	268.9*	134.9*		
	(3.49)	(2.56)	(3.74)										
15.	0.06	0.03**		0.13*		0.017	8.61*	874	6.21*	371.6*		185.8*	
	(3.89)	(2.49)		(2.93)									
16.	0.06	0.03*			0.16*	0.019	9.71*	874	6.92*	296.4*			148*
	(3.57)	(2.63)			(3.26)								

Table 5.11 Regression Results—Maharahstra (Ordinary Least Square With Log) Dependent Variable = ΔLC

	Constant	ΔLY	ΔLVC	ΔLBC	ΔLEC	R^2	F*	No of Obs.	F* ΔLY=0	F* ΔLVC=1 or ΔLBC =1 or ΔLEC =1	F* ΔLY=0, ΔLVC =1	F* ΔLY=0, ΔLBC =1	F* ΔLY=0, ΔLEC =1
							Aggregate						
1.	0.02	0.02*				0.006	30.1*	4640	30.1*				
	(5.2)	(5.5)											
2.	0.01	0.01*	0.85*			0.208	609.7*	4640	21.2*	35.1*	26.9*		
	(2.69)	(4.6)	(34.4)										
3.	0.01	0.01*		0.82*		0.257	801.1*	4640	13.7*	73.3*		41.6*	
	(2.7)	(3.7)		(39.5)									
4.	0.01	0.02*			0.66*	0.156	425.2*	4640	23.1*	210.4*			113.8*
	(3.20)	(4.8)			(28.5)								
							AAY						
5.	0.02	0.03*				0.011	10.8*	888	10.8*				
	(1.95)	(3.29)											
6.	0.01	0.02**	0.98*			0.245	144.5*	888	4.68**	0.12	2.4***		
	(0.63)	(2.16)	(16.6)										
7.	0.00	0.02**		0.81*		0.288	180.5*	888	5.84*	18.4*		11.4*	
	(0.50)	(2.42)		(18.6)									
8.	0.01	0.02**			0.61*	0.142	73.4*	888	4.17*	54.7*			28.1*
	(0.87)	(2.04)			(11.6)								
							BPL						
9.	0.03	0.03*				0.008	25.2*	2846	25.2*				
	(4.80)	(5.02)											
10.	0.01	0.02*	0.70*			0.166	284.5*	2846	19.3*	96.2*	55.9*		
	(3.07)	(4.39)	(23.2)										
11.	0.01	0.02*		0.84*		0.197	348.9*	2846	14.6*	24.3*		18.3*	
	(2.33)	(3.82)		(25.8)									
12.	0.02	0.02*			0.58*	0.137	223.7*	2846	21.3*	215.8*			116.5*
	(3.36)	(4.61)			(20.5)								
							APL						
13.	-0.02	0.01				0.002	2.40	906	2.40				
	(1.57)	(1.55)											
14.	0.00	0.01	1.19*			0.307	201.7*	906	2.14	10.48*	6.41*		
	(0.24)	(1.46)	(20.0)										
15.	0.01	0.00		0.81*		0.357	252.4*	906	0.29	27.9*		13.9*	
	(1.37)	(0.54)		(22.4)									
16.	0.01	0.01			0.97*	0.236	139.2*	906	2.37	0.19			1.26
	(0.72)	(1.5)			(16.5)								

Table 5.12 Regression Results—Uttarakhand (Ordinary Least Square With Log) Dependent Variable = ΔLC

	Constant	ΔLY	ΔLVC	ΔLBC	ΔLEC	R^2	F*	No of Obs.	F* ΔLY=0	F* ΔLVC=1 or ΔLBC =1 or ΔLEC =1	F* ΔLY=0, ΔLVC =1	F* ΔLY=0, ΔLBC =1	F* ΔLY=0, ΔLEC =1
							Aggregate						
1.	-0.02	0.02*				0.011	51.5*	4737	51.5*				
	(-4.9)	(7.17)											
2.	-0.01	0.02*	0.78*			0.140	386.9*	4737	29.5*	56.3*	39.8*		
	(-1.8)	(5.4)	(26.7)										
3.	-0.01	0.015*		0.69*		0.142	391.7*	4737	25.5*	151.4*		83.2*	
	(-2.56)	(5.05)		(26.9)									
4.	-0.01	0.02*			0.67*	0.133	358.5*	4737	30.9*	153.7*			87.3*
	(-2.44)	(5.56)			(25.7)								
							AAY						
5.	-0.01	0.02*				0.006	7.01*	954	7.01*				
	(-1.20)	(2.65)											
6.	0.002	0.01***	0.81*			0.119	65.2*	954	3.72***	6.59*	4.8*		
	(0.28)	(1.93)	(11.1)										
7.	-0.004	0.01		0.61*		0.107	58.3*	954	2.61	44.1*		22.4*	
	(-0.42)	(1.62)		(10.4)									
8.	0.001	0.02**			0.72*	0.121	65.4*	954	4.14**	18.6*			10.8*
	(0.12)	(2.03)			(11.1)								
							BPL						
9.	-0.02	0.02*				0.014	40.7*	2831	40.7*				
	(-3.5)	(6.38)											
10.	-0.01	0.01*	0.74*			0.149	248.2*	2831	16.9*	53.9*	32.1*		
	(-1.09)	(4.11)	(21.2)										
11.	-0.01	0.01*		0.74*		0.156	261.9*	2831	16.5*	60.1*		34.8*	
	(-1.80)	(4.06)		(21.8)									
12.	-0.01	0.02*			0.66*	0.144	236.4*	2831	18.1*	112.6*			60.7*
	(-1.83)	(4.25)			(20.6)								
							APL						
13.	-0.04	0.02*				0.007	7.40*	952	7.40*				
	(-3.79)	(2.72)											
14.	-0.02	0.02*	0.86*			0.145	81.5*	952	10.3*	3.8***	7.22*		
	(-2.35)	(3.21)	(12.4)										
15.	-0.02	0.02*		0.66*		0.147	82.9*	952	6.76*	40.5*		23.2*	
	(-2.16)	(2.6)		(12.5)									
16.	-0.02	0.02*			0.66*	0.118	63.1*	952	9.01*	30.0*			19.7*
	(-2.5)	(3.00)			(10.9)								

Note: * significant at 1%, ** significant at 5%, significant at 10%.

The results of the regressions were mixed for different states and categories. The value of income coefficient was near to zero and value of the village/ethnic/beneficiary consumption near to unity in most of the cases. These results are consistent with the implications of risk sharing. In explaining the change in household consumption, the change in aggregate consumption entered with a coefficient one while change in household income had a zero coefficient. However, the value of 't' test presented in the parenthesis pointed out that the household income was significant in most of the states and categories. The coefficient of household income was insignificant for the APL category in Delhi and Jharkhand (without log). In addition to these two states, coefficient was not significant in the case of log equations in Maharashtra among APL and Madhya Pradesh among BPL households. Significant value of household income in all other cases indicates that the changes in household consumption were idiosyncratic. The coefficients of village/ethnic/beneficiary consumption, however, were highly significant in all the states and all categories without any exception both without and with log supporting the hypothesis of risk sharing. On the basis of the F-test, the full risk sharing implications could not be accepted for any of the state or any category of households. The hypothesis was rejected mostly at one per cent significance level. Thus, on the one hand, individual consumption was found co-moving along with the aggregate village consumption supporting the hypothesis of risk sharing. On the other hand, coefficient of individual income was found highly significant indicating individual consumption was a function of individual income, thereby leaving the households vulnerable in the face of fluctuating income due to natural calamities and other idiosyncratic factors.

Comparing among different categories, the value of coefficient of individual income was generally same across different categories. However, value of group consumption across village or beneficiary or ethnicity varied across different household categories. The value of the coefficient was higher for APL households compared to BPL/AAY households for both without and with log in all the states except Kerala. The higher values of combined consumption for APL households indicate that economically better-off household were better insured compared to lower income strata households belonging to BPL and AAY categories. Our results also enable us to find out the *modus operandi* of informal group insurance at village or sub-village categories. It is seen from the results that the coefficient of group consumption for village, beneficiary and ethnic groups was significant in all the states and in both the cases of with and without log. However, the value of R^2 was highest in the case of economic grouping or beneficiary consumption (DBC) followed by ethnic grouping (DEC) and village grouping (DVC). These results support the earlier literature by Morduch (1991) who found that food consumption appeared to be well insured for some castes, suggesting that the right model may be the one where neighbours insure each other against dire events but are left to cope individually in the face of minor shocks. Our results suggest that rather than insurance being at the village level, it was more convincing among the sub-groups, either based on economic stratification or based on ethnic or caste grounds. We also estimated a model grouping consumption across various ethnic and economic groups at the broader state level rather than within a village under these sub-categories. The results were not significant as R^2 was significantly small compared to the results presented above. Therefore, these results are not reported here. Finally we have estimated our equations only for food instead of taking total expenditure (food + non-food). The results are presented in the Annexure Tables A-5.1 to A-5.6 (without log) and A-5.7 to A-5.12 (with log). It is seen from the tables that results of food were not significantly different from that of total expenditure presented above.

It was mentioned in our econometric model that the disturbance term includes both preference shocks and measurement errors from the data. Unbiased estimation of the coefficients requires a zero correlation between the disturbance term and the right hand side variables of aggregate consumption and household income. However, our results do not correct for possible correlation between household income and the disturbance. Nonetheless, a bias of the coefficient on aggregate consumption can be avoided by testing a modified version of the first differenced specification:

$$\Delta c^j_t - \Delta C^a_t = \beta_0 + \beta_1 \Delta Y^j_t + u^j_t \qquad \text{(v)}$$

The change in aggregate (village) consumption is simply subtracted from the change in household consumption so that a unit coefficient on aggregate (village) consumption is imposed. The right hand side now has individual income and any other variable like household size, etc. The risk sharing model in this format predicts zero coefficients for the individual income. In addition, we can add changes in aggregate (village) income among the explanatory variables to find out, along with risk sharing in consumption if some income transfer is taking place from the aggregate (village) sources towards individual households. The results for this exercise are presented in Table 5.13.[6] The table displays the values of the coefficients and

6. Households' size and number of earning members are taken as additional determinants. However, the values are not reported in the table.

their 't' values. F-ratios testing whether the coefficients of household income and aggregate income are significantly different from zero or not are also presented (separately) in the table.

The results further verify our earlier assertion that the risk sharing within the periphery of village was not taking place as coefficient of individual income was in most of the cases significantly different from zero. It is seen from the F-ratio of individual income that the hypothesis was rejected for all the category of households in Delhi, Kerala, Maharashtra and Uttarakhand, without any exception. The hypothesis, however, could not be rejected in the case of all categories in Jharkhand and among AAY and BPL in Madhya Pradesh. The F-ratio for aggregate (village) income tests slow whether income transfer was happening among household within the periphery of village. The test was not rejected in most of the cases indicating absence of income transfer, which further verifies the hypothesis of idiosyncratic shocks for most of our selected households. The coefficient of aggregate income was found positive only in the case of BPL households in Jharkhand and Uttarakhand and APL households in Kerala. However, even in these cases value of the coefficient was insignificant.

Table 5.13: The Incidence of Idiosyncrasy and Net Direct of Transfer of Sources (Dependent Variable = $\Delta C - \Delta VC$)

	Δ Individual Income	't' Value	Δ Village Income	't' Value	F-Ratio Individual Income	F-Ratio Village Income	R^{-2}	F
				Delhi				
State	0.01	(4.6)	-0.01	-(1.7)	21.06*	3.02***	0.01	15.74
AAY	0.01	(2.3)	-0.01	-(0.9)	5.17*	0.87	0.01	3.01
BPL	0.01	(4.0)	0.00	-(0.9)	15.81*	0.84	0.01	7.54
APL	0.01	(1.7)	-0.02	-(1.3)	2.96***	1.70	0.01	2.62
				Jharkhand				
State	0.02	(4.6)	-0.02	-(1.6)	20.74*	2.57	0.004	5.54
AAY	0.02	(1.4)	-0.05	-(1.9)	2.10	3.48**	0.004	1.97
BPL	0.03	(5.5)	0.00	(0.0)	30.73	0.00	0.01	8.84
APL	0.01	(0.8)	-0.08	-(1.7)	0.63	2.94***	0.004	0.86
				Kerala				
State	0.02	(10.6)	-0.02	-(3.6)	112.15*	13.09*	0.02	29.45
AAY	0.02	(3.6)	-0.03	-(2.0)	13.18*	4.03**	0.01	3.76
BPL	0.02	(6.5)	-0.03	-(4.0)	42.77*	16.17*	0.02	12.91
APL	0.03	(5.7)	0.01	(0.4)	32.41*	0.15	0.04	10.70
				Madhya Pradesh				
State	0.05	(4.3)	-0.06	-(1.2)	18.30*	1.40	0.003	4.63
AAY	-0.03	-(1.1)	-0.04	-(1.0)	1.22	1.03	0.000	0.95
BPL	0.00	(0.3)	-0.10	-(2.1)	0.08	4.37**	0.000	1.13
APL	0.08	(2.8)	0.15	(0.8)	7.68*	0.59	0.01	2.37
				Maharashtra				
State	0.02	(7.9)	-0.02	-(2.6)	62.74*	6.86*	0.01	15.82
AAY	0.02	(2.3)	-0.01	-(0.5)	5.16**	0.28	0.002	1.53
BPL	0.02	(4.5)	-0.02	-(2.5)	20.70*	6.20*	0.01	5.82
APL	0.03	(4.4)	-0.04	-(1.1)	18.95*	1.30	0.02	4.90
				Uttarakhand				
State	0.01	(5.2)	-0.01	-(1.2)	26.92*	1.51	0.005	7.08
AAY	0.04	(4.7)	-0.01	-(0.7)	22.42*	0.50	0.02	5.75
BPL	0.01	(3.3)	0.00	(0.1)	10.79*	0.01	0.003	3.47
APL	0.02	(3.2)	-0.05	-(1.8)	10.00*	3.22***	0.01	2.87

Note: * significant at 1%, ** significant at 5%, significant at 10%.

In summary, our tests suggest that selected households were not fully insured against idiosyncratic income risks. The rejection of the full insurance model was for all the states and all the category of households. The full insurance was earlier refuted by Townsend (1994), Udry (1994), Morduch (1990) and Deaton (1992). The value of aggregate consumption coefficient was found near to unity along with near zero value of the coefficient of household income. These results indicate some possibility of partial risk sharing activities between households either within the same village, within their same ethnic groups or within same economic strata groups. However, the possibility of insurance among same economic strata and same ethnic groups was more strong compared to insurance at the aggregate village level. These results are also valid from the socio-economic viewpoint. It is a well known fact that Indian society is strongly divided on caste and creed lines. The people in a particular caste/group prefer to transact within their own ethnic group and these facts lend support to our above findings that risk sharing groups are more closely knit on the ethnic or caste basis. The implications of these results are quite significant. Government is running various schemes/programmes including the targeted public distribution system designed specifically to reduce the risk factor present in rural incomes. The stated aim of such programmes is often to provide a safety net to the rural poor. Our results support the fact that such programmes are not being targeted adequately as the poorest of the poor (the AAY) households remained the most vulnerable. The results of this chapter strengthen the case for improved targeting and making some provision for the public insurance for the poorest of the poor.

Table A-5.1 Only Food—Delhi (Without Log) Dependent Variable = ΔConsumption Food

	Constant	ΔY	ΔVC	ΔBC	ΔEC	R^2	F*	No of Obs.	F* ΔY=0	F* ΔVC=1 or ΔBC=1 or ΔEC=1	F* ΔY=0, ΔVC=1	F* ΔY=0, ΔBC=1	F* ΔY=0, ΔEC=1
							Aggregate						
1.	8.17	0.01*				0.003	13.3*	5000	13.3*				
	(2.0)	(3.7)											
2.	12.53	0.04*	0.32*			0.091	251*	5000	12.0*	2224.8*	1116.0*		
	(3.2)	(3.5)	(22.1)										
3.	21.88	0.00*		0.43*		0.172	517*	5000	10.6*	1828.2*		916.7*	
	(5.9)	(3.3)		(31.9)									
4.	20.67	0.01*			0.39*	0.119	334*	5000	13.67*	1605.2*			807*
	(5.4)	(3.8)			(25.6)								
							AAY						
5.	36.45	0.02				0.000	0.41	1000	0.41				
	(4.7)	(0.6)											
6.	39.13	0.01	0.18*			0.039	20.4*	1000	1.65	900.4*	459.5*		
	(5.1)	(1.29)	(6.4)										
7.	27.68	0.00		0.39*		0.125	71.3*	1000	0.02	324.0*		162.2*	
	(3.8)	(0.2)		(11.9)									
8.	44.26	0.00			0.25*	0.621	33.0*	1000	1.22	569.4*			287.6*
	(5.8)	(1.1)			(8.1)								
							BPL						
9.	17.8	0.01*				0.007	20.7*	2985	20.8*				
	(3.7)	(4.6)											
10.	22.45	0.08*	0.32*			0.111	186.5*	2985	21.2*	1633.3*	825.2*		
	(4.9)	(4.6)	(18.7)										
11.	26.02	0.01*		0.48*		0.178	322.6*	2985	15.7*	711.6*		359.9*	
	(5.9)	(3.9)		(24.9)									
12.	29.21	0.01*			0.38*	0.139	240.8*	2985	21.5*	1206.7*			611.1*
	(6.5)	(4.6)			(21.4)								
							APL						
13.	-48.08	0.00				0.000	0.36	1015	0.36				
	(-4.0)	(0.6)											
14.	-43.31	-0.00	0.49*			0.117	67.51*	1015	0.07	145.6*	73.5*		
	(-3.6)	(-0.3)	(11.6)										
15.	0.79	0.00		0.34*		0.168	102.4*	1015	0.62	558.9*		279.9*	
	(0.1)	(0.8)		(14.3)									
16.	-27.47	0.00			0.51**	0.131	75.56*	1015	0.14	136.7*			68.4*
	(-2.4)	(0.4)			(12.3)								

Table A-5.2 Only Food—Jharkhand (Without Log) Dependent Variable = ΔConsumption Food

	Constant	ΔY	ΔVC	ΔBC	ΔEC	R^2	F*	No of Obs.	F* ΔY=0	F* ΔVC=1 or ΔBC=1 or ΔEC=1	F* ΔY=0, ΔVC=1	F* ΔY=0, ΔBC=1	F* ΔY=0, ΔEC=1
							Aggregate						
1.	-20.45	0.01*				0.002	9.12*	5000	9.12*				
	(-4.1)	(3.0)											
2.	-11.16	0.01*	0.46*			0.103	285.8	5000	8.34*	780.6*	393.6*		
	(-1.2)	(2.9)	(23.7)										
3.	-9.14	0.01*		0.56*		0.232	755.8*	5000	11.5*	993.9*		502.6*	
	(-2.1)	(3.4)		(38.7)									
4.	-11.26	0.01**			0.46**	0.116	323.0*	5000	5.70**	905.0*			453.6*
	(-2.4)	(2.4)			(25.2)								
							AAY						
5.	-27.0	0.00				0.000	0.17	1000	0.17				
	(2.7)	(0.4)											
6.	-20.04	-0.00	0.34*			0.058	31.2*	1000	0.00	229.4*	115.1*		
	(-1.9)	(-0.0)	(7.9)										
7.	-15.20	-0.00		0.44*		0.109	60.9*	1000	0.12	199.1*		100.5*	
	(-1.5)	(-0.4)		(11.0)									
8.	-19.01***	-0.00			0.31*	0.061	32.1*	1000	0.04	304.6*			153.6*
	(-1.7)	(-0.2)			(8.0)								
							BPL						
9.	-15.53	0.02*				0.009	28.1*	3205	28.1*				
	(-3.1)	(5.3)											
10.	-6.13	0.02*	0.44*			0.146	274.3*	3205	28.6*	814.5*	419.3*		
	(-1.3)	(5.4)	(22.7)										
11.	-5.65	0.02*		0.57*		0.219	451.2*	3205	15.5*	503.9*		254.8*	
	(-1.3)	(3.9)		(29.4)									
12.	-8.09	0.02*			0.46*	0.157	295.8*	3205	24.5*	756.3*			386.7*
	(-1.7)	(4.9)			(23.7)								
							APL						
13.	-30.97	-0.00				0.000	0.05	795	0.05				
	(-1.6)	(-0.2)											
14.	-20.21	-0.00	0.66*			0.092	40.3*	795	0.00	23.5*	11.7*		
	(-1.1)	(-0.0)	(8.9)										
15.	-17.34	0.01		0.57*		0.314	181.4*	795	2.20	202*		104.9*	
	(-1.1)	(1.5)		(19.0)									
16.	-13.99	-0.00			0.57*	0.111	49.34*	790	0.07	56.9*			28.5*
	(-0.8)	(-0.3)			(9.9)								

Table A-5.3 Only Food—Kerala (Without Log) Dependent Variable = ΔConsumption Food

	Constant	ΔY	ΔVC	ΔBC	ΔEC	R^2	F*	No of Obs.	F* ΔY=0	F* ΔVC=1 or ΔBC =1 or ΔEC =1	F* ΔY=0, ΔVC =1	F* ΔY=0, ΔBC =1	F* ΔY=0, ΔEC =1
							Aggregate						
1.	-40.38	0.01*				0.008	42.20*	5000	42.20*				
	(-7.9)	(6.5)											
2.	-41.69	0.001*	0.27*			0.041	106.9*	5000	44.11*	1197.9*	621.7*		
	(-8.4)	(6.6)	(13.0)										
3.	-24.04	0.01*		0.31*		0.083	227.0*	5000	54.35*	2014.5*		1045.6*	
	(-4.9)	(7.4)		(20.2)									
4.	-24.46	0.01*			0.31*	0.074	196.7*	5000	50.34*	1769.2*			914.7*
	(-4.9)	(7.1)			(18.6)								
							AAY						
5.	-38.23	0.01**				0.005	5.9**	1005	5.9**				
	(-3.7)	(2.4)											
6.	-39.90	0.01**	0.39*			0.082	45.7*	1005	6.2**	208.0*	106.9*		
	(-4.0)	(2.5)	(9.2)										
7.	-20.11	0.01*		0.36*		0.142	82.9*	1005	13.7*	523.5*		277.9*	
	(-2.1)	(3.7)		(12.6)									
8.	21.28	0.01*			0.33*	0.081	43.4*	985	7.6*	335.4*			172.3*
	(-2.1)	(2.8)			(8.9)								
							BPL						
9.	-31.25	0.01*				0.007	22.1*	3005	22.1*				
	(-5.1)	(4.7)											
10.	-32.5	0.01*	0.28*			0.045	71.7*	3005	26.6*	801.6*	419.5*		
	(-5.4)	(5.2)	(10.9)										
11.	-15.45	0.01*		0.39*		0.109	183.7*	3005	38.9*	804.6*		436.3*	
	(-2.6)	(6.2)		(18.5)									
12.	-14.3	0.01*			0.34*	0.093	152.3*	2980	32.8*	1059.6*			556.2*
	(-2.4)	(5.7)			(16.7)								
							APL						
13.	-70.40	0.01*				0.011	11.5*	990	11.5*				
	(-5.1)	(3.4)											
14.	-71.29	0.01*	0.14**			0.017	8.7*	990	10.8*	216.4*	111.8*		
	(-5.2)	(3.3)	(2.4)										
15.	-56.48	0.01*		0.15*		0.029	15.2*	990	10.6*	599.7*		302.7*	
	(-4.0)	(3.3)		(4.3)									
16.	-58.03	0.01*			0.22*	0.039	20.1*	980	11.3*	372.1*			190.2*
	(-4.3)	(3.4)			(5.3)								

Table A-5.4 Only Food—Madhya Pradesh (Without Log) Dependent Variable = ΔConsumption Food

	Constant	ΔY	ΔVC	ΔBC	ΔEC	R^2	F*	No of Obs.	F* ΔY=0	F* ΔVC=1 or ΔBC =1 or ΔEC =1	F* ΔY=0, ΔVC =1	F* ΔY=0, ΔBC =1	F* ΔY=0, ΔEC =1
							Aggregate						
1.	52.59 (10.1)	0.00 (1.4)				0.000	1.9*	5000	1.9*				
2.	48.12 (9.4)	0.00 (1.0)	0.10* (11.8)			0.027	70.8*	5000	1.1	10480.9*	5241.2*		
3.	50.32 (9.7)	0.00 (1.0)		0.05* (8.3)		0.014	35.0*	5000	1.0	300034.4*		15040.1*	
4.	49.47 (9.6)	0.00 (1.1)			0.06* (10.0)	0.020	50.9*	5000	1.1	23775.0*			11892.1*
							AAY						
5.	59.68 (6.7)	-0.01 (-1.3)				0.002	1.7	975	1.7				
6.	57.05 (6.5)	-0.01*** (-1.7)	0.06* (4.4)			0.021	10.4*	975	2.9***	4110.3*	2082.9*		
7.	48.86 (5.5)	-0.01 (-1.5)		0.18* (6.9)		0.048	24.7*	975	2.3	1028.4*		516.9*	
8.	56.87 (6.4)	-0.01 (-1.5)			0.04* (3.9)	0.017	8.5*	975	2.2	8117.4*			4077.4*
							BPL						
9.	54.37 (8.9)	0.01** (2.4)				0.002	5.9**	3055	5.9**				
10.	50.21 ((8.3)	0.01** (2.1)	0.10* (9.3)			0.029	46.3*	3055	4.5**	7553.4*	3777.2*		
11.	49.58 (8.2)	0.01* (2.3)		0.09* (9.5)		0.031	48.2*	3055	5.4*	9610.1*		4805.5*	
12.	51.89 (8.6)	0.01** (2.2)			0.06* (8.1)	0.023	35.9*	3030	4.9*	18820.6*			9412.4*
							APL						
13.	40.56 (2.5)	0.00 (0.2)				0.000	0.06	970	0.06				
14.	32.74 (2.0)	0.00 (0.2)	0.16* (6.1)			0.037	18.7*	970	0.02	928.2*	464.1*		
15.	39.9 (2.4)	0.00 (0.1)		0.02** (2.4)		0.006	2.9**	970	0.01	10998.9*		5518.9*	
16.	34.9 (2.1)	0.00 (0.1)			0.10* (4.9)	0.024	11.9*	950	0.00	1788.6*			894.9*

Table A-5.5 Only Food—Maharashtra (Without Log) Dependent Variable = ΔConsumption Food

	Constant	ΔY	ΔVC	ΔBC	ΔEC	R^2	F*	No of Obs.	F* ΔY=0	F* ΔVC=1 or ΔBC =1 or ΔEC =1	F* ΔY=0, ΔVC =1	F* ΔY=0, ΔBC =1	F* ΔY=0, ΔEC =1
						Aggregate							
1.	5.89	0.02*				0.015	74.1*	5000	74.1*				
	(1.2)	(8.6)											
2.	-8.06	0.02*	0.55*			0.148	434.6*	5000	61.1*	544.4*	294.2*		
	(-1.8)	(97.8)	(27.9)										
3.	-7.1	0.01*		0.51*		0.233	757.8*	5000	48.2*	1320.8*		669.5*	
	(1.7)	(6.9)		(37.7)									
4.	-3.32	0.02*			0.36*	0.102	280.5*	4940	67.9*	1496.7*			770.7*
	(-0.7)	(8.2)			(21.8)								
						AAY							
5.	7.7	0.04*				0.024	23.8*	965	23.8*				
	(0.8)	(4.8)											
6.	-8.26	0.03*	0.61*			0.249	159.1*	965	16.9*	116.6*	63.5*		
	(-1.0)	(4.1)	(16.9)										
7.	-7.35	0.03*		0.73*		0.431	364.28*	965	13.8*	90.0*		48.9*	
	(-1.0)	(3.7)		(26.2)									
8.	1.6	0.04*			0.20*	0.089	46.2*	945	18.1*	1067.6*			534.5*
	(0.2)	(4.3)			(8.2)								
						BPL							
9.	7.36	0.02*				0.010	31.2*	3020	31.2*				
	(1.4)	(5.6)											
10.	-1.56	0.02*	0.35*			0.089	146.3*	3020	29.1*	887.4*	454.3*		
	(-0.3)	(5.4)	(16.1)										
11.	-7.41	0.01*		0.51*		0.122	210.4*	3020	21.8*	346.2*		179.2*	
	(-1.5)	(0.0)		(19.6)									
12.	0.36	0.01*			0.28*	0.071	115.9*	2990	27.4*	1277.5*			648.9*
	(0.1))	(5.2)			(14.2)								
						APL							
13.	-0.59	0.02*				0.019	19.7*	1015	19.7*				
	(-0.0)	(4.4)											
14.	-28.5	0.01*	1.10*			0.268	185.6*	1015	11.5*	3.1***	7.9*		
	(2.1)	(3.4)	(18.6)										
15.	-9.9	0.01*		0.46*		0.299	215.5*	1015	13.3*	539.3*		271.4*	
	(-0.8)	(3.7)		(20.1)									
16.	-19.6*	0.01*			0.87*	0.225	145.8*	1005	16.9*	5.7*			10.7*
	(-1.4)	(4.1)			(16.3)								

Table A-5.6 Only Food—Uttarakhand (Without Log) Dependent Variable = ΔConsumption Food

	Constant	ΔY	ΔVC	ΔBC	ΔEC	R^2	F*	No of Obs.	F* ΔY=0	F* ΔVC=1 or ΔBC =1 or ΔEC =1	F* ΔY=0, ΔVC =1	F* ΔY=0, ΔBC =1	F* ΔY=0, ΔEC =1
							Aggregate						
1.	-8.32	0.01*				0.009	43.6*	5000	43.6*				
	(-1.8)	(6.6)											
2.	-0.98	0.01*	0.42*			0.149	435.7*	5000	31.8*	1519.9*	766.6*		
	(0.2)	(5.6)	(28.7)										
3.	4.27	0.01*		0.37*		0.124	352.5*	5000	35.9*	1893.6*		955.9*	
	(1.0)	(6.0)		(25.6)									
4.	7.49	0.01*			0.46*	0.150	436.3*	4935	31.5*	1125.2*			570.7*
	(1.7)	(5.6)			(28.7)								
							AAY						
5.	-7.80	0.05*				0.067	61.7*	1025	61.7*				
	(-0.8)	(7.9)											
6.	-1.06	0.04*	0.37*			0.178	110.9*	1025	50.5*	456.2*	240.4*		
	(-0.1)	(7.1)	(12.3)										
7.	5.01	0.04*		0.46 *		0.169	104.2*	1025	40.3*	195.3*		106.2*	
	(0.6)	(6.4)		(11.8)									
8.	8.78	0.04*			0.41*	0.182	112.2*	1010	43.1*	309.8*			163.9*
	(1.0)	(6.6)			(12.5)								
							BPL						
9.	-4.05	0.01*				0.005	15.1*	2960	15.1*				
	(-0.7)	(3.9)											
10.	3.26	0.00*	0.43*			0.162	285.9*	2960	8.0*	989.8*	495.4*		
	(0.6)	(2.8)	(23.5)										
11.	13.19	0.00**		0.63*		0.225	430.9*	2960	5.9**	298.1*		149.9*	
	(2.6)	(2.4)		(29.0)									
12.	11.07	0.00*			0.49*	0.176	312.1*	2935	8.4*	638.9*			320.7*
	(2.1)	(2.9)			(24.6)								
							APL						
13.	-24.36	0.01*				0.017	17.7*	1015	17.7*				
	(-2.0)	(4.2)											
14.	-16.57	0.01*	0.46*			0.133	77.4*	1015	17.8*	187.6*	101.5*		
	(-1.4)	(4.2)	(11.6)										
15.	-14.35	0.01*		0.17*		0.062	33.2*	1015	19.0*	1133.8*		577.8*	
	(-1.2)	(4.4)		(6.9)									
16.	-7.96	0.01*			0.41*	0.109	60.4*	990	17.6*	217.4*			116.5*
	(-0.7)	(4.2)			(10.1)								

Table A-5.7 Only Food—Delhi (With Log) Dependent Variable = ΔConsumption Food

	Constant	ΔLY	ΔLVC	ΔLBC	ΔLEC	R^2	F*	No of Obs.	F* ΔLY=0	F* ΔLVC=1 or ΔLBC =1 or ΔLEC =1	F* ΔLY=0, ΔLVC =1	F* ΔLY=0, ΔLBC =1	F* ΔLY=0, ΔLEC =1
							Aggregate						
1.	0.01	0.00				0.000	1.6*	4254	1.6				
	(2.7)	(1.3)											
2.	002	0.00	0.57*			0.102	242*	4254	0.1	274.1*	137.2*		
	(5.9)	(0.2)	(21.9)										
3.	0.01	0.00		0.59*		0.142	352*	4254	0.0	352.3*		222.3*	
	(4.9)	(0.1)		(26.5)									
4.	0.16	0.00			0.50*	0.097	227*	4254	0.2	444.3*			222.3*
	(5.2)	(0.5)			(21.3)								
							AAY						
5.	0.04	-0.01				0.002	2.20	839	2.20				
	(4.9)	(-1.5)											
6.	0.04	-0.01	0.34*			0.035	15.45*	839	2.3	104.3*	53.3*		
	(5.8)	(-1.5)	(5.4)										
7.	0.03	-0.01**		0.49*		0.096	44.64*	839	4.5**	97.57*		52.5*	
	(4.1)	(2.1)		(9.3)									
8.	0.04	-0.01			0.34*	0.040	17.40*	839	1.94	117.7*			59.5*
	(5.8)	(-1.4)			(5.7)								
							BPL						
9.	0.01	0.01*				0.004	10.35*	2559	10.35*				
	(3.3)	(3.2)											
10.	0.23	0.01***	0.62*			0.129	190.7*	2559	3.75***	142.7*	71.9*		
	(6.3)	(1.9)	(19.2)										
11.	0.02	0.01**		0.63*		0.151	228.1*	2559	4.01**	154.3*		77.81*	
	(5.0)	(2.0)		(21.1)									
12.	0.12	0.01**			0.52*	0.116	167.8*	2559	4.82**	264.9*			132.9*
	(5.4)	(2.2)			(17.9)								
							APL						
13.	-0.03	-0.00				0.001	0.72	856	0.72				
	(-4.8)	(-0.9)											
14.	-0.02	-0.01	0.67*			0.147	73.85*	856	1.5	34.44*	18.12*		
	(-3.8)	(-1.2)	(12.1)										
15.	-0.01	-0.00		0.53*		0.152	76.4*	856	0.54	115.2*		57.8*	
	(-1.6)	(-0.7)		(12.3)									
16.	-0.02	-0.00			0.57*	0.135	65.9*	856	1.3	76.9*			39.3*
	(-3.8)	(-1.1)			(11.5)								

Table A-5.8 Only Food—Jharkhand (With Log) Dependent Variable = ΔConsumption Food

	Constant	ΔLY	ΔLVC	ΔLBC	ΔLEC	R^2	F*	No of Obs.	F* ΔLY=0	F* ΔLVC=1 or ΔLBC =1 or ΔLEC =1	F* ΔLY=0, ΔLVC =1	F* ΔLY=0, ΔLBC =1	F* ΔLY=0, ΔLEC =1
							Aggregate						
1.	-0.14	-0.00				0.000	0.07	4942	0.07				
	(-3.4)	(-0.3)											
2.	-0.01***	-0.00	0.49*			0.071	187.3	4942	0.03	413.3*	206.6*		
	(-1.9)	(-0.2)	(19.4)										
3.	0.01	-0.11		0.51*		0.103	284.1*	4942	0.12	538.3*		269.2*	
	(-1.9)	(-0.3)		(23.8)									
4.	-0.01	-0.00			0.44*	0.067	177.3*	4942	0.08	578.2*			289.1*
	(-2.1)	(-0.3)			(18.8)								
							AAY						
5.	-0.03	-0.00				0.000	0.02	994	0.02				
	(-2.4)	(-0.1)											
6.	-0.02	-0.00	0.40*			0.037	19.11*	994	0.01	83.9*	41.9*		
	(-1.9)	(-0.1)	(6.2)										
7.	-0.02***	-0.00		0.36*		0.047	24.25*	994	0.08	154.4*		77.3*	
	(-1.8)	(-0.3)		(6.9)									
8.	-0.02**	-0.00			0.35*	0.037	18.79*	994	0.01	133.9*			66.9*
	(-1.9)	(-0.1)			(6.1)								
							BPL						
9.	-0.01	0.01				0.000	0.84	3171	0.84				
	(-1.9)	(0.9)											
10.	-0.00	0.00	0.52*			0.087	150.1*	3171	0.48	257.3*	128.73*		
	(-0.8)	(0.7)	(17.3)										
11.	-0.00	0.00		0.55*		0.109	194.1*	3171	0.22	264.4*		132.2*	
	(-0.7)	(0.5)		(19.7)									
12.	-0.01	0.00			0.46*	0.076	128.2*	3171	0.53	363.5*			181.9*
	(-1.0)	(0.7)			(15.9)								
							APL						
13.	-0.02	-0.01***				0.004	3.07***	777	307***				
	(-1.7)	(-1.8)											
14.	-0.01	-0.01	0.46*			0.071	29.74*	777	1.68	77.30*	38.90*		
	(-0.9)	(-1.3)	(7.5)										
15.	-0.01	-0.01		0.56*		0.201	97.56*	777	1.16	119.9*		60.07*	
	(-1.1)	(-1.1)		(13.8)									
16.	-0.01	-0.01			0.50*	0.099	42.15*	772	2.29	80.02*			40.72*
	(-0.9)	(-1.5)			(9.0)								

Table A-5.9 Only Food—Kerala (With Log) Dependent Variable = ΔConsumption Food

	Constant	ΔLY	ΔLVC	ΔLBC	ΔLEC	R^2	F*	No of Obs.	F* ΔLY=0	F* ΔLVC=1 or ΔLBC =1 or ΔLEC =1	F* ΔLY=0, ΔLVC =1	F* ΔLY=0, ΔLBC =1	F* ΔLY=0, ΔLEC =1
							Aggregate						
1.	-0.04	0.02*				0.004	18.9*	4668	18.9*				
	(-8.1)	(4.4)											
2.	-0.02	0.02*	0.52*			0.075	189.0*	4668	33.2*	314.1*	181.2*		
	(-4.5)	(5.7)	(18.9)										
3.	-0.02	0.02*		0.48*		0.087	223.1*	4668	31.7*	519.9*		283.3*	
	(-5.0)	(5.6)		(20.6)									
4.	-0.02	0.02*			0.43*	0.066	161.7*	4668	29.2*	524.1*			283.5*
	(-5.2)	(5.4)			(17.4)								
							AAY						
5.	-0.34	0.03**				0.005	4.7**	942	4.7**				
	(-3.1)	(2.2)											
6.	0.01	0.03**	0.77*			0.132	71.5*	942	5.4**	11.6*	8.5*		
	(-0.9)	(2.3)	(11.7)										
7.	-0.02	0.03*		0.54*		0.147	80.9*	942	6.9*	112.7*		60.6*	
	(-1.5)	(2.6)		(12.5)									
8.	-0.02	0.02***			0.54*	0.077	38.7*	922	3.6***	52.1*			27.3*
	(-1.7)	(1.9)			(8.5)								
							BPL						
9.	-0.03	0.02				0.003	9.31*	2826	9.31*				
	(-5.3)	(3.1)											
10.	-0.01	0.03*	0.56*			0.089	138.4*	2826	20.3*	166.0*	98.6*		
	(-2.2)	(4.5)	(16.3)										
11.	-0.02	0.03*		0.55*		0.097	153.2*	2826	21.21*	203.9*		118.8*	
	(-3.0)	(4.6)		(17.2)									
12.	-0.02	0.03*			0.50*	0.086	131.1*	2805	19.9*	247.9*			140.3*
	(-2.7)	(4.5)			(15.8)								
							APL						
13.	-0.06	0.02**				0.006	5.3**	900	5.3**				
	(-6.1)	(2.3)											
14.	-0.05	0.02**	0.12**			0.011	5.0*	900	6.1**	216.4*	114.8*		
	(-5.6)	(2.5)	(2.2)										
15.	-0.05	0.02**		0.13**		0.013	5.8*	900	5.6**	257.9*		132.6*	
	(-5.4)	(2.4)		(2.5)									
16.	-0.05	0.02**			0.16*	0.018	8.2*	890	6.3**	288.8*			149.9*
	(-5.5)	(2.5)			(3.3)								

Table A-5.10 Only Food—Madhya Pradesh (With Log) Dependent Variable = ΔConsumption Food

	Constant	ΔLY	ΔLVC	ΔLBC	ΔLEC	R^2	F*	No of Obs.	F* ΔLY=0	F* ΔLVC=1 or ΔLBC =1 or ΔLEC =1	F* ΔLY=0, ΔLVC =1	F* ΔLY=0, ΔLBC =1	F* ΔLY=0, ΔLEC =1
							Aggregate						
1.	0.09	-0.01				0.001	2.7	4675	2.7				
	(14.4)	(-1.6)											
2.	0.08	-0.02*	0.20*			0.023	56.0*	4675	7.6*	1707.0*	879.5*		
	(13.2)	(-2.8)	(10.5)										
3.	0.08	-0.01*		0.21*		0.028	66.5*	4675	6.9*	1806.8*		923.4*	
	(12.9)	(-2.6)		(11.4)									
4.	0.08	-0.01*			0.02*	0.026	61.9*	4675	7.2*	1876.8*			962.2*
	(12.8)	(-2.7)			(11.0)								
							AAY						
5.	0.12	-0.06*				0.013	11.9*	911	11.9*				
	(7.6)	(-3.5)											
6.	0.11	-0.06*	0.20*			0.030	14.2*	911	15.5*	265.4*	150.4*		
	(7.2)	(-3.9)	(4.0)										
7.	0.09	-0.06*)		0.33*		0.052	25.0*	911	14.3*	159.3*		88.9*	
	(6.1)	(-3.8)		(6.1)									
8.	0.11	-0.06*			0.19*	0.030	13.9*	896	14.5*	278.8*			152.9*
	(6.9)	(-3.8)			(4.0)								
							BPL						
9.	0.08	-0.01				0.000	0.9*	2890	0.9				
	(10.9)	(-1.0)											
10.	0.07	-0.01**	0.22*			0.028	41.7*	2890	3.9**	1033.6*	532.4*		
	(9.9)	(-1.9)	(9.1)										
11.	0.07	-0.01***		0.22*		0.031	46.8*	2890	2.8***	1149.5*		583.01	
	(9.7)	(-1.7)		(9.6)									
12.	0.07	-0.01**			0.22*	0.033	49.2*	2868	3.9**	1174.4*			602.6*
	(9.6)	(-1.9)			(9.9)								
							APL						
13.	0.07	0.01				0.001	0.7	874	0.7				
	(5.5)	(0.8)											
14.	0.06	0.00	0.16*			0.019	8.5*	874	0.2	440.9*	221.8*		
	(4.9)	(0.4)	(4.0)										
15.	0.07	0.00		0.10*		0.009	3.7**	874	0.2	620.9*		315.4*	
	(5.4)	(0.4)		(2.6)									
16.	0.06	0.00*			0.15 *	0.017	7.4*	862	0.2	474.2*			238.4*
	(4.9)	(0.5)			(3.8)								

Table A-5.11 Only Food—Maharashtra (With Log) Dependent Variable = ΔConsumption Food

	Constant	ΔLY	ΔLVC	ΔLBC	ΔLEC	R^2	F*	No of Obs.	F* ΔLY=0	F* ΔLVC=1 or ΔLBC =1 or ΔLEC =1	F* ΔLY=0, ΔLVC =1	F* ΔLY=0, ΔLBC =1	F* ΔLY=0, ΔLEC =1
							Aggregate						
1.	0.01	0.02*				0.006	29.6*	4640	29.6*				
	(1.1)	(5.4)											
2.	-0.01	0.02*	0.70*			0.148	402.4*	4640	21.4*	138.5*	77.7*		
	(-1.3)	(4.6)	(27.7)										
3.	-0.01	0.01*		0.70*		0.197	567.9*	4640	14.7*	193.3*		100.9*	
	(-1.6)	(3.8)		(33.2)									
4.	-0.00	0.02*			0.55*	0.114	294.6*	4587	20.9*	372.3*			192.9*
	(-0.9)	(4.6)			(23.6)								
							AAY						
5.	0.01	0.03*				0.011	9.8*	888	9.8*				
	(0.5)	(3.1)											
6.	-0.01	0.02**	0.89*			0.220	124.8*	888	4.2**	3.9**	3.7**		
	(-0.9)	(2.0)	(15.4)										
7.	-0.01	0.02**		0.79*		0.301	190.9*	888	4.9**	24.6*		13.9*	
	(-1.3)	(2.2)		(19.2)									
8.	-0.01	0.02***			0.55*	0.132	66.1*	873	3.5***	83.5*			42.1*
	(-0.7)	(1.9)			(11.1)								
							BPL						
9.	0.01	0.02*				0.007	20.7*	2846	20.7*				
	(0.9)	(4.6)											
10.	-0.00	0.02*	0.51*			0.087	134.7*	2846	16.0*	222.1*	116.5*		
	(0.6)	(4.0)	(15.7)										
11.	-0.01	0.02*		0.68*		0.125	202.1*	2846	12.3*	82.3*		45.3*	
	(-1.3)	(3.5)		(19.5)									
12.	-0.00	0.02*			0.43*	0.074	113.1*	2828	17.3*	347.6*			180.2*
	(0.3)	(4.2)			(14.3)								
							APL						
13.	0.00	0.01**				0.004	3.9**	906	3.9**				
	(0.4)	(1.5)											
14.	-0.01	0.01**	1.11*			0.333	225.5*	906	3.9**	4.5**	4.3**		
	(-1.3)	(1.9)	(21.1)										
15.	-0.00	0.01		0.67*		0.307	199.7*	906	1.3	94.7*		47.5*	
	(-0.1)	(1.1)		(19.9)									
16.	-0.01	0.01***			0.92*	0.266	161.7*	896	2.8***	2.2			2.4***
	(-0.7)	(1.7)			(17.8)								

Table A-5.12 Only Food—Uttarakhand (With Log) Dependent Variable = ΔConsumption Food

	Constant	ΔLY	ΔLVC	ΔLBC	ΔLEC	R^2	F*	No	F* of Obs.	F* ΔLY=0	F* ΔLVC=1 or ΔLBC =1 or ΔLEC =1	F* ΔLY=0, ΔLVC =1	F* ΔLY=0, ΔLBC =1	ΔLY=0, ΔLEC =1
							Aggregate							
1.	-0.00	0.02*				0.011	50.2*	4737	50.2*					
	(-0.7)	(7.1)												
2.	0.01	0.02*	0.64*			0.107	284.3*	4737	30.6*	160.0*	90.1*			
	(2.2)	(5.5)	(22.7)											
3.	0.01	0.02*		0.58*		0.113	302.1*	4737	26.7*	293.2*		152.8*		
	(1.6)	(5.2)		(23.4)										
4.	0.01	0.02*			0.55*	0.099	258.6*	4674	32.0*	314.6*			166.4*	
	(1.7)	(5.7)			(21.5)									
							AAY							
5.	-0.00	0.03*				0.011	10.5*	954	10.5*					
	(-0.1)	(3.2)												
6.	0.01	0.02*	0.72*			0.099	52.4*	954	6.9*	14.4*	9.9*			
	(1.3)	(2.6)	(9.7)											
7.	0.01	0.02**		0.59*		0.107	57.2*	954	5.1**	47.5*		24.8*		
	(0.7)	(2.3)		(10.1)										
8.	0.01	0.02*			0.61*	0.095	48.9*	939	7.3*	34.5*			19.9*	
	(1.2)	(2.7)			(9.3)									
							BPL							
9.	0.00	0.02*				0.010	29.2*	2831	29.2*					
	(0.2)	(5.4)												
10.	0.01	0.01*	0.64*			0.119	191.9*	2831	10.9*	110.1*	57.0*			
	(2.6)	(3.3)	(18.7)											
11.	0.01	0.01*		0.68*		0.142	234.1*	2831	9.6*	94.5*		49.0*		
	(2.1)	(3.1)		(20.8)										
12.	0.01*	0.01*			0.57*	0.118	187.8*	2808	11.6*	185.3*			94.2*	
	(2.0)	(3.4)			(18.5)									
							APL							
13.	-0.02	0.02*				0.011	10.9*	952	10.9*					
	(-1.8)	(3.3)												
14.	-0.01	0.02*	0.58*			0.092	48.0*	952	13.3*	45.4*	29.9*			
	(-0.6)	(3.7)	(9.2)											
15.	-0.01	0.02*		0.38*		0.071	36.2*	952	10.2*	165.5*		86.8*		
	(-0.7)	(3.2)		(7.8)										
16.	-0.01	0.02*			0.42*	0.068	33.7*	927	12.3*	111.2*			62.2*	
	(-0.9)	(3.5)			(7.5)									

Note: * significant at 1%, ** significant at 5%, significant at 10%.

6 Performance of Targeted Public Distribution System

Errors of Inclusion and Exclusion

6.1 Introduction

In the previous three chapters, we have provided the details of income and consumption pattern and their relationship for the selected AAY, BPL and APL households. In a number of recent studies, it has been highlighted that there are large-scale errors in the identification of BPL (and AAY) families, low off-take of food grains by the poor and there are weaknesses in the delivery system.[1] In the light of our observed per capita income and consumption of the below poverty households, it becomes essential to check the authenticity of identification of the beneficiaries and to further explore these issues in the light of information we have collected through our sample survey. This chapter deals with the matters related to efficiency of the targeted public distribution system. The chapter is divided into five sections. The first section presents household entitlement for PDS grains and the system of delivery of food grains to the households. The next section presents indicators related to performance of PDS through our qualitative questions on the distribution of grains through fair price shops and the quality of grains distributed through PDS. Section 3 presents the criteria followed by State Governments in issuing BPL and AAY cards. We also compare the official poverty line with the income earned by our households at the below poverty level. Section 4 presents the issues related to identification of BPL and AAY households. The extent of error in the identification of below poverty households is measured among our six selected states. In the last section, we have enumerated the amount of diversion of food for the categories of AAY, BPL and APL in the six states under study.

6.2 Household Entitlement and the Amount of Grains Distributed

Tables 6.1 to 6.6 present the statistics related to household entitlement and the number of instalment preferred/received by the selected households during the reference year 2006 for wheat and rice in the six states. Similarly, Tables 6.7 to 6.12 present data related to entitlement not withdrawn despite availability and the reasons thereof during the reference year. In Chapter 4 we presented actual quantity of cereals received by the households from the PDS shops. In order to seek the households' perception about their entitlement, we asked them how much wheat and rice they were entitled to get from the PDS shops. On an average, households' perceptions were reasonably close in Delhi, Jharkhand, Kerala and Uttarakhand while some dissimilarities were observed in Maharashtra and Madhya Pradesh. Nevertheless, households were mostly found to be aware about their entitlement of 35 kgs of total cereals while proportion of wheat and rice differed across households. To our question, in how many instalments during a month they were allowed to lift their entitled quantity, upto 90 per cent households in all the categories and in all the states, except Kerala, responded that they were allowed once in a month. In Kerala, more than 70 per cent households among all the categories replied that they were allowed more than two instalments in a month to lift their entitled quantity of both rice as well as wheat. About the households' choice, a majority of households in all the states, except Kerala also expressed their preference for one instalment. However, against the tradition of supplying food only once in a month, around 25 to 35 per cent AAY and BPL households in Delhi, Madhya Pradesh, Maharashtra and Uttarakhand and 40 per cent of them in Jharkhand expressed their desire to obtain food twice a month. In Kerala, overwhelming majority expressed their choice as also they obtained their entitlements more than twice a month.

1. In our our evaluation study of Phase I, we highlighted some of these issues, e.g., the excess cards, wrong identification, diversion of cereals, etc. For more on these issues, see e.g., Planning Commission (2005), Radhakrishna and Subbarao (1997) and ORG (2005).

Table 6.1 Entitlement and Delivery under TPDS during 2006 (Delhi)

	Quantity Entitled (kgs)	No. of Instalments Allowed (Per cent)				Your Preferred Instalments (Per cent)				No. of Months Entitlement not Obtained during Last Year by the HHs who Obtained Irregular Supply				Reasons for not Obtaining Entitlement by such HHs (Per cent)		
		1	2	>2	No Response	1	2	>2	No Response	1	2	>2	No Response	No Explanation Given	Less Supply to the FPS	No Response
AAY																
Rice	10.00	100.00				65.17	34.83			0.00	0.00	0.00	100.00		100.00	
Wheat	25.00	100.00				65.36	34.64			0.00	100.0	0.00	0.00		100.00	
BPL																
Rice	10.00	99.72	0.28			76.26	23.74			100.0	0.00	0.00	0.00	75.00	25.00	
Wheat	25.00	99.63	0.37			75.66	24.34			83.33	4.17	12.50		35.29	64.71	
APL																
Rice	10.00	99.19	0.81			93.44	6.56			52.94	17.65	29.41		30.77	69.23	
Wheat	25.00	99.20	0.80			92.74	7.26			55.00	10.00	35.00		42.86	52.38	4.76

Table 6.2 Entitlement and Delivery under TPDS during 2006 (Jharkhand)

	Quantity Entitled (kgs)	No. of Instalments allowed (Per cent)				Your Preferred Instalments (Per cent)				No. of Months Entitlement Not Obtained during Last Year by the HHs who Obtained Irregular Supply				Reasons for Not Obtaining Entitlement by such HHs (Per cent)		
		1	2	>2	No Response	1	2	>2	No Response	1	2	>2	No Response	No Explanation Given	Less Supply to the FPS	No Response
AAY																
Rice	21.00	88.89	11.11			60.13	39.24	0.63		30.77	20.00	49.23		52.54	47.46	0.00
Wheat	14.00	88.77	11.23			59.49	39.87	0.63		25.00	23.33	51.67		56.90	43.10	0.00
BPL																
Rice	20.00	92.66	7.34			59.43	39.24	1.33		19.16	17.44	63.40		41.00	59.00	0.00
Wheat	9.00	92.45	7.55			57.29	41.25	1.46		14.56	28.03	57.41		38.02	61.98	0.00
APL																
Rice	26.00	100.00	0.00			12.50	87.50			12.50	25.00	62.50		20.00	80.00	0.00
Wheat	9.00	100.00	0.00							25.00	62.50	12.50		16.67	83.33	0.00

Table 6.3 Entitlement and Delivery under TPDS during 2006 (Kerala)

	Quantity Entitled (kgs)	No. of Instalments Allowed (Per cent)				Your Preferred Instalments (Per cent)				No. of Months Entitlement Not Obtained during Last Year by the HHs who Obtained Irregular Supply				Reasons for Not Obtaining Entitlement by such HHs (Per cent)		
		1	2	>2	No Response	1	2	>2	No Response	1	2	>2	No Response	No Explanation Given	Less Supply to the FPS	No Response
AAY																
Rice	35.00	4.44		95.55		1.20		98.80		8.93	19.64	71.43		77.59	17.24	5.17
Wheat		20.00		80.00				100.00		33.33	0.00	66.67		33.33	0.00	66.67
BPL																
Rice	19.00	12.36	1.35	86.30		2.22		97.78		15.11	8.44	76.45		88.31	6.49	5.20
Wheat	6.00	25.61	2.44	71.95		14.22	10.43	75.35		15.22	3.48	81.30		62.50	30.77	6.73
APL																
Rice	26.00	8.18		91.83			4.92	95.08		16.95	8.47	74.58		75.00	13.89	11.11
Wheat	9.00	15.58		84.41		8.16	4.08	87.76		15.28	4.17	80.55		55.81	20.93	23.26

Table 6.4 Entitlement and Delivery under TPDS during 2006 (Madhya Pradesh)

	Quantity Entitled (kgs)	No. of Instalments Allowed (Per cent)				Your Preferred Instalments (Per cent)				No. of Months Entitlement Not Obtained during Last Year by the HHs who Obtained Irregular Supply				Reasons for Not Obtaining Entitlement by such HHs (Per cent)		
		1	2	>2	No Response	1	2	>2	No Response	1	2	>2	No Response	No Explanation Given	Less Supply to the FPS	No Response
AAY																
Rice	2.00	95.27			4.73	67.44	26.74	1.74	4.07	12.90	8.06	79.04		56.00	34.67	9.33
Wheat	33.00	96.59			3.41	66.29	28.57	1.71	3.43	14.49	13.04	72.47		53.85	38.46	7.69
BPL																
Rice	5.00	97.56	0.17		2.27	76.57	20.80	0.35	2.27	25.40	9.52	65.08		60.52	35.16	4.32
Wheat	30.00	97.67	0.36			76.48	21.18	0.36	1.97	26.95	11.82	61.23		55.58	41.85	2.58
APL																
Rice	5.00	100.00				92.86	7.14			0.00	0.00	100.00		50.00	50.00	0.00
Wheat	30.00	100.00				81.25	18.75		1.97	33.33	11.11	55.56		28.57	71.43	0.00

Table 6.5 Entitlement and Delivery under TPDS during 2006 (Maharashtra)

	Quantity Entitled (kgs)	No. of Instalments Allowed (Per cent)				Your Preferred Instalments (Per cent)				No. of Months Entitlement Not Obtained during Last Year by the HHs who Obtained Irregular Supply				Reasons for Not Obtaining Entitlement by such HHs (Per cent)		
		1	2	>2	No Response	1	2	>2	No Response	1	2	>2	No Response	No Explanation Given	Less Supply to the FPS	No Response
AAY																
Rice	28.00	86.85	0.47		12.68	51.90	35.24		12.86	48.51	19.80	31.69		44.85	27.94	27.21
Wheat	7.00	85.78	1.47		12.75	55.00	32.00		13.00	42.05	27.27	30.68		41.18	26.05	32.77
BPL																
Rice	28.00	86.95			13.05	58.59	27.98		13.43	38.59	24.00	37.41		48.71	29.52	21.77
Wheat	7.00	85.86	0.86		13.29	60.11	26.07		13.82	35.38	31.20	33.42		48.84	27.22	23.94
APL																
Rice	10.00	85.71			14.29	78.57	7.14			62.50	12.50	25.00		66.67	8.33	25.00
Wheat	25.00	91.67			8.33	83.33	8.33		8.33	57.14	14.29	28.57		50.00	25.00	25.00

Table 6.6 Entitlement and Delivery under TPDS during 2006 (Uttarakhand)

	Quantity Entitled (kgs)	No. of Instalments Allowed (Per cent)				Your Preferred Instalments (Per cent)				No. of Months Entitlement Not Obtained during Last Year by the HHs who Obtained Irregular Supply				Reasons for Not Obtaining Entitlement by such HHs (Per cent)		
		1	2	>2	No Response	1	2	>2	No Response	1	2	>2	No Response	No Explanation Given	Less Supply to the FPS	No Response
AAY																
Rice	25.00	100.00				73.60	26.40		14.29	85.42		14.58		67.24	32.76	0.00
Wheat	10.00	99.47	0.53			74.19	25.81			75.00	4.17	20.83		57.89	42.11	0.00
BPL																
Rice	25.00	99.21	0.79			80.16	19.84			76.61	7.26	16.13		71.79	28.21	0.00
Wheat	10.00	99.02	0.98			78.84	21.16			85.19	11.11	3.70		68.42	31.58	0.00
APL																
Rice	24.00	97.67	2.33			92.68	7.32			57.14	28.57	14.29		33.33	66.67	0.00
Wheat	11.00	95.45	4.55			92.86	7.14			61.54	15.38	23.08		57.14	42.86	0.00

Table 6.7 Entitlement not Purchased Despite Availability under TPDS during 2006 (Delhi)

	Entitled Qty. not Purchased at least Once during the last Year (%)	Reasons by such Households for not Lifting Entitlement (%)									
		Inferior Quality	No Difference in Price	Preference for Local Variety	Instalments not Allowed	Standing in Queue a Problem	FPS not Accessible	Grains Purchased from Other Food Programmes	Self Production	Scarcity of Income	Lack of Information
AAY											
Rice	0.50	50.00	0.00	0.00	0.00	0.00	0.00	0.00	0.00	0.00	50.00
Wheat	0.50	50.00	0.00	0.00	0.00	0.00	0.00	0.00	0.00	0.00	50.00
BPL											
Rice	0.17	25.00	25.00	0.00	25.00	0.00	0.00	0.00	0.00	0.00	25.00
Wheat	0.17	33.33	0.00	0.00	33.33	0.00	0.00	0.00	0.00	0.00	33.33
APL											
Rice	11.33	48.15	11.11	0.00	0.00	0.00	18.52	0.00	0.00	0.00	22.22
Wheat	11.82	38.46	15.38	0.00	0.00	0.00	23.08	0.00	0.00	0.00	22.08

Table 6.8 Entitlement not Purchased Despite Availability under TPDS during 2006 (Jharkhand)

	Entitled Qty. not Purchased at least Once during the Last Year (%)	Reasons by such Households for not Lifting Entitlement (%)									
		Inferior Quality	No Difference in Price	Preference for Local Variety	Instalments not Allowed	Standing in Queue a Problem	FPS not Accessible	Grains Purchased from Other Food Programmes	Self Production	Scarcity of Income	Lack of Information
AAY											
Rice	0.00	-	-	-	-	-	-	-	-	-	-
Wheat	0.00	-	-	-	-	-	-	-	-	-	-
BPL											
Rice	5.77	0.00	0.00	0.00	10.53	2.63	28.95	15.79	42.11	0.00	0.00
Wheat	4.37	0.00	0.00	0.00	17.86	10.71	0.00	0.00	0.00	14.29	57.14
APL											
Rice	2.52	0.00	0.00	0.00	0.00	0.00	0.00	0.00	75.00	25.00	0.00
Wheat	0.63	0.00	0.00	0.00	0.00	100.00	0.00	0.00	0.00	0.00	0.00

Table 6.9 Entitlement not Purchased Despite Availability under TPDS during 2006 (Kerala)

	Entitled Qty. not Purchased at least Once during the Last Year (%)	Reasons by such Households for not Lifting Entitlement (%)									
		Inferior Quality	No Difference in Price	Preference for Local Variety	Instalments not Allowed	Standing in Queue a Problem	FPS not Accessible	Grains Purchased from Other Food Programmes	Self Production	Scarcity of Income	Lack of Information
AAY											
Rice	1.49	100.00	0.00	0.00	0.00	0.00	0.00	0.00	0.00	0.00	0.00
Wheat	1.99	100.00	0.00	0.00	0.00	0.00	0.00	0.00	0.00	0.00	0.00
BPL											
Rice	1.33	80.00	20.00	0.00	0.00	0.00	0.00	0.00	0.00	0.00	0.00
Wheat	6.82	34.29	2.86	0.00	0.00	0.00	0.00	0.00	0.00	0.00	62.86
APL											
Rice	40.40	95.06	2.47	1.23	0.00	0.00	0.00	0.00	0.00	0.00	1.23
Wheat	45.96	79.78	3.37	1.12	0.00	0.00	0.00	0.00	0.00	0.00	15.73

Table 6.10 Entitlement not Purchased Despite Availability under TPDS during 2006 (Madhya Pradesh)

	Entitled Qty. not Purchased at least Once during the Last Year (%)	Reasons by such Households for fot Lifting Entitlement (%)									
		Inferior Quality	No Difference in Price	Preference for Local Variety	Instalments not Allowed	Standing in Queue a Problem	FPS not Accessible	Grains Purchased from Other Food Programmes	Self Production	Scarcity of Income	Lack of Information
AAY											
Rice	3.08	0.00	0.00	0.00	0.00	0.00	0.00	0.00	0.00	100.00	0.00
Wheat	2.56	0.00	0.00	0.00	0.00	0.00	0.00	0.00	0.00	100.00	0.00
BPL											
Rice	5.73	7.89	2.63	5.26	2.63	0.00	0.00	0.00	13.16	50.00	18.42
Wheat	5.07	0.00	0.00	6.45	0.00	0.00	0.00	0.00	16.13	61.29	16.13
APL											
Rice	0.00	-	-	-	-	-	-	-	-	-	-
Wheat	0.00	-	-	-	-	-	-	-	-	-	-

Table 6.11 Entitlement not Purchased despite Availability under TPDS during 2006 (Maharashtra)

	Entitled Qty. not Purchased at least Once during the Last Year (%)	Reasons by such Households for not Lifting Entitlement (%)									
		Inferior Quality	No Difference in Price	Preference for Local Variety	Instalments not Allowed	Standing in Queue a Problem	FPS not Accessible	Grains Purchased from Other Food Programmes	Self Production	Scarcity of Income	Lack of Information
AAY											
Rice	3.11	0.00	0.00	83.33	0.00	0.00	0.00	0.00	0.00	16.67	0.00
Wheat	2.07	0.00	0.00	75.00	0.00	0.00	0.00	0.00	0.00	25.00	0.00
BPL											
Rice	2.48	6.25	0.00	0.00	0.00	12.50	43.75	0.00	6.25	31.25	0.00
Wheat	2.48	6.25	0.00	0.00	0.00	12.50	43.75	0.00	6.25	31.25	0.00
APL											
Rice	0.00	-	-	-	-	-	-	-	-	-	-
Wheat	0.00	-	-	-	-	-	-	-	-	-	-

Table 6.12 Entitlement not Purchased Despite Availability under TPDS during 2006 (Uttarakhand)

	Entitled Qty. not Purchased at least Once during the Last Year (%)	Reasons by such Households for not Lifting Entitlement (%)									
		Inferior Quality	No Difference in Price	Preference for Local Variety	Instalments not Allowed	Standing in Queue a Problem	FPS not Accessible	Grains Purchased from Other Food Programmes	Self Production	Scarcity of Income	Lack of Information
AAY											
Rice	2.44	0.00	0.00	0.00	0.00	0.00	0.00	0.00	0.00	100.00	0.00
Wheat	1.46	0.00	0.00	0.00	0.00	0.00	0.00	0.00	0.00	100.00	0.00
BPL											
Rice	2.53	11.11	0.00	0.00	0.00	11.11	0.00	0.00	0.00	66.67	11.11
Wheat	3.55	7.14	0.00	0.00	0.00	0.00	0.00	0.00	0.00	42.86	50.00
APL											
Rice	2.96	28.57	14.29	0.00	0.00	0.00	0.00	0.00	0.00	0.00	57.14
Wheat	2.46	28.57	14.29	0.00	0.00	0.00	0.00	0.00	0.00	0.00	57.14

In Chapter 4 we presented the amount of cereals received and the percentage of households receiving their entitlement from the fair price shops under the TPDS. In this section, we further try to check the regularity of the cereal distribution among the households and to find out the reasons as given to the households by the shop owners for not supplying regular food to them. We further tried to know for those households who did not receive regular supply, what was the frequency of the same during the reference year. A majority of those households who did not receive regular entitlements indicated that they did not obtain supply for more than two months during the last calendar year in Jharkhand, Kerala and Madhya Pradesh. A majority of such households in Delhi, Maharashtra and Uttarakhand, however, expressed that they did not obtain regular supply only once during the reference year. In Jharkhand, a majority of the AAY households not receiving regular supply pointed out that they were not being given any explanation by the fair price shop owners for not supplying entitlement, while a majority among the BPL and APL households pointed out that the reason given to them by the FPS was supply not received from the godown. In Kerala and Madhya Pradesh, a majority of such households indicated that they were not given any explanation for not being supplied the entitled food while rest of the households (not receiving regular supply) indicated less supply at the FPS. In rest of the states, households quoted no explanation given by the FPS for irregular supply.

Against the trends of households not being supplied the entitlement, it was also observed that in some cases respondents did not lift their entitlement even though supply was available at the FPS. The frequency of such households was not very high among the selected states. The incidence was found among the APL households in Delhi and Kerala. Among BPL, it occurred in Jharkhand and Madhya Pradesh. The number of such households in AAY was almost negligible in all the selected states. In Delhi, a majority of these APL households indicated inferior quality as the reason for not lifting the entitlement while a few others quoted lack of information (about the timings) of its availability. Similarly in Kerala, overwhelming majority of these APL households indicated inferior quality for not lifting their entitlement. In Jharkhand, majority of the above-mentioned BPL households indicated lack of information, inaccessibility of the FPS and self-production as the reasons for not lifting their entitlement. In Madhya Pradesh, majority of such BPL households indicated scarcity of income for not lifting their entitlement. Scarcity of income was also mentioned as a reason by AAY and BPL households, although miniscule in numbers, who did not lift their quantity in Uttarakhand. Apart from these reasons there were other reasons like inferior quality at the FPS, preference for the local variety, home produced food available with the households, etc., quoted by few other households who did not lift their entitlement in the selected states.

6.3 Performance of PDS—Qualitative Facts

In addition to quantitative information on entitlement, prices and lifting of food grains and other essentials from the PDS, we also collected some qualitative facts about the performance of the PDS in the selected states. The data on qualitative information is summarised in this section. Tables 6.13 to 6.18 present facts related to PDS performance in terms of adherence to the prescribed norms, underweighment of the grains distributed and questions related to consumer satisfaction. Tables 6.19 to 6.24 present qualitative facts related to PDS specifically for the two main food crops, namely rice and wheat. To the question of adherence to the prescribed opening time and keeping the outlet opened for stipulated number of days by the FPS shopkeepers, around 90 per cent of all category of households were satisfied with the opening time and numbers of days the shop remains opened in Delhi, Kerala and Uttarakhand. Similarly, around 80 per cent households in Maharashtra and Madhya Pradesh were satisfied with the openings of the FPS shops and number of days food was being distributed. In Jharkhand, however, 25 per cent BPL households and more than 10 per cent AAY households faced problems in drawing their entitlement because of improper opening times of the FPS shops. Similarly, around 25 per cent APL households and above 10 per cent AAY and BPL households in Madhya Pradesh and Maharashtra indicated the prescribed timings of the FPS shop as poor or very poor. Majority of the households disapproved the perception that cereals being supplied through the fair price shops were being underweighed. Less than 10 per cent households in Uttarakhand, Maharashtra and Madhya Pradesh (among all categories) were of the opinion that there was serious problem of food weighment at the FPS. In other states, around 25 per cent of AAY and BPL households in Delhi, 15 per cent APL households in Jharkhand and 30 per cent AAY and BPL households in Kerala expressed some fear of underweighment of grains at the FPS.

To a question whether the shop owners indulged in diverting food to the open market or involved in black marketing, a majority of the selected households expressed their inability to answer this question directly. A majority of them replied to this question that they could not say anything on this issue. Only 5 per cent households in Delhi, Maharashtra and Uttarakhand answered that the shop owners were very frequently or frequently indulging in diverting food to the open market. In Jharkhand, around 20 per cent households answered that shopkeepers often indulge in such activities, while another 20 per cent answered that they indulge in such activities sometimes. In Kerala, around 18 per cent households were of the view that shopkeepers divert food sometimes while same number of households in Madhya Pradesh opined that they do so very oftenly. Against these trends, an overwhelming majority (85 per cent) among the AAY and APL households in Uttarakhand pointed out that shopkeepers indulge in food diversions sometimes.

Table 6.13 Qualitative Questions Related to TPDS (Delhi)

	AAY	BPL	APL
Q1: How do you rate adherence to the prescribed time of PDS outlet w.r.t. opening of the shop?			
Very good	0.00	1.09	0.79
Good	52.91	53.65	46.46
Satisfactory	46.03	43.08	48.03
Poor	1.06	2.18	4.72
Very poor	0.00	0.00	0.00
Q2: How do you rate adherence to the prescribed days of PDS outlet w.r.t. opening of the shop?			
Very good	0.00	1.08	0.79
Good	53.44	53.72	46.46
Satisfactory	45.50	43.03	48.03
Poor	1.06	2.01	4.72
Very poor	0.00	0.00	0.00
No response	0.00	0.15	0.00
Q3: Do they underweigh grains while distributing?			
Yes	21.93	25.16	39.20
No	78.07	74.84	60.80
Q4: What is your perception about diversion of grains by ration shop owner?			
Very frequently	0.53	0.77	1.57
Frequently	4.23	3.10	11.02
Never	13.76	7.89	9.45
Sometimes	0.00	0.00	0.79
Cannot say	79.89	87.62	76.38
No response	1.59	0.62	0.79
Q5: Are you satisfied with the quality of service at the FPS?			
Yes	82.51	74.37	56.45
No	17.49	25.63	43.55
Q6: If not what were is the reasons?			
Rude behaviour of the owner	11.11	23.26	0.00
Mismanagement in the shop	88.89	76.74	87.50
Preference given to known people in supply of grains	0.00	0.00	12.50
Q7: If the quality of service/grains is bad, do you know to whom to complain?			
Yes	7.41	5.92	15.13
No	92.59	94.08	84.87
Q8: Have you ever complained during the last year?			
Yes	1.64	0.90	0.00
No	98.36	99.10	100.00
Q9: Have you observed improvement in quality of service/grains after the complaint?			
Yes	1.82	1.01	0.00
No	98.18	98.99	100.00

Table 6.14 Qualitative Questions Related to TPDS (Jharkhand)

	AAY	BPL	APL
Q1: How do you rate adherence to the prescribed time of PDS outlet w.r.t. opening of the shop?			
Very good	3.52	2.00	15.00
Good	26.63	14.62	25.00
Satisfactory	57.79	58.15	60.00
Poor	10.05	22.00	0.00
Very poor	2.01	3.23	0.00
Q2: How do you rate adherence to the prescribed days of PDS outlet w.r.t. opening of the shop?			
Very good	3.50	1.69	9.52
Good	28.00	15.95	28.57
Satisfactory	56.50	57.06	47.62
Poor	9.50	21.93	9.52
Very poor	2.00	3.37	0.00
No response	0.50	0.00	4.76
Q3: Do they underweigh grains while distributing?			
Yes	7.65	9.55	15.00
No	92.35	90.45	85.00
Q4: What is your perception about diversion of grains by ration shop owner?			
Very frequently	4.00	7.82	9.52
Frequently	14.00	15.03	14.29
Never	13.50	7.67	19.05
Sometimes	23.00	23.31	9.52
Cannot say	43.00	44.17	33.33
No response	2.50	1.99	14.29
Q5: Are you satisfied with the quality of service at the FPS?			
Yes	79.40	65.89	50.00
No	20.60	34.11	50.00
Q6: If not what is the reason?			
Rude behaviour of the owner	23.08	20.69	11.11
Mismanagement in the shop	38.46	59.48	66.67
Preference given to known people in supply of grains	38.46	19.83	22.22
Q7: If the quality of service/grains is bad, do you know to whom to complain?			
Yes	12.06	15.19	20.00
No	87.94	84.81	80.00
Q8: Have you ever complained during the last year?			
Yes	11.54	20.37	40.00
No	88.46	79.63	60.00
Q9: Have you observed improvement in quality of service/grains after the complaint?			
Yes	0.00	0.00	0.00
No	100.00	100.00	100.00

Table 6.15 **Qualitative Questions Related to TPDS (Kerala)**

	AAY	BPL	APL
Q1: How do you rate adherence to the prescribed time of PDS outlet w.r.t. opening of the shop?			
Very good	20.53	12.83	8.18
Good	18.42	16.43	27.27
Satisfactory	57.37	65.93	57.27
Poor	3.16	4.81	6.36
Very poor	0.53	0.00	0.91
Q2: How do you rate adherence to the prescribed days of PDS outlet w.r.t. opening of the shop?			
Very good	19.27	12.67	7.21
Good	25.00	17.82	23.42
Satisfactory	51.04	63.17	59.46
Poor	3.13	4.75	8.11
Very poor	0.52	0.00	0.90
No response	1.04	1.58	0.90
Q3: Do they underweigh grains while distributing?			
Yes	27.81	29.98	16.36
No	72.19	70.02	83.64
Q4: What is your perception about diversion of grains by ration shop owner?			
Very frequently	1.56	1.39	0.90
Frequently	3.65	3.96	4.50
Never	3.13	2.38	4.50
Sometimes	18.23	18.81	10.81
Cannot say	70.31	71.49	75.68
No response	3.13	1.98	3.60
Q5: Are you satisfied with the quality of service at the FPS?			
Yes	72.58	74.14	73.64
No	27.42	25.86	26.36
Q6: If not what is the reason?			
Rude behaviour of the owner	13.51	2.99	5.56
Mismanagement in the shop	67.57	65.67	66.67
Preference given to known people in supply of grains	18.92	31.34	27.78
Q7: If the quality of service/grains is bad, do you know to whom to complain?			
Yes	1.60	1.61	4.67
No	98.40	98.39	95.33
Q8: Have you ever complained during the last year?			
Yes	0.00	0.00	0.00
No	100.00	100.00	100.00
Q9: Have you observed improvement in quality of service/grains after the complaint?			
Yes	0.00	16.67	0.00
No	100.00	83.33	100.00

Table 6.16 **Qualitative Questions Related to TPDS (Madhya Pradesh)**

	AAY	BPL	APL
Q1: How do you rate adherence to the prescribed time of PDS outlet w.r.t. opening of the shop?			
Very good	1.52	0.50	
Good	13.64	12.61	16.67
Satisfactory	65.15	65.21	54.17
Poor	11.62	10.25	4.17
Very poor	8.08	11.43	25.00
Q2: How do you rate adherence to the prescribed days of PDS outlet w.r.t. opening of the shop?			
Very good	1.51	0.82	0.00
Good	22.11	23.23	15.63
Satisfactory	58.29	55.85	46.88
Poor	9.55	6.92	0.00
Very poor	8.04	11.37	18.75
No response	0.50	1.81	18.75
Q3: Do they underweigh grains while distributing?			
Yes	7.58	7.41	7.69
No	92.42	92.59	92.31
Q4: What is your perception about diversion of grains by ration shop owner?			
Very frequently	11.56	12.03	6.25
Frequently	4.02	5.11	0.00
Never	7.54	7.91	3.13
Sometimes	4.02	4.78	6.25
Cannot say	70.85	67.87	65.63
No response	2.01	2.31	18.75
Q5: Are you satisfied with the quality of service at the FPS?			
Yes	73.63	73.93	84.00
No	26.37	26.07	16.00
Q6: If not what is the reason?			
Rude behaviour of the owner	11.86	14.57	0.00
Mismanagement in the shop	64.41	63.32	60.00
Preference given to known people in supply of grains	23.73	22.11	40.00
Q7: If the quality of service/grains is bad, do you know to whom to complain?			
Yes	1.67	1.54	0.00
No	98.33	98.46	100.00
Q8: Have you ever complained during the last year?			
Yes	16.67	16.67	0.00
No	83.33	83.33	100.00
Q9: Have you observed improvement in quality of service/grains after the complaint?			
Yes	0.00	2.53	0.00
No	100.00	97.47	100.00

Table 6.17 **Qualitative Questions Related to TPDS (Maharashtra)**

	AAY	BPL	APL
Q1: How do you rate adherence to the prescribed time of PDS outlet w.r.t. opening of the shop?			
Very good	1.98	0.32	7.69
Good	36.63	31.01	38.46
Satisfactory	50.00	56.01	30.77
Poor	10.89	12.03	23.08
Very poor	0.50	0.63	0.00
Q2: How do you rate adherence to the prescribed days of PDS outlet w.r.t. opening of the shop?			
Very good	1.49	0.16	0.00
Good	36.14	31.01	38.46
Satisfactory	50.99	56.01	30.77
Poor	10.89	12.18	23.08
Very poor	0.50	0.63	0.00
No response	0.00	0.00	7.69
Q3: Do they underweigh grains while distributing?			
Yes	9.41	8.54	0.00
No	90.59	91.46	100.00
Q4: What is your perception about diversion of grains by ration shop owner?			
Very frequently	0.50	0.95	0.00
Frequently	2.48	3.64	0.00
Never	11.88	11.23	7.69
Sometimes	2.48	2.06	0.00
Cannot say	82.67	82.12	84.62
No response	0.00	0.00	7.69
Q5: Are you satisfied with the quality of service at the FPS?			
Yes	84.08	83.55	61.54
No	15.92	16.45	38.46
Q6: If not what is the reason?			
Rude behaviour of the owner	16.13	20.00	20.00
Mismanagement in the shop	58.06	59.17	80.00
Preference given to known people in supply of grains	25.81	20.83	0.00
Q7: If the quality of service/grains is bad, do you know to whom to complain?			
Yes	1.00	1.28	
No	99.00	98.72	100.00
Q8: Have you ever complained during the last year?			
Yes	0.00	0.00	0.00
No	100.00	100.00	100.00
Q9: Have you observed improvement in quality of service/grains after the complaint?			
Yes	0.00	0.00	0.00
No	100.00	100.00	100.00

Table 6.18 Qualitative Questions Related to TPDS (Uttarakhand)

	AAY	BPL	APL
Q1: How do you rate adherence to the prescribed time of PDS outlet w.r.t. opening of the shop?			
Very good	0.00	0.73	2.08
Good	28.06	23.05	10.42
Satisfactory	70.92	74.05	87.50
Poor	1.02	1.63	0.00
Very poor	0.00	0.54	0.00
Q2: How do you rate adherence to the prescribed days of PDS outlet w.r.t. opening of the shop?			
Very good	1.02	1.45	0.00
Good	25.00	20.15	12.50
Satisfactory	72.45	75.68	87.50
Poor	1.02	1.81	0.00
Very poor	0.00	0.36	0.00
No response	0.51	0.54	0.00
Q3: Do they underweigh grains while distributing?			
Yes	3.09	2.79	2.22
No	96.91	97.21	97.78
Q4: What is your perception about diversion of grains by ration shop owner?			
Very frequently	0.00	1.27	0.00
Frequently	4.08	4.54	8.33
Never	11.22	6.72	2.08
Sometimes	84.69	0.36	83.33
Cannot say	0.00	86.39	0.00
No response	0.00	0.73	6.25
Q5: Are you satisfied with the quality of service at the FPS?			
Yes	98.95	95.12	97.83
No	1.05	4.88	2.17
Q6: If not what is the reason?			
Rude behaviour of the owner	12.50	28.13	0.00
Mismanagement in the shop	87.50	53.13	0.00
Preference given to known people in supply of grains	0.00	18.75	100.00
Q7: If the quality of service/grains is bad, do you know to whom to complain?			
Yes	2.63	2.98	4.44
No	97.37	97.02	95.56
Q8: Have you ever complained during the last year?			
Yes	0.00	3.57	0.00
No	100.00	96.43	100.00
Q9: Have you observed improvement in quality of service/grains after the complaint?			
Yes	0.00	2.63	0.00
No	100.00	97.37	100.00

Table 6.19 Qualitative Questions Related to TPDS for Rice and Wheat (Delhi)

	AAY	BPL	APL	AAY	BPL	APL
Q1: Is the local variety of grains considerably different from the PDS variety?						
	Rice			*Wheat*		
Yes	20.21	17.45	33.60	20.21	18.22	33.87
No	79.79	82.55	66.40	79.79	81.78	66.13
Q2: Do you strongly prefer the local variety of grains to the PDS variety?						
	Rice			*Wheat*		
Yes	7.61	9.92	24.00	7.57	9.92	24.00
No	92.39	90.08	76.00	92.43	90.08	76.00
Q3: Do they underweigh grains while distributing?						
	Rice			*Wheat*		
Yes	1.59	2.50	2.38	1.59	2.94	2.36
No	98.41	97.50	97.62	98.41	96.75	96.85
					0.31	0.79
Q4: If 'Yes' to above, what is the proportion?						
	Rice			*Wheat*		
<5%	5.26	3.45	0.00	5.26	3.28	0.00
5% to 10%	89.47	94.83	100.00	89.47	95.08	100.00
10% to 15%	5.26	1.72	0.00	5.26	1.64	0.00
15% to 20%	0.00	0.00	0.00	0.00	0.00	0.00
>20%	0.00	0.00	0.00	0.00	0.00	0.00
No response	0.00	0.00	0.00	0.00	0.00	0.00
Q5: Are you satisfied with the quality of grains?						
	Rice			*Wheat*		
Yes	98.41	98.14	96.06	97.88	99.07	96.06
No	0.53	0.77	3.15	1.06	0.77	3.15
No response	1.06	1.08	0.79	1.06	0.15	0.79
Q6: If 'No' to above, how is the quality?						
	Rice			*Wheat*		
Presence of impurities	0.53	0.77	0.79	0.53	0.77	0.79
Rotten	1.59	2.94	2.36	1.59	2.94	2.36
Inferior quality	0.00	0.00	0.00	0.00	0.00	0.00
Broken grains	0.00	0.00	0.00	0.00	0.00	0.00
Insect infested supply	0.00	0.15	0.00	0.00	0.15	0.00
Colour is not good	0.00	0.00	0.00	0.00	0.00	0.00
Taste is not good	0.00	0.15	0.00	0.00	0.15	0.00
Foul smell	0.00	0.00	0.00	0.00	0.00	0.00
Moisture content is more	0.00	0.00	0.00	0.00	0.00	0.00
No response	97.88	95.98	96.85	97.88	95.98	96.85
Q7: How do you rate the performance of TPDS with respect to supply of grains during times of distress?						
	Rice			*Wheat*		
Very good	0.53	1.24	1.60	0.53	1.24	1.60
Good	84.04	81.99	77.60	83.96	82.02	77.60
Satisfactory	15.43	16.61	16.00	15.51	16.59	16.00
Poor	-	0.16	4.80	-	0.16	4.80

Table 6.20 **Qualitative Questions Related to TPDS for Rice and Wheat (Jharkhand)**

	AAY	BPL	APL	AAY	BPL	APL
Q1: Is the local variety of grains considerably different from the PDS variety?						
	Rice			*Wheat*		
Yes	38.00	37.02	66.67	37.50	35.02	55.56
No	62.00	62.98	33.33	62.50	64.98	44.44
Q2: Do you strongly prefer the local variety of grains to the PDS variety?						
	Rice			*Wheat*		
Yes	27.50	31.90	61.11	26.00	30.09	55.56
No	72.50	68.10	38.89	74.00	69.91	44.44
Q3: Do they underweigh grains while distributing?						
	Rice			*Wheat*		
Yes	5.53	6.61	16.67	5.53	6.92	16.67
No	94.47	93.39	83.33	94.47	93.08	83.33
No response						
Q4: If 'Yes' to above, what is the proportion?						
	Rice			*Wheat*		
<5%	23.08	10.64	0.00	23.08	10.20	0.00
5% to 10%	46.15	21.28	33.33	46.15	24.49	33.33
10% to 15%	23.08	59.57	66.67	23.08	57.14	66.67
15% to 20%	7.69	2.13	0.00	7.69	2.04	0.00
>20%	0.00	6.38	0.00	0.00	6.12	0.00
No response	0.00	0.00	0.00	0.00	0.00	0.00
Q5: Are you satisfied with the quality of grains?						
	Rice			*Wheat*		
Yes	88.38	81.36	50.00	88.89	82.28	61.11
No	11.62	18.64	50.00	11.11	17.72	38.89
Q6: If 'No' to above, how is the quality?						
	Rice			*Wheat*		
Presence of impurities	24.00	32.52	37.50	25.00	27.19	16.67
Rotten	8.00	17.07	-	8.33	16.67	16.67
Inferior quality	56.00	43.09	62.50	58.33	48.25	66.67
Broken grains	12.00	3.25	-	4.17	1.75	-
Insect infested supply	-	1.63	-	-	1.75	-
Colour is not good	-	0.81	-	4.17	4.39	-
Taste is not good	-	0.81	-	-	-	-
Foul smell	-	0.00	-	-	-	-
Moisture content is more	-	0.81	-	-	-	-
Q7: How do you rate the performance of TPDS with respect to supply of grains during times of distress?						
	Rice			*Wheat*		
Very good	4.00	3.83	16.67	4.02	3.69	16.67
Good	25.50	18.40	33.33	25.13	18.43	33.33
Satisfactory	57.50	54.75	38.89	57.79	54.99	38.89
Poor	13.00	18.71	11.11	13.07	18.59	11.11
Very poor	-	4.29	-	-	4.30	-

Table 6.21 **Qualitative Questions Related to TPDS for Rice and Wheat (Kerala)**

	AAY	BPL	APL	AAY	BPL	APL
Q1: Is the local variety of grains considerably different from the PDS variety?						
	Rice			*Wheat*		
Yes	97.88	97.20	92.38	93.75	97.72	86.15
No	2.12	2.80	7.62	6.25	2.28	13.85
Q2: Do you strongly prefer the local variety of grains to the PDS variety?						
	Rice			*Wheat*		
Yes	97.35	99.00	92.38	100.00	98.98	86.36
No	2.65	1.00	7.62	0.00	1.02	13.64
Q3: Do they underweigh grains while distributing?						
	Rice			*Wheat*		
Yes	31.22	30.46	22.86	46.15	25.63	16.67
No	68.78	69.54	77.14	53.85	74.37	83.33
Q4: If 'Yes' to above, what is the proportion?						
	Rice			*Wheat*		
<5%	10.53	14.29	11.76	0.00	6.25	16.67
5% to 10%	73.68	71.43	64.71	50.00	75.00	66.67
10% to 15%	13.16	12.70	23.53	0.00	18.75	16.67
15% to 20%	0.00	0.00	0.00	0.00	0.00	0.00
>20%	2.63	1.59	0.00	50.00	0.00	0.00
No response	0.00	0.00	0.00	0.00	0.00	0.00
Q5: Are you satisfied with the quality of grains?						
	Rice			*Wheat*		
Yes	53.97	60.60	61.90	62.50	68.78	72.31
No	46.03	39.40	38.10	37.50	31.22	27.69
Q6: If 'No' to above, how is the quality?						
	Rice			*Wheat*		
Presence of impurities	31.82	27.69	23.68	14.29	13.68	5.88
Rotten	6.82	4.10	2.63	-	4.27	-
Inferior quality	4.55	1.54	-	-	1.71	-
Broken grains	35.23	44.10	50.00	14.29	47.86	58.82
Insect infested supply	-	0.51	-	-	-	-
Colour is not good	5.68	9.23	5.26	-	16.24	29.41
Taste is not good	12.50	9.74	13.16	28.57	9.40	-
Foul smell	2.27	1.03	-	-	1.71	-
Moisture content is more	1.14	2.05	5.26	42.86	5.13	5.88
Q7: How do you rate the performance of TPDS with respect to supply of grains during times of distress?						
	Rice			*Wheat*		
Very good	7.94	4.40	5.71	25.00	5.33	7.58
Good	26.98	28.40	26.67	31.25	29.44	31.82
Satisfactory	58.73	61.80	61.90	43.75	58.88	53.03
Poor	6.35	4.80	5.71	-	5.58	7.58
Very poor	-	0.60	-	-	0.76	-

Table 6.22 Qualitative Questions Related to TPDS for Rice and Wheat (Madhya Pradesh)

	AAY	BPL	APL	AAY	BPL	APL
Q1: Is the local variety of grains considerably different from the PDS variety?						
	Rice			*Wheat*		
Yes	43.08	43.55	33.33	48.73	45.97	33.33
No	56.92	56.45	66.67	51.27	54.03	66.67
Q2: Do you strongly prefer the local variety of grains to the PDS variety?						
	Rice			*Wheat*		
Yes	43.01	44.37	29.17	41.24	39.43	25.00
No	56.99	55.63	70.83	58.76	60.57	75.00
Q3: Do they underweigh grains while distributing?						
	Rice			*Wheat*		
Yes	6.12	6.38	0.00	6.70	6.83	0.00
No	93.88	93.62	100.00	93.30	93.17	100.00
Q4: If 'Yes' to above, what is the proportion?						
	Rice			*Wheat*		
<5%	15.38	15.00	0.00	61.29	66.06	100.00
5% to 10%	15.38	32.50	0.00	9.68	14.68	0.00
10% to 15%	61.54	50.00	0.00	25.81	18.35	0.00
15% to 20%	7.69	0.00	0.00	3.23	0.00	0.00
>20%	0.00	2.50	0.00	0.00	0.92	0.00
No response	0.00	0.00	100.00	0.00	0.00	0.00
Q5: Are you satisfied with the quality of grains?						
	Rice			*Wheat*		
Yes	85.64	88.09	100.00	76.27	81.51	100.00
No	14.36	11.91	-	23.73	18.30	-
No response					0.19	-
Q6: If 'No' to above, how is the quality?						
	Rice			*Wheat*		
Presence of impurities	37.93	50.70	-	44.26	42.77	100.00
Rotten	27.59	19.72	-	39.34	43.98	-
Inferior quality	6.90	1.41	-	3.28	0.60	-
Broken grains	3.45	-	-	1.64	0.60	-
Insect infested supply	-	-	-	-	-	-
Colour is not good	20.69	16.90	-	9.84	6.02	-
Taste is not good	3.45	7.04	-	1.64	4.22	-
Foul smell	-	1.41	-	-	0.60	-
Moisture content is more	-	2.82	-	-	1.20	-
No response	-	-	100.00	-	-	-
Q3: How do you rate the performance of TPDS with respect to supply of grains during times of distress?						
	Rice			*Wheat*		
Very good	-	-	-	-	-	-
Good	11.28	14.92	8.33	11.80	16.96	8.70
Satisfactory	45.13	42.03	54.17	39.89	39.69	52.17
Poor	18.97	20.51	-	20.79	21.39	-
Very poor	24.62	22.54	37.50	27.53	21.97	39.13
No response	-	0.22	-	-	0.66	-

Table 6.23 Qualitative Questions Related to TPDS for Rice and Wheat (Maharashtra)

	AAY	BPL	APL	AAY	BPL	APL
Q1: Is the local variety of grains considerably different from the PDS variety?						
	Rice			*Wheat*		
Yes	45.77	47.78	63.64	53.00	59.90	72.73
No	54.23	52.22	36.36	47.00	40.10	27.27
Q2: Do you strongly prefer the local variety of grains to the PDS variety?						
	Rice			*Wheat*		
Yes	45.77	46.83	63.64	53.77	58.48	72.73
No	54.23	53.17	36.36	46.23	41.52	27.27
Q3: Do they underweigh grains while distributing?						
	Rice			*Wheat*		
Yes	2.97	3.16	0.00	2.97	3.32	8.33
No	97.03	96.84	84.62	97.03	96.52	91.67
No response			15.38		0.16	
Q4: If 'Yes' to above, what is the proportion?						
	Rice			*Wheat*		
<5%	1.98	1.58	0.00	1.99	1.74	0.00
5% to 10%	0.99	1.74	0.00	1.00	1.74	0.00
10% to 15%	0.00	0.16	0.00	0.00	0.16	0.00
15% to 20%	0.00	0.00	0.00	0.00	0.00	0.00
>20%	0.00	0.00	0.00	0.00	0.00	0.00
No response	97.03	96.52	100.00	97.01	96.35	100.00
Q5: Are you satisfied with the quality of grains?						
	Rice			*Wheat*		
Yes	83.17	82.44	50.00	72.77	68.83	41.67
No	16.34	17.41	41.67	26.73	30.70	50.00
No response	0.50	0.16	8.33	0.50	0.47	8.33
Q6: If 'No' to above, how is the quality?						
	Rice			*Wheat*		
Presence of impurities	5.45	4.91	33.33	9.41	5.54	33.33
Rotten	2.48	1.42	-	2.48	1.58	-
Inferior quality	-	0.79	-	0.50	1.11	-
Broken grains	4.95	5.70	8.33	4.95	5.70	8.33
Insect infested supply	-	0.63	-	-	0.63	-
Colour is not good	4.46	2.69	-	11.39	13.45	-
Taste is not good	-	2.06	-	1.49	3.64	-
Foul smell	-	-	-	-	-	-
Moisture content is more	-	-	-	-	-	-
No response	81.68	81.80	58.33	69.80	68.35	58.33
Q3: How do you rate the performance of TPDS with respect to supply of grains during times of distress?						
	Rice			*Wheat*		
Very good	6.44	4.11	9.09	6.47	4.12	9.09
Good	41.09	36.23	18.18	40.80	36.29	18.18
Satisfactory	35.64	34.97	36.36	35.82	34.87	36.36
Poor	8.42	14.24	9.09	8.46	14.26	9.09
Very poor	8.42	10.44	27.27	8.46	10.46	27.27

Table 6.24 Qualitative Questions Related to TPDS for Rice and Wheat (Uttarakhand)

	AAY	BPL	APL	AAY	BPL	APL
Q1: Is the local variety of grains considerably different from the PDS variety?						
	Rice			*Wheat*		
Yes	70.10	74.44	95.45	69.43	73.04	95.45
No	29.90	25.56	4.55	30.57	26.96	4.55
Q2: Do you strongly prefer the local variety of grains to the PDS variety?						
	Rice			*Wheat*		
Yes	71.50	76.21	97.67	70.53	74.70	97.62
No	28.50	23.79	2.33	29.47	25.30	2.38
Q3: Do they underweigh grains while distributing?						
	Rice			*Wheat*		
Yes	2.04	1.28	2.27	2.07	1.39	2.22
No	97.96	98.72	97.73	97.93	98.61	97.78
Q4: If 'Yes' to above, what is the proportion?						
	Rice			*Wheat*		
<5%	16.67	6.25	0.00	23.08	6.25	0.00
5% to 10%	83.33	93.75	100.00	76.92	93.75	100.00
10% to 15%	0.00	0.00	0.00	0.00	-	0.00
15% to 20%	0.00	0.00	0.00	0.00	0.00	0.00
>20%	0.00	0.00	0.00	0.00	0.00	0.00
No response	0.00	0.00	0.00	0.00	0.00	0.00
Q5: Are you satisfied with the quality of grains?						
	Rice			*Wheat*		
Yes	98.45	96.88	100.00	98.96	97.81	100.00
No	1.55	3.12	-	1.04	2.19	-
Q6: If 'No' to above, how is the quality?						
	Rice			*Wheat*		
Presence of impurities	75.00	36.84	0.00	75.00	43.75	0.00
Rotten	25.00	31.58	0.00	25.00	37.50	0.00
Inferior quality	0.00	5.26	0.00	0.00	6.25	0.00
Broken grains	0.00	15.79	0.00	0.00	0.00	0.00
Insect infested supply	0.00	5.26	0.00	0.00	0.00	0.00
Colour is not good	0.00	5.26	0.00	0.00	0.00	0.00
Taste is not good	0.00	0.00	0.00	0.00	6.25	0.00
Foul smell	0.00	0.00	0.00	0.00	0.00	0.00
Moisture content is more	0.00	0.00	0.00	0.00	6.25	0.00
No response	0.00	0.00	100.00	0.00	0.00	100.00
Q3: How do you rate the performance of TPDS with respect to supply of grains during times of distress?						
	Rice			*Wheat*		
Very good	1.02	0.55	4.44	1.03	0.60	4.44
Good	53.06	52.38	35.56	52.06	49.80	35.56
Satisfactory	44.39	42.86	57.78	45.36	45.02	57.78
Poor	1.02	4.21	2.22	1.03	4.58	2.22
Very poor	0.51	0.00	0.00	0.52	0.00	0.00

Were the consumers satisfied with the quality of services offered at the FPS, more than 70 per cent households among AAY and BPL and more than 50 per cent among APL replied yes in all the six selected states. To those households who were not satisfied, we asked why were they not satisfied? A majority of dissatisfied households in Delhi, Kerala, Madhya Pradesh, Maharashtra and Uttarakhand were of the opinion that there was mismanagement at the fair price shops. In Jharkhand, dissatisfied households were equally divided on the reasons namely, rude behaviour, mismanagement and preference given to the known people by the shop owners. Among the APL households, around 12 per cent in Delhi, 22 per cent in Jharkhand, 28 per cent in Kerala, 40 per cent in Madhya Pradesh and all the dissatisfied households in Uttarakhand pointed out that they were being discriminated as shop owners were giving preference to their own known people. These views are important specifically for the APL households as among this section of people, shop owners had discretion while distributing food whereas the entitled food for the other two categories was fully targeted and shop owners had less choice during distribution. In almost all the states, majority of the households were not knowing whom to complain if the quality of grains offered from PDS was really bad. Above 80 per cent households in the selected states responded that they did not know how and where to complain. Even those who knew where to complain, around 80 to 90 per cent of them never complained on getting a bad quality during the last one year in all the states without any exception. Those 10 per cent households who indicated that they did complain for the same, even they argued that they did not observe any improvement in the quality and they were not knowing how to get their problem redressed.

On the specific questions of quality and variety of wheat and rice distributed through PDS, a majority of households in Delhi, Jharkhand and Madhya Pradesh responded that there was no significant difference between the PDS and local varieties. In Kerala and Uttarakhand, a majority of households stated that PDS rice and wheat varieties were considerably different from the local varieties available. Similarly, in Maharashtra, the households indicated that wheat variety from the PDS was different from the market. Except Kerala and Uttarakhand, households in all other states indicated that they did not have any strong preference for local varieties and they could consume PDS varieties of wheat and rice. Only in Kerala and Uttarakhand, selected people preferred local variety over the PDS grains. A related question was posed whether the households liked the quality of the grains supplied and if not, what was the lacuna in the grains supplied through PDS. Above 95 per cent households (all categories) were satisfied with the quality of grains supplied in Delhi and Uttarakhand. In Maharashtra, above 70 per cent households among AAY and BPL and above 40 per cent households among APL were satisfied with the grain quality. In Madhya Pradesh, more than 70 per cent households were okay with the quality of grains across all the categories. In Kerala, 30 to 40 per cent households (all categories) and 40 per cent APL households in Jharkhand were dissatisfied with the quality of grains supplied through the PDS. Those who were not satisfied, a majority of them in Kerala reasoned that there were impurities in the grain and the grain supplied were broken. Another significant number indicated that taste of the grains was not good. In Jharkhand, more than 50 per cent of the dissatisfied households indicated inferior quality of the grains and around 25 per cent pointed out presence of impurities in the grains supplied. In Madhya Pradesh, dissatisfied households indicated presence of impurities, colour of the grains not good, rotten grains and inferior quality of the grains as the main reasons for their outcries. The other problems indicated by the household in the selected states was, foul smell, high moisture content in the grains, etc.

On the question of underweighment of the grains, we tried to find out what was the extent of such activities. A majority of those households who answered that underweighment was happening were of the opinion that it was 5 to 10 per cent in all states, except Madhya Pradesh where the extent was indicated up to 15 per cent. Finally, to our question of how the households rate the performance of TPDS during the periods of distress, an overwhelming majority (around 80 per cent) in Delhi indicated it as good while less than 5 per cent rated it as poor. In Jharkhand, around 80 per cent were of the opinion that it was good or satisfactory while 20 per cent indicated it either poor or very poor. In Kerala, the proportion of households who rated it very good, good or satisfactory exceeded 90 per cent while less than 10 per cent indicated it as poor. In Madhya Pradesh, those who rated it poor or very poor averaged around 40 to 45 per cent while equal number of them indicated it as satisfactory. In Maharashtra, the households answering poor or very poor performance averaged around 20 to 25 per cent while more than 30 per cent rated it as good. Last and the least, Uttarakhand fared far better like in the case of Delhi, where only less than 5 per cent rated it poor or very poor while more than 50 per cent were of the view that performance of PDS during distress was good and another 40 per cent indicated it as satisfactory.

6.4 Criterion Fixed for Identification of BPL and AAY Families

For the identification of BPL and AAY families, State Governments follow the guidelines issued by the Ministry of Rural Development, Government of India. Ministry of Rural Development conducts a below poverty line (BPL) Census at the beginning of each Five Year Plan. The basic objective of this census is to identify the households living below the poverty line who could be assisted under various anti-poverty programmes implemented by the Ministry. With a view to improving the methodology for identification of BPL households in the BPL Census for the 10th Five Year Plan (2002-03 to 2006-07), the Ministry of Rural Development had constituted an Expert Group, comprising administrators, academicians, planners and representatives of the states of Assam, Kerala, Orissa, Rajasthan and Uttar Pradesh. The Expert Group made a number of important recommendations for improvement in the design and content of the BPL Census to be conducted for the 10th Five Plan period. The new criterion proposed to adopt a normative approach for identification of the rural poor by introducing a 'score-based ranking' based on relative deprivations revealed by certain socio-economic indicators in contrast to the 'income approach' adopted in BPL Census, 1992 and 'expenditure approach' adopted in 1997. In the new approach, 13 cardinal indicators, *viz.*: (i) size group of operational holdings, (ii) type of house, (iii) availability of normal clothing, (iv) food security, (v) sanitation, (vi) ownership of consumer durable, (vii) literacy status, (viii) status in labour force (ix) means of livelihood, (x) status of children, (xi) type of indebtedness, (xii) reasons for migration from household, (xiii) preference for assistance for various government programmes were identified for which scores were assigned on a relative scale. However, in addition to the above cardinal indicators, some non-scorable variables were also used for categorisation of the households into 'very poor', 'poor', 'not-so-poor' and 'non-poor'. The State Governments were given flexibility to decide the cut-off score for identifying and sub-categorisation of the households into various groups. The cut-off score could be uniform or could be varying within a state depending on the ground realities.

For classifying people into AAY, BPL and APL among our selected states, the State Governments were following different criterion in different states. Mostly it was the cut-off income limit that was being followed for classifying people below and above poverty line. In addition to income criterion, some State Governments also had few additional exclusion criteria like families having assets such as tractors, tillers, four or two wheelers, colour TV, telephone, etc. The identification criterion followed by the State Governments in our selected states are given in Table 6.25.

The beneficiaries under the Schemes of below poverty line, Antyodaya Anna Yojana and Annapurna Yojana in Delhi are finalised by the Circle Advisory Committee consisting of area MLA as chairman, members of Municipal Corporation, Food and Supplies Officer of the concerned Circle and seven members nominated by the chairman. The entire population of National Capital Territory of Delhi has been divided into the following categories for the purpose of proper supply and distribution of food and other essentials under the TPDS system. In Maharashtra, to keep the affluent families away from PDS food and to curb diversion of food grains and instead provide more food grains to the needy families, the State Government introduced tricoloured ration card scheme w.e.f., 1st May 1999. While yellow ration card is meant for the below poverty households and is issued to the families having annual income upto Rs. 15000, saffron card is issued to households having annual income between Rs. 15001 to one lakh and white ration card is issued to the families having an annual income of Rs. 1 lakh and above. Any member of the family possessing a four wheeler or the family aggregately holding more than 4 hectares irrigated land are issued a white ration card. Identification of below poverty households in Kerala, Madhya Pradesh and Uttarakhand is done on the basis of BPL survey 2002. In Jharkhand, the criterion for the identification is adopted from its erstwhile state of Bihar.

The income norms fixed by the State Governments (Table 6.25) were generally less than the estimates obtained from the Planning Commission based on the 61st Round National Sample Survey as given in Table 6.26. However, in addition to the cut-off income in few states there were some additional indicators, like in Maharashtra, along with Rs. 15000 annual income, a household should not own a telephone or a four wheeler and should have more than a specified irrigated/unirrigated land. Therefore, while making comparison of official poverty line with our own estimates, we compare only the Planning Commission cut-off with our observed income/expenditure estimates. The income limit set by the Planning Commission was based on the actual expenditure incurred by a household, which was worked out using the National Sample Survey Data (61st Round). Planning Commission have used this income to work out the percentage of poor existing in different states during the period

2. These income estimates are updated for the next year by the Planning Commission using the price index as a deflator. However, the Planning Commission's current estimates are for the year 2004-05. To make the official cut-off comparable with our estimates, we have updated the Planning Commission cut-off by using consumer price index for agricultural labourers for the rural areas and consumer price index for the industrial workers for the urban areas. As our estimates belong to the calendar year 2006, we have updated the official figures for the year 2006-07.

2004-05.[2] Therefore, for the sake of comparison, henceforth, we will use the Planning Commission cut-off figures. It is to be pointed out here that our sample consists of 80 per cent of rural households and 20 per cent of urban households. To make the official figures comparable with our observed income, we have updated the Planning Commission cut-off for rural and urban areas up to 2006-07. Further, we have calculated a weighted average of the official cut-off income for the year 2006-07.[3]

Table 6.25 Criterion Adopted by the State Governments for BPL and AAY Cardholders

States	Criteria
Delhi	*Above Poverty Line:* Families having total family income above Rs. 24200 per annum are given APL cards. A total of 22 lakh such families are covered under the TPDS scheme in Delhi.
	Below Poverty Line: Families having total family income below Rs. 24200 have been identified under this category. Under this scheme, a total of 3.82 lakh families are covered.[4]
	Antyodaya *Anna Yojana (AAY):* Households with disabled adult and no assured means of subsistence, landless labours, marginal farmers, artisans, craft man, widows, terminally ill person, etc.
Jharkhand	*Below Poverty Line:* Annual income should be less than Rs. 20000 (with the new circular while the previous circular of 1997 being Rs. 11500). Besides, the families should not own any vehicle, etc. These criterion are based on erstwhile Bihar, while after formation of Jharkhand, the State Government followed the same old criterion.
Kerala	As per Rural Development Department. List provided by *gram panchayats*.
Madhya Pradesh	*Below Poverty Line:* BPL Census 2002 based on a 'score-based ranking' of each household with 13 scorable indicators indicating their quality of life based on both economic and social indicators. Those families whose income level is below poverty line as per Indian government norms. The final authority rests with Rural Development Department and elected members of the village council in rural areas and local administrative department in the urban areas.
	Antyodaya Anna Yojana (AAY): Those families whose income level is nil or negligible (Indian government norms); Most of the cases widow, deprived, older aged, divorcee, separated, etc., should be preferred for the AAY category. Families from the bottom list of BPL should be chosen for issuing an AAY card.
Maharashtra	*Below Poverty Line:* Families having annual income up to Rs. 15000. None of the members in the family should be a doctor or lawyer or architect or chartered accountant. None of the members in the family should be professional tax payer, sales tax payer or income tax payer or eligible to pay such tax. The family should not possess residential telephone. The family should not possess four wheeler vehicle. All the persons in the family should not hold total two hectare rainfed or one hectare semi-irrigated or half hectare irrigated (double in drought affected *talukas*) land.
	Antyodaya Anna Yojana (AAY): The poorest of the poor households from the BPL list are entitled for the AAY card.
Uttarakhand	*Below Poverty Line:* The income limit fixed for the BPL cut out is Rs. 9000 only. This criteria was fixed by the Uttar Pradesh government. However, after formation of Uttarakhand, the new State Government adopted the same criterion. In the recent years, the State Government has conducted a BPL Survey. However, identification of below and above poverty households based on BPL survey was still under process at the time of our field survey. Therefore, it is difficult to say that identification of the poor people was based on cut-out income or based on the cardinal indicators of the BPL survey.
	Antyodaya Anna Yojana (AAY): The requisite number should be chosen from the BPL list as those families who are the poorest in the list. The concerned authorities are desired to choose these families from the bottom of the BPL list.

comparing our observed income for BPL with that of the weighted average of Planning Commission estimates (updated for the year 2006-07), it is seen from Figure 6.1 that our observed household income was above the official cut-off income in the well-off states namely, Delhi and Kerala. The observed figures were close to the official cut-off for the other better-off state namely, Maharashtra. In comparatively poor states, *viz.*, Madhya Pradesh, Jharkhand and Uttarakhand, our observed income was much less than the official cut-off. However, it is notable that our survey income is the average income of all the selected BPL households in each state. The actual distribution of BPL income will lie just above or below this income. On the other hand, the Planning Commission income belonged to the cut-off income that provides the upper limit for the poverty line. Those households who are just below or equal to this income, they would fall in the BPL list. In the former three states, even our estimated average income for BPL was above or equal to the official cut-off income for poverty. To know how many households were truly above or below poverty compared to the official estimates, we would have to look at the actual distribution of

3. The weighted average (Planning Commission) of the cut-off income is calculated by providing 80 per cent weight for the rural areas and 20 per cent for the urban areas.

4. As on 13/11/2007, Food Supply and Consumer Affairs Department, Government of National Capital Territory, Delhi.

income among our selected households, the analysis that is done in the next section. However, from this comparison it becomes clear that the identification process followed by the states had certain flaws in their mechanism.

Table 6.26 Comparison between Official Income and our Observed Income (Rs. per Household per Annum)

State	Cut-off as per Planning Commission's Norms (Updated for the year 2006-07)			Average Income as Observed by our Survey Data: Based on Annual Estimates		Average Income as Observed by our Survey Data: Based on Monthly Estimates	
	Rural	Urban	Weighted Average*	AAY	BPL	AAY	BPL
Delhi	30353	45332	33349	28376	37835	28038	35516
Jharkhand	28887	33565	29823	15586	17893	21317	22362
Kerala	26553	35572	28356	43504	47114	46533	48005
Madhya Pradesh	25558	43965	29239	12614	16144	20644	23811
Maharashtra	25374	49618	30223	20393	28874	22245	29649
Uttarakhand	36521	48867	38990	17451	27581	23425	30971

Note: 1. The Planning Commission (2004-05) estimates are based on NSS 61st Round data for expenditure class-wise distribution of persons (based on URP-consumption, that is, consumption data collected from 30-day recall period for all items).

2. The Planning Commission poverty line is given in terms of per capita monthly income. The household income estimates are calculated using the household size data as given in 'Census of India 2001, Analytical Report on Housing Amenities', Office of the Registrar General and Census Commissioner, New Delhi, India.

3. The latest Planning Commission Poverty Line estimates are available for the year 2004-05. We have updated the Planning Commission cut-off using consumer price index for agricultural labourers for the rural cut-off and consumer price index for industrial workers for the urban cut-off.

4. * As our sample is drawn with 80 per cent weight for the rural areas and 20 per cent for the urban, the same weight is used to work out the poverty line for the sake of comparison.

Figure 6.1 Comparison of Official Cut-off with our Observed Household Income for Below Poverty

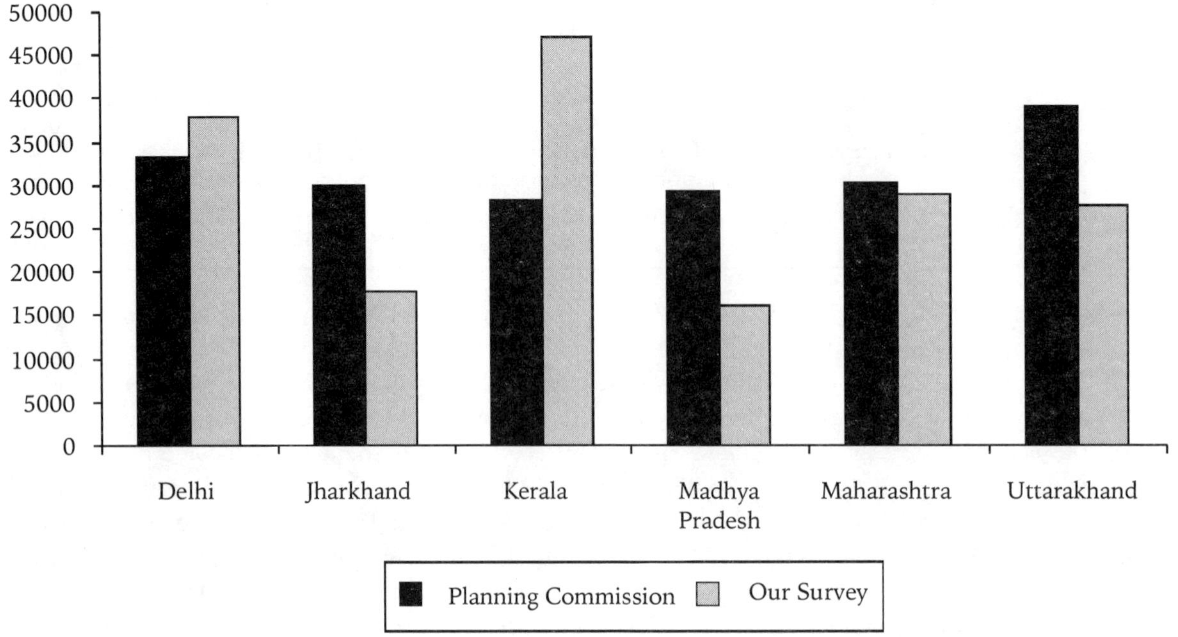

6.5 Identification Problems—Errors of Targeting[5]

Cornia and Stewart (1993) in their pioneer research work on principles of targeting pointed out two errors of targeting namely, errors of omission of the poor from the scheme (exclusion error) and errors of inclusion of the non-poor (inclusion error). In statistical analysis, these two types of errors correspond to Type I and Type II errors. In terms of efficiency of the targeting mechanism, exclusion error refers to a situation where scheme fails to reach the target population. Cornia and Stewart describe this as an F-mistake indicating a failure in the prime objective of the intervention. The inclusion error refers to a situation where intervention reaches to the non-target population. This they called as E-mistake indicating excessive coverage. The measurement of the two errors of targeting is important to understand whether and to what extent the benefits of TPDS are reaching the target group.

Table 6.27 Identification Matrix: E and F-Mistakes

	Poor	Non-Poor	Total
All covered by subsidy scheme	P^c	N^c(E-mistake, Inclusion error)	M^c
All non-covered by subsidy scheme	P^{nc}(F-mistake, Exclusion error)	N^{nc}	M^{nc}
Total	P	N	M

F-mistake consists of exclusion of poor and is represented by P^{nc}. Dividing these numbers by the target population (P^{nc}/P) gives us the extent of F-mistake, which is a good measure of how far a scheme is failing in its primary intention to reach the target group. E-mistake, on the other hand, consists of non-poor covered and is represented by N^c. Dividing these numbers by the non-target population (N^c/N) gives us the extent of E-mistake, which also indicates the extra cost of the excess coverage.

In our Phase I report, we presented incidences of excess card issued/unidentified families as well as inclusion/exclusion errors among all the states and at the all India level, using data from various secondary sources. In order to avoid repetition, we reproduce the results on incidence of excess cards, unidentified families and inclusion/exclusion errors only among our six selected states in Tables 6.28 and 6.29. The number of excess cards issued in our selected states were highest around 12 lakh in Madhya Pradesh, 10 lakh in Maharashtra and around 5 lakh in Uttarakhand. In the other three states, number of cards issued were less than that of existing families. The extent of unidentified families was highest around 25 lakh in Jharkhand and 4 lakh in Delhi. In the case of identification errors, excessive targeting or inclusion error (E) was much higher than the exclusion error or failure of targeting the poor (F). A very high amount of exclusion error (poor getting left out) was observed only in Uttarakhand (28 per cent) among our selected states. The inclusion of non-poor in the subsidised food was a serious problem and it was observed up to 18 per cent in Kerala and 5 to 7 per cent in Maharashtra, Jharkhand and Madhya Pradesh.

6.6 Authenticity of Identification and Diversion of PDS Food

In order to check the authenticity of a particular category card held by a household, we have to look into the distribution of observed income and expenditure per capita of the same household. We compare the per capita income and expenditure of the selected AAY, BPL and APL households with the Planning Commission's cut-off expenditure criterion to validate whether the card they hold is true or false. In other words, if we re-designate the households as below or above poverty following the Planning Commission cut-off, then how many households would stand faulty in their present category. Table 6.30 provides such estimates for all the six selected states. However, it was not possible to check AAY identification, i.e., how many truly lied in the class of AAY and how many of them should have been in the BPL class, as there was no criterion fixed for that class neither by the Planning Commission nor by Central or any State Government. The only criterion for selecting AAY household was that they should come from the lowest income group among the BPL household list.

5. In our evaluation of Phase I Report, we have discussed the details of the two types of errors based on Cornia and Stewart (1993). In the present analysis, we only provide the definition of inclusion and exclusion errors. For details on error of targeting, refer to our Phase I report on PDS.

Table 6.28 Number of Excess Cards Issued and the Number of Unidentified Households (Status as on 29.09.2006)

State/UT	AAY Cards Issued[1] (Lakhs)	BPL Cards Issued[1] (Lakhs)	APL Cards Issued[1] (Lakhs)	Total Cards Issued (Lakhs)	Projected No. of HH in 2006[2] (Lakhs)	Excess Cards Issed (Lakhs)	Unindentified HH (Lakhs)
Delhi	0.56	3.82	21.96	26.34	30.97		4.63
Jharkhand	7.27	16.68	5.15	29.10	54.01		24.91
Kerala	5.96	14.91	47.52	68.39	68.99		0.60
Madhya Pradesh	15.64	36.4	82.27	134.31	121.73	12.58	
Maharashtra	19.84	53.15	148.34	221.33	211.19	10.14	
Uttarakhand	1.51	3.47	17.66	22.64	17.40	5.24	

Source: 1. Govt. of India, Ministry of Consumer Affairs, Food and Public Distribution, Dept. of Food and Public Distribution, New Delhi.

2. Calculated using population figures of 1991 and 2001 and household size of 2001 as given in 'Census of India 2001, Analytical Report on Housing Amenities' Office of the Registrar General and Census Commissioner, New Delhi, India.

Table 6.29 Inclusion and Exclusion Errors in Identification (Status as on 29.09.2006)

State/UT	Projected No. of HH in 2006 (Lakh)	Per cent Population Below Poverty Line[1]	Projected BPL HH in 2006 (Lakh)	BPL Cards Issued (Including AAY) (Lakh)	Projected APL HH in 2006	F-mistake (Exclusion Error)	E-Mistake (Inclusion Error)
Delhi	30.97	14.7	4.55	4.38	26.42	3.78	
Jharkhand	54.01	40.3	21.77	23.95	32.24		6.77
Kerala	68.99	15	10.35	20.87	58.64		17.94
Madhya Pradesh	121.73	38.3	46.62	52.04	75.11		7.21
Maharashtra	211.19	30.7	64.83	72.99	146.35		5.57
Uttarakhand	17.40	39.6	6.89	4.98	10.51	27.73	

Source: 1. Planning Commission, Govt. of India, 2004. The percentage below poverty is calculated by the Planning Commission using Uniform Recall Period consumption in which the consumer expenditure data for all the items are collected from 30-day recall period.

The results of Table 6.30 should be read in the following way. Among the AAY and BPL categories as given in the table, those households that are in the below percentage, are confirmed by the Planning Commission cut-off and these households are rightly designated as below poverty households. Similarly, among the APL families, those who appear in the above percentage are truly designated as above poverty households. However, those households among the AAY and BPL categories, who fall in the above percentage, are the controversial cases as following the Planning Commission criterion, they should have been designated as APL households. In technical terms, these households come under the inclusion error (E-mistake), as they are wrongly included in the BPL (or AAY) list whereas they should have been excluded from this list. The inclusion error highlights the extra cost that TPDS system is bearing because of wrong identification. On the other extreme, those APL households who appear in the below percentage are wrongly designated as APL households, whereas they should have been issued either a BPL or AAY card (can not say definitely, to which category they belong to) as they are the cases of below poverty. In technical terms, this is the case of exclusion error (F-mistake), whereby the concerned authorities have failed in meeting the basic objective of striking the target group. The consequences of exclusion error are more ominous than the inclusion error. Whereas the occurrence of inclusion mistake raises the cost of the subsidy scheme, occurrence of exclusion mistake indicates failure in fulfiling the basic objective of the subsidy scheme, i.e., to target the poor in the TPDS system.

Table 6.30 The Percentage of Selected Households Below and Above the Cut-off Income of Poverty Line as Defined by the Planning Commission

	Income Criterion[1]			Expenditure Criterion[1]		
	AAY	BPL	APL	AAY	BPL	APL
			Delhi			
% Below	46.50	36.85	**16.75***	83.50	82.75	**51.23***
% Above	**53.50****	**63.15****	83.25	**16.50****	**17.25****	48.77
			Jharkhand			
% Below	68.00	71.61	**58.49***	95.50	94.70	**83.65***
% Above	**32.00****	**28.39****	41.51	**4.50****	**5.30****	16.35
			Kerala			
% Below	25.87	19.63	**16.67***	94.03	89.35	**70.20***
% Above	**74.13****	**80.37****	83.33	**5.97****	**10.65****	29.80
			Madhya Pradesh			
% Below	67.18	64.16	**42.78***	94.36	94.27	**76.29***
% Above	**32.82****	**35.84****	57.22	**5.64****	**5.73****	23.71
			Maharashtra			
% Below	58.55	60.10	**37.93***	94.30	96.36	**60.10***
% Above	**41.45****	**39.90****	62.07	**5.70****	**3.64****	39.90
			Uttarakhand			
% Below	76.10	75.84	**39.41***	97.56	97.97	**77.34***
% Above	**23.90****	**24.16****	60.59	**2.44****	**2.03****	22.66

Note: 1. The income and expenditure per capita as observed by our selected households in our survey data.

2. The bold figures indicate that these households are issued a wrong card. The figures shown with ** are the cases of E-mistake (inclusion error) and that of * are the cases of F-mistake (exclusion error).

Looking at the extent of incidence of inclusion and exclusion errors among our selected households, it is clearly evident from the data that the percentage of inclusion error was quite high if one compares observed income with that of Planning Commission cut-off. On the other hand, the extent of exclusion error was more if one followed the observed expenditure with that of the Planning Commission cut-off. Following income criterion, the inclusion error was up to 80 per cent in Kerala, above 50 per cent in Delhi, around 40 per cent in Maharashtra and between 20 to 40 per cent in Jharkhand, Madhya Pradesh and Uttarakhand. With respect to expenditure criterion, the exclusion error was more than 80 per cent in Jharkhand, 70 to 80 per cent in Kerala, Madhya Pradesh and Uttarakhand and 50 to 60 per cent in Delhi and Maharashtra. The more serious problem was the wrong identification of AAY households who should have been issued an APL card instead. Their proportion was around 70 per cent in Kerala, around 50 per cent in Delhi, 40 per cent in Maharashtra and 20-30 per cent in the rest of the three selected states. Divergent number of errors based on observed income and expenditure of the households raises a doubt whether the households' income and expenditure move hand in hand in the long run. As Planning Commission's estimates of below poverty households are based on per capita expenditure (drawn from the NSS consumption estimates), there seems to be a serious doubt on such numbers if one follows income criterion instead, as households' savings seems to be positive in the long run.

In the incidence of mis-targeting, it is implicit that the food is being diverted to the non-poor due to identification problems. Even though food is being distributed and a very high percentage of households were found getting food in majority of states, it was actually being diverted to non-target population as has been indicated by showing the extent of occurrence of inclusion and exclusion errors among our selected sample. However, in addition to such diversions, there was some proportion of food that was not being actually distributed among any of the households but it was shown in the state records as uplifted. Therefore, we can presume that food grains not distributed but withdrawn from the state accounts are being diverted to the black market or in the open market or may be distributed among the non-poor people at a higher price.

In this section, we try to measure the extent of diversion of wheat and rice in our selected states. For arriving at the state level figures, we assume here that the percentage of households (six months average) obtaining amount of wheat and rice from the PDS in our sample, on an average, prevails over the whole state. Similarly, we assume that the quantity of wheat and rice received by the sample households for the six months sample period on an average also as the quantity for the whole state. With these assumptions, we calculate the total grains actually distributed through the PDS in our selected states using the total number of cards issued during 2006 (as on 6th September) given by the Ministry of Food. We compare the distributed wheat and rice in our selected states with the total off-take as obtained from the secondary sources. The amount of diversion of rice and wheat in our six selected states is presented in Table 6.31.

It is evident from the data that in the case of AAY rice, no diversion was observed in Maharashtra, Uttarakhand and Madhya Pradesh. In Delhi and Jharkhand, some diversion was found but the volume of diversion was very small almost negligible in Delhi (only 1.6 per cent) and less than 5 per cent in Jharkhand. In Kerala, however, diversion of rice was noticed up to 19 per cent. In the case of AAY wheat, diversions were noticed in four of the six selected states. No mismatch was found in the distribution and off-take of wheat for AAY households in Uttarakhand and Kerala and like in the case of rice, diversion of wheat was also small, less than 5 per cent in Delhi. Diversion was up to 16 per cent in Jharkhand and Madhya Pradesh and less than 10 per cent in Maharashtra. Among BPL households, the extent of diversion of food was highest, especially for wheat. In BPL rice, no diversion was noticed in Uttarakhand, Maharashtra, Kerala and Jharkhand while in Delhi, diversion was less than 5 per cent. Thus, in the BPL quota of rice, significant diversions were found only in Madhya Pradesh. The extent of rice diversion was 19 per cent in that state. In the case of BPL wheat, as mentioned above diversion was observed in all the selected states, except Delhi. Diversion of wheat was less than 10 per cent in Jharkhand, 18-20 per cent in Maharashtra and Kerala and around 30 per cent in Madhya Pradesh and Uttarakhand.

Among above poverty households, no diversion was observed for rice while in the case of wheat, significant diversions were found only in Jharkhand and Kerala. Although diversion exceeded 50 per cent for wheat in Jharkhand, the volume of off-take for above poverty was much lower compared to the volume lifted for below poverty and for Antyodaya households. It was less than $1/10^{th}$ quantity of grains lifted under APL as compared to BPL and AAY lifting. In Kerala, wheat diversion under APL was up to 13 per cent while it was less than 5 per cent in Uttarakhand. Delhi was the only state where almost the whole amount uplifted was distributed among the households as no diversions were observed in the case of APL while diversion in BPL and AAY were almost negligible. Last and the least, Annexure Table A-6.1 presents off-take as a percentage of allocation in the selected states. It is evident from the table that off-take percentage was very high in the category of AAY households in all the states without any exception. In the case of BPL, off-take of rice was especially low in Jharkhand during all the three years for which data is presented. The off-take percentage of APL rice was almost negligible in Jharkhand, Madhya Pradesh and Maharashtra, reconfirming our assertion that grains were not being distributed in the APL in these states.

Thus, diversion of food for the APL category was not very high except the case of wheat in Jharkhand and Kerala. However, in the former case uplifting of wheat was very small while in the latter case diversion was less than 15 per cent. In the case of AAY, diversion of rice was found in Kerala and diversion of wheat was found in Madhya Pradesh and Jharkhand. In all the three cases, diversion was less than 20 per cent. In the case of BPL, diversion of grains was more widespread across the selected states. Diversion was up to 30 per cent for wheat in Madhya Pradesh and Uttarakhand, around 20 per cent in Kerala and Maharashtra for wheat and Madhya Pradesh for rice and less than 10 per cent for wheat in Jharkhand and rice in Delhi. Thus, except, the case of wheat for APL in Jharkhand, diversion were less than 30 per cent in all the selected states and for all the categories. From the above discussion, one can conclude that distribution of grains was found satisfactory in Delhi while some improvement is needed in the system in the other selected states. However, the identification of appropriate target group remains an illusive task in all the states under study including that of Delhi.

Table 6.31 Diversion of Food (Rice and Wheat) in the Selected States

	Delhi	Jharkhand	Kerala	Madhya Pradesh	Maharashtra	Uttarakhand
AAY						
Rice						
Total cards issued in the state (lakh)	0.56	7.27	5.96	15.64	19.84	1.51
Percentage of beneficiaries receiving grain from FPS	97.80	91.30	97.10	83.20	96.30	98.00
Monthly amount received by the beneficiaries (kgs)	9.82	21.77	29.21	6.30	16.94	23.24
Total distributed grains per annum in the state (tonnes)	6454	173398	202783	98374	388385	41269
Total off-take of grains by the state in 2005-06 (tonnes)	6561	180250	249313	94681	343321	31702
Percentage of diversion to off-take	1.63	3.80	18.66	0.00	0.00	0.00
Wheat						
Total cards issued in the state (lakh)	0.56	7.27	5.96	15.64	19.84	1.51
Percentage of beneficiaries receiving grain from FPS	98.10	90.30	5.70	89.30	94.90	95.90
Monthly amount received by the beneficiaries (kgs)	23.84	12.62	5.30	25.28	14.25	9.80
Total distributed grains per annum in the state (tonnes)	15716	99417	2160	423688	321962	17030
Total off-take of grains by the state in 2005-06 (tonnes)	16323	119016	0	509306	355432	15702
Percentage of diversion to off-take	3.72	16.47	0.00	16.81	9.42	0.00
BPL						
Rice						
Total cards issued in the state (lakh)	3.82	16.68	14.91	36.4	53.15	3.47
Percentage of beneficiaries receiving grain from FPS	95.60	66.00	97.50	74.10	96.70	93.00
Monthly amount received by the beneficiaries (kgs)	9.78	24.22	18.90	8.08	14.47	23.49
Total distributed grains per annum in the state (tonnes)	42859	319960	329705	261524	892441	90965
Total off-take of grains by the state in 2005-06 (tonnes)	44340	274117	314083	322600	734576	83967
Percentage of diversion to off-take	3.34	0.00	0.00	18.93	0.00	0.00
Wheat						
Total cards issued in the state (lakh)	3.82	16.68	14.91	36.4	53.15	3.47
Percentage of beneficiaries receiving grain from FPS	99.00	74.60	83.50	78.00	94.00	85.50
Monthly amount received by the beneficiaries (kgs)	23.96	9.38	4.70	15.12	12.38	10.01
Total distributed grains per annum in the state (tonnes)	108734	140062	70217	515144	742221	35638
Total off-take of grains by the state in 2005-06 (tonnes)	102141	153855	86943	726990	902641	50698
Percentage of diversion to off-take	0.00	8.97	19.24	29.14	17.77	29.71
APL						
Rice						
Total cards issued in the state (lakh)	21.96	5.15	47.52	82.27	148.34	17.66
Percentage of beneficiaries receiving grain from FPS	69.20	6.10	67.10	8.20	6.60	26.40
Monthly amount received by the beneficiaries (kgs)	9.14	24.03	21.77	11.97	16.56	22.22
Total distributed grains per annum in the state (tonnes)	166673	9059	832988	96902	194556	124314
Total off-take of grains by the state in 2005-06 (tonnes)	95786	812	180737	24634	46892	40484
Percentage of diversion to off-take	0.00	0.00	0.00	0.00	0.00	0.00
Wheat						
Total cards issued in the state (lakh)	21.96	5.15	47.52	82.27	148.34	17.66
Percentage of beneficiaries receiving grain from FPS	77.40	7.90	49.70	8.40	8.40	27.90
Monthly amount received by the beneficiaries (kgs)	21.90	12.20	5.98	19.23	17.02	9.95
Total distributed grains per annum in the state (tonnes)	446682	5956	169479	159471	254494	58830
Total off-take of grains by the state in 2005-06 (tonnes)	282479	13100	195032	112018	123048	61876
Percentage of diversion to off-take	0.00	54.53	13.10	0.00	0.00	4.92

Table A-6.1 Percentage of Off-take of Rice and Wheat under TPDS

		2004-05			2005-06			2006-07		
		BPL	APL	AAY	BPL	APL	AAY	BPL	APL	AAY
Delhi	Rice	91.5	34.1	79.4	97.6	19.0	94.9	99.5	32.0	98.5
	Wheat	97.5	43.9	86.9	97.9	35.1	95.0	98.3	77.2	98.0
Jharkhand	Rice	33.8	1.6	81.0	38.6	0.4	88.8	53.5	0.5	98.3
	Wheat	63.8	21.1	83.3	82.6	28.4	97.3	81.9	34.0	97.6
Kerala	Rice	101.6	6.7	94.7	97.6	4.2	96.9	98.9	13.3	100.4
	Wheat	100.6	38.5	-	99.6	59.5	-	100.2	80.1	-
Madhya Pradesh	Rice	100.4	0.9	93.2	96.6	1.3	98.1	95.8	3.5	92.2
	Wheat	91.0	0.9	93.7	103.2	7.6	94.9	99.9	33.0	93.0
Maharashtra	Rice	82.7	0.7	85.5	83.2	0.9	90.8	82.1	2.8	86.1
	Wheat	87.5	1.8	90.7	87.9	3.7	87.3	88.8	19.8	81.8
Uttarakhand	Rice	101.3	5.5	144.7	100.3	9.9	71.7	84.1	19.1	75.8
	Wheat	100.2	4.8	94.9	106.4	24.3	79.6	102.1	81.6	88.1

7 Functioning of the Fair Price Shops

7.1 Introduction

The principal chore of distribution of grains entitled for the poor remains with the fair price shops (FPS) operating at the village/sub-village or group of village level under the monitoring of various authorities including that of Civil Supplies Department. The efficiency of the distribution system essentially depends on the working of these FPSs in their various operations. This chapter assesses the functioning of the fair price shops, their monitoring, transparency and financial viability. The facts presented here are based on a separate questionnaire designed specially for the FPS and carried out during the longitudinal field survey. In total, 150 fair shops, one each for our selected village was surveyed. The selected fair price shop was the one that was catering to our selected households in each village. In the cases where more than one shop was operating in the village, we selected the one that encompassed the maximum number of our selected households. Discussion of this chapter is divided into 10 sections. The next section presents the profile of the fair price shops, their management and general functioning. Section 3 presents the issues that deal with entitlement of households from the PDS. The fourth section is devoted to the issues related to lifting of quota by the FPS. Section 5 discusses transparency in the functioning of the FPSs. The next section presents the monitoring system followed by a section on the stocking pattern at the FPS. Section 8 presents pattern of distribution of grains among the consumers by the FPS, followed by a section that puts forth the issues related to mode of transportation of grains. The chapter is concluded by a section that compares prices of grains as revealed by the FPS owners with the price paid by the consumers.

7.2 Profile of Fair Price Shops

The selected fair price shops were mostly individually owned. The owners were mostly educated. A majority of them were educated up to higher secondary or graduation level. In Delhi, 20 per cent shop owners were educated up to secondary level and rest all of them were higher secondary or above (Table 7.1). In Jharkhand, half of the selected shopkeepers were educated up to secondary and rest were higher secondary or above. Similarly, in Kerala, Madhya Pradesh and Maharashtra, a majority of the shopkeepers were educated upto 12th standard or above. In Uttarakhand, around two-third of the selected shop owners were educated up to 10th standard. However, in none of the cases, shopkeepers were found illiterate or literate without formal education. The PDS shops were generally exclusive for that purpose while in Uttarakhand around 36 per cent shopkeepers were also doing other retailing business in the same shop. The ownership status was individual, except in Madhya Pradesh and Maharashtra, where 84 and 36 per cent shopkeepers, respectively were running as cooperatives. In Kerala, around 12 per cent of the selected shops were run under cooperative ownership. In rest of the states, mostly shops were in the individual capacity. Table 7.2 presents details about location and opening time of the shops. The shops in majority of the cases were located in a periphery of around 5 to 20 kilometres from the godown from where the grains were being lifted. However, in Delhi and Madhya Pradesh, about one-third of the selected shops were located at more than 25 kilometres distance from the godown and thereby freight charges for transporting grains would be higher for these shopkeepers. To the question of how many days the shop owners were keeping the shop opened for distribution of grains among the households, a majority of them replied more than 15 days. During these days shops were opened the whole day for this activity in all the states except Jharkhand. In the latter state, all the shopkeepers distributed grains only in the forenoon during the opening days of PDS that too varied from more than 15 days to less than a day.

Table 7.1 Profile of Fair Price Shop (%)

	Delhi	Jharkhand	Kerala	Madhya Pradesh	Maharashtra	Uttarakhand
Educational qualifications of the shop owner						
Literate without formal schooling	0.00	4.00	0.00	0.00	0.00	0.00
Upto primary	4.00	20.00	4.00	0.00	24.00	24.00
Upto secondary	16.00	28.00	28.00	8.00	24.00	40.00
Upto higher secondary	44.00	20.00	40.00	68.00	20.00	12.00
Above higher secondary	36.00	28.00	24.00	24.00	32.00	24.00
Illiterate	0.00	0.00	4.00	0.00	0.00	0.00
Type of shop						
Only PDS	88.00	92.00	88.00	96.00	100.00	64.00
PDS cum retailer	12.00	8.00	12.00	0.00	0.00	36.00
PDS cum wholesaler	0.00	0.00	0.00	4.00	0.00	0.00
No response	0.00	0.00	0.00	0.00	0.00	0.00
Ownership status						
Individual	96.00	96.00	88.00	12.00	64.00	100.00
Joint	0.00	4.00	0.00	4.00	0.00	0.00
Government	0.00	0.00	0.00	0.00	0.00	0.00
Cooperative	4.00	0.00	12.00	84.00	36.00	0.00
Corporation	0.00	0.00	0.00	0.00	0.00	0.00
NGO	0.00	0.00	0.00	0.00	0.00	0.00
Gram panchayat	0.00	0.00	0.00	0.00	0.00	0.00
Others	0.00	0.00	0.00	0.00	0.00	0.00

Table 7.2 Location and Functioning of the Shop

	Delhi	Jharkhand	Kerala	Madhya Pradesh	Maharashtra	Uttarakhand
Proximity of lifting godown from the ration shop						
Within 5 kms	20.00	16.67	40.00	16.67	4.00	28.00
5-10 kms	8.00	33.33	28.00	25.00	24.00	28.00
10-25 kms	36.00	37.50	28.00	29.17	56.00	44.00
>25 kms	36.00	12.50	4.00	29.17	16.00	0.00
No response	0.00	0.00	0.00	0.00	0.00	0.00
For how many days does your shop remain open in a month?						
Only 1 day	4.17	16.67	0.00	0.00	0.00	4.00
Upto 5 days	0.00	0.00	0.00	8.70	4.00	0.00
5-10 days	0.00	4.17	0.00	17.39	8.00	0.00
11-15 days	0.00	20.83	4.00	13.04	8.00	0.00
>15 days	95.83	58.33	96.00	60.87	80.00	96.00
What is the opening time of your shop?						
Forenoon	0.00	100.00	0.00	0.00	12.00	0.00
Afternoon	0.00	0.00	0.00	4.00	0.00	0.00
Evening	0.00	0.00	4.00	8.00	16.00	4.00
Whole day	100.00	0.00	96.00	88.00	72.00	96.00
No response	0.00	0.00	0.00	0.00	0.00	0.00

7.3 Entitlement According to FPS

The household entitlement for grains was fixed on the monthly basis. The entitlement was fixed at 35 kgs per household, irrespective of the family size, which was confirmed by the surveyed fair price shop owners in all the categories, except Kerala and Jharkhand. In Kerala, almost all the fair price shop owners indicated 25 kgs of cereals (rice + wheat) as entitlement for the category of BPL households. In the case of Jharkhand, no entitlement was shown for the category of APL households. Looking at the distribution between rice and wheat (Table 7.3), it is clear from the mode values shown in the table[1] that in Delhi, entitlement was fixed as 25 kgs of wheat + 10 kgs of rice in all the three categories. In Jharkhand, entitlement was fixed at 14 kgs of wheat + 21 kgs of rice in AAY and 9 kgs of wheat + 26 kgs of rice for the BPL households. In Kerala, entitlement was fixed as 35 kgs of rice alone for AAY, 6 kgs of wheat + 19 kgs of rice for BPL and 9 kgs of wheat + 26 kgs of rice for the APL households. In Madhya Pradesh, entitlement was fixed at 33 kgs of wheat + 2 kgs of rice for AAY, 30 kgs of wheat + 5 kgs rice for BPL and 25 kgs of wheat + 10 kgs of rice for the APL households. In Maharashtra and Uttarakhand both, 10 kgs of wheat + 25 kgs of rice was fixed uniformly for all the categories. The mean values shown in the above table are very close to the mode values except in Madhya Pradesh and Maharashtra where in the latter case, mean values are more equitable towards the distribution of wheat and rice and in the former case the proportion of rice is 6 kgs, instead of 2 kgs in the case of AAY households. The households obtaining PDS grains as shown in Chapter 4 verify the entitlement pattern as indicated by the fair price shop owners as discussed above.

Table 7.3 Monthly Entitlement according to FPS (in Kgs)

	Wheat			Rice		
	AAY	BPL	APL	AAY	BPL	APL
			Mean			
Delhi	25.00	25.00	25.00	10.00	10.00	10.00
Jharkhand	13.71	9.47	-	21.29	25.57	-
Kerala	-	5.52	8.72	35.00	19.48	25.24
Madhya Pradesh	28.08	20.12	23.44	6.92	14.88	11.69
Maharashtra	16.76	16.76	17.35	18.24	18.24	17.65
Uttarakhand	10.04	10.00	10.00	24.96	25.00	25.00
			Mode			
Delhi	25.00	25.00	25.00	10.00	10.00	10.00
Jharkhand	14.00	9.00	-	21.00	26.00	-
Kerala	-	6.00	9.00	35.00	19.00	26.00
Madhya Pradesh	33.00	30.00	25.00	2.00	5.00	10.00
Maharashtra	10.00	10.00	10.00	25.00	25.00	25.00
Uttarakhand	10.00	10.00	10.00	25.00	25.00	25.00

7.4 Households Catered and Amount of Grains Lifted and Distributed by the FPS

Every cardholder is registered with a fair price shop from where the cardholder draws his/her entitlement. The registration of cards is compulsory even for the above poverty households, although all above poverty households do not obtain grains from the FPS. Table 7.4 presents the average number of cards registered with fair price shops in each state for AAY, BPL and APL

1. Mode values indicate the highest frequency whereas average values are affected by the lower and upper bounds.

categories. In the AAY category, the maximum number of cards registered per FPS occurred in Madhya Pradesh while in the other two categories, the highest cards were found in Delhi. On an average, around 1.4 thousand households (including the APL households) were registered with every FPS in Delhi. In Madhya Pradesh, the number of households registered was more than a thousand, while in other selected states, number of cards registered varied between four to seven hundred. Nonetheless, the actual number of households catered by fair price shops were far less than the registered number of cards because the highest number of cards registered in all the states belonged to that of APL and given the fact that percentage of APL population served through PDS grains was very low in the selected states (see Chapter 4). The coefficient of variation across time indicates fluctuations in the number of households registered over time in each category. The small value of the coefficients in the selected states points out almost fixed number of ration cards exclusively for each category registered with the FPS across six months of survey period. However, the value of the coefficient was quite high across FPSs, indicating varying number of households catered by fair price shops in different villages. Thus, number of households catered by each fair price shop although varied across space but their numbers remained constant over time during the survey period.

Table 7.4 Number of Households Catered by the Selected Fair Price Shops

		Delhi	Jharkhand	Kerala	Madhya Pradesh	Maharashtra	Uttarakhand
January	AAY	46	80	47	158	80	31
	BPL	313	145	168	336	220	103
	APL	998	242	402	613	381	307
February	AAY	46	80	50	165	80	31
	BPL	313	145	156	340	219	155
	APL	1009	242	401	616	381	307
March	AAY	46	80	50	171	80	31
	BPL	313	145	155	335	221	103
	APL	1015	242	403	616	381	308
April	AAY	46	80	58	175	80	31
	BPL	313	145	155	310	221	103
	APL	1018	242	405	558	380	308
May	AAY	47	80	50	175	83	31
	BPL	313	145	155	335	217	101
	APL	1021	242	405	523	382	308
June	AAY	47	80	50	164	86	31
	BPL	313	145	155	335	210	99
	APL	1028	242	406	550	382	308
Average	AAY	46	80	51	168	82	31
	BPL	313	145	157	332	218	111
	APL	1015	242	403	579	381	308
	Total	1374	467	611	1079	681	450
COV Across Time							
6 months period	AAY	0.66	0.00	7.04	3.99	2.73	0.80
	BPL	0.02	0.00	3.16	3.22	1.99	19.63
	APL	1.03	0.00	0.44	7.05	0.21	0.12
COV Across FPS							
25 fair price shops	AAY	111.08	60.4	57.4	110.9	61.4	107.9
	BPL	74.03	39.6	53.7	80.6	39.8	127.4
	APL	62.65	36.4	36.9	159.0	116.1	105.5

In addition to the number of households catered by each FPS, it is interesting to know how much grains were handled (lifted and distributed) by the selected fair price shops. Table 7.5 presents average quantity of grains lifted from the godown and distributed by the FPS on monthly basis (average of six month) as well as the amount handled during the calendar year 2006. The table also presents the grains distributed as a percentage of the amount lifted.[2] The statistics reveals that on an average, every FPS in Delhi lifted and distributed more than 200 quintals of wheat and less than 100 quintals of rice among all categories of households every month. In Jharkhand and Uttarakhand, the distribution of wheat and rice, on an average amounted to 20 and 40 quintals, respectively. In Kerala and Maharashtra, the quantity distributed averaged around 20 to 30 quintals of wheat and 50 to 60 quintals of rice. In Madhya Pradesh, the quantity distributed was less than Delhi but more than other selected states. It averaged around 85 quintals of wheat and 35 quintals of rice. Looking at the percentage of grains distributed to that of grains lifted, it is seen from the table that on an average, grains distributed matched with grains lifted, as percentage was less than hundred in some cases but exceeded hundred in other cases. Considering 35 kgs cereals as entitlement for each registered card, the amount of grains entitled on the basis of number of households registered was quite close to the amount of grains distributed by each FPS, except the case of above poverty households. In the latter case, the wedge between the total entitlement and grains distributed was quite high, pointing out the fact that all the registered households in the case of APL were not being served through PDS grains.

Table 7.5 The Average Amount of Grains Lifted and Distributed by Selected FPS (Quintals)

	Wheat						Rice					
	Lifted		Distributed		Percentage Distributed		Lifted		Distributed		Percentage Distributed	
	Monthly	2006	Monthly	2006	Monthly	2006	Monthly	2006	Monthly	2006	Monthly	2006
Delhi												
AAY	10.3	123.8	10.2	123.9	99.4	100.0	4.1	50.8	4.1	50.0	98.6	98.3
BPL	79.4	813.0	79.9	885.1	100.6	108.9	37.9	354.6	34.3	325.9	90.4	91.9
APL	107.6	1413.0	110.2	1407.5	102.5	99.6	43.6	542.6	46.2	521.7	106.1	96.1
Jharkhand												
AAY	10.6	126.9	10.2	116.8	95.9	92.1	17.4	184.6	17.5	194.8	100.8	105.5
BPL	12.0	134.7	12.5	114.4	104.8	84.9	22.4	237.4	21.6	225.6	96.7	95.0
APL	0.0	0.0	0.0	0.0	-	-	0.0	0.0	0.0	0.0	-	-
Kerala												
AAY	0.0	0.0	0.9	5.8	-	-	17.2	273.6	18.0	213.6	105.1	78.1
BPL	7.1	93.0	7.9	90.8	112.2	97.6	25.9	317.5	24.8	296.1	95.8	93.3
APL	11.9	139.8	10.7	149.7	90.4	107.1	14.2	182.5	13.0	188.7	91.3	103.4
Madhya Pradesh												
AAY	43.8	441.7	45.1	455.3	102.9	103.1	7.0	92.1	6.7	89.3	96.5	97.0
BPL	33.5	488.4	34.4	527.6	102.8	108.0	24.9	277.4	23.7	253.0	95.0	91.2
APL	4.4	43.2	5.9	44.8	134.0	103.7	6.5	30.1	5.9	132.5	90.8	439.7
Maharashtra												
AAY	9.6	107.3	9.5	109.8	99.3	102.3	16.7	149.7	15.8	142.4	94.9	95.2
BPL	19.0	311.8	20.5	308.0	107.9	98.8	32.1	313.2	31.2	305.0	97.2	97.4
APL	1.1	8.1	1.1	6.3	102.5	77.3	0.7	4.8	0.9	5.2	123.1	109.1
Uttarakhand												
AAY	3.4	36.5	3.4	35.9	99.5	98.4	8.0	81.9	9.7	77.1	121.6	94.1
BPL	11.3	130.2	10.4	143.7	92.3	110.4	24.4	278.9	22.7	301.7	92.7	108.2
APL	9.6	66.6	9.7	79.8	100.5	119.9	4.3	29.5	4.3	35.3	100.7	119.8

2. These figures are based on the data collected from each selected fair price shop through an FPS questionnaire.

7.5 Lifting of Quota and Disposal of Remaining Stocks

During the last year, were there any instances when the FPS had lifted less than the allocated quota from the godown? More than 70 per cent of owners replied yes to this question in all the states except in Uttarakhand, where only 20 to 25 per cent shop owners replied yes to the above question. Above 70 per cent shop owners in Delhi, Kerala and Maharashtra pointed out that their lifted quota was less than the allotted quota which was more than 10 times during the last calendar year. An overwhelming majority of shop owners in Delhi and Maharashtra pointed out less availability of grains at godown as the main reason for lifting less than the allotted quota. In Jharkhand, Kerala and Uttarakhand, on the other hand, shop owners pointed out lack of demand of grains as the reason for not lifting their allotted quota. Among other reasons for not lifting, bad quality of grains was pointed out by a majority of shop owners in Madhya Pradesh. On the question of volume of grains not lifted during the last year (2006), the shop owners quoted that the average quantity of wheat was above 500 but less than 1000 quintals in Delhi, Madhya Pradesh and Maharashtra and less than 200 quintals in Kerala. In Jharkhand and Uttarakhand, the amount quoted was negligible. In the case of rice, the quantity not lifted during the calendar year 2006 exceeded 500 quintals in Kerala while it was less than 500 quintals in other states, except the case of Uttarakhand where the quantity of rice not lifted was just negligible.

Against the phenomenon of lifting less than the allotted quota from godown, fair price shops were also left with undistributed grains in many instances. Around 20 to 40 per cent of the interviewed shop owners accepted that sometimes entitlement was not lifted by some of the beneficiaries. To our question, how they were disposing off the unlifted stock, an overwhelming majority of them replied that they adjusted it in the next month supply, while only 15 per cent in Kerala and Madhya Pradesh pointed out that they distributed more grains to the beneficiaries while there was not even a single reply saying that they sold undistributed stocks in the open market. We tried to find out the volume of such undistributed stock. The amount of undistributed stock was not very high for both wheat as well as rice. Undistributed wheat and rice on an average ranged between 5 to 10 quintals each, in Jharkhand and Kerala and less than 5 quintals each, in the remaining selected states for the calendar year 2006.

Table 7.6 Instances of Lifting Less than Quota by FPS from Godown

	Delhi	Jharkhand	Kerala	Madhya Pradesh	Maharashtra	Uttarakhand
			Wheat			
Were there instances during the 2006 when lifting by FPS from godown was less than the allotted quota?						
Yes	76.00	76.00	70.83	88.00	92.00	20.00
No	24.00	24.00	29.17	12.00	8.00	80.00
If 'Yes' to above, how many times the lifted quota was less than the allotted quota during 2006?						
Never	5.26	0.00	0.00	4.76	8.33	0.00
1-5 times	15.79	26.32	0.00	0.00	20.83	25.00
5-10 times	5.26	47.37	4.76	66.67	0.00	25.00
>10 times	73.68	26.32	95.24	28.57	70.83	50.00
What were the reasons for not lifting the grains?						
Less availability at godown	78.95	36.84	0.00	0.00	50.00	0.00
Insufficient opening stock	0.00	0.00	0.00	0.00	0.00	25.00
Due to poor demand	21.05	52.63	85.71	33.33	45.83	75.00
Lack of money	0.00	0.00	0.00	0.00	0.00	0.00
Bad quality	0.00	10.53	14.29	66.67	4.17	0.00
Others	0.00	0.00	0.00	0.00	0.00	0.00
Average quantity not lifted in 2006 (quintals)	690	34	180	853	510	8.08

contd...

...contd...

	Delhi	Jharkhand	Kerala	Madhya Pradesh	Maharashtra	Uttarakhand
			Rice			
Are there instances during the 2006 when lifting by FPS from godown was less than the allotted quota?						
Yes	64.00	84.00	75.00	84.00	87.50	24.00
No	36.00	16.00	25.00	16.00	12.50	76.00
If 'Yes' to above, how many times the lifted quota was less than the allotted quota during 2006?						
Never	0.00	0.00	0.00	9.09	0.00	0.00
1-5 times	12.50	28.57	0.00	0.00	31.82	20.00
5-10 times	12.50	47.62	4.55	68.18	0.00	40.00
>10 times	75.00	23.81	95.45	22.73	68.18	40.00
What were the reasons for not lifting the grains?						
Less availability at godown	68.75	38.10	0.00	4.55	54.55	0.00
Insufficient opening stock	0.00	0.00	0.00	0.00	0.00	20.00
Due to poor demand	31.25	42.86	90.91	22.73	45.45	80.00
Lack of money	0.00	4.76	0.00	0.00	0.00	0.00
Bad quality	0.00	14.29	9.09	72.73	0.00	0.00
Others	0.00	0.00	0.00	0.00	0.00	0.00
Average quantity not lifted in 2006 (Quintals)	491	211	769	294	359	33

Table 7.7 **Disposal of Remaining Stock**

	Delhi	Jharkhand	Kerala	Madhya Pradesh	Maharashtra	Uttarakhand
			Wheat			
Are there any instances during 2006 when your shop was left with some stock undistributed?						
Yes	8.00	40.00	70.83	32.00	36.00	21.74
No	92.00	60.00	29.17	68.00	64.00	78.26
If 'Yes' to above, how did you dispose off the remaining stock?						
Adjusted in next month	100.00	100.00	85.71	83.33	90.00	100.00
Gave more to consumer	0.00	0.00	14.29	16.67	10.00	0.00
Sold in open market	0.00	0.00	0.00	0.00	0.00	0.00
Others	0.00	0.00	0.00	0.00	0.00	0.00
Average quantity of undistributed stock in 2006 (quintals)	1.04	6.04	4.59	0.50	1.93	1.39
			Rice			
Are there any instances during 2006 when your shop was left with some stock undistributed?						
Yes	12.00	40.00	95.45	25.00	37.50	21.74
No	88.00	60.00	4.55	75.00	62.50	78.26
If 'Yes' to above, how did you dispose off the remaining stock?						
Adjusted in next month	100.00	100.00	100.00	100.00	100.00	100.00
Gave more to consumer	0.00	0.00	0.00	0.00	0.00	0.00
Sold in open market	0.00	0.00	0.00	0.00	0.00	0.00
Others	0.00	0.00	0.00	0.00	0.00	0.00
Average quantity of undistributed stock in 2006 (quintals)	5.49	7.32	9.39	3.54	3.07	2.10

7.6 Records of Transparency

The information dissemination at the gross root level is the key for any system to run in an efficient way. As with any other system, performance of PDS also depends on the level of awareness of the beneficiaries as well as the transparency maintained at the fair price shops. Keeping proper records, displaying the list of beneficiaries and their amount of entitlement, the timings of the distribution of grains, price etc., keep the consumers vigilant. We propounded some questions related to transparency to the FPS owners and the details provided by them are summarised in Tables 7.8 and 7.9. To the question whether the FPS shops keep records of their transactions, almost all the interviewed shop owners answered yes. On the type of records maintained, more than 90 per cent were of the opinion that they kept all the details of stocks handled as well as lifting details from the godown and distribution of grains among the beneficiaries by the number of cards and the total grains distributed of a particular commodity. To the question whether they just keep the records with themselves or do they display the information related to price, stock and the number of cards registered with the FPS on the notice board for public information, almost all of them pointed out that they displayed all the information for the information of the beneficiaries.

Table 7.8 Maintenance of Records

	Delhi	Jharkhand	Kerala	Madhya Pradesh	Maharashtra	Uttarakhand
Do you maintain updated records?						
Yes	100.00	100.00	100.00	100.00	96.00	100.00
No	0.00	0.00	0.00	0.00	4.00	0.00
If 'Yes' to above, what type of records do you maintain?						
Stock details						
Yes	100.00	100.00	100.00	96.00	96.00	100.00
No	0.00	0.00	0.00	4.00	4.00	0.00
Lifting details (Commodity wise)						
Yes	100.00	100.00	100.00	100.00	96.00	96.00
No	0.00	0.00	0.00	0.00	4.00	4.00
Distribution details (Commodity wise)						
Yes	100.00	100.00	100.00	96.00	96.00	96.00
No	0.00	0.00	0.00	4.00	4.00	4.00
Distribution details (Card status wise)						
Yes	100.00	100.00	100.00	100.00	96.00	100.00
No	0.00	0.00	0.00	0.00	4.00	0.00
Display of prices of stock						
Yes	100.00	100.00	100.00	96.00	96.00	100.00
No	0.00	0.00	0.00	4.00	4.00	0.00
Display of stock						
Yes	100.00	100.00	100.00	92.00	96.00	100.00
No	0.00	0.00	0.00	8.00	4.00	0.00
Ration card register						
Yes	100.00	100.00	100.00	92.00	92.00	100.00
No	0.00	0.00	0.00	8.00	8.00	0.00

On further details of transparency, we tried to find out how systematically FPS were functioning, which were run mostly by the private owners. A majority of the shop owners in all the states, except Maharashtra indicated that they had displayed the list of beneficiaries outside the shop for public knowledge. They also opined that along with the list of beneficiaries, the amount of entitlement in each case and the scale of issue and the retail price at which food was being distributed were also displayed. Along with these details, shop owners also claimed that they were keeping the beneficiaries updated about the timings of opening and closing of the shop and stocks of essential commodities received and distributed. On the question whether they displayed the name and address of the authority for redressal of consumers' grievances, a majority of them replied yes. However, on cross checking from the households, the replies of the shop owners were not found consistent and there were two opposite views on many of the above questions. Last and the least, do the shop owners provide samples of food they distribute among the consumers? Majority of the shopkeepers replied that they keep all the samples on display.

Table 7.9 Records of Transparency

	Delhi	Jharkhand	Kerala	Madhya Pradesh	Maharashtra	Uttarakhand
List of BPL and AAY beneficiaries						
Yes	84.00	100.00	92.00	92.00	44.00	76.00
No	16.00	0.00	4.00	8.00	56.00	24.00
No response	0.00	0.00	4.00	0.00	0.00	0.00
Entitlement of essential commodities						
Yes	100.00	100.00	100.00	96.00	92.00	96.00
No	0.00	0.00	0.00	4.00	8.00	4.00
Scale of issue						
Yes	100.00	100.00	100.00	96.00	96.00	100.00
No	0.00	0.00	0.00	4.00	4.00	0.00
Retail issue price						
Yes	100.00	100.00	100.00	100.00	96.00	100.00
No	0.00	0.00	0.00	0.00	4.00	0.00
Timings of opening and closing of the FPS						
Yes	100.00	100.00	100.00	100.00	76.00	100.00
No	0.00	0.00	0.00	0.00	24.00	0.00
Stock of essential commodities received during the month						
Yes	96.00	100.00	100.00	100.00	92.00	100.00
No	4.00	0.00	0.00	0.00	8.00	0.00
Opening and closing stock of essential commodities						
Yes	96.00	100.00	92.00	96.00	92.00	96.00
No	4.00	0.00	4.00	4.00	8.00	0.00
No response	0.00	0.00	4.00	0.00	0.00	4.00
The authority for redressal of grievances/lodging complaints w.r.t. quality and quantity of essential commodities under the PDS						
Yes	96.00	68.00	68.00	91.67	84.00	76.00
No	4.00	16.00	8.00	8.33	8.00	24.00
No response	0.00	16.00	24.00	0.00	8.00	0.00
Availability of sample on display						
Display all samples	64.00	100.00	64.00	76.00	48.00	20.00
Display some samples	20.00	0.00	28.00	12.00	8.00	64.00
No sample display	16.00	0.00	8.00	8.00	44.00	16.00
No response	0.00	0.00	0.00	4.00	0.00	0.00

7.7 Monitoring System of the FPS

For the monitoring of the FPS functioning, there were multiple authorities that were supposed to check the functioning of the FPS and also could check the samples of grain being sold to the beneficiaries. Such authority was vested with the *gram panchayat* or its designated committee, vigilance committee from the block or district officials or the government officials from the Civil Supplies Department. Among our selected shop owners, almost all shop owners in all the states, except Madhya Pradesh pointed out Civil Supplies Department as the main monitoring authority for their distribution of grains. In Madhya Pradesh, a majority of the shop owners indicated District Vigilance Committee as the monitoring authority who inspected their shops. Panchayat Committee was also monitoring FPS in few cases. A few shop owners in Kerala replied that their shops were never monitored by any authority. To the question, what was the frequency of such inspection, a majority of shop keepers replied atleast once in a month's time period while a significant number of them in Madhya Pradesh and Maharashtra indicated that it was done on a quarterly basis.

Table 7.10 Monitoring of FPS Functioning

	Delhi	Jharkhand	Kerala	Madhya Pradesh	Maharashtra	Uttarakhand
		(Priority I)				
Who monitors the FPS						
Panchayat committee/designated authority by the *panchayat* or village	0.00	0.00	0.00	4.00	4.00	0.00
Vigilance committee from the block/district level	4.00	0.00	0.00	60.00	0.00	0.00
Government officials/civil supply departments	92.00	100.00	96.00	36.00	96.00	100.00
Nobody monitors	0.00	0.00	4.00	0.00	0.00	0.00
Others	4.00	0.00	0.00	0.00	0.00	0.00
No response	0.00	0.00	0.00	0.00	0.00	0.00
		(Priority II)				
Who monitors the FPS						
Panchayat committee/designated authority by the *panchayat* or village	0.00	68.00	24.00	4.00	8.00	52.00
Vigilance committee from the block/district level	4.00	24.00	20.00	4.00	12.00	4.00
Government officials/civil supply departments	4.00	0.00	0.00	4.00	0.00	0.00
Nobody monitors	0.00	0.00	0.00	0.00	0.00	0.00
Other	0.00	0.00	0.00	0.00	0.00	0.00
No response	92.00	8.00	56.00	88.00	80.00	44.00
What is the frequency of your inspection?						
Atleast once in a month	92.00	100.00	86.36	40.00	40.00	84.00
Four times in a year	8.00	0.00	13.64	44.00	48.00	4.00
Two times in a year	0.00	0.00	0.00	8.00	4.00	0.00
Once in a year	0.00	0.00	0.00	8.00	4.00	0.00
Did not visit last one year	0.00	0.00	0.00	0.00	0.00	0.00
Never	0.00	0.00	0.00	0.00	0.00	4.00
No response	0.00	0.00	0.00	0.00	4.00	8.00

7.8 Stocking Pattern at the FPS

What was the pattern of fair price shops lifting food from the godowns and distributing it among the beneficiaries. A majority of shop owners in Kerala, Madhya Pradesh and Uttarakhand indicated first or second week of the distributing month as the time for receiving their stock from the godown. In Delhi, Jharkhand and Maharashtra, a majority indicated that they do not get any such date to receive their stock from the godown. Therefore, in the latter three states, shop owners had to keep ready to lift their grains whenever they received orders from the godown without having any pre-set date and time period, which caused a great inconvenience for these shop owners. After receiving the release order from the godowns, the shop owners were given sufficient time (two to three weeks) to lift their grains in Delhi, Jharkhand and Maharashtra. However, in Kerala, 96 per cent shop owners indicated that they had to lift their grains within three days of releasing order while a majority of shop owners in Madhya Pradesh and Uttarakhand pointed out a week's time for the same.

Table 7.11 Frequency of Lifting Ration from Godowns

	Delhi	Jharkhand	Kerala	Madhya Pradesh	Maharashtra	Uttarakhand
When do you receive lifting/release order for lifting stock for FPS for current month?						
On a fixed date during a month	8.00	4.00	20.00	12.00	16.00	4.00
First week of distributing month	40.00	20.00	56.00	56.00	8.00	8.00
After first week of distributing month	4.00	16.00	12.00	16.00	24.00	68.00
Not get any such order	48.00	60.00	0.00	4.00	52.00	16.00
No response	0.00	0.00	12.00	12.00	0.00	4.00
		Wheat				
How many days are you allowed/actually to lift stock after receiving/releasing order?						
Less than 3 days	20.00	0.00	96.00	8.00	16.00	0.00
3 to 7 days	4.00	12.00	0.00	68.00	16.00	96.00
8 to 15 days	4.00	36.00	0.00	4.00	64.00	0.00
More than 15 days	72.00	52.00	0.00	16.00	4.00	0.00
No response	0.00	0.00	4.00	4.00	0.00	4.00
		Rice				
How many days are you allowed/actually to lift stock after receiving/releasing order?						
Less than 3 days	20.00	0.00	96.00	8.00	16.00	0.00
3 to 7 days	4.00	12.00	0.00	68.00	16.00	96.00
8 to 15 days	4.00	36.00	0.00	4.00	64.00	0.00
More than 15 days	72.00	52.00	0.00	16.00	4.00	0.00
No response	0.00	0.00	4.00	4.00	0.00	4.00

To our question whether the stocks were readily available when they visited the godown, a majority of the shopkeepers in almost all the states replied that stocks were always or mostly available. However, 30 per cent shop owners in Jharkhand pointed out that stocks were rarely available while 4 per cent in Jharkhand and Kerala pointed out that stocks were never available on their first entry whenever they visited the godown. To the question whether after getting the release order, whether or not the shopkeepers were getting their quota in a single lot, a majority of them replied only sometimes they received their quota in a single lot. A majority in Kerala and Maharashtra indicated that they receive their quota in a single lot always, while majority in Delhi, Jharkhand, Madhya Pradesh and Uttarakhand pointed out that they receive their quota in a single lot only sometimes. Twenty per cent shop owners in Maharashtra opined that they never received their quota in a single lot that increased their transportation cost.

7.9 Pattern of Distribution among the Consumers

Generally PDS grains are distributed among consumers on the monthly basis. However, the distribution pattern may vary in different states due to local customs and requirements. Among our selected states, some of the FPS shop owners pointed out that they are distributing grains weekly and fortnightly. The percentage of shop owners who indicated weekly distribution among the consumers was quite high (84 per cent) in Kerala. Twenty per cent of selected shopkeepers in Jharkhand and 16 per cent in Madhya Pradesh also indicated weekly distribution. However, majority of the shop owners in Delhi, Madhya Pradesh,

Maharashtra and Uttarakhand followed the monthly distribution pattern. In Jharkhand, majority of them pointed out that their distribution depends on the availability of stocks from the godown. To another question of how frequently the shop runs stock out situation, majority of FPS owners indicated that they never run out of stock, while a few of them from Jharkhand and Uttarakhand indicated once or twice (less than five times) in a year. To the question, how oftenly they have to pay bribe to receive their allocated quota from the godown, almost all selected shop owners except Jharkhand said they never paid any bribe. On the other hand, all selected shop owners from Jharkhand and around 15 per cent from Maharashtra answered that they always or most of the times paid bribe to receive their quota from the godown.

Table 7.12 Availability of Stocks at Godowns

	Delhi	Jharkhand	Kerala	Madhya Pradesh	Maharashtra	Uttarakhand
			Wheat			
Readiness of stock availability at the godowns during 2006						
Always available	16.00	16.00	72.00	36.00	44.00	24.00
Mostly available	84.00	44.00	24.00	56.00	56.00	76.00
Rarely available	0.00	36.00	0.00	0.00	0.00	0.00
Never available	0.00	4.00	4.00	0.00	0.00	0.00
No response	0.00	0.00	0.00	8.00	0.00	0.00
How often you get the total allotted stock in a single lot after receiving releasing order						
Always	32.00	40.00	68.00	32.00	68.00	28.00
Sometimes	64.00	60.00	32.00	60.00	12.00	72.00
Never	4.00	0.00	0.00	0.00	20.00	0.00
No response	0.00	0.00	0.00	8.00	0.00	0.00
			Rice			
Readiness of stock availability at the godowns during 2005-06						
Always available	16.00	16.00	72.00	36.00	44.00	36.00
Mostly available	84.00	44.00	24.00	56.00	56.00	64.00
Rarely available	0.00	36.00	0.00	0.00	0.00	0.00
Never available	0.00	4.00	4.00	0.00	0.00	0.00
No response	0.00	0.00	0.00	8.00	0.00	0.00
How often you get the total allotted stock in a single lot after receiving releasing order						
Always	32.00	40.00	68.00	32.00	68.00	40.00
Sometimes	64.00	60.00	28.00	60.00	12.00	60.00
Never	4.00	0.00	0.00	0.00	20.00	0.00
No response	0.00	0.00	4.00	8.00	0.00	0.00

7.10 Mode of Transportation of Grains

For transporting grains from the godown to the fair price shop, almost all shop owners in Jharkhand, Kerala, Uttarakhand and majority of them from Maharashtra pointed out that they had to make their own arrangements. Majority of the shop owners in Delhi pointed out that grains were delivered to the FPS through Civil Supply Department or through Food Corporation of India. In Madhya Pradesh, an overwhelming majority indicated that grains were delivered at the FPS by the godown owner. The mode of transportation used for this purpose was truck or tempo in almost all the states among majority of the shops. In Jharkhand, 36 per cent of them used tractor/trolley to lift the grains while 8 per cent in Jharkhand indicated using rickshaw with load carrier. In Uttarakhand, 12 per cent shop owners pointed using animal back for fetching their allocated grains because of the hilly terrain in that state. To the question who bears the transportation cost, overwhelming majority in all the selected states, except Madhya Pradesh replied that it was borne out by the FPS. In Madhya Pradesh, majority of the shop owners pointed out that transportation cost was borne by some other agency and not by the FPS. In some cases, transportation cost was paid by the FPS, but they were reimbursed the same either at the time of lifting of grains or later. The reimbursement cases were found in Maharashtra. It was learned through the surveyed shop owners that in most of the cases, food grains were being stored in the *kuccha/pucca* houses, as there was no provision for scientific storage or warehouse at the FPS. Only in Delhi around 8 per cent shop owners replied that they were using a scientific storage/ warehouse to store the grains. As a consequence, up to 10 per cent of the grains stored in the shop were getting spoiled in some cases, or their quality was deteriorated by the time the grains were lifted by the consumer.

Table 7.13 Frequency of Distribution to Consumer

	Delhi	Jharkhand	Kerala	Madhya Pradesh	Maharashtra	Uttarakhand
			Wheat			
What was the frequency of distribution of stock to the consumers during 2006?						
Weekly	0.00	20.00	84.00	16.00	0.00	0.00
Fortnightly	0.00	0.00	0.00	16.00	0.00	4.00
Monthly	88.00	24.00	0.00	60.00	100.00	96.00
Once in 2 months	0.00	0.00	0.00	4.00	0.00	0.00
Once in 3-6 months	0.00	0.00	0.00	0.00	0.00	0.00
Depending on the availability of items	12.00	56.00	12.00	0.00	0.00	0.00
Not lifted	0.00	0.00	0.00	0.00	0.00	0.00
No response	0.00	0.00	4.00	4.00	0.00	0.00
			Rice			
What was the frequency of distribution of stock to the consumers during 2006?						
Weekly	0.00	20.00	84.00	16.00	0.00	0.00
Fortnightly	0.00	0.00	0.00	16.00	0.00	4.00
Monthly	88.00	24.00	0.00	60.00	100.00	96.00
Once in 2 months	0.00	0.00	0.00	4.00	0.00	0.00
Once in 3-6 months	0.00	0.00	0.00	0.00	0.00	0.00
Depending on the availability of items	12.00	56.00	12.00	0.00	0.00	0.00
Not lifted	0.00	0.00	0.00	0.00	0.00	0.00
No response	0.00	0.00	4.00	4.00	0.00	0.00
			Wheat			
How often did you face stock out situation during 2006?						
Once in a year	8.00	44.00	0.00	4.00	40.00	28.00
Less than 5 times in year	0.00	32.00	0.00	8.00	4.00	0.00
5 to 10 times in a year	16.00	24.00	0.00	0.00	16.00	0.00
More than 10 times in year	0.00	0.00	0.00	8.00	0.00	0.00
Never	76.00	0.00	100.00	80.00	40.00	72.00
			Rice			
How often did you face stock out situation during 2006?						
Once in a year	8.00	40.00	0.00	4.00	40.00	24.00
Less than 5 times in year	0.00	20.00	0.00	8.00	4.00	0.00
5 to 10 times in a year	16.00	40.00	0.00	0.00	16.00	0.00
More than 10 times in year	0.00	0.00	0.00	8.00	0.00	0.00
Never	76.00	0.00	100.00	80.00	40.00	76.00

contd...

...contd...

	Delhi	Jharkhand	Kerala	Madhya Pradesh	Maharashtra	Uttarakhand
			Wheat			
Have you ever paid bribe for lifting commodities from godowns?						
Paid bribe all the times	0.00	92.00	0.00	0.00	16.00	0.00
Paid bribe most of the times	0.00	8.00	0.00	0.00	0.00	0.00
Paid bribe sometimes	0.00	0.00	0.00	0.00	0.00	0.00
Never paid	100.00	0.00	100.00	100.00	84.00	100.00
			Rice			
Have you ever paid bribe for lifting commodities from godowns?						
Paid bribe all the times	0.00	92.00	0.00	0.00	16.00	0.00
Paid bribe most of the times	0.00	8.00	0.00	0.00	0.00	0.00
Paid bribe sometimes	0.00	0.00	0.00	0.00	0.00	0.00
Never paid	100.00	0.00	100.00	100.00	84.00	100.00

Table 7.14 Lifting and Transportation

	Delhi	Jharkhand	Kerala	Madhya Pradesh	Maharashtra	Uttarakhand
Who makes the transportation arrangements for grains from godown to the FPS?						
Own arrangements	0.00	100.00	84.00	0.00	68.00	96.00
Delivered by *panchayat*	0.00	0.00	0.00	20.00	0.00	4.00
Delivered by godown owner	4.00	0.00	0.00	72.00	4.00	0.00
Delivered by Civil Supplies Department	56.00	0.00	4.00	4.00	24.00	0.00
Delivered by Food Corporation of India	24.00	0.00	4.00	0.00	0.00	0.00
Delivered by the State Government	0.00	0.00	0.00	4.00	0.00	0.00
Others	16.00	0.00	8.00	0.00	0.00	0.00
No response	0.00	0.00	0.00	0.00	4.00	0.00
What mode of transportation is used for transporting commodities to FPS?						
Truck	100.00	88.00	68.00	92.00	36.00	88.00
Bus	0.00	0.00	4.00	4.00	0.00	0.00
Tempo/Van/Matador	0.00	48.00	28.00	4.00	76.00	0.00
Tractor trolley	0.00	36.00	0.00	4.00	0.00	8.00
Auto rickshaw	0.00	0.00	4.00	0.00	0.00	0.00
Animal drawn vehicle	0.00	0.00	0.00	0.00	0.00	0.00
Rickshaw with load carrier	0.00	8.00	0.00	0.00	0.00	0.00
Boats	0.00	0.00	0.00	0.00	0.00	0.00
Animal back	4.00	0.00	0.00	0.00	0.00	12.00
Head load	0.00	0.00	0.00	0.00	0.00	0.00
Any other	0.00	0.00	0.00	0.00	0.00	0.00

Table 7.15 Transportation Charges

	Delhi	Jharkhand	Kerala	Madhya Pradesh	Maharashtra	Uttarakhand
Who bears transportation cost?						
FPS	100.00	96.00	88.00	12.00	68.00	92.00
Panchayati raj institutions	0.00	4.00	8.00	4.00	0.00	0.00
Civil Supplies Departments	0.00	0.00	0.00	0.00	28.00	0.00
Food Corporation of India (FCI)	0.00	0.00	0.00	0.00	0.00	0.00
Any other agency	0.00	0.00	4.00	76.00	0.00	0.00
Jointly	0.00	0.00	0.00	0.00	0.00	0.00
No response	0.00	0.00	0.00	0.00	0.00	8.00
Do you get reimbursement from the government?						
Yes	0.00	0.00	0.00	0.00	40.00	4.00
No	100.00	100.00	100.00	100.00	32.00	80.00
No response	0.00	0.00	0.00	0.00	28.00	16.00
In what proportion you get reimbursement?						
50:50	-	-	-	-	60.00	0.00
25:75	-	-	-	-	0.00	0.00
75:25	-	-	-	-	30.00	0.00
Any other ratio	-	-	-	-	0.00	100.00
No response	-	-	-	-	10.00	0.00

Table 7.16 Storage of Food Grains by FPS

	Delhi	Jharkhand	Kerala	Madhya Pradesh	Maharashtra	Uttarakhand
Where do you store food grains?						
Scientific storage/warehouse	8.00	0.00	0.00	0.00	0.00	0.00
***Pucca* house**	92.00	52.00	100.00	76.00	88.00	100.00
***Kuchha* house**	0.00	48.00	0.00	20.00	8.00	0.00
Other means	0.00	0.00	0.00	4.00	4.00	0.00
What is the percentage of food grains damaged in the store?						
Average percentage of grains	2.34	8.20	1.31	0.64	0.57	0.66

7.11 Prices Charged by the FPS

Last and the least, we tried to recheck the prices at which the food grains were being supplied to the households from the FPS. We collected retail prices at which food was being sold to the beneficiaries from the fair price shops during our survey period. The price details as given by the fair price shops are summarised in Table 7.17. It is seen from the mode of prices that almost all fair price shop owners in all the states, stated that they were supplying wheat at the rate of Rs. 2 per kg and rice at Rs. 3 per kg to the AAY households. The only exception was Kerala, where wheat was sold at par with the rice (Rs. 3 per kg). The mode prices as calculated for the households (in Chapter 4) were quite close to the mode prices calculated below for the fair price shops. However, if we compare the mean prices of the households (Chapter 4) with the calculated mean prices below for the FPS, it is visible from the comparison that the mean prices for FPS were generally lower than the mean prices revealed by the household analysis, although difference is less than a rupee in almost all the cases. However, the difference clearly indicates that some households were bearing slightly higher price than that indicated by the shop owners (the stipulated prices). Probably in some cases where transportation cost was fully borne by the shop owners, the latter tried to recover a part of the cost through passing-out some proportion of the cost to the consumers. The table also presents coefficient of variation of FPS prices across time and across various fair price shops for each of the AAY, BPL and APL categories. Like in the case of beneficiaries catered (as discussed above), coefficient of variation for FPS prices was miniscule across time but quite significant across various fair price shops. This indicates that prices remained constant over time for the same FPS but fluctuated across fair price shops in each state.

Table7.17 Prices of PDS Commodities as Quoted by the FPS

	Wheat			Rice		
	AAY	BPL	APL	AAY	BPL	APL
			Mean			
Delhi	2.00	4.65	6.81	3.08	6.20	8.86
Jharkhand	2.06	5.01	-	3.11	6.63	-
Kerala	3.00	3.01	6.69	3.04	3.08	8.83
Madhya Pradesh	2.09	5.00	6.78	2.97	6.45	8.65
Maharashtra	2.00	5.00	6.94	2.99	5.97	9.32
Uttarakhand	2.00	4.88	6.72	3.13	6.36	8.50
			Median			
Delhi	2.00	4.65	6.80	3.00	6.15	9.00
Jharkhand	2.00	5.00	-	3.00	6.50	-
Kerala	3.00	3.00	6.70	3.00	3.00	8.90
Madhya Pradesh	2.00	5.00	7.00	3.00	6.50	9.20
Maharashtra	2.00	5.00	7.00	3.00	6.00	9.50
Uttarakhand	2.00	4.75	6.68	3.00	6.38	8.69
			Mode			
Delhi	2.00	4.65	6.80	3.00	6.15	9.00
Jharkhand	2.00	5.00	-	3.00	6.50	-
Kerala	3.00	3.00	6.70	3.00	3.00	8.90
Madhya Pradesh	2.00	5.00	7.00	3.00	6.50	9.20
Maharashtra	2.00	5.00	7.00	3.00	6.00	9.50
Uttarakhand	2.00	4.65	6.60	3.00	6.15	8.45
			COV Across Time			
Delhi	0.00	0.23	0.50	2.80	1.37	1.39
Jharkhand	0.00	0.01	-	2.33	1.76	-
Kerala	-	1.31	0.20	2.06	3.96	1.20
Madhya Pradesh	3.76	2.00	2.22	0.69	1.12	0.37
Maharashtra	0.00	0.00	1.96	0.55	0.81	2.77
Uttarakhand	0.00	2.44	0.05	3.73	2.58	1.85
			COV Across FPS			
Delhi	0.00	1.16	2.44	15.98	7.13	10.01
Jharkhand	10.49	5.19	-	14.51	9.46	-
Kerala	-	6.11	1.26	11.35	22.05	6.15
Madhya Pradesh	27.86	9.04	14.13	5.44	6.26	18.17
Maharashtra	0.00	0.00	5.18	2.74	4.31	6.73
Uttarakhand	0.00	12.37	7.28	23.17	12.73	12.60

8 Concluding Remarks and Suggestions

8.1 Introduction

Department of Food and Public Distribution, Government of India started a series of concurrent evaluations of the targeted public distribution system. This volume is based on the second evaluation in that series. The main objective of the evaluation study was to examine the extent to which food grains disbursed under TPDS were actually reaching the BPL and AAY categories of population in the country and to identify the incidence as well as the mode of irregularities in the system.

8.2 Main Findings

Pattern of Income and its Major Constituents

Keeping into account the main objectives of evaluation, 80 per cent sample was drawn from the below poverty households and only 20 per cent sample belonged to the above poverty households. The demographic profile of the households indicates that the majority of the households belonged to scheduled caste, scheduled tribe or other backward castes. In the case of above poverty households, although percentage of forward castes' households was comparatively higher but the majority still belonged to the SC, ST and OBCs. The dominance of the latter three classes in the sample was apparently because of the preference given to the district/block where maximum numbers of below poverty cards were issued.

Occupation structure was significantly different among below and above poverty households. Whereas above poverty households depended mostly on agriculture/livestock, regular salaried jobs and on employment in self-business to eke out their daily earnings, below poverty households depended mostly on casual earnings in non-agriculture, farming activities or as migrant workers. As higher number of APL households depended on salary and self-business, they had assured regular earnings. Whereas, BPL and AAY households were more vulnerable as they did not have any regular means of employment and in most of the cases they were not employed for the whole month. However, comparing occupation structure within BPL and AAY households, no significant differences appeared in the pattern of occupation of these two categories. A majority of working members of AAY and BPL households depended on ad hoc means of income as they were engaged in wage earnings, mostly in non-agricultural activities. Among other minor occupations, public work programmes, work in common property resources, other self-construction works and working as a migrant workers were the activities that engaged households sporadically across all the three categories in the six states.

In all the six states, income was highest for the APL households and lowest for the AAY households without any exception. On an average, the selected AAY households earned around Rs. 43 thousand in Kerala, 28 thousand in Delhi, 20 thousand in Maharahstra and around 15 thousand in other three states, namely Uttarakhand, Jharkhand and Madhya Pradesh from all sources during the calendar year 2006. Among the BPL households, average earnings during the year were Rs. 47 thousand in Kerala, 38 thousand in Delhi, 28 to 29 thousand in Maharashtra and Uttarakhand, while Jharkhand and Madhya Pradesh were at the bottom with 18 and 16 thousand, respectively. For the above poverty households, average earnings topped in Delhi at Rs. 80 thousand, followed by Kerala and Maharashtra with Rs. 63 to Rs. 66 thousand, respectively. Uttarakhand lay in the middle with slightly above Rs. 50 thousand and Madhya Pradesh and Jharkhand remained at the bottom with an average income of Rs. 33 and 28 thousand, respectively. Differences in household income among different categories were lowest in Kerala and Jharkhand and higest in Delhi and Maharashtra. On an average, BPL income was 30 per cent higher compared to

AAY income while APL income was around twice that of BPL income and thrice that of AAY income among all the selected states.

Comparing the sources of income across different activities, wage income, income from self-employment (non-agriculture) and income from salary/pension were the major activities that contributed a lion's share in the aggregate household income. Among different categories, wage income from non-agricultural activities dominated with its share in total income of AAY and BPL households. In the case of APL households, it was income from the regular employment in salary that contributed the major amount in most of the states. Significant share of wages in BPL and AAY income further verifies results on occupational distribution. In the case of above poverty households, in consonance with the occupational structure, earnings from salary/pension and self-employment in non-agriculture constituted the highest share in income of these households in all the states without any exception. For the BPL and AAY households, salary/pension and self-employment income were the other sources of earnings. The transfer earnings from the family members who migrated temporarily constituted a significant share especially among the AAY and BPL households in two states, namely Madhya Pradesh and Jharkhand. Income from dividends, hiring-out assets and rents were the minor source for all the three category of households in all the six states.

The coefficient of variation indicates the dispersion of income across various households for the respective economic activities. Dispersion of income across households was highest for agriculture/livestock in most of the cases. High variability of agricultural and livestock income is quite natural because of the seasonal nature of these activities. For other activities, dispersion was lowest for salary, followed by wage income and self-employment earnings. Although the number of people engaged in salary and casual earnings was quite large, these two activities had lowest dispersion in income across the households. These statistics indicate that wage and fixed salary differential across households were far less than the earnings through agriculture and self-employment. The higher dispersion for agriculture and self-employment could be the result of the variation that takes place due to differences in land area cultivated and the amount of capital invested by the households in business and other activities.

The observed monthly income estimates compare very well with the annual income. On an average, monthly income for AAY, BPL and APL categories was quite closer to the annual income. The monthly income estimates were slightly less than the annual income in Jharkhand, Madhya Pradesh and Uttarakhand while they were pretty close to that of annual income for all the categories in Delhi, Kerala and Maharashtra. Nonetheless, in the former three states also, the differences between the two were not very high and significant. Monthly income across the six states further verifies our earlier findings on the ranking of different states in terms of household income. Like in annual income, Delhi and Kerala were on top in monthly income while Madhya Pradesh and Jharkhand lay at the bottom, leaving Maharashtra and Uttarakhand in the middle similar to as was observed in the case of annual income. The distribution across different economic activities was almost same as was discussed in the case of annual income. The major constituent of monthly income was wage from the non-agriculture sector in the case of AAY and BPL households, except Maharashtra where agriculture wages contributed the highest share. In the case of APL households, salary and income from self-employment contributed the major share in their case.

Comparison of our below poverty income data with the Planning Commission poverty cut-off revealed that our income estimates were more or less very close to that of Planning Commission. Our BPL income estimates were above the official poverty line in Delhi, Kerala and Maharashtra based on both annual estimates as well as monthly estimates. In Madhya Pradesh, our BPL estimates based on monthly income were almost equal to the official figure for rural areas, while annual BPL income was less than that of official figure. In Uttarakhand and Jharkhand, our BPL income based on annual as well as monthly was less than that of official poverty line. However, it is worth mentioning that the official poverty line income is the upper bound cut-off, whereas our estimated income is only the average income.

Pattern of Consumption—Food and Non-Food

On an average, per capita cereal consumption was more or less in consonance with the 1200 calorie norm, i.e., total cereal consumption was around 10.5 kgs in Delhi, Madhya Pradesh, Maharashtra and Uttarakhand. It far exceeded the 1200 calorie-norm in Jharkhand where average consumption of cereal was found 13.5 kgs while it was much lower than the norm, around 8.5 kgs in Kerala. In Jharkhand, all categories of households had much above the minimum requirement norm while in Kerala, all categories fell short of this target. Among the cereals, wheat and rice constituted the principal share while coarse grains were minor cereals. Wheat was the major cereal consumed in Delhi with average consumption of 7.7 kgs and in Madhya Pradesh with average quantity of 6 kgs. Rice occupied the principal place in Kerala and Jharkhand with an average quantity of 7.8 kgs and 11.4 kgs, respectively. In the other two states namely, Maharashtra and Uttarakhand, both wheat and rice were consumed almost in the same ratio. The other coarse cereals consumed namely, *jowar*, *bajra*, maize, barley and *ragi* were around 1.5 kgs in Maharashtra and 1 kg in Madhya Pradesh. In the other four states coarse cereal consumption was almost negligible. At the overall, average cereal consumption in the six states was around 11 kgs, that varied from 8.6 kgs in Kerala, between 10 to 11 kgs in Delhi, Madhya Pradesh and Maharashtra each, a little more than 11 kgs in Uttarakhand and the amount was maximum 13.5 kgs in Jharkhand.

Comparing total cereal consumption in the selected states from our survey data with that of NSS, our average cereal consumption was slightly less than the latest round of NSS (2004-05) survey in Kerala, Madhya Pradesh and Uttarakhand. It was slightly higher in rest of the three states, namely Delhi, Jharkhand and Maharashtra. However, the difference in the consumption between our survey data and the respective NSS data was generally less than 10 per cent. The food basket of an average Indian is diversifying with their rising income and improved living standards. The diversification of consumption from cereals and pulses towards edible oils, milk and high value products was visible from the trends presented by our survey data. Comparing the three categories of household, the quantity of cereals consumed by AAY households was generally higher than that of BPL and APL households. On the other hand, the quantity of edible oils, sugar and milk consumed was much higher for APL households as compared to BPL and AAY households in all the states without any exception.

Comparing variability in the food consumption among different categories, consumption variation was higher among the below poverty households compared to the above poverty households. Higher variation in food consumption by the poor households puts forth the question of affordability of food by such people and raises the need for some sort of income insurance for them. Among AAY households, coefficient of variation was high for milk in almost all the states, indicating its high cost for the poor that was beyond purchasing capacity of the AAY households. At the overall, coefficient of variation of consumption over time was lower than that of coefficient of variation in income supporting the well-documented phenomenon of consumption smoothing by the households.

Monthly per capita food consumption expenditure varied between Rs. 150 to Rs. 300 among our selected households. Although expenditure was lowest for the AAY households and highest for the APL households in all the states, the wedge between these three classes was not too wide. The consumption expenditure of BPL households was around 15 per cent higher against their AAY counterparts while it was 35 per cent higher in the case of APL households against that of BPL households. The wedge between APL and AAY households was little wider whereby the consumption expenditure of former was more than 50 per cent higher compared to the latter. Comparing the six selected states, the consumption expenditure was highest in Delhi, followed by Uttarakhand, Maharashtra, Kerala, Jharkhand and Madhya Pradesh in the descending order. Comparing food and non-food expenditure, the latter was less than total food expenditure in all the states without any exception and that was consistent with the all India NSS data. On an average, the distribution of food and non-food expenditure for all the categories and all the states was in the range of 60-70 per cent for food and 30-40 per cent for non-food. Among the non-food items, education and health involved the highest expenditure in almost all the states. Education was followed by fuel and light, clothing, other items (toiletry, entertainment, intoxicants, transport and other services) and footwear. Looking at the spread of total consumption expenditure across the selected states, total consumption expenditure for all categories topped in Delhi (Rs. 476), followed by Kerala (Rs. 415), Uttarakhand (Rs. 388), Maharashtra (Rs. 380) while Madhya Pradesh and Jharkhand were on the bottom with per capita consumption expenditure around Rs. 300 and 283, respectively.

Last and the least, comparing the variability in food and non-food expenditure, the coefficient of variation was significantly higher for the non-food commodities as compared to food items in all the states and in all the categories. On an average, coefficient of variation was less than 100 per cent in the case of food items while it averaged around 150 to 200 per cent in the non-food items. Among food items, variability was higher in the case of milk and milk products, poultry and meat, fruits and vegetables and spices. In the case of non-food items, variability was higher for all items compared to food items because of wide differences in the use of such items among the selected households, as we have clubbed households in each category, irrespective of the fact whether they belong to rural or urban areas.

Delivery under TPDS

The pattern of disbursement of PDS commodities through fair price shops indicated that in Delhi and Madhya Pradesh, wheat distribution dominated while rice was the principal cereal distributed in Kerala, Uttarakhand and Jharkhand. In Maharashtra, both these cereals were distributed nearly in the same proportion. The quantity of total cereals distributed among the AAY households averaged around 33 kgs in Delhi, Jharkhand and Uttarakhand and around 30 kgs in the other three states namely, Maharashtra, Madhya Pradesh and Kerala. The coverage of population was quite impressive with more than 98 per cent of household surveyed in the AAY category in Delhi and Uttarakhand, around 97 per cent in Kerala and Maharashtra, 93 per cent in Jharkhand and around 91 per cent in Madhya Pradesh. Thus, more than 90 per cent of the targeted Antyodaya families obtained 30 kgs or more of rice and wheat during the six month of survey period without any exception in the six selected states. In the case of BPL, the distributed quantity was closer to stipulated quantity only in two states namely, Delhi and Uttarakhand. In Delhi, 33 kgs cereals were distributed covering 99 per cent of the selected families, while in Uttarakhand 32 kgs cereals were distributed among 94 per cent households. In other selected states, in Maharashtra, 26 kgs of cereals were distributed among 98 per cent of the selected households, while in Kerala, 98 per cent of BPL households obtained 23 kgs of cereals (mainly rice). Jharkhand and Madhya Pradesh were relatively less efficient in delivery as only 79 per cent population obtained 29 kgs of cereals in Jharkhand and in Madhya Pradesh, 81 per cent BPL households obtained only 22 kgs of rice and wheat. Delhi and Kerala made exceptions in the APL targeting (more than 70 per cent) who obtained 30 and 24 kgs of cereals, respectively. In Uttarakhand, around one-third of the selected households obtained around 29 kgs of cereals. In rest of the three states namely, Jharkhand, Maharashtra and Madhya Pradesh, APL targeting remained only nominal as less than 10 per cent of them obtained 20-25 kgs of cereals. Sugar and kerosene oil were the other commodities that were distributed in the selected states mostly on the universal basis. Besides these four commodities, some selected households in Delhi also reported obtaining some quantity of pulses at some concessional prices during one or two months of the survey period.

Looking at the share of food provided by the PDS and that purchased through the open market, the ratio of PDS to market was around two-third to one-third for the combination of wheat and rice in the case of AAY households in Delhi, Kerala, Maharashtra and Uttarakhand. It was slightly higher than 50 per cent for the PDS in Madhya Pradesh and slightly less than 50 per cent in Jharkhand. In the case of other below poverty households, the ratio of PDS to market (for cereals) was 60/40 in Delhi, Kerala, Maharashtra and around 50/50 in Uttarakhand. In Madhya Pradesh, the ratio was measured one-third to two-third and in Jharkhand, it was slightly more than 40/60. Share of PDS in consumption of sugar was quite divergent while in the case of kerosene oil, more than 90 per cent of its demand was met by the PDS in the selected states including that of above poverty households.

A pertinent question to ask is to what extent the food subsidy is being passed on to the poor in the form of lower prices of food and other essentials. It was shown by the data that our observed mode price for Antyodaya families was exactly equal to the stipulated price in all the selected states except Kerala, where price was Rs. 3 per kg for both the cereals. In the case of BPL households, the mode price charged for rice was in the range of Rs. 6 to Rs. 7 per kg, except Kerala where it was Rs. 3 per kg. Price charged for wheat in all other states for the BPL households was uniformly Rs. 5 per kg. Comparing mode prices with the more common average, namely the mean, the statistics indicated that mean prices were more or less equal to the mode prices in all the states for both wheat as well as rice. Mean prices were slightly higher for AAY households in Jharkhand and for BPL households in Maharashtra and Uttarakhand. Nonetheless, the difference between the mean and mode prices was only miniscule, not only for wheat and rice but also for kerosene oil and sugar. Thus, households below poverty obtained their entitlement at a price that was quite closer to the stipulated price.

Insurance against the Income Risks

We tested the hypothesis of consumption insurance by the households against the unforeseen income risks using regression tools on our penal data. Our test results suggested that our selected households were not fully insured against idiosyncratic income risks. The rejection of the full insurance model was for all the states and all the category of households. However, regression results indicated some possibility of partial risk sharing activities between households either within the same village or within their same ethnic groups. The implications of these results are quite significant. Government is running various schemes/programmes including the targeted public distribution system designed specifically to reduce the risk factor present in rural incomes. The stated aim of such programmes is often to provide a safety net to the rural poor. Our results support the fact that such programmes are not being targeted adequately as the poorest of the poor (the AAY) households remain the most vulnerable. The results of this chapter strengthen the case for improved targeting and making some provision for the public insurance for the poorest of the poor.

Performance of TPDS on Qualitative Issues

To quantify the performance of PDS system, we collected information on entitlement, prices and other related aspects. In addition to such quantitative information we also collected qualitative information on various aspects of PDS. The findings on qualitative aspects are summarised in the following lines. On an average, households' perceptions about their entitlement were reasonably close to the actual amount received in Delhi, Jharkhand, Kerala and Uttarakhand while some differences were observed in Maharashtra and Madhya Pradesh. A majority of those households who did not receive regular entitlements indicated that they did not obtain supply for more than two months during the last calendar year. In Jharkhand, a majority of the AAY households not receiving regular supply pointed out that they were not given any explanation by the fair price shop owners for not supplying entitlement, while a majority among the BPL and APL households pointed out that the reason given to them by the FPS was supply not received from the godown. In Kerala and Madhya Pradesh, a majority of such households indicated that they were not given any explanation for not being supplied the entitled food while rest of the households indicated less supply at the FPS. The frequency of households not lifting food despite availability was not very high among the selected states. However, incidence was disturbing in Jharkhand and Madhya Pradesh where some BPL households did not lift their entitlement because of scarcity of income.

To the question of adherence to the prescribed opening time and keeping the outlet opened for stipulated number of days by the FPS shopkeepers, 25 per cent BPL households in Jharkhand and same number of APL households in Madhya Pradesh and Maharashtra faced problems in drawing their entitlement because of improper opening timings of the FPS shops. Majority of the households disapproved the perception that cereals being supplied through the fair price shops were being underweighed. To a question whether the shop owners indulged in diverting food to the open market or involved in black marketing, a majority of the selected households expressed their inability to answer this question directly. In Jharkhand, around 20 per cent households answered that shopkeepers often indulge in such activities, while another 20 per cent answered that they indulge in such activities sometimes. Were the consumers satisfied with the quality of services offered at the FPS, more than 70 per cent households among AAY and BPL and more than 50 per cent among APL replied yes in all the six selected states. A majority of dissatisfied households in Delhi, Kerala, Madhya Pradesh, Maharashtra and Uttarakhand were of the opinion that there was mismanagement at the fair price shops. In almost all the states, majority of the households were not knowing whom to complain if the quality of grains offered from PDS was really bad. On the specific questions of quality and variety of wheat and rice distributed through PDS, a majority of households in Delhi, Jharkhand and Madhya Pradesh responded that there was no significant difference between the PDS and local varieties. In Kerala and Uttarakhand, a majority of households stated that PDS rice and wheat varieties were considerably different from the local varieties available. Similarly, in Maharashtra, the households indicated that wheat variety from the PDS was different from the market. Except, Kerala and Uttarakhand, households in all other states indicated that they did not have any strong preference for local varieties and they could consume PDS varieties of wheat and rice. In Kerala, 30 to 40 per cent households (all categories) and 40 per cent APL households in Jharkhand were dissatisfied with the quality of grains supplied through the PDS. Those who were not satisfied, a majority of them in Kerala reasoned that there were impurities in the grain and grain supplied were broken. Another significant numbers indicated that the taste of the grains was not good. In Jharkhand, more than 50 per cent of the dissatisfied households indicated inferior quality of the grains and around 25 per cent pointed out presence of impurities in the grains supplied. On the question of underweighment of the grains, we tried to find out what was the extent of such activities. A majority of those households who answered that underweighment was happening were of the opinion that it was 5 to 10 per cent. Finally, to our question of how the households rate the performance of TPDS during the periods of distress, an overwhelming majority (around 80 per cent) in Delhi and Uttarakhand indicated it as good while less than 5 per cent rated it as poor. In Jharkhand, around 80 per cent were of the opinion that it was good or satisfactory while 20 per cent indicated it either poor or very poor. In Kerala, the proportion of households who rated it very good, good or satisfactory exceeded 90 per cent while less than 10 per cent indicated it as poor. In Madhya Pradesh, those who rated it poor or very poor averaged around 40 to 45 per cent while equal number of them indicated it as satisfactory. In Maharashtra, the households answering poor or very poor performance averaged around 20 to 25 per cent while more than 30 per cent rated it as good.

Identification Problems—Errors of Targeting

Using data from various secondary sources, we calculated incidences of excess card issued/unidentified families as well as inclusion/exclusion errors among all the states and at the all India level. The number of excess cards issued in our selected states were highest, around 12 lakh in Madhya Pradesh, 10 lakh in Maharashtra and around 5 lakh in Uttarakhand. In the other three states, number of cards issued were less than that of existing families. The extent of unidentified families was highest around 25 lakh in Jharkhand and 4 lakh in Delhi. In the case of identification errors, excessive targeting or inclusion error (E) was much higher than the exclusion error or failure of targeting the poor (F). A very high amount of exclusion error (poor getting left out) was observed only in Uttarakhand (28 per cent) among our selected states. The inclusion of non-poor in the subsidised food was a serious problem and it was observed up to 18 per cent in Kerala and 5 to 7 per cent in Maharashtra, Jharkhand and Madhya Pradesh.

We compared the per capita income and expenditure of the selected AAY, BPL and APL households with the Planning Commission's cut-off expenditure criterion to validate whether the card they held is true or false. Following the income criterion, the inclusion error was up to 80 per cent in Kerala, above 50 per cent in Delhi, around 40 per cent in Maharashtra and between 20 to 40 per cent in Jharkhand, Madhya Pradesh and Uttarakhand. With respect to expenditure criterion, the exclusion error was more than 80 per cent in Jharkhand, 70 to 80 per cent in Kerala, Madhya Pradesh and Uttarakhand and 50 to 60 per cent in Delhi and Maharashtra. The more serious problem was the wrong identification of AAY households who should have been issued an APL card instead. Their proportion was around 70 per cent in Kerala, around 50 per cent in Delhi, 40 per cent in Maharashtra and 20-30 per cent in the rest of the three selected states.

Diversion of Wheat and Rice

In the incidence of mis-targeting, it is implicit that the food is being diverted to the non-poor due to identification problems. However, in addition to such diversions, there was some proportion of food that was not being actually distributed among any of the households but it was shown in the state records as uplifted. In the case of AAY rice, no diversion was observed in Maharashtra, Uttarakhand and Madhya Pradesh. In Delhi and Jharkhand, the volume of diversion was less than 5 per cent. In Kerala, however, diversion of rice was noticed up to 19 per cent. In the case of AAY wheat, diversions were noticed in four of the six selected states and its volume was up to 16 per cent in Jharkhand and Madhya Pradesh and less than 10 per cent in Maharashtra. Among BPL households, the extent of diversion of food was highest, especially for wheat while in the case of rice, the extent of diversion was 19 per cent in Madhya Pradesh. In wheat, diversion was observed in all the selected states, except Delhi. Diversion of wheat was less than 10 per cent in Jharkhand, 18-20 per cent in Maharashtra and Kerala and around 30 per cent in Madhya Pradesh and Uttarakhand. Among above poverty households, no diversion was observed for rice while in the case of wheat significant diversions were found only in Jharkhand and Kerala. Thus, Delhi was the only state where almost whole amount uplifted was distributed among the households as no diversions were observed in the case of APL while diversion in BPL and AAY were almost negligible. In the other states, except the case of wheat for APL in Jharkhand, diversion were less than 30 per cent in all the selected states and for all the categories. From the above discussion, one can conclude that distribution of grains was found satisfactory in Delhi while some improvement is needed in the system in the other selected states. However, the identification of appropriate target group remains an illusive task in all the states under study including that of Delhi.

Functioning of the Fair Price Shops

To assess the functioning of fair price shops a separate questionnaire was designed. The conclusive remarks on FPS functioning are presented here. The shops in all the cases were located in a periphery of around 5 to 20 kilometres from the godown from where the grains were being lifted. A majority of the shopkeepers were keeping their shop opened to supply grains for more than 15 days and shop was opened the whole day in majority of cases for the convenience of the beneficiaries. The household entitlement for grains was fixed on the monthly basis. The entitlement was fixed at 35 kgs per household, irrespective of the family size, which was confirmed by the surveyed fair price shop owners in all the categories, except Kerala and Jharkhand. In Kerala, almost all the fair price shop owners indicated 25 kgs of cereals (rice + wheat) as entitlement for the category of BPL households. In the case of Jharkhand, no entitlement was shown for the category of APL households. The entitlement indicated by the FPS owners was almost same as was indicated by the households interviewed.

In the AAY category, the maximum number of cards registered per FPS occurred in Madhya Pradesh while in the other two categories, the highest cards were found in Delhi. Looking at the percentage of grains distributed to that of grains lifted, on an average, grains distributed matched with grains lifted. More than 70 per cent of owners replied yes to the question whether during the last year there were any instances when the FPS had lifted less than the allocated quota from the godown. An overwhelming majority of shop owners in Delhi and Maharashtra pointed out less availability of grains at godown as the main reason for lifting less than the allotted quota. In Jharkhand, Kerala and Uttarakhand, on the other hand, shop owners pointed out lack of demand of grains as the reason for not lifting their allotted quota. Fair price shops were also left with undistributed grains in many instances. A majority of the shopkeepers pointed out that they adjust the unlifted grains in the next month supply, while only 15 per cent in Kerala and Madhya Pradesh pointed out that they distribute more grains to the beneficiaries.

We propounded some questions related to transparency to the FPS owners. Almost all the interviewed shop owners answered yes to the question whether the FPS shops keep records of their transactions. On the type of records maintained, more than 90 per cent were of the opinion that they kept all the details of stocks handled as well as lifting details from the godown and distribution of grains among the beneficiaries by the number of cards and the total grains distributed of a particular commodity. Almost all of shop owners pointed out that they displayed all the information to the beneficiaries. On the question whether they displayed the name and address of the authority for redressal of consumers' grievances, a majority of them replied yes. However, on cross checking from the households, the replies of the shop owners were not found consistent.

For the monitoring of the FPS functioning, there were multiple authorities that were supposed to check the functioning of the FPS and also could check the samples of grain being sold to the beneficiaries. Among our selected shop owners, almost all shop owners in all the states, except Madhya Pradesh pointed out Civil Supplies Department as the main monitoring authority for their distribution of grains. In Madhya Pradesh, a majority of the shop owners indicated District Vigilance Committee as the monitoring authority who inspected their shops. Panchayat Committee was also monitoring FPS in few cases. A few shop owners in Kerala replied that their shops were never monitored by any authority.

To our question whether the stocks were readily available when they visited the godown, a majority of the shopkeepers in almost all the states replied that stocks were always or mostly available. However, 30 per cent shop owners in Jharkhand pointed out that stocks were rarely available while 4 per cent in Jharkhand and Kerala pointed out that stocks were never available on their first entry whenever they visited the godown. Among our selected states, some of the FPS shop owners pointed out that they are distributing grains weekly and fortnightly. The percentage of shop owners who indicated weekly distribution among the consumers was quite high (84 per cent) in Kerala. In Jharkhand, majority of them pointed out that their distribution depends on the availability of stock from the godown. To another question of how frequently the shop runs stock-out situation, majority of FPS owners indicated that they never run out of stock, while a few of them from Jharkhand and Uttarakhand indicated once or twice (less than five times) in a year. To the question, how oftenly they have to pay bribe to receive their allocated quota from the godown, almost all selected shop owners except Jharkhand said they never paid any bribe. All selected shop owners from Jharkhand, however, answered that they always or most of the times paid bribe to receive their quota from the godown.

For transporting grains from the godown to the fair price shop, almost all shop owners in Jharkhand, Kerala, Uttarakhand and majority of them from Maharashtra pointed out that they had to make their own arrangements. Majority of the shop owners in Delhi pointed out that grains were delivered to the FPS through Civil Supply Department or through Food Corporation of India. The mode of transportation used for this purpose was truck or tempo in almost all the states among majority of the shops. To the question who bears the transportation cost, overwhelming majority in all the selected states, except Madhya Pradesh replied that it was borne out by the FPS. In some cases, transportation cost was paid by the FPS but they were reimbursed the same either at the time of lifting of grains or later. The reimbursement cases were found in Maharashtra. It was learned through the surveyed shop owners that in most of the cases, food grains were being stored in the *kuccha/pucca* houses, as there was no provision for scientific storage or warehouse at the FPS. Only in Delhi around 8 per cent shop owners replied that they were using a scientific storage/warehouse to store the grains. As a consequence, up to 10 per cent of the grains stored in the shop were getting spoiled in some cases, or their quality was deteriorated by the time the grains were lifted by the consumer.

Almost all fair price shop owners in all the states, indicated that they were supplying wheat at the rate of Rs. 2 per kg and rice at Rs. 3 per kg to the AAY households. The only exception was Kerala, where wheat was sold at par of rice (Rs. 3 per kg). Comparing mean prices of the households with that of fair price shops, it was seen that the mean prices for FPS were generally lower than the mean prices obtained from the household analysis, although difference was less than a rupee in almost all the cases. However, the difference clearly indicates that some households were bearing slightly higher prices than that indicated by the shop owners (the stipulated prices). Probably in some cases where transportation cost was fully borne by the shop owners, the latter tried to recover a part of their cost through switching out some proportion of the cost to the consumers.

8.3 Summing Up

Like in the previous volume, the evaluation findings for this set of six selected states about the efficiency of the PDS system are mixed ones. The performance of PDS in terms of providing food to the poor was quite satisfactory in Delhi and Uttarakhand where nearly 35 kgs of cereals were distributed to more than 98 per cent targeted groups. In Kerala and Maharashtra, although coverage of targeted groups was above 96 per cent but the cereals distributed were far less than 35 kgs. Madhya Pradesh and Jharkhand, fell short of target, both in terms of targeting population and the amount of cereals distributed. In these two states, only 80 per cent of BPL households were supplied 22 and 28 kgs of cereals, respectively. The gross irregularities were found in terms of huge identification errors and some incidences of diversion of food, especially in the case of BPL households. The basic criterion for the identification of AAY was that it should be meant for those people who are not able to have two square meals a day. In our questionnaire we posed this question to all our households (did they have days without two square meals per day in a month during the last one year?). The responses of the households are summarised in Table 8.1 below. It is clear from the results that on an average less than 15 per cent AAY households answered yes to the above question. Similarly, we have summarised the amount of assets held by our selected households in Table 8.2. The data clearly indicates that the average assets holding for AAY households were very high in almost all the selected states.

Table 8.1 Percentage of the Population Who Remained Without Two Square Meals a Day in a Month

State	Percentage of Households
AAY	
Delhi	12.5
Jharkhand	7.5
Kerala	3.0
Madhya Pradesh	1.0
Maharashtra	8.8
Uttarakhand	15.6
BPL	
Delhi	17.1
Jharkhand	4.4
Kerala	2.3
Madhya Pradesh	4.7
Maharashtra	9.8
Uttarakhand	17.6
APL	
Delhi	19.7
Jharkhand	0.6
Kerala	9.6
Madhya Pradesh	1.0
Maharashtra	8.9
Uttarakhand	17.2

Table 8.2 Assets Holdings (Rs. per Household)

	Delhi	Jharkhand	Kerla	Madhya Pradesh	Maharashtra	Uttarakhand
			AAY			
Land	0	16202	32376	8262	12982	16303
House property	53000	21870	70149	16250	38550	38555
Agricultural imp & livestock	150	1781	1118	759	820	1030
Consumer assets	3138	1132	3860	339	1166	1173
Business assets	314	12	90	21	1968	989
Ornaments	380	1409	7541	1679	3312	571
Utensils	1401	700	1231	1029	1296	966
Others	0	4	0	15	21	0
Total	58383	43110	116365	28354	60115	59587
			BPL			
Land	2742	28393	38769	17676	36258	22973
House property	66164	25273	84692	19476	49669	48311
Agricultural imp & livestock	62	3031	1135	2090	1394	3395
Consumer assets	4442	1853	5352	1785	2435	1764
Business assets	2302	308	440	175	3751	2296
Ornaments	619	2229	10420	2643	4163	1316
Utensils	1685	812	1277	1124	1732	1358
Others	2	6	0	38	43	439
Total	78018	61905	142085	45007	99445	81852
			APL			
Land	2709	52232	41404	49227	70443	82759
House property	2660099	57796	144949	48822	96552	74877
Agricultural imp & livestock	0	4351	384	17387	8076	4291
Consumer assets	32512	7836	14676	5773	10458	9116
Business assets	34283	11123	2556	4415	3094	2626
Ornaments	1820	8987	31630	8324	12385	3838
Utensils	3286	1323	2122	2441	2168	1812
Others	0	31	0	51	115	40
Total	2734709	143679	237721	136440	203291	179359

The issue of gross failure of identification of the right beneficiaries, as was also found in the previous volume of the study raises the question whether it is right methodology to identify poor families on the basis of income cut-off, identified through household expenditure as is practiced by the Planning Commission. There is a huge difference between the per capita income and per capita consumption expenditure presented and analysed in details in both the volumes. The difference is natural given the fact that Indian economy is growing at a very fast pace (around 8 to 9 per cent) and gross domestic savings touched around 35 per cent during 2006-07. The gap between the household income and household expenditure for the six months of survey period (in terms of savings/dis-savings) is presented in Table 8.3. It is seen from the table that in all the three categories, gap between income and consumption not only was positive but also was quite significant. The volume ranged between 25 to 50 per cent in all the categories including that of Antyodaya families. This highlights the fact that it is inappropriate to proxy income from the consumption expenditure. In our analysis, we saw that dispersion in household income was much higher compared to household consumption across our three categories of households. The consumption expenditure varied much less compared to the variation in income. Therefore, when we compare our observed income and consumption expenditure with the official cut-off, huge differences appear in the extent of inclusion and exclusion errors.

However, devising some alternate criterion as cut-off income/expenditure or some other method for the identification of poor is not going to be an easy task. A voice is raised from some quarters in favour of replacing the procurement and distribution system by food stamps whereby subsidy is transferred to the poor by means of stamps rather than handling the huge amount of food stocks. However, the international experience suggests the system of food stamps is also wrought with huge amount of inclusion and exclusion errors (see Annexure A-8.1). Even if we switch to the system of food stamp, the problem of wrong identification is going to increase rather than decrease. Another major problem that food stamps programme might have to face is the misuse of food stamps whereby poor people use stamps to buy commodities other than food or resell stamps to better-off people in lure of money. Finally Table 8.4 presents ranking of 12 states in terms of performance according to different indicators.

8.4 Policy Suggestions

Given the ground reality, it would not be possible to improve the PDS system unless the consumer, especially the poorest ones are made aware of their rights. The whole problem of identification error arises because of lack of information/unawareness of the poor about the fixation criteria for the AAY or BPL or any other welfare schemes for that matter. The people in the lower strata are by and large, unaware of the method that is being followed in fixing up the entitlement for holding an AAY, BPL or APL card. The following steps might help in bringing more awareness among the poor and improving the functioning of the PDS system in overall meeting the targets.

Display the Criterion Followed in Fixing Up the Entitlement

It should be made mandatory on the part of the *gram panchayat*/civil supply authorities to display the main criterion followed for issuing a BPL or AAY card. The information should be written in the local language and it should be displayed on the notice board at the *panchayat* office as well as on all other important places, like school, primary health care centre, *choupal*, etc. It should also be made mandatory on the part of the *panchayat* to propagate the criterion among the villagers through a campaign or mass information system usually used for disseminating important information among the villagers.

Display the Entitled Quantity and Price for AAY and BPL Households

It should be made mandatory for the *panchayat* to educate people about the entitlement of grains fixed for the BPL and AAY households as well as the stipulated price. The mass information system should be used to keep the villagers informed and updated about the entitlement and price of grains as well as the grains received from the godown by FPS and timing of distribution of grains among the beneficiaries. This can also be done with the help of primary and secondary schools running within the village by educating the kids about the criterion followed in issuing cards and entitlement and price of grains for the AAY and BPL households. There is a need to include this within the curriculum of the schools. The medium of mass awareness, e.g., local language newspapers, regional radio and television stations can also be used for spreading general awareness about the criterion and the entitlement among the public.

Display the Criterion and Entitlement on the FPS and on the Ration Card

It would also help to educate the villagers to a great extent if the list of beneficiaries (AAY and BPL cardholders) is displayed on a notice board outside each and every fair price shop. In addition to beneficiary list, the information related to entitlement for each category, price of grains, the total amount of stock received from godown and distributed among the beneficiaries should be displayed in local language on daily basis. The criterion as well as entitlement and price information should also be printed on the back of the ration card.

Make the Monitoring Compulsory and Punish the Culprit Including the Panchayats

It is essential to monitor the process of identification of card holding. At present, identification is done by the district/block supply officers on the recommendations of the concerned *panchayat* or local bodies in the village and urban areas, respectively. However, this power of identification is indisposed in most of the cases. There is no authority that cross checks the identification.

In the given circumstances, a large number of inclusion and exclusion errors are found as is confirmed by the results of this study. Even if the irregularities are observed at some level, there is no provision for any action against the authorities that have done wrong identification either deliberately or due to lack of proper information. Nonetheless, it becomes compulsory to make the system more full proof by making the provision of bringing the concerned officials as well as that of the *panchayat* or local bodies to book if such irregularities come into picture. It would be more appropriate if there are multiple authorities cross checking the identification.

Open a Grievance Cell for the Poor

In some cases, it has been observed that there is a nexus between the FPS owner, civil supplies inspector and the *sarpanch* in the village. There is a dire need to break this nexus. This can be done by taking various actions like, frequent monitoring of the FPS; opening up one grievance cell in every village or in a group of villages where people can lodge their complaints related to PDS; circulation of clear rules and regulations related to identification, entitlement, prices and quality norms and its mass publicity among the public; evaluation of PDS functioning in the village by a peer group within the village, including the headmaster/school teachers, doctor at the community health centre and other more aware members that may include some of the members from the *panchayat*, excluding the *sarpanch*. In order to provide incentives for efficiency those who are working honestly and more efficiently should be rewarded including that of village *panchayats* as well as fair price shops.

Make the FPS More Viable by Giving them Higher Margin

In many cases it was observed that fair price shops were neither being provided with any transportation facility nor their transportation cost from godown to the fair price shop was being refunded. By and large, the fair price shop owners were of the opinion that if they did not pass on the transportation cost to the consumers, they would end up bearing huge losses. In many other cases, lower net margin also led the fair price shop owners to indulge in unfair means and black marketing. In order to improve efficiency and remove corruption in the system, it becomes compulsory to provide incentives to the FPS by giving them better margin between their purchase and sale price.

Computerisation of Records for Cross Checking

All business at fair price shops and supply godowns was done on manual basis. In such a system, it becomes very difficult to cross check the records to maintain the transparency in the system. In the long run, it is highly desirable to computerise the whole system and prepare a network whereby all FPS and civil supply godowns should be connected online. This will bring more efficiency and transparency in the system.

Multi-tier Checking of the Quality of Grains Supplied

The grains supplied from godown to the FPS and ultimately to the consumers should be inspected at multi stages. A large number of households surveyed pointed out defects in the quality of grains supplied through fair price shops. In some of the cases even households were not buying their entitlements because of poor quality of the grains supplied.

Strengthening the Role of NGOs in Combating Corruption

NGOs can play a significant role in ensuring that FPS owners do not indulge in diverting PDS food to the open market or in black marketing. There are many examples whereby NGOs using Right to Information Act helped poor people in obtaining their entitled quantity at the stipulated price. Other means of awareness should also be used for spreading information among the poor people. Ignorance has been one of the major causes of diversion. More awareness regarding entitlements, prices stipulated by the Government for rice and wheat can be spread through street plays and documentary movies. These can be based on the real life instances. Also, information such as the prices stipulated by the Government must be there on the ration card so that each person can ensure that he/she is not being cheated.

Table 8.3 Gap in Consumption and Income as a Percentage of Income for the Selected Households

	Month 1	Month 2	Month 3	Month 4	Month 5	Month 6	Average
				AAY			
Delhi	43.70	45.98	24.50	34.69	30.21	23.06	34.51
Jharkhand	34.85	32.93	40.75	35.46	35.50	40.69	36.77
Kerla	59.25	53.53	66.54	64.23	65.63	62.69	62.11
Madhya Pradesh	52.07	50.25	47.52	43.68	46.11	43.03	46.81
Maharashtra	44.61	43.67	33.70	41.19	37.45	41.66	40.54
Uttarakhand	35.59	34.47	39.33	45.18	36.07	40.50	38.69
				BPL			
Delhi	45.65	44.76	33.22	38.85	30.42	28.18	37.52
Jharkhand	35.29	30.83	31.45	28.26	27.00	30.00	30.57
Kerla	58.29	52.25	63.09	65.74	63.67	59.51	60.58
Madhya Pradesh	44.23	41.26	38.35	28.38	41.65	40.79	39.03
Maharashtra	43.33	43.63	28.51	39.46	34.19	37.17	38.00
Uttarakhand	37.19	34.87	36.52	42.66	34.46	38.05	37.40
				APL			
Delhi	51.77	44.14	38.14	49.77	45.40	40.45	45.53
Jharkhand	34.15	28.98	28.72	26.69	26.48	33.53	29.83
Kerla	53.72	46.50	53.62	55.00	57.29	55.08	53.58
Madhya Pradesh	43.15	34.78	51.76	21.73	38.73	48.13	40.14
Maharashtra	48.63	50.01	8.85	47.45	45.22	44.67	43.13
Uttarakhand	46.65	37.60	53.93	60.44	44.86	52.59	50.24

Table 8.4 Ranking of the 12 Selected States According to their Performance under TPDS

Indicators	Raj.	Chh.	Bih.	UP	Asm.	Miz.	Del.	Jha.	Ker.	MP	Mah.	Utrk.
Delivery - AAY	8	3	12	4	11	10	1	7	6	9	5	2
Delivery - BPL	5	3	12	7	11	8	1	9	4	10	6	2
Price efficiency	8	4	12	7	10	11	1	9	6	5	2	3
Quality satisfaction	7	3	12	10	5	11	4	9	6	8	2	1
Excess cards issued	11	6	1	12	7	5	1	1	1	10	9	8
Inclusion errors	9	7	10	5	11	12	6	2	8	3	4	1
Exclusion errors	5	6	3	4	1	2	7	12	8	11	9	10
Food diversion - AAY	1	1	12	4	5	11	6	10	9	8	7	1
Food diversion - BPL	1	9	11	6	10	8	2	3	5	12	4	7

Note: 1. The ranking is based on PDS performance for AAY and BPL households.

2. The ranking indicates 1 for best performance and 12 for worst performance.

Source: Own calculations.

Annexure

Annexure A-8.1: Food Stamp Programmes in Jamaica, Honduras and Sri Lanka: An Assessment[1]

In 1984, Jamaica switched from an expensive general food subsidy to a food stamp programme. The programme targeted four categories of vulnerable groups: pregnant and lactating women, children under six years of age, individuals who already qualify for poverty relief and public social assistance (mostly the elderly and the handicapped) and low-income single-parent or poor households. Food stamps are legal tender, and can be used to purchase cornmeal, rice, powdered skim milk, dark sugar, flour and meat. The value of the stamps is J$45 for pregnant and lactating women, J$60 for persons receiving poverty relief and public assistance and single-person households and J$105 for multiple-headed households. Registration of recipients at a primary health clinic is necessary; stamps are issued every two months and can be collected in public areas (e.g., police stations, churches, etc.).

Overall, the programme is relatively well-targeted. Linking benefits to other requirements such as registration at clinics has considerably reduced inclusion errors, though some benefits certainly reach the upper quintiles. Thus, as of 1991-92, while there is a severe shortfall in the registration of pregnant and lactating women, single-person households and poor households have exceeded registration targets, implying substantial inclusion errors. Presumably, the relatively higher value of benefits to households may have encouraged the non-poor to enter the programme. Although the rolls have been "cleaned" since the introduction of the scheme (once in 1987 and again in 1989) and recipients means tested repeatedly, the system does not yet have exit mechanisms that are better defined and implemented. Although the poor were favoured, the share of benefits across quintiles did not become progressive over time. According to the survey of Living Conditions Report of 1991, the poorest 40 per cent of the population comprised 58.2 per cent of the beneficiaries—about the same as previous years. The main problem is the under-coverage of pregnant and lactating women—the most vulnerable group. The reason: the procedures for registration at health clinics is complicated and far from automatic: implementation programmes persisted at all stages from application to registration to disbursement. Weak coordination between the staff of the Ministry of Labour and the Ministry of Health, and shortage of staff in the latter, have been cited as the main reasons for the observed deficiencies.

Honduras provides another example of a delivery system that promoted self-targeting. In 1993, Honduras implemented a food stamp programme that distributed stamps through schools and health centres. Under the Women Head of Household Coupon Program, food stamps are distributed through schools to poor mothers and their children attending grades one through three and who are shown to be at risk of malnutrition. In addition, at schools where the results of the annual nutrition survey shows a high incidence of malnutrition equal to or higher than 60 per cent, all first graders are eligible for the programme. Food stamps are distributed three times a year, and are estimated to cover 20 per cent of household food expenditures. Food stamps are also delivered through health centres in the maternal Child Coupon Program. The target group are low-income children under five and pregnant and lactating mothers. The intervention is concentrated on the earliest stages of infancy and childhood, and includes assistance to pregnant mothers to improve the changes of reaching children before malnutrition causes permanent damage. Beneficiaries must meet health surveillance requirements in order to maintain eligibility. The programme also provides nutrition education and involves the private sector.

Successful dissemination of information has resulted in 100 per cent of merchants accepting the coupons. Local commercial banks are also willing to redeem coupons directly; this leaves no room for merchants to demand "servicing fees" in redeeming coupons against goods. Beneficiaries can redeem coupons form commercial banks within four months of their issue (with redemption not contingent on purchasing of food). The programme has been relatively more cost-effective than other nutrition programmes in reducing poverty, and it has been widely accepted by participating retailers and banks.

In 1979, Sri Lanka replaced a four-decade old quantity rationing system by a food stamp scheme. Prior to this change, food subsidies accounted for about 5 per cent of GDP or 15 per cent of total government expenditure. After the switch to food stamps, the share of food subsidies in GDP and as a per cent of total government spending fell to 1.3 per cent and 3 per cent, respectively. Two features of this food stamp programme have considerably reduced its effectiveness in helping the most vulnerable households. First, the value of food stamps was not indexed to inflation. The immediate consequence is an erosion in the real value of transfer as staple food prices (rice in particular) escalated soon after the switch to a food stamp programme. Second, the principal method for identifying eligible households was self-reported household income. The value of stamps was adjusted for household composition: each member older than 12 would receive stamps worth Rs. 15; each child between ages 8 and 12 would receive stamps worth Rs. 20 and each child less than 8 years would receive stamps worth Rs. 25.

1. *Sources.* R. Radhakrishna and K. Subbarao (1997). "India's Public Distribution System, A National and International Perspective," World Bank *Discussion Paper* No. 380. Washington, D.C.: World Bank;

   Edirisinghe, N. (1987) *The Food Stamp Scheme in Sri Lanka: Costs, Benefits and Options for Modification.* (Washington D.C.], [international Food Policy Research Institute.);

   H. Alderman (1991), "Food Subsidies and the Poor" in G. Psacharopoulos ed. *Essays on Poverty and Equity and Growth.* Oxford University Press;

   D. Sahn and H. alderman (1995) "The Effect of Food Subsidies on Labor Supply in Sri Lanka", in D. van de Walle and K. Nead (Eds.) *Public Spending and the Poor.* Baltimore and London: the Johns Hopkins University Press.

The information requirements for administering and monitoring the programme were formidable. To ensure proper targeting of the programme, it was necessary to continuously monitor incomes as well as household composition. Not surprisingly, household incomes were under-reported. Whereas the poverty ratio in the country was less than 30 per cent, over 50 per cent of the households were covered under the food stamp programme inclusion error was significant. A large share of food stamp outlay "leaked" to the upper income households which reduced the cost effectiveness of the programme. Assuming that the responsibility of the government was to ensure adequate nutrition only to the lowest quintile, the cost to the government of providing a given amount of calories to the households in the lowest income quintile was 250 per cent of the cost the households themselves would have incurred. Evidence suggests that the generous coverage may have enhanced the "real economic cost" of the programme, as it may have reduced labour supply at margin.

The impact of the food stamp programme on the nutritional status of children would depend on the pattern of intra-household food allocation. A special survey of 480 children revealed that, controlling for all other factors, an increase in income due to food stamps increased the calories consumption of children by 5.4 per cent, whereas the calorie consumption of all other members of the households increased by 10 per cent. The implication is: if the objective is to protect the nutritional status of children in very poor households, a nutrition programme directly targeted to such children would have perhaps proved a more effective intervention than the food stamp programme.

Thus, the switch from quantity ratios to food stamps did result in a reduced fiscal burden to the government, and enhanced the viability of the private sector in the food grain retail system. Yet the switch did not guarantee better targeting, nor did it protect the welfare of the most vulnerable. The lessons: (a) It is not enough to switch from one programme to another; it is important to get the design of the programme right to avoid inclusion and exclusion errors; and (b) Before a change is initiated, it is useful to first decide on which objective is to be realised from a programme, consider all potential alternatives and then select the most cost-effective option.

References

Alderman, H. and Paxson, C. (1994). "Do the Poor Insure? A Synthesis of the Literature on Risk and Consumption in Developing Countries", in E. Bacha (ed.), *Economics in a Changing World*, Vol. 4; Proceedings of the 10th World Congress of the International Economic Association, Moscow, *Development, Trade and the Environment*, IEA Conference Volume No. 110; New York: St. Martin's Press; London: Macmilan Press in association with the International Economic Association.

———. (1992). "Do the Poor insure? A Synthesis of the Literature on Risk and Consumption in Developing Countries", Policy Research, *Working Paper* No.108. Washington D.C.: The World Bank.

Cornia, G.A. and Frances Stewart (1993). "Two Errors of Targeting", in M. Lipton and J. van der Gaag (ed), *Including the Poor*. Washington DC: World Bank.

Deaton, A. (1990). "On Risk, Insurance, Intra Village Consumption Smoothing, Research Program in Development Studies". Unpublished Manuscript, Princeton University.

———. (1992). "Saving and Income Smoothing in Cote d'Ivoire", *Mimeo*, Princeton University.

Delgado, *et al.* (1999). "Livestock to 2020: The Next Food Revolution", Food, Agriculture and The Environment *Discussion Paper* 28, International Food Policy Research Institute, Washington D.C., U.S.A.

Douthwaite, R. (1999). *The Growth Illusion: How Economic Growth has Enriched the Few, Impoverished the Many and Endangered the Planet.* New Society Publishers.

Fafchamps, M. (1992). "Solidarity Networks in Pre Industrial Societies: Rational Peasants With a Moral Economy", *Economic Development and Cultural Change* 41: 147-76.

Grimard, F. (1997). "Household Consumption Smoothing Through Ethnic Ties: Evidence from Cote d'Ivoire", *Journal of Development Economics* 41: 391-422.

Grosh, M.E, (1992). "The Jamaican Food Stamps Program: A Case Study in Targeting", *Food Policy* 17(1): 23-40.

Gulati, I.S. and T.N. Krishnan (1975). "Public Distribution and Procurement of Foodgrains: A Proposal", *Economic and Political Weekly* 10. May 24.

Government of NCT Delhi, *Economic Survey of Delhi, 2005-06*, Planning Department, Government of National Capital Territory of Delhi.

Government of Kerala (2004), *Economic Review 2004: An Overview*, Department of Planning and Economic Affairs, Government of Kerala, *http://www.kerala.gov.in/dept_planning/er/chapter1.pdf*

———. (2006). *Towards an entitlement-based approach to Poverty Reduction: Development and Application of Entitlement Index.* Government of Kerala.

Hari, K.S. and K.P. Kannan (2002). "Kerala's Gulf Connection: Emigration, Remittances and their Macro Economic Impact", *Working Paper* No. 328, Centre for Development Studies, Trivandrum.

Heinberg, R. (2004). *Powerdown: Options and Actions for a Post-Carbon World.* New Society Publishers.

Jalan, J. and Ravallion, M. (1999). "Are the Poor Less Well Insured? Evidence on Vulnerability to Income Risk in Rural China", *Journal of Development Economics* 58: 61-81.

Johnston, B.F. (1953). *Japanese Food Management in World War II.* California: Stanford University Press.

Mace, B.J. (1991). "Full Insurance in the Presence of Aggregate Uncertainty", *Journal of Political Economy* 99(5): 928-56.

Maitra, P. (1998). "Consumption Smoothing in Rural Punjab in the Green Revolution Years", *Indian Economic Review* 33(2): 185-96.

———. (2003). "Are the Poor More Vulnerable to Income Shocks? An Analysis of Consumption Insurance in Rural India", in Raghbendra Jha (ed.), *Indian Economic Reforms*. New York: Palgrave, Macmillan.

Mooij, Jos (2001). "Food and Power in Bihar and Jharkhand: PDS and Its Functioning", *Economic and Political Weekly*, August 25.

———. (1999). *Food Policy and the Indian State: The Public Distribution System in South India.* Delhi: Oxford University Press.

Morduch, J. (1995). "Income Smoothing and Consumption Smoothing", *Journal of Economic Perspectives* 9(3): 103-14.

———. (1990). "Consumption Smoothing Across Space: Testing for Village Level Responses to Risk", Unpublished Manuscript, Harvard University.

———. (1991). "Risk and Welfare in Developing Countries", Unpublished Ph.D. Dissertation, Department of Economics, Harvard University.

Murty, K.N. (1999). "Decomposition of Changes in Cereals Demand into its Components in Semi-Arid Tropical Area", Paper presented at the 35th Indian Econometrics Society Meeting held at the Department of Economics,University of Rajasthan, Jaipur, March 11-13.

Nasurudeen *et al.* (2006). "The Dynamics and Inequality of Nutrient Consumption in India", *Indian Journal of Agricultural Economics.*

Negi, S.S. (1991). *Himalayan Rivers, Lakes and Glaciers.* New Delhi: Indus Publishing Company.

NSSO (1993-94). "Consumption of Some Important Commodities in India", National Sample Survey Organisation, Government of India, March, Report No. 404.

———. (1999-2000). "Consumption of Some Important Commodities in India", National Sample Survey Organisation, Government of India, July, Report No. 461.

———. (2004-05). "Level and Pattern of Consumer Expenditure", National Sample Survey Organisation, Government of India, December, Report No. 508.

ORG (2005). *Evaluation Study of Targeted Public Distribution System and Antodaya Anna Yojana*. New Delhi: ORG Centre for Social Research.

Pinstrup (1991). "Targeted Nutrition Interventions", *Food and Nutrition Bulletin* 13(3): 161-169.

Planning Commission (2005). *Performance Evaluation of Targeted Public Distribution System (TPDS)*. New Delhi: Programme Evaluation Organisation, Planning Commission, Government of India.

Platteau, J.P. (1991). "Traditional System of Social Security and Hunger Insurance: Some Lessons from the Evidence Pertaining to Third World Village Societies", in Ahmad, E. Dreze, J., Sen, A.K. (Eds). *Social Security in Developing Countries*. Oxford: Oxford University Press.

Radhakrishna, R. (2002). *India Development Report 2002*. Kirit S. Parikh and R. Radhakrishna (Eds). Oxford University Press.

Radhakrishna R. and C. Ravi (1991). *Food Demand Projection For India*. Hyderabad: Centre For Economic and Social Studies.

Radhakrishna R. and K. Subbarao (1997). "India's Public Distribution System: A National and International Perspective", World Bank *Discussion Paper* No. 380, Washingron D.C: World Bank.

Rajan, S.I. and K.C. Zachariah (2005). "Unemployment in Kerala at the Turn of the Century: Insights from CDS Gulf Migration Studies", Centre for Development Studies, Trivandrum.

Ray (2005). *Analysis of Changes in Food Consumption and their Implications for Food Security and Undernourishment: The Indian Experience in the 1990s*. University of Tasmania.

Rosenzweig, M.R. (1988). "Risk, Implicit Contracts and the Family in Rural Areas of Low-Income Countries", *The Economic Journal* 98: 1148-1170.

Rosenzweig, M.R. and O. Stark (1989). "Consumption Smoothing, Migration and Marriage: Evidence from Rural India", *Journal of Political Economy* 97(4): 905-27.

Saran, Ram (1975). "Management of Mass Consumption Goods Distribution With Special Reference to Foodgrains", *Agricultural Situation in India*. 20, January.

Shenoy, B.R. (1974). *PL 480 Aid and India's Food Problem*. New Delhi: Affiliate East West Press.

Tharamanalam, J. (2005), "The Perils of Social Development Without Economic Growth: The Development Debate of Kerala, India", *Political Economy for Environment Planners, http://www.infra.kth.se/courses/1H1142?Kerala_paper_4pdf*

Townsend, R.M. (1994). "Risk and Insurance in Village India", *Econometrica* 62(3): 539-91.

———. (1995). "Consumption Insurance: An Evaluation of Risk Bearing Systems in Low Income Countries", *Journal of Economic Perspectives* 9(3): 83-102.

Tyagi, D.S. (1990). *Managing India's Food Economy: Problems and Alternatives*. New Delhi: Sage Publications.

Udry, C. (1994). "Risk, Insurance and Default in a rural credit market: an Empirical Investigation in Northern Nigeria", Unpublished Manuscript. Northwestern University.

World Health Organization (2003). *Diet Nutrition and the Prevention of Chronic Diseases*. Technical Report Series 916. Geneva.